BMW | 3 AND 5 SERIES
1989-93 REPAIR MANUAL

CHILTON'S

President, Chilton Enterprises	David S. Loewith
Senior Vice President	Ronald A. Hoxter
Publisher and Editor-In-Chief	Kerry A. Freeman, S.A.E.
Executive Editors	Dean F. Morgantini, S.A.E., W. Calvin Settle, Jr., S.A.E.
Managing Editor	Nick D'Andrea
Special Products Manager	Ken Grabowski, A.S.E., S.A.E.
Senior Editors	Jacques Gordon, Michael L. Grady, Debra McCall, Kevin M. G. Maher, Richard J. Rivele, S.A.E., Richard T. Smith, Jim Taylor, Ron Webb
Project Managers	Martin J. Gunther, Will Kessler, A.S.E., Richard Schwartz
Production Manager	Andrea Steiger
Product Systems Manager	Robert Maxey
Director of Manufacturing	Mike D'Imperio
Editor	Benjamin E. Greisler, S.A.E.

CHILTON BOOK COMPANY

ONE OF THE **DIVERSIFIED PUBLISHING COMPANIES,**
A PART OF **CAPITAL CITIES/ABC, INC.**

Manufactured in USA
© 1994 Chilton Book Company
Chilton Way, Radnor, PA 19089
ISBN 0-8019-8427-0
Library of Congress Catalog Card No. 92-054907
3456789012   5432109876

Contents

Contents

SAFETY NOTICE

Proper service and repair procedures are vital to the safe, reliable operation of all motor vehicles, as well as the personal safety of those performing repairs. This manual outlines procedures for servicing and repairing vehicles using safe, effective methods. The procedures contain many NOTES, CAUTIONS, and WARNINGS which should be followed along with standard procedures to eliminate the possibility of personal injury or improper service which could damage the vehicle or compromise its safety.

It is important to note that the repair procedures and techniques, tools and parts for servicing motor vehicles, as well as the skill and experience of the individual performing the work vary widely. It is not possible to anticipate all of the conceivable ways or conditions under which vehicles may be serviced, or to provide cautions as to all of the possible hazards that may result. Standard and accepted safety precautions and equipment should be used when handling toxic or flammable fluids, and safety goggles or other protection should be used during cutting, grinding, chiseling, prying, or any other process that can cause material removal or projectiles.

Some procedures require the use of tools specially designed for a specific purpose. Before substituting another tool or procedure, you must be completely satisfied that neither your personal safety, nor the performance of the vehicle will be endangered.

Although information in this manual is based on industry sources and is complete as possible at the time of publication, the possibility exists that some car manufacturers made later changes which could not be included here. While striving for total accuracy, Chilton Book Company cannot assume responsibility for any errors, changes or omissions that may occur in the compilation of this data.

PART NUMBERS

Part numbers listed in this reference are not recommendation by Chilton for any product by brand name. They are references that can be used with interchange manuals and aftermarket supplier catalogs to locate each brand supplier's discrete part number.

SPECIAL TOOLS

Special tools are recommended by the vehicle manufacturer to perform their specific job. Use has been kept to a minimum, but where absolutely necessary, they are referred to in the text by the part number of the tool manufacturer. These tools can be purchased, under the appropriate part number, from your dealer or regional distributor, or an equivalent tool can be purchased locally from a tool supplier or parts outlet. Before substituting any tool for the one recommended, read the SAFETY NOTICE at the top of this page.

ACKNOWLEDGMENTS

The Chilton Book Company expresses appreciation to BMW of North America, Robert D. Mitchell, BMW NA Corporate Communications, Valerie Klabouch, BMW NA Press Fleet Coordinator, Bavarian Specialties, King of Prussia, PA, Zygmunt Motors, Doylestown, PA and the members of the BMW Car Club of America for their generous assistance in producing this manual.

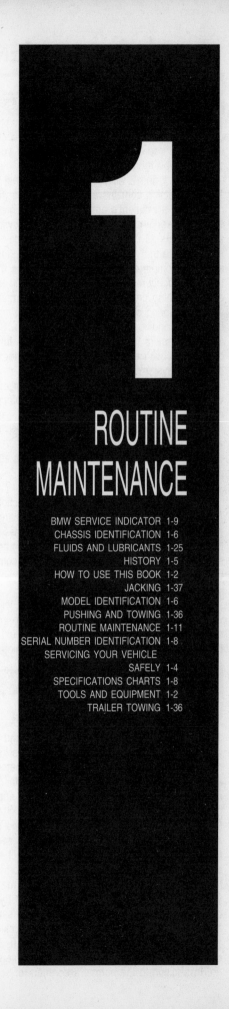

1

ROUTINE
MAINTENANCE

HOW TO USE THIS BOOK

Chilton's Total Car Care Manual for the BMW is intended to teach you more about the inner working of your automobile and save you money on its upkeep.

Sections 1 and 2 will probably be the most frequently used. The first section contains all the information that may be required at a moment's notice. Aside from giving the location of various serial numbers and the proper towing instructions, it also contains all the information on basic day-to-day maintenance that you will need to ensure good performance and long component life. Section 2 contains the necessary tune-up procedures to assist you not only in keeping the engine running properly and at peak performance levels, but also in restoring some of the more delicate components to operating condition in the event of a failure. Sections 3 through 10 cover repairs (rather than maintenance) for various portions of your car, with each section covering either separate systems or related systems.

In general, there are 3 things a proficient mechanic has which must be allowed for when a non-professional does work on his/her car. These are:

1. A sound knowledge of the construction of the parts he is working with; their order of assembly, etc.

2. A knowledge of potentially hazardous situations; particularly how to prevent them.

3. Manual dexterity.

This manual provides step-by-step instructions and illustrations whenever possible. Use them carefully and wisely — don't just jump headlong into disassembly. When there is doubt about being able to readily reassemble something, make a careful drawing of the component before taking it apart. Assemblies always look simple when everything is still attached.

'CAUTIONS,' 'WARNINGS' and 'NOTES' will be provided where appropriate to help prevent you from injuring yourself or damaging your car. Consequently, you should always read through the entire procedure before beginning the work so as to familiarize yourself with any special problems which may occur during the given procedure. Since no number of warnings could cover every possible situation, you should work slowly and try to envision what is going to happen in each operation ahead of time.

When it comes to tightening bolts and connections, there is generally a slim area between too loose to properly seal or resist vibration and so tight as to risk damage or warping. When dealing with major engine parts, or with any aluminum component, it pays to buy a torque wrench and go by the recommended figures.

When reference is made in this book to the 'right side' or the 'left side' of the car, it should be understood that the positions are always to be viewed from the front seat. This means that the left side of the car is the driver's side and the right side is the passenger's side. This will hold true throughout the book, regardless of how you might be looking at the car at the time.

We have attempted to eliminate the use of special tools whenever possible, substituting more readily available hand tools. However, in some cases, the special tools are necessary. These tools can usually be purchased from your local BMW dealer, from an automotive parts store or specialty mail order house.

Always be conscious of the need for safety in your work. Never get under a car unless it is firmly supported by jackstands or ramps. Never smoke near, or allow flame to get near the battery or the fuel system. Keep your clothing, hands and hair clear of the fan and pulleys when working near the engine if it is running. Most importantly, try to be patient, even in the midst of an argument with a stubborn bolt; reaching for the largest hammer in the garage is usually a cause for later regret and more extensive repair. Also note that using a tool too small for the job will end in frustration just as well. As you gain confidence and experience, working on your car will become a source of pride and satisfaction.

TOOLS AND EQUIPMENT

▶ **See Figure 1**

It would be impossible to catalog each and every tool that you may need to perform all the operations included in this book. It would also not be wise for the amateur to rush out and buy an expensive set of tools on the theory that he may need one of them at some time. The best approach is to proceed slowly, gathering together a good quality set of those tools that are used most frequently. Don't be mislead by the low cost of bargain tools. It is far better to spend a little more for quality, name brand tools. Forged wrenches, 6- or 12-point sockets and fine-tooth ratchets are by far preferable to their less expensive counterparts. As any good mechanic can tell you, there are few worse experiences than trying to work on a car or truck with bad tools. Your monetary savings will be far outweighed by frustration and mangled knuckles.

Begin accumulating those tools that are used most frequently; those associated with routine maintenance and tune-up. In addition to the normal assortment of screwdrivers and pliers, you should have the following tools for routine maintenance jobs:

1. Metric wrenches, sockets and combination open end/box end wrenches
2. Jackstands for support
3. Oil filter wrench
4. Oil filler spout or funnel
5. Ball pein hammer
6. Hydrometer for checking the battery
7. A low flat pan for draining fluids
8. Lots of rags for wiping up the inevitable mess
9. Hand cleaner

In addition to these items there are several others which are not absolutely necessary, but handy to have around. These include a transmission funnel and filler tube, a drop light on a long cord, an adjustable wrench and a pair of slip joint pliers.

A more advanced set of tools, suitable for tune-up work, can be drawn up easily. While the tools are slightly more sophisticated, they need not be outrageously expensive. The key to

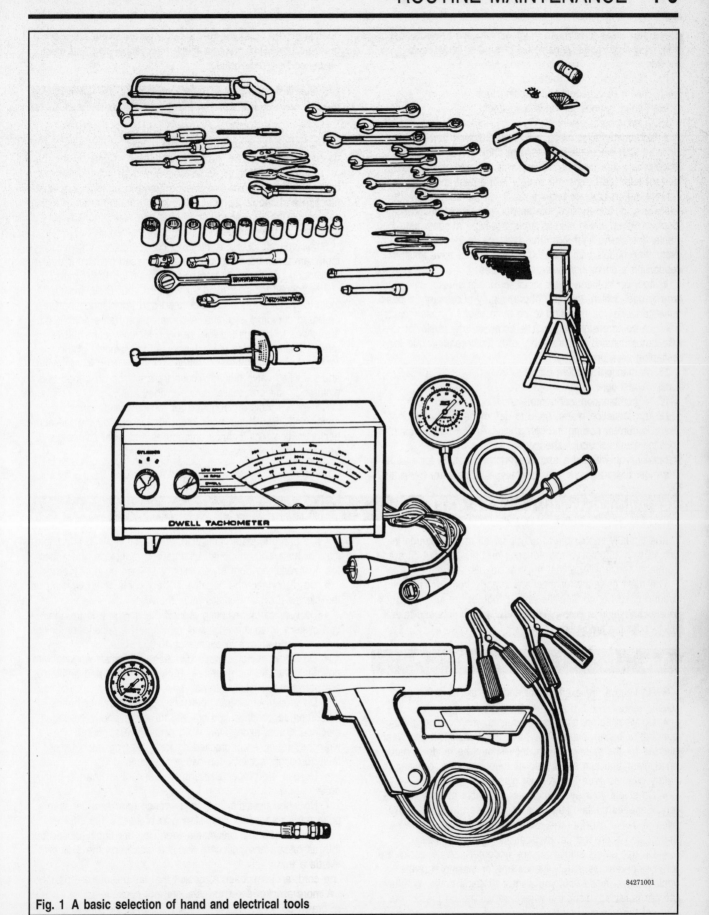

84271001

Fig. 1 A basic selection of hand and electrical tools

these purchases is to make them with an eye towards adaptability and wide range. A basic list of tune-up tools could include:

10. Tachometer/dwell meter
11. Spark plug gauge and gapping tool
12. Feeler gauges for valve adjustment
13. Timing light

A tachometer/dwell meter will allow checking tune-up work on cars with electronic ignition. The choice of a timing light should be made carefully. A light which works on the DC current supplied by the car battery is the best choice; it should have a xenon tube for brightness. Since all models have an electronic ignition system, the timing light should have an inductive pickup which clamps around the No. 1 spark plug cable (the timing light illustrated has one of these pickups). Note that models with the M50 engine do not have ignition leads and a timing light will be of no use.

In addition to these basic tools, there are several other tools and gauges which, though not particularly necessary for basic tune-up work, you may find to be quite useful. These include:

14. A compression gauge. The screw-in type is slower to use but eliminates the possibility of a faulty reading due to escaping pressure
15. A manifold vacuum gauge
16. A test light
17. A combination volt-ohmmeter
18. An induction meter, used to determine whether or not there is current flowing through a wire. An extremely helpful tool for electrical troubleshooting.

Finally, you will find a torque wrench necessary for all but the most basic of work. The beam-type models are perfectly adequate. The click-type (breakaway) torque wrenches are more accurate, but are also much more expensive and must be periodically recalibrated.

Special Tools

Normally, the use of special factory tools is avoided for repair procedures, since these are not readily available for the do-it-yourself mechanic. When it is possible to perform the job with more commonly available tools, it will be pointed out, but occasionally, a special tool was designed to perform a specific function and should be used. Before substituting another tool, you should be convinced that neither you safety nor the performance of the vehicle will be compromised.

Some special tools are available commercially from major tool manufacturers. Others can be purchased from your dealer or through companies that specialize in selling BMW parts.

The special tools required for work on your BMW include tools for rebuilding the cylinder head and troubleshooting the on-board computer systems. A compression frame permits all the valves to be opened fully at once for easy camshaft removal. There are also guide pins used for removal of the rocker shaft assembly, and various punches used in removing and installing valve guides. These tools will be described and pictured in the procedures to which they apply.

No special tools are required for routine maintenance or minor work. BMW has made great strides in reducing the number of routine maintenance procedures and what still needs to be done has been made simpler to complete.

SERVICING YOUR VEHICLE SAFELY

It is virtually impossible to anticipate all of the hazards involved with automotive maintenance and service, but care and common sense will prevent most accidents.

The rules of safety for mechanics range from 'don't smoke around gasoline,' to 'use the proper tool for the job.' The trick to avoiding injuries is to develop safe work habits and take every possible precaution.

Dos

• Do keep a fire extinguisher and first aid kit within easy reach.

• Do wear safety glasses or goggles when cutting, drilling, grinding or prying, even if you have 20/20 vision. If you wear glasses for the sake of vision, they should be made of hardened glass that can serve also as safety glasses, or wear safety goggles over your regular glasses.

• Do shield your eyes whenever you work around the battery. Batteries contain sulfuric acid. In case of contact with the eyes or skin, flush the area with water or a mixture of water and baking soda and get medical attention immediately.

• Do use safety stands for any undercar service. Jacks are for raising vehicles, safety stands are for making sure the vehicle stays raised until you want it to come down. Whenever the car is raised, block the wheels remaining on the ground and set the parking brake.

• Do use adequate ventilation when working with any chemicals or hazardous material. Like carbon monoxide, the asbestos dust resulting from brake lining wear can be hazardous.

• Do disconnect the negative battery cable when working on the electrical system unless told otherwise.

• Be very careful working around the engine and the ignition system when the engine is running. The secondary ignition system can generate in excess of 40,000 volts.

• Do follow manufacturer's directions whenever working with potentially hazardous materials. Both brake fluid and antifreeze are poisonous if taken internally.

• Do properly maintain your tools. Loose hammer heads, mushroomed punches and chisels, frayed or poorly grounded electrical cords, excessively worn screwdrivers, spread wrenches (open end), cracked sockets, slipping ratchets, or faulty droplight sockets can cause accidents.

• Do use the proper size and type of tool for the job being done.

• Do when possible, pull on a wrench handle rather than push on it, and adjust your stance to prevent a fall.

• Do be sure that adjustable wrenches are tightly closed on the nut or bolt and pulled so that the face is on the side of the fixed jaw.

• Do select a wrench or socket that fits the nut or bolt. The wrench or socket should sit straight, not cocked.

- Do strike squarely with a hammer; avoid glancing blows.
- Do set the parking brake and block the drive wheels if the work requires the engine running.
- Do use a fender cover to protect the finish of the car.

Don'ts

- Don't run an engine in a garage or anywhere else without proper ventilation — EVER! Carbon monoxide is poisonous; it takes a long time to leave the human body and you can build up a deadly supply of it in your system by simply breathing in a little every day. You may not realize you are slowly poisoning yourself. Always use power vents, windows, fans or open the garage door.
- Don't work around moving parts while wearing a necktie or other loose clothing. Short sleeves are much safer than long, loose sleeves; hard-toed shoes with neoprene soles protect your toes and give a better grip on slippery surfaces. Jewelry such as watches, fancy belt buckles, beads or body adornment of any kind is not safe working around a car. Long hair should be hidden under a hat or cap.
- Don't use pockets for tool boxes. A fall or bump can drive a screwdriver deep into your body. Even a wiping cloth hanging from the back pocket can wrap around a spinning shaft or fan.
- Don't smoke when working around gasoline, cleaning solvent or other flammable material.
- Don't smoke when working around the battery. When the battery is being charged, it gives off explosive hydrogen gas.
- Don't use gasoline to wash your hands; there are excellent soaps available. Gasoline removes all the natural oils from the skin so that bone dry hands will suck up oil and grease.
- Don't service the air conditioning system unless you are equipped with the necessary tools and training. The refrigerant, R-12 or R-134a, is extremely cold when compressed, and when released into the air will instantly freeze any surface it contacts, including your eyes. Although the refrigerant is normally non-toxic, R-12 becomes a deadly poisonous gas in the presence of an open flame. One good whiff of the vapors from burning refrigerant can be fatal.

HISTORY

BMW (Bavarian Motor Works) began its life in 1916 as a builder of aircraft engines (called the 'Bavarian Aircraft Works'), although the name was changed to the present one only a year later. The company logo which still appears several places on each car represents a propeller spinning against a blue sky. Thus, the high performance associated with BMW engines has its origin in the necessity to minimize weight in an aircraft. BMW's first car was a licensed version of the Austin Seven produced by the Dixi automobile works which BMW purchased in 1928.

In 1933, BMW produced its first in-house design, the BMW 303. This model series began two BMW traditions which are well known — the 6-cylinder engine and twin kidney grills. By the end of the 30's, BMW was making the famous and still beautiful 328, which featured an engine using a light alloy head, with V-type overhead valves and hemi-head combustion chambers.

BMW's history as a major manufacturer of performance cars was eclipsed by the destruction of the Munich plant in World War II. The 50's were dominated by the extremes — the too-large 501, and the Isetta with a BMW motorcycle engine propelling it. Neither brought much profit to the company.

In 1959 Dr. Herbert Quant invested heavily in the company to save it from a sale of assets. In 1961, the 1500 was introduced, in the tradition of the later models. This 'Neue Klasse' of 4-cylinder sports sedans has become recognized for its high output, low displacement and fuel efficient engine and light and compact chassis-body, which offers excellent road holding and braking.

First introduced to the North American continent as the 1.6 liter 1600, the 2 door versions of the 'Neue Klasse' cars struck a chord with the motoring cognoscente. A year later in 1968 the first of the 2 liter 2002's rolled of the ships and into the driveways and racetracks. These were the cars that gave BMW a foothold in the North American market and practically invented the 'sports sedan' segment that BMW has dominated ever since. With the introduction of the 530i in 1975, BMW began to be associated with luxury-performance cars as well as sports sedans.

New models were introduced, the 320i and 528i, replacing the 2002 and 530. These models brought BMW from the 70's into the 80's. Early in the decade, the E30 chassis 318i replaced the 320i and the E32 chassis 528e/533i replaced the 528i. The E30 chassis, with varying engine displacements existed up into the 90's, with the super fast, homologation special M3 as the pinnacle of the chassis.

The E32 chassis, also with varying engine displacements, existed up to 1988 when it was replaced by the E34 chassis 535i. In 1992 the M5 was upgraded to 310 horsepower with handling and brakes to match. The year 1992 also brought the introduction of the E36 chassis 325i and 318i, taking the target of the sports sedan market to new heights.

Practically no other marque has had such loyalty from its owners. The popularity of the 2002 sparked the formation of the BMW Car Club of America in the late 60's. Fully active in the early 70's, the club expanded and brought services and driving events to its members. Presently BMW CCA holds membership in excess of 30,000. From social events to drivers schools, 2002's to M5's, the BMW CCA has brought additional enjoyment to the owners of The Ultimate Driving Machine.

BMW cars take to the racetrack with aplomb. The advanced chassis and engines that make BMW's so good on the road, translate into winning on the racetrack. From parking lot autocross and road course racetracks to the forest roads of special stage PRO Rally, BMW's of all vintages can be found in the Winners Circle.

MODEL IDENTIFICATION

BMW identifies models by the vehicle badging. The 3 digit car 'name' as it appears on the trunklid is a code for the series and the engine displacement of that vehicle.

84271002

Fig. 2 310 HP of the "Ultimate Driving Machine"

The first digit represents the series of the vehicle. A 325i would be a 3 series vehicle as a 525i would be a 5 series vehicle. Knowing the series of the vehicle is of use when ordering parts and to identify what chassis it is.

The second and third digits represent the engine displacement of the vehicle. The 325i has a 2.5 liter engine and a 318i has a 1.8 liter engine. The 525i has a 2.5 liter engine and a 535i has a 3.5 liter engine. Note that these digits represent a rounded off number and not an exact engine size. Use the engine identification chart to determine exactly the displacement of the engine in your car.

On the M cars, the badging is different from the standard BMW naming system. The M3 and M5 are limited production vehicles produced by the Motorsport division of BMW AG. The M represents the Motorsport parentage and the 3 or 5 represents the series on which it was based. The M3, based on the E30 3 series vehicle uses an engine based on early BMW Formula 1 efforts. The M5 uses an engine pulled almost directly from the M1 supercar.

CHASSIS IDENTIFICATION

When dealing with BMW vehicles, it is often more convenient and apt to describe them by their chassis designation. Chassis designation is done via an E number. This book covers 2 chassis versions of the 3 series, the E30 and the E36. There is 1 chassis covered in the 5 series, the E34. Check the charts to identify the chassis designation of your vehicle.

The reason it is more convenient to use the chassis designation in certain instances is that there is overlap of the 3 series vehicles in the early 1990's. For example, in a given year, there were two 325i's. They used different chassis' (E30 and E36) and different engines (M20 and M50), but the same name designations. To keep from confusing the 2 vehicles, use of the chassis designation pinpoints the car in question.

VEHICLE IDENTIFICATION

Year	Model	Engine Displacement Liters (cc)	Engine Series Identification	Chassis Identification	No. of Cylinders	Engine Type
1989	325i	2.5 (2494)	M20B25	E30	6	OHC
	325iC	2.5 (2494)	M20B25	E30	6	OHC
	325iX	2.5 (2494)	M20B25	E30	6	OHC
	M3	2.3 (2302)	S14B23	E30	4	16V DOHC
	525i	2.5 (2494)	M20B25	E34	6	OHC
	535i	3.5 (3430)	M30B35	E34	6	OHC
1990	325i	2.5 (2494)	M20B25	E30	6	OHC
	325iC	2.5 (2494)	M20B25	E30	6	OHC
	325iX	2.5 (2494)	M20B25	E30	6	OHC
	M3	2.3 (2302)	S14B23	E30	4	16V DOHC
	525i	2.5 (2494)	M20B25	E34	6	OHC
	535i	3.5 (3430)	M30B35	E34	6	OHC
1991	318i	1.8 (1796)	M42B18	E30	4	16V DOHC
	318iC	1.8 (1796)	M42B18	E30	4	16V DOHC
	318iS	1.8 (1796)	M42B18	E30	4	16V DOHC
	325i	2.5 (2494)	M20B25	E30	6	OHC
	325iC	2.5 (2494)	M20B25	E30	6	OHC
	325iX	2.5 (2494)	M20B25	E30	6	OHC
	M3	2.3 (2302)	S14B23	E30	4	16V DOHC
	525i	2.5 (2494)	M50B25	E34	6	24V DOHC
	535i	3.5 (3430)	M30B35	E34	6	OHC
	M5	3.6 (3535)	S38B36	E34	6	24V DOHC
1992-93	318i	1.8 (1796)	M42B18	E36	4	16V DOHC
	318iS	1.8 (1796)	M42B18	E36	4	16V DOHC
	318iC	1.8 (1796)	M42B18	E30	4	16V DOHC
	325i	2.5 (2494)	M50B25	E36	6	24V DOHC
	325iS	2.5 (2494)	M50B25	E36	6	24V DOHC
	325iC	2.5 (2494)	M20B25	E30	6	OHC
	525i	2.5 (2494)	M50B25	E34	6	24V DOHC
	525iT	2.5 (2494)	M50B25	E34	6	24V DOHC
	535i	3.5 (3430)	M30B35	E34	6	OHC
	M5	3.6 (3535)	S38B36	E34	6	24V DOHC

OHC—Overhead Camshaft
DOHC—Double Overhead Camshaft

84271058

SERIAL NUMBER IDENTIFICATION

Vehicle

♦ **See Figures 3, 4 and 5**

On the E36 3 series and the E34 5 series, the vehicle identification chassis number is stamped in the body, under the hood next to the right side wiper arm. On the E30 3 series, the vehicle identification chassis number is stamped on the right side of the heater cowl.

The vehicle identification chassis number is also printed on a sticker in the left side door jamb on all vehicles. The vehicle identification chassis number is also visible on a plate mounted to the dash near the middle of the windshield.

Most vehicles have the vehicle identification chassis number stamped into body parts, the engine and the transmission. This is for identification and to help prevent vehicle theft.

Engine

The engine number can be found in different places depending on engine. On 4 cylinder engines, the number is stamped on the intake side of the crankcase. On 6 cylinder engines, the number is stamped on a pad at the clutch end of the crankcase.

Transmission

ENGINE IDENTIFICATION

Year	Model	Engine Displacement Liters (cc)	Engine Series Identification	Fuel System ①	No. of Cylinders	Engine Type
1989	325i	2.5 (2494)	M20B25	M1.3	6	OHC
	325iC	2.5 (2494)	M20B25	M1.3	6	OHC
	325iX	2.5 (2494)	M20B25	M1.3	6	OHC
	M3	2.3 (2302)	S14B23	M1.2②	4	16V DOHC
	525i	2.5 (2494)	M20B25	M1.3	6	OHC
	535i	3.5 (3430)	M30B35	M1.3	6	OHC
1990	325i	2.5 (2494)	M20B25	M1.3	6	OHC
	325iC	2.5 (2494)	M20B25	M1.3	6	OHC
	325iX	2.5 (2494)	M20B25	M1.3	6	OHC
	M3	2.3 (2302)	S14B23	M1.2②	4	16V DOHC
	525i	2.5 (2494)	M20B25	M1.3	6	OHC
	535i	3.5 (3430)	M30B35	M1.3	6	OHC
1991	318i	1.8 (1796)	M42B18	M1.7	4	16V DOHC
	318iC	1.8 (1796)	M42B18	M1.7	4	16V DOHC
	318iS	1.8 (1796)	M42B18	M1.7	4	16V DOHC
	325i	2.5 (2494)	M20B25	M1.3	6	OHC
	325iC	2.5 (2494)	M20B25	M1.3	6	OHC
	325iX	2.5 (2494)	M20B25	M1.3	6	OHC
	M3	2.3 (2302)	S14B23	M1.2②	4	16V DOHC
	525i	2.5 (2494)	M50B25	M3.1	6	24V DOHC
	535i	3.5 (3430)	M30B35	M1.3	6	OHC
	M5	3.6 (3535)	S38B36	M1.2②	6	24V DOHC
1992-93	318i	1.8 (1796)	M42B18	M1.7	4	16V DOHC
	318iS	1.8 (1796)	M42B18	M1.7	4	16V DOHC
	318iC	1.8 (1796)	M42B18	M1.7	4	16V DOHC
	325i	2.5 (2494)	M50B25	M3.1	6	24V DOHC
	325iS	2.5 (2494)	M50B25	M3.1	6	24V DOHC
	325iC	2.5 (2494)	M20B25	M1.3	6	OHC
	525i	2.5 (2494)	M50B25	M3.1	6	24V DOHC
	525iT	2.5 (2494)	M50B25	M3.1	6	24V DOHC
	535i	3.5 (3430)	M30B35	M1.3	6	OHC
	M5	3.6 (3535)	S38B36	M1.2②	6	24V DOHC

OHC—Overhead Camshaft
DOHC—Double Overhead Camshaft
① Digital Motor Electronic
② Motorsport Motronics

84271059

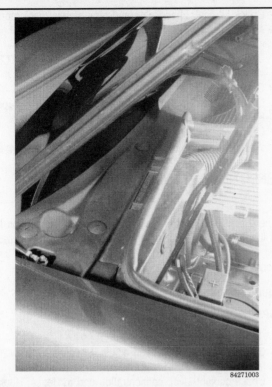

84271003

Fig. 3 Location of the vehicle ID number under the hood

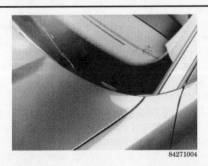

84271004

Fig. 4 The vehicle ID number is located on the drivers side of the instrument panel

The manual transmission number is on a label affixed to the upper portion of the bellhousing. The label is located just be-

84271005

Fig. 5 Location of the vehicle ID number in the door jamb

hind the flat portion cast at the bellhousing to engine block mounting face.

The automatic transmission number is on a label affixed to the side of the casing. The label is located between the shift lever and bracket.

Drive Axle

The drive axle ratio is stamped on a tag attached to the axle housing cover. Return this tag to its original location whenever the cover is removed and replaced.

Transfer Case

The transfer case of the 325iX has an identification label affixed to the upper side of the unit. The label is positioned on the case in front of the case vent.

BMW SERVICE INDICATOR

General Description

The BMW Service Indicator is the row of LEDs in the instrument panel. There are 5 LEDs colored green and 1 each red and yellow. The Service Indicator is designed to monitor the usage of the car and inform the driver of when service is needed. The Service Indicator takes information from the various sensors on the engine and vehicle, such as the engine speed, vehicle speed and coolant temperature, computes the way the car is being driven and decides when the next service

is due. This method of service interval determination strikes the proper balance of driving style, vehicle longevity and economy with the need for service.

A vehicle that is driven mainly on the highway, at steady speeds will not need servicing as often as a vehicle driven on short, city style trips. To base oil changes and other services strictly on mileage or time does not take the variability of driving style into consideration. This can lead to servicing at too long of intervals, thus lessening the service life of the car, or at too short of intervals, leading to wasted money and lessening the economy of owning a BMW.

Too short of intervals will not hurt the car in any way, and it is recommended to increase the service intervals if severe conditions are encountered, such as towing, competition use, drivers schools or extreme weather, hot or cold. The standard of 3 months or 3000 miles for oil changes still isn't a bad idea.

Operation

▶ **See Figure 6**

The Service Indicator will light on starting the car. A row of green LEDs will illuminate when the ignition is switched ON. The Service Indicator is extinguished once the engine is started and no service is due. There are 5 green LEDs and as they count down from 5 to 1, they are indicating that it is getting closer to a service. When it is time for a service, the yellow LED will illuminate along with the inscription 'OIL' or 'INSPECTION' and will stay illuminated while the engine is running. If the car is not serviced within the maintenance interval, a red LED will illuminate along with the yellow LED and the inscription. If the red LED is illuminated, try to avoid driving the car and have the service performed immediately.

Types of Service

The 2 types of service are OIL and INSPECTION. Each indicates what is to be done to the vehicle to satisfy the service needs.

OIL SERVICE

The oil service is fairly obvious in its nature. The vehicle is telling you it needs to have the oil changed; this is a requirement. There should be other items checked during the oil service to ensure a long vehicle life and proper operation. Regardless of what the Service Indicator says, do not exceed 10,000 miles between oil changes.
- Change the oil and filter while at operating temperature.
- Reset the Service Indicator

At the time of the oil service, the following operations should be performed:
- Check the steering linkage, box, flexible joint coupling, oil level and all connections.
- Check the brake pads, rotors, hoses, connections, parking brakes and cables.
- Check tires for pressure and tread wear patterns.

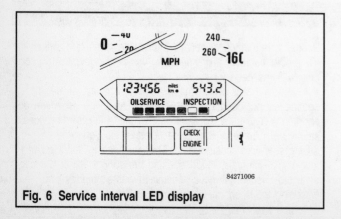

84271006

Fig. 6 Service interval LED display

- Check all lights, headlights and aim, warning indicators, turn signals, back-up lights, glove and map lights, and check the operation of the horns.
- Check wipers, washer fluid level and spray pattern. Check the intensive washer fluid level.
- Check the seatbelts for damage.
- Clean the cassette player heads, pinch roller and capstan.
- Road test.
- Clean injectors, if necessary.
- Wash and clean the interior and exterior of the vehicle.

INSPECTION SERVICE

There are 2 inspection services aptly named Inspection I and Inspection II. They are performed alternately. Keep records of when an inspection is done, so the proper inspection can be completed when due.

Required Services

INSPECTION I

- Check for any diagnostic codes.
- Check valve clearance and adjust if necessary on M20 and M30 engines.
- Check coolant level, concentration and for leaks. Replace every 2 years.
- Check steering gear for leaks and maintain fluid level.
- Check brake and clutch fluid level. Change fluid at least every 2 years.
- Check washer fluid and intensive washer fluid level.
- Check battery electrolyte level.
- Check operation of air conditioning system.
- Clean and lubricate all bearing points of the throttle linkage.
- Reset the Service Indicator.
- Change the oil and filter while at operating temperature.
- Check for leakage at the transmission and differentials.
- Change the automatic transmission fluid.
- Check the fuel tank and lines for damage and leaks.
- Check exhaust system for damage and leaks.
- Check steering for free-play and centering.
- Check the brake pads, rotors, calipers and emergency brake.
- Check the tightness of the M5 wheel air vane ring bolts, 6 ft. lbs. (8 Nm).
- Check steering linkage and suspension components.
- Check tire condition and pressure.
- Check wipers.
- Check seatbelts.
- Lubricate all body hinges, catches and latches.
- Check all lights and headlight aim.
- Check hydraulic fluid level on self leveling suspension with the suspension fully lifted.
- Change the microfilter for the ventilation system.
- Road test.

INSPECTION II

- All items in Inspection I.
- Check the condition and tension of all drive belts. Tension the belts if necessary, except the serpentine belt on the M50 engine.

- Replace the spark plugs. Not to exceed 40,000 miles between changes.
- Check the automatic transmission fluid level.
- Every other Inspection II or every 4 years, whichever comes first, replace the timing belt on the M20 engine.
- Replace the air filter or every 2 years, whichever comes first. Replace more often if needed. Not to exceed 40,000 miles between changes.
- Replace the ASC+T inlet filter (535i with ASC+T).
- Change manual transmission lubricant.
- Change transfer case lubricant (325iX).
- Change rear differential lubricant.
- Change front differential lubricant (325iX).
- Check CV joint boots.
- Check parking brake linings.
- Replace fuel filter. Not to exceed 40,000 miles between changes.
- Check clutch disc.
- Check condition of body structure.

Additional Services

The oxygen sensor must be replaced every 50,000 miles, except on the 1993 318i and 325i. The oxygen sensor should be changed every 60,000 miles on the 318i and every 100,000 miles on the 325i. This is to ensure proper operation of the engine management system and to keep emissions to a minimum. This maintenance interval is a strictly mileage based interval as driving habits and time do not affect the deterioration of the oxygen sensor.

Service Indicator

The Service Indicator must be reset after the service is completed. This will restore the Service Indicator to its baseline and it will start to calculate the new service interval.

A special tool is required to reset the lights. The tool is available from the dealer, specialty retailers and mail order. It is not difficult to use, but it can be pricey. If you do not decide to purchase the tool, it is sometimes possible to borrow the tool from a local BMW club or have your dealer or local shop reset the lights for a nominal fee.

ROUTINE MAINTENANCE

▶ **See Figures 7, 8, 9, 10, 11, 12, 13, 14 and 15**

Air Cleaner

REMOVAL & INSTALLATION

Filter Element

E30 318i, 318is AND 318iC

1. Loosen the hose clamp at the air flow meter. Disconnect the hose at the air flow meter.
2. Remove the air flow meter electrical connection by rotating the outer ring and pulling off.

PROCEDURE

The following procedures are for use with the BMW reset tool. Other tools will be similar or identical in operation. Follow the instructions that come with the unit you are using.

Be sure that you are doing the correct reset procedure for the correct service. If the wrong button, OIL SERVICE or INSPECTION is depressed, it cannot be corrected. This will not harm anything, but it will make the service interval incorrect.

After Inspection Service

1. Turn OFF all electrical accessories.
2. Turn ON the ignition, but do not start the engine.
3. Install the reset tool and adapter, if necessary, on the diagnosis socket.
4. Push and hold the red colored INSPECTION button. The green lamp illuminates.
5. The red lamp will illuminate after approximately 3 seconds, then extinguish after approximately 12 seconds.
6. Let go of the INSPECTION button. The green light will extinguish.
7. Check that all 5 green LEDs are lit and the other LEDs are out.

After Oil Service

1. Turn OFF all electrical accessories.
2. Turn ON the ignition, but do not start the engine.
3. Install the reset tool and adapter, if necessary, on the diagnosis socket.
4. Push and hold the green colored OIL SERVICE button. The green lamp illuminates.
5. The yellow lamp will illuminate after approximately 10 seconds, then extinguish after approximately 3 seconds.
6. Let go of the OIL SERVICE button. The green light will extinguish.
7. Check that all 5 green LEDs are lit and the other LEDs are out.

3. Unsnap the 4 clips securing the upper portion of the air cleaner assembly to the lower assembly.
4. Lift the upper portion of the air cleaner assembly up and out of the engine compartment. Handle the air flow meter with care.
5. Remove the air filter element. Clean the lower plenum of the air cleaner assembly as it tends to collect large pieces of dirt and leaves.

To install:
6. Install the new element in the lower portion of the air cleaner. The element will be marked as to the correct position with an arrow pointing in the direction of air flow or by some other means.
7. Replace the upper portion of the air cleaner assembly. Be sure that the air filter element seals the upper and lower sections completely. If not, check that you are using the cor-

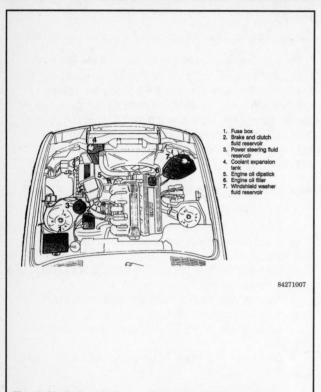

1. Fuse box
2. Brake and clutch fluid reservoir
3. Power steering fluid reservoir
4. Coolant expansion tank
5. Engine oil dipstick
6. Engine oil filler
7. Windshield washer fluid reservoir

84271007

Fig. 7 Underhood view — E30 318i, 318iS and 318iC w/M42 engine

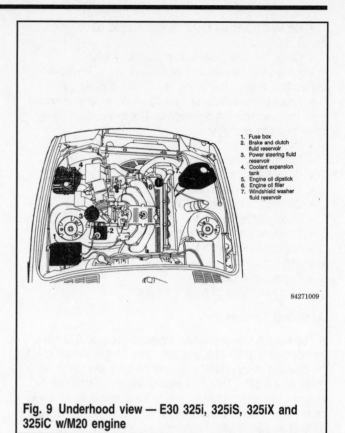

1. Fuse box
2. Brake and clutch fluid reservoir
3. Power steering fluid reservoir
4. Coolant expansion tank
5. Engine oil dipstick
6. Engine oil filler
7. Windshield washer fluid reservoir

84271009

Fig. 9 Underhood view — E30 325i, 325iS, 325iX and 325iC w/M20 engine

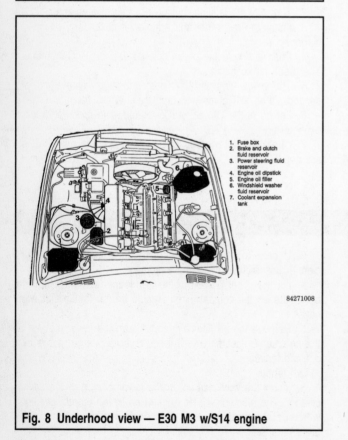

1. Fuse box
2. Brake and clutch fluid reservoir
3. Power steering fluid reservoir
4. Engine oil dipstick
5. Engine oil filler
6. Windshield washer fluid reservoir
7. Coolant expansion tank

84271008

Fig. 8 Underhood view — E30 M3 w/S14 engine

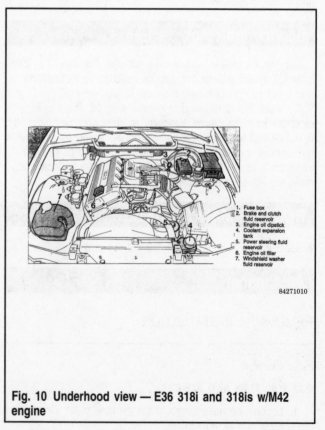

1. Fuse box
2. Brake and clutch fluid reservoir
3. Engine oil dipstick
4. Coolant expansion tank
5. Power steering fluid reservoir
6. Engine oil filler
7. Windshield washer fluid reservoir

84271010

Fig. 10 Underhood view — E36 318i and 318is w/M42 engine

rect element or that the element is properly installed in the housing.

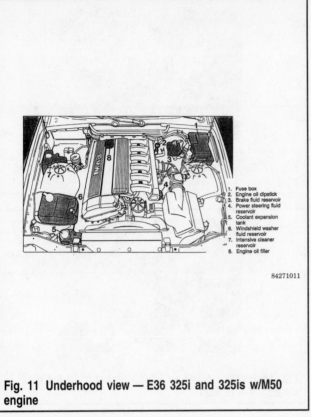

1. Fuse box
2. Engine oil dipstick
3. Brake fluid reservoir
4. Power steering fluid reservoir
5. Coolant expansion tank
6. Windshield washer fluid reservoir
7. Intensive cleaner reservoir
8. Engine oil filler

84271011

Fig. 11 Underhood view — E36 325i and 325is w/M50 engine

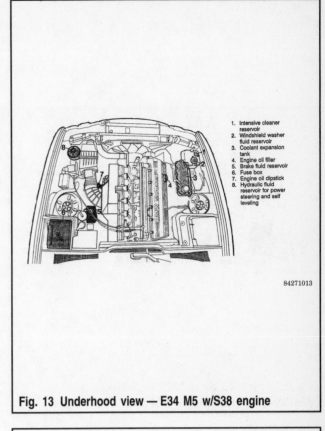

1. Intensive cleaner reservoir
2. Windshield washer fluid reservoir
3. Coolant expansion tank
4. Engine oil filler
5. Brake fluid reservoir
6. Fuse box
7. Engine oil dipstick
8. Hydraulic fluid reservoir for power steering and self leveling

84271013

Fig. 13 Underhood view — E34 M5 w/S38 engine

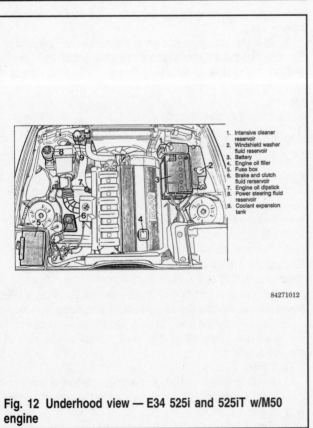

1. Intensive cleaner reservoir
2. Windshield washer fluid reservoir
3. Battery
4. Engine oil filler
5. Fuse box
6. Brake and clutch fluid reservoir
7. Engine oil dipstick
8. Power steering fluid reservoir
9. Coolant expansion tank

84271012

Fig. 12 Underhood view — E34 525i and 525iT w/M50 engine

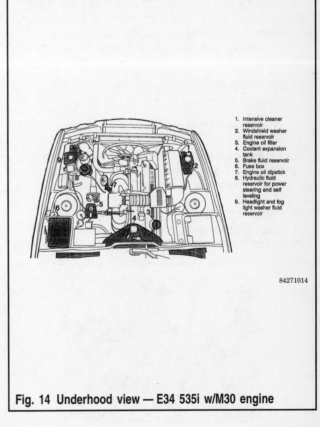

1. Intensive cleaner reservoir
2. Windshield washer fluid reservoir
3. Engine oil filler
4. Coolant expansion tank
5. Brake fluid reservoir
6. Fuse box
7. Engine oil dipstick
8. Hydraulic fluid reservoir for power steering and self leveling
9. Headlight and fog light washer fluid reservoir

84271014

Fig. 14 Underhood view — E34 535i w/M30 engine

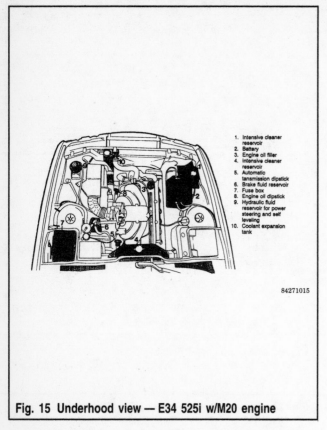

1. Intensive cleaner reservoir
2. Battery
3. Engine oil filler
4. Intensive cleaner reservoir
5. Automatic transmission dipstick
6. Brake fluid reservoir
7. Fuse box
8. Engine oil dipstick
9. Hydraulic fluid reservoir for power steering and self leveling
10. Coolant expansion tank

Fig. 15 Underhood view — E34 525i w/M20 engine

8. Snap the clips into place. Connect the air flow meter electrical connection by aligning the marks on the connectors and rotating the outer ring until it locks into place.

9. Connect the hose to the air flow meter and tighten the hose clamp.

E36 318i AND 318iS

▶ **See Figures 16, 17 and 18**

1. Unsnap the 4 clips holding the upper section of the air cleaner to the lower.

2. Lift the upper section to remove the air filter element.

3. Remove the air filter element. Clean the lower plenum of the air cleaner assembly as it tends to collect large pieces of dirt and leaves.

To install:

4. Install the new element in the lower portion of the air cleaner. The element will be marked as to the correct position

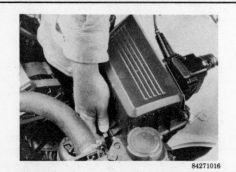

Fig. 16 Unclipping the air cleaner fasteners — E36 318i

Fig. 17 Separating the halves of the air cleaner — E36 318i

Fig. 18 Removing the air filter element from the air cleaner — E36 318i

with an arrow pointing in the direction of air flow or by some other means.

5. Replace the upper portion of the air cleaner assembly. Be sure that the air filter element seals the upper and lower sections completely. If not, check that you are using the correct element or that the element is properly installed in the housing.

6. Snap the clips into place.

E30 325i, 325iX, 325iC AND M3

1. Loosen the hose clamp at the air flow meter. Disconnect the hose at the air flow meter.

2. Remove the air flow meter electrical connection by depressing the clip and pulling off. Remove the 2 nuts securing the air cleaner to the bracket. Cut off the wire tie holding the electrical lead, if equipped.

3. Remove the air cleaner from the engine compartment. Unsnap the 4 clips securing the upper portion of the air cleaner assembly to the lower assembly.

4. Lift the upper portion of the air cleaner assembly off the lower section. Handle the air flow meter with care.

5. Remove the air filter element. Clean the lower plenum of the air cleaner assembly as it tends to collect large pieces of dirt and leaves.

To install:

6. Install the new element in the lower portion of the air cleaner. The element will be marked as to the correct position with an arrow pointing in the direction of air flow or by some other means.

7. Replace the upper portion of the air cleaner assembly. Be sure that the air filter element seals the upper and lower sections completely. If not, check that you are using the cor-

rect element or that the element is properly installed in the housing.

8. Snap the clips into place. Replace the assembly in the engine compartment. Connect the air flow meter electrical connection and press until it locks in place. Install a new wire tie. Tighten the nuts securing the air cleaner to the bracket.

9. Connect the hose to the air flow meter and tighten the hose clamp.

E36 325i AND 325iS

▶ **See Figures 19 and 20**

1. Pull up on the air filter element cover and remove the filter.

2. Clean the interior of the air cleaner housing of dirt and leaves.

3. Install the new element. Be sure the element is installed in the correct direction as marked on the element.

4. Replace the element cover by snapping into place.

E34 525i WITH M20 ENGINE

1. Loosen the hose clamp at the air flow meter. Disconnect the hose at the air flow meter.

2. Remove the air flow meter electrical connection by depressing the clip and pulling off.

3. Unsnap the 4 clips securing the upper portion of the air cleaner assembly to the lower assembly.

4. Lift the upper portion of the air cleaner assembly up and out of the engine compartment. Handle the air flow meter with care.

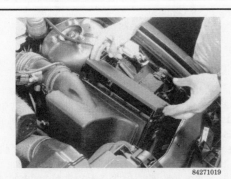

84271019

Fig. 19 Unclipping the air cleaner fasteners — E36 325i

84271020

Fig. 20 Removing the air filter element from the air cleaner — E36 325i

5. Remove the air filter element. Clean the lower plenum of the air cleaner assembly as it tends to collect large pieces of dirt and leaves.

To install:

6. Install the new element in the lower portion of the air cleaner. The element will be marked as to the correct position with an arrow pointing in the direction of air flow or by some other means.

7. Replace the upper portion of the air cleaner assembly. Be sure that the air filter element seals the upper and lower sections completely. If not, check that you are using the correct element or that the element is properly installed in the housing.

8. Snap the clips into place. Connect the air flow meter electrical connection by aligning connectors and pressing together until it locks into place.

9. Connect the hose to the air flow meter and tighten the hose clamp.

E34 525i WITH M50 ENGINE

1. Loosen the hose clamp holding the hose to the air flow meter. Disconnect the hose from the air flow meter.

2. Remove the nuts holding the air cleaner to the bracket and push the unit back to gain some clearance.

3. Unsnap the 4 clips holding the halves of the air cleaner. Separate the halves.

4. Remove the air filter element and clean the interior of the housing of dirt and leaves.

To install:

5. Install the new element in the air cleaner. The element will be marked as to the correct position with an arrow pointing in the direction of air flow or by some other means.

6. Press together the sections of the air cleaner assembly. Be sure that the air filter element seals the upper and lower sections completely. If not, check that you are using the correct element or that the element is properly installed in the housing.

7. Snap the clips into place. Install the 2 nuts holding the air cleaner to the bracket.

8. Connect the hose to the air flow meter and tighten the hose clamp.

535i

1. Loosen the hose clamp at the air flow meter. Disconnect the hose at the air flow meter.

2. Unsnap the 6 clips securing the upper portion of the air cleaner assembly to the lower assembly.

3. Lift the upper portion of the air cleaner assembly up.

4. Remove the air filter element. Clean the lower plenum of the air cleaner assembly as it tends to collect large pieces of dirt and leaves.

To install:

5. Install the new element in the lower portion of the air cleaner. The element will be marked as to the correct position with an arrow pointing in the direction of air flow or by some other means.

6. Replace the upper portion of the air cleaner assembly. Be sure that the air filter element seals the upper and lower sections completely. If not, check that you are using the correct element or that the element is properly installed in the housing.

7. Snap the clips into place.

8. Connect the hose to the air flow meter and tighten the hose clamp.

E34 M5

▶ See Figure 21

1. Remove the nuts holding the air cleaner to the bracket and push the unit back to gain some clearance.
2. Unsnap the 4 clips holding the halves of the air cleaner. Separate the halves.
3. Remove the air filter element and clean the interior of the housing of dirt and leaves.

To install:
4. Install the new element in the air cleaner. The element will be marked as to the correct position with an arrow pointing in the direction of air flow or by some other means.
5. Press together the sections of the air cleaner assembly. Be sure that the air filter element seals the sections completely. If not, check that you are using the correct element or that the element is properly installed in the housing.
6. Snap the clips into place. Install the 2 nuts holding the air cleaner to the bracket.

Fuel Filter

REMOVAL & INSTALLATION

Filter Canister

> **✳✳CAUTION**
>
> Gasoline is very dangerous and can cause explosion and fire if exposed to an ignition source. Keep all flame and sparks away from the vehicle during servicing otherwise personal injury or property damage can occur. Gasoline can also cause personal discomfort if it is allowed to contact the skin for any period of time. Flush area with water if exposed to gasoline.

E30 3 SERIES

The fuel filter is located near the fuel pump at the rear axle of the vehicle. A set of fuel line block off clamps are needed for this procedure. They are available at most automotive parts stores at reasonable prices.

1. Install the fuel line block off clamps on both the inlet and outlet lines to the fuel filter. This will prevent fuel from leaking out of the hoses once the filter is removed.
2. Loosen the clamps holding the body of the fuel filter. Loosen the fuel line clamps.
3. Use a container to catch the fuel left in the filter and remove the hoses from the filter. Remove the filter.

To install:
4. Note the direction of flow of the new filter and install in the clamps.
5. Attach the fuel lines to the correct ends of the filter and tighten the hose clamps.
6. Tighten the filter body clamps and remove the fuel line clamps. Check the area for leaks.

E36 318i AND 318iS

The fuel filter is located on the left side front frame rail. A set of fuel line block off clamps are needed for this procedure. They are available at most automotive parts stores at reasonable prices.

1. Install the fuel line block off clamps on both the inlet and outlet lines to the fuel filter. This will prevent fuel from leaking out of the hoses once the filter is removed.
2. Loosen the fuel line clamps. Use a container to catch the fuel left in the filter and remove the hoses from the filter, top hose first.
3. Remove the filter by loosening the clamp bolt and prying the clamp apart.

To install:
4. Note the direction of flow of the new filter and install the filter. Tighten the clamp bolt.
5. Attach the fuel lines to the correct ends of the filter and tighten the hose clamps.
6. Check the area for leaks.

E36 325i AND 325iS

▶ See Figure 22

The fuel filter is located on the left side front frame rail. A set of fuel line block off clamps are needed for this procedure. They are available at most automotive parts stores at reasonable prices.

1. Remove the dust cover by loosening the hose clamps.
2. Install the fuel line block off clamps on both the inlet and outlet lines to the fuel filter. This will prevent fuel from leaking out of the hoses once the filter is removed.

84271021

Fig. 21 Air cleaner assembly — E34 M5

84271022

Fig. 22 Fuel filter on the left frame rail — E35 325i

3. Loosen the fuel line clamps. Use a container to catch the fuel left in the filter and remove the hoses from the filter, top hose first.

4. Loosen the clamp holding the body of the fuel filter. Remove the filter by pulling down and out.

To install:

5. Note the direction of flow of the new filter and install in the clamp.

6. Attach the fuel lines to the correct ends of the filter and tighten the hose clamps.

7. Remove the fuel line clamps. Check the area for leaks.

E34 5 SERIES

▶ **See Figure 23**

The fuel filter is located near the rear axle of the vehicle. A set of fuel line block off clamps are needed for this procedure. They are available at most automotive parts stores at reasonable prices.

1. Install the fuel line block off clamps on both the inlet and outlet lines to the fuel filter. This will prevent fuel from leaking out of the hoses once the filter is removed.

2. Loosen the clamp holding the body of the fuel filter. Loosen the fuel line clamps.

3. Use a container to catch the fuel left in the filter and remove the hoses from the filter. Remove the filter. Remove the rubber ring from the filter.

To install:

4. Note the direction of flow of the new filter and install in the clamp. Be sure to fit the rubber ring from the old filter on the new unit.

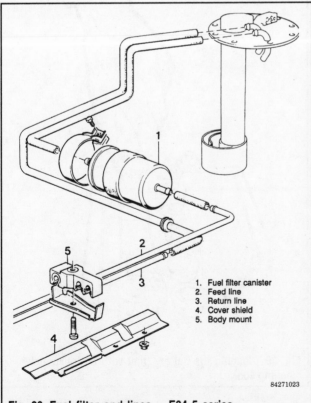

1. Fuel filter canister
2. Feed line
3. Return line
4. Cover shield
5. Body mount

84271023

Fig. 23 Fuel filter and lines — E34 5 series

5. Attach the fuel lines to the correct ends of the filter and tighten the hose clamps.

6. Tighten the filter body clamp and remove the fuel line clamps. Check the area for leaks.

PCV System and Evaporative Canister

All engines use a sealed PCV system that does not allow fresh air into the crankcase. This means the crankcase is under vacuum at all times and any leak in the system is a vacuum leak. It is important to make sure all hoses are in good condition and the dipstick is firmly sealed in the tube. No other maintenance is required, though visually checking the system for damaged hoses and leaks is recommended.

The fuel evaporation system consists of an expansion tank, carbon canister, fuel filler cap, solenoid activated purge valve and connecting lines and hoses. The filler cap is a check valve that allows air into the tank but will not allow vapors out. No scheduled maintenance is required, though visually checking the system for damaged hoses and leaks is recommended.

Battery

LOCATION

The battery in your vehicle can be mounted in a variety of locations depending on the model, engine or chassis style, convertible or hardtop. The battery is mounted underhood on the right side on the 318is, 325iC and the 525i. The battery is mounted under the rear seat on the 535i and M5. The battery is mounted in the trunk on the right side, under the trunk liner, on the 318i, 325i and M3.

When the battery is mounted under the rear seat cushion, the cushion can be removed by pulling up on the front edge and removing from the vehicle. Be sure that the seat cushion is secure when it is replaced so it doesn't become dislodged in a sudden stop. Be sure the vent tube is not crimped when replacing the cushion.

GENERAL MAINTENANCE

▶ **See Figure 24**

The original equipment battery installed in your BMW is a maintenance free, non-sealed unit. This means that even though the unit should never need fluid in its useful life, the level can be checked and replenished if severe service made the addition of fluid necessary.

If the car is not driven much, or is used for stop and restart type of driving, the battery may not have an opportunity to be recharged by the alternator. With the high usage of on-board electronics and the associated high electrical load, it is important to keep the battery in a fully charged state. If many short trips are anticipated, that would leave the battery low, either change your route of travel to include some highway driving to allow the battery to charge or use a trickle charger installed in the manner intended by its manufacturer.

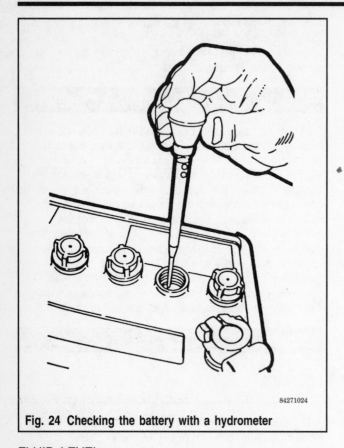

Fig. 24 Checking the battery with a hydrometer

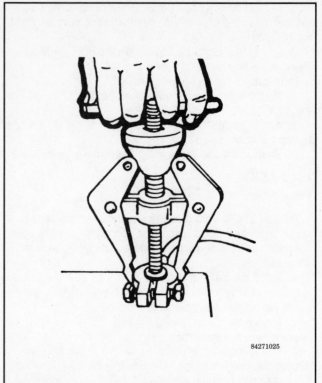

Fig. 25 Using a terminal puller to remove a stuck battery terminal

FLUID LEVEL

Clean the top of the battery before removing the cell caps. With the battery exposed and the cell caps removed, the fluid level should be 0.2 in. (5mm) above the plates or at the level marker visible in the opening, if equipped. Fluid should not need replenishing in general use, but extended periods of hot weather use can lower the level. Fill the cells with distilled water, only. Do not fill the cells with battery acid!

If water is added during freezing weather, the car should be driven several miles to allow the electrolyte and water to mix. Otherwise the battery could freeze.

CABLES AND CLAMPS

▶ See Figures 25, 26 and 27

Once a year, the battery terminals and the cable clamps should be cleaned. Loosen the clamps and remove the cable, negative cable first. On batteries with posts on top, the use of a puller specially made for that purpose is recommended. These are inexpensive, and available in auto parts stores.

Clean the cable clamps and the battery terminals with a wire brush, until all corrosion, grease, etc. is removed and the metal is shiny. It is especially important to clean the inside of the clamp thoroughly, since a small deposit of foreign material or oxidation will prevent a sound electrical connection and inhibit either starting or charging. Special tools are available for cleaning these parts, one type for conventional batteries and another type for side terminal batteries. Get the type for your battery; all BMW's are equipped with top post batteries.

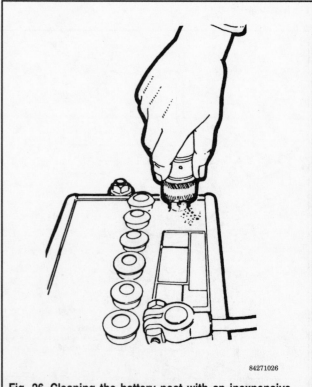

Fig. 26 Cleaning the battery post with an inexpensive cleaning tool

Before installing the cables, loosen the battery hold-down clamp or strap, remove the battery and check the battery tray.

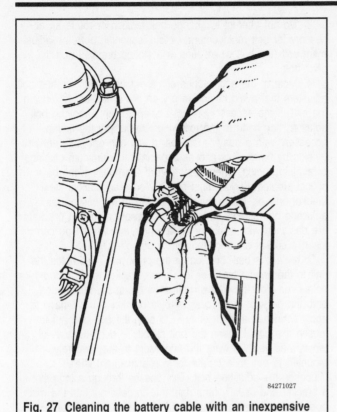

Fig. 27 Cleaning the battery cable with an inexpensive cleaning tool

Clear it of any debris, and check it for soundness. Rust should be wire brushed away, and the metal given a coat of anti-rust paint. Replace the battery and tighten the hold-down clamp or strap securely, but be careful not to over tighten, which will crack the battery case.

After the clamps and terminals are clean, reinstall the cables, negative cable last, do not hammer on the clamps to install. Tighten the clamps securely, but do not distort them. Give the clamps and terminals a thin external coat of grease after installation, to retard corrosion. Replace the vent tube, if equipped.

Check the cable at the same time that the terminals are cleaned. If the cable insulation is cracked or broken, or if the ends are frayed, the cable should be replaced with a new cable of the same length and gauge.

❊❊CAUTION

Keep flame or sparks away from the battery; it gives off explosive hydrogen gas. Battery electrolyte contains sulfuric acid. If you should splash any on your skin or in your eyes, flush the affected area with plenty of clear water; if it lands in your eyes, get medical help immediately.

TESTING SPECIFIC GRAVITY(EXCEPT SEALED MAINTENANCE FREE BATTERIES)

At least once a year, check the specific gravity of the battery. It should be between 1.20 and 1.26 at room temperature.

The specific gravity can be checked with the use of a hydrometer, an inexpensive instrument available from many sources, including auto parts stores. The hydrometer has a squeeze bulb at one end and a nozzle at the other. Battery electrolyte is sucked into the hydrometer until the float is lifted from its eat. The specific gravity is then read by noting the position of the float. Generally, if after charging, the specific gravity between any 2 cells varies more than 50 points (0.050), the battery is bad and should be replaced.

It is not possible to check the specific gravity in this manner on sealed ('maintenance free') batteries. Instead, the indicator built into the top of the case must be relied on to display any signs of battery deterioration. If the indicator is dark, the battery can be assumed to be OK. If the indicator is light, the specific gravity is low, and the battery should be charged or replaced.

CHARGING

The battery on your BMW can be charged without removing the battery from the vehicle. On vehicles with the battery mounted underhood, connect the charging leads directly to the battery posts. On vehicles with the battery mounted in the trunk or under the rear seat cushion, connect the positive charging lead to the remote positive terminal under the hood and the negative lead to the engine lifting bracket.

❊❊CAUTION

Never charge a frozen battery! The battery may explode and cause personal harm. Allow the battery to thaw before charging.

➡**Charging must be done with the engine not running and turned OFF. Do not 'quick charge' or use a higher voltage than the battery is rated as this can damage the battery and electrical system.**

REPLACEMENT

When it becomes necessary to replace the battery, select a battery with a rating equal to or greater than the battery originally installed. Deterioration, embrittlement and just plain aging of the battery cables, starter motor, and associated wires makes the battery's job harder in successive years. The slow increase in electrical resistance over time makes it prudent to install a new battery with an equal or greater capacity than the old one. Never use a battery with less capacity.

When replacing the battery, remove the negative cable first, then the positive. Remove the hold-down strap bolt and remove the battery. Install the battery and tighten the hold-down strap bolt. Connect the positive cable, then the negative. Be sure the vent tube is not blocked or crimped.

JUMP STARTING

◗ **See Figure 28**

Follow the procedure listed in your owners manual. Be sure that before you disconnect the cables, return the engine speed to idle, turn on the rear defogger, the headlights and the

Fig. 28 Remote positive battery terminal used for jump starting

heater fan to help absorb the voltage spike that can occur during disconnection. This will help prevent possible damage to the electrical system.

Belts

INSPECTION

Belts should be inspected for both tension and condition at intervals of 12,500 miles (20,000 km) and shortly after replacement. Belt tension is checked by applying pressure (about 10-15 lbs.) with your thumb midway between 2 pulleys. The belt should deflect (stretch) about ½-¾" for each 10" of distance between pulley centers. The belt should spring tight, not sagging or having play, but not so tight that it requires tremendous effort to get a slight deflection. Excessive belt tension may wear the bearings of the accessory being driven, or may stretch and crack the belt, while insufficient tension will cause slippage and glazing.

Inspect the belt for separation between the outer surface and the Vee, and for radial cracks, which usually begin at the inner surface. The driving surfaces should be rough, slightly cross-hatched because they are fabric covered. If the surface is perfectly smooth, the belt has slipped, and this has caused overheating. A glazed belt cannot offer a sufficient amount of friction to carry the load without excessive tension. Belts which show cracks or glazing should be replaced.

REPLACEMENT

Vee-Type

▶ See Figure 29

1. Replace belts with the proper part. A belt of the wrong length will have to be pried on if too short, a procedure that will seriously damage the belt even before it turns around once, or which may prevent sufficient tightening to compensate for wear long before the belt has really worn out. If you must use a belt that is just a little too short, you might be able to avoid stretching it during installation by completely dismounting the driven accessory, working the belt around the pulleys, and then remounting the accessory.

2. Replace the multiple belts in sets only, as work belts stretch and mixing stretched belts with new ones will prevent even division of the load.

3. Do not attempt to change belt tension or rotate an accessory for belt replacement without loosening both the adjustment bolt (the bolt which runs in a slotted bracket) and the pivot bolt.

4. Most of the accessories come equipped with toothed bolt adjusters that avoid having to pry on the accessory to tension the belt. If the accessory is not equipped with a toothed bolt adjuster, pay heed to the following: Do not pry the driven accessory with a heavy metal bar if you can get sufficient belt tension by hand. This applies especially to aluminum castings or air/fluid pumps, where distortion of the housing can be a critical problem. If you must pry, pry on a substantial steel bracket only or, failing that, on the part of the casting the adjusting bolt screws into. Some accessory mounting brackets are designed with a slot or square hole into which you can insert a socket drive for tensioning purposes.

To replace a belt, first locate the pivot bolt. This holds the unit to the engine block or to a short bracket which has only a hole — no slot. If the pivot bolt does not use a nut welded onto the back of the accessory or a bracket you will have to apply wrenches at both ends — to both the bolt and nut to loosen this bolt. Loosen the bolt slightly — don't release all tension, as you will want the accessory to stay securely mounted to get an accurate tension adjustment later.

Loosen the adjusting bolt. This passes through a long slot in a bracket and usually runs right into threads cut into the main body of the accessory. Now, all belt tension will be gone.

Move the accessory all the way toward the engine, and pull off the belt. Position the new belt around all the pulleys. Make sure it tracks in all the pulley grooves and, if there are multiple pulleys or pulleys and belts involved, make sure the belt runs in pulleys which are directly in line with one another.

Be ready to tighten the adjusting bolt. Pull or pry the accessory away from the engine until the tension is correct (see above), and then tighten the adjusting bolt. Finally, tighten the pivot bolt. If the accessory is equipped with a toothed adjusting bolt, rotate the bolt with a wrench to obtain the adjustment. No prying will be required.

➡**When installing a new belt (one run less than 10 minutes) put a little extra tension on it to allow for stretch and seating in the pulley Vees during break-in. About 30-40 percent extra tension will do. Instead of deflecting as much as ¾", the belt should deflect a little less than ½" for each 10" of distance between the pulley centers. Recheck tension of new belts several days after installation in case of stretch.**

Fig. 29 Adjuster bolt on the alternator — E36 318i shown

Multi-Vee Type

◗ **See Figures 30 and 31**

1. Before removing the belt, take note of the routing of the belt over the pulleys. If there is not a diagram on an underhood sticker, draw a diagram of the routing. This will be of great help when replacing the belt.

2. Remove the pulley covers, if equipped and insert a hex key in the tensioner pulley. Rotate the pulley clockwise to release the tension in the belt.

3. Remove the belt from the pulleys.

4. When replacing the belt, be sure that the belt is fully seated in the grooves and it is in the proper routing arrangement.

5. Release the tensioning pulley.

Worn hoses will feel brittle, the lower hose may be permanently narrowed at one point from suction, or may appear frayed or cracked. New hoses will be springy and pliable yet firm, the rubber surface will be solid and smooth, and there will be no evidence of string reinforcements showing through.

Hoses

REPLACEMENT

1. Remove the splash guard from under the vehicle. Put a bucket of about 2 gallons capacity under the radiator drain. Remove the drain plug.

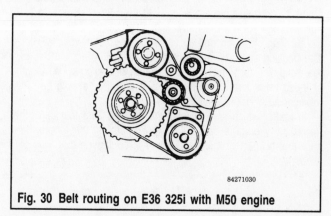

84271030

Fig. 30 Belt routing on E36 325i with M50 engine

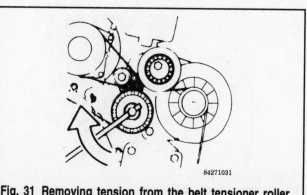

84271031

Fig. 31 Removing tension from the belt tensioner roller

2. If a heater hose is being replaced, turn the rotary heater control to 'Warm' and allow any water contained in the heater core and hoses to drain.

3. Loosen the clamps at both ends of the hoses. Work the hose ends off the radiator or heater core and engine block connections.

4. Install the new hose in reverse order. If the hose has bends molded into it, make sure to position the hose so that it does not become crimped at these points. Also, install new factory style hose clamps onto the hose from both ends before sliding hose ends onto connections. Position the clamps so they are accessible once the hose is installed. Make sure hoses slide all the way onto the connectors. Make sure you then slide the clamps over the lips on the connectors but not all the way at the ends of the hoses.

5. Tighten the clamps securely, and then refill the cooling system.

Air Conditioning Systems

SAFETY WARNINGS

R-12 and other chlorofluorocarbon refrigerants, when released into the atmosphere, may contribute to the depletion of the ozone layer of the upper atmosphere. Ozone filters out damaging ultraviolet radiation from the sun.

Consult the laws in your area before attempting service on the air conditioning system in your vehicle. In some states it is illegal to perform repairs involving refrigerant unless the work is done by a certified technician.

The air conditioner is filled with refrigerant R-12 or R-134a, which produces very high pressure even when the system is not operating. Not only can a component broken by mishandling, crack or break explosively, but the escaping refrigerant will immediately drop to -27°F (-33°C), causing severe frostbite to any part of the body exposed nearby. The problem is worsened by the fact that refrigerant systems employ thin sections of light alloys to transfer heat efficiently — thus, components are readily damaged by inexperienced mechanics.

Thus, we recommend that you make no attempt whatever to repair any component on the air conditioning system. If a refrigerant component must be moved to gain access to another part, we recommend you leave at least the part of the job involving the refrigerant component to someone with the specialized training, tools, and experience to handle the job safely. However, if you are going to work on the system yourself, you must be very careful and use common sense before making any repairs.

SYSTEM INSPECTION

Once a year, before hot weather sets in, it is advisable to check the refrigerant charge in the air conditioner system. This may be accomplished on R-12 filled systems by looking at the sight glass located in the engine compartment. First, wipe the sight glass clean with a cloth wrapped around the eraser end of a pencil. Have a friend operate the air conditioner controls while you look at the sight glass. Have your friend set the dash panel control to **MAX** cooling. Start the engine and idle at 1500 rpm. While looking at the sight glass, signal your friend to turn the blower switch to the **HIGH** position. If a few bubbles appear immediately after the blower is turned on and then disappear, the system is sufficiently charged with refrigerant. If, on the other hand, there are a large amount of bubbles after the blower has operated for a few seconds, then the system is in need of additional refrigerant. If no bubbles appear at all, then there is either sufficient refrigerant in the system, or it is bone dry. The way to clear this question up is to have your friend turn the unit **OFF** and **ON** (engine running at 1500 rpm) about every 10 seconds or so while you look at the sight glass. This will cycle the magnetic clutch. If the system is properly charged, bubbles will appear in the sight glass a few seconds after the unit is turned off and disappear when it is turned on although they may linger awhile in extremely hot weather. If no bubbles appear when the unit is in the **OFF** position, then the system should be serviced by an authorized dealer and checked for leaks. Do not operate the unit if you suspect that the refrigerant has leaked out.

Check the radiator and condenser for clogging by bugs and road debris. If the fins of the radiator and condenser are blocked, heat cannot be transferred from the fins to the airstream. Clean the debris from the fins to restore the airflow.

DISCHARGING AND CHARGING

BMW recommends the use of their special charging and recovery system for both R-12 and R-134a systems. The unit is manufactured by BEHR and is designed for use by a trained technician. If your vehicle requires the air conditioning system to be discharged and later charged, let a trained and certified technician perform the work.

Windshield Wipers

Intense heat from the sun, snow, and ice, road oils and the chemicals used in windshield washer solvent combine to deteriorate the rubber wiper refills. The refills should be replaced about twice a year or whenever the blades begin to streak or chatter.

WIPER REFILL REPLACEMENT

▶ **See Figures 32 and 33**

Normally, if the wipers are not cleaning the windshield properly, only the refill has to be replaced. The blade and arm usually require replacement only in the event of damage. It is not necessary (except on new Tridon® refills) to remove the arm or the blade to replace the refill (rubber part), though you may have to position the arm higher on the glass. You can do this by turning the ignition switch ON and operating the wipers. When they are positioned where they are accessible, turn the ignition switch OFF.

There are several types of refills and your vehicle could have any kind, since aftermarket blades and arms may not use exactly the same type refill as the original equipment.

Most Anco® styles use a release button that is pushed down to allow the refill to slide out of the yoke jaws. The new refill slides in and locks in place.

Some Trico® refills are removed by locating where the metal backing strip or the refill is wider. Insert a small screwdriver blade between the frame and metal backing strip. Press down to release the refill from the retaining tab.

Other Trico® blades are unlocked at one end by squeezing 2 metal tabs, and the refill is slid out of the frame jaws. When the new refill is installed, the tabs will click into place, locking the refill.

The polycarbonate type is held in place by a locking lever that is pushed downward out of the groove in the arm to free the refill. When the new refill is installed, it will lock in place automatically.

The Tridon® refill has a plastic backing strip with a notch about 1″ (25mm) from the end. Hold the blade (frame) on a hard surface so that the frame is tightly bowed. Grip the tip of the backing strip and pull up while twisting counterclockwise. The backing strip will snap out of the retaining tab. Do this for the remaining tabs until the refill is free of the arm. The length of these refills is molded into the end and they should be replaced with identical types.

No matter which type of refill you use, be sure that all of the frame claws engage the refill. Before operating the wipers, be sure that no part of the metal frame is contacting the windshield.

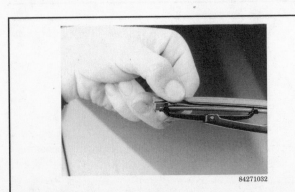

84271032

Fig. 32 Wiper blade mounting

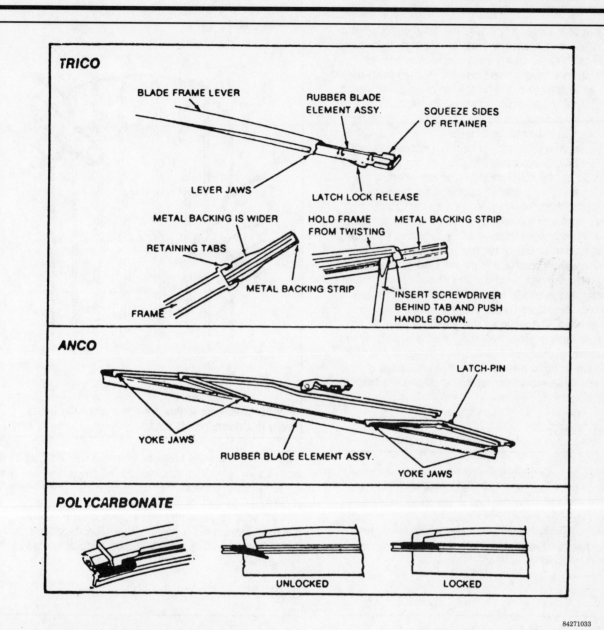

Fig. 33 Different types of wiper blade mounting

Tires and Wheels

TIRE ROTATION

BMW does not recommend rotating the tires. Due to the design of the suspension, the front tires tend to wear on the outside edge and the rear tires wear on the inside edge. When the tires are rotated front to back, the ground contact patch is reversed, resulting in less contact patch area. This can adversely affect the handling, road holding and braking performance of the vehicle.

There is not much to be gained in terms of tire life by rotation, but if you wish to rotate the tires, do so every 3000 miles (5000 km) at maximum. If the period of time between rotations is extended, greater adverse effects in terms of handling, road holding and braking performance of the vehicle can be expected.

Rotation must be accomplished by keeping the tires in the same rotation orientation. This means the tires must be kept on the same side of the vehicle. If the spare is to be included in the rotation, do so from the start as to keep the wear on the spare relative to that of the other tires.

TIRE DESIGN

As every vehicle covered in this book came stock with radial design tires and bias ply tires are all but a memory, a simple reminder that bias ply and radial tires should never be used together should suffice. The BMW car was designed to use radial tires and the use of bias ply tires would adversely affect the handling, road holding and braking ability of the vehicle.

There is a wide range of tires available for your car ranging from all-season mud and snow tread tires, to high performance spirited driving oriented tires. New tire technology has advanced to where everyday street tires can offer as much performance as yesterdays racing tires, while offering wet weather grip, a comfortable ride and a long tread life. Discussions with your tire retailer can put you on the right track as to the type of tire to buy that will match your needs.

When buying new tires, stick to the stock size tire as recommended by BMW. If the tire size is changed, the performance of the vehicle can be compromised along with affecting the ABS braking system. Maintain the same size tires on all corners of the car. With different sized tires on the car, varying wheel speeds, due to the differing tire circumferences, will confuse the ABS controller and affect its performance. If you desire to change the wheels or tire size, check with your dealer for recommendations, practical value and legal considerations.

When purchasing new tires, buy tires of the same or higher speed rating as the original equipment tires. If the tires are replaced with lower speed rated tires, the vehicle dynamics could be effected. The argument that you don't travel as fast as the tire is rated is not a valid one. There is more to speed rating than what speed you travel. Speed ratings involve the tires ability to dissipate heat and thus the way the tire is constructed. These factors control the behavior of the tire and vehicle.

TIRE STORAGE

Mark the tires with the location on the car from which they came off. This will keep the rotations correct when they are replaced on the car. Store the tires at the proper inflation pressure if they are mounted on wheels. Keep them in a cool dry place, laid on their sides. If the tires are stored in the garage or basement, do not let them stand on a concrete floor; set them on strips of wood.

TIRE INFLATION

▶ See Figures 34 and 35

For the best performance from your tires, check the inflation pressure at least every 2 weeks. It is better to check every week. If the tire pressure is incorrect, driving performance, braking and handling will be affected. Keep an accurate pressure gauge in your glove compartment.

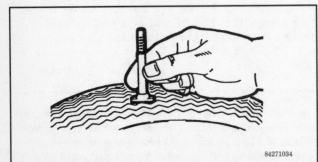

84271034

Fig. 34 Checking the tread depth with an inexpensive gauge

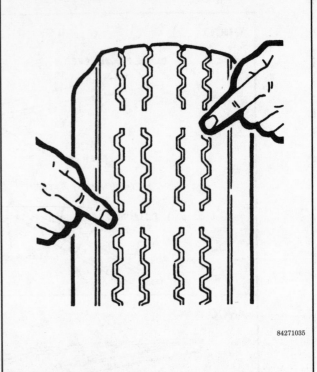

84271035

Fig. 35 Treadwear indicators show when the tire is worn to its serviceable limit

Be sure to check the pressure when the tires are cold as a warm tire will give false readings. As the tire temperature goes up, so does the pressure. For every 18°F (10°C) the pressure is raised 1.5 psi (0.1 bar).

Match your tire pressure to your planned load. Increase the pressure to counteract a heavy load. Follow the guide provided by BMW in the owners manual and on a sticker located on the vehicle itself.

CARE OF WHEELS

Most BMW vehicles are equipped with alloy wheels. Care must be taken when cleaning the wheels. Use only a product formulated for cleaning alloy wheels. Do not use a product containing abrasives, strong acids or alkalis. Do not use water heated to more than 140°F (60°C). Follow the instructions provided with the cleaning product.

Use brushes designed to be used on alloy wheels. These brushes have soft bristles that will not scratch the surface of the wheel. If the wheel is very dirty, allow the cleaning solution to work into the dirt, scrub with the brush and hose off the dirt.

Do not use brake dust shields mounted between the wheel and hub. These shields can block the flow of brake cooling air and cause overheating of the rotor. Differences in materials can cause the lug bolts to loosen when the expansion and contraction rates of the materials vary. To prevent build-up of brake dust on the wheels, wash the wheels often.

Wash the wheels frequently to prevent road dirt, salt and brake dust from corroding the wheels. If contaminants are allowed to sit on the wheel and bake into it with the heat from the brakes, the wheel can become stained. Wash the wheels often to prevent this.

CHANGING TIRES

1. With the car still on the ground, set the parking brake and put the car in PARK or 1st gear.
2. Place the supplied chock under the rear wheel on the opposite side of the vehicle.
3. On vehicles with the cross spoke type wheels, remove the lug cover with the supplied wrench. Turn the wrench counterclockwise to remove.
4. Loosen the lug bolts. Place the jack in the jacking point. Make sure the ground underneath the jack is stable enough to support the weight of the vehicle. Place a board under the jack on soft ground.

5. Raise the vehicle enough to provide space to fit the spare.

❊❊CAUTION

Do not go under the car while it is supported solely by the tire changing jack. The jack can slip and fall causing personal injury or death.

6. Remove the lug bolts and remove the tire. A tire that has been run on while flat can be hot.
   To install:
7. Place the centering pin in one of the bolt holes. Place the wheel on the hub over the centering pin. Replace the lug bolts, removing the centering pin after at least one lug bolt is in place. Snug the bolts.
8. Lower the car and torque the lug bolts to 81 ft. lbs. (110 Nm). Replace the lug cover on cross spoke wheels.

FLUIDS AND LUBRICANTS

Fluid Disposal

Used fluids such as engine oil, transmission fluid, antifreeze and brake fluid are hazardous wastes and must be disposed of properly. Before draining any fluids, consult with the local authorities; in many areas, waste oil, etc. is being accepted as a part of recycling programs. A number of service stations and auto parts stores are also accepting waste fluids for recycling.

Be sure of the recycling center's policies before draining any fluids, as many will not accept different fluids that have been mixed together.

Fuel and Engine Oil Recommendations

OIL

▶ **See Figure 36**

The SAE (Society of Automotive Engineers) grade number indicates the viscosity of the engine oil and thus its ability to lubricate at a given temperature. The lower the SAE grade number, the lighter the oil; the lower the viscosity, the easier it is to crank the engine in cold weather.

Oil viscosities should be chosen from those oils recommended for the lowest anticipated temperature during the oil change interval.

Multi-viscosity oils (10W-30, 20W-50, etc.) offer the important advantage of being adaptable to temperature extremes. They allow easy starting at low temperatures, yet they give good protection at high speeds and engine temperatures. This is a decided advantage in changeable climates or in long distance touring.

The API (American Petroleum Institute) designation indicates the classification of engine oil used under certain given operating conditions. Only oils designated for use 'Service SF' or 'Service SG' should be used. Never use oils rated lower, though it is acceptable to use oils rated for use in diesel

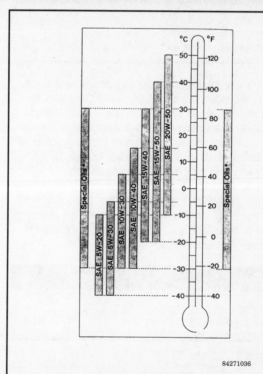

84271036

Fig. 36 Recommended oil viscosity for temperature range. Synthetic oils are considered 'Special Oils' by BMW

engines as long as the oil has a SF or SG gasoline rating also. Oils of the SF/SG type perform a variety of functions inside the engine in addition to their basic function as a lubricant. Through a balanced system of metallic detergents and polymeric dispersants, the oil prevents the formation of high and low temperature deposits and also keeps sludge and particles of dirt in suspension. Acids, particularly sulfuric acid, as well as other by-products of combustion, are neutralized. Both the SAE grade number and the API designation can be found on top of the oil can.

For recommended oil viscosities, refer to the chart.

✳✳WARNING

Non-detergent or straight mineral oils should not be used in your car.

Do not use engine oil additives, as today's oils perform all the tasks necessary to maintain the internal condition of the engine. Modern synthetic oils can provide additional engine protection due to the superior lubricating properties of these oils. Low friction synthetic oils are rated in the same way as standard oils, so all the guidelines, service and viscosity ratings used for standard oils apply to synthetics. Use low friction synthetic oils approved by BMW. Your dealer can provide you with an up to date list of approved synthetic low friction oils.

✳✳WARNING

Do not use low friction oils in the M5. Check with your BMW dealer for use of low friction oils in the M3. Use only a API SF, SAE 15W-40 or 15W-50 oil in these models.

FUEL

The use of a fuel too low in octane (a measurement of anti-knock quality) will result in spark knock. Since many factors such as altitude, terrain, air temperature and humidity affect operating efficiency, knocking may result even though the recommended fuel is being used. If persistent knocking occurs, it may be necessary to switch to a high grade of fuel. Continuous or heavy knocking may result in engine damage.

The use of 87 AKI (Anti Knock Index) gasoline is acceptable in the 535i, the 1991 525i, the 325iC and the 1991 325i. Use 90 AKI gasoline in all other vehicles. Note, these are minimum ratings and it is acceptable to use higher rated fuels. Always use a brand name, premium fuel.

Engine

OIL LEVEL CHECK

▶ **See Figures 37, 38 and 39**

The oil level must be checked on a regular basis. Running the engine low on oil may result in catastrophic engine failure at worst and lessened service life at best.

The most accurate oil level readings are done with the car level and with the oil cold, though it may be more convenient to check the oil at fill-ups with the engine warm. The level will read slightly higher with a warm engine once the oil has drained back into the crankcase, but the change will be minimal.

Every time you stop for fuel, check the engine oil as follows:
1. Make sure the car is parked on level ground.
2. Checking the oil immediately after stopping will lead to a false reading. Wait a few minutes after turning off the engine to allow the oil to drain back into the crankcase.

Fig. 37 Pulling the dipstick to check the oil

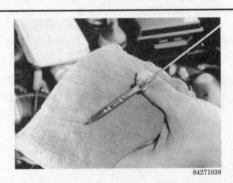

Fig. 38 The oil level should be between the 2 marks

Fig. 39 Adding oil through a funnel to prevent spills

3. Open the hood and locate the dipstick on the left side of the engine compartment. Pull the dipstick from its tube, wipe it clean and then reinsert it.

4. Pull the dipstick out again and, holding it horizontally, read the oil level. The oil should be between the 2 marks on the dipstick. If the oil is below the upper mark, but still above the lower mark, the level is acceptable. When the oil has reached the lower mark, add oil of the proper viscosity through the capped opening in the top of the cylinder head cover.

5. Replace the dipstick and check the oil level again after adding any oil. Be careful not to overfill the crankcase. Approximately 1.1 quarts (1 liter) of oil will raise the level from the lower mark to the upper mark. Excess oil will generally be consumed at an accelerated rate and can damage the engine or at the least increase the output of pollutants..

OIL AND FILTER CHANGE

BMW cars can be equipped with 2 styles of oil filter. One is the familiar spin-on cartridge type and the other is a housing enclosed full flow element. The types are easy to identify. If there is a cast aluminum housing with a bolt through the top center, towards the front of the engine, it is the full flow element type. The spin-on cartridge type is easy to recognize on the side of the engine block.

Use only a BMW approved filter or its commercial market equivalent. Use only a high grade filter as it is there to protect a high grade engine. Some low grade filters do not fit correctly and may cause the filter housing not to seal correctly. Always use new O-rings when changing the oil filter and replace the oil pan plug crush washer.

Spin-On Cartridge

▶ **See Figures 40, 41, 42 and 43**

Prolonged and repeated skin contact with used engine oil, with no effort to remove the oil, may be harmful. Always follows these simple precautions when handling used motor oil: 1. Avoid prolonged skin contact with used motor oil.   2. Remove oil from skin by washing thoroughly with soap and water or waterless hand cleaner. Do not use gasoline, thinners or other solvents.   3. Avoid prolonged skin contact with oil-soaked clothing.

1. Run the engine until it reaches normal operating temperature.

2. Jack up the front of the car and support it on safety stands.

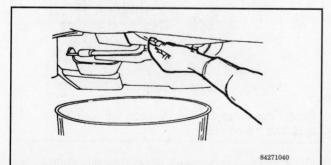

Fig. 40 Keep an inward pressure as you remove the drain plug to keep oil from leaking out of the threads

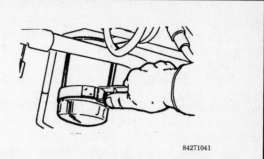

Fig. 41 Use a strap wrench to ease the removal of the old oil filter

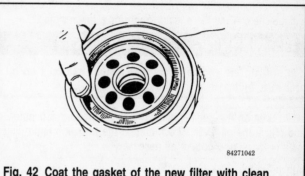

Fig. 42 Coat the gasket of the new filter with clean engine oil

Fig. 43 Install the new filter by hand only. Do not use a wrench

3. Slide a drain pan of at least 150% of the capacity of the oil sump under the oil pan.

4. Loosen the drain plug with a proper sized wrench. It normally will be 17mm or 19mm. Turn the plug out by hand. By keeping an inward pressure on the plug as you unscrew it, oil won't escape past the threads and you can remove it without being burned by hot oil.

5. Allow the oil to drain completely and then install the drain plug with a new crush washer. Don't overtighten the plug, or you'll be buying a new pan or a trick replacement plug for stripped threads. Torque the 17mm plug to 22-26 ft. lbs. (30-36 Nm). Torque the 19mm plug to 43-46 ft. lbs. (59-64 Nm)

6. Using a strap wrench, remove the oil filter. Keep in mind that it's holding about 1 quart of dirty, hot oil.

7. Empty the old filter into the drain pan and dispose of the filter.

8. Using a clean rag, wipe off the filter adapter on the engine block. Be sure that the rag doesn't leave any lint which could clog an oil passage.

9. Coat the rubber gasket on the filter with fresh oil. Fill the oil filter with fresh oil as much as possible. Spin it onto the engine by hand; when the gasket touches the adapter surface, give it another ¹/₂-³/₄ turn or as printed on the filter housing. No more, or you'll squash the gasket and it will leak.

10. Refill the engine with the correct amount of fresh oil. See the 'Capacities' chart.

11. Check the oil level on the dipstick. It is normal for the level to be a bit above the full mark. Start the engine and allow it to run at 2500 rpm for a few seconds until the oil lamp extinguishes. Allow the engine to run for a few minutes.

✳✳WARNING

Do not run the engine under load until it has built up oil pressure, indicated when the oil light goes out.

12. Shut off the engine, allow the oil to drain for a minute, and check the oil level. Check around the filter and drain plug for any leaks, and correct as necessary.

Full Flow Element

◆ **See Figures 44, 45, 46 and 47**

Prolonged and repeated skin contact with used engine oil, with no effort to remove the oil, may be harmful. Always follows these simple precautions when handling used motor oil: 1. Avoid prolonged skin contact with used motor oil. 2. Remove oil from skin by washing thoroughly with soap and water or waterless hand cleaner. Do not use gasoline, thinners or other solvents. 3. Avoid prolonged skin contact with oil-soaked clothing.

1. Run the engine until it reaches normal operating temperature.

2. Jack up the front of the car and support it on safety stands.

3. Loosen the oil filter housing bolt with a wrench. The oil in the housing will drain into the oil pan.

4. Remove the cover from the housing. Remove the old O-rings from the bolt and the filter cover. Check that the filter cover O-ring did not stick to the filter housing.

5. Remove the filter element from the housing. Allow the excess oil to drain from the element into the drain pan. Dispose of the element properly.

6. Slide a drain pan of at least 150% of the capacity of the oil sump under the oil pan.

7. Loosen the drain plug with a proper sized wrench. It normally will be 17mm or 19mm. Turn the plug out by hand. By keeping an inward pressure on the plug as you unscrew it, oil won't escape past the threads and you can remove it without being burned by hot oil.

8. Allow the oil to drain completely and then install the drain plug with a new crush washer. Don't overtighten the plug, or you'll by buying a new pan or a trick replacement plug for stripped threads. Torque the 17mm plug to 22-26 ft. lbs. (30-36 Nm). Torque the 19mm plug to 43-46 ft. lbs. (59-64 Nm)

Fig. 44 Removing the bolt to loosen the oil filter housing cover

Fig. 45 Removing the bolt will allow the oil to drain back into the oil pan

9. Place the new element in the filter housing, correct side up. It should be marked on the filter element.

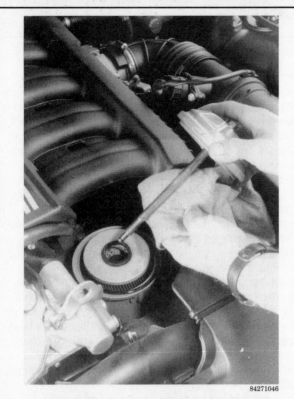

Fig. 46 Be careful not to lose the O-ring seals

Fig. 47 Allow the filter to drain before removing to prevent spills

10. Coat the O-rings with fresh oil and install the housing cover. Torque the bolt to 20-24 ft. lbs. (27-33 Nm).

11. Refill the engine with the correct amount of fresh oil. See the 'Capacities' chart.

12. Check the oil level on the dipstick. It is normal for the level to be a bit above the full mark. Start the engine and allow it to run at 2500 rpm for a few seconds until the oil lamp extinguishes. Allow the engine to run for a few minutes.

✳✳WARNING

Do not run the engine under load until it has built up oil pressure, indicated when the oil light goes out.

13. Shut off the engine, allow the oil to drain for a minute, and check the oil level. Check around the filter and drain plug for any leaks, and correct as necessary.

Manual Transmission

FLUID RECOMMENDATIONS

BMW recommends the use of non-hypoid GL4 SAE 80 in all models except the M5 and the 1993 318i and 325i. In the M5 and 1993 318i and 325i, use Dexron®II ATF.

➡Due to running production changes, the lubricant in your transmission may be a different type than what is listed here or in your owners manual. The recommended fluid for the transmission installed in your vehicle will be specified on a tag on the transmission body.

Synthetics can offer easier shifting in cold weather and greater protection from wear, but can sometimes cause noisier operation and they may not be compatible with all transmissions. If you wish to use a synthetic manual transmission lubricant, check with your BMW dealer for suggestions and details.

LEVEL CHECK

▶ See Figure 48

1. With the car parked on a level surface or raised and supported in a level position, remove the filler plug from the side of the transmission housing.

2. If the lubricant begins to trickle out of the hole, there is enough and you need not go any further. Otherwise, carefully

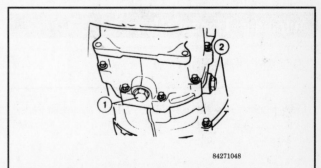

Fig. 48 Remove fill plug 2 before drain plug 1 when checking the manual transmission lubricant level

insert your finger (watch out for sharp threads) and check to see if the lubricant is up to the edge of the hole.

3. If not, add lubricant through the hole until the level is at the edge of the hole. Most gear lubricants come in a plastic squeeze bottle with a nozzle; making additions simple. You can also use a common kitchen baster. Use standard non hypoid-type gear oil — SAE 80 in all models except the M5 and the 1993 318i and 325i. In the M5 and 1993 318i and 325i use Dexron®II ATF.

➡Due to running production changes, the lubricant in your transmission may be a different type than what is listed here or in your owners manual. The recommended fluid for the transmission installed in your vehicle will be specified on a tag on the transmission body.

4. Replace the filler plug, run the engine and check for leaks.

DRAIN AND REFILL

1. The lubricant must be hot before it is drained. Drive the car until the engine reaches normal operating temperature.

2. Remove the filler plug to provide a vent. Be sure to remove this first. If the fluid is drained and trouble is encountered removing the fill plug, the car will be out of service until a method to remove the stuck fill plug is found.

3. Place a large container underneath the transmission and then remove the 17mm drain plug.

4. Allow the lubricant to drain completely. Clean the magnetic drain plug of any excessive metal particles and replace it; tighten it until it is just snug.

5. Fill the transmission with standard API GL4 non hypoid-type gear oil — SAE 80W in all models except the M5 and the 1993 318i and 325i. In the M5 and 1993 318i and 325i use Dexron®II ATF. Refer to the 'Capacities' chart for the correct amount of lubricant.

➡Due to running production changes, the lubricant in your transmission may be a different type than what is listed here or in your owners manual. The recommended fluid for the transmission installed in your vehicle will be specified on a tag on the transmission body.

6. When the lubricant level is up to the edge of the filler hole, replace the filler plug. Drive the car for a few minutes, stop, and check for any leaks.

Automatic Transmission

FLUID RECOMMENDATION

BMW recommends the use of DEXRON®II automatic transmission fluid (ATF). Check the level at Inspections as indicated by the Service Indicator.

FLUID LEVEL CHECK

▶ **See Figure 49**

Most of us are familiar with the ATF dipstick found at the back of the engine compartment. On some BMW vehicles, use of the dipstick has been discontinued. The transmission fluid is checked and added through a pipe plug on the side of the transmission sump pan. The procedure to check and change the fluid is similar to that of a manual transmission equipped vehicle.

Check the automatic transmission fluid level at Inspection intervals. The dipstick can be found in the rear of the engine compartment. The fluid level should be checked only when transmission is hot (normal operating temperature). The transmission is considered hot after about 20 miles (30 km) of highway driving.

1. Park the car on a level surface with the engine idling. Shift the transmission into Neutral and set the parking brake.

2. Remove the dipstick, wipe it clean and then reinsert it firmly. some models have locking dipsticks that require the top of the dipstick to be tilted to unlock. Be sure that it has been pushed all the way in. Remove the dipstick again and check the fluid level while holding it horizontally. With the engine running, the fluid level should be between the 2 marks on the dipstick.

3. If the fluid level is below the second mark, add DEXRON®II automatic transmission fluid through the dipstick tube. This is easily done with the aid of a funnel. Check the level often as you are filling the transmission. Be extremely careful not to overfill it. Overfilling will cause slippage, seal damage and overheating. Approximately one pint of ATF will raise the fluid level from one mark to the other.

➡Always use DEXRON®II ATF. The use of ATF Type F or any other fluid will cause severe damage to the transmission. The fluid on the dipstick should always be a bright red color, If it is discolored (brown or black) or smells burnt, serious transmission troubles, probably due to overheating, should be suspected. The transmission should be inspected by a qualified technician to locate the cause of the burnt fluid.

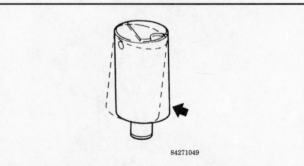

84271049

Fig. 49 Tilt the top of the automatic transmission dipstick to unlock

DRAIN AND REFILL

▶ **See Figures 50 and 51**

1. Raise and safely support the vehicle in a level plane. Place a drain pan under the transmission sump. Remove the dipstick on vehicles so equipped. On vehicles with locking dipsticks, tilt the top of the dipstick to unlock.

2. Loosen and remove the oil filler tube from the sump pan if not equipped with a drain plug. Be ready to catch fluid as it drains.

3. Remove the sump pan drain plug and catch the draining fluid.

4. Attach the oil filler tube, if disconnected, and torque to 71 ft. lbs. (98 Nm).

5. Replace the gasket or crush washer on the drain plug and torque to 11-12 ft. lbs. (15-17 Nm) for transmissions with

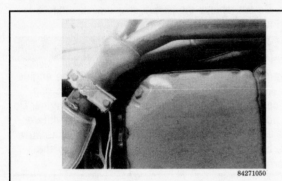

84271050

Fig. 50 Automatic transmission drain plug

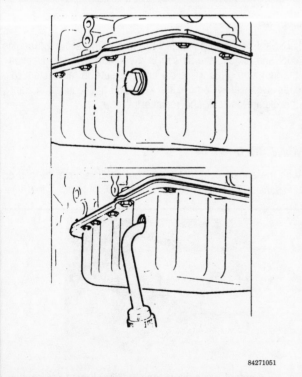

84271051

Fig. 51 Automatic transmission fill plug when not equipped with a dipstick

an M10 drain plug or 29-33 ft. lbs. (40-46 Nm) for transmissions with an M18 drain plug.

6. Fill the transmission with the proper amount of DEXRON®II automatic transmission fluid through the dipstick tube on vehicles with dipsticks or through the fill plug on transmissions without a dipstick. The transmission will take approximately 3.2 quarts (3.0 liters) of ATF.

7. Check the fluid level once completed.

PAN AND FILTER SERVICE

1. Raise and safely support the vehicle in a level plane. Place a drain pan under the transmission sump. Remove the dipstick on vehicles so equipped. On vehicles with locking dipsticks, tilt the top of the dipstick to unlock.

2. Loosen and remove the oil filler tube from the sump pan if not equipped with a drain plug. Be ready to catch fluid as it drains.

3. Remove the sump pan drain plug and catch the draining fluid.

4. Note the positions of the pan holder at each bolt and loosen and remove the bolts.

5. Remove the pan and gasket. Remove the screws from the filter. Note their positions. Check that the O-ring from the filter did not stick to the transmission valve body.

6. Install the new filter and O-ring. Replace the screws in their original positions.

7. Clean the pan and magnets. Replace the pan gasket and install the pan on the transmission. Replace the pan holders and bolts at their original positions. Torque to 4.5-5.0 ft. lbs. (6-7 Nm).

8. Attach the oil filler tube, if disconnected, and torque to 71 ft. lbs. (98 Nm).

9. Replace the gasket or crush washer on the drain plug and torque to 11-12 ft. lbs. (15-17 Nm) for transmissions with a M10 drain plug or 29-33 ft. lbs. (40-46 Nm) for transmissions with a M18 drain plug.

10. Fill the transmission with the proper amount of DEXRON®II automatic transmission fluid through the dipstick tube on vehicles with dipsticks or through the fill plug on transmissions without a dipstick. The transmission will take approximately 3.2 quarts (3.0 liters) of ATF.

11. Check the fluid level once completed.

Transfer Case

FLUID RECOMMENDATION

The transfer case contains 0.53 quarts (0.5 liters) of DEXRON®II ATF. This is the factory recommended fluid to use in the transfer case.

LEVEL CHECK

Remove the filler plug on the side of the transfer case. The fluid should be level with the bottom of the filler plug hole.

Torque M14 and M24 plugs to 22-25 ft. lbs. (30-35 Nm).
Torque M18 plugs to 14-18 ft. lbs. (20-25 Nm).

DRAIN AND REFILL

The transfer case has a drain plug that is removed to drain the fluid. To fill the transfer case, open the filler plug located on the top edge of the case and add the fluid. The fluid should flow from the filler hole when it is full. Torque M14 and M24 plugs to 22-25 ft. lbs. (30-35 Nm). Torque M18 plugs to 14-18 ft. lbs. (20-25 Nm).

Drive Axle

LEVEL CHECK

Front and Rear Axles

1. With the car on a level surface, remove the filler plug from the side of the differential.
2. If the oil begins to trickle out of the hole, there is enough. Otherwise, carefully insert your finger (watch out for sharp threads) into the hole and check that the oil is up to the bottom edge of the filler hole.
3. If not, add oil through the hole until the level is at the edge of the hole. Most gear oils come in a plastic squeeze bottle with a nozzle; making additions is simple. You can also use a common kitchen baster. Use only standard GL-5 hypoid-type gear oil, SAE 90.

DRAIN AND REFILL

1. Park the car on a level surface and set the parking brake.
2. Remove the filler plug.
3. Place a large container underneath the rear axle. Remove the drain plug at the bottom of the differential and allow all lubricant to drain into the pan.
4. When all lubricant has drained out, clean and replace the drain plug. Use a new crush washer. Torque to 40 ft. lbs. (55 Nm) on the rear axle and 14 ft. lbs. (20 Nm) on the front axle.
5. Refill with GL-5 hypoid-type gear oil, SAE 90 until it runs out of the fill hole. Replace the filler plug and torque to 40 ft. lbs. (55 Nm). Run the car and check for leaks.

Cooling System

BMW recommends that the coolant be changed every 2 years. Collect your used coolant in a clean pan, do not allow any other fluids to mix with it, and return it to a recycling facility or shop. Do not drain the coolant on the ground or pour it into a sewer.

FLUID RECOMMENDATIONS

BMW recommends that an ethylene glycol based antifreeze coolant be used. Stay with a name brand that is compatible with aluminum and is nitrate and amino free. The coolant should be a 50/50 mix to achieve protection to -35°F. (-37°C.). Any concentration in excess of 50/50 will actually reduce the effectiveness of the fluid as a heat transfer medium.

LEVEL CHECK

▶ **See Figures 52, 53 and 54**

BMW vehicles are equipped with translucent coolant expansion tanks. There will be marks indicating 'MAX' and/or 'COLD' levels. There is no need to remove the fill cap from the expansion tank. Do not remove the fill cap unless coolant needs to be added to the system.

✳✳CAUTION

Do not remove the expansion tank fill cap with the engine still hot. Allow the engine to cool, then remove the cap. Coolant can ignite if spilled onto an overheated engine. Do not add coolant to a hot engine. The temperature differential between the hot metal and the cold coolant can cause warpage, boiling splash back and other damage to the engine or personal injury.

ADDING COOLANT

Except M5

If coolant needs to be added to the system, allow the engine to cool and remove the fill cap in a counterclockwise direction to the first stop. This will allow any pressure in the system to escape. Completely remove the cap, add the required coolant to the expansion tank and replace the cap.

M5

ENGINE COLD

With the engine cold, not warm, but cold, remove the cap on the expansion tank and top up to the 'COLD' mark. If the

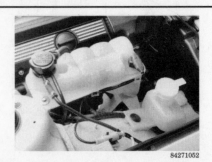

Fig. 52 Coolant expansion tank is translucent for easy level checks

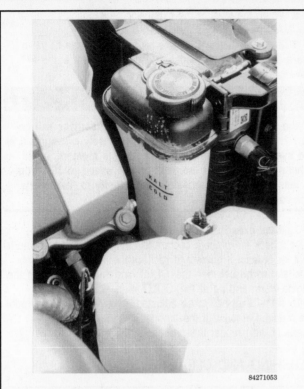

Fig. 53 Integral coolant expansion tank is translucent for easy level checks

Fig. 54 Bleeder is located next to radiator cap. Check the radiator cap gaskets when removed

system required more than 1.1 quarts (1 liter), follow the Engine Warm procedure.

ENGINE WARM

If the engine is warm with the temperature gauge reading in the lower third of its range, follow this procedure. Do not attempt to fill the system until the temperature gauge is reading in the lower third of its range.

✳✳CAUTION

The M5 cooling system is a pressurized system and requires a specific method of adding coolant. If the fill cap is removed while the engine is still warm, above the one third mark on the temperature gauge, a risk of scalding and severe burns exists.

1. Allow the engine to cool until the temperature gauge is in the lower third of its range.
2. Turn the cap counterclockwise to the first stop and allow any pressure to escape. Remove the cap fully.
3. Fill the expansion tank to the 'MAX' marking.
4. Start the engine and press the side and window defroster button on the climate control panel.
5. Loosen the cooling system bleeder valve located near the remote positive battery connection. Allow any air to escape and tighten.
6. Refill the expansion tank to the 'MAX' mark and run the engine at 2500 rpm.
7. When the level in the expansion tank steadies itself at the 'MAX' mark, replace the fill cap.
8. If the expansion tank is equipped with an air fill valve, use a tire pump to pressurize the cooling system at the fill valve on the expansion tank to 7 psi (0.5 bar).

✳✳WARNING

If the system is not pressurized, engine damage will occur. The system is designed to be precisely pressurized. If the system cannot be pressurized at the moment, avoid driving the vehicle or limit the engine speed to 3000 rpm or less until the first possible opportunity to restore the pressure.

9. If the expansion tank is not equipped with an air fill valve, check the present coolant level, then allow the engine to cool for at least 6 hours and recheck the level. The coolant level should be between the 'COLD' and 'MAX' marks with the engine warm and be at the 'COLD' mark when cold.
10. If the level has to be adjusted, remove the cap and add the required amount. If the amount was in excess of 1.1 quarts (1 liter) repeat this procedure.

DRAIN AND REFILL

1. Allow the engine to cool completely. Turn the cap counterclockwise to the first stop and allow any pressure to escape. Remove the cap fully.
2. Loosen the bleeder screw on the radiator on vehicles with integrally mounted expansion tanks.
3. Remove the splash shield from under the vehicle to access the radiator drain plug.

4. Remove the drain plug and catch the used coolant in a clean container. Return the used coolant to a recycling facility or shop.

5. Replace the drain plug and tighten to 1.1-1.9 ft. lbs. (1.5-3.0 Nm).

6. Add a 50/50 mix of coolant to the expansion tank and bleed the system.

SYSTEM BLEEDING

The cooling system must be bled to remove air from the coolant passages. If the system is not bled, hot spots can form leading to overheating and engine damage.

INTEGRAL EXPANSION TANK SYSTEMS

These systems have the expansion tank as part of the radiator assembly. It is the vertically mounted, translucent tank on the side of the radiator.

1. With the expansion tank filled with coolant mix, run the engine to operating temperature. Set the heater controls to WARM and engine speed to fast idle.

2. Loosen the radiator mounted bleeder screw. Allow coolant to run out of the bleeder until a solid stream of coolant and no air is coming out. Keep the expansion tank full during this step. Tighten the bleeder screw.

3. Turn OFF the engine, but keep the ignition switch in the **ON** position. On vehicles with a thermostat housing bleeder screw, open the screw and allow coolant to run out of the bleeder until a solid stream of coolant and no air is coming out. Keep the expansion tank full during this step. Tighten the bleeder screw to 4.5-7.0 ft lbs. (6-10 Nm).

4. Start the engine and run at 2500 rpm. The coolant level will drop to the 'COLD' mark on the expansion tank or close to it, indicating that residual air has been purged from the system.

5. Replace the expansion tank cap.

REMOTE EXPANSION TANK SYSTEMS

EXCEPT M5

1. With the expansion tank filled with coolant mix, run the engine to operating temperature. Set the heater controls to WARM and engine speed to fast idle.

2. Loosen the thermostat housing mounted bleeder screw. Allow coolant to run out of the bleeder until a solid stream of coolant and no air is coming out. Do not allow the expansion tank to run dry during this step. Tighten the bleeder screw to 4.5-7.0 ft lbs. (6-10 Nm).

3. Fill the expansion tank to the 'COLD' mark. Replace the tank cap.

M5

1. Fill the expansion tank to the 'MAX' marking.

2. Start the engine and press the side and window defroster button on the climate control panel.

3. Loosen the cooling system bleeder valve located near the remote positive battery connection. Allow any air to escape and tighten.

4. Refill the expansion tank to the 'MAX' mark and run the engine at 2500 rpm.

5. When the level in the expansion tank steadies itself at the 'MAX' mark, replace the fill cap.

6. If the expansion tank is equipped with an air fill valve use a tire pump to pressurize the cooling system at the fill valve on the expansion tank to 7 psi (0.5 bar).

❄❄WARNING

If the system is not pressurized, engine damage will occur. The system is designed to be precisely pressurized. If the system cannot be pressurized at the moment, avoid driving the vehicle or limit the engine speed to 3000 rpm or less until the first possible opportunity to restore the pressure.

7. If the expansion tank is not equipped with an air fill valve, check the present coolant level, then allow the engine to cool for at least 6 hours and recheck the level. The coolant level should be between the 'COLD' and 'MAX' marks with the engine warm and be at the 'COLD' mark when cold.

8. If the level has to be adjusted, remove the cap and add the required amount. If the amount was in excess of 1.1 quarts (1 liter) repeat this procedure.

FLUSHING AND CLEANING

With the use of electrically actuated heater valves and bi-zone heater cores, it is not easy or advisable to cut hoses to mount a flushing tee. Drain the system, add clear water, bleed the system and run the engine to flush the system of old coolant. Drain the system, add fresh coolant and bleed the system. This will get rid of most of the old coolant and keep the cooling system in good shape. It is important to change the coolant on a regular basis, every 2 years, as this will prevent corrosion from building up and creating the need for cleaning the cooling system.

Clutch and Brake Master Cylinder

The clutch and brake master cylinders share a fluid reservoir. Note that a leaking clutch slave or master cylinder will lower the reservoir level just as easily as a leaking brake hydraulic system.

BMW recommends that the brake fluid be changed and the system bled every 2 years. It may be wise to increase that interval to once a year for increased protection from hydraulic system damage. If the vehicle is used for sporting purposes, it is wise to change the fluid after each event.

FLUID RECOMMENDATION

Use only high quality, name brand DOT 4 brake fluid. Use tightly sealed small containers to refill the reservoir. Large containers offer a false economy. A large container that has been opened will absorb moisture and ruin the fluid. Only use large containers when performing major work on the brake or clutch hydraulic systems and the entire contents will be used at once.

Tightly cap any container to prevent moisture from being absorbed into the brake fluid.

LEVEL CHECK

▶ **See Figure 55**

Wipe the reservoir cap and surrounding area clean. Make sure the level is up to the full marker (the reservoir is translucent). If necessary, add DOT 4 specification fluid that is brand new (do not attempt to reuse fluid). Be careful not to drop any dirt into the fluid, and avoid spilling fluid on the paint work, or wipe it up immediately if it spills.

Power Steering

FLUID RECOMMENDATIONS

All vehicles except the M5 use automatic transmission fluid (ATF) as the power steering fluid. Use DEXRON®II type ATF.

The M5 has a self leveling suspension that shares a hydraulic fluid reservoir with the power steering system. Use the hydraulic fluid printed on the reservoir. DO NOT use ATF, brake fluid or engine oil.

LEVEL CHECK

▶ **See Figures 56 and 57**

On vehicles other than the M5, stop the engine and remove the dipstick from the power steering reservoir. The dipstick is part of the reservoir cap and is removed by turning the cap. Wipe the dipstick and replace in the reservoir. Remove and check the level. Check that the level is between the marks on the dipstick and add fluid as necessary. Run the engine and recheck the fluid level. With the engine not running, the fluid level may rise above the marks on the dipstick, but this is normal.

On the M5, stop the engine and remove the top of the reservoir. Press and release the brake pedal until the fluid level stops rising. It may take 10 or more pumps. The level of the fluid should be 0.4 in. (10mm) from the top of the reservoir. Add the proper hydraulic fluid as printed on the reservoir. If the vehicle is loaded, do not fill totally to the top. Screw the reservoir top in place.

Fig. 55 Brake fluid level should be between the MIN and MAX marks

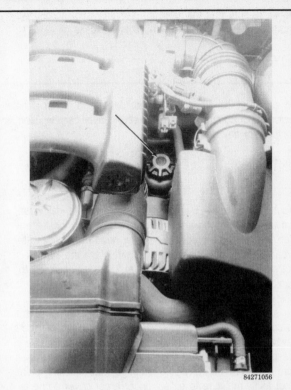

Fig. 56 Power steering fluid reservoir with the dipstick as part of the cap

Fig. 57 Power steering and self leveling system hydraulic fluid reservoir

Body Maintenance and Lubrication

LOCK CYLINDERS

Apply graphite lubricant sparingly through the key slot. Insert the key and operate the lock several times to be sure that the lubricant is worked into the lock cylinder.

DOOR HINGES, LATCHES, STRIKERS AND CATCHES

Spray a light oil lubricant on the hinge pivot points to eliminate any binding conditions. Open and close the door several times to be sure that the lubricant is evenly and thoroughly distributed. Wipe the joint to remove any excess oil.

BODY DRAIN HOLES

Be sure that the drain holes in the doors and rocker panels are cleared of obstruction. A small screwdriver can be used to clear them of any debris.

PAINT

Wash the car either by hand or in an automatic car wash. Rinse the car first with a light stream of water to loosen any dirt on the painted surfaces. Soak any dead bugs with water and car washing solution, then wipe off. Wash the car out of direct sunlight as waterspots can form if water is allowed to evaporate from the painted surfaces.

Use only waxes with carnauba or synthetic formulations. Keep a good coat of wax on the car to protect the surface from contaminants. Use only high quality paint care products as available through your dealer or specialty boutique.

Wash the car often in the winter months to keep road salt off the car. Touch up any paint damage with matching paint. Do not allow moisture to collect under a car cover if one is used.

UNDERHOOD

The engine compartment should be cleaned and treated once a year. This will clean away any accumulated dirt, grease and oil that may be hiding leaks or other problems. A clean engine runs cooler and makes routine maintenance more pleasurable.

GLASS

Interior glass surfaces can be cleaned with a commercial cleaner or a one to one mixture of water and white vinegar. Do not use any cleaner containing an abrasive. Exterior glass and lenses can be cleaned with water and car washing solution or with the same mixture used for the interior glass.

RUBBER SEALS AND TRIM

Clean with water and treat with silicone spray. A commercial rubber treatment can also be used. Do not use harsh solvents as these will damage the rubber.

SEATBELTS

Wash the seatbelts with soap and water. Keep the seatbelts fully extended until they dry completely. Never allow the seatbelts to retract while still wet.

UPHOLSTERY

Use a product designed for the seating surfaces your car has. If you have a cloth interior, brush the nap of the fabric after cleaning to restore the pile. Wipe down leather seats with a wool or cotton cloth that is slightly moist. Dry the leather and treat it with a leather care product.

TRAILER TOWING

BMW of North America does not recommend using your BMW to tow trailers. In Europe, towing equipment is made available for various BMW models, but due to regulatory and litigious matters, BMW NA has chosen not to recommend trailer towing.

PUSHING AND TOWING

If your car needs to be towed, the best method is by flatbed. The risk of body damage or drive axle and transmission damage is reduced by using a flatbed. If a flatbed is not available, have the car towed by a wheel lift type tow truck. Do not tow the vehicle with a bumper lift type tow truck or severe damage to the bodywork will occur.

If the car is equipped with automatic transmission, a few special precautions must be taken to prevent the transmission from being damaged. The car must be towed with the selector lever in the **NEUTRAL** position. The car may be towed a maximum distance of 30 miles (50 km) at a maximum towing speed of 25-30 mph. If the car must be towed a greater distance then stated above, either the driveshaft must be disconnected or an additional 2.1 pts. of DEXRON®II must be added to the transmission (to be drained immediately after towing).

If the vehicle needs to be pulled out of mud or sand, use a nylon tow strap to pull the vehicle out. All vehicles are equipped with tow eyes or attachment points for screw-in tow eyes. The screw-in tow eye is located in the toolkit. The tow eyes or attachment points are located behind panels in the front and back of the vehicle. Pry the panel off to expose the tow eye or attachment point. Screw in the tow eye fully and tightly. Do not tow with the tow eye loose.

It is recommended not to push your BMW. Due to height differences in bumpers and the possibility of damaging the energy absorption bumper, do not push your car.

JACKING

Do not use the tire changing jack to work on the vehicle. Use a hydraulic floor jack rated for the weight of the vehicle. BMW supplies a wheel chock with each vehicle. Use the wheel chock whenever raising the car.

The vehicle should be jacked up only using the factory jacking points. The jacking points along the rocker panel are marked with indents in the metal. Chock the wheel opposite the corner being raised. Pad the jack saddle with a rubber pad or a block of wood. Use jackstands to support the car. Do not go under the car with the car supported only by the jack.

On the E36 3 series, the jacking points for a garage jack are located directly below the openings for the tire changing jack and are raised platforms on the underside of the body.

✳✳CAUTION

The car must be secure on the jack and the jackstands at all times during the lifting phase or when stationary. If the car is not stable and secure, the car may fall, damaging the vehicle and causing personal injury or death.

TORQUE SPECIFICATIONS

Component	U.S.	Metric
Automatic transmission oil filler tube	71 ft. lbs.	98Nm
Automatic transmission oil pan bolts	4.5–5.0 ft. lbs.	6–7 Nm
Front axle drain plug	14 ft. lbs.	20 Nm
Front axle fill plug	40 ft. lbs.	55 Nm
Lug bolts	81 ft. lbs.	110 Nm
Manual transmission drain plug		
M10:	11–12 ft. lbs.	15–17 Nm
M18:	29–33 ft. lbs.	40–46 Nm
Oil pan drain plug		
17mm:	22–26 ft. lbs.	30–36 Nm
19mm:	43–46 ft. lbs.	59–64 Nm
Oil filter housing cover	20–24 ft. lbs.	27–33 Nm
Radiator drain plug	1.1–1.9 ft. lbs.	1.5–3.0 Nm
Rear axle drain plug	40 ft. lbs.	55 Nm
Rear axle fill plugs	40 ft. lbs.	55 Nm
Thermostat housing bleeder screw	4.5–7.0 ft. lbs.	6–10 Nm
Transfer case drain and fill plugs		
M14:	22–25 ft. lbs.	30–35 Nm
M18:	14–18 ft. lbs.	20–25 Nm
M24:	22–25 ft. lbs.	30–35 Nm
Wheel air vane ring bolts		
M5:	6 ft. lbs.	8 Nm

84271061

CAPACITIES

Year	Model	Engine ID/VIN	Engine Displacement Liters (cc)	Engine Crankcase with Filter (qts.)	Transmission (pts.)			Transfer Case (pts.)	Drive Axle (pts.)		Fuel Tank (gal.)	Cooling System (qts.)
					4-Spd	5-Spd	Auto.		Front	Rear		
1989	325i	M20B25	2.5 (2494)	4.5	—	2.6	6.4	—	—	3.6	16.4	11.0
	325iC	M20B25	2.5 (2494)	4.5	—	2.6	6.4	—	—	3.6	16.4	11.0
	325iX	M20B25	2.5 (2494)	4.5	—	2.6	6.4	2	1.5	3.6	16.4	11.0
	M3	S14B23	2.3 (2302)	4.6	—	3.0	—	—	—	3.6	14.5	10.0
	525i	M20B25	2.5 (2494)	5.0	—	2.6	6.4	—	—	3.6	21.1	10.6
	535i	M30B35	3.5 (3430)	6.1	—	2.6	6.4	—	—	4.0	21.1	12.7
1990	325i	M20B25	2.5 (2494)	4.5	—	2.6	6.4	—	—	3.6	16.4	11.0
	325iC	M20B25	2.5 (2494)	4.5	—	2.6	6.4	—	—	3.6	16.4	11.0
	325iX	M20B25	2.5 (2494)	4.5	—	2.6	6.4	2	1.5	3.6	16.4	11.0
	M3	S14B23	2.3 (2302)	4.6	—	3.0	—	—	—	3.6	14.5	10.0
	525i	M20B25	2.5 (2494)	5.0	—	2.6	6.4	—	—	3.6	21.1	11.0
	535i	M30B35	3.5 (3430)	6.1	—	2.6	6.4	—	—	4.0	21.1	12.7
1991	318i	M42B18	1.8 (1796)	5.26	—	2.5	—	—	—	1.9	14.5	6.9
	318iC	M42B18	1.8 (1796)	5.26	—	2.5	—	—	—	1.9	14.5	6.9
	318iS	M42B18	1.8 (1796)	5.26	—	2.5	—	—	—	1.9	14.5	6.9
	325i	M20B25	2.5 (2494)	4.5	—	2.6	6.4	—	—	3.6	16.4	11.0
	325iC	M20B25	2.5 (2494)	4.5	—	2.6	6.4	—	—	3.6	16.4	11.0
	325iX	M20B25	2.5 (2494)	4.5	—	2.6	6.4	2	1.5	3.6	16.4	11.0
	M3	S14B23	2.3 (2302)	4.6	—	3.0	—	—	—	3.6	14.5	10.0
	525i	M50B25	2.5 (2494)	6.1	—	2.2	6.4	—	—	3.6	21.4	11.0
	535i	M30B35	3.5 (3430)	6.1	—	2.6	6.4	—	—	4.0	21.4	12.7
	M5	S38B36	3.6 (3535)	6.1	—	2.6	—	—	—	4.0	21.4	14.0
1992-93	318i	M42B18	1.8 (1796)	5.26	—	2.5	6.4	—	—	2.5	17.0	6.9
	318iS	M42B18	1.8 (1796)	5.26	—	2.5	6.4	—	—	2.5	17.0	6.9
	318iC	M42B18	1.8 (1796)	5.26	—	2.5	—	—	—	1.9	14.5	6.9
	325i	M50B25	2.5 (2494)	6.9	—	2.5	6.4	—	—	3.6	17.0	11.1
	325iS	M50B25	2.5 (2494)	6.9	—	2.5	6.4	—	—	3.6	17.0	11.1
	325iC	M20B25	2.5 (2494)	4.5	—	2.6	6.4	—	—	3.6	16.4	11.0
	525i	M50B25	2.5 (2494)	6.1	—	2.2	6.4	—	—	3.6	21.4	11.7
	525iT	M50B25	2.5 (2494)	6.1	—	2.2	6.4	—	—	3.6	21.4	11.7
	535i	M30B35	3.5 (3430)	6.1	—	2.6	6.4	—	—	4.0	21.4	12.7
	M5	S38B36	3.6 (3535)	6.1	—	2.6	—	—	—	4.0	21.4	14.0

84271060

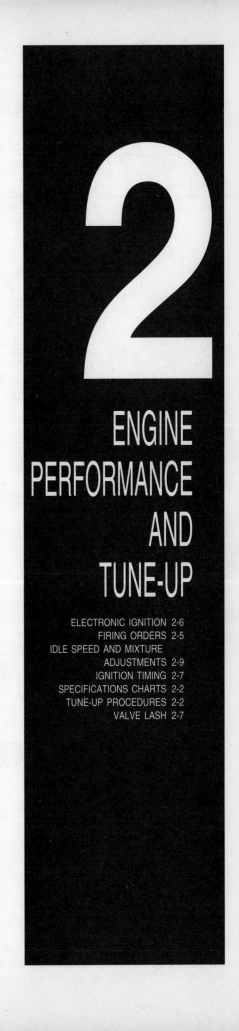

2

ENGINE PERFORMANCE AND TUNE-UP

TUNE-UP PROCEDURES

GASOLINE ENGINE TUNE-UP SPECIFICATIONS

Year	Engine ID/VIN	Engine Displacement Liters (cc)	Spark Plugs Gap (in.) ①	Ignition Timing (deg.)		Fuel Pump (psi)	Idle Speed (rpm)		Valve Clearance ③	
				MT	AT		MT	AT	In.	Ex.
1989	S14B23	2.3 (2302)	0.024	②	②	43	880	—	0.012	0.012
	M20B25	2.5 (2494)	0.027	②	②	43	760	760	0.010	0.010
	M30B35	3.5 (3430)	0.027	②	②	43	800	800	0.012	0.012
1990	S14B23	2.3 (2302)	0.024	②	②	43	880	—	0.012	0.012
	M20B25	2.5 (2494)	0.027	②	②	43	760	760	0.010	0.010
	M30B35	3.5 (3430)	0.027	②	②	43	800	800	0.012	0.012
1991	M42B18	1.8 (1796)	0.027	②	②	43	850	850	Hyd.	Hyd.
	S14B23	2.3 (2302)	0.024	②	②	43	880	—	0.012	0.012
	M20B25	2.5 (2494)	0.027	②	②	43	760	760	0.010	0.010
	M50B25	2.5 (2494)	0.027	②	②	50	700	700	Hyd.	Hyd.
	M30B35	3.5 (3430)	0.027	②	②	43	800	800	0.012	0.012
	S38B36	3.6 (3535)	0.024	②	②	43	970	—	0.012	0.012
1992–93	M42B18	1.8 (1796)	0.027	②	②	43	850	850	Hyd.	Hyd.
	M20B25	2.5 (2494)	0.027	②	②	43	760	760	0.010	0.010
	M50B25	2.5 (2494)	0.027	②	②	50	700	700	Hyd.	Hyd.
	M30B35	3.5 (3430)	0.027	②	②	43	800	800	0.012	0.012
	S38B36	3.6 (3535)	0.024	②	②	43	970	—	0.012	0.012

NOTE: The lowest cylinder pressure should be within 75% of the highest cylinder pressure reading. For example, if the highest cylinder is 134 psi, the lowest should be 101. Engine should be at normal operating temperature with throttle valve in the wide open position.
The underhood specifications sticker often reflects tune-up specification changes in production. Sticker figures must be used if they disagree with those in this chart.
Hyd.—Hydraulic
① With Triangle Ground Electrode—0.036 in.   ② Motronic Injection System—Refer to Underhood   ③ All Valve Specifications are with Engine Cold
     Emission Decal

84272024

The tune-up as once known is obsolete. With the present electronic engine controls, the need to manually adjust the operating parameters of the ignition system has been done away with. The Digital Motor Electronics (DME) engine control system your car is equipped with, monitors the operation of the engine with sensors and automatically adjusts the operating parameters as the engine runs. This leads to better fuel economy, less exhaust emissions and better engine performance. The days of adjusting timing, mixture and idle speed are over. The tune-up on your car consists of changing the spark plugs and inspecting the rest of the system.

Spark Plugs

REMOVAL & INSTALLATION

Except M50 and M42 Engines

1. Make sure the ignition is OFF. Replace one spark plug at a time, so as not to confuse which spark plug wires go on which spark plugs.
2. Pull spark plug wire off of the spark plug. Pull only on the boot; do not pull on the wire itself otherwise the wire and connector can be damaged.
3. Use a spark plug socket and extension, and place over the spark plug. Loosen the spark plug just a little. If compressed air is available, remove the spark plug socket and

blow out the spark plug hole. This will prevent dirt from falling into the engine, but is not necessary.
4. Remove the spark plug the rest of the way. Inspect the tip for signs of damage.
To install:
5. Gap the new plug if necessary. Some spark plugs come pregapped and should not be gapped. Lightly coat the threads of the spark plug with anti-seize compound, unless directed otherwise on the spark plug packaging.
6. Place the spark plug in the socket and place in the spark plug hole.
7. Turn the socket by hand until the spark plug seats. Do not use a wrench, to prevent crossthreading. The spark plug should thread in easily by hand. If it doesn't't, check the threads for dirt.
8. Using a torque wrench, tighten to 14-22 ft. lbs. (20-30 Nm). If a torque wrench is not available, tighten until the crush washer is felt to crush and the spark plug feels snug.
9. Replace the spark plug wire on the spark plug.

M50 Engine

▶ See Figures 1, 2, 3, 4, 5, 6, 7, 8, 9 and 10

1. Make sure the ignition is OFF. Remove the oil filler cap.
2. Remove the plugs from the valve cover cladding.
3. Remove the nuts securing the valve cover cladding and remove the cladding. Place a clean rag in the oil filler to prevent anything from falling in the engine. It may be necessary to remove the fuel injector rail cover to remove the clad-

Fig. 1 Removing the valve cover cladding plugs — M50 engine

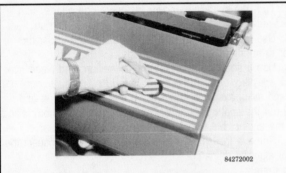

Fig. 2 Remove the plugs — M50 engine

Fig. 3 Removing the valve cover cladding mounting nuts — M50 engine

Fig. 4 Removing the valve cover cladding. Remove the oil filler cap first — M50 engine

Fig. 5 Coil packs exposed — M50 engine

Fig. 6 Flip down the coil pack connector locking bar — M50 engine

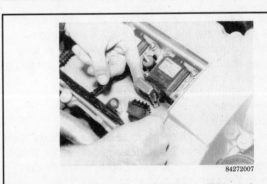

Fig. 7 Disconnecting the coil pack — M50 engine

Fig. 8 Removing the coil pack securing nuts — M50 engine

ding. The fuel injector rail cover is removed in the same method as the valve cover cladding.

4. Release the clips for the coil pack connectors.

5. Remove the nuts holding the coil packs.

6. Pull up to remove the coil packs and to expose the spark plug holes.

Fig. 9 Removing the coil pack by pulling up — M50 engine

Fig. 10 Removing the spark plug — M50 engine

7. Use a spark plug socket and extension, and place over the spark plug. Loosen the spark plug just a little. If compressed air is available, remove the spark plug socket and blow out the spark plug hole. This will prevent dirt from falling into the engine, but is not necessary.

8. Remove the spark plug the rest of the way. Inspect the tip for signs of damage.

To install:

9. Gap the new plug if necessary. Some spark plugs come pregapped and should not be gapped. Lightly coat the threads of the spark plug with anti-seize compound, unless directed otherwise on the spark plug packaging.

10. Place the spark plug in the socket and place in the spark plug hole.

11. Turn the socket by hand until the spark plug seats. Do not use a wrench, to prevent crossthreading. The spark plug should thread in easily by hand. If it doesn't't, check the threads for dirt.

12. Using a torque wrench, tighten to 14-22 ft. lbs. (20-30 Nm). If a torque wrench is not available, tighten until the crush washer is felt to crush and the spark plug feels snug.

13. Replace the coil packs on the spark plugs and tighten the nuts. Connect the harness connector and lock down the connector bar.

14. Replace the valve cover cladding and fuel injector rail cover. Replace the oil filler cap and the nuts securing the cladding. Replace the cladding plugs by snapping in.

M42 Engine

▶ **See Figures 11 and 12**

1. Make sure the ignition is OFF.

Fig. 12 Removing the spark plug wires with the supplied tool — M42 engine

2. Turn the spark plug cover fasteners one quarter turn clockwise and remove. Remove the cover by pulling up.

3. Use the spark plug wire pulling tool found under the cover to remove the spark plug leads.

4. Use a spark plug socket and extension, and place over the spark plug. Loosen the spark plug just a little. If compressed air is available, remove the spark plug socket and blow out the spark plug hole. This will prevent dirt from falling into the engine, but is not necessary.

5. Remove the spark plug the rest of the way. Inspect the tip for signs of damage.

To install:

6. Gap the new plug if necessary. Some spark plugs come pregapped and should not be gapped. Lightly coat the threads of the spark plug with anti-seize compound, unless directed otherwise on the spark plug packaging.

7. Place the spark plug in the socket and place in the spark plug hole.

8. Turn the socket by hand until the spark plug seats. Do not use a wrench, to prevent crossthreading. The spark plug should thread in easily by hand. If it doesn't, check the threads for dirt.

9. Using a torque wrench, tighten to 14-22 ft. lbs. (20-30 Nm). If a torque wrench is not available, tighten until the crush washer is felt to crush and the spark plug feels snug.

10. Replace the spark plug wire and press down to seat it. Snap the cover into place being sure to have replaced the spark plug wire pulling tool first.

11. Replace the cover fasteners and secure by turning one quarter turn counterclockwise.

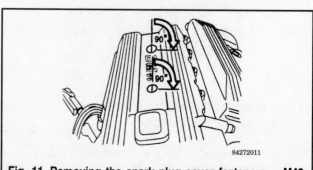

Fig. 11 Removing the spark plug cover fasteners — M42 engine

Spark Plug Wires

▶ See Figure 13

The spark plug wires are routed in a tube or ducting. The spark plug leads can be replaced as a unit with the tubing or individually. Unplug the spark plug wires at the distributor cap for engines with a distributor or at the coil pack on the M42 engine. The M50 engine has no spark plug wires as the coils sit directly on top of the spark plugs. Mark the leads as each one is disconnected to correctly refit the wires. Original equipment wires and distributor caps are marked with the cylinder number, making the installation easy.

Unclip the spark plug wire duct or tube and remove the wire. Replace the wire in the same routing as the old wire. Be sure

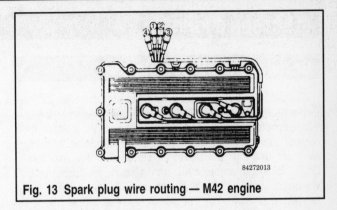

Fig. 13 Spark plug wire routing — M42 engine

to match the wire number with the distributor cap number or coil pack number. Snap the ducting or tubing together.

FIRING ORDERS

▶ See Figures 14, 15, 16 and 17

➡To avoid confusion, remove and tag the wires one at a time, for replacement.

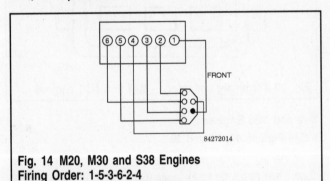

Fig. 14 M20, M30 and S38 Engines
Firing Order: 1-5-3-6-2-4
Distributor Rotation: Clockwise

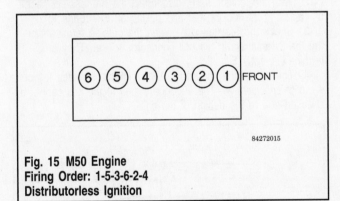

Fig. 15 M50 Engine
Firing Order: 1-5-3-6-2-4
Distributorless Ignition

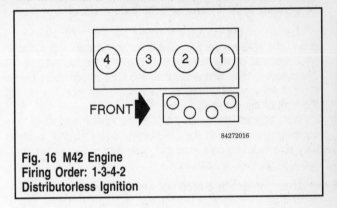

Fig. 16 M42 Engine
Firing Order: 1-3-4-2
Distributorless Ignition

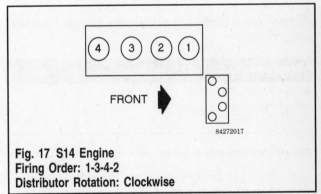

Fig. 17 S14 Engine
Firing Order: 1-3-4-2
Distributor Rotation: Clockwise

ELECTRONIC IGNITION

Description and Operation

All ignition and fuel injection functions are controlled by the Digital Motor Electronics (DME) control unit. Ignition timing is fully electronically controlled; there is no vacuum advance or manual adjustment. Ignition functions are calculated from internal maps and from the same sensors used for fuel injection. On vehicles with an automatic transmission, the control unit will retard ignition timing briefly when the transmission is about to shift up or down. For this reason, there is a data link between the DME control unit and the transmission control unit.

➡ **For complete testing of the Digital Motor Electronics (DME) system and sensors, refer to Section 4, Emission Controls. Descriptions and testing of the DME system will be covered under Electronic Engine Controls.**

Variations of this ignition system are used on different engines. The M42 engine uses distributorless ignition with a coil pack mounted on the inner fender. The M50 engine uses distributorless ignition with a coil mounted above each spark plug. Most of the remaining engines use a distributor mounted on the front of the camshaft.

On all engines, the primary side of the ignition system is completely contained in the DME control unit. Only the secondary side including coils, cap and rotor, high tension wires and spark plugs may be serviced.

➡ **Never connect or disconnect any ignition system or control unit wiring with the ignition switch ON. Never use an ohmmeter with the ignition switch ON. Improper test methods can instantly and permanently damage electronic components.**

Testing

IGNITION COIL

Except M42 and M50 Engines

1. With the ignition OFF, disconnect the ignition lead from the coil tower. Disconnect the primary wires from the screw terminals on the coil. Note that the terminals are marked with a 1 and 15. The center tower terminal is called 4.
2. Use an ohmmeter and check the resistance between the 2 screw terminals, 1 and 15. The resistance should be 0.45-0.55 ohms.
3. Use an ohmmeter and check the resistance between the terminals, 4 and 15. The resistance should be 5400-6600 ohms.
4. Replace the coil if not in specification.

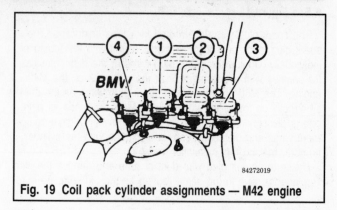

Fig. 19 Coil pack cylinder assignments — M42 engine

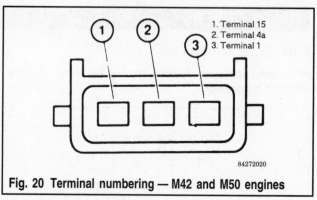

1. Terminal 15
2. Terminal 4a
3. Terminal 1

Fig. 20 Terminal numbering — M42 and M50 engines

M42 and M50 Engines
▶ **See Figures 18, 19 and 20**

1. On the M50 engine, remove the valve cover cladding as done when removing spark plugs. On the M42 engine, pull off the coil pack cover.
2. With the ignition OFF, disconnect the harness connector by releasing the locking bar and pulling off the connector.
3. Check the resistance between the outside terminals of the the 3 terminals in the coil connector socket. They are terminals 1 and 15.
4. The resistance should be 0.4-0.8 ohms. Replace the coil if out of specification. The secondary side of the coil cannot be checked due to the design of the coil.

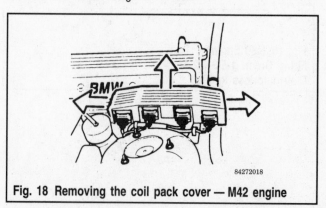

Fig. 18 Removing the coil pack cover — M42 engine

Parts Replacement

DISTRIBUTOR CAP AND ROTOR

Check the cap and rotor for signs of burning, carbon tracks or excessive corrosion on the terminals. Do not try to clean the terminals. The cap and rotor should be replaced at the same time.

1. Make sure the ignition is OFF.

2. To prevent scraping the skin off your knuckles on the radiator fins, slide a thin piece of cardboard or equivalent down between the radiator and the fan.

3. Remove the ignition lead cover from the distributor cap. If not already marked, tag the ignition leads for later installation.

4. Pull off the ignition leads from the distributor cap.

5. Remove the screws from the distributor cap and remove the cap. Check the condition of the distributor cap seal and replace if necessary.

6. Unscrew the 3mm hexhead bolts holding the rotor and remove the rotor.

To install:

7. Place the new rotor on the shaft and tighten the hexhead bolts to 1.9-2.1 ft. lbs. (2.6-3.0 Nm).

8. Replace the distributor cap and seal. Tighten the mounting screws.

9. Replace the ignition leads on the proper terminals and clip the cover into place. Remove the cardboard from between the radiator and fan.

IGNITION TIMING

The ignition timing on BMW vehicles is not adjustable. Even checking the timing would be an effort in futility as the timing is automatically adjusted by the DME control unit as engine conditions change. As a result the timing can be anywhere in a range as determined by the DME and not at any one stationary point that could be checked.

VALVE LASH

All BMW gasoline engines except for the S14 and S38 dual overhead camshaft designs and the hydraulic lifter equipped M42 and M50, are equipped with an overhead camshaft operating the intake and exhaust valves through rocker arm linkage.

Valve lash on these engines should be adjusted at intervals determined by the Service Interval lights. See Section 1 and your service manual. It is important to adjust the lash to make up for wear in the valve train, which will cause noisy valve operation and reduced power, or, in some cases, excessive tightness in the valve train, which can cause the valves to burn and may even reduce compression. The BMW features a unique adjuster design that makes it easy to hold the required dimension while tightening the locknut; thus, valve adjustment is unusually easy.

Except S14 and S38 Engines

▶ **See Figures 21 and 22**

1. Make sure the engine is as cold as possible. It need not actually sit overnight, but must be cool to the touch — under 95°F (35°C). Several hours should be allowed for cooling if the engine started out at operating temperature.

2. Remove the valve cover. This will require, in some cases, removal of the air cleaner or main air intake hose, and disconnecting the PCV line or other vacuum lines. Note that the valve cover is secured to the cylinder head by cap nuts, while bolts attach it to the timing cover on the front of the engine. Make sure you remove all the fasteners. Then, lift the cover straight out.

3. The engine must be rotated to a position that will ensure that there will be no closing effect from the camshaft when the valves are adjusted. This requests a different position for the adjustment of each cylinder. The figure lists the cylinder to be

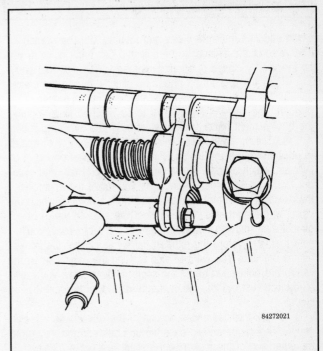

Fig. 21 Checking the valve lash between the valve stem and the rocker arm adjusting eccentric — M20 and M30 engines

adjusted in the first (left hand) column, and the cylinder whose valves must be watched while positioning the engine in the right hand column. Cylinders are numbered from front to rear, 1 through 4 or 1 through 6. The engine may be rotated by rolling the car in third gear (if it is equipped with a manual transmission) or by installing a socket wrench on the bolt

4 CYLINDER ENGINES

TO ADJUST CYLINDER:	PUT THIS CYLINDER AT OVERLAP POSITION
1	4
3	2
4	1
2	3

6 CYLINDER ENGINES

TO ADJUST CYLINDER:	PUT THIS CYLINDER AT OVERLAP POSITION
1	6
5	2
3	4
6	1
2	5
4	3

84272022

Fig. 22 Valve lash adjusting sequence

which attaches the front pulley and rotating with the wrench. The valve of the cylinder to be adjusted (left hand column) will be in the fully closed position, compression TDC, so that you can wiggle the rockers up and down slightly, feeling the clearance in the valve train, when the engine is in the proper position. The valve in the cylinder to be watched while rotating the engine (right hand column) must be in the overlap position. At this position, both valves will be slightly open. For example, to position the engine for adjustment of the valves on No. 1 cylinder, watch cylinder No. 4 on 4-cylinder engines, and cylinder No. 6 on 6-cylinder engines. As you rotate the engine in the direction of normal rotation, you'll note a point at which the valve on the right side of the engine (the exhaust valve) begins closing (moving upward). If you crank very slowly, you'll note that, just before the exhaust valve has closed, the intake begins opening. You want to stop rotating the engine when the valves are both open about the same amount. Now, you are ready to adjust cylinder No. 1, as described in the next 2 steps.

4. Check the clearances on one of the valves with a feeler gauge. The gauge should pass through between the valve and the outer end of the rocker with a slight resistance (don't check between the camshaft and rocker, at the center of the engine). If there is any doubt about the clearance, check with the gauges equivalent, thicker and thinner by 0.002 in. If the specification is, for example, 0.12 in., and the 0.012 in. gauge passes through snugly, and the 0.014 gauge feels tight while a 0.010 gauge slips through easily, the valve is adjusted correctly. If the clearance is not right, insert the bent wire tool (these may be purchased at an automotive supply store or you can make one yourself with a piece of coat hanger) into the small hole in the adjusting cam, which is located in the outer end of the rocker arm. Then, use a 10mm wrench to loosen

the adjusting locknut, also located on the end of the rocker. Rotate the adjusting cam with the wire as you slide the gauge between the cam and valve. When the gauge will go in between the valve and adjusting cam and can be slid back and forth with just a slight resistance, hold the position of the cam with the adjusting wire and then tighten the locknut.

5. Recheck the clearance to make sure it has not changed — if the minimum and maximum dimension gauges behave as described in the step above, the adjustment is correct.

6. Repeat the adjustment for the other valve on cylinder No. 1, located directly across from the one already adjuster.

7. Rotate the engine to the next cylinder listed in the left hand column of the figure, watching the valve of the cylinder listed in the right hand column. When the engine is positioned for this cylinder, adjust the valves for it as described in Steps 4, 5 and 6. Then, proceed with the next cylinder in the left hand column in the same way, until all 4- or 6-cylinders have had their valves adjuster.

8. Replace the valve cover using a new gasket. Tighten the cover cap nuts or bolts a very little at a time and alternately in order to bring the cam cover down onto the gasket evenly in all areas. Be careful not to overtighten the cover cap nuts/bolts. Torque to 6-7 ft. lbs. (8-10 Nm).

9. Reconnect all disconnected hoses and, if necessary, replace the air cleaner.

S14 and S38 Engines

▶ See Figure 23

➡ To perform this procedure, a special tool is needed to depress the valves against spring pressure to gain access to the valve adjusting discs. Use BMW Tool 11 3 170 or equivalent. Also needed are: compressed air to lift valve adjusting discs that must be replaced out of the valve tappet; an assortment of adjusting discs of various thicknesses and a precise outside micrometer.

1. Make sure the engine is overnight cold. Remove the rocker cover.

2. Turn the engine until the No. 1 cylinder intake valve cams are both straight up. The intake cam is labeled A on the head.

3. Slide a flat feeler gauge in between each of the cams and the adjacent valve tappet. Check to see if the clearance is within the specified range. If it is, proceed with checking the remaining clearances as described starting in Step 8. If not,

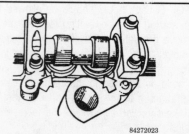

84272023

Fig. 23 Turn the valve buckets so the notches are in this orientation before checking adjustment — S14 and S38 engines

switch gauges and measure the actual clearance. When actual clearance is achieved, proceed with Steps 4-7.

4. Turn the tappets so the grooves machined into their edges are aligned as shown. Looking at the valves from the center of the engine, the right hand tappet's groove should be at about 5 o'clock and the left hand tappet's groove should be at about 7 o'clock. Use the end of the special tool required for the camshaft involved — in this case the A or intake camshaft (the exhaust camshaft end is labeled E on the engine and tool). Slide the proper end of the tool, going from the center of the engine outward, under the cam, with the heel of the tool pivoting on the inner side of the camshaft valley. Force the handle downward until the handle rests on the protrusion on the center of the cylinder head.

5. Use compressed air to pop the disc out of the tappet. Read the thickness dimension on the disc.

6. Determine the thickness required as follows:

a. If the valve clearance is too tight, try the next thinner disc.

b. If the valve clearance is too loose, try the next thicker disc.

7. Slip the thinner or thicker disc into the tappet with the letter facing downward. Rock the valve spring depressing tool out and remove it. Then, recheck the clearance. Change the disc again, if necessary, until the clearance falls within the specified range.

8. Turn the engine in firing order sequence (1-5-3-6-2-4 for the 6-cylinder engines or, for the M3, 1-3-4-2), turning the crankshaft forward ⅓ of a turn each time to get the intake cams to the upward position for each cylinder. Measure the clearance as in Step 3 and, if it is outside the specified range, follow Steps 4-7 to adjust either or both valves. Repeat this for all the intakes, and then turn the engine until No. 1 cylinder exhaust valves are upward.

9. Follow the same sequence for all the exhaust valves, going through the firing order, checking clearance as described in Step 3 and adjusting the valves as in Steps 4-7. Note that it is necessary, however, to use the opposite end of the special tool — the end marked E to depress the exhaust valves.

10. When all the clearances are in the specified range, replace the cam cover, start the engine, and check for leaks.

IDLE SPEED AND MIXTURE ADJUSTMENTS

The idle speed is controlled with a motor operated rotary valve. The motor is double wound and can be driven in both directions. Power is supplied from the main DME relay anytime the ignition switch is **ON**. The control unit selects which of 2 ground circuits to complete, opening or closing the valve as required to maintain the programmed idle speed. Further idle speed control is accomplished through very fine ignition timing adjustments. This allows very fast idle speed control; turning on the air conditioner at idle will produce almost no momentary drop in idle speed.

Idle speed and idle CO cannot be adjusted or changed. If the either is incorrect and the valve works properly, look for a vacuum leak, clogged air cleaner or fuel injection problems. Adjusting any screws on the throttle body is unnecessary and will not change the idle speed or mixture. The DME unit will adjust for any changes made.

TORQUE SPECIFICATIONS

Component	U.S.	Metric
Distributor rotor 3mm bolts	1.9–2.1 ft. lbs.	2.6–3.0 Nm
Spark plugs	14–22 ft. lbs.	20–30 Nm
Valve cover nuts	6–7 ft. lbs.	8–10 Nm

84272025

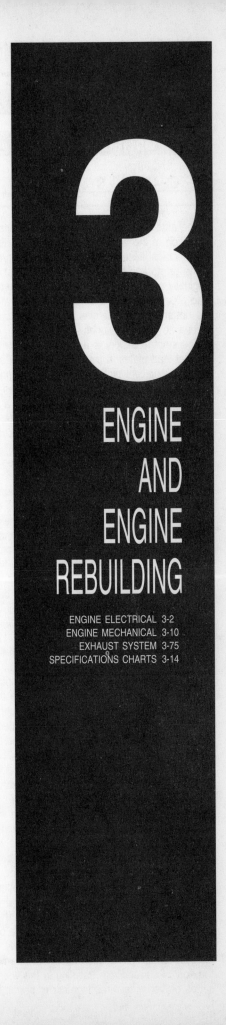

3

ENGINE AND ENGINE REBUILDING

ENGINE ELECTRICAL

Basic Operating Principles

THE CHARGING SYSTEM

The automobile charging system provides electrical power for operation of the vehicle's ignition and starting systems and all the electrical accessories. The battery serves as an electrical surge or storage tank, sorting (in chemical form) the energy originally produced by the engine-driven generator. The system also provides a means of regulator generator output to protect the battery from being overcharged and to avoid excessive voltage to the accessories.

The storage battery is a chemical device incorporating parallel lead plates in a tank containing a sulfuric acid-water solution. Adjacent plates are slightly dissimilar, and the chemical reaction of the 2 dissimilar plates produces electrical energy when the battery is connected to a load such as the starter motor. The chemical reaction is reversible, so that when the generator is producing a voltage (electrical pressure) greater than that produced by the battery, electricity is forced into the battery, and the battery is returned to its fully charged state.

The vehicle's generator is driven mechanically, through Vee-belts, by the engine crankshaft. It consists of 2 coils of fine wire, one stationary (the 'stator') , and one movable ('the rotor'). The rotor may also be known as the 'armature,' and consist of fine wire wrapped around an iron core which is mounted on a shaft. The electricity which flows through the 2 coils of wire (provided initially by the battery in some cases) creates an intense magnetic field around both rotor and stator, and the interaction between the 2 fields creates voltage, allowing the generator to power the accessories and charge the battery.

There are 2 types of generators; the earlier is the direct current (DC) type. The current produced by the DC generator is generated in the armature and carried off the spinning armature by stationary brushes contacting the commutator. The commutator is a series of smooth metal contact plates on the end of the armature. The commutator plates, which are separated from one another by a very short gap, are connected to the armature circuits so that current will flow in one direction only in the wires carrying the generator output. The generator stator consists of 2 stationary coils of wire which draw some of the output current of the generator to form a powerful magnetic field and create the interaction of fields which generates the voltage. The generator field is wired in series with the regulator.

Your BMW uses an alternating current generator, or 'alternator' because they are more efficient, can be rotated at higher speeds, and have fewer brush problems. In an alternator, the field rotates while all the current produced passes only through the stator windings. The brushes bear against continuous slip rings rather than a commutator. This causes the current produced to periodically reverse the direction of its flow. Diodes (electrical one-way switches) block the flow of current from traveling in the wrong direction. A series of diodes is wired together to permit the alternating flow of the stator to be converted to a pulsating, but uni-directional flow at the alternator output. The alternator's field is wired in series with the voltage regulator.

The regulator precisely controls the voltage. It senses the voltage being produced by the alternator and varies the voltage to maintain the proper range of operation. The regulator is built into the body of the alternator.

BATTERY AND STARTING SYSTEM

The battery is the first link in the chain of mechanisms which work together to provide cranking of the automobile engine. In most modern cars, the battery is a lead-acid electro-chemical device consisting of 6 2-volt (2V) subsections connected in series so the unit is capable of producing approximately 12V of electrical pressure. Each subsection, or cell, consist of a series of positive and negative plates held a short distance apart in a solution of sulfuric acid and water. The 2 types of plates are of dissimilar metals. This causes a chemical reaction to be set up, and it is this reaction which produces current flow from the battery when its positive and negative terminals are connected to an electrical appliance such as a lamp or motor. The continued transfer of electrons would eventually convert the sulfuric acid in the electrolyte to water, and make the 2 plates identical in chemical composition. As electrical energy is removed from the battery, its voltage output tends to drop. Thus, measuring battery voltage and battery electrolyte composition are 2 ways of checking the ability of the unit to supply power. During the starting of the engine, electrical energy is removed from the battery. However, if the charging circuit is in good condition and the operating conditions are normal, the power removed from the battery will be replaced by the alternator. Generally, the major power supply cable that leaves the battery goes directly to the starter, while other electrical system needs are supplied by a smaller cable. During the starter operation, power flows from the battery to the starter and is sending electrons back through the battery, reversing the normal flow, and restoring the battery to its original chemical state.

The battery and starting motor are linked by very heavy electrical cables designed to minimize resistance to the flow of electrons. The return current flows through the car's frame and the battery's negative ground strap.

The starting motor is a specially designed, direct current electric motor capable of producing a very great amount of power for its size. One thing that allows the motor to produce a great deal of power is its tremendous rotating speed. It drives the engine through a small pinion gear (attached to the starter's armature), which drives the very large flywheel ring gear at a reduced speed. Another factor allowing it to produce so much power is that only intermittent operation is required of it. Thus, little allowance for air circulation is required, and the windings can be built into a very small space.

The starter solenoid is a magnetic device which employs the small current supplied by the starting switch circuit if the ignition switch. This magnetic action moves a plunger which mechanically engages the starter and electrically closes the heavy switch which connects it to the battery. The starting switch circuit consists of the starting switch contained within the ignition switch, a transmission neutral safety switch or clutch pedal switch, and the wiring necessary to connect these with the starter solenoid or relay.

A pinion, which is a small gear, is mounted to a one-way drive clutch. This clutch is splined to the starter armature shaft. When the ignition switch is moved to the **START** position, the solenoid plunger slides the pinion toward the flywheel ring gear via a collar and spring. If the teeth on the pinion and flywheel match properly, the pinion will engage the flywheel immediately. If the gear teeth butt one another, the spring will be compressed and will force the gears to mesh as soon as the starter turns far enough to allow them to do so. As the solenoid plunger reaches the end of its travel, it closes the contacts that connect the battery and starter and then the engine is cranked.

As soon as the engine starts, the flywheel ring gear begins turning fast enough to drive the pinion at an extremely high rate of speed. At this point, the one-way clutch begins allowing the pinion to spin faster than the starter shaft so that the starter will not operate at excessive speed. When the ignition switch is released from the starter position, the solenoid is de-energized, and a spring contained within the solenoid assembly pulls the gear out of mesh and interrupts the current flow to the starter.

Alternator

PRECAUTIONS

Several precautions must be observed with alternator equipped vehicles to avoid damaging the unit. They are as follows:

• If the battery is removed for any reason, make sure it is reconnected with the correct polarity. Reversing the battery connections will result in damage to the electrical system.

• When utilizing a booster battery as a starting aid, always connect it as follows: positive to positive, and negative (booster battery) to a good ground on the engine.

• Never use a fast charger as a booster to start vehicles.

• When servicing the battery with a charger, always disconnect the battery cables.

• Do not short across or ground any of the terminals on the alternator.

• Turn off the ignition switch and then disconnect the battery terminals when performing any service on the electrical system or charging the battery.

• Disconnect the battery ground cable if arc welding is to be done on any part of the vehicle.

TESTING

When faced with the possibility of a charging system problem, there are certain tests that can help find the cause. Before embarking on a tear down of the entire charging system, check the obvious. Many charging system problems are caused by bad connections that are either loose or dirty. Many times just going over all the battery, alternator and cable connections can solve a problem.

Check the battery for the correct electrolyte fluid level. Check that the battery cable connections are not corroded and are tight. Clean and tighten the connections if necessary. Refer to Section 1 for battery procedures.

Check the alternator belt for tightness and proper tensioning. If the belt is slipping, the alternator will not be able to put out a full charge. Check the belt for signs of slippage and glazing. Do not use belt preparations to cure slippage or glazing; replace the belt with new if necessary.

If the alternator light does not illuminate when the ignition key is turned to the **ON** position, check the indicator bulb. Disconnect the D+/61 wire from the alternator, it will be marked on the alternator body. Ground this wire with the ignition key turned to the **ON** position. If the alternator light does not come on, check the indicator bulb and related wiring. If the bulb does light, there is most likely an internal problem with the alternator.

If the alternator light comes on with the ignition switch in the **OFF** position, there is an internal problem with the alternator. The diodes are damaged and the alternator should be rebuilt, replaced or have the diode plate replaced.

If the alternator lights comes on or glows with the engine running, check the alternator charging voltage and amperage. With the engine running at 1500 rpm, the voltage should be 13.5-14.2 volts. The amperage measured with an inductive meter clipped over the battery cable or a non-inductive meter connected as instructed by the manufacturer, should be at least 15 amps. If the amperage is low, switch on the high beams and other heavy current users. The amperage should go up with each device turned on. If the amperage stays the same, the alternator is not charging and should be replaced.

If the alternator light is not illuminated while the engine is running but the alternator still does not charge the battery or doesn't charge it enough, check the connections at the alternator and battery. Check the condition of the battery, alternator belt and wiring. If no obvious cause is found, check the alternator charging voltage and amperage as above. Replace the alternator if the voltage or amperage is incorrect.

If no problems with the charging system or alternator can be found, the cause of the problem will most likely be the battery. Replace the battery as necessary.

BELT TENSION ADJUSTMENT

The fan belt tension is adjusted by moving the alternator on the slack adjuster bracket. The belt tension is adjusted to a deflection of approximately ½ inch under moderate thumb pressure in the middle of its longest span. On many engines, the position of the top of the alternator is adjusted via a bolt that is geared to the bracket. This bolt is turned to position the alternator and determine tension, and then is locked in position with a lock bolt. On engines with a serpentine belt, the self tensioner will automatically adjust the tension.

REMOVAL & INSTALLATION

▶ **See Figures 1, 2, 3 and 4**

1. Disconnect the negative battery cable. Remove the air cleaner assembly. Remove the fan and cowl on the M5, 525i with M50 engine and 325i with M50 engine.

2. Disconnect the wires from the rear of the alternator, marking them for installation. Note that there is a ground wire on some vehicles. On the E30 325i and M3, it may be easier to remove the alternator mounting bolts, turn it, and then remove the wires.

3. Loosen the hose clamp on the alternator cooling duct, if equipped. Remove the cooling duct.

4. Loosen the lock bolt, turn the tensioning bolt so as to eliminate belt tension and then remove the belt. Remove the bolts and remove the alternator.

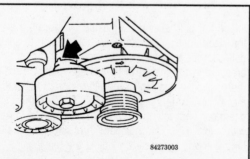

Fig. 1 Alternator mounting showing the adjuster bolts — E36 318i shown

Fig. 2 Loosening the serpentine belt on M50 engine

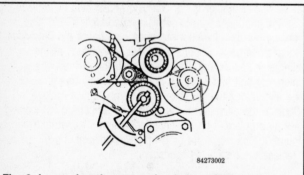

Fig. 3 The tab on the tensioner must be fit into the slot on M50 engines

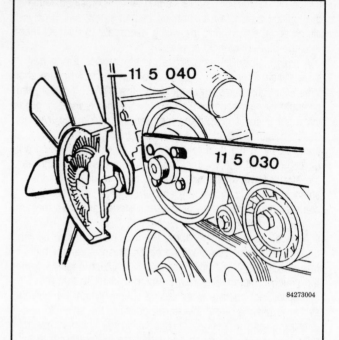

Fig. 4 Removing the fan by holding the pulley with tool 11 5 030 or equivalent and turning the left hand threads of the fan nut with tool 11 5 040 or equivalent

To install:

5. Install the alternator in position and install the retaining bolts.

6. The tensioning bolt on the front of the alternator must be turned so as to tension the belt, using a torque wrench, until the torque is approximately 5 ft. lbs. (7 Nm). Then, hold the adjustment with one wrench while tightening the locknut at the rear of the unit. Make sure, if the unit has a ground wire on the alternator, it has been reconnected.

7. Replace the fan and cowl. Install the air cleaner and connect the hoses. Install the alternator cooling duct. Connect the wires to the alternator.

Starter

▶ **See Figure 5**

TESTING

The starter can be inspected for incorrect operation through visual and operational means. A series of simple checks can help locate the problem with the starting system. The starter consists of 2 main parts, the solenoid and the starter motor. The solenoid engages the starter pinion and acts a high current switch for the starter motor. Note that there is a thick battery cable leading to the solenoid and a braided copper lead going from the solenoid into the motor body. There is a smaller wire going from the ignition switch to the 50 terminal of the solenoid. This is the control signal that actuates the solenoid which in turn passes the larger current from the battery to the starter motor via the braided copper lead.

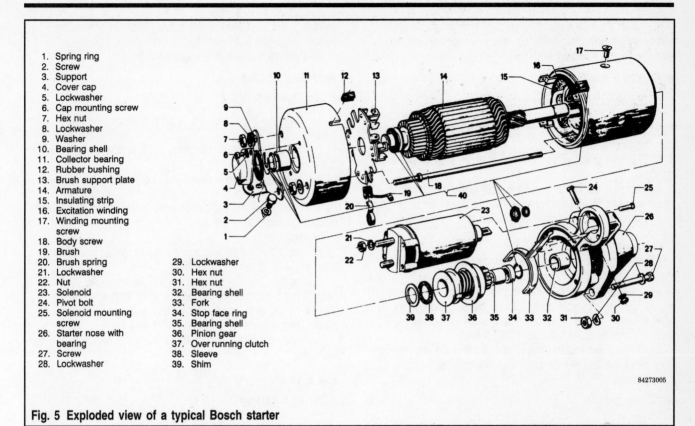

1. Spring ring
2. Screw
3. Support
4. Cover cap
5. Lockwasher
6. Cap mounting screw
7. Hex nut
8. Lockwasher
9. Washer
10. Bearing shell
11. Collector bearing
12. Rubber bushing
13. Brush support plate
14. Armature
15. Insulating strip
16. Excitation winding
17. Winding mounting screw
18. Body screw
19. Brush
20. Brush spring
21. Lockwasher
22. Nut
23. Solenoid
24. Pivot bolt
25. Solenoid mounting screw
26. Starter nose with bearing
27. Screw
28. Lockwasher
29. Lockwasher
30. Hex nut
31. Hex nut
32. Bearing shell
33. Fork
34. Stop face ring
35. Bearing shell
36. Pinion gear
37. Over running clutch
38. Sleeve
39. Shim

84273005

Fig. 5 Exploded view of a typical Bosch starter

If the starter will not operate at all, check the condition of the battery. The starter needs a good strong charge to operate correctly. Jump start the car in the proper sequence. If the starter operates, check the charging system for faults. If the starter still will not operate, check that all the connections from the battery to the starter are intact and clean. Check that battery voltage is present at the thick cable connection on the solenoid.

If all the connections are clean and tight to the starter, including the engine ground strap, check that the solenoid is getting the start signal from the ignition switch. Check that battery voltage is present at terminal 50 on the solenoid when the ignition switch is turned. If voltage is present, then the solenoid or starter is bad. The solenoid and starter is typically replaced as a unit.

If the solenoid clicks when the ignition switch is turned, but the starter does not crank, check that the copper braid from the starter motor to the solenoid is intact and the connection is tight. If the connection is clean and tight, check if battery voltage is present at the copper braid when the ignition switch is turned. If voltage is present, the starter is bad. If no voltage present, the solenoid is bad.

If the starter cranks slowly, check the condition of the battery and cable connections. This condition is typically caused by a low charge on the battery or high resistance cable connections. Clean all the cable connections and charge the battery. If this doesn't help, it is possible that the front bearing in the starter nose is binding. Replace the starter in this case.

Visual checks of the starter body can show a loose solenoid. Sometimes the solenoid mounting bolts can work loose causing the solenoid to back off from the starter body. This will cause incomplete engagement of the pinion and hard starting.

When the starter is removed, check the pinion gear teeth for chips and wear. Replace the starter if the pinion is damaged. The pinion can be damaged if the starter is engaged while the engine is running or if the starter grinds on engagement. Check the condition of the flywheel ring gear if the pinion is found to be damaged. The ring gear tends to get damaged as the pinion is damaged.

REMOVAL & INSTALLATION

E30 3 Series

WITH M42 ENGINE

1. Disconnect the negative battery terminal. Remove the air cleaner assembly and the hose leading to the throttle body.
2. Remove the intake manifold support. Mark the electrical connectors on the lead duct and disconnect.
3. Move the lead duct towards the side of the engine compartment to access the starter.
4. Mark and remove the wires from the starter. Remove the starter mounting nuts and remove the starter.
   To install:
5. Install the starter and tighten the mounting nuts and bolts to 34-36 ft. lbs. (47-50 Nm).
6. Connect the wires to the original locations on the solenoid. If the battery cable connection is all metal, torque to 3.6-4.4 ft. lbs. (5-6 Nm). If the battery cable connection is plastic, torque to 0.7-1.1 ft. lbs. (1.0-1.5 Nm).
7. Replace the lead duct and connect the electrical connector in their original positions. Be sure the rubber grommets are installer correctly to prevent water from entering the lead duct.

8. Install the intake manifold support and tighten to 15-17 ft. lbs. (20-24 Nm). Install the air cleaner assembly and connect the negative battery terminal.

WITH M20 ENGINE

1. Disconnect the negative battery terminal.

2. Remove the air cleaner assembly. Drain the coolant and disconnect the heater hoses to allow the starter to be removed from the engine compartment.

3. Disconnect the wires from the solenoid after noting their locations.

4. Remove the starter mounting nuts at the bell housing. You may need to use a curved wrench to reach the upper nut.

5. Remove the rear mounting bracket and remove the starter.

To install:

6. Install the starter and tighten the mounting nuts and bolts to 34-36 ft. lbs. (47-50 Nm).

7. Connect the wires to the original locations on the solenoid. If the battery cable connection is all metal, torque to 3.6-4.4 ft. lbs. (5-6 Nm). If the battery cable connection is plastic, torque to 0.7-1.1 ft. lbs. (1.0-1.5 Nm).

8. Connect the heater hoses, fill and bleed the cooling system. Install the air cleaner assembly. Connect the negative battery terminal.

WITH S14 ENGINE

1. Disconnect the negative battery terminal.

2. Remove the intake manifold assembly. Drain the coolant and disconnect the coolant return pipe to allow the starter to be removed from the engine compartment.

3. Disconnect the wires from the solenoid after noting their locations.

4. Remove the starter mounting nuts at the bell housing. You may need to use a curved wrench to reach the upper nut.

5. Remove the rear mounting bracket and remove the starter.

To install:

6. Install the starter and tighten the mounting nuts and bolts to 34-36 ft. lbs. (47-50 Nm).

7. Connect the wires to the original locations on the solenoid. If the battery cable connection is all metal, torque to 3.6-4.4 ft. lbs. (5-6 Nm). If the battery cable connection is plastic, torque to 0.7-1.1 ft. lbs. (1.0-1.5 Nm).

8. Connect the coolant return line, fill and bleed the cooling system. Install the intake manifold assembly. Connect the negative battery terminal.

E36 3 Series

WITH M42 ENGINE

1. Disconnect the negative battery terminal. Mark and remove the wires from the solenoid.

2. Remove the upper starter bolt from inside the engine compartment.

3. From under the car remove the lower starter bolt. Remove the starter from the car.

To install:

4. Install the starter and tighten the mounting nuts and bolts to 34-36 ft. lbs. (47-50 Nm).

5. Connect the wires to the original locations on the solenoid. If the battery cable connection is all metal, torque to

3.6-4.4 ft. lbs. (5-6 Nm). If the battery cable connection is plastic, torque to 0.7-1.1 ft. lbs. (1.0-1.5 Nm).

6. Connect the negative battery terminal.

WITH M50 ENGINE

▶ **See Figures 6 and 7**

1. Disconnect the negative battery terminal. Remove the air cleaner assembly.

2. Remove the intake manifold. Mark and remove the wires from the solenoid.

3. Remove the upper starter bolt from inside the engine compartment.

4. From under the car remove the lower starter bolt. Remove the starter from the car.

To install:

5. Install the starter and tighten the mounting nuts and bolts to 34-36 ft. lbs. (47-50 Nm).

6. Connect the wires to the original locations on the solenoid. If the battery cable connection is all metal, torque to 3.6-4.4 ft. lbs. (5-6 Nm). If the battery cable connection is plastic, torque to 0.7-1.1 ft. lbs. (1.0-1.5 Nm).

7. Install the intake manifold. Connect the negative battery terminal.

E34 5 Series

WITH M20 ENGINE

1. Disconnect the negative battery terminal.

2. Disconnect the wires from the solenoid after noting their locations.

3. Remove the starter mounting nuts at the bell housing. You may need to use a curved wrench to reach the upper nut.

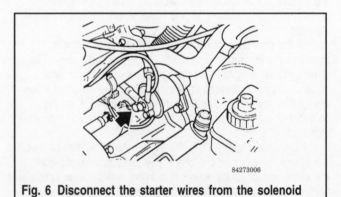

Fig. 6 Disconnect the starter wires from the solenoid

Fig. 7 Upper starter mounting bolt

To install:

4. Install the starter and tighten the mounting nuts and bolts to 34-36 ft. lbs. (47-50 Nm).

5. Connect the wires to the original locations on the solenoid. If the battery cable connection is all metal, torque to 3.6-4.4 ft. lbs. (5-6 Nm). If the battery cable connection is plastic, torque to 0.7-1.1 ft. lbs. (1.0-1.5 Nm).

6. Connect the negative battery terminal.

WITH M50 ENGINE

1. Disconnect the negative battery terminal. Disconnect the alternator cooling duct and remove the air cleaner assembly. Remove the intake manifold.

2. Disconnect the wires from the solenoid after noting their locations.

3. Remove the starter mounting nuts at the bell housing. You may need to use a curved wrench to reach the upper nut.

To install:

4. Install the starter and tighten the mounting nuts and bolts to 34-36 ft. lbs. (47-50 Nm).

5. Connect the wires to the original locations on the solenoid. If the battery cable connection is all metal, torque to 3.6-4.4 ft. lbs. (5-6 Nm). If the battery cable connection is plastic, torque to 0.7-1.1 ft. lbs. (1.0-1.5 Nm).

6. Install the intake manifold, alternator cooling duct and the air cleaner assembly. Connect the negative battery terminal.

WITH M30 ENGINE

1. Disconnect the negative battery terminal. Remove the screws from the coolant expansion tank and move to the side to gain better access to the mounting bolts.

2. Disconnect the wires from the solenoid after noting their locations.

3. Remove the starter mounting nuts at the bell housing. You may need to use a curved wrench to reach the upper nut.

To install:

4. Install the starter and tighten the mounting nuts and bolts to 34-36 ft. lbs. (47-50 Nm).

5. Connect the wires to the original locations on the solenoid. If the battery cable connection is all metal, torque to 3.6-4.4 ft. lbs. (5-6 Nm). If the battery cable connection is plastic, torque to 0.7-1.1 ft. lbs. (1.0-1.5 Nm).

6. Connect the negative battery terminal.

WITH S38 ENGINE

1. Disconnect the negative battery terminal. Remove the intake manifold.

2. Disconnect the wires from the solenoid after noting their locations.

3. Remove the starter mounting nuts at the bell housing. You may need to use a curved wrench to reach the upper nut.

To install:

4. Install the starter and tighten the mounting nuts and bolts to 34-36 ft. lbs. (47-50 Nm).

5. Connect the wires to the original locations on the solenoid. If the battery cable connection is all metal, torque to 3.6-4.4 ft. lbs. (5-6 Nm). If the battery cable connection is plastic, torque to 0.7-1.1 ft. lbs. (1.0-1.5 Nm).

6. Install the intake manifold, alternator cooling duct and the air cleaner assembly. Connect the negative battery terminal.

SOLENOID REPLACEMENT

It is most common to replace the starter and solenoid as an assembly. Finding a replacement solenoid is not as easy as finding a complete new or rebuilt starter. If the solenoid is worn, chances are that the starter motor has an equivalent amount of wear. Replacing both as an assembly reduces the chance of having problems with the starter motor soon after replacing the solenoid.

1. Remove the starter.

2. Disconnect the copper braid lead from the solenoid terminal. Be careful not to twist and pull on the lead as the nut is removed.

3. Remove the 2 or 3 screws at the nose end of the solenoid.

4. Remove the solenoid. Be careful not to lose the spring in the solenoid.

To install:

5. Install the solenoid onto the body of the starter. Coat the threads of the screws with threadlocker compound and tighten.

6. Connect the copper braid lead to the solenoid terminal. Be careful not to twist or pull on the lead as the nut is tightened.

7. Install the solenoid.

Sending Units and Sensors

REMOVAL & INSTALLATION

Coolant Temperature Sensor

M42 ENGINE (FOR DME)

▶ See Figure 8

The coolant temperature sensor for the DME unit is located in the cylinder head below and just behind the front engine lifting loop.

1. Pull off the sensor connector.

2. Remove the crankcase breather hose from the valve cover.

84273008

Fig. 8 DME coolant temperature sensor — M42 engine mounted in E36 318i

3. Use a crowsfoot wrench on an extension and unscrew the sensor.

4. Install the sensor with a new crush washer and tighten to 11 ft. lbs. (15 Nm).

M42 ENGINE (FOR GAUGE)

▶ See Figures 9, 10, 11 and 12

The coolant temperature sensor for the temperature gauge is located on the cylinder head further back from the DME temperature sensor. It is below the second intake port.

1. Remove the air cleaner assembly and the crankcase breather hose.

2. Remove the intake manifold support and pull the wire duct forward.

3. Disconnect the sender and remove using a crowsfoot wrench on an extension.

To install:

4. Install the sensor with a new crush washer and tighten to 12.5-13.5 ft. lbs. (17-19 Nm).

5. Replace the lead duct and connect the electrical connector in their original positions. Be sure the rubber grommets are installed correctly to prevent water from entering the lead duct.

6. Install the intake manifold support and tighten to 15-17 ft. lbs. (20-24 Nm). Install the air cleaner assembly and the crankcase breather hose.

M20 AND M30 ENGINES

The coolant temperature sensors are located on the coolant outlet on the left side of the engine. This is the junction of the coolant hoses where the coolant flows to the engine block. The DME coolant temperature sensor has a blue colored con-

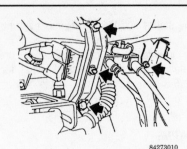

Fig. 10 Intake manifold support mounting bolts on M42 engine

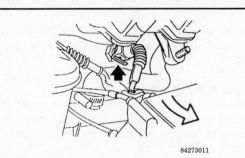

Fig. 11 Pull the electric wire duct forward to expose the coolant temperature sensor on the M42 engine

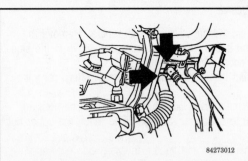

Fig. 12 Make sure the rubber seals are in place on the M42 engine when replacing the wire duct

nector body. The gauge temperature sensor is typically colored brown.

1. Pull off the sensor connector.

2. Use a crowsfoot wrench on an extension and unscrew the sensor.

3. Install the sensor with a new crush washer and tighten to 12.5-13.5 ft. lbs. (17-19 Nm).

M50 ENGINE

On the M50 engine, the coolant temperature sensors are located under the intake manifold on the engine. The forwardmost sensor is the DME sensor and the rear sensor is for the temperature gauge.

1. Pull off the sensor connector.

2. Use a crowsfoot wrench on an extension and unscrew the sensor.

3. Install the sensor with a new crush washer and tighten to 12.5-13.5 ft. lbs. (17-19 Nm).

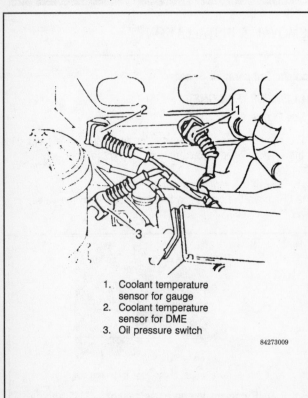

1. Coolant temperature sensor for gauge
2. Coolant temperature sensor for DME
3. Oil pressure switch

Fig. 9 Sensor locations on the M42 engine

S14 ENGINE

The coolant temperature sensors on the S14 engine are located in the coolant pipe above the exhaust side of the engine. The rear sensor services the DME and the forward services the temperature gauge.

1. Pull off the sensor connector.
2. Use a crowsfoot wrench on an extension and unscrew the sensor.
3. Install the sensor with a new crush washer and tighten to 12.5-13.5 ft. lbs. (17-19 Nm).

S38 ENGINE

▶ See Figure 13

The coolant temperature sensors on the S38 engine are located in the coolant pipe above the exhaust side of the engine and in the thermostat housing. The unit in the coolant pipe is the DME sensor and the unit in the thermostat housing is for the temperature gauge.

1. Pull off the sensor connector.
2. Use a crowsfoot wrench on an extension and unscrew the sensor.
3. Install the sensor with a new crush washer and tighten to 12.5-13.5 ft. lbs. (17-19 Nm).

Fig. 13 Temperature gauge sensor mounted on the thermostat housing on the S38 engine

Oil Pressure Switch

LOCATIONS

M20 engine: The oil pressure switch is located on the engine block near the oil filter. **M30 engine:** The oil pressure switch is located on the oil filter housing. It is on the upper side of the base. **M42 engine:** The oil pressure switch is located on the oil filter housing. It is on the back side of the base.

M50 engine: The oil pressure switch is located on the oil filter housing. It is on the back side of the base behind the line fittings. **S14 engine:** The oil pressure switch is located on the oil filter adapter housing. **S38 engine:** The oil pressure switch is located on the oil filter housing. It is on the upper side of the base. The temperature sender for the temperature gauge is mounted sideways below the pressure switch.

REMOVAL & INSTALLATION

1. Remove the electrical connector.
2. Loosen and remove the switch.
3. Install the sender with a new crush washer and tighten to 22-29 ft. lbs. (30-40 Nm) for the M20 and M30 engines. Tighten to 17-22 ft. lbs. (24-31 Nm) for the M42 engine. On the M50, S14 and S38 engines tighten to 12-17 ft. lbs. (17-23 Nm).
4. Connect the electrical lead.

Electric Fan Switch

▶ See Figure 15

The electric fan switch is located on the radiator body. The tightening torque is 9.5-10 ft. lbs. (13-14 Nm).

Coolant Level Sensor

There is a coolant level sensor located in the coolant expansion tank. On expansion tanks mounted separate from the radiator, the sensor is mounted through the top tank. On integral radiator mounted expansion tanks it is mounted in the bottom of the expansion tank.

Oil Level Sensor

The is an oil level sensor mounted in the oil pan. It is accessible either at the top of the oil pan extension or through the bottom of the oil pan depending on the chassis and engine combination.

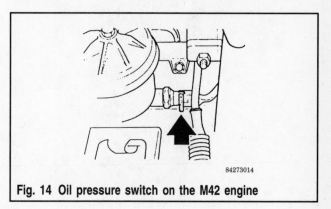

Fig. 14 Oil pressure switch on the M42 engine

ENGINE MECHANICAL

Description

▶ **See Figures 16, 17, 18, 19 and 20**

BMW has engineered some of the finest engines in the world. The repertoire of BMW produced engines include automotive, motorcycle, marine, industrial and, of course, aircraft units. The concept of refined, no compromise design has given BMW a reputation for high performance, high reliability and high efficiency engines.

All BMW engines covered in this book have iron blocks and aluminum heads. Intelligent design has made the iron block lightweight while providing the rigidity that any good motor requires. The aluminum head reduces the weight of the engine while providing good heat conductance. The aluminum head is designed to be very rigid and warp resistant.

The M20 and M30 engines are a single overhead camshaft design with 2 valves per cylinder. The M20 engine uses a timing belt to drive the camshaft, while the M30 engine uses a timing chain for the same chore. These engines share similar architecture with the original Neue Klasse 4 cylinder engines designed in the early 1960's. These engines are still considered a goal of reliability and smoothness for other manufacturers to meet.

The cylinder heads employ valves located in an inverted Vee pattern, allowing the use of hemispherical combustion chambers for optimum, swirl assisted combustion with minimum heat transfer to the cylinder head. This kind of combustion chamber also allows for use of the largest possible valves. The valves are actuated by a single, nitride hardened overhead camshaft.

Since they are not located directly below the shaft, they are actuated via light alloy rockers. This makes valve adjustment procedure very simple-the only special tool required is a simple piece of wire. Valve adjustments are made via a unique cam, located in the end of the rocker arm and in effect, pinched between sections of it. Since the adjusting cams are separate from the adjusting lockbolts and nuts, and since the lockbolts are prevented from turning via a flat at one end, it is easy to tighten down on the adjustment mechanism without changing the clearance. This minimizes the time required in performing the adjustment. Other engine features that prolong life are the use of chromium plated rings and valve stems, and forged connecting rods.

The M42 4 cylinder and M50 6 cylinder engines are double overhead camshaft design engines. Introduced in the early 1990's these 4 valve per cylinder designs boosted the performance, fuel efficiency and driveability of the vehicles in which they were installed. These engines were designed to be minimum maintenance engines. The hydraulic valve lash adjusters eliminated the need for periodic valve adjustment and the timing chain eliminated any need to change a timing belt. The ignition system has no distributor so there is no distributor cap or rotor to replace. The M50 has a racing inspired coil-over-sparkplug ignition system that totally dispenses with sparkplug wires.

The famous M-cars feature two of the most driver satisfying engines ever to make their way from racing car to street car. Both the S14 and S38 are double overhead camshaft design, 4 valve per cylinder engines with adjustable valves. Differing from almost every other production automotive engine, the S14 and S38 enjoy the use of a separate throttle plate for each cylinder. The individual intake runners make a very racy sound which is not surprising since the engines come straight from racing backgrounds. Redlines above 7000 rpm and the willingness to spin at such speeds all day long show the engineering expertise and spirit built into the M-car engines.

Engine Overhaul Tips

Most engine overhaul procedures are fairly standard. In addition to specific parts replacement procedures and complete specifications for your individual engine, this section also is a guide to accepted rebuilding procedures. Examples of standard rebuilding practice are shown and should be used along with specific details concerning your particular engine.

Competent and accurate machine shop services will ensure maximum performance, reliability and engine life.

In most instances it is more profitable for the do-it-yourself mechanic to remove, clean and inspect the component, buy the necessary parts and deliver these to a shop for actual machine work.

On the other hand, much of the rebuilding work (crankshaft, block, bearings, piston rods, and other components) is well within the scope of the do-it-yourself mechanic.

Keep in mind while performing the work, that the engine was built with pride and precision at the BMW factory and best results will come from performing the rebuilding work with the same level of pride and precision. The process is enjoyable and the end result will be satisfying.

84273015

Fig. 15 Electric fan switch and coolant level sensor on an integral expansion tank radiator

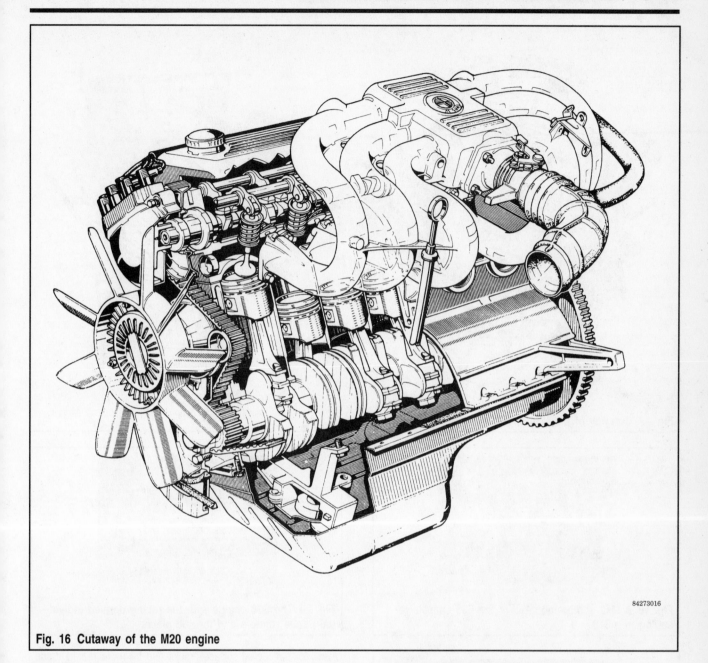

84273016

Fig. 16 Cutaway of the M20 engine

TOOLS

The tools required for an engine overhaul or parts replacement will depend on the depth of your involvement. With a few exceptions, they will be the tools found in a mechanic's tool kit (see Section 1). More in-depth work will require any or all of the following:

- A dial indicator (reading in thousandths) mounted on a universal base
- Micrometers and telescope gauges
- Jaw and screw-type pullers
- Scraper
- Valve spring compressor
- Ring groove cleaner
- Piston ring expander and compressor
- Ridge reamer
- Cylinder hone or glaze breaker
- Plastigage®
- Engine stand
- Valve compression fixture (M20 and M30 engines)

Many can be rented for a one-time use from a local parts jobber or tool supply house specializing in automotive work.

Occasionally, the use of special tools is called for. See the information on Special Tools and Safety Notice in the front of this book before substituting another tool.

INSPECTION TECHNIQUES

Procedures and specifications are given in this section for inspecting, cleaning and assessing the wear limits of most major components. Other procedures such as Magnaflux® and Zyglo® can be used to locate material flaws and stress cracks. Magnaflux® is a magnetic process applicable only to

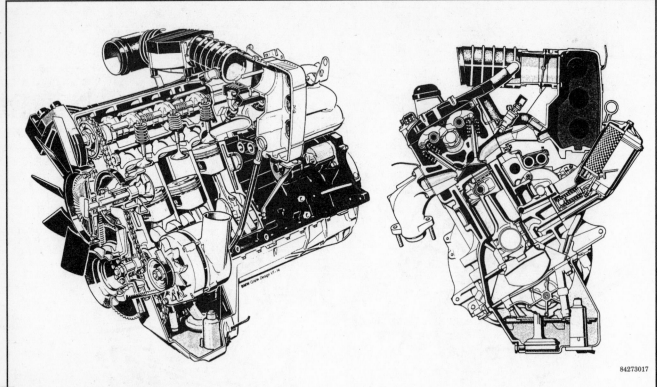

Fig. 17 Cutaway of the M30 engine

Fig. 18 A M42 engine mounted in the E36 chassis resulting in a 318i

Fig. 19 A M50 engine mounted in the E36 chassis resulting in a 325i

ferrous materials. The Zyglo® process coats the material with a fluorescent dye penetrant and can be used on any material

Fig. 20 The S38 engine with the racing derived individual intake runners and throttle plates

Check for suspected surface cracks can be more readily made using spot check dye. The dye is sprayed onto the suspected area, wiped off and the area sprayed with a developer. Cracks will show up brightly. These checks are available at any machine shop.

OVERHAUL TIPS

The cylinder head, timing covers and other engine parts are constructed with aluminum. Observe the following precautions when handling aluminum parts:
• Never hot tank aluminum parts (the caustic hot tank solution will eat the aluminum.
• Remove all aluminum parts (timing covers, oil filter housings, etc.) from engine parts prior to the tanking.
• Clean all threaded holes before installing a bolt or stud.

• Always coat threads lightly with engine oil or anti-seize compounds before installation, to prevent seizure.

• Never over-torque bolts or spark plugs especially in aluminum threads.

Stripped threads in any component can be repaired using any of several commercial repair kits (Heli-Coil®, Microdot®, Keenserts®, etc.).

When assembling the engine, any parts that will be frictional contact must be prelubed to provide lubrication at initial start-up, such as the camshaft. Any product specifically formulated for this purpose can be used, but engine oil is not recommended as a prelube.

When semi-permanent (locked, but removable) installation of bolts or nuts is desired, threads should be cleaned and coated with Loctite® or other similar, commercial threadlocker.

REPAIRING DAMAGED THREADS

Several methods of repairing damaged threads are available. Heli-Coil®, Keenserts® and Microdot® are among the most widely used. All involve basically the same principle — drilling out stripped threads, tapping the hole and installing a prewound insert — making welding, plugging and oversize fasteners unnecessary.

Two types of thread repair inserts are usually supplied: a standard type for most Metric Course and Metric Fine thread sizes and a spark lug type to fit most spark plug port sizes. Consult the individual manufacturer's catalog to determine exact applications. Typical thread repair kits will contain a selection of prewound threaded inserts, a tap (corresponding to the outside diameter threads of the insert) and an installation tool. Spark plug inserts usually differ because they require a tap equipped with pilot threads and a combined reamer/tap section. Most manufacturers also supply blister-packed thread repair inserts separately in addition to a master kit containing a variety of taps and inserts plus installation tools.

Before effecting a repair to a threaded hole, remove any snapped, broken or damaged bolts or studs. Penetrating oil can be used to free frozen threads; the offending item can be removed with locking pliers or with a screw or stud extractor. After the hole is clear, the thread can be repaired, as listed in the manufacturers instructions.

Checking Engine Compression

A noticeable lack of engine power, excessive oil consumption and/or poor fuel mileage measured over an extended pe-riod are all indicators of internal engine war. Worn piston rings, scored or worn cylinder bores, blown head gaskets, sticking or burnt valves and worn valve seats are all possible culprits here. A check of each cylinder's compression will help you locate the problems.

As mentioned in the Tools and Equipment section of Section 1, a screw-in type compression gauge is more accurate that the type you simply hold against the spark plug hole, although it takes slightly longer to use. It's worth it to obtain a more accurate reading.

1. Warm up the engine to normal operating temperature.
2. Remove all spark plugs.
3. Disconnect the DME relay.
4. Fully open the throttle either by operating the throttle linkage by hand or by having an assistant floor the accelerator pedal.
5. Screw the compression gauge into the no.1 spark plug hole until the fitting is snug.

➡**Be careful not to crossthread the plug hole. On aluminum cylinder heads use extra care, as the threads in these heads are easily ruined.**

6. Then, while you read the compression gauge, ask the assistant to crank the engine two or three times in short bursts using the ignition switch.
7. Read the compression gauge at the end of each series of cranks, and record the highest of these readings. Repeat this procedure for each of the engine's cylinders. Compare the highest reading of each cylinder to the others.

The cylinder pressures should be within 7 psi of one another. The cylinder pressure will typically be centered around 150 psi. Do not look for a specific value, but for a consistency across the cylinders. If the results are even, the engine is in good condition.

8. If a cylinder is unusually low, pour a tablespoon of clean engine oil into the cylinder through the spark plug hole and repeat the compression test. If the compression comes up after adding the oil, it appears that the cylinder's piston rings or bore are damaged or worn. If the pressure remains low, the valves may not be seating properly (a valve job is needed), or the head gasket may be blown near that cylinder. If compression in any two adjacent cylinders is low, and if the addition of oil doesn't help the compression, there is leakage past the head gasket. Oil and coolant water in the combustion chamber can result from this problem. There may be evidence of water droplets on the engine dipstick when a head gasket has blown.

GENERAL ENGINE SPECIFICATIONS

Year	Engine ID/VIN	Engine Displacement Liters (cc)	Fuel System Type	Net Horsepower @ rpm	Net Torque @ rpm (ft. lbs.)	Bore × Stroke (in.)	Compression Ratio	Oil Pressure @ rpm
1989	M20B25	2.5 (2494)	M1.3	168 @ 5800	164 @ 4300	3.31 × 2.95	8.8:1	18 @ Idle
	M30B35	3.5 (3430)	M1.3	208 @ 5700	225 @ 4000	3.62 × 3.39	9.0:1	18 @ Idle
	S14B23	2.3 (2302)	M1.2①	192 @ 6750	170 @ 4750	3.68 × 3.31	10.5:1	18 @ Idle
1990	M20B25	2.5 (2494)	M1.3	168 @ 5800	164 @ 4300	3.31 × 2.95	8.8:1	18 @ Idle
	M30B35	3.5 (3430)	M1.3	208 @ 5700	225 @ 4000	3.62 × 3.39	9.0:1	18 @ Idle
	S14B23	2.3 (2302)	M1.2①	192 @ 6750	170 @ 4750	3.68 × 3.31	10.5:1	18 @ Idle
1991	M20B25	2.5 (2494)	M1.3	168 @ 5800	164 @ 4300	3.31 × 2.95	8.8:1	18 @ Idle
	M30B35	3.5 (3430)	M1.3	208 @ 5700	225 @ 4000	3.62 × 3.39	9.0:1	18 @ Idle
	M42B18	1.8 (1796)	M1.7	134 @ 6000	127 @ 4600	3.31 × 3.19	10.0:1	18 @ Idle
	M50B25	2.5 (2494)	M3.1	189 @ 5900	181 @ 4700	3.31 × 2.95	10.0:1	28 @ Idle
	S14B23	2.3 (2302)	M1.2①	192 @ 6750	170 @ 4750	3.68 × 3.31	10.5:1	18 @ Idle
	S38B36	3.6 (3535)	M1.2①	310 @ 6900	266 @ 4750	3.68 × 3.39	10.0:1	18 @ Idle
1992–93	M20B25	2.5 (2494)	M1.3	168 @ 5800	164 @ 4300	3.31 × 2.95	8.8:1	18 @ Idle
	M30B35	3.5 (3430)	M1.3	208 @ 5700	225 @ 4000	3.62 × 3.39	9.0:1	18 @ Idle
	M42B18	1.8 (1796)	M1.7	134 @ 6000	127 @ 4600	3.31 × 3.19	10.0:1	18 @ Idle
	M50B25	2.5 (2494)	M3.1	189 @ 5900	181 @ 4700	3.31 × 2.95	10.0:1	28 @ Idle
	S38B36	3.6 (3535)	M1.2①	310 @ 6900	266 @ 4750	3.68 × 3.39	10.0:1	18 @ Idle

NOTE: Horsepower and torque are SAE net figures. They are measured at the rear of the transmission with all accessories installed and operating. Since the figures vary when a given engine is installed in different models, some are representative rather than exact.
① Motorsport Motronic

84273113

CAMSHAFT SPECIFICATIONS

All measurements given in inches.

Year	Engine ID	Engine Displacement Liters (cc)	Journal Diameter	Lobe Height	Bearing Clearance	Camshaft End Play
1989	M20B25	2.5 (2494)	NA	NA	NA	0.008
	M30B35	3.5 (3430)	NA	NA	NA	0.0012–0.0071
	S14B23	2.3 (2302)	1.1811	1.721	0.0011–0.0021	0.004–0.006
1990	M20B25	2.5 (2494)	NA	NA	NA	0.008
	M30B35	3.5 (3430)	NA	NA	NA	0.0012–0.0071
	S14B23	2.3 (2302)	1.1811	1.721	0.0011–0.0021	0.004–0.006
1991	M20B25	2.5 (2494)	NA	NA	NA	0.008
	M30B25	3.5 (3430)	NA	NA	NA	0.0012–0.0071
	M42B18	1.8 (1796)	NA	1.8755–1.8803	0.0008–0.0021	0.006–0.013
	M50B25	2.5 (2494)	NA	In. 1.8755–1.8803 Ex. 1.8401–1.8449	0.0008–0.0021	0.006–0.013
	S14B23	2.3 (2302)	1.1811	1.721	0.0011–0.0021	0.004–0.006
	S38B36	3.6 (3535)	1.1811	1.736	0.0011–0.0021	0.004–0.006
1992–93	M20B25	2.5 (2494)	NA	NA	NA	0.008
	M30B35	3.5 (3430)	NA	NA	NA	0.0012–0.0071
	M42B18	1.8 (1796)	NA	1.8755–1.8803	0.0008–0.0021	0.006–0.013
	M50B25	2.5 (2494)	NA	In. 1.8755–1.8803 Ex. 1.8401–1.8449	0.0008–0.0021	0.006–0.013
	S38B36	3.6 (3535)	1.1811	1.736	0.0011–0.0021	0.004–0.006

NA—Not available

84273114

CRANKSHAFT AND CONNECTING ROD SPECIFICATIONS

All measurements are given in inches.

Year	Engine ID/VIN	Engine Displacement Liters (cc)	Crankshaft				Connecting Rod		
			Main Brg. Journal Dia.	Main Brg. Oil Clearance	Shaft End-play	Thrust on No.	Journal Diameter	Oil Clearance	Side Clearance
1989	M20B25	2.5 (2494)	2.3622	0.0012–0.0027	0.0031–0.0064	6	1.7707–1.7713	0.0008–0.0022	NA
	M30B35	3.5 (3430)	2.3616	0.0008–0.0018	0.0033–0.0068	4	1.8888–1.8894	0.0008–0.0022	NA
	S14B23	2.3 (2302)	2.1653	0.0012–0.0027	0.0033–0.0068	3	1.8888–1.8894	0.0012–0.0027	NA
1990	M20B25	2.5 (2494)	2.3622	0.0012–0.0027	0.0031–0.0064	6	1.7707–1.7713	0.0008–0.0022	NA
	M30B35	3.5 (3430)	2.3616	0.0008–0.0018	0.0033–0.0068	4	1.8888–1.8894	0.0008–0.0022	NA
	S14B23	2.3 (2302)	2.1653	0.0012–0.0027	0.0033–0.0068	3	1.8888–1.8894	0.0012–0.0027	NA
1991	M20B25	2.5 (2494)	2.3622	0.0012–0.0027	0.0031–0.0064	6	1.7707–1.7713	0.0008–0.0022	NA
	M30B35	3.5 (3430)	2.3616	0.0008–0.0018	0.0033–0.0068	4	1.8888–1.8894	0.0008–0.0022	NA
	M42B18	1.8 (1796)	2.3616	0.0008–0.0023	0.0031–0.0064	4	1.7719–1.7726	0.0008–0.0022	NA
	M50B25	2.5 (2494)	2.3616	0.0008–0.0023	0.0031–0.0064	6	1.7721–1.7727	0.0008–0.0022	NA
	S14B23	2.3 (2302)	2.1653	0.0012–0.0027	0.0033–0.0068	3	1.8888–1.8894	0.0012–0.0027	NA
	S38B36	3.6 (3535)	2.3622	0.0012–0.0027	0.0033–0.0068	4	1.8888–1.8894	0.0008–0.0022	NA
1992-93	M20B25	2.5 (2494)	2.3622	0.0012–0.0027	0.0031–0.0064	6	1.7707–1.7713	0.0008–0.0022	NA
	M30B35	3.5 (3430)	2.3616	0.0008–0.0018	0.0033–0.0068	4	1.8888–1.8894	0.0008–0.0022	NA
	M42B18	1.8 (1796)	2.3616	0.0008–0.0023	0.0031–0.0064	4	1.7719–1.7726	0.0008–0.0022	NA
	M50B25	2.5 (2494)	2.3616	0.0008–0.0023	0.0031–0.0064	6	1.7721–1.7727	0.0008–0.0022	NA
	S38B36	3.6 (3535)	2.3622	0.0012–0.0027	0.0033–0.0068	4	1.8888–1.8894	0.0008–0.0022	NA

NA—Not available

84273115

VALVE SPECIFICATIONS

Year	Engine ID/VIN	Engine Displacement Liters (cu. in.)	Seat Angle (deg.)	Face Angle (deg.)	Spring Test Pressure (lbs. @ in.)	Spring Installed Height (in.)	Stem-to-Guide ① Clearance (in.)		Stem Diameter (in.)	
							Intake	Exhaust	Intake	Exhaust
1989	M20B25	2.5 (2494)	45	NA	NA	NA	0.031	0.031	0.2756	0.2756
	M30B35	3.5 (3430)	45	NA	NA	NA	0.031	0.031	0.3150	0.3150
	S14B23	2.3 (2302)	45	NA	NA	NA	0.025	0.031	0.2756	0.2756
1990	M20B25	2.5 (2494)	45	NA	NA	NA	0.031	0.031	0.2756	0.2756
	M30B35	3.5 (3430)	45	NA	NA	NA	0.031	0.031	0.3150	0.3150
	S14B23	2.3 (2302)	45	NA	NA	NA	0.025	0.031	0.2756	0.2756
1991	M20B25	2.5 (2494)	45	NA	NA	NA	0.031	0.031	0.2756	0.2756
	M30B35	3.5 (3430)	45	NA	NA	NA	0.031	0.031	0.3150	0.3150
	M42B18	1.8 (1796)	45	NA	NA	NA	0.020	0.020	0.2756	0.2756
	M50B25	2.5 (2494)	45	NA	NA	NA	0.020	0.020	0.2756	0.2756
	S14B23	2.3 (2302)	45	NA	NA	NA	0.025	0.031	0.2756	0.2756
	S38B36	3.6 (3535)	45	NA	NA	NA	0.025	0.031	0.2756	0.2756
1992-93	M20B25	2.5 (2494)	45	NA	NA	NA	0.031	0.031	0.2756	0.2756
	M30B35	3.5 (3430)	45	NA	NA	NA	0.031	0.031	0.3150	0.3150
	M42B18	1.8 (1796)	45	NA	NA	NA	0.020	0.020	0.2756	0.2756
	M50B25	2.5 (2494)	45	NA	NA	NA	0.020	0.020	0.2756	0.2756
	S38B36	3.6 (3535)	45	NA	NA	NA	0.025	0.031	0.2756	0.2756

NA—Not available
① See text for procedure

84273116

PISTON AND RING SPECIFICATIONS

All measurements are given in inches.

Year	Engine ID/VIN	Engine Displacement Liters (cc)	Piston Clearance	Ring Gap			Ring Side Clearance		
				Top Compression	Bottom Compression	Oil Control	Top Compression	Bottom Compression	Oil Control
1989	M20B25	2.5 (2494)	0.0004–0.0016	0.0080–0.0200	0.0080–0.0200	0.0080–0.0200	0.0016–0.0031	0.0012–0.0027	0.0008–0.0020
	M30B35	3.5 (3430)	0.0008–0.0020	0.0080–0.0180	0.0160–0.0250	0.0120–0.0240	0.0016–0.0028	0.0012–0.0024	0.0008–0.0022
	S14B23	2.3 (2302)	0.0012–0.0024	0.0118–0.0217	0.0118–0.0217	0.0100–0.0200	0.0024–0.0035	0.0024–0.0035	0.0008–0.0020
1990	M20B25	2.5 (2494)	0.0004–0.0016	0.0080–0.0200	0.0080–0.0200	0.0080–0.0200	0.0016–0.0031	0.0012–0.0027	0.0008–0.0020
	M30B35	3.5 (3430)	0.0008–0.0020	0.0080–0.0180	0.0160–0.0250	0.0120–0.0240	0.0016–0.0028	0.0012–0.0024	0.0008–0.0022
	S14B23	2.3 (2302)	0.0012–0.0024	0.0118–0.0217	0.0118–0.0217	0.0100–0.0200	0.0024–0.0035	0.0024–0.0035	0.0008–0.0020
1991	M20B25	2.5 (2494)	0.0004–0.0016	0.0080–0.0200	0.0080–0.0200	0.0080–0.0200	0.0016–0.0031	0.0012–0.0027	0.0008–0.0022
	M30B35	3.5 (3430)	0.0008–0.0020	0.0080–0.0180	0.0160–0.0250	0.0120–0.0240	0.0016–0.0028	0.0012–0.0024	0.0008–0.0022
	M42B18	1.8 (1796)	0.0004–0.0016	0.0080–0.0160	0.0080–0.0160	0.0080–0.0180	0.0008–0.0020	0.0008–0.0020	0.0008–0.0022
	M50B25	2.5 (2494)	0.0004–0.0016	0.0080–0.0160	0.0080–0.0160	0.0080–0.0180	0.0008–0.0020	0.0008–0.0020	0.0008–0.0022
	S14B23	2.3 (2302)	0.0012–0.0024	0.0118–0.0217	0.0118–0.0217	0.0100–0.0200	0.0024–0.0035	0.0024–0.0035	0.0008–0.0020
	S38B36	3.6 (3535)	0.0012–0.0024	0.0118–0.0217	0.0118–0.0217	0.0100–0.0200	0.0024–0.0035	0.0024–0.0035	0.0008–0.0020
1992-93	M20B25	2.5 (2494)	0.0004–0.0016	0.0080–0.0200	0.0080–0.0200	0.0080–0.0200	0.0016–0.0031	0.0012–0.0027	0.0008–0.0022
	M30B35	3.5 (3430)	0.0008–0.0020	0.0080–0.0180	0.0160–0.0250	0.0120–0.0240	0.0016–0.0028	0.0012–0.0024	0.0008–0.0022
	M42B18	1.8 (1796)	0.0004–0.0016	0.0080–0.0160	0.0080–0.0160	0.0080–0.0180	0.0008–0.0020	0.0008–0.0020	0.0008–0.0022
	M50B25	2.5 (2494)	0.0004–0.0016	0.0080–0.0160	0.0080–0.0160	0.0080–0.0180	0.0008–0.0020	0.0008–0.0020	0.0008–0.0022
	S38B36	3.6 (3535)	0.0012–0.0024	0.0118–0.0217	0.0118–0.0217	0.0100–0.0200	0.0024–0.0035	0.0024–0.0035	0.0008–0.0020

84273117

TORQUE SPECIFICATIONS
All readings in ft. lbs.

Year	Engine ID/VIN	Engine Displacement Liters (cc)	Cylinder Head Bolts	Main Bearing Bolts	Rod Bearing Bolts	Crankshaft Damper Bolts	Flywheel Bolts	Manifold Intake	Manifold Exhaust	Spark Plugs	Lug Nut
1989	M20B25	2.5 (2494)	②	42–46	⑦	281–309	82–94	16–18	⑤	14–22	65–79
	M30B35	3.5 (3430)	③	42–46	38–41	311–325	82–94	16–18	⑤	14–22	65–79
	S14B23	2.3 (2302)	①	④	⑧	311–325	82–94	6.5–8.0	6.5–8.0	14–22	65–79
1990	M20B25	2.5 (2494)	②	42–46	⑦	281–309	82–94	16–18	⑤	14–22	65–79
	M30B35	3.5 (3430)	③	42–46	38–41	311–325	82–94	16–18	⑤	14–22	65–79
	S14B23	2.3 (2302)	①	④	⑧	311–325	82–94	6.5–8.0	6.5–8.0	14–22	65–79
1991	M20B25	2.5 (2494)	②	42–46	⑦	281–309	82–94	16–18	⑤	14–22	65–79
	M30B35	3.5 (3430)	③	42–46	38–41	311–325	82–94	16–18	⑤	14–22	65–79
	M42B18	1.8 (1796)	⑥	④	⑦	217–231	82–94	10–12	17–18	14–22	65–79
	M50B25	2.5 (2494)	⑥	④	⑦	281–309	82–94	10–12	14	14–22	65–79
	S14B23	2.3 (2302)	①	④	⑧	311–325	82–94	6.5–8.0	6.5–8.0	14–22	65–79
	S38B36	3.6 (3535)	①	④	⑧	⑨	82–94	⑩	6.5–8.0	14–22	65–79
1992–93	M20B25	2.5 (2494)	②	42–46	⑦	281–309	82–94	16–18	⑤	14–22	65–79
	M30B35	3.5 (3430)	③	42–46	38–41	311–325	82–94	16–18	⑤	14–22	65–79
	M42B18	1.8 (1796)	⑥	④	⑦	217–231	82–94	10–12	17–18	14–22	65–79
	M50B25	2.5 (2494)	⑥	④	⑦	281–309	82–94	10–12	14	14–22	65–79
	S38B36	3.6 (3535)	①	④	⑧	⑨	82–94	⑩	6.5–8.0	14–22	65–79

① Step 1: 35–37 ft. lbs.
  Step 2: 57–59 ft. lbs.
  Step 3: wait 15 minutes
  Step 4: 71–73 ft. lbs.
② Hex Head Bolts
    Step 1: 29–33 ft. lbs.
    Step 2: wait 15 minutes
    Step 3: 43–47 ft. lbs.
    Step 4: run engine 25 minutes
    Step 5: +25–30 degree turn
  Torx Head Bolts
    Step 1: 22 ft. lbs.
    Step 2: +90 degree turn
    Step 3: +90 degree turn
③ Step 1: 42–44 ft. lbs.
  Step 2: wait 20 minutes
  Step 3: run engine 25 minutes
  Step 4: +30–40 degree turn
④ Step 1: 14–18 ft. lbs.
  Step 2: +47–53 degree turn
⑤ Step 1: coat the upper row of bolts with thread sealer
  Step 2: 16–18 ft. lbs.
⑥ Step 1: 24 ft. lbs.
  Step 2: +90–95 degree turn
  Step 3: +90–95 degree turn
  Note: M50B25 engine with 6mm torx: 7.2 ft. lbs. maximum
⑦ Step 1: 14 ft. lbs.
  Step 2: +70 degree turn
⑧ Step 1: 7 ft. lbs.
  Step 2: 22 ft. lbs.
  Step 3: +60–62 degree turn
⑨ Step 1: 43 ft. lbs.
  Step 2: +60 degree turn
  Step 3: +60 degree turn
  Step 4: +30 degree turn
⑩ 6mm Bolts: 6.5–8.0 ft. lbs.
  8mm Bolts: 14–17 ft. lbs.

84273118

Engines

REMOVAL & INSTALLATION

E30 3 Series

WITH M42 ENGINE

1. Disconnect the battery ground cable. Remove the transmission and remove the engine splash guard. Disconnect the gas spring and prop rod and support hood safely in the fully open position.

2. Remove the fan cowl by turning the expansion rivets on the left and right sides. Lift the cowl up and out of the engine compartment.

3. Hold the fan pulley while unscrewing the fan nut from the shaft. The shaft uses left hand threads; turn the nut counterclockwise to unscrew.

4. Drain the coolant from the engine block. Disconnect the bottom hose from the radiator expansion tank, the engine coolant hoses and the heater hoses from the splash wall. Drain all coolant into clean containers for reuse or proper disposal.

5. Disconnect the air flow meter electrical plug and loosen the hose clamp and mounting screws. Lift the air sensor with the air cleaner up and out of the engine compartment.

6. Unclip the throttle cable and pull the cable out with the rubber holder.

7. Disconnect the fuel lines taking note of their positions. Pull off the vent hose to the filter for tank venting.

8. Disconnect the vacuum fitting at the brake booster.

9. Remove the ignition leads from the coil. Unscrew the connections at the alternator and starter. Disconnect the 2 plugs from the electrical duct. Remove the plug from the throttle valve potentiometer located at the throttle neck. Pull off the tank venting valve plug located next to the air cleaner. Disconnect the fuel injector plug located at the end of the electrical duct near to the fuel pipes. Pull off the idle speed control connector at the rear of the intake manifold. Disconnect the oil pressure switch electrical connection.

10. Unscrew the front and rear intake manifold supports.

11. Remove the electrical duct from the engine. Disconnect the coolant temperature senders for the gauge and the DME.

12. Disconnect the electrical duct and wiring harness on the engine and lay it off to the side of the engine.

13. Use a suitable lifting yoke to attach to the engine lifting eyes. Unscrew the motor mounts and the engine ground strap. Lift out the engine.

To Install:

14. Lower engine into engine compartment. Fasten the motor mounts and the ground strap.

15. Attach the engine wiring harness and electrical duct. Make sure that the rubber grommets on the duct are clipped in correctly. Connect the leads to the 2 coolant sensors and the oil pressure switch.

16. Fasten the front and rear intake manifold supports.

17. Connect the idle speed control plug, the fuel injector plug, the tank venting valve plug, the throttle valve potentiometer plug and the electrical lead duct plugs.

18. Reconnect the starter and the alternator. Attach the ignition leads to the coil in the proper order.

19. Refit the vacuum connection to the brake booster. Reconnect the tank vent hose and the fuel hoses. The upper fuel hose is the return line and the bottom is the feed line.

20. Attach the throttle cable and its holder. Replace the air cleaner and air flow meter assembly. Attach the electrical connector to the air flow meter.

21. Connect the heater hoses, engine coolant hoses and the radiator expansion tank hose.

22. Install the fan using tool 11 5 040 or equivalent. Torque the nut to 29 ft. lbs. (40 Nm). If using the tool set the torque wrench to 22 ft. lbs. (30 Nm); the additional length of the tool multiplies the torque to achieve 29 ft. lbs. (40 Nm) at the nut.

23. Replace the fan cowl taking care to engage the tabs at the right and left.

24. Replace the splash guard and the transmission. Reconnect the hood prop rod and gas spring.

25. Add the proper coolant mixture and bleed the cooling system.

26. Connect the battery leads and check all fluid levels before starting the engine.

WITH S14 ENGINE

▶ See Figure 21

1. Disconnect the negative battery cable. Remove the transmission.

2. Remove the splash guard from underneath the engine. Put a drain pan underneath and then drain coolant from both the radiator and block.

3. Loosen the hose clamps at either end of the air intake hose leading to the air intake sensor. Pull off the hose. Then, pull both electrical connectors off the air cleaner/airflow sensor unit. Remove both mounting nuts and remove the unit.

4. Disconnect the accelerator and cruise control cables. Unscrew the nuts mounting the cable housing mounting bracket and set the housings and bracket aside.

5. Loosen the clamp and disconnect the brake booster vacuum hose.

6. Loosen the clamp and disconnect the other end of the booster vacuum hose at the manifold. Remove the nut from the intake manifold brace.

7. Loosen the hose clamp and disconnect the air intake hose at the manifold. Then, remove all the nuts attaching the manifold assembly to the outer ends of the intake throttle necks and remove the assembly.

8. Put a drain pan underneath and then loosen the hose clamps and disconnect the coolant expansion tank hoses. Disconnect the engine ground strap.

9. Disconnect the ignition coil high tension lead. Then, label and disconnect the plugs on the front of the block. Remove the nut fastening another lead farther forward of the plugs and move the lead aside so it will not interfere with engine removal.

10. Label and disconnect the plugs from the rear of the alternator. Label the additional leads and then remove the nuts and disconnect those leads. It's best to reinstall nuts once the leads are removed to keep them from being mixed up.

11. Remove the cover for the electrical connectors from the starter. Label the leads and then remove the attaching nuts and disconnect them. Reinstall the nuts.

12. There is a wire running to a connector on the oil pan to warn of low oil level. Pull off the connector, unscrew the car-

rier for the lead, and then pull the lead out from above. Pull off the connectors near where the lead for the low oil warning system ran and unclip the wires from the carrier.

13. Find the vacuum hose leading to the fuel pressure regulator. Pull it off. Label and then disconnect the plugs. Unscrew the mounting screw for the electrical lead connecting with the top of the block and remove the lead and its carrier.

14. There is a vacuum hose connecting with one of the throttle necks. Disconnect it and pull it out of the intake manifold bracket. Pull off the electrical connector. Pull out the rubber retainer, and then pull the idle speed control out and put it aside. The engine wiring harness is located nearby. Take it out of its carriers.

15. All the fuel injectors are plugged into a common plate. Carefully and evenly pull the plate off the injectors, pull it out past the pressure regulator, and lay it aside.

16. Loosen the clamp and then disconnect the PCV hose. Label and then disconnect the fuel lines connecting the injector circuit. Put a drain pan underneath and then disconnect the heater hose from the cylinder head.

17. Loosen the clamp near the throttle necks and then pull the engine wiring harness out and put it aside. Put a drain pan underneath and then disconnect the heater hose that connects to the block.

18. Loosen the mounting clamp for the carbon canister, slide it out of the clamp, and place it aside with the hoses still connected.

19. Note the routing of the oil cooler lines where they connect at the base of the oil filter. Label them if necessary. Put a drain pan underneath and then unscrew the flared connectors for the lines.

20. Unbolt and remove the fan. Store it in an upright position. Remove the radiator.

21. Support the power steering pump. Remove the adjusting bolt and disconnect and remove the belt. Then, remove the nuts and bolts on which the unit hinges. Pull the unit aside and hang it so there will not be strain on the hoses.

22. Remove the adjusting bolt for the air conditioning compressor and disconnect and remove the belt. Then, remove the nut at one end of the hinge bolt and pull the bolt out, suspending the compressor.

23. Remove the through-bolts to disconnect the engine hood supports and then open the hood and support it securely.

24. Suspend the engine with a suitable lifting device. Then, remove the nuts for the engine mounting bolts. The mounts are on the axle carrier and the nut is at the top on the left and on the bottom on the right. Then, carefully lift the engine

84273021

Fig. 21 Air conditioner compressor mounting bolts on the S14 engine

out of the compartment, avoiding contact between it and the components remaining in the vehicle.

To install:

25. Keep these points in mind during installation:

   a. Torque the engine mounting bolts to 32.5 ft. lbs. (44 Nm).

   b. Adjust the belt tension for the air conditioning compressor and power steering pump drive belts to give ½-¾ inch deflection.

   c. Torque the oil cooler line flare nuts to 25 ft. lbs. (34 Nm)

   d. When reconnecting the intake manifold to the throttle necks, inspect and, if necessary, replace the O-rings. Torque the mounting nuts to 6.5 ft. lbs. (9 Nm).

26. Reverse the procedures used for removal and lower the engine into the engine compartment. When the engine is positioned, the guide pin must fit in the bore of the axle carrier. Torque the mounting bolts on the front axle carrier (small bolt) to 18-20 ft. lbs. (25-27 Nm); the larger bolt to 31-35 ft. lbs. (40-47 Nm). The mount-to-bracket bolts are torqued to 31-35 ft. lbs. (40-47 Nm).

27. Install the intake manifold assembly and connect the fuel lines, use new hose clamps to connect the fuel lines to the fuel filter. Connect all of the multi-prong plugs and all vacuum hoses.

28. Connect the accelerator cable and cruise control cable to the throttle body and adjust the accelerator cable and cruise control cable.

29. Install the coolant recovery tank, use a new hose clamp on the coolant expansion tank.

30. Install the air cleaner and reconnect all electrical plugs. Connect and install the relays in the relay box.

31. Reconnect the wiring to the main control unit and install the idle control unit.

32. Install the air conditioning compressor and power steering pump, properly route the accessory drive belt. Adjust the belt tension.

33. Install the radiator and connect the hoses.

34. Install the transmission.

35. Install the hood support and lower the hood.

36. Make sure all fluid levels are correct before starting the engine. Bleed air from the cooling system.

WITH M20 ENGINES

1. Disconnect the negative battery cable. Remove the transmission.

2. Without disconnecting hoses, loosen and remove the power steering pump bolts and remove the pump and belts and support the pump out of the way.

3. Remove the drain plug and remove the coolant from the radiator. Then, remove the radiator. Unbolt and remove the fan from the engine. Store it in an upright position.

4. Without disconnecting hoses, remove the mounting bolts that run through the compressor body and remove the air conditioner compressor and drive belt and support the compressor out of the way.

5. Remove the through-bolts to disconnect the engine hood supports and then open the hood and support it securely.

➡**The hood must be propped in a secure manner. If it falls during work serious injury could result.**

6. Disconnect the accelerator cable. If the vehicle has cruise control, disconnect the cruise control cable. If the vehicle has an automatic transmission, disconnect the throttle cable leading to the transmission.

7. Pull the large, multi-prong plug off the airflow sensor (an integral part of the air cleaner). Loosen the clamp and disconnect the air intake hose at the airflow sensor. Remove the mounting nuts and remove the air cleaner/airflow sensor unit.

8. Disconnect the coolant expansion tank hose. Disconnect the large, multi-prong connector near the air intake hose.

9. The diagnosis plug is a large, screw-on connector located near the thermostat and associated hoses. Unscrew and disconnect this connector.

10. Disconnect the large coolant hoses connecting to the thermostat.

11. Make sure the engine is cold. Place a metal container under the connection to collect fuel; then, disconnect the fuel line at the connection right near the thermostat housing by unscrewing it. Unfasten the fuel line clip about a foot away from this connection.

12. Disconnect the electrical plugs near the diagnosis plug connector. Disconnect the bracket for the dipstick guide tube.

13. Remove the bolts which attach the water pipes going to the engine to mounting brackets.

14. Disconnect the heater hoses at the heater core (near the firewall). Remove the coolant hose running to the top of the block.

15. Place a metal container under the connection to collect fuel; then, disconnect the remaining fuel hose supplying the engine injectors. Disconnect the electrical connectors.

16. Remove the bolt from the mounting brace connecting with the cylinder head.

17. Mark and then disconnect the electrical leads from the starter. Unbolt the starter and lift it out from above.

18. Place a metal container under the connection to collect fuel; then, disconnect the fuel pipe that runs right near the starter.

19. Label electrical connectors on the alternator. Then, pull off the rubber caps for the connectors which are attached with nuts and remove the nuts and any washers. Disconnect the plug-on connector.

20. Disconnect the electrical leads for the coil. Loosen the clips attaching the leads under the distributor and pull the harness away to the left. Disconnect the oil pressure sending unit.

21. Place a drain pan underneath the connections and then disconnect the oil cooler pipes at the crankcase by unscrewing the flare nut fittings.

22. Take the cover off the relay box. Then, lift out the relays and their mounting sockets. Place the relays and associated wiring on top of the engine so they will come out with it.

23. Loosen the mounting clamp and then remove the carbon canister. There is a plate to which a number of electrical leads are connected. Remove the mounting screws and move the plate aside so it will clear the dipstick guide tube when the engine is removed.

24. Remove the 2 bolts that fasten the wiring harness to the firewall. Then, disconnect the engine ground strap.

25. Remove both engine mount through-bolts. Lift out the engine with a suitable hoist, using hooks at front and rear.

To install:

26. Reverse the procedures used for removal and lower the engine into the engine compartment. When the engine is positioned, the guide pin must fit in the bore of the axle carrier. Torque the mounting bolts on the front axle carrier (small bolt) to 18-20 ft. lbs. (25-27 Nm); the larger bolt to 31-35. The mount-to-bracket bolts are torqued to 31-35 ft. lbs. (40-47 Nm). Engine-to-bracket mounts are torqued to (small bolt) 16-17 ft. lbs. (22-23 Nm); (large bolt) 31-35 ft. lbs. (40-47 Nm).

27. Connect the fuel lines, use new hose clamps to connect the fuel lines to the fuel filter. Connect all of the multi-prong plugs and all vacuum hoses.

28. Connect the accelerator cable and cruise control cable to the throttle body and adjust the accelerator cable and cruise control cable.

29. Install the coolant recovery tank, use a new hose clamp on the coolant expansion tank.

30. Install the air cleaner and reconnect all electrical plugs. Connect and install the relays in the relay box.

31. Reconnect the wiring to the main control unit and install the idle control unit.

32. Install the air conditioning compressor and power steering pump, properly route the accessory drive belt. Adjust the belt tension.

33. Install the radiator and connect the hoses.

34. Install the transmission.

35. Install the hood support.

36. Make sure all fluid levels are correct before starting the engine. Bleed air from the cooling system.

E36 3 Series

WITH M42 ENGINE

1. Disconnect the battery ground cable. Remove the transmission and remove the engine splash guard. Press the hinge so it goes over center and support hood safely in the fully open position.

2. Remove the fan cowl by turning the expansion rivets on the left and right sides. Lift the cowl up and out of the engine compartment. Disconnect the air conditioner compressor without removing the lines. Suspend of to one side.

3. Hold the fan pulley while unscrewing the fan nut from the shaft. The shaft uses left hand threads; turn the nut counterclockwise to unscrew.

4. Drain the coolant from the engine block. Disconnect the bottom hose from the radiator expansion tank, the engine coolant hoses and the heater hoses from the splash wall. Drain all coolant into clean containers for reuse or proper disposal.

5. Disconnect the air flow meter electrical plug and loosen the hose clamp and mounting screws. Lift the air sensor with the air cleaner up and out of the engine compartment.

6. Remove the air intake duct and disconnect the idle speed control hose. Disconnect the wire holders from the duct.

7. Unbolt the power steering reservoir. Unbolt the power steering pump and support without tension on the hose. Do not disconnect the hoses. Secure the power steering reservoir off to the side.

8. Flip up the throttle linkage cover on the throttle body. Unscrew the holder and disconnect the cable from the linkage.

9. Mark the locations of the fuel feed and return hoses. the upper hose is the return line. Disconnect the hoses and plug.

Disconnect the vacuum line from the brake booster. Plug the opening to prevent dirt from entering.

10. Remove the grill from the air intake cowl at the base of the windshield. Remove the electrical lead tray. Remove the screws on the right side cowl holder bracket and the screw on the left side. Remove the cowl from the engine compartment.

11. Remove the ignition leads from the spark plugs. Disconnect the wiring from the alternator and the starter. Disconnect the cylinder ID sensor and the pulse sender located just behind the oil filter housing. Disconnect the idle speed control and remove from the holder.

12. Disconnect the throttle position sensor lead, oil pressure sender and the tank venting valve connector. Unbolt the fuel line holder and the intake manifold support. Loosen the clamp holding the pipe to the intake support.

13. Unscrew the intake support from the electrical lead duct. Disconnect the temperature sensors under the intake manifold. Unplug the fuel injectors and disconnect the electric lead duct from the engine. Place off to the side.

14. Disconnect the coolant hose from the transfer pipe on the side of the engine.

15. Connect an engine lifting yoke to the lifting tabs at the front and rear of the engine. Disconnect the ground strap and motor mounts. Remove the engine.

➡ **Do not invert the engine for longer than 10 minutes total or the hydraulic valve lash compensators will drain. This will render the compensators useless and will require replacement.**

To install:

16. Install the engine in the car. Connect the ground strap and torque the engine mounts to 30 ft. lbs. (42 Nm).

17. Connect the coolant hose to the transfer pipe. Replace the injector electrical lead duct and connect the injectors. Replace the electric lead duct on the intake support and replace the intake support. Connect the temperature sensors under the intake manifold. Attach the fuel line holder.

18. Connect the tank venting valve, the throttle position sender, the oil pressure switch and the idle speed control. Install the idle speed control in its holder. Connect the cylinder ID sender and the pulse sender. Connect the starter and alternator. Connect the ignition leads.

19. Install the air cowl, bracket and grill. Connect the brake booster vacuum line and the fuel hoses. The upper hose is the fuel return line. Connect the throttle cable and holder.

20. Install the power steering pump and reservoir. Install the air intake duct and the air cleaner assembly. Connect the idle speed line and the electrical leads. Connect the air flow sensor.

21. Connect the coolant hoses. Install the fan, fan cowl and the air conditioner compressor. Install the hood and transmission. Install the splash guard and fill the engine fluids.

22. Connect the battery, start the car, bleed the coolant and check for leaks.

WITH M50 ENGINE

▶ See Figure 22

1. Disconnect the battery ground cable. Remove the transmission and remove the engine splash guard. Press the hinge so it goes over center and support hood safely in the fully open position.

84273022

Fig. 22 Engine mount and exhaust flanges on M50 engine installed in the E36 chassis

2. Disconnect the air mass sensor plug and loosen the air intake duct hose clamp. Remove the air cleaner assembly. Disconnect the hoses for the idle speed control and the crankcase breather.

3. Unscrew and remove the ducting for the alternator. Pull out the fan cowl expansion rivets and remove the cowl upwards. Hold the pulley with tool 11 5 030 or equivalent, and unscrew the fan clockwise. Remove the fan and keep upright.

4. Drain the coolant from the block at the plug accessible through the exhaust manifold. Remove the upper and lower radiator hoses from the radiator. Disconnect the coolant level switch and the automatic transmission cooler lines. Plug the cooler lines. Disconnect the right side hose and the temperature sensor.

5. Insert a tool into the radiator support clips and press down on the tab. Pull back on the radiator to release it. Remove the radiator. Disconnect the heater hoses from the heater and heater valve.

6. Remove the grill from the air intake cowl at the base of the windshield. Remove the electrical lead tray. Remove the screws on the right side cowl holder bracket and the screw on the left side. Remove the cowl from the engine compartment.

7. Unscrew the fastener from the throttle cable cover and pull the cover forward and off. Unclip the cable and pull the cable out with the rubber holder.

8. Pull the vacuum fitting from the brake booster and plug the openings.

9. Remove the engine and intake manifold covers. Unscrew the bolt holding the ground strap on the front lifting eye. Replace the bolt before lifting the engine.

10. Unscrew the 2 bolts holding the plug plate and pull off the plug plate. Be careful not to damage the rubber seals. Take off the ignition coil electrical plugs. Remove the plug plate complete with the electrical leads.

11. Remove the cylinder head vent hose and pull off the air temperature sensor plug. Remove the tank venting hose and the throttle heating hoses from the throttle body. Remove the throttle valve switch plug. Unclip the idle speed control valve mounted on the manifold. Disconnect the fuel hoses from the pipes.

12. Unscrew the hardware holding the intake manifold to the cylinder head. Remove the intake manifold taking care not to drop anything into the exposed ports.

13. Disconnect the plugs from the temperature sensor, temperature gauge, the oil pressure switch and the idle speed control valve. Disconnect the cylinder identifying sender plug (black) and the pulse sender plug (gray) for the DME. Unscrew the oxygen sensor plug in the holder.

14. Remove the electric leads from the alternator and the starter. Unscrew the electrical lead tray and place the engine wiring harness to the side.

15. Loosen the drive belt for the power steering pump and the air conditioner compressor by turning their respective tensioners clockwise. This will release the tension on the belt and allow the belt to be removed.

16. Unbolt the power steering pump and place to the side without disconnecting the hoses. Unbolt the air conditioner compressor and place to the side without disconnecting the lines.

17. Attach a lifting fixture to the engine lifting hooks. Unscrew the engine mounts and ground strap. Lift the engine out of the vehicle being careful of the front radiator mount.

To Install:

18. Lower the engine into the vehicle and attach the motor mounts and ground strap.

19. Install the power steering pump and the air conditioner compressor. Install the drive belts.

20. Replace the wiring harness and electrical lead tray on the engine. Connect the leads to the starter and alternator. Screw in the plug for the oxygen sensor holder. Connect the leads for the cylinder identifying sender, the DME pulse sender, the temperature sensor, the temperature gauge sender, the oil pressure switch and the idle speed control valve.

21. Install the intake manifold making sure that the intake seals are intact. Replace the intake seals if any signs of deterioration are evident.

22. Attach the fuel lines. The upper line is the return and the lower is the feed.

23. Attach the idle speed control valve hose located on the manifold.

24. Connect the throttle valve switch plug, the throttle valve heating lines and the tank vent line.

25. Connect the air temperature sensor plug and attach the cylinder head venting hoses.

26. Reconnect the plugs for the ignition coils and mount the plug plate. Attach the ground strap to the front lifting eye.

27. Replace the engine and manifold covers. Connect the line to the brake booster.

28. Reconnect the throttle cable and cover. Install the air intake cowl at the base of the windshield.

29. Connect the heater hoses to the valve and inlet. Remount the radiator by pressing down on the mounting clips to fasten. Check that the lower mounts are in place. Connect the temperature switch plug for the air conditioner and replace the trim panel. Connect the cooling system hoses and the automatic transmission lines. Use new seals on the transmission lines and tighten to 13-15 ft. lbs. (18-21 Nm). Make sure the block coolant plug is in place and tight.

30. Install the fan using tool 11 5 040 or equivalent wrench and holding too 11 5 030 or equivalent. Torque the nut to 29 ft. lbs. (40 Nm). If using the tool set the torque wrench to 22 ft. lbs. (30 Nm); the additional length of the tool multiplies the torque to achieve 29 ft. lbs. (40 Nm) at the nut. Replace the radiator cowling into its mounting slots and press in the rivets.

31. Install the alternator air ducting. Connect the idle speed and crankcase breather hose to the air intake duct. Replace the air cleaner assembly and connect the electrical plug.

32. Install the transmission and fill and bleed the cooling system. Connect the battery and install the splash shield. Check all fluids before starting engine.

5 Series

WITH M20 ENGINE

1. Allow the engine to cool. Disconnect the battery cable from the battery, negative side first. Open the hood to the widest position possible and secure in place.

2. Remove the splash shield from under the car. Drain the coolant and remove the fan and radiator.

3. Remove the transmission.

4. Disconnect the throttle cable and the cruise control cable. Disconnect the cable brackets from the intake manifold.

5. Loosen and remove the electrical and air connections to the air cleaner assembly. Remove the air cleaner assembly and air flow meter.

6. Disconnect the coolant hoses from the engine. Mark the feed and return fuel line connections. Remove the fuel lines, catching any excess fuel.

7. Disconnect the idle speed control. Remove the brake booster vacuum line and plug the opening.

8. Disconnect the heater hoses and the vacuum line going into the passenger compartment. Disconnect the heater coolant pipe.

9. Disconnect the leads from the ignition coil and the oil pressure switch. Place the electrical lead duct from under the distributor to the left side of the engine.

10. If equipped, disconnect the oil cooler lines from the engine and place to the side. Plug the lines to prevent oil from leaking out and to keep any contaminants from inside the lines.

11. Disconnect the starter and the alternator. Disconnect the plug located behind the alternator.

12. Disconnect the DME sensors and the other engine sensors. Disconnect the engine harness and place off to the side.

13. Disconnect the ground strap. Connect an engine lifting sling to the engine.

14. Disconnect the left engine mount from above and the right side mount from under the car. Lift the engine out of the car.

To install:

15. Install the engine and tighten the motor mounts to 32.5 ft. lbs. (45 Nm). Install the ground strap.

16. Install the engine wiring harness and connect the sensors and hoses. Connect the DME sensors. Connect the alternator and starter. Connect the plug located behind the alternator.

17. Install the oil cooler lines, if equipped. Tighten to 22-29 ft. lbs. (30-40 Nm).

18. Connect the ignition coil. Connect the coolant lines and pipes. Connect the vacuum line going into the passenger compartment.

19. Install the idle speed control and the brake booster vacuum line. Connect the radiator hoses and the fuel lines to the previously marked locations.

20. Install the air cleaner and the air flow meter. Connect the air ducts and the electrical connections.

21. Install the throttle cables and the bracket. Install the air conditioner compressor and the power steering pump. Tension the belts.

22. Install the radiator and connect the hoses.

23. Install the transmission.

24. Install the hood support.

25. Make sure all fluid levels are correct before starting the engine. Bleed air from the cooling system.

WITH M50 ENGINE

1. Disconnect the battery terminals, negative side first, and remove the battery, if mounted in engine compartment. Unscrew and remove the battery tray. Remove the transmission.

2. Loosen the clamp on the cooling duct to the alternator and remove the duct.

3. Disconnect the plug to the air flow meter and loosen the clamps to the air cleaner duct. Unscrew the mounting bolts and remove the air cleaner assembly.

4. Pull out the expansion rivets that hold the fan cowl. Remove the cowl by pulling up out of the engine compartment.

5. Hold the fan pulley while unscrewing the fan nut from the shaft. The shaft uses left hand threads; turn the nut counterclockwise to unscrew.

6. Drain the coolant from the block. The drain plug is located between the exhaust manifolds. Disconnect the coolant hoses from the radiator and remove the coolant level switch plug. On automatic transmission equipped vehicles remove the oil lines to the radiator and plug.

7. Disconnect the bottom radiator hose and remove the trim panel from the right side of the engine compartment to expose the side of the radiator and the air conditioner condenser.

8. Pull the plug off of the air conditioner temperature switch.

9. Remove the radiator supporting clips by inserting a small prybar down from above into the slot and pulling back. Pull the radiator free from the clip. Remove the radiator from the vehicle.

10. Disconnect the heater hoses from the heater valve and the heater.

11. Unscrew the fastener from the throttle cable cover and pull the cover forward and off. Unclip the cable and pull the cable out with the rubber holder.

12. Pull the vacuum fitting from the brake booster and plug the openings.

13. Remove the engine and intake manifold covers. Unscrew the bolt holding the ground strap on the front lifting eye. Replace the bolt before lifting the engine.

14. Unscrew the 2 bolts holding the plug plate and pull off the plug plate. Be careful not to damage the rubber seals. Take off the ignition coil electrical plugs. Remove the plug plate complete with the electrical leads.

15. Remove the cylinder head vent hose and pull off the air temperature sensor plug. Remove the tank venting hose and the throttle heating hoses from the throttle body. Remove the throttle valve switch plug. Unclip the idle speed control valve mounted on the manifold. Disconnect the fuel hoses from the pipes.

16. Unscrew the hardware holding the intake manifold to the cylinder head. Remove the intake manifold taking care not to drop anything into the exposed ports.

17. Disconnect the plugs from the temperature sensor, temperature gauge, the oil pressure switch and the idle speed control valve. Disconnect the cylinder identifying sender plug (black) and the pulse sender plug (gray) for the DME. Unscrew the oxygen sensor plug in the holder.

18. Remove the electric leads from the alternator and the starter. Unscrew the electrical lead tray and place the engine wiring harness to the side.

19. Loosen the drive belt for the power steering pump and the air conditioner compressor by turning their respective tensioners clockwise. This will release the tension on the belt and allow the belt to be removed.

20. Unbolt the power steering pump and place to the side without disconnecting the hoses. Unbolt the air conditioner compressor and place to the side without disconnecting the lines.

21. Attach a lifting fixture to the engine lifting hooks. Unscrew the engine mounts and ground strap. Lift the engine out of the vehicle being careful of the front radiator mount.

To Install:

22. Lower the engine into the vehicle and attach the motor mounts and ground strap.

23. Install the power steering pump and the air conditioner compressor. Install the drive belts.

24. Replace the wiring harness and electrical lead tray on the engine. Connect the leads to the starter and alternator. Screw in the plug for the oxygen sensor holder. Connect the leads for the cylinder identifying sender, the DME pulse sender, the temperature sensor, the temperature gauge sender, the oil pressure switch and the idle speed control valve.

25. Install the intake manifold making sure that the intake seals are intact. Replace the intake seals if any signs of deterioration are evident.

26. Attach the fuel lines. The upper line is the return and the lower is the feed.

27. Attach the idle speed control valve hose located on the manifold.

28. Connect the throttle valve switch plug, the throttle valve heating lines and the tank vent line.

29. Connect the air temperature sensor plug and attach the cylinder head venting hoses.

30. Reconnect the plugs for the ignition coils and mount the plug plate. Attach the ground strap to the front lifting eye.

31. Replace the engine and manifold covers. Connect the line to the brake booster.

32. Reconnect the throttle cable and cover.

33. Connect the heater hoses to the valve and inlet. Remount the radiator by pressing down on the mounting clips to fasten. Check that the lower mounts are in place. Connect the temperature switch plug for the air conditioner and replace the trim panel. Connect the cooling system hoses and the automatic transmission lines.

34. Install the fan using tool 11 5 040 or equivalent. Torque the nut to 29 ft. lbs. (40 Nm). If using the tool set the torque wrench to 22 ft. lbs. (30 Nm); the additional length of the tool multiplies the torque to achieve 29 ft. lbs. (40 Nm) at the nut. Replace the radiator cowling.

35. Replace the air cleaner assembly and connect the electrical plug. Install the transmission and fill and bleed the cooling system. Install the battery tray and battery. Check all fluids before starting engine.

WITH M30 ENGINE

1. Allow the engine to cool. Disconnect the battery cable from the battery, negative side first. Open the hood to the widest position possible and secure in place.

2. Remove the splash shield from under the car. Drain the coolant and remove the radiator.

3. Remove the transmission.

4. Remove the nut holding the transmission oil cooler lines to the engine oil pan.

5. Loosen and remove the drive belts to the power steering pump and the air conditioner compressor. Remove the bolts holding the pump and compressor to the engine and remove them from the engine, keeping the lines connected. Wire the pump and compressor out of the way and without any tension on the hoses.

6. Disconnect the hoses from the coolant expansion tank. remove the screws on the side of the expansion tank and remove the expansion tank from the engine compartment.

7. Disconnect the heater hoses from the heater control valve and the heater inlet pipe.

8. Pull off the connections to the ignition coil. Remove the air cleaner assembly. Disconnect and remove the idle speed control from the intake duct.

9. Disconnect the harness to the air flow meter. Disconnect the ducting to the air flow meter and remove along with the crankcase breather vacuum line.

10. On non-ASC equipped cars, disconnect the cruise control cable and the throttle cable at the throttle. Remove the cable mounting bracket. If equipped with ASC, remove the connector to the throttle control unit as there will be no throttle cable to disconnect.

11. Disconnect the leads to the starter. Disconnect the 2 electrical connectors in the starter area. Disconnect the oil level sender leads and the alternator connections. Remove the air duct to the alternator.

12. Disconnect the tank venting valve and the hose to the carbon canister.

13. Mark the feed and return fuel lines. Disconnect the lines and catch any spilled fuel.

14. Disconnect the vacuum line from the brake booster and plug the opening. Disconnect the harness connections to the temperature sensors and DME sensors.

15. Disconnect the ground strap and make a check for any remaining lines or electrical leads still attached.

16. Attach a lifting sling to the engine. Remove the engine mount nuts and bolts and lift the engine from the engine bay.

To install:

17. Install the engine into the engine compartment. Torque the engine mounts to 32.5 ft. lbs. (45 Nm). Connect the ground strap.

18. Connect the brake booster vacuum line, the temperature sensors and the DME sensors.

19. Connect the fuel lines to the proper locations as previously marked. Connect the tank venting valve and the carbon canister line. Attach the alternator leads and the cooling duct.

20. Connect the starter leads and the electrical connector in the starter area. Connect the oil level sender leads.

21. Connect the throttle cable and the cruise control cable and bracket. Install the air flow sensor and the crankcase breather line.

22. Install the idle speed control to the air intake duct. Install the air cleaner assembly.

23. Connect the heater lines to the heater control valve and the heater inlet pipe. Install the coolant expansion tank and connect the lines.

24. Install the air conditioner compressor and power steering pump. Adjust the belt tensions.

25. Connect the automatic transmission oil cooling lines to the bracket on the engine oil pan.

26. Install the transmission and the radiator. Fill the cooling system and check the engine fluids. Install the splash shield and connect the battery.

27. Run the engine and check for leaks. Bleed the cooling system.

WITH S38 ENGINE

➡ If the engine is to be disassembled the vibration damper nut MUST be removed from the engine before the engine is removed. This is due to the fact the nut is torqued to approximately 578 ft. lbs. (800 NM) and is almost impossible to remove once the engine has been removed from the engine compartment.

1. Disconnect the battery negative cable. Then, disconnect the positive cable. Remove the windshield washer jets from the hood and place off to the side. Scribe matchmarks and then remove the hood.

2. Remove the transmission with tool 23 1 330 or equivalent.

3. Remove the radiator along with the oil cooler and fan cowling. Remove the fan by using tool 11 5 030, or equivalent to hold the pulley stationary while unscrewing the lefthand threads of the fan with tool 11 5 040 or equivalent.

4. Remove the alternator cooling duct.

5. Support the power steering pump. Remove the mounting bolts and then hang the pump out of the way in a position that will not put stress on the hoses.

6. Support the air conditioning compressor. Remove the mounting bolts and then hang the compressor out of the way in a position that will not put stress on the hoses.

7. If the engine is going to be disassembled and the vibration damper must be removed, turn the engine so the TDC mark on the tooth wheel faces straight down. Attach tool 11 2 240, or equivalent to the pulley with all 8 of the 8x20mm bolts. The mounting pattern is asymmetrical and the tool can only be mounted one way. The tool is designed so it bears against the right side of the subframe and provide the counteroffers to the removal torque of the vibration damper bolt.

8. Disconnect the ground strap and the engine mounts.

9. Remove the headlight cover piece and disconnect the harness from the air cleaner and air flow meter assembly. Remove the mounting hardware and the air ducts. Disconnect the air temperature sensor. Remove the air cleaner and air flow meter assembly.

10. Disconnect the throttle cables and the holder brackets.

11. Disconnect the coolant lines at the coolant expansion tank. Remove the coolant expansion tank. Disconnect the heater coolant hoses at the heater inlet and the heater control valve.

12. Tilt the engine as far forward as possible and support with a wooden block. Disconnect the brake booster vacuum line and plug the opening.

13. Disconnect the air pump intake hose at the air cleaner.

14. Mark the fuel feed and return lines. Disconnect the fuel lines and the tank venting valves located near the base of the engine oil dipstick.

15. Disconnect the starter leads at the remote positive terminal. Lift of the cover directly behind the remote positive terminal. Remove the electric lead covers along the top of the engine and at the rear of the engine compartment. Remove the electronics box cover screw and cover.

16. Mark and disconnect the leads from the ignition coil. Disconnect the ground lead behind the ignition coil. Disconnect the engine electric harness from the holders and disconnect the DME and the 2 multi-pin connectors in the electronic box.

17. Remove the 3 relays still connected to the sockets in the electronics box. Disconnect the connectors and the temperature sensor. Remove the relay holder and the control unit located beneath it. Remove the plug.

18. Remove the grommet holder and pull the harness out with the grommet. Place the harness that will stay with the car and not come out with the engine up on the firewall and secure.

19. Disconnect the engine plug and the diagnosis connector. Remove the holder and place the wiring harness out of the way after loosening the straps.

20. Attach an engine lifting sling. The rear chain should be placed between the intake and the check valve. Lift the engine out of the engine compartment.

To install:

21. Install the engine in the engine compartment and tilt as far forward as possible and block into place. Install the wiring harness into the original positions and secure. Install the diagnostic socket and the engine plug.

22. Install the harness, control unit and the rubber grommet back into the electronics box. Install the grommet holder and the relay holder. Connect the multi-pin connector and the temperature sensor. Connect the positive lead.

23. Connect the ignition coil and the ground strap. Install the cover on the electronics box and in the engine compartment.

24. Connect the tank venting valve at the base of the oil dipstick. Connect the fuel lines to the original positions. Connect the air pump inlet hose to the air cleaner.

25. Connect the vacuum line to the brake booster. Tilt the engine back to the original position. Connect the heater hoses and install the coolant expansion tank.

26. Connect the throttle cables. Install the air cleaner assembly and the air flow meter. Connect the air temperature sensor.

27. Tighten the motor mounts to 30 ft. lbs. (42 Nm). Connect the ground strap.

28. Install the air conditioning compressor and the power steering pump. Tension the belts. Install the alternator cooling duct.

29. Install the fan with tool 11 5 040 or equivalent, and tighten to 29 ft. lbs. (40 Nm). Set the torque wrench to 22 ft. lbs. (30 Nm) if using the BMW tool. Hold the pulley still with tool 11 5 030 or its equivalent.

30. Install the transmission and the radiator with oiler cooler. Tighten the oil cooler lines to 22-29 ft. lbs. (30-40 Nm).

31. Install the hood and the washer jets. Fill and check the engine fluids. Bleed the cooling system and check for leaks.

Rocker Arm (Valve) Cover

REMOVAL & INSTALLATION

E30 3 Series

WITH M42 ENGINE

▶ See Figures 23 and 24

1. Remove the spark plug valley cover from the valve cover. The 2 fasteners are rotated 90 degrees and the cover is pulled out.

2. Unplug the spark plug leads. Remove the 2 screws holding the ignition lead loom and place the loom off to the side.

3. Disconnect the crankcase breather hose from the valve cover. Remove the 15 bolts along the edges and in the center of the valve cover.

➡**The mounting bolts pass through rubber isolators. Check that all the isolators are in place and did not drop into the cylinder head when removed. Check the condition of the isolators and replace as necessary.**

4. Check the condition of the valve cover gasket and replace as necessary.

To install:

5. Clean the mating areas of the cylinder head and the valve cover. Install the valve cover gasket.

6. Place the valve cover on the cylinder head. Check that all the isolators are in place at the bolt holes. Check the gasket is properly fitted at the rear of the cylinder head.

84273023

Fig. 23 Remove the entire ignition lead loom before removing the valve cover on the M42 engine

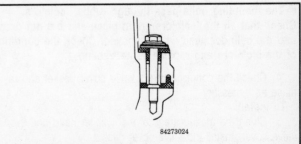

84273024

Fig. 24 The M42 and M50 engine valve cover is mounted via rubber isolators that must be kept in position during installation

7. Torque the 15 bolts 6-7 ft. lbs. (8-10 Nm) in a crisscrossing pattern to evenly tighten.

8. Connect the crankcase breather hose. Install the ignition lead loom and replace the spark plug leads. Install the spark plug valley cover.

WITH M20 ENGINE

1. Disconnect the intake manifold to valve cover brace.
2. Disconnect the crankcase breather hose.
3. Remove the 8 nuts holding the cover. Remove the cover and gasket.

To install:

4. Clean the mating flanges of the cylinder head and the valve cover. Install the new gasket on the cylinder head.
5. Attach the ground strap at the rear stud and install the ignition lead loom.
6. Tighten the 8 nuts in a crisscross pattern starting at the center of the valve cover. Torque to 6-7 ft. lbs. (8-10 Nm).
7. Connect the crankcase breather hose. Install the intake manifold support and torque to 15-17 ft. lbs. (20-24 Nm).

WITH S14 ENGINE

1. Disconnect the crankcase breather hose.
2. Remove the 2 bolts holding the ignition lead loom. Disconnect the spark plug leads and place the loom off to the side.
3. Remove the 18 nuts holding the valve cover.

To install:

4. Clean the mating flanges of the cylinder head and the valve cover. Install the new gasket on the cylinder head.
5. Tighten the 18 nuts in a crisscross pattern starting at the center of the valve cover. Torque to 6-7 ft. lbs. (8-10 Nm).
6. Connect the crankcase breather hose. Install the spark plug lead and the ignition lead loom bolts.

E36 3 Series

WITH M42 ENGINE

1. Remove the spark plug valley cover from the valve cover. The 2 fasteners are rotated 90 degrees and the cover is pulled out.
2. Unplug the spark plug leads. Remove the 2 screws holding the ignition lead loom and place the loom off to the side.
3. Disconnect the crankcase breather hose from the valve cover. Remove the 15 bolts along the edges and in the center of the valve cover.

➡**The mounting bolts pass through rubber isolators. Check that all the isolators are in place and did not drop into the cylinder head when removed. Check the condition of the isolators and replace as necessary.**

4. Check the condition of the valve cover gasket and replace as necessary.

To install:

5. Clean the mating areas of the cylinder head and the valve cover. Install the valve cover gasket.
6. Place the valve cover on the cylinder head. Check that all the isolators are in place at the bolt holes. Check the gasket is properly fitted at the rear of the cylinder head.
7. Torque the 15 bolts 6-7 ft. lbs. (8-10 Nm) in a crisscrossing pattern to evenly tighten.

8. Connect the crankcase breather hose. Install the ignition lead loom and replace the spark plug leads. Install the spark plug valley cover.

WITH M50 ENGINE

1. Make sure the ignition is OFF. Remove the oil filler cap.
2. Remove the plugs from the valve cover cladding.
3. Remove the nuts securing the valve cover cladding and remove the cladding. Place a clean rag in the oil filler to prevent anything from falling in the engine. It may be necessary to remove the fuel injector rail cover to remove the cladding. The fuel injector rail cover is removed in the same method as the valve cover cladding.
4. Release the clips for the coil pack connectors and disconnect.
5. Remove the nuts holding the coil packs. Pull up to remove the coil packs.
6. Pull out the crankcase breather connector.
7. Remove the 10 bolts holding the valve cover.

➡**The mounting bolts pass through rubber isolators. Check that all the isolators are in place and did not drop into the cylinder head when removed. Check the condition of the isolators and replace as necessary.**

8. Check the condition of the valve cover gasket and replace as necessary.

To install:

9. Clean the mating areas of the cylinder head and the valve cover. Install the valve cover gasket.
10. Place the valve cover on the cylinder head. Check that all the isolators are in place at the bolt holes. Check the gasket is properly fitted at the rear of the cylinder head.
11. Torque the 15 bolts 6-7 ft. lbs. (8-10 Nm) in a crisscrossing pattern to evenly tighten.
12. Connect the crankcase breather hose. Install the ignition coils and tighten the nuts. make sure the ground strap is attached. Connect the coil pack connectors and install the valve cover cladding and injector cladding.

E34 5 Series

WITH M20 ENGINE

1. Disconnect the intake manifold to valve cover brace.
2. Disconnect the crankcase breather hose.
3. Remove the 8 nuts holding the cover. Remove the cover and gasket.

To install:

4. Clean the mating flanges of the cylinder head and the valve cover. Install the new gasket on the cylinder head.
5. Attach the ground strap at the rear stud and install the ignition lead loom.
6. Tighten the 8 nuts in a crisscross pattern starting at the center of the valve cover. Torque to 6-7 ft. lbs. (8-10 Nm).
7. Connect the crankcase breather hose. Install the intake manifold support and torque to 15-17 ft. lbs. (20-24 Nm).

WITH M30 ENGINE

▶ **See Figure 25**

1. Disconnect the crankcase breather hose.
2. Disconnect the ignition lead loom from the valve cover.

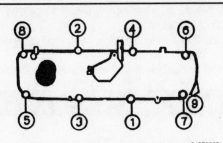

Fig. 25 On the M30 engine, tighten the valve cover bolts in this order to prevent warping.

3. Remove the 9 nuts holding the cover. Remove the cover and gasket.

To install:

4. Clean the mating flanges of the cylinder head and the valve cover. Install the new gasket on the cylinder head.

5. Attach idle speed at the stud.

6. Tighten the 8 nuts in a crisscross pattern starting at the center of the valve cover. Torque to 6-7 ft. lbs. (8-10 Nm).

7. Connect the crankcase breather hose. Install the ignition lead loom.

WITH M50 ENGINE

1. Make sure the ignition is OFF. Remove the oil filler cap.

2. Remove the plugs from the valve cover cladding.

3. Remove the nuts securing the valve cover cladding and remove the cladding. Place a clean rag in the oil filler to prevent anything from falling in the engine. It may be necessary to remove the fuel injector rail cover to remove the cladding. The fuel injector rail cover is removed in the same method as the valve cover cladding.

4. Release the clips for the coil pack connectors and disconnect.

5. Remove the nuts holding the coil packs. Pull up to remove the coil packs.

6. Pull out the crankcase breather connector.

7. Remove the 10 bolts holding the valve cover.

➡ **The mounting bolts pass through rubber isolators. Check that all the isolators are in place and did not drop into the cylinder head when removed. Check the condition of the isolators and replace as necessary.**

8. Check the condition of the valve cover gasket and replace as necessary.

To install:

9. Clean the mating areas of the cylinder head and the valve cover. Install the valve cover gasket.

10. Place the valve cover on the cylinder head. Check that all the isolators are in place at the bolt holes. Check the gasket is properly fitted at the rear of the cylinder head.

11. Torque the 15 bolts 6-7 ft. lbs. (8-10 Nm) in a crisscrossing pattern to evenly tighten.

12. Connect the crankcase breather hose. Install the ignition coils and tighten the nuts. make sure the ground strap is attached. Connect the coil pack connectors and install the valve cover cladding and injector cladding.

WITH S38 ENGINE

1. Disconnect the crankcase breather hose.

2. Remove the 2 bolts holding the ignition lead loom. Disconnect the spark plug leads and place the loom off to the side.

3. Remove the 24 nuts holding the valve cover.

To install:

4. Clean the mating flanges of the cylinder head and the valve cover. Install the new gasket on the cylinder head.

5. Tighten the 24 nuts in a crisscross pattern starting at the center of the valve cover. Torque to 6-7 ft. lbs. (8-10 Nm).

6. Connect the crankcase breather hose. Install the spark plug lead and the ignition lead loom bolts.

Rocker Arms/Shafts

INSPECTION

Check the rocker shafts for scoring and wear at the rocker arm pivot points. Check the shaft oiling holes for clogging and varnish. Check the bushing in the rocker arm for wear. Check the adjuster eccentric for flatspots. Check the iron pad for wear and looseness. If the iron pad is loose, it will make a ticking or tapping noise when the engine is running.

REMOVAL & INSTALLATION

M20 Engine

The cylinder head must be removed before the rocker arm shafts can be removed. Support the head so it can not move around on the bench.

1. Disconnect the negative battery cable. Remove the cylinder head.

2. Mount the head on a suitable holding fixture.

3. Remove the camshaft sprocket bolt and remove the camshaft distributor adapter and sprocket. Reinstall the adapter on the camshaft.

4. Adjust the valve clearance to the maximum allowable on all valves.

5. Remove the front and rear rocker shaft plugs and lift out the thrust plate.

6. Remove the spring-clips from the rocker arms by lifting them off.

7. Remove the exhaust side rocker arm shaft:

a. Set the No. 6 cylinder rocker arms at the valve overlap position (rocker arms parallel), by rotating the camshaft through the firing order.

b. Push in on the front cylinder rocker arm and then turn the camshaft in the direction of the intake rocker shaft, using a ½ inch drive breaker bar and a deep well socket to fit over the camshaft adapter. Slide each rocker arm to one side as it develops sufficient clearance away from its actuating camshaft and the valve it actuates. Rotate the camshaft until all of the rocker arms are relaxed.

c. Remove the rocker arm shaft by driving it out or pulling it out.

8. Remove the intake side rocker arm shaft:

a. Turn the camshaft in the direction of the exhaust rocker arm.

b. Use a deep well socket and ½ inch drive breaker bar on the camshaft adapter to turn the camshaft. Slide each rocker arm to one side as it develops sufficient clearance away from its actuating camshaft and the valve it actuates. Rotate the camshaft until all of the rocker arms are relaxed.

c. Remove the rocker arm shaft.

9. Install the rocker arm shafts by reversing the removal procedure. Keep the following points in mind:

a. The large oil bores in the rocker shafts must be installed downward, toward the valve guides and the small oil bores and grooves for the guide plate face inward toward the center of the head.

b. The straight sections of the spring clamps must fit into the grooves in the rocker arm shafts.

c. The guide plate must fit into the grooves in the rocker arm shafts.

d. Adjust the valve clearance.

M30 Engine

▶ See Figure 26

1. Disconnect the negative battery cable. Remove the cylinder head.

2. Remove the camshaft.

3. Remove the retaining bolts and remove the end cover from the rear of the cylinder head. Slide the thrust rings and rocker arms rearward and remove the snaprings from the rocker arm shafts.

4. Install dowel pins part No. 11 1 063 or equivalent to keep the rocker shafts from turning. Then, remove the rocker shaft oil plugs from the front of the rocker shafts. These require a hex head wrench. Remove the dowel pins. If the rocker shafts have welded plugs, the shafts will have to be pressed out of the head with a tool such as 11 3 050 or equivalent.

❋❋CAUTION

There is considerable force on the springs positioning the rockers. They may pop out. Be cautious and wear safety glasses.

5. Install a threaded slide hammer into the end of the rocker shafts and remove.

To install:

6. The rocker arms, springs, washers, thrust rings and shafts should be examined and worn parts replaced. Special attention should be given to the rocker arm camshaft followers. If these are loose, replace the arm assembly. The valves can be removed, repaired or replaced, as necessary, while the shafts and rocker arms are out of the cylinder head.

7. Install the rocker arms in position, noting the following procedures:

a. Design changes of the rocker arms and shafts have occurred with the installation of a bushing in the rocker arm and the use of 2 horizontal oil flow holes drilled into the rocker shaft for improved oil supply. Do not mix the previously designed parts with the later design.

b. When installing the rocker arms and components to the rocker shafts, install locating pins in the cylinder head bolt bores to properly align the rocker arm shafts. The order of installation is: spring, washer, rocker arm, thrust washer,

snapring. Note also that newer, short springs may be used with the older design.

c. Install sealer on the rocker arm shaft retaining plugs and rear cover.

8. Install the camshaft and adjust the valve clearance.

Thermostat

REMOVAL & INSTALLATION

M20 Engine

1. Partially drain the coolant. Save the coolant in sealed containers if being reused or dispose of safely.

2. Remove the 3 bolts on the thermostat housing located at the intake side of the engine.

3. Pull the thermostat housing off and remove the thermostat. Note the positioning of the thermostat.

To install:

4. Replace the thermostat with the support bar facing out. Replace the O-ring.

5. Install the thermostat housing and torque the bolts to 6-7 ft. lbs. (8-10 Nm).

6. Fill the cooling system with coolant mixture and bleed.

M30 Engine

1. Partially drain the coolant. Save the coolant in sealed containers if being reused or dispose of safely.

2. Remove the 4 bolts on the thermostat housing located at the intake side of the engine.

3. Pull the thermostat housing off and remove the thermostat. Note the positioning of the thermostat.

To install:

4. Replace the thermostat with the support bar facing out. Replace the O-ring.

5. Install the thermostat housing and torque the bolts to 6-7 ft. lbs. (8-10 Nm).

6. Fill the cooling system with coolant mixture and bleed.

M42 Engine

1. Partially drain the coolant. Save the coolant in sealed containers if being reused or dispose of safely.

2. Remove the 4 bolts on the thermostat housing located at the front of the cylinder head. It may be necessary to remove the hoses from the housing first if the housing can't be pulled forward enough.

3. Pull the thermostat housing off and remove the thermostat. Note the positioning of the thermostat.

To install:

4. Replace the thermostat with the support bar facing out. Replace the O-ring and gasket.

5. Install the thermostat housing and torque the bolts to 6-7 ft. lbs. (8-10 Nm).

6. Fill the cooling system with coolant mixture and bleed.

M50 Engine

1. Partially drain the coolant. Save the coolant in sealed containers if being reused or dispose of safely.

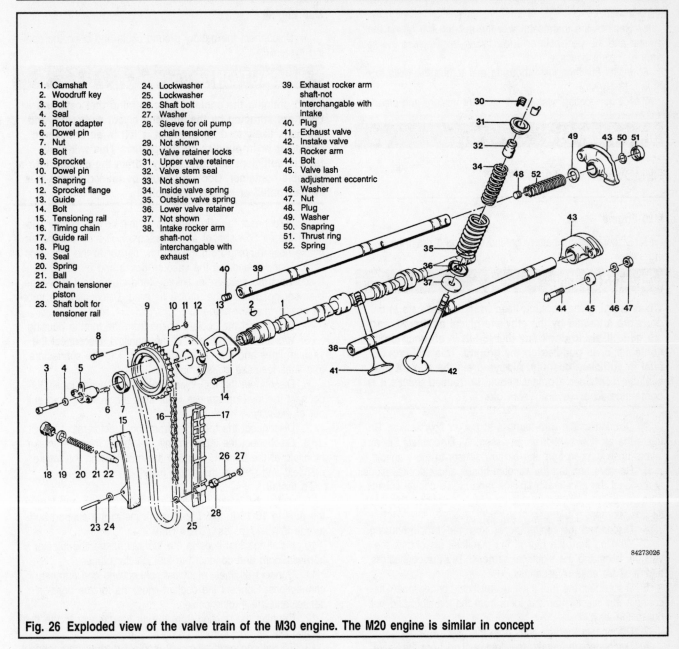

1. Camshaft
2. Woodruff key
3. Bolt
4. Seal
5. Rotor adapter
6. Dowel pin
7. Nut
8. Bolt
9. Sprocket
10. Dowel pin
11. Snapring
12. Sprocket flange
13. Guide
14. Bolt
15. Tensioning rail
16. Timing chain
17. Guide rail
18. Plug
19. Seal
20. Spring
21. Ball
22. Chain tensioner piston
23. Shaft bolt for tensioner rail
24. Lockwasher
25. Lockwasher
26. Shaft bolt
27. Washer
28. Sleeve for oil pump chain tensioner
29. Not shown
30. Valve retainer locks
31. Upper valve retainer
32. Valve stem seal
33. Not shown
34. Inside valve spring
35. Outside valve spring
36. Lower valve retainer
37. Not shown
38. Intake rocker arm shaft-not interchangable with exhaust
39. Exhaust rocker arm shaft-not interchangable with intake
40. Plug
41. Exhaust valve
42. Instake valve
43. Rocker arm
44. Bolt
45. Valve lash adjustment eccentric
46. Washer
47. Nut
48. Plug
49. Washer
50. Snapring
51. Thrust ring
52. Spring

Fig. 26 Exploded view of the valve train of the M30 engine. The M20 engine is similar in concept

2. Remove the 4 bolts on the thermostat housing and the 1 nut holding the engine lifting hook located at the front of the cylinder head. It may be necessary to remove the hoses from the housing first if the housing can't be pulled forward enough.

3. Pull the thermostat housing off and remove the thermostat. Note the positioning of the thermostat.

To install:

4. Replace the thermostat with the support bar facing out and the vent hole or arrow facing up. Replace the O-ring and gasket.

5. Install the thermostat housing and torque the bolts to 6-7 ft. lbs. (8-10 Nm).

6. Fill the cooling system with coolant mixture and bleed.

S14 Engine

1. Drain the coolant. Save the coolant in sealed containers if being reused or dispose of safely.

2. Loosen the hose clamps holding the thermostat at the exhaust side of the engine. Place a drain pan under the thermostat to catch the coolant that will drain out.

3. Remove the thermostat.

4. Install the thermostat using new clamps. Fill the cooling system and bleed.

S38 Engine

1. Partially drain the coolant. Save the coolant in sealed containers if being reused or dispose of safely.

2. Disconnect the hoses from the thermostat housing located on the exhaust side of the engine.

3. Remove the 5 screws holding the thermostat housing.

4. Pull the thermostat housing off and remove the thermostat. Note the positioning of the thermostat.

To install:

5. Replace the thermostat with the support bar facing the engine and the vent hole or arrow facing up. Replace the seal on the coolant passage.

6. Install the thermostat housing and torque the bolts to 6-7 ft. lbs. (8-10 Nm).

7. Fill the cooling system with coolant mixture and bleed.

Intake Manifold

REMOVAL & INSTALLATION

M20 Engine

1. Disconnect the battery ground cable and drain the cooling system.

✳✳CAUTION

When draining the coolant, keep in mind that cats and dogs are attracted by the ethylene glycol antifreeze, and are quite likely to drink any that is left in an uncovered container or in puddles on the ground. This will prove fatal in sufficient quantity. Always drain the coolant into a sealable container. Coolant should be reused unless it is contaminated or several years old.

2. Disconnect the wire harness at the air flow sensor. Remove the air flow sensor as an assembly. Disconnect the air intake hose running from the air flow sensor to the manifold.

3. Remove and tag the vacuum hoses and electrical plugs. Disconnect the accelerator linkage (and cruise control linkage, if so-equipped) from the throttle housing. Disconnect the throttle position sensor harness.

4. Disconnect the coolant hoses from the throttle housing.

5. Working from the rear of the manifold, disconnect the vacuum lines and the electrical harness. Tag the connectors and lines for ease of assembly.

6. Disconnect the fuel injector electrical connections. Disconnect the injector harness loom from the manifold and pull out of the way.

7. Disconnect the fuel lines from the injector rail.

8. Disconnect the intake manifold support from the valve cover. Remove the nuts holding the intake manifold and remove the intake manifold.

To install:

9. Install the intake manifold with new gaskets and torque the nuts to 16-18 ft. lbs. (22-25 Nm). Install the support and torque to 15-17 ft. lbs. (20-24 Nm).

10. Install the fuel lines to the fuel rail. Install the injector harness loom and connect the fuel injector plugs.

11. Connect all lines, electrical connections and harness connections. Connect the coolant lines, the throttle position sensor and the throttle cables.

12. Connect the ducting from the air flow sensor to the throttle and the air flow sensor.

13. Fill the cooling system with coolant mixture and connect the negative battery terminal.

M30 Engine

1. Disconnect the battery ground cable and drain the cooling system.

✳✳CAUTION

When draining the coolant, keep in mind that cats and dogs are attracted by the ethylene glycol antifreeze, and are quite likely to drink any that is left in an uncovered container or in puddles on the ground. This will prove fatal in sufficient quantity. Always drain the coolant into a sealable container. Coolant should be reused unless it is contaminated or several years old.

2. Disconnect the wire harness at the air flow sensor. Remove the air flow sensor as an assembly. Disconnect the air intake hose running from the air flow sensor to the manifold.

3. Remove and tag the vacuum hoses and electrical plugs. Disconnect the accelerator linkage (and cruise control linkage, if so-equipped) from the throttle housing. Disconnect the throttle position sensor harness.

4. Disconnect the coolant hoses from the throttle housing.

5. Working from the rear of the manifold, disconnect the vacuum lines and the electrical harness. Tag the connectors and lines for ease of assembly.

6. Disconnect the fuel injector electrical connections. Disconnect the injector harness loom from the manifold and pull out of the way.

7. Disconnect the fuel lines from the injector rail.

8. Disconnect the intake manifold support from the intake manifold at the bottom. Remove the nuts holding the intake manifold and remove the intake manifold.

To install:

9. Install the intake manifold with new gaskets and torque the nuts to 16-18 ft. lbs. (22-25 Nm). Install the support and torque to 15-17 ft. lbs. (20-24 Nm).

10. Install the fuel lines to the fuel rail. Install the injector harness loom and connect the fuel injector plugs.

11. Connect all lines, electrical connections and harness connections. Connect the coolant lines, the throttle position sensor and the throttle cables.

12. Connect the ducting from the air flow sensor to the throttle and the air flow sensor.

13. Fill the cooling system with coolant mixture and connect the negative battery terminal.

M42 Engine

♦ See Figures 27, 28, 29, 30, 31, 32 and 33

1. Disconnect the battery ground cable. Remove the air duct to the throttle body.

2. Disconnect the rear mounting bracket and remove the hose.

3. Loosen the front mounting bracket and remove the nut directly under the throttle body.

4. Remove the 9 mounting bolts and lift off the upper manifold section. Pull the hose off the fuel pressure regulator at the same time.

5. Pull the plug plate off the fuel injectors and remove the clamp.

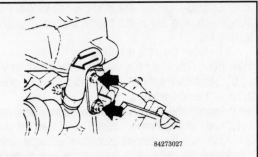

Fig. 27 The rear brace and hose on the M42 engines intake manifold

Fig. 31 Replace the gasket and check the dowel sleeves before replacing the upper section of the intake manifold — M42 engine

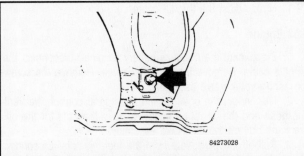

Fig. 28 Remove the this nut when removing the upper section of the M42 engines intake manifold

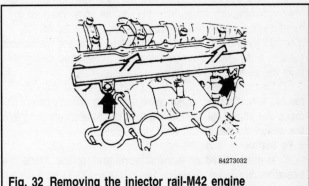

Fig. 32 Removing the injector rail-M42 engine

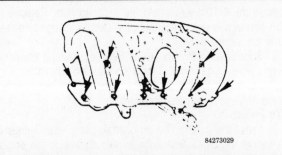

Fig. 29 Remove the these bolts when removing the upper section of the M42 engines intake manifold

Fig. 33 Remove these bolts to remove the lower intake manifold — M42 engine

To install:

7. Check the sleeves on the studs. Replace the manifold gasket and install the lower manifold section. Torque to 10-12 ft. lbs. (13-17 Nm).

8. Lubricate the injector seals with a slight film of oil and install the injector rail. Install the plug plate and clamp.

9. Connect the fuel pressure regulator vacuum line and install the upper manifold section with a new gasket. Torque to 10-12 ft. lbs. (13-17 Nm).

10. Tighten the nut directly under the throttle body. It may be necessary to bend the tab against the throttle body.

11. Connect the front and rear braces. Connect the hose to manifold. Connect the air duct to the throttle body. Connect the negative battery terminal.

M50 Engine

1. Disconnect the negative battery cable and drain the coolant to a level below that of the throttle housing. Unscrew the

Fig. 30 Lift off the upper section of the intake manifold and remove the vacuum hose — M42 engine

6. Remove the injector rail with the fuel injectors attached. Remove the 5 bolts holding the lower manifold section and remove the manifold.

fastener from the throttle cable cover and pull the cover forward and off. Unclip the cable and pull the cable out with the rubber holder.

2. Pull the vacuum fitting from the brake booster and plug the openings.

3. Remove the engine and intake manifold covers. Unscrew the bolt holding the ground strap on the front lifting eye. Replace the bolt before lifting the engine.

4. Unscrew the 2 bolts holding the plug plate and pull off the plug plate. Be careful not to damage the rubber seals. Take off the ignition coil electrical plugs. Remove the plug plate complete with the electrical leads.

5. Remove the cylinder head vent hose and pull off the air temperature sensor plug. Remove the tank venting hose and the throttle heating hoses from the throttle body. Remove the throttle valve switch plug. Unclip the hose mounted on the manifold for the idle speed control valve. Mark and disconnect the fuel hoses from the pipes near the throttle and disconnect from the pipe on the subframe.

6. Disconnect the manifold support braces. Unscrew the hardware holding the intake manifold to the cylinder head. Remove the intake manifold taking care not to drop anything into the exposed ports.

To install:

7. Inspect the intake manifold seals and replace. Install the intake manifold and torque to 14-17 ft. lbs. (20-24 Nm). Install the intake manifold supports.

8. Connect the fuel hoses near the throttle body and the subframe. The rear line is the return line and the front line is the feed.

9. Install the hose for the idle speed control by pushing it into the manifold. Connect the throttle switch plug and the throttle heating hoses. Connect the air temperature sensor.

10. Clip in the crankcase vent hose connector. Plug in the ignition coil harness connectors. Install the plug plate and the ground strap. Install the covers, brake booster vacuum line and the throttle cables.

11. Fill the cooling system with coolant, connect the air intake duct and the negative battery terminal.

S14 Engine

➡**A Torx nut driver is needed to perform this operation.**

1. Disconnect the negative battery cable. Remove the cap nuts at the outer ends of the 4 throttle necks. Then remove the mounting nuts underneath.

2. Make sure the engine has cooled off. Loosen the hose clamps for the air intake lines and for the fuel lines where they connect with the injector fuel rail. Collect fuel in a metal container.

3. Disconnect the throttle cable.

4. Pull off the intake manifold. Remove the crankcase ventilation hose running to it from the crankcase. Then, remove the manifold and place it aside. Use a new crankcase ventilation hose during installation.

5. Pull off the throttle valve switch plug.

6. Pull the fuel pressure regulator vacuum hose off the pressure regulator.

7. Remove the 2 mounting bolts for the injector pipe. Then, carefully lift off the pipe and injectors. Remove the clips holding the connectors to the injectors and pull the plug plate off the injectors.

8. Unscrew the nut attaching the ball joint at the end of the throttle actuating rod to the throttle linkage. Supply a new self-locking nut.

9. Remove the nuts attaching the throttle necks to the cylinder head. Then, remove the 4 throttle necks as an assembly.

10. Separate the throttle neck assemblies by pulling them apart at the connecting pipe.

11. Inspect the O-rings in the connecting pipe and at the outer ends of the throttle necks. Replace as necessary.

12. Reverse the removal procedure to install. Use the new throttle linkage self-locking nut and the new crankcase ventilation hose.

13. Torque the nuts attaching the throttle necks to the head and the intake manifold to the throttle necks to 6.5-8.0 ft. lbs. (9-11 Nm). Adjust the throttle cable.

S38 Engine

1. Disconnect the negative battery terminal. Disconnect the throttle cable. Remove the air intake hose. Remove the screws on each throttle valve assembly.

2. Disconnect the hose for the idle speed control, the venting hose and the oil return hose. Remove the nuts for the oil trap and pull off the air intake assembly.

3. Pull off the plug plate from the fuel injectors. Disconnect the fuel lines from the fuel rail. Pull of the intermediate plug for the idle speed control. Remove the fuel rail with the fuel injectors.

4. Disconnect the vacuum hoses after noting the routing. Remove the 6 10mm nuts and the 9 13mm nuts. Remove the shaft connection nut. Disconnect the throttle linkage and remove the throttle bodies.

5. Separate the throttle bodies by disconnecting the connecting pipes. Check the O-rings on the pipe. Clean the throttle shafts before pulling out of the bores and do not use tools on the shaft or it may be damaged.

To install:

6. Install the throttle bodies together using new O-rings on the connecting pipes. Install the throttle bodies on the engine using new gaskets. Tighten the 10mm nuts to 6.5-8.0 ft. lbs. (9-11 Nm) and the 13mm nuts to 14-17 ft. lbs. (20-24 Nm).

7. Route and connect the vacuum hoses. Install the shaft connection nut and the throttle linkage. Install the fuel rail and the fuel connections. Connect the intermediate plug and the injector plug plate.

8. Check the O-rings on the air intake assembly and attach the pins at the bottom of the assembly. Install the air intake assembly.

9. Connect the oil return hose, the idle speed hose and the venting hose. Install the air intake duct and install the screws at each throttle. Connect the negative battery terminal.

Exhaust Manifold

REMOVAL & INSTALLATION

M20 Engine

1. Disconnect the negative battery terminal.

2. With the exhaust system cool, disconnect the exhaust pipes from the manifolds. Remove the 3 nuts on each flange

connection and lower the exhaust pipes. Support the exhaust system. Make sure the oxygen sensor wire is not being stretched.

3. Remove the nuts securing the manifolds to the cylinder head. Remove the manifolds.

To install:

4. Clean the mounting surfaces on the manifolds and the cylinder head. Check the condition of the studs and replace if necessary.

5. Install the new exhaust manifold heat shield gaskets and install the manifolds. Torque the nuts to 16-18 ft. lbs. (22-25 Nm). Use new copper nuts.

6. Connect the exhaust pipes to the manifolds using new gaskets. Connect the negative battery terminal. Start engine and check for leaks.

M30 Engine

1. Disconnect the negative battery terminal.

2. With the exhaust system cool, disconnect the exhaust pipes from the manifolds. Remove the 2 nuts on each flange connection and lower the exhaust pipes. Support the exhaust system. Make sure the oxygen sensor wire is not being stretched.

3. Remove the nuts securing the manifolds to the cylinder head. Remove the manifolds.

To install:

4. Clean the mounting surfaces on the manifolds and the cylinder head. Check the condition of the studs and replace if necessary.

5. Install the new exhaust manifold heat shield gaskets and install the manifolds. Torque the nuts to 16-18 ft. lbs. (22-25 Nm). Use new copper nuts.

6. Connect the exhaust pipes to the manifolds. Connect the negative battery terminal. Start engine and check for leaks.

M42 Engine

▶ **See Figures 34 and 35**

1. Disconnect the negative battery terminal.

2. With the exhaust system cool, disconnect the exhaust pipe from the manifold. Remove the 4 nuts on the flange connection and lower the exhaust pipes. Support the exhaust system. Make sure the oxygen sensor wire is not being stretched.

3. Remove the nuts securing the manifold to the cylinder head. Remove the manifolds.

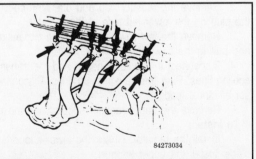

Fig. 34 Remove these bolts when removing the exhaust manifold — M42 engine

84273034

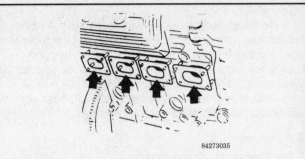

84273035

Fig. 35 Make sure the graphite side of the exhaust manifold gasket faces the cylinder head

To install:

4. Clean the mounting surfaces on the manifolds and the cylinder head. Check the condition of the studs and replace if necessary.

5. Install the new exhaust manifold gaskets with the graphite side towards the cylinder head and install the manifolds. Torque the nuts to 16-18 ft. lbs. (22-25 Nm). Use new nuts and anti-seize.

6. Connect the exhaust pipe to the manifolds. Connect the negative battery terminal. Start engine and check for leaks.

M50 Engine

1. Disconnect the negative battery terminal.

2. With the exhaust system cool, disconnect the exhaust pipe from the manifold. Remove the 3 nuts on each flange connection and lower the exhaust pipes. Support the exhaust system. Make sure the oxygen sensor wire is not being stretched.

3. Remove the nuts securing the manifold to the cylinder head. Remove the manifolds.

To install:

4. Clean the mounting surfaces on the manifolds and the cylinder head. Check the condition of the studs and replace if necessary.

5. Install the new exhaust manifold gaskets with the graphite side towards the cylinder head and install the manifolds. Torque the nuts to 16-18 ft. lbs. (22-25 Nm). Use new nuts and anti-seize.

6. Connect the exhaust pipe to the manifolds. Connect the negative battery terminal. Start engine and check for leaks.

S14 Engine

1. Disconnect the negative battery cable. With the engine cool, remove the coolant drain plug from the block. Remove the 2 electrical connectors from the front of the coolant manifold that runs along the exhaust side of the engine. Disconnect the radiator hose from the front of this pipe. Then, remove all the mounting bolts for this pipe and remove it. Inspect the O-rings and replace any that are worn or damaged.

2. Disconnect the exhaust pipe at the manifold flange. Remove the heat shields from under the engine.

3. Remove the mounting nuts at the cylinder head and remove the manifold.

4. Clean all gasket material from the surfaces of the manifold and head and replace the gaskets.

To install:

5. To install, position the manifold on the head, torquing the manifold bolts to 6.5-7.0 ft. lbs. (9 Nm) and the coolant pipe mounting bolts to 7.5-8.5 ft. lbs. (11 Nm). Torque the bolts at the flange attaching manifold and exhaust pipe first to 22-25 ft. lbs. (30-34 Nm) and then to 36-40 ft. lbs. (48-54 Nm). Make sure to refill the cooling system with fresh anti-freeze/water mix and bleed the cooling system.

S38 Engines

▶ **See Figures 36, 37 and 38**

1. Disconnect the negative battery cable. Remove the exhaust system. Drain the coolant below the level of the head. Disconnect the right side engine mount and ground strap.

2. Disconnect the air injection pipe and the heat shield. Remove the fan cowl and coolant expansion tank. Remove the air pump air filter housing.

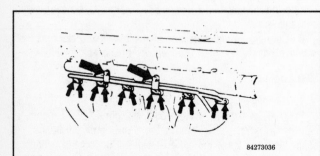

Fig. 36 Removing the air injection pipe on the S38 engine

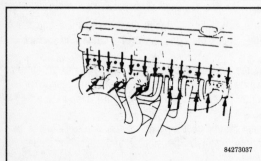

Fig. 37 Exhaust manifold mounting locations on the S38 engine

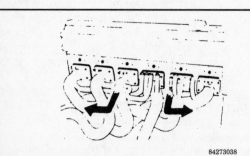

Fig. 38 To remove the manifold halves, pull outwards then apart on the S38 engine

3. Lift the right side of the engine as far as possible without damaging any connections.

4. Remove the heat shield holder and the air injection pipe. It may be necessary to use an universal joint on an extension. There is a mounting tab at cylinder number 1.

5. Disconnect the sensor plugs on the coolant pipe. Remove the coolant pipe.

6. Remove the exhaust manifold nuts and pull of the studs. Push the rear manifold back and pull the front manifold. Remove the rear manifold.

To install:

7. Clean the manifold mounting surfaces of the manifold and cylinder head. Install new gaskets with the graphite surface towards the cylinder head.

8. Install the manifolds. Place the manifolds in the reverse order of removal. Torque the nuts 6.5-8.0 ft. lbs. (9-11 Nm).

9. Replace the O-rings and install the coolant pipe. Torque to 8.0-8.5 ft. lbs. (11-12 Nm). Replace the air injection pipe gaskets and the air injection pipe. Torque to 25-33 ft. lbs. (35-45 Nm).

10. Install the heat shield. Lower the engine. Install the air pump filter, coolant expansion tank and the fan cowl. Connect the air injection pipe and tighten to 25-33 ft. lbs. (35-45 Nm). Install the heat shield holder.

11. Connect the ground strap and the engine mount. Torque to 30 ft. lbs. (42 Nm). Install the exhaust system and fill the cooling system. Connect the negative battery terminal.

Radiator

REMOVAL & INSTALLATION

❈❈CAUTION

Ethylene glycol coolant can be dangerous to animals and small children if ingested in enough quantity. Even a small amount can kill a pet and cause sickness in a child. Keep children and pets away from coolant.

E30 3 Series

WITH M42 ENGINE

1. Disconnect the negative battery terminal. Allow the engine to cool completely.

2. Remove the radiator cap and drain the cooling system at the plug on the lower left side of the radiator.

3. Remove the fan cowl by pulling the expansion rivets out and pulling the cowl out.

4. Disconnect the radiator hoses and the transmission oil cooling lines. Plug the transmission lines. Disconnect the sensor electrical leads.

5. Remove the upper radiator support and the radiator.

To install:

6. Install the radiator. Check the lower supports are in place. Install the upper support.

7. Connect the electrical leads and the transmission lines. Tighten the connections to 13-15 ft. lbs. (18-21 Nm).

8. Install the radiator hoses with new clamps. Install the radiator cowl by pushing the rivets in. Tighten the drain plug

and fill with coolant mixture. Connect the negative battery terminal. Start the engine, bleed the system and check for leaks.

WITH M20 AND S14 ENGINE

1. Disconnect the negative battery terminal. Allow the engine to cool completely.

2. Remove the expansion tank cap.

3. Remove the fan cowl by pulling the expansion rivets out and pulling the cowl out. Remove the splash shield if necessary and drain the cooling system at the plug on the lower left side of the radiator.

4. Disconnect the radiator hoses, vent hose and the transmission oil cooling lines. Plug the transmission lines. Disconnect the sensor electrical leads.

5. Remove the upper radiator support and the radiator.

To install:

6. Install the radiator. Check the lower supports are in place. Install the upper support.

7. Connect the electrical leads and the transmission lines. Tighten the connections to 13-15 ft. lbs. (18-21 Nm).

8. Install the radiator hoses with new clamps. Install the radiator cowl by pushing the rivets in. Tighten the drain plug and fill with coolant mixture. Connect the negative battery terminal. Start the engine, bleed the system and check for leaks.

E36 3 Series

▶ See Figures 39 and 40

The E36 chassis 3 series use a radiator with an integral expansion tank. The expansion tank is mounted to the radiator and has hash marks along the side to indicate level.

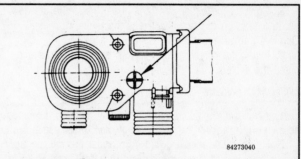

Fig. 40 The arrow marks the bleeder screw on the integral expansion tank radiators

WITH M42 ENGINE

1. Allow the engine to cool completely. Loosen the bleeder screw on the radiator expansion tank next to the radiator cap.

2. Remove the splash guard from under the car. Loosen the drain plug and catch the coolant in a container.

3. Disconnect the upper radiator hose and catch the coolant. Disconnect the temperature switch. Disconnect the lower radiator hose and catch any coolant.

4. Pull out the rivets and remove the fan cowl. Disconnect the lower expansion tank hose. Disconnect the automatic transmission oil cooling lines and plug.

5. Unlock the radiator holding clips by inserting a tool in the opening and pressing down. Remove the radiator.

To install:

6. Install the radiator on the mounts and press into the clips until the spline engagement stops.

7. Connect the electrical leads and the transmission lines. Tighten the connections to 13-15 ft. lbs. (18-21 Nm).

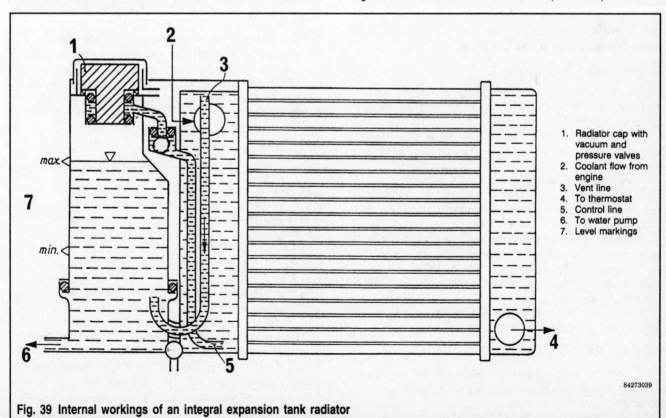

1. Radiator cap with vacuum and pressure valves
2. Coolant flow from engine
3. Vent line
4. To thermostat
5. Control line
6. To water pump
7. Level markings

Fig. 39 Internal workings of an integral expansion tank radiator

8. Connect the expansion tank hose. Install the fan cowl into the slots on the radiator. Press the rivets in to lock. Connect the radiator hoses.

9. Install the splash shield, fill with coolant mixture and bleed the system.

WITH M50 ENGINE

1. Allow the engine to cool completely. Loosen the bleeder screw on the radiator expansion tank next to the radiator cap.

2. Remove the splash guard from under the car. Loosen the drain plug and catch the coolant in a container. Pull the connector off the level sender. Remove the air guide upper section and disconnect from the alternator cooling duct. Remove the cooling duct.

3. Disconnect the upper radiator hose and catch the coolant. Disconnect the temperature switch. Disconnect the lower radiator hose and catch any coolant.

4. Pull out the rivets and remove the fan cowl. Disconnect the lower expansion tank hose. Disconnect the automatic transmission oil cooling lines and plug.

5. Unlock the radiator holding clips by inserting a tool in the opening and pressing down. Remove the radiator.

To install:

6. Install the radiator on the mounts and press into the clips until the spline engagement stops.

7. Connect the electrical leads and the transmission lines. Tighten the connections to 13-15 ft. lbs. (18-21 Nm).

8. Connect the expansion tank hose. Install the fan cowl into the slots on the radiator. Press the rivets in to lock. Connect the radiator hoses. Install the alternator cooling duct and guide.

9. Install the splash shield, fill with coolant mixture and bleed the system.

E34 5 Series

▶ **See Figures 41, 42, 43, 44 and 45**

WITH M20 AND M50 ENGINES

1. Allow the engine to cool completely. Remove the expansion tank cap and the splash shield. Drain the coolant into a container.

2. Disconnect the radiator hoses. Remove the right headlight cover. Disconnect the temperature switch plug. Disconnect the automatic transmission cooling oil lines and plug.

3. Pull out the rivets and push back the fan cowl.

4. Unlock the radiator holding clips by inserting a tool in the opening and pressing down. Remove the radiator.

To install:

5. Install the radiator into the mounts and press into the upper clips until the spline engagement sound stops.

6. Install the fan cowl rivets. Connect the electrical leads and the transmission lines. Tighten the connections to 13-15 ft. lbs. (18-21 Nm).

7. Install the right headlight cover. Connect the radiator hoses. Fill and bleed the system.

WITH M30 AND S38 ENGINES

1. Allow the engine to cool completely. Remove the expansion tank cap and the splash shield. Drain the coolant into a container.

2. Disconnect the radiator hoses and expansion tank hose. Remove the right headlight cover. Disconnect the temperature switch plug. Disconnect the automatic transmission cooling oil lines and plug.

3. Pull out the rivets and push back the fan cowl.

4. Unlock the radiator holding clips by inserting a tool in the opening and pressing down. Remove the radiator.

To install:

5. Install the radiator into the mounts and press into the upper clips until the spline engagement sound stops.

6. Install the fan cowl rivets. Connect the electrical leads and the transmission lines. Tighten the connections to 13-15 ft. lbs. (18-21 Nm).

7. Install the right headlight cover. Connect the radiator hoses and the expansion tank hose. Fill and bleed the system.

Engine Oil Cooler

REMOVAL & INSTALLATION

▶ **See Figure 46**

1. On the 5 series, remove the radiator.

2. Disconnect the oil lines from the oil cooler.

3. On the 5 series, spread the clips on the cooler mount to remove. Unplug the temperature sensors and remove out to the left.

4. On the 3 series, unscrew the mounts to remove.

5. Install in reverse order. Torque the fittings to 18.0-21.5 ft. lbs. (25-30 Nm). Check the engine oil level and fill.

Engine Fan

The engine cooling fan is driven by a belt and is bolted to the water pump. A temperature and engine speed sensitive clutch is used to limit the drag imposed on the engine by the fan. With the engine stopped, if the fan is seized, turns too freely or can be moved in a fore-aft manner, the fan clutch should be replaced.

REMOVAL & INSTALLATION

1. Hold the pulley with tool 11 5 030 or equivalent. The tool is designed to be bolted to 2 of the pulley bolts and to provide the resistance to allow the fan to be unscrewed from the pulley.

2. Unscrew the fan clockwise. Remove the fan and keep upright. The fan cowl may need to be removed. Be careful of the radiator fins.

3. Remove the fan from the fan clutch. Install the fan clutch bolts and torque to 6-7 ft. lbs. (8-10 Nm).

4. Install the fan using tool 11 5 040 or equivalent wrench and holding tool 11 5 030 or equivalent. Torque the nut to 29 ft. lbs. (40 Nm). If using the tool set the torque wrench to 22 ft. lbs. (30 Nm); the additional length of the tool multiplies the torque to achieve 29 ft. lbs. (40 Nm) at the nut.

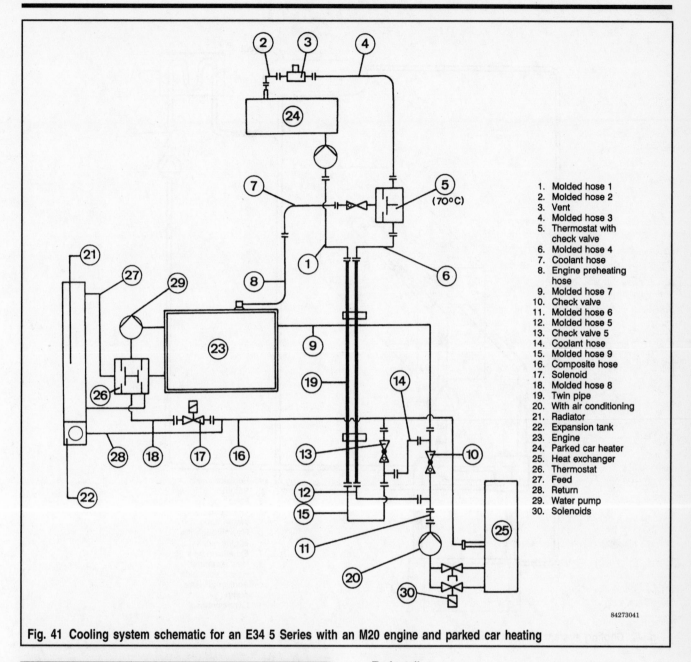

1. Molded hose 1
2. Molded hose 2
3. Vent
4. Molded hose 3
5. Thermostat with check valve
6. Molded hose 4
7. Coolant hose
8. Engine preheating hose
9. Molded hose 7
10. Check valve
11. Molded hose 6
12. Molded hose 5
13. Check valve 5
14. Coolant hose
15. Molded hose 9
16. Composite hose
17. Solenoid
18. Molded hose 8
19. Twin pipe
20. With air conditioning
21. Radiator
22. Expansion tank
23. Engine
24. Parked car heater
25. Heat exchanger
26. Thermostat
27. Feed
28. Return
29. Water pump
30. Solenoids

84273041

Fig. 41 Cooling system schematic for an E34 5 Series with an M20 engine and parked car heating

Auxiliary Cooling Fan

REMOVAL & INSTALLATION

E30 3 Series

1. Disconnect the negative battery terminal. Remove the radiator. Remove the grilles.
2. Loosen and remove the bolts holding the air conditioning condenser. Do not disconnect the refrigerant lines.
3. Remove the trim panel behind the left side headlight. Disconnect the fan plug and remove the mounting nuts.
4. Pull back the condenser and remove the fan from above.

To install:

5. Install the cooling fan and tighten the nuts. Plug in the connector.
6. Install the trim panel behind the headlight. Install the condenser mounting bolts.
7. Install the radiator and the grilles. Connect the negative battery terminal.

E36 3 Series

1. Remove the air duct from above the radiator. There are 5 mounting screws.
2. Remove the splash shield from under the vehicle.
3. Disconnect the fan electrical plug. Remove the 3 fan mounting bolts.
4. Pull the fan forward and out.

To install:

5. Install the fan and tighten the mounting bolts. Plug in the electrical connector.

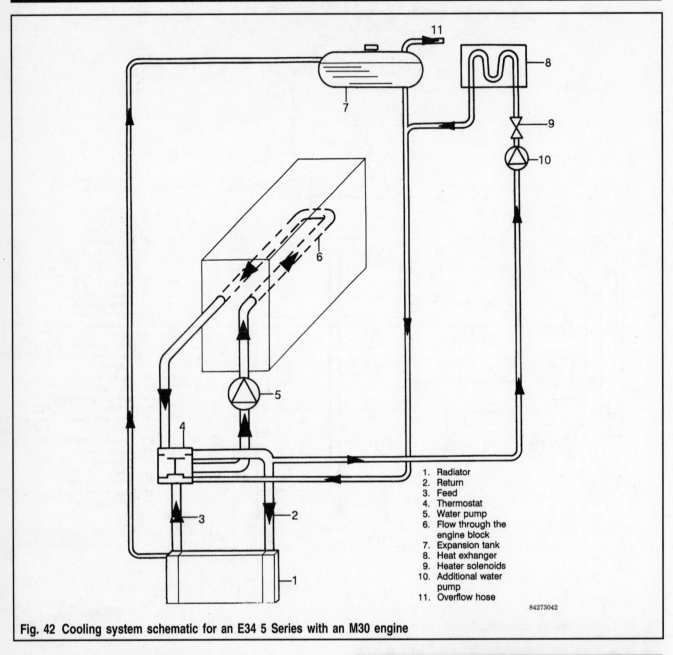

1. Radiator
2. Return
3. Feed
4. Thermostat
5. Water pump
6. Flow through the engine block
7. Expansion tank
8. Heat exhanger
9. Heater solenoids
10. Additional water pump
11. Overflow hose

84273042

Fig. 42 Cooling system schematic for an E34 5 Series with an M30 engine

6. Install the splash shield and the air duct.

E34 5 Series

1. Remove the front bumper. Remove the center double kidney grille.

2. Remove the mounting screws for the right horn and the cooling coil for the power steering. Move and support out of the way. Remove the right side headlight grille.

3. Disconnect the fan electrical plug. Remove the mounting bolts and pull the fan out from below.

To install:

4. Install the fan and tighten the mounting nuts. Connect the electrical plug.

5. Install the horn, cooling coil and the right side headlight grille.

6. Install the kidney grille and the bumper.

Water Pump

REMOVAL & INSTALLATION

M20 Engine

▶ See Figure 47

1. Disconnect the negative battery cable. Drain the cooling system.

2. Remove the distributor cap and rotor. Remove the rotor adapter, the dust shield and the distributor housing.

3. Remove the fan. The fan must be held stationary with tool 11 5 030 or some sort of flat blade cut to fit over the hub and drilled to fit over 2 of the studs on the front of the pulley. Remove the fan coupling nut; left hand thread-turn clockwise to remove.

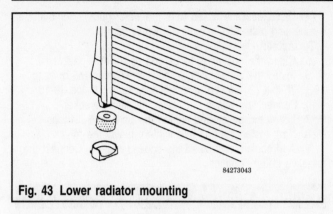

Fig. 43 Lower radiator mounting

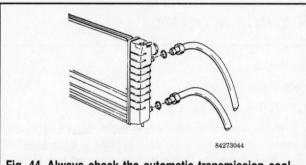

Fig. 44 Always check the automatic transmission cooling line connection seals

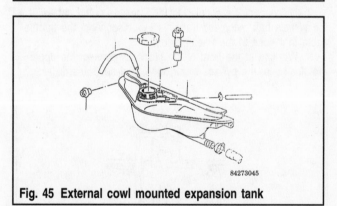

Fig. 45 External cowl mounted expansion tank

4. Remove the belt and pulley.

5. Remove the rubber guard and distributor and or upper timing belt cover.

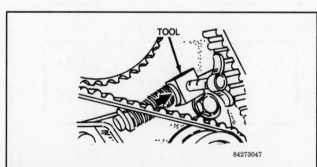

Fig. 47 Compress the timing belt tensioner spring and clamp with tool 11 5 010 or equivalent

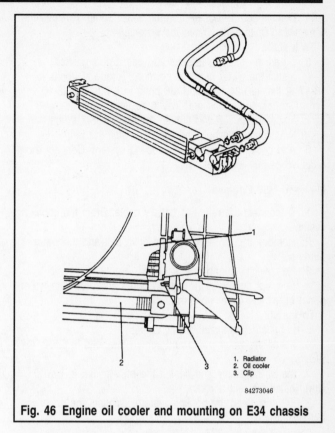

1. Radiator
2. Oil cooler
3. Clip

Fig. 46 Engine oil cooler and mounting on E34 chassis

6. Compress the timing tensioner spring and clamp pin with the proper tool.

➡**Observe the installed position of the tensioner spring pin on the water pump housing for reinstallation purposes.**

7. Remove the water hoses, remove the 3 water pump bolts and remove the pump.

To install:

8. Clean the gasket surfaces and use a new gasket.

9. Install the water pump in position. Note the position of the tensioner spring pin. Torque M8 bolts to 16-17 ft. lbs. (20-24 Nm) and M6 bolts to 6-7 ft. lbs. (8-10 Nm). Connect the hoses.

10. Release the tensioner from the holding pin. Install the upper timing cover. Install the pulley and tighten the bolts to 6-7 ft. lbs. (8-10 Nm). Install the belt and tighten.

11. Install the fan, distributor housing and dust shield. Tighten the rotor adapter to 39-47 ft. lbs. (55-65 Nm). Install the rotor, O-ring and cap.

12. Add coolant and bleed the cooling system. Connect the negative battery terminal.

M30 Engine

1. Disconnect the negative battery cable. Drain the cooling system.

2. Remove the fan. The fan must be held stationary with tool 11 5 030 or some sort of flat blade cut to fit over the hub and drilled to fit over 2 of the studs on the front of the pulley. Remove the fan coupling nut; left hand thread-turn clockwise to remove.

3. Remove the belt and pulley. Remove the engine lifting bracket.

4. Disconnect the hoses from the water pump. Remove the 6 mounting bolts and remove the water pump.

To install:

5. Clean the gasket surfaces and use a new gasket.

6. Install the water pump in position. Torque M8 bolts to 16-17 ft. lbs. (20-24 Nm) and M6 bolts to 6-7 ft. lbs. (8-10 Nm). Connect the hoses and install the lifting bracket.

7. Install the pulley and tighten the bolts to 6-7 ft. lbs. (8-10 Nm). Install the belt and tighten. Install the fan.

8. Add coolant and bleed the cooling system. Connect the negative battery terminal.

M42 and M50 Engines

1. Disconnect the negative battery cable. Drain the cooling system.

2. Remove the fan. Remove the drive belt and the water pump pulley.

3. Remove the pump mounting bolts.

4. Screw 2 bolts into the tapped bores and press the water pump out of the cover uniformly.

To install:

5. Lubricate and install a new O-ring.

6. Install the water pump and tighten the bolts to 6.5 ft. lbs. (9 Nm).

7. Install the pulley and tighten the bolts to 6.5 ft. lbs. (9 Nm). Install the belt and fan.

8. Fill and bleed the cooling system. Connect the negative battery terminal.

S14 Engine

1. Disconnect the negative battery cable. Drain the cooling system.

2. Remove the fan. The fan must be held stationary with tool 11 5 030 or some sort of flat blade cut to fit over the hub and drilled to fit over 2 of the studs on the front of the pulley. Remove the fan coupling nut; left hand thread-turn clockwise to remove.

3. Remove the belt and pulley.

4. Disconnect the hoses from the water pump. Remove the 7 mounting bolts and remove the water pump.

To install:

5. Clean the gasket surfaces and use a new gasket.

6. Install the water pump in position. Torque M8 bolts to 16-17 ft. lbs. (20-24 Nm) and M6 bolts to 6-7 ft. lbs. (8-10 Nm). Connect the hoses.

7. Install the pulley and tighten the bolts to 6-7 ft. lbs. (8-10 Nm). Install the belt and tighten. Install the fan.

8. Add coolant and bleed the cooling system. Connect the negative battery terminal.

S38 Engine

1. Disconnect the negative battery cable. Drain the cooling system.

2. Remove the fan. The fan must be held stationary with tool 11 5 030 or some sort of flat blade cut to fit over the hub and drilled to fit over 2 of the studs on the front of the pulley. Remove the fan coupling nut; left hand thread-turn clockwise to remove.

3. Remove the air cleaner assembly with the air flow meter. Remove the belt and pulley. Remove the engine lifting bracket.

4. Disconnect the hoses from the water pump. Remove the 6 mounting bolts and remove the water pump.

To install:

5. Clean the gasket surfaces and use a new gasket.

6. Install the water pump in position. Torque M8 bolts to 16-17 ft. lbs. (20-24 Nm) and M6 bolts to 6-7 ft. lbs. (8-10 Nm). Connect the hoses and install the lifting bracket.

7. Install the pulley and tighten the bolts to 6-7 ft. lbs. (8-10 Nm). Install the belt and tighten. Install the fan.

8. Add coolant and bleed the cooling system. Connect the negative battery terminal.

Cylinder Head

REMOVAL & INSTALLATION

M20 Engine
▶ See Figures 48 and 49

MOUNTED IN E30 3 SERIES

1. Disconnect the negative battery cable. Make sure the engine is cool. Disconnect the exhaust pipes at the manifold and at the transmission clamp. Remove the drain plug at the bottom of the radiator and drain the coolant. Drain the engine oil.

2. Disconnect the accelerator and cruise control cables. If the vehicle has automatic transmission, disconnect the throttle cable that goes to the transmission.

3. Working at the front of the block, disconnect the upper radiator hose, the bypass water hose, and several smaller

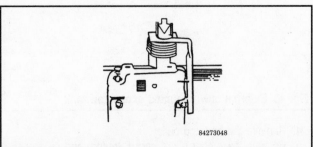

84273048

Fig. 48 To release the vent tube on the M20 engine, the collar must be held down with tool 11 1 290 or equivalent

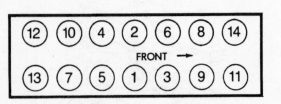

84273049

Fig. 49 Head bolt torque order — M20 engine

water hoses. Remove the diagnosis plug located at the front corner of the manifold. Remove the bracket located just underneath. Disconnect the fuel line and drain the contents into a metal container for safe disposal.

4. Working on the air cleaner/airflow sensor, disconnect the vacuum hoses, labeling them if necessary. Disconnect all electrical connectors and unclip and remove the wiring harness. There is a relay located in an L-shaped box near the strut tower. Disconnect and remove it. Unclamp and remove the air hose. Remove the mounting nuts and remove the assembly.

5. Disconnect the hose at the coolant overflow tank. Disconnect the idle speed positioner vacuum hose and then remove the positioner from the manifold.

6. If equipped with 4 wheel drive, disconnect the vacuum hose from the servo mounted on the manifold.

7. Place a drain pan underneath and then disconnect the water connections at the front of the intake manifold. Disconnect the electrical connector.

8. Disconnect the heater water hoses. Press down on the vent tube collar and install the special tool or a similar device to retain the collar in the unlocked position. Disconnect the vent tube and inspect its O-ring seal, replacing it, if necessary.

9. Unbolt the dipstick tube at the manifold. Remove the fuel hose bracket at the cylinder head. Make sure the engine is cold. Then, place a metal container under the connection and disconnect the fuel hose at the connection.

10. Disconnect the high tension lead from the coil. Disconnect and remove the coolant expansion tank.

11. If equipped with 4 wheel drive, disconnect the intake manifold vacuum hose leading the servo that engages 4 wheel drive.

12. Disconnect the fuel injector connectors at all 6 injectors, as well as the 2 additional electrical connectors to sensors on the head. Disconnect the oil pressure sending unit connector. Then, unfasten the carriers and remove this wiring harness toward the left side of the vehicle.

13. Disconnect the coil high tension wire and disconnect the high tension wires at the plugs. Then, disconnect the tube in which the wires run at the camshaft cover. Disconnect the PCV hose. Then, remove the retaining nuts and remove the camshaft cover.

14. Turn the crankshaft so the TDC line is aligned with the indicator and the valves of No. 6 cylinder are in overlapping, slightly open position.

15. Remove the distributor cap. Then, unscrew and remove the rotor. Unscrew and remove the adapter just underneath the rotor. Remove the cover underneath the adapter. Check its O-ring and replace it, if necessary.

16. Remove the distributor mounting bolts and the protective cover.

17. These engines are equipped with a rubber drive and timing belt. Remove the belt covers. To loosen belt tension, loosen the tension roller bracket pivot bolt and adjusting slot bolt. Push the roller and bracket away from the belt to release the tension, hold the bracket in this position, and tighten the adjusting slot bolt to retain the bracket it this position.

18. Remove the timing belt.

➡ **Make sure to avoid rotating both the engine and camshaft from this point onward.**

19. Remove the cylinder head mounting bolts in exact reverse order of the proper tightening sequence. Then, remove the cylinder head.

To install:

20. Install the head with a new gasket. Check that all passages line up with the gasket holes. Clean the threads on the head bolts and coat with a light coating of oil. Keep oil out of the bolt cavities in the head or the head could be cracked or proper torquing affected.

21. Torque bolts in a crisscross pattern staring at the center of the head and working towards the end. If equipped with hex head bolts, torque to 29-34 ft. lbs. (40-45 Nm). Wait 15 minutes then torque to 43-47 ft. lbs. (60-65 Nm). After the installation is completed, run the engine for 25 minutes and give the bolts a final turn of 25-30 degrees. If equipped with Torx bolts, torque to 22 ft. lbs. (30 Nm), turn 90 degrees, then complete with an additional 90 degrees. Do not wait or run engine. Adjust the valves.

22. Clean both cylinder head and block sealing surfaces thoroughly with a hardwood scraper. Inspect the surfaces for flatness.

23. Complete the installation by reversing all removal procedures. Torque the head bolts starting from the center and move in a crisscross fashion to the ends of the head. Make sure to refill the engine oil pan and cooling system with proper fluids and to bleed the cooling system.

24. Replace the gaskets for the exhaust system connections, if necessary. Coat the studs with the proper sealant. Note that the plugs for the DME reference mark and speed signals should be connected so the gray plug goes to the socket with a ring underneath.

➡**Align the timing marks when installing the timing belt. The crankshaft sprocket mark must point at the notch in the flange of the front engine cover. The camshaft sprocket arrow must point at the alignment mark on the cylinder head. Also, the No. 1 piston must be at TDC of the compression stroke. BMW recommends that the timing belt be replaced every time the cylinder head is removed and the belt is disturbed as a consequence. Tension the belt.**

25. Start the engine and run it until it is hot. Stop the engine and again remove the camshaft cover. Using an angle gauge, retorque the head bolts to specification. Reinstall the camshaft cover.

MOUNTED IN E34 5 SERIES

1. Unbolt the exhaust pipe connections at the manifold and at the transmission pipe clamp. Disconnect the negative battery cable.

2. Remove the splash shield from under the engine. With the engine cool, remove the drain plugs from the bottom of the radiator and block. Drain the engine oil.

3. Disconnect the throttle and cruise control cables at the throttle lever. Unbolt the cable housing retainer and remove the housing and cables.

4. Loosen the hose clamp and disconnect the air inlet hose from the air flow sensor.

5. The unit on the opposite side of the intake hose from the air cleaner contains the idle speed control valve, which must be removed next. Loosen the hose clamps and pull off the hoses. Disconnect the electrical connector. Remove the

mounting nut and then pull the idle speed control out of the air intake hose.

6. Disconnect and plug the brake booster vacuum line.

7. Disconnect the radiator hoses, the heater hoses and the fuel lines. Mark the lines for ease of installation.

8. Disconnect the venting valve vacuum line and electrical connector from under the intake manifold. Disconnect the connections on the plug plate located under the intake manifold and remove the plug plate.

9. Remove the fan. Lift out the expansion rivets on either side and remove the fan shroud.

10. Disconnect the throttle body coolant hoses. Loosen the mount for the engine oil dipstick.

11. Disconnect the plugs near the thermostat housing. Loosen the hose clamps and pull off the coolant hoses.

12. Disconnect the plug in the line leading to the oxygen sensor. Disconnect the other plugs.

13. Disconnect the fuel supply and return lines, collecting fuel in a metal container for safe disposal.

14. Disconnect the fuel pipe running along the cylinder head, near the manifold. Pull off the electrical connector at the throttle body. Remove the caps, then remove the attaching bolts and remove the wiring harness carrier and harness for the fuel injectors.

15. Disconnect the coil high tension lead. Disconnect the high tension wires at the plugs. Then, remove the mounting nuts and remove the carrier for the high tension wires from the head.

16. Remove the timing belt. The timing belt must be replaced anytime it is removed or the tensioner loosened.

17. Remove the heater hose from the cylinder head. Press down on the venting pipe collar and lock into position. Remove the valve cover. Check for any remaining connections that may have been missed.

18. Remove the head bolts in a crisscross pattern starting from the ends towards the center. Lift off the head.

19. Make checks of the lower cylinder head and block deck surface to make sure they are true. Install a new head gasket, making sure all bolt, oil, and coolant holes line up. Use a 0.3mm thicker gasket, if the head has been machined.

To install:

20. Apply a very light coating of oil to the head bolts. Don't let oil get into the bolt holes or apply excessive amounts of oil, or torque could be incorrect and the block could crack. Use the type of bolt without a collar. Install the bolts, finger tight.

21. Torque bolts in a crisscross pattern staring at the center of the head and working towards the end. If equipped with hex head bolts, torque to 29-34 ft. lbs. (40-45 Nm). Wait 15 minutes then torque to 43-47 ft. lbs. (60-65 Nm). After the installation is completed, run the engine for 25 minutes and give the bolts a final turn of 25-30 degrees. If equipped with Torx bolts, torque to 22 ft. lbs. (30 Nm), turn 90 degrees, then complete with an additional 90 degrees. Do not wait or run engine. Adjust the valves.

22. Connect the venting pipe and release the collar. Connect the heater hose on the cylinder head. Connect the throttle body coolant hoses and install the wiring harnesses and injector plugs. Connect the sensors and vacuum lines.

23. Install a new timing belt. Never reuse a timing belt. Install the fan and cowl.

24. Connect the fuel lines, air intake hoses, vacuum lines, idle air control and throttle cables.

25. Fill the engine with fluids and bleed the coolant system. Connect the exhaust system and the negative battery terminal.

M30 Engine

▶ See Figure 50

1. Unbolt the exhaust pipe connections at the manifold and at the transmission pipe clamp. Disconnect the negative battery cable.

2. Remove the splash shield from under the engine. With the engine cool, remove the drain plugs from the bottom of the radiator and block. Drain the engine oil.

3. Remove the fan. Lift out the expansion rivets on either side and remove the fan shroud.

4. Loosen the hose clamp and disconnect the air inlet hose. Remove the mounting nut and remove the air cleaner.

5. The unit on the opposite side of the intake hose from the air cleaner contains the idle speed control valve, which must be removed next. Loosen the hose clamps and pull off the hoses. Disconnect the electrical connector. Remove the mounting nut and then pull the idle speed control out of the air intake hose.

6. Pull off the retainers for the airflow sensor, and then pull the unit off its mountings, disconnecting the vacuum hose from the PCV system at the same time.

7. Working on the coolant expansion tank, disconnect the electrical connector. Remove the nuts on both sides. Loosen their clamps and then disconnect all hoses and remove the tank.

8. Disconnect the heater hoses at both the control valve and at the heater core. Remove the valve, if needed.

9. Disconnect the throttle and cruise control cables at the throttle lever. Unbolt the cable housing retainer and remove the housing and cables.

10. Disconnect the plugs near the thermostat housing. Loosen the hose clamps and pull off the coolant hoses.

11. Disconnect the plug in the line leading to the oxygen sensor. Disconnect the other plugs.

12. Disconnect the fuel supply and return lines, collecting fuel in a metal container for safe disposal.

13. Disconnect the fuel pipe running along the cylinder head, near the manifold. Pull off the electrical connector at the throttle body. Remove the caps, then remove the attaching bolts and remove the wiring harness carrier and harness for the fuel injectors.

14. Disconnect the coil high tension lead. Disconnect the high tension wires at the plugs. Then, remove the mounting

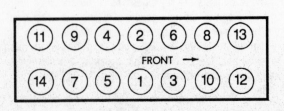

Fig. 50 Head bolt torque order — M30 engine

nuts and remove the carrier for the high tension wires from the head.

15. Remove the attaching nuts for the camshaft cover and remove it.

16. Turn the engine until the timing marks are at TDC and the No. 6 valves are at overlap, both slightly open, position.

17. Remove the upper timing case cover. Remove the timing chain tensioner piston.

18. Remove the upper timing chain sprocket bolts and pull the sprocket off, holding it upward and then supporting it securely so the relationship between the chain and sprockets top and bottom will not be lost.

19. Disconnect the upper radiator hose at the thermostat housing. Remove the bolts and remove the support for the intake manifold.

20. Remove the cylinder head bolts in the opposite of numbered order. Then, install 4 special pins part No. 11 1 063 or equivalent. This is necessary to keep the rocker arm shafts from moving. Then, lift off the head.

21. Make checks of the lower cylinder head and block deck surface to make sure they are true. Install a new head gasket, making sure all bolt, oil, and coolant holes line up. Use a 0.3mm thicker gasket, if the head has been machined.

To install:

22. Apply a very light coating of oil to the head bolts. Don't let oil get into the bolt holes or apply excessive amounts of oil, or torque could be incorrect and the block could crack. Use the type of bolt without a collar. Install the bolts, finger tight.

23. Torque bolts 1-6 in the correct order to 42-44 ft. lbs. (57-60 Nm). Remove the pins holding the rocker shafts in place. Now, complete the first stage of torquing by torquing bolts 7-14 in the correct order, to the same specification. Wait 20 minutes. Torque to 57-59 ft. lbs. (78-82 Nm). Once the procedure is completed, run the engine for 25 minutes. Tighten the bolts, in the correct order, with a torque angle gauge 30-40 degrees, using special tool 11 2 110 or equivalent.

24. Reinstall the timing sprocket to the camshaft. Make sure the camshaft is in proper time, that new lock plates are used, and that nuts are properly torqued. Install the tensioner piston.

25. When reinstalling the timing cover, make sure to apply a liquid sealer to the joints between upper and lower timing covers. The remainder of installation is the reverse of removal. Note these points:

a. Adjust throttle, speed control, and accelerator cables. Inspect and if necessary replace the exhaust manifold gasket.

b. When reinstalling the cylinder block coolant plug, coat it with sealer. Make sure to refill the cooling system and bleed it. Make sure to refill the oil pan with the correct amount of oil.

c. Install the timing chain so the down pin on the camshaft sprocket is at the 8 o'clock when its tapped bores are at right angles to the engine. Torque the sprocket bolts to 6.5-7.5 ft. lbs. (8-10 Nm).

d. Check the camshaft cover gasket, replacing, as necessary. Tighten camshaft cover bolts in the order shown. Torque the bolts to 6.5-7.5 ft. lbs. (8-10 Nm).

e. When reinstalling the fan shroud, make sure all guides are located properly.

f. Coat the tapered portion of the exhaust pipe connection flange with the proper sealant. Torque the attaching nuts to 4.5 ft. lbs. (6 Nm) and loosen 1½ turns.

M42 Engine

▶ **See Figure 51**

1. Disconnect the negative battery cable. Remove the intake manifold and the exhaust manifold.

2. Remove the ignition coil cover and pull off the spark plug connectors.

3. Remove the complete ignition leads. Remove the cylinder head cover.

4. Disconnect the coolant hoses and remove the position sensor.

5. Remove the thermostat housing and thermostat. Unscrew the upper timing case cover.

6. Rotate the engine in the direction of the rotation until the camshaft peaks of the intake and exhaust camshafts for cylinder No. 1 face each other. The arrows on the sprocket face up.

7. Remove the chain tensioner. Remove the upper chain guide, chain guide bolt on the right side and the sprockets.

8. Remove the cylinder head bolts from the outside to the inside in several steps using the proper tool.

9. Remove the cylinder head. Clean the sealing surfaces on the cylinder head and the crankcase.

To install:

10. Clean the new head bolts and the bores of the cylinder block. Do not allow oil or contaminants to fill the bores. Use a 0.012 inch (0.3mm) thicker gasket if the head was machined. Install a new gasket for the timing case at the front of the cylinder head.

11. If the valve train or camshafts were removed, wait 30 minutes between the time of mounting the camshafts and mounting the head. This will allow the hydraulic lash adjusters to bleed down and prevent the valves from contacting the pistons.

12. Install a new head gasket in the proper orientation as marked on the gasket. Check the condition of the guide dowels in the cylinder deck. Torque the new head bolts in a crisscross pattern starting at the center of the head and working towards the ends. Tighten to 24 ft. lbs. (33 Nm), then turn 93 degrees, then finish with a final turn of 93 degrees.

13. Install tool 11 2 300 or equivalent, to hold the crank at TDC. Install tool 11 3 240 or equivalent, to hold the camshafts in proper alignment. If the camshafts have to be turned so much that the valves in cylinders 1 or 4 start to open, turn the crank 90 degrees in the direction of engine rotation. Turn the camshafts and install the tool, then rotate the crankshaft back to TDC. This will prevent the valves from striking the pistons.

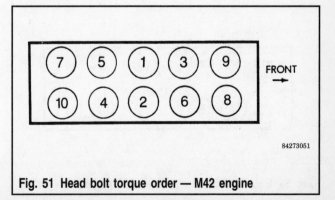

84273051

Fig. 51 Head bolt torque order — M42 engine

14. Install the camshaft sprockets with the arrows pointing up. Torque to 10-12 ft. lbs. (13-17 Nm). Install the timing chain, timing guide bolt on the right side and the upper chain guide.

15. If not installing a new tensioner piston, knock the outer sleeve of the tensioner piston so the piston is released from the sleeve. Assemble the tensioner with the spring, the piston and the snaprings in position. Place in a vice and press together until both snaprings engage. If the piston starts to extend, the procedure must be done again. The compressed tensioner will be 2.697 inch (68.5mm).

16. Install the tensioner into its bore and tighten the plug to 17-19 ft. lbs. (23-27 Nm). Push the tensioner rail against the tensioner to release the tensioner piston.

17. Remove the camshaft holding tool and the crankshaft holding tool. Install the front timing upper cover with new gaskets and fill the gaps with non hardening sealer. Press down on the cover to align it with the cylinder head. Install the bolts and torque to 6-7 ft. lbs. (8-10 Nm) for M6 bolts and 15-17 ft. lbs. (20-22 Nm) for M8 bolts.

18. Use a new gasket and install the thermostat housing. Make sure the vent on the thermostat faces up. Torque to 6-7 ft. lbs. (8-10 Nm). Install the position sensor. Connect the coolant hose. Install the valve cover and ignition leads. Install the manifolds. Fill and bleed the cooling system. Change the oil and fill to the proper level.

M50 Engine

▶ **See Figure 52**

1. If engine is not already removed from the vehicle, disconnect the negative battery cable and drain the engine coolant. Remove the intake manifold and throttle valve. Disconnect the exhaust pipes and the oxygen sensor wire. Remove the exhaust manifolds. Remove the thermostat housing and engine lifting eye.

2. Pull off the connectors for the ignition coils and remove the coils. Unscrew the cylinder heads cover and remove. Remove the sender from the head and the electrical lead duct.

3. Remove the upper timing case cover and the camshaft cover. Crank the engine in the direction of rotation so that the intake and exhaust camshaft peaks for cylinder No.1 face each other. Hold the camshafts in place with tool 11 3 240 or equivalent. With the camshafts in this alignment the arrows on the sprockets will be facing up. Remove the valve cover mounting studs. Lock the flywheel in place to prevent movement of the crankshaft.

4. Unscrew the chain tensioner and carefully remove. There is a spring contained within the tensioner and may eject out if care is not taken.

5. Press down on the upper chain tensioner and lock it into place using tool 11 3 290 or equivalent. Unscrew the transfer timing chain sprockets and pull the 2 off together with the chain. Remove the upper chain tensioner and the lower chain guide. Pull off the main timing chain sprocket along with the chain. Use a bent piece of wire to hold the chain from falling down into the engine. Do not rotate the engine after this point or the valve timing will be disturbed when the engine is reassembled.

6. Unscrew the bolts on the head at the ends of the cams. Using a proper sized Torx® bit or tool 11 2 250 loosen the cylinder head bolts in several steps. Use an outside to inside pattern to prevent warpage. On production heads the bolt washers are locked into place while on replacement heads the washers are loose. Keep track of the bolt washers.

To Install:

7. If the camshafts have been removed and reinstalled a waiting period dependent on the ambient temperature is necessary before mounting the cylinder head on the engine. At room temperature wait 4 minutes to allow the lifters to compress fully. At temperatures down to 50° F.(10° C.) wait 11 minutes. At temperatures lower than 50° F.(10° C.) wait 30 minutes. This is to prevent contact between the valves and the piston tops. The engine may not be cranked under the same condition for a period of 10 minutes at room temperature; 30 minutes for temperatures down to 50° F.(10° C.); 75 minutes for temperatures below 50° F.(10° C.).

8. Clean all mounting surfaces and check the head for warpage. Take care not to drop any pieces of gasket or dirt into the oil or coolant passages. Check the condition of the head locating dowel sleeves.

9. Place a new head gasket on the engine block over the locating dowels and gently place the head on the engine. Align the head with the dowel sleeves and check that the head sits flat on the engine.

10. Cylinder head bolts may only be used once. Lightly oil the threads of the new cylinder head bolts. Check that the head bolt washers are in place and install the bolts. Torque the head bolts in 3 steps; Step 1: 24 ft. lbs. (33 Nm), Step 2 and 3: 93 degree torque angle. Torque the center bolts first and go out in a diagonal pattern.

11. Align main timing chain and sprocket on the camshaft so that the arrow faces up. The bolt holes in the camshaft should be on the left sides of the sprocket slots. This will allow the tensioner to take up the slack in the chain and rotate the gear to the counterclockwise position.

12. Install the upper chain tensioner and the lower chain guide. Install the transfer timing gears and chain on the camshafts with the arrows facing up. Make sure that the pulse sender is installed on the intake cam. Do not tighten the sprocket bolts.

13. Install the lower timing chain tensioner with the groove in a vertical position. Use a new sealing ring and torque to 29 ft. lbs. (40 Nm).

14. Release the upper timing chain tensioner and torque the sprocket bolts to 16 ft. lbs. (22 Nm).

15. Install the valve cover mounting studs and remove the flywheel lock. Install the camshaft cover and the timing case covers using new gaskets. Install the lifting eye and the electri-

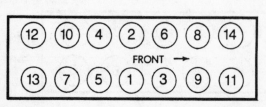

84273052

Fig. 52 Head bolt torque order — M50 engine

cal lead duct. Install the camshaft sensor with a new seal if needed.

16. Install the valve cover using new gaskets if necessary. Check that the gasket seats correctly all the way around the seating area.

17. Install the ignition coils and connect the electrical leads to each coil.

18. Install the thermostat with the arrow or vent facing up with a new O-ring. Install the thermostat housing with a new gasket. Install the intake manifold and throttle valve. Install the exhaust manifolds. Change the oil and check all fluid levels.

S14 Engine

▶ See Figures 53 and ?

1. Disconnect the negative battery cable. Remove the splash guard from under the engine. Put drain pans underneath and remove the drain plugs from both the radiator and block to drain all coolant.

2. Loosen the hose clamps for the air intake hose located next to the radiator and then remove the hose. Disconnect the electrical connectors for the airflow sensor. Then, remove the attaching nuts and remove the air cleaner/ airflow sensor unit.

3. Disconnect the accelerator and cruise control cables. Unbolt the cable mounting bracket and move the cables and bracket aside.

4. Remove the attaching nut, pull off the clamp, and then detach the vacuum hose from the brake booster.

5. Loosen the hose clamp and remove the air intake hose from the intake manifold. Remove the nut from the manifold brace.

6. Loosen the clamp and disconnect the other end of the booster vacuum hose at the manifold. Remove the nut from the intake manifold brace.

7. Loosen the hose clamp and disconnect the air intake hose at the manifold. Then, remove the nuts attaching the manifold assembly to the outer ends of the intake throttle necks and remove the assembly.

8. Put a drain pan underneath and loosen the hose clamps and disconnect the coolant expansion tank hoses. Disconnect the engine ground strap.

9. Disconnect the ignition coil high tension lead. Label and then disconnect the plugs on the front of the block. Remove the nut fastening the lead farther forward of the plugs and move the lead aside so it will not interfere with cylinder head removal.

10. Find the vacuum hose leading to the fuel pressure regulator. Pull it off. Label and then disconnect the 2 plugs. Un-

screw the mounting screw for the electrical lead connecting with the top of the block and remove the lead and its carrier.

11. There is a vacuum hose connecting with one of the throttle necks. Disconnect it and pull it out of the intake manifold bracket. Pull off the electrical connector. Pull out the rubber retainer, and then pull the idle speed control out and put it aside. The engine wiring harness is located nearby. Take it out of its carriers.

12. All the fuel injectors are plugged into a common plate. Carefully and evenly pull the plate off the injectors, pull it out past the pressure regulator, and lay it aside.

13. Loosen the clamp and then disconnect the PCV hose. Label and then disconnect the fuel lines connecting with the injector circuit. Put a drain pan underneath and then disconnect the heater hose from the cylinder head.

14. Loosen the clamp near the throttle necks and then pull the engine wiring harness out and put it aside. Put a drain pan underneath and then disconnect the heater hose that connects to the block.

15. Remove the bolts from the flanges connecting the exhaust pipes to the exhaust manifold. Provide new gaskets and self-locking nuts. Disconnect the oxygen sensor plug.

16. Put a drain pan underneath and then disconnect the radiator hoses from the pipe at the front of the block.

17. Pull off the spark plug connectors. Remove the nuts from the camshaft cover, located just to one side of the row of spark plugs. Remove the ignition lead tube. Remove the remaining nuts and remove the camshaft cover. Provide new gaskets.

18. It is not necessary to remove the timing chain completely, but it is necessary to remove the camshaft cover, front covers for the camshaft drive sprockets, the upper guide rail for the timing chain and then turn the engine to TDC firing position for No. 1. Remove the timing chain tensioner. Note the relationship between the chain and both the crankshaft and camshaft sprockets, and then remove both camshaft drive sprockets. Leave the chain in a position that will not interfere with removal of the head and which will minimize disturbing its routing through the areas on the front of the block.

19. Remove the camshafts.

20. Remove the camshaft followers one at a time, keeping them in exact order for installation in the same positions.

21. Remove the bolts, some are accessible from below, that retain the timing case to the head at the front, the timing case houses the lifters and the camshaft lower bearing saddles. Note that one bolt, on the right side of the vehicle, is longer and retains the shaft for the upper timing chain tensioning rail.

22. Remove the coolant pipe that runs along the left/rear of the block. Remove one bolt at the left/front of the block that is located outside the camshaft cover. Then, go along in the area under the camshaft cover and remove all the remaining bolts for the timing case. Remove the timing case.

23. Remove the hex bolts fastening the head to the block at the front. These are located outside the camshaft cover and just behind the water pump drive belt. Then, remove the head bolts located under the camshaft cover in reverse order of the cylinder head torque sequence.

To install:

24. BMW does not recommend machining the head. Make checks of the lower cylinder head and block deck surface to make sure they are true. Clean both cylinder head and block sealing surfaces thoroughly. Lubricate the head bolts with a

| 8 | 6 | 2 | 4 | 10 | FRONT → |
| 9 | 3 | 1 | 5 | 7 | |

84273053

Fig. 53 Head bolt torque order — S14 engine

light coating of engine oil. Make sure there is no oil or dirt in the bolt holes in the block. Install a new head gasket, making sure all bolt, oil, and coolant holes line up. Install the bolts as follows:

    a. Torque them in the correct order to 35-37 ft. lbs. (47-50 Nm).

    b. Then torque them in order to 57-59 ft. lbs. (80-82 Nm).

    c. Wait 15 minutes.

    d. Torque them, in order, to 71-73 ft. lbs. (96-100 Nm).

    e. Remember to reinstall the bolts that go outside the cylinder head cover and fasten the front of the head to the block at front and rear.

25. BMW recommends checking the fit of each tappet in the timing case, by performing the following procedure:

    a. Measure a tappet's outside diameter with a micrometer. Then, zero an inside micrometer at this exact dimension.

    b. Then, use the inside micrometer to measure the tappet bore that corresponds to this particular tappet. If the resulting measurement is 0.0001-0.0026 inch the tappet may be reused. If it is worn past this dimension, replace it with a new one. If the tappet is being replaced, repeat steps a and b to make sure it will now meet specifications. If the bore were to be worn so much that even a new tappet would not restore clearance to specification, it would be necessary to replace the timing case.

    c. Repeat for all the remaining tappets. Make sure to measure each tappet and its corresponding bore only.

26. The remaining steps of installation are the reverse of the removal procedure. Note the following:

    a. Before remounting the timing case, replace the O-ring in the oil passage located at the left/front of the block. Also, check the O-rings in the tops of the spark plug bores and replace these as necessary.

    b. Install the timing case and torque the bolts in several stages. The smaller (M7) bolts are torqued to 10-12 ft. lbs. (14-16 Nm); the larger (M8) bolts are torqued to 14.5-15.5 ft. lbs. (19-21 Nm). Install each tappet back into the same bore.

    c. When bolting the exhaust pipes to the flange at the manifold, use new gaskets and self-locking nuts and torque the nuts to 36 ft. lbs. (48 Nm).

    d. When reinstalling the intake manifold, check and, if necessary, replace the O-rings where the manifold tubes connect to the throttle necks. Torque the nuts to 6.5 ft. lbs. (8 Nm).

    e. Make sure to refill the radiator and bleed the cooling system.

S38 Engine

▶ **See Figure 54**

The engine must be removed to perform this procedure. Remove the engine and set it up on an engine stand.

1. The engine should be mounted on an engine stand and have the intake and exhaust manifolds removed. Remove the camshafts. Remove the tappets and store in the order in which they were removed.

2. Remove the pipe that runs along the front of the engine and remove the bolts at the front of the camshaft case. Remove the bolts in and along the camshaft case.

3. Remove the bolts at the front of the cylinder head. Remove the cylinder head bolts starting at the ends of the head and working towards the center in a crisscross fashion.

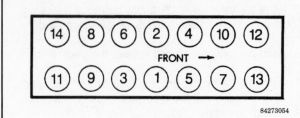

Fig. 54 Head bolt torque order — S38 engine

To install:

4. BMW does not recommend having the head machined. Make checks of the lower cylinder head and block deck surface to make sure they are true. Lubricate the head bolts with a light coating of engine oil. Make sure there is no oil or dirt in the bolt holes in the block. Install a new head gasket, making sure all bolt, oil, and coolant holes line up.

5. Replace the O-ring in the head at the right/rear where the coolant pipe comes up from the block. Coat the pipe with a suitable sealer.

6. Install the head onto the block. Install the head bolts and tighten in a crisscross fashion starting in the center and working towards the ends. Torque first to 34.5-37.5 ft. lbs. (48-52 Nm), then to 56.5-59.5 ft. lbs. (78-82 Nm). Wait 15 minutes then torque to 71-73 ft. lbs. (98-102 Nm).

7. When installing the timing case, replace the O-rings in the small oil passages in the ends of the head. Inspect the O-rings in the center of the block and replace them if necessary. Coat all sealing surfaces with a sealer. Tighten the bolts evenly, torquing the smaller (M7) bolts to 10-12 ft. lbs. (14-17 Nm) and the larger (M8) bolts to 14.5-15.5 ft. lbs. (19-21 Nm). Install all lifters back into the same bores.

8. Install the camshafts.

9. Reroute the timing chain, as necessary, and remount the drive sprockets for the camshaft. Install the tensioning rail that goes at the top of the timing chain.

10. Install the front cover.

11. Continue to reverse the removal procedure. Note these points:

    a. When reinstalling the intake manifold, inspect the O-rings and replace, as necessary.

    b. Refill the cooling system with an appropriate antifreeze/water mix and bleed the cooling system.

CLEANING, INSPECTION AND RESURFACING

▶ **See Figure 55**

Chip carbon away from the valve heads, combustion chambers and ports by using a chisel made of hardwood. Remove the remaining deposits with a stiff brush or a brush attachment for a hand drill.

➡**Aluminum is very soft and is easily damaged. Be very careful not to damage the head. Make sure that the deposits are actually removed, rather than just burnished.**

Fig. 55 Check for warpage of the cylinder head by placing a straightedge across the mounting face in these 3 orientations

Clean the remaining cylinder head components in an engine cleaning solvent. Do not remove the protective coating from the valve springs.

✳✳CAUTION

As all BMW cylinder heads are made out of aluminum, NEVER 'hot tank' the cylinder head as is a common process with cast iron heads.

Place a straight-edge across the gasket surface of the cylinder head. On double overhead camshaft engines, check the camshaft bearing housing surfaces in addition to the gasket surface. Using feeler gauges, determine the clearance at the center of the straight-edge. If warpage exceeds 0.0012 inch (0.03mm) over the total length, the cylinder head will require resurfacing. BMW does not recommend resurfacing the S14 and S38 engines cylinder heads. It is acceptable to clean the surface with a whetstone, but the heads should not be ground.

The maximum amount of material removed must not exceed 0.012 inch (0.3mm). The head must be replaced if more material needs to be removed. Head gaskets with an additional thickness of 0.012 inch (0.3mm) are available to restore the compression ration to standard after the head has been reground.

➡If warpage exceeds the manufacturer's tolerance for material removal, the cylinder head must be replaced.

Cylinder head resurfacing should be performed by a reputable machine shop in your area. You will need to give the machine shop the stripped head and the front cover. The front cover needs to be machined at the same time as the cylinder head to keep the heights consistent.

Valves

✳✳CAUTION

Never use old valves as punches or any other type of tool. The valve may crack and break if struck causing personal injury. Some exhaust valves, such as those installed in the M42 and M50 engines are sodium filled. Do not cut the valve stems or throw them into a standard waste container for disposal. Take the old valves to a

BMW dealer or machine shop for proper disposal. Sodium is extremely reactive and can be an explosion hazard if exposed to air and water.

REMOVAL & INSTALLATION

▶ **See Figures 56, 57, 58 and 59**

It is understood that the cylinder head has been removed before performing valve removal. On all engines the camshafts must be removed. The rocker shafts and rocker arms must be removed on M20 and M30 engine.

1. The factory BMW valve spring compressor and removal tool mounts the cylinder head on a support tray with projections that fit into the combustion chamber. This supports the valves as the springs are compressed and the retainers removed. The BMW tool number for the spring compressor is 11

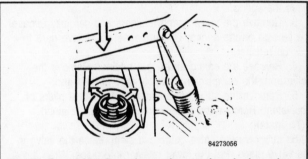

Fig. 56 Removing the valve spring retainer locks using the BMW valve spring compressor

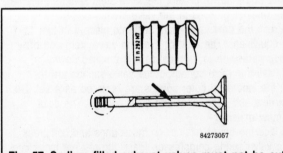

Fig. 57 Sodium filled exhaust valves must not be cut open or throw away with standard scrap. Return to a machine shop or BMW dealer for disposal

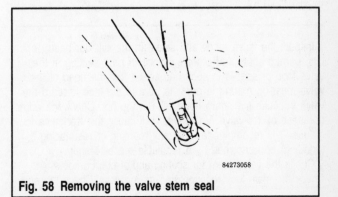

Fig. 58 Removing the valve stem seal

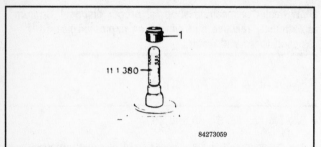

84273059

Fig. 59 Using protection for the valve stem seal when sliding over the end of the valve stem. Use the BMW tool or equivalent

1 060. There is a different number for the support tray for each engine. Consult with your dealer if you wish to use the factory tools.

2. If an aftermarket tool is used, safely and securely support the head while placing the valve spring compressor. Compress the spring.

3. Remove the valve spring retainers and carefully release the tension on the spring. Use a magnet to retrieve hard to pick up retainers.

4. Remove the spring and upper retainer. Remove the valve from the combustion chamber side of the head.

5. Remove the valve stem seal with a removal pliers or equivalent. Remove the lower spring washer or retainer.

To install:

6. Lubricate the valve guide and stem. Place the valve in the valve guide. Put the lower retainer into place. Wrap the end of the valve stem with thin tape or use BMW tool 11 1 340 (M30), 11 1 350 (M20), 11 1 360 (S14 and S38), 11 1 380 (M42 and M50) to protect the valve stem seal as it is slid over the retainer grooves in the valve stem.

7. Press the new valve stem seal into place with tool 11 1 200 or equivalent. The tool fits over the valve stem and provides even pressure to the seal as it is pressed down.

8. Install the valve springs. If the valve springs are replaced, the inner and outer springs are replaced as a set. Do not mix new and used inner and outer springs. The color codes must match.

9. Place the upper retainer on the springs and compress with the valve spring compressor. Place the retainer locks into the grooves. Release the compressor slowly to make sure the retainers are in place.

INSPECTION

Inspect the valve faces and seats (in the cylinder head) for pits, burned spots and other evidence of poor seating. If the valve face or seat is in such bad shape that the head of the valve must be ground in order to true up the face, discard the valve because the sharp edge will run too hot. Check the edge thickness of the valve. Valve wear will cause this thickness to reduce. It is recommended that any reaming or resurfacing (grinding) be performed by a reputable machine shop.

Check the valve stem for scoring and/or burned spots. Check the stem lock retainer grooves for wear. Check the end of the stem for wear. If not noticeably scored or damaged, clean the valve stem with a suitable solvent to remove all gum and varnish. Clean the valve guides using a suitable solvent

Check the valve for signs of bending or piston contact. If a valve has contacted a piston, there will be a telltale mark on the piston crown if the engine is still operational. If there has been piston contact, it is a good bet that the valve is bent. Replace the valve and guide.

Clean the valve face and valve seat in the head. Invert the head and place the valves into the guides. Fill the combustion chamber with gasoline and check for leakage into the ports. If leakage exists, the valve seat and valve face should be refaced to ensure seating.chart of valve edge thicknesses will be included in rebuilding chart

REFACING

If the valves need to be refaced, replacing the valves is the best bet. If the valves are to be refaced, refer the job to a reputable machine shop. The valves and the valve seats should be machined at the same time so the proper relationship of the seats can be maintained.

If after refacing the seats leak gasoline as tested above, lap the valves.

1. Clean the valve face and seat. Lubricate the valve stem and insert in the head.

2. Place a fine lapping compound on the valve seat and place the lapping tool on the valve head. The lapping tool is a stick with a suction cup to attach to the valve. The valve is rotated with the stick.

3. Rotate the valve back and forth, lifting the valve of its seat every so often.

4. Once a fine finish is achieved, remove the valve and clean all traces of lapping compound off. Clean the cylinder head of all traces of lapping compound. Check for leakage.

➡ **All compound must be cleaned and removed as the lapping compound is extremely abrasive and will quickly wear any moving parts it contacts.**

Valve Stem Seals

REPLACEMENT

1. Remove the valve spring and valve.

2. Remove the valve stem seal with a removal pliers or equivalent.

3. Lubricate the valve guide and stem. Place the valve in the valve guide. Put the lower retainer into place. Wrap the end of the valve stem with thin tape or use BMW tool 11 1 340 (M30), 11 1 350 (M20), 11 1 360 (S14 and S38), 11 1 380 (M42 and M50) to protect the valve stem seal as it is slid over the retainer grooves in the valve stem.

4. Press the new valve stem seal into place with tool 11 1 200 or equivalent. The tool fits over the valve stem and provides even pressure to the seal as it is pressed down.

5. Install the spring.

Valve Springs

REMOVAL & INSTALLATION

It is understood that the cylinder head has been removed before performing valve spring removal. On all engines the camshafts must be removed. The rocker shafts and rocker arms must be removed on M20 and M30 engine.

1. The factory BMW valve spring compressor and removal tool mounts the cylinder head on a wooden support tray with projections that fit into the combustion chamber. This supports the valves as the springs are compressed and the retainers removed. The BMW tool number for the spring compressor is 11 1 060. There is a different number for the wooden support tray for each engine. Consult with your dealer if you wish to use the factory tools.

2. If an aftermarket tool is used, safely and securely support the head while placing the valve spring compressor. Compress the spring.

3. Remove the valve spring retainers and carefully release the tension on the spring. Use a magnet to retrieve hard to pick up retainers.

4. Remove the spring and upper retainer. Remove the valve from the combustion chamber side of the head.

To install:

5. Install the valve springs. If the valve springs are replaced, the inner and outer springs are replaced as a set. Do not mix new and used inner and outer springs. The color codes must match.

6. Place the upper retainer on the springs and compress with the valve spring compressor. Place the retainer locks into the grooves. Release the compressor slowly to make sure the retainers are in place.

INSPECTION

The valve springs on BMW engines are of high quality and are capable of operating at high engine speeds. They should be replaced with original equipment units or specially made aftermarket units.

Line all the springs up. Check that they are all the same height. Place the springs against a straight edge. Check that they are straight and aren't twisted or bent.

Replace the inner and outer springs as a set. The springs must be a matched set and have the same color code.

Valve Seats

The valve seats should be inspected in the same manner and at the same time as the valves. If the valve seats need to be replaced, refer the job to a reputable machine shop. Seat replacement involves heating the head to as much as 300° F. (150° C.) and chilling the seats to as low as -240° F. (-150° C.), not a job for the do-it-yourselfer. The seat would also need to be machined after installation. BMW valves and valve seats tend to be very rugged and long wearing. Usually a valve job will return the seats to usable condition.

Valve Guides

REMOVAL & INSTALLATION

The valve guides are shrunk-fit into the cylinder head. Therefore, this procedure is best left to a qualified automotive machine shop. The procedure is included here for reference purposes.

The valve guides on the M42, M50, S14 and S38 engines typically are not replaced if they are worn, though they can be if necessary. These guides are reamed for an oversized valve stem and a replacement valve used with the appropriately oversized stem.

1. Remove the cylinder head.

2. Using a suitable valve spring compressor, compress the spring and remove the split keepers. Remove the spring and check it against specifications.

3. Check the valve stem-to-valve clearance by holding the valve stem end flush with the end of the valve guide and rocking it sideways.

4. If the clearance is excessive, the guide must be driven out (into the combustion chamber) with a drift of the proper diameter and replaced.

5. To install new valve guide, the cylinder head must be heated to so the new guide can be pressed in without excessive pressure. The guide is then pressed in. BMW special tool 11 1 20 (or the like), incorporates a recess which provides the proper protrusion.

STEM TO GUIDE CLEARANCE CHECKING

▶ **See Figure 60**

1. The head should be disassembled so the valve can be moved by hand. Remove the valve spring.

2. Clean the valve guide and the valve stem. Lightly lubricate the valve stem and insert it into the valve guide.

3. Install a dial indicator with the push rod parallel with the cylinder head deck.

4. Place the end of the valve stem flush with the end of the valve guide on the cam side of the head.

5. Place the tip of the dial indicator on the edge of the valve and measure the distance the valve can move back and forth. This is the guide rocking measurement as BMW calls it or the stem to guide clearance as Chilton calls it.

84273060

Fig. 60 Checking the stem to guide clearance with a dial indicator

6. If the measurement is greater than recommended, have the valve guides replaced and reamed for the existing valves or have the guides reamed oversized to match new valves with oversized valve stems. The valve guides on the M42, M50, S14 and S38 engines typically are not replaced if they are worn, though they can be if necessary. These guides are reamed for an oversized valve stem and a replacement valve used with the appropriately oversized stem.

Valve Lifters and Rocker Arms

REMOVAL & INSTALLATION

The M20 and M30 single overhead camshaft engines use rocker arms that are removed in the process of removing the rockershafts. To remove the rockershafts, it is impossible not to remove the rocker arms. See rockershaft/arm removal in this section.

The double overhead camshaft engines use a direct valve actuation through a bucket and shim as on the S14 and S38 engines or a hydraulic lash adjuster as one the M42 and M50 engines.

The bucket and shim lifters on the S14 and S38 engines are removed after the camshafts have been removed. Mark their locations and lift them from their bores. The lifters must be replaced in the original positions. Measure the lifter bore with an inside micrometer and the outside diameter of the lifter with an outside micrometer. The difference should be 0.0010-0.0026 inch (0.025-0.066mm).

The hydraulic lifters in the M42 and M50 engines are kept in the bearing plates for most operations. They can be held in place using BMW tool 11 3 250 or equivalent. Check the lifters for scoring and wear.

Oil Pan

REMOVAL & INSTALLATION

E30 3 Series

WITH M42 ENGINE

▶ **See Figures 61 and 62**

1. Disconnect the negative battery cable. Raise and safely support the vehicle.
2. Drain the engine oil. Disconnect the air cleaner and the heater hoses at the firewall. Remove the fan and fan cowl. Remove the dipstick tube and idle speed control.
3. Disconnect the exhaust pipe at the manifold and at the transmission mount. Disconnect the engine mounts. Disconnect the power steering pump and the reservoir at the support arm.
4. Lift the engine to provide clearance for the pan removal. Remove the lower oil pan mounting bolts and take off the lower oil pan. Remove the upper section oil pan bolts and the oil pump intake. Remove the upper oil pan.
5. Clean the mounting surfaces and install a new gasket. Fill the holes at the corners of the gasket where the covers, block and pan join with non-hardening sealer.

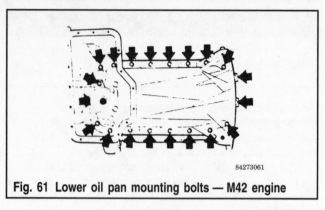

Fig. 61 Lower oil pan mounting bolts — M42 engine

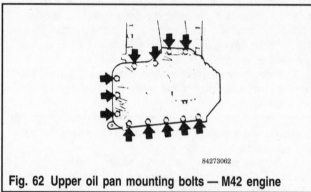

Fig. 62 Upper oil pan mounting bolts — M42 engine

6. The installation is the reverse of the removal procedure. Install the upper pan and tighten the mounting bolts to 6.5 ft. lbs. (9 Nm). Install the lower pan and tighten the mounting bolts to 6.5 ft. lbs. (9 Nm).

WITH M20 ENGINE

1. Disconnect the negative battery cable. Raise the vehicle and support it. Drain the engine oil. On the 325iX remove the front subframe and differential.
2. Remove the front lower splash guard, if necessary.
3. Disconnect the electrical terminal from the oil sending unit.
4. Remove the power steering gear from the front axle carrier.
5. Remove the flywheel cover reinforcement.
6. Remove the oil pan bolts and lower the oil pan. Remove the oil pump bolts and take out the oil pump and oil pan.
7. Install the oil pan, paying attention to the following points:
   a. Clean the gasket surfaces and use a new gasket on the oil pan.
   b. Torque M8 bolts to 13-15 ft. lbs. (18-22 Nm) and M6 bolts to 6.5-8.0 ft. lbs. (9-11 Nm).
   c. Coat the joints on the ends of the front engine cover with a non-hardening sealing compound.
   d. Install the sending unit wire and the engine oil. If the power steering gear was removed, make sure to refill and bleed this system.

WITH S14 ENGINE

1. Remove the dipstick. Remove the splash guard from underneath the engine. Raise and safely support the vehicle.

2. Remove the drain plug and drain the oil. Unscrew all the bolts for the lower oil pan and remove it.

3. Remove the oil pump.

4. Remove the lower flywheel housing cover by removing the 3 bolts at the bottom of the flywheel housing and the 2 bolts in the cover just ahead of the flywheel housing.

5. Disconnect the oil level sending unit plug. Unbolt the oil pan bracket. Disconnect the ground lead. Loosen its clamp and disconnect the crankcase ventilation hose.

6. Remove the oil pan bolts and remove the upper oil pan. Clean all sealing surfaces. Supply a new gasket and the coat the joints where the timing case cover and block meet with a brush-on sealant. Install the pan and torque the bolts evenly to 7 ft. lbs. (10 Nm).

7. Reverse the remaining removal procedures to install, cleaning all sealing surfaces and using a new gasket on the lower pan, also. Torque the lower pan bolts, also, to 7 ft. lbs. (10 Nm).

8. Install the oil pan drain plug, torquing to 24 ft. lbs. (33 Nm). Refill the oil pan with the required amount of approved oil. Start the engine and check for leaks.

E36 3 Series

WITH M42 ENGINE

▶ See Figures 61 and 62

1. Disconnect the negative battery cable. Raise and safely support the vehicle.

2. Drain the engine oil. Disconnect the air cleaner and the heater hoses at the firewall. Remove the fan and fan cowl. Remove the dipstick tube and idle speed control.

3. Disconnect the exhaust pipe at the manifold and at the transmission mount. Disconnect the engine mounts. Disconnect the power steering pump and the reservoir at the support arm.

4. Lift the engine to provide clearance for the pan removal. Remove the lower oil pan mounting bolts and take off the lower oil pan. Remove the upper section oil pan bolts and the oil pump intake. Remove the upper oil pan.

5. Clean the mounting surfaces and install a new gasket. Fill the holes at the corners of the gasket where the covers, block and pan join with non-hardening sealer.

6. The installation is the reverse of the removal procedure. Install the upper pan and tighten the mounting bolts to 6.5 ft. lbs. (9 Nm). Install the lower pan and tighten the mounting bolts to 6.5 ft. lbs. (9 Nm).

WITH M50 ENGINE

1. Disconnect the negative battery terminal. Raise and safely support the car. Drain the oil. Remove the exhaust system. Place the hood in the full upright position.

2. Remove the air cleaner assembly with the air flow sensor. Remove the alternator cooling air duct assembly. Remove the air intake cowl for the heater. Remove the fan and fan cowl. Release the radiator from the clips at the top.

3. Remove the dipstick tube. Loosen the power steering fluid reservoir from its mounts and pull forward. Remove the engine belt. Remove the power steering pump and air conditioner compressor from the engine and support them with wire. Do not disconnect the lines.

4. Remove the upper nuts on the engine mounts. Loosen the lower nuts on the engine mounts by 4 turns. Lift the

engine carefully up as far as possible without damaging any hoses, wires or components.

5. Remove the oil pan bolts and lower the pan. Remove the oil pump sprocket nut with left hand threads and pull the sprocket off the shaft. Remove the oil pump pickup support bolts and the oil pump mounting bolts. Remove the oil pump and oil pan.

To install:

6. Clean all mounting surfaces. Apply non-hardening sealer to the block, cover and pan joints. Install a new gasket and place the pan into position.

7. Install the oil pump. Torque the mounting bolts to 15-17 ft. lbs. (20-24 Nm). Torque the sprocket nut to 18-22 ft. lbs. (25-30 Nm).

8. Install the oil pan and torque the M8 bolts to 13-15 ft. lbs. (18-22 Nm) and M6 bolts to 6.5-8.0 ft. lbs. (9-11 Nm).

9. Lower the engine and torque the M8 nuts to 16 ft. lbs. (22 Nm) and M10 nuts to 30 ft. lbs. (40 Nm). Make sure the ground strap is attached.

10. Install the power steering pump and air conditioning compressor. Install the engine belt, power steering reservoir, dipstick tube, fan and fan cowl. Attach the radiator, air intake duct and alternator cooling duct. Install the air cleaner assembly.

11. Fill the engine with oil and install the exhaust system.

E34 5 Series

WITH M20 ENGINE

1. Disconnect the negative battery cable. Raise the vehicle and support it. Drain the engine oil.

2. Remove the front lower splash guard, if necessary.

3. Disconnect the electrical terminal from the oil sending unit.

4. Remove the power steering gear from the front axle carrier.

5. Remove the flywheel cover reinforcement.

6. Remove the oil pan bolts and lower the oil pan. Remove the oil pump bolts and take out the oil pump and oil pan.

7. Install the oil pan, paying attention to the following points:

   a. Clean the gasket surfaces and use a new gasket on the oil pan.

   b. Torque M8 bolts to 13-15 ft. lbs. (18-22 Nm) and M6 bolts to 6.5-8.0 ft. lbs. (9-11 Nm).

   c. Coat the joints on the ends of the front engine cover with a non-hardening sealing compound.

   d. Install the sending unit wire and the engine oil. If the power steering gear was removed, make sure to refill and bleed this system.

WITH M30 AND S38 ENGINES

1. Disconnect the negative battery cable. Loosen the hose clamp for the air intake hose. Remove the mounting nut for the air cleaner, and remove the air cleaner. Remove the fan and shroud.

2. Disconnect the electrical plug and overflow hose from the coolant expansion tank. Be careful not to kink the hose. Remove the mounting nuts and remove the tank.

3. Remove the splash guard for the power steering pump. Loosen the locknut for the pump adjustment and remove the through bolt that mounts the pump lower bracket (which con-

tains the adjustment mechanism) to the block. Swing the bracket aside. Unscrew the bolt attaching the power steering pump lines to the block and shift them aside too.

4. Disconnect the oil pipe holder. Raise and safely support the vehicle. Remove the oil pan drain plug and drain the oil.

5. Remove the bracket for the exhaust pipes.

6. Disconnect the ground strap from the engine. Remove the nuts and washers attaching the engine to the mounts on both sides.

7. Attach an engine lifting sling to the hooks at either end of the cylinder head. Lift the engine as necessary for clearance.

8. Remove all oil pan mounting bolts and remove the pan.

To install:

9. Clean both sealing surfaces and supply a new gasket. Coat the 4 joints, between the block and timing case cover at the front and the block and rear main seal housing cover at the rear, with a proper sealer. Install the oil pan bolts and torque them to 6.5-7.5 ft. lbs. (9 Nm).

10. Reverse the remaining procedures to install the oil pan. Torque the engine mount nuts to 31-34 ft. lbs. (42-47 Nm). Refill the oil pan with the required amount and type of oil.

WITH M50 ENGINE

1. Disconnect the negative battery terminal. Raise and safely support the car. Drain the oil. Remove the exhaust system. Place the hood in the full upright position.

2. Remove the air cleaner assembly with the air flow sensor. Remove the alternator cooling air duct assembly. Remove the air intake cowl for the heater. Remove the fan and fan cowl. Release the radiator from the clips at the top.

3. Remove the dipstick tube. Loosen the power steering fluid reservoir from its mounts and pull forward. Remove the engine belt. Remove the power steering pump and air conditioner compressor from the engine and support them with wire. Do not disconnect the lines.

4. Remove the upper nuts on the engine mounts. Loosen the lower nuts on the engine mounts by 4 turns. Lift the engine carefully up as far as possible without damaging any hoses, wires or components.

5. Remove the oil pan bolts and lower the pan. Remove the oil pump sprocket nut with left hand threads and pull the sprocket off the shaft. Remove the oil pump pickup support bolts and the oil pump mounting bolts. Remove the oil pump and oil pan.

To install:

6. Clean all mounting surfaces. Apply non-hardening sealer to the block, cover and pan joints. Install a new gasket and place the pan into position.

7. Install the oil pump. Torque the mounting bolts to 15-17 ft. lbs. (20-24 Nm). Torque the sprocket nut to 18-22 ft. lbs. (25-30 Nm).

8. Install the oil pan and torque the M8 bolts to 13-15 ft. lbs. (18-22 Nm) and M6 bolts to 6.5-8.0 ft. lbs. (9-11 Nm).

9. Lower the engine and torque the M8 nuts to 16 ft. lbs. (22 Nm) and M10 nuts to 30 ft. lbs. (40 Nm). Make sure the ground strap is attached.

10. Install the power steering pump and air conditioning compressor. Install the engine belt, power steering reservoir, dipstick tube, fan and fan cowl. Attach the radiator, air intake duct and alternator cooling duct. Install the air cleaner assembly.

11. Fill the engine with oil and install the exhaust system.

Oil Pump

REMOVAL

M20 Engine

1. Remove the oil pan to expose the oil pump.

2. Remove the oil pump mounting bolts and the oil pump support mounting bolts.

3. Lower the oil pump and the drive shaft.

M30 Engine

1. Remove the oil pan to expose the oil pump.

2. Remove the sprocket mounting nut and pull the sprocket from the shaft. The nut is left hand threaded.

3. Remove the oil pump mounting bolts.

4. Lower the oil pump.

M42 Engine

▶ **See Figure 63**

1. The oil pump is part of the timing case. It is necessary to remove the front timing cover, timing chain and sprockets to access the timing case.

2. Remove the front cover, timing chain, guides and sprockets. The oil pump is integral to the timing case.

3. Remove the 4 bolts to remove the oil pump cover. Be careful not to drop the inner and outer rotors.

M50 Engine

1. Remove the lower oil pan to expose the oil pump. Remove the upper oil pan mounting bolts.

2. Remove the sprocket mounting nut and pull the sprocket from the shaft. The nut is left hand threaded.

3. Remove the oil pump mounting bolts.

4. Lower the oil pump and pan.

S14 and S38 Engines

1. Remove the oil pan to expose the oil pump.

2. Remove the sprocket mounting nut and pull the sprocket from the shaft. The nut is left hand threaded.

3. Remove the oil pump mounting bolts and the oil pump support mounting bolts.

4. Lower the oil pump.

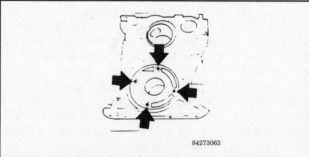

84273063

Fig. 63 Oil pump cover mounting bolts in the timing cover — M42 engine

INSPECTION

Except M42 Engine

Check that the oil pump turns freely and without binding. Check that the oil pump pickup screen is not clogged. Check the condition of the drive sprocket on chain driven pumps.

While the pumps can be disassembled and checked for wear, it is more common to replace the oil pump if it has seen long service. If the pump is to be disassembled, be sure that new gaskets are available before disassembling the pump body.

If the drive sprocket is found to be worn as indicated by pointy teeth, replace the chain at the same time. The sprocket and the chain will wear at the same rate. In cases of severe wear, the crankshaft gear may need to be replaced also. This will require the crankshaft to be removed.

Depress the oil pressure relief valve washer and remove the snapring. Measure the free length of the spring and check that the piston can move freely. The valve is contained in the body of the oil pump.

M42 Engine

▶ See Figure 64

1. Remove the timing case.
2. Remove the cover from the pump rotors. Make note of the positioning of the rotors.
3. Measure the play between the pump body and the outer rotor; outer rotor and inner rotor. The distance should be 0.005-0.008 inch (0.12-0.20mm).
4. The marks on the rotors face up and the rotors should be placed in the original orientation as removed. Replace the cover assembly and tighten to 6-7 ft. lbs. (8-10 Nm).
5. Depress the oil pressure relief valve washer and remove the snapring. Measure the free length of the spring and check that the piston can move freely.
6. Replace the timing case.

INSTALLATION

M20 Engine

1. Replace the oil pump drive shaft bearing:
   a. Remove the clamp bolt holding the pump drive shaft. This is located on the side of the engine where the distributor used to be mounted on non-DME equipped vehicles.

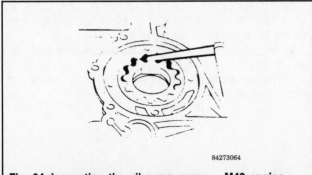

Fig. 64 Inspecting the oil pump gears — M42 engine

84273064

b. Pull the cover with the gear out of the bore. Check the condition of the O-ring and replace if necessary.
   c. Use BMW tool 11 1 310 or equivalent, to drive out the needle bearing out through the top of the bore.
   d. Lubricate the new needle bearing with grease and install with BMW tool 11 1 300 or equivalent. Drive the bearing into the bore until fully seated.
   e. Install the gear and cover.
2. Fill the oil pump pressure side with oil.
3. Install the oil pump and guide the drive shaft up into the drive gear. Torque the bolts to 15-17 ft. lbs. (20-24 Nm).

M30, M50, S14 and S38 Engines

1. Install the oil pump on the engine. Tighten the pump to block bolts, then the support bolts. Torque the bolts to 15-17 ft. lbs. (20-24 Nm).
2. Place the pump drive chain around the drive sprocket and slide over the pump shaft. Torque the nut to 18-21 ft. lbs. (25-29 Nm).
3. Check the slack in the drive chain. The chain should have slight play when depressed with thumb pressure.
4. If the chain is too loose, add oil pump mounting shims between the pump and engine block mounting. The shims are available at your dealer or parts supplier. Match the bore in the shim with the bore in the block.

M42 Engine

The oil pump in the M42 engine is integral with the timing case.
1. Replace the gasket and install the timing case. The lubrication spray nozzle faces the bolt.
2. Replace the timing chain and sprockets. Install the timing covers.

Crankshaft Hub/Damper

REMOVAL & INSTALLATION

M20 Engine

1. Remove the fan and radiator. Remove the belts and water pump pulley. Remove the vibration damper bolts and remove the damper and pulley.
2. Remove the timing belt covers and belt.
3. Hold the hub with BMW tool 11 2 150 or equivalent. Remove the center bolt and the collar.
4. Replace the bolt in the threaded hole about 3 turns. Use a gear puller that has arms that will thread into the holes to remove the hub.
5. If the engine has a 2 piece hub, place the bolt back into the center hole about 3 turns and remove the sprocket using a similar puller as used to remove the first piece.

To install:
6. Install the hub and sprocket with the lettering facing outwards. Check the crankshaft key is in place.
7. Hold the hub with BMW tool 11 2 150 or equivalent. Torque the center bolt to 281-309 ft. lbs. (390-430 Nm).
8. Install the timing belt. Use a new timing belt. Install the belt covers.

9. Install the vibration damper and pulley, matching the alignment pin. Torque the bolts to 16.5-17.5 ft. lbs. (22-24 Nm).

10. Install the water pump pulley and tighten the bolts to 6-7 ft. lbs. (8-10 Nm). Install the belts and tighten. Install the fan and radiator. Fill the radiator with coolant mixture.

M30 Engine

1. Remove the fan and radiator. Remove the belts. Remove the vibration damper bolts and remove the damper and pulley.

2. Hold the hub with BMW tool 11 2 220 or equivalent, or lock the flywheel. Remove the center bolt and the collar.

3. Replace the bolt in the threaded hole about 3 turns. Use a gear puller that has arms that will thread into the holes to remove the hub.

To install:

4. Install the hub and check the crankshaft key is in place.

5. Hold the hub with BMW tool 11 2 220 or equivalent. Torque the center bolt to 311-325 ft. lbs. (430-450 Nm).

6. Install the vibration damper and pulley, matching the alignment pin. Torque the bolts to 16.5-17.5 ft. lbs. (22-24 Nm).

7. Install the belts and tighten. Install the fan and radiator. Fill the radiator with coolant mixture.

M42 Engine

1. Remove the fan and radiator. Remove the belts. Remove the vibration damper bolts and remove the damper and pulley.

2. Hold the hub or lock the flywheel. Remove the center bolt and the collar.

3. Replace the bolt in the threaded hole about 3 turns. Use a gear puller that has arms that will thread into the holes to remove the hub.

To install:

4. Install the hub and check the crankshaft key is in place. The collar part of the washer faces the hub.

5. Hold the hub or lock the flywheel. Torque the center bolt to 224 ft. lbs. (310 Nm).

6. Install the vibration damper and pulley, matching the alignment pin. Torque the bolts to 16.5-17.5 ft. lbs. (22-24 Nm).

7. Install the belts and tighten. Install the fan and radiator. Fill the radiator with coolant mixture.

M50 Engine

1. Remove the fan and radiator. Remove the belts. Remove the vibration damper bolts and remove the damper and pulley.

2. Hold the hub or lock the flywheel. Remove the center bolt and the collar.

3. Replace the bolt in the threaded hole about 3 turns. Use a gear puller that has arms that will thread into the holes to remove the hub.

To install:

4. Check the condition of the cover seal. Replace if necessary. Install the hub and check the crankshaft key is in place. The collar part of the washer faces the hub.

5. Hold the hub or lock the flywheel. Torque the center bolt to 296 ft. lbs. (410 Nm).

6. Install the vibration damper and pulley, matching the alignment pin. Torque the bolts to 16.5-17.5 ft. lbs. (22-24 Nm).

7. Install the belts and tighten. Install the fan and radiator. Fill the radiator with coolant mixture.

S14 Engine

1. Remove the fan and radiator. Remove the belts.

2. Hold the hub by locking the flywheel. Remove the center bolt.

3. Gently tap the pulley from the crankshaft. Do not use a gear puller or hit it with a hammer, otherwise the pulley can be distorted.

To install:

4. Check the condition of the cover seal. Replace if necessary. Install the pulley and check the crankshaft key is in place.

5. Hold the hub by locking the flywheel. Torque the center bolt to 311-325 ft. lbs. (430-450 Nm).

6. Install the belts and tighten. Install the fan and radiator. Fill the radiator with coolant mixture.

S38 Engine

The damper and hub should be removed while the engine is still in the car. The hub is held with such a high torque on the nut that it would be impractical to hold the engine on a stand while trying to loosen of tighten the nut. The procedure calls for using a brace that bolts to the hub and wedges against the front subframe. This provides the counter torque necessary.

1. Remove the fan and radiator. Remove the belts.

2. Turn the engine so the TDC mark on the tooth wheel faces straight down. Attach tool 11 2 240, or equivalent to the pulley with all 8 of the 8x20mm bolts. The mounting pattern is asymmetrical and the tool can only be mounted one way. The tool is designed so it bears against the right side of the subframe and provide the counteroffers to the removal torque of the vibration damper bolt.

3. Remove the nut. Remove the hub and damper. Remove the damper from the hub.

To install:

4. Check the condition of the cover seal. Replace if necessary. Install the hub and check the crankshaft key is in place.

5. With the tool 11 2 240 or equivalent in place, torque the nut to 43 ft. lbs. (60 Nm). Then turn the nut 60 degrees, then another 60 degrees and finish with a 30 degree turn.

6. Remove the tool and tighten the damper bolts to 17 ft. lbs. (23 Nm).

7. Replace the belts, fan and radiator. Fill the radiator with coolant mixture.

Timing Belt Front Cover

REMOVAL & INSTALLATION

M20 Engine

The M20 engine is equipped with a timing belt, as opposed to a timing chain as is usual BMW style. The distributor guard plate is actually the upper timing belt cover.

1. Disconnect the negative battery cable. Remove the distributor cap and rotor. Remove the inner distributor cover and seal.

2. Remove the 2 distributor guard plate attaching bolts and one nut. Remove the rubber guard and take out the guard plate (upper timing belt cover).

3. Rotate the crankshaft to set No. 1 piston at TDC of its compression stroke.

➡At TDC of No. 1 piston compression stroke, the camshaft sprocket arrow should align directly with the mark on the cylinder head.

4. Remove the radiator.

5. Remove the lower splash guard and take off the alternator, power steering and air conditioning belts.

6. Remove the crankshaft pulley and vibration damper.

7. If equipped with a 2 piece hub, hold the crankshaft hub from rotating with the proper tool. Remove the crankshaft hub bolt.

8. Install the hub bolt into the crankshaft about 3 turns and use the proper gear puller, to remove the crankshaft hub.

9. Remove the bolt from the engine end of the alternator bracket. Loosen the alternator adjusting bolt and swing the bracket out of the way.

10. Lift out the TDC transmitter and set it aside.

11. Remove the remaining bolt and lift off the lower timing belt protective cover.

12. Loosen the timing belt tensioner roller bolts and push the roller in to remove the belt. Remove the intermediate shaft sprocket bolt and the sprocket.

13. Loosen the oil pan bolts and remove the 3 front pan bolts that go into the timing cover. Use a thin blade to loosen the oil pan gasket from the cover. Remove the 6 bolts holding the cover and remove from the engine.

To install:

14. Remove the oil pan and replace the gasket using non-hardening sealer at the joints. Replace the seals in the cover if necessary. Install the timing cover with new gaskets and tighten the M6 bolts to 6-7 ft. lbs. (8-10 Nm) and the M8 bolts to 15-17 ft. lbs. (20-24 Nm). Tighten the oil pan M6 bolts to 6.5-8.0 ft. lbs. (9-11 Nm) and the M8 bolts to 13-15 ft. lbs. (18-22 Nm).

15. Install the intermediate shaft sprocket and timing belt. Tighten the belt.

16. Install the lower timing protective cover and tighten the bolt. Install the TDC sender.

17. Replace the alternator bracket. Install the crankshaft hub and torque the nut to 281-309 ft. lbs. (390-430 Nm).

18. Install the vibration damper and pulley. Torque the bolts to 17 ft. lbs. (23 Nm).

19. Install the upper cover and nut. Install the rubber guard. Check the condition of the O-ring and install the upper cover. Install the rotor and distributor cap.

20. Install the accessories and belts. Install the splash shield and fill the cooling system with coolant mixture. Bleed the cooling system.

OIL SEAL REPLACEMENT

1. Disconnect the negative battery cable. Remove the front engine cover.

2. Press the 2 radial oil seals out of the front engine cover.

3. Install the oil seals flush with the front engine cover using the proper tools.

4. Install the front engine cover. Connect the negative battery cable.

Timing Chain Cover

REMOVAL & INSTALLATION

M30 Engine

1. Disconnect the negative battery cable. Remove the cylinder head cover. Remove the distributor cap, rotor and rotor adapter.

2. Drain the coolant to below the level of the thermostat and remove the thermostat housing cover.

3. Remove the mounting bolts and note the lengths and positions of the bolts. Remove the upper timing case cover.

4. Remove the fan, vibration damper and hub. Remove the water pump pulley. The power steering pump must be removed, leaving the pump hoses connected and supporting the pump out of the way but so the hoses are not stressed.

5. Remove the piston which tensions the timing chain, working carefully because of very high spring pressure.

6. Detach the TDC position sender.

7. Loosen all the oil pan bolts, and then unscrew all the bolts from the lower timing case cover, noting their lengths for reinstallation in the same positions. Carefully, use a sharp bladed tool to separate the gasket at the base of the lower timing cover. Then, remove the cover.

To install:

8. Check the condition of the oil pan gasket; replace if necessary. To install the lower cover, first coat the joints of the oil pan and block with sealer. Put it into position on the block, using new gaskets.

9. Install the tensioning piston with the conical end of the spring against the plug. Install all bolts; then tighten the lower front cover bolts evenly; finally, tighten the oil pan bolts evenly. Torque the timing cover M6 bolts to 6-7 ft. lbs. (8-10 Nm) and the M8 bolts to 15-17 ft. lbs. (20-24 Nm). Tighten the oil pan M6 bolts to 6.5-8.0 ft. lbs. (9-11 Nm) and the M8 bolts to 13-15 ft. lbs. (18-22 Nm).

10. To bleed the tensioner, fill the tensioner pocket where the piston contacts the tensioner rail with oil. Loosen the plug a few threads and move the tensioner rail back and forth until oil comes out of the plug threads and resistance is felt. Tighten the plug to 21-29 ft. lbs. (30-40 Nm).

11. Inspect the hub of the vibration damper. If the hub is scored, install the radial seal so the sealing lip is in front of or to the rear of the scored area. Lubricate the seal with oil and install it with a sealer installer.

12. Install the pulley/damper and torque the bolt to specifications. When installing, make sure the key and keyway are properly aligned. Install the TDC transmitter and its mounting bracket.

13. Install the power steering pump and water pump pulley. Reinstall and tension all belts.

14. Just before installing the upper timing case cover, check the condition of that area of the head gasket. It will usually be in good condition. If it should show damage, it must be replaced.

15. Before installing the upper cover, use sealer to seal the joint between the back of the lower timing cover and block at the top. On some vehicles, there are sealer wells which are to be filled with sealer. If these are present, fill them carefully. Install new gaskets. Check the seal at the distributor drive and replace it, if necessary.

16. Note that the top bolt on the driver's side and the bottom bolt on the passenger's side are longer. Tighten the 2 bolts that run down into the lower timing cover first to finger tight; torque the 6 bolts, then torque the bottom bolts. Torque the timing cover M6 bolts to 6-7 ft. lbs. (8-10 Nm) and the M8 bolts to 15-17 ft. lbs. (20-24 Nm).

17. Inspect the sealing O-rings and replace, as necessary. Make sure the bolt at the center of the rotor has its seal in place and torque to 16-17 ft. lbs. (22-24 Nm). Install the rotor and distributor cap.

18. Install the cylinder head cover. Install the thermostat and housing with a new O-ring. Fill the cooling system with coolant and bleed.

M42 Engine

1. Remove the ignition leads and valve cover. Remove the cam position sender on the upper cover. Drain the coolant and remove the thermostat housing. Remove the thermostat.

2. Remove the 11 bolts holding the upper timing cover. Remove the cover carefully to avoid damaging the head gasket.

3. Remove the radiator, fan, belts and water pump pulley. The water pump does not need to be removed to remove the lower cover.

4. Remove the damper and the crankshaft hub.

5. Remove the 21 bolts and remove the cover.

To install:

6. Check the engine block dowel sleeves. Install new gaskets on the cover. Check the condition of the radial seals and replace if necessary.

7. Install the cover and torque the M6 bolts to 6-7 ft. lbs. (8-10 Nm) and the M8 bolts to 15-17 ft. lbs. (20-24 Nm).

8. Install the crankshaft hub and damper. Install the water pump pulley and belts. Install the fan and radiator.

9. Place sealer at the head gasket to cover joints. Place the upper cover with new gaskets. Install 2 bolts and press the upper cover into place by wedging down against the camshaft sprocket. Torque the M6 bolts to 6-7 ft. lbs. (8-10 Nm) and the M8 bolts to 15-17 ft. lbs. (20-24 Nm).

10. Install the valve cover and ignition leads. Install the thermostat and cover. Install the cam position sender. Fill the cooling system with coolant mixture and bleed.

M50 Engine

1. Remove the ignition coils and valve cover. Drain the coolant and remove the thermostat housing. Remove the thermostat.

2. Remove the 8 bolts holding the upper timing cover. Remove the cover carefully to avoid damaging the head gasket.

3. Remove the radiator, fan, belts and water pump pulley. The water pump does not need to be removed to remove the lower cover.

4. Remove the damper and the crankshaft hub.

5. Remove the 13 bolts and remove the cover.

To install:

6. Check the engine block dowel sleeves. Install new gaskets on the cover. Check the condition of the radial seals and replace if necessary.

7. Install the cover and torque the M6 bolts to 6-7 ft. lbs. (8-10 Nm) and the M8 bolts to 15-17 ft. lbs. (20-24 Nm).

8. Install the crankshaft hub and damper. Install the water pump pulley and belts. Install the fan and radiator.

9. Place the upper cover with new gaskets. Torque the M6 bolts to 6-7 ft. lbs. (8-10 Nm) and the M8 bolts to 15-17 ft. lbs. (20-24 Nm).

10. Install the valve cover and ignition coils. Install the thermostat and cover. Fill the cooling system with coolant mixture and bleed.

S14 Engine

1. Disconnect the negative battery cable. Drain the cooling system through the bottom of the radiator. Remove the radiator and fan.

2. Disconnect all electrical plugs, remove the attaching nuts, and remove the air cleaner and airflow sensor.

3. Note and, if necessary, mark the wiring connections. Then, disconnect all alternator wiring. Unbolt the alternator and remove it and the drive belt.

4. Unbolt the power steering pump. Remove the belt and then move the pump aside, supporting it out of the way but in a position where the hoses will not be stressed.

5. Remove the 3 bolts from the bottom of the bell housing and the 2 bolts below it which fasten the reinforcement plate in place.

6. Remove the drain plug and drain the oil from the lower oil pan. Then, remove the lower oil pan bolts and remove the lower pan.

7. Remove the 3 bolts fastening the bottom of the front cover to the front of the oil pan. Loosen all the remaining oil pan bolts so the pan may be shifted downward just slightly to separate the gasket surfaces.

8. Remove the water pump. Remove the center bolt and use a puller to remove the crankshaft pulley.

9. Remove the piston for the timing chain tensioner.

10. Remove the bolts attaching the top of the front cover to the cylinder head. Then, remove all the bolts fastening the cover to the block.

11. Run a sharp bladed tool carefully between the upper surface of the oil pan gasket and the lower surface of the front

cover to separate them without tearing the gasket. If the gasket is damaged, remove the oil pan and replace it.

To install:

12. Before reinstalling the cover, use a file to break or file off flashing at the top/rear of the casting on either side so the corner is smooth. Replace all gaskets, coating them with silicone sealer. Where gasket ends extend too far, trim them off. Apply sealer to the area where the oil pan gasket passes the front of the block.

13. Slide the cover straight on to avoid damaging the seal. Install all bolts in their proper positions. Coat the 3 bolts fastening the front cover to the upper oil pan with the proper sealant.

14. Tighten the bolts at the top, fastening the lower cover to the upper cover first. Then, tighten the remaining front cover bolts and, finally, the oil pan bolts to 7 ft. lbs. (9 Nm). Torque the M6 bolts to 6-7 ft. lbs. (8-10 Nm) and the M8 bolts to 15-17 ft. lbs. (20-24 Nm). Inspect the sealing O-rings and replace, as necessary. If it uses the DME distributor with the screw-off type rotor, make sure the bolt at the center of the rotor has its seal in place and that it is installed with a sealer designed to prevent the bolt from backing out.

15. Torque the oil drain plug to 24 ft. lbs. (32 Nm) and both upper and lower oil pan bolts to 7 ft. lbs. (10 Nm).

16. Reverse the remaining portions of the removal procedures, making sure to fill and bleed the cooling system and to refill the oil pan with the correct oil.

S38 Engine

1. Disconnect the negative battery cable. Pull out the plug and remove the wiring leading to the airflow sensor. Loosen the hose clamp and disconnect the air intake hose. Remove the mounting nut and remove the air cleaner and airflow sensor as an assembly.

2. Remove the radiator and fan. Remove the damper and hub.

3. Remove the pipe that runs across in front of the front cover. Remove the mounting bolts and remove the water pump pulley.

4. Loosen the top/front mounting bolt for the alternator. Remove the lower/front bolt. Loosen the 2 side bolts. Swing the alternator aside.

5. Remove the power steering pump mounting bolts. Make sure to retain the spacer that goes between the pump and oil pan. Swing the pump aside and support it so the hoses will not be under stress.

6. Remove the bolts at the top, fastening the lower front cover to the upper front cover. Remove the bolts at the bottom, fastening the lower cover to the oil pan. Loosen the remaining oil pan mounting bolts.

7. Run a sharp bladed tool carefully between the upper surface of the oil pan gasket and the lower surface of the front cover to separate them without tearing the gasket.

8. Loosen and remove the remaining front cover mounting bolts, noting the locations of the TDC sending unit on the upper/right side of the engine and the suspension position sending unit on the upper left. Also, keep track of the bolts that mount these accessories, as their lengths are slightly different. Remove the timing cover, pulling it off squarely.

To install:

9. Before reinstalling the cover, use a file to break or file off flashing at the top/rear of the casting on either side so the corner is smooth. Replace all gaskets, coating them with silicone sealer. Where gasket ends extend too far, trim them off. Apply sealer to the area where the oil pan gasket passes the front of the block.

10. Slide the cover straight on to avoid damaging the seal. Install all bolts in their proper positions. Tighten the bolts at the top, fastening the lower cover to the upper cover first. Then, tighten the remaining front cover bolts and, finally, the oil pan bolts. Torque the M6 bolts to 6-7 ft. lbs. (8-10 Nm) and the M8 bolts to 15-17 ft. lbs. (20-24 Nm). Inspect the sealing O-rings and replace as necessary. If it uses the DME distributor with the screw-off type rotor, make sure the bolt at the center of the rotor has its seal in place and that it is installed with a sealer designed to prevent the bolt from backing out.

11. Complete the installation procedure, making sure to refill and bleed the cooling system.

Timing Belt Replacement

REMOVAL & INSTALLATION

▶ **See Figures 65, 66, 67 and 68**

M20 Engine

The M20 engine is the only engine covered in this manual that is equipped with a timing belt as opposed to a timing chain. A timing belt has the advantage of being a quieter method of driving the camshaft as compared to the timing

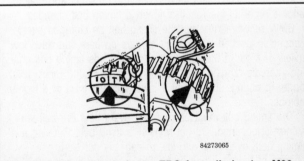

84273065

Fig. 65 Setting the engine to TDC for cylinder 1 — M20 engine

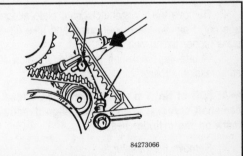

84273066

Fig. 66 Releasing the tension on the spring for the timing belt roller — M20 engine

Fig. 67 Checking the alignment of the timing marks before installing the timing belt — M20 engine

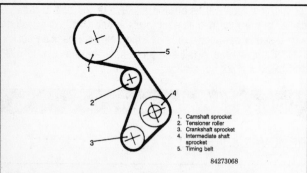

1. Camshaft sprocket
2. Tensioner roller
3. Crankshaft sprocket
4. Intermediate shaft sprocket
5. Timing belt

84273068

Fig. 68 Timing belt arrangement — M20 engine

chain. The disadvantage is that the timing belt must be changed on a regular basis, or risk having the belt break and causing severe engine damage. If the belt breaks, the valve timing will be off compared to the piston timing. This will cause the valves to hang open and contact the pistons on the next engine revolution. Bent valves, damaged pistons and major engine repair is the result of ignoring timing belt changes.

BMW recommends that the timing belt be changed every second Inspection II, or every 4 years on cars that have low mileage. Most of the rest of the industry has timing belt changing intervals ranging from 40,000 miles to 60,000 miles. It is better to change the belt at a lower mileage than at a higher number.

The timing belt must be replaced every time the belt tensioner is loosened. Do not reinstall a used belt. Reusing a timing belt, even one with low mileage, is not worth the chance of having a belt break and damaging the engine.

1. Disconnect the negative battery cable. Remove the distributor cap and rotor. Remove the inner distributor cover and seal.

2. Remove the 2 distributor guard plate attaching bolts and one nut. Remove the rubber guard and take out the guard plate (upper timing belt cover).

3. Rotate the crankshaft to set No. 1 piston at TDC of its compression stroke.

➡️**At TDC of No. 1 piston compression stroke, the camshaft sprocket arrow should align directly with the mark on the cylinder head.**

4. Remove the radiator.

5. Remove the lower splash guard and take off the alternator, power steering and air conditioning belts.

6. Remove the crankshaft pulley and vibration damper.

7. If equipped with a 2 piece hub, hold the crankshaft hub from rotating with the proper tool. Remove the crankshaft hub bolt.

8. Install the hub bolt into the crankshaft about 3 turns and use the proper gear puller, to remove the crankshaft hub.

9. Remove the bolt from the engine end of the alternator bracket. Loosen the alternator adjusting bolt and swing the bracket out of the way.

10. Lift out the TDC transmitter and set it aside.

11. Remove the remaining bolt and lift off the lower timing belt protective cover.

12. Loosen the timing belt tensioner roller bolts and push the roller. Tighten the upper bolt with the roller pushed in. Remove the belt.

To install:

13. Check the alignment of the mark on the camshaft sprocket with the mark on the cylinder head. Check that the crankshaft sprocket mark aligns with the notch in the timing case.

14. Install the new timing belt by starting at the crankshaft sprocket and continuing in reverse direction of engine rotation.

15. Loosen the upper timing belt tensioner roller bolt. The spring tension should be enough to move the roller. Turn the engine 1 revolution in the direction of rotation using the crankshaft bolt to tension the belt. Check that the timing marks align exactly at the camshaft sprocket and the crankshaft sprocket. Tighten the roller bolts, top bolt first, then the bottom bolt.

16. Install the lower timing protective cover and tighten the bolt. Install the TDC sender.

17. Replace the alternator bracket. Install the crankshaft hub and torque the nut to 281-309 ft. lbs. (390-430 Nm).

18. Install the vibration damper and pulley. Torque the bolts to 17 ft. lbs. (23 Nm).

19. Install the upper cover and nut. Install the rubber guard. Check the condition of the O-ring and install the upper cover. Install the rotor and distributor cap.

20. Install the accessories and belts. Install the splash shield and fill the cooling system with coolant mixture. Bleed the cooling system.

21. Apply a sticker showing the date and mileage of the belt change on the engine.

Timing Chain

REMOVAL & INSTALLATION

M30 Engine

1. Remove the upper and lower timing chain covers.

2. Turn the engine in the direction of rotation and set cylinder number 1 to TDC.

3. Loosen and remove the camshaft sprocket bolts and remove with the chain. Do not rotate the engine with the timing chain removed.

4. Guide the chain out of the tensioner rails and off the lower sprocket.

To install:

5. Inspect the sprockets for wear and replace if necessary. The bottom sprocket is shrunk on the crankshaft and it is best left to a machine shop to replace. The machine shop will heat

the sprocket evenly and pull it off the crankshaft and install it in a similar fashion. The camshaft sprocket is replaced simply with a new unit.

6. Install the new chain and the camshaft sprocket. The dowel pin will located at the lower left when looking at it from the front. The bolt holes will be aligned straight up and down, side to side.

7. Replace the bolt lock plates if equipped and torque the bolts to 6.5-7.5 ft. lbs. (9-11 Nm). Fold the lock plates up.

8. Replace the lower and upper timing covers.

M42 Engine

▶ **See Figures 69, 70, 71, 72 and 73**

1. Disconnect the negative battery cable. Drain the coolant.
2. Disconnect the coolant hoses and remove the position sensor.

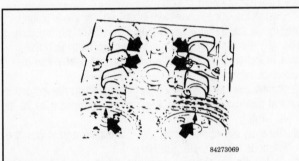

Fig. 69 Setting the camshafts to TDC of cylinder 1 — M42 engine

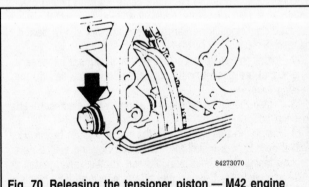

Fig. 70 Releasing the tensioner piston — M42 engine

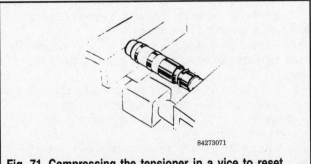

Fig. 71 Compressing the tensioner in a vice to reset it — M42 engine

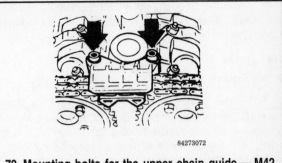

Fig. 72 Mounting bolts for the upper chain guide — M42

Fig. 73 Once the tensioner is installed, it must be released by pressing back on the tensioner rail — M42 engine

3. Remove the thermostat housing and thermostat. Unscrew the upper timing case cover.

4. Remove the crankshaft hub and the lower timing cover.

5. Rotate the engine in the direction of the rotation until the camshaft peaks of the intake and exhaust camshafts for cylinder No. 1 face each other. The arrows on the sprocket face up.

6. Remove the chain tensioner. Remove the upper chain guide, chain guide bolt on the right side and the sprockets.

7. Remove the lower timing chain guide from under the crankshaft sprocket and lift out the timing chain.

   To install:

8. Install tool 11 2 300 or equivalent, to hold the crank at TDC. Install tool 11 3 240 or equivalent, to hold the camshafts in proper alignment. If the camshafts have to be turned so much that the valves in cylinders 1 or 4 start to open, turn the crank 90 degrees in the direction of engine rotation. Turn the camshafts and install the tool, then rotate the crankshaft back to TDC. This will prevent the valves from striking the pistons.

9. Install the camshaft sprockets with the arrows pointing up. Torque to 10-12 ft. lbs. (13-17 Nm). Install the timing chain, timing guide bolt on the right side and the upper and lower chain guides.

10. If not installing a new tensioner piston, knock the outer sleeve of the tensioner piston so the piston is released from the sleeve. Assemble the tensioner with the spring, the piston and the snaprings in position. Place in a vice and press together until both snaprings engage. If the piston starts to extend, the procedure must be done again. The compressed tensioner will be 2.697 inch (68.5mm).

11. Install the tensioner into its bore and tighten the plug to 17-19 ft. lbs. (23-27 Nm). Push the tensioner rail against the tensioner to release the tensioner piston.

12. Install the lower and upper timing covers, crankshaft hub, belts and accessories. Fill and bleed the cooling system. Check the engine oil.

M50 Engine

▶ **See Figures 74, 75 and 76**

1. Remove the upper timing case cover and the camshaft cover. Crank the engine in the direction of rotation so that the intake and exhaust camshaft peaks for cylinder No.1 face each other. Hold the camshafts in place with tool 11 3 240 or equivalent. With the camshafts in this alignment the arrows on the sprockets will be facing up. Remove the valve cover mounting studs. Lock the flywheel in place to prevent movement of the crankshaft.

2. Unscrew the chain tensioner and carefully remove. There is a spring contained within the tensioner and may eject out if care is not taken.

Fig. 74 Inserting the clip to hold the tensioner in the released position — M50 engine

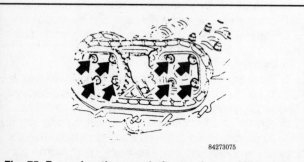

Fig. 75 Removing the camshaft sprockets — M50 engine

Fig. 76 Removing the upper chain tensioner — M50 engine

3. Press down on the upper chain tensioner and lock it into place using tool 11 3 290 or equivalent. Unscrew the transfer timing chain sprockets and pull the 2 off together with the chain. Remove the upper chain tensioner and the lower chain guide. Pull off the main timing chain sprocket along with the chain. Use a bent piece of wire to hold the chain from falling down into the engine. Do not rotate the engine after this point or the valve timing will be disturbed when the engine is reassembled.

4. Remove the lower timing chain cover and fold the tensioner rails down. Remove the timing chain.

To Install:

5. Install the timing chain on the lower sprocket and on the upper sprocket.

6. Align main timing chain and sprocket on the camshaft so that the arrow faces up. The bolt holes in the camshaft should be on the left sides of the sprocket slots. This will allow the tensioner to take up the slack in the chain and rotate the gear to the counterclockwise position.

7. Install the upper chain tensioner and the lower chain guide. Install the transfer timing gears and chain on the camshafts with the arrows facing up. Make sure that the pulse sender is installed on the intake cam. Do not tighten the sprocket bolts.

8. Install the lower timing chain tensioner with the groove in a vertical position. Use a new sealing ring and torque to 29 ft. lbs. (40 Nm).

9. Release the upper timing chain tensioner and torque the sprocket bolts to 16 ft. lbs. (22 Nm).

10. Install the lower timing cover and accessories. Install the upper timing cover.

11. Install the valve cover mounting studs and remove the flywheel lock. Install the camshaft cover and the timing case covers using new gaskets. Install the lifting eye and the electrical lead duct. Install the camshaft sensor with a new seal if needed.

12. Install the valve cover using new gaskets if necessary. Check that the gasket seats correctly all the way around the seating area.

13. Install the ignition coils and connect the electrical leads to each coil.

14. Install the thermostat with the arrow or vent facing up with a new O-ring. Install the thermostat housing with a new gasket. Install the intake manifold and throttle valve. Install the exhaust manifolds. Change the oil and check all fluid levels.

S14 Engine

1. Disconnect the negative battery cable. Remove the valve cover and lower timing case cover.

2. Remove the distributor cap, rotor and rotor adapter. Remove the distributor housing and the intake camshaft end cover.

3. Remove the socket head bolts holding the upper timing chain guide. Turn the engine in the direction of rotation to TDC of cylinder number 1. Do not move the position of the engine from this point on.

4. Remove the timing tensioner piston. There is strong spring pressure behind the plug.

5. Unfold the sprocket bolt lock plate and remove the sprocket bolts. Remove the sprockets.

6. Remove the 2 snaprings for the guide rail, which is located on the left (driver's) side of the engine.

7. Pull the guide rail forward and then turn it up to free it from the chain.

To install:

8. Install the timing chain and the guide rail. Install the guide rail snaprings. Place the chain around the lower sprocket

9. Engage the chain with the intake side (E) sprocket with the marks aligned. Turn the intake side (E) sprocket in the direction opposite to normal rotation to tension the timing chain on that side. Bolt this sprocket and the lock plates onto the front end of the intake camshaft. Prevent the camshaft from rotating and torque the bolts to 6-7 ft. lbs. (8-10 Nm). Fold the lock plates up.

10. Engage the timing marks with the mark on the exhaust side (A) sprocket and install the sprocket and lock plates onto the front end of the exhaust camshaft. Use the distributor rotor adapter to keep the sprocket from turning, and torque the bolts to 6-7 ft. lbs. (8-10 Nm). Fold the lock plates up. Make sure the timing chain has stayed in time.

11. Slide the chain tensioner piston into its cylinder. Install a new seal. Now install the spring with the conical end out. Install the cap which retains the spring. Add oil to the well where the piston contacts the tensioner rail. Loosen the nipple on the plug and keep adding oil until oil runs out of the nipple. Close the nipple and torque the cap to 29 ft. lbs. (40 Nm).

12. Turn the engine 1 revolution in the normal direction of rotation. Recheck the timing. With the crankshaft at TDC, one groove on each camshaft faces inward and another on each faces the cast boss on the bearing cap.

13. Install the upper timing chain guide. Check and adjust the guide so the chain is centered in the guide.

14. Install the timing case cover, distributor housing, distributor rotor adapter, rotor and distributor cap. Install the camshaft end cover and valve cover.

S38 Engine

1. Disconnect the negative battery cable. Remove the valve cover and lower timing case cover. Remove the water pump.

2. Remove the distributor cap, rotor and rotor adapter. Remove the distributor housing and the intake camshaft end cover.

3. Remove the socket head bolts holding the upper timing chain guide. Turn the engine in the direction of rotation to TDC of cylinder number 1. Do not move the position of the engine from this point on.

4. Remove the timing tensioner piston. There is strong spring pressure behind the plug.

5. Unfold the sprocket bolt lock plate and remove the sprocket bolts. Remove the sprockets.

6. Remove the 2 guide pins for the guide rail, which is located on the left (driver's) side of the engine. They are removed by using the flats on the base of the pins as a place to put the wrench. There may be washers under the flats; be careful not to loose them down into the oil pan.

7. Pull the guide rail forward and then turn it up to free it from the chain.

To install:

8. Install the timing chain, guide pins and the guide rail. Place the chain around the lower sprocket

9. Engage the chain with the intake side (E) sprocket with the marks aligned. Turn the intake side (E) sprocket in the direction opposite to normal rotation to tension the timing chain on that side. Bolt this sprocket and the lock plates onto the front end of the intake camshaft. Prevent the camshaft from rotating and torque the bolts to 6-7 ft. lbs. (8-10 Nm).

10. Engage the timing marks with the mark on the exhaust side (A) sprocket and install the sprocket and lock plates onto the front end of the exhaust camshaft. Use the distributor rotor adapter to keep the sprocket from turning, and torque the bolts to 6-7 ft. lbs. (8-10 Nm). Make sure the timing chain has stayed in time.

11. Slide the chain tensioner piston into its cylinder. Install a new seal. Now install the spring with the conical end out. Install the cap which retains the spring. Add oil to the well where the piston contacts the tensioner rail. Loosen the nipple on the plug and keep adding oil until oil runs out of the nipple. Close the nipple and torque the cap to 29 ft. lbs. (40 Nm).

12. Turn the engine 1 revolution in the normal direction of rotation. Recheck the timing. With the crankshaft at TDC, one groove on each camshaft faces inward and another on each faces the cast boss on the bearing cap.

13. Install the upper timing chain guide. Check and adjust the guide so the chain is centered in the guide.

14. Install the timing case cover, water pump, distributor housing, distributor rotor adapter, rotor and distributor cap. Install the camshaft end cover and valve cover.

Camshaft

REMOVAL & INSTALLATION

M20 Engine

▶ See Figures 77 and 78

1. Remove the cylinder head.
2. Remove the rocker shaft and rocker arms.
3. Remove the bolts holding the camshaft retainer and slide out the camshaft. Be careful not to damage the bearing surfaces while pulling out.

To install:

4. Slide the camshaft carefully into to the cylinder head.
5. Check the seals and replace if necessary.
6. Install the camshaft retainer, rocker arms and rocker shafts.

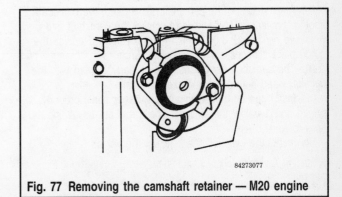

84273077

Fig. 77 Removing the camshaft retainer — M20 engine

Fig. 78 Removing the camshaft — M20 engine

M30 Engine

1. Disconnect the negative battery cable. Remove the oil line from the top of the cylinder head.

→**Observe the location of the seals when removing the hollow oil line studs. Install new seals in the same position.**

2. Remove the cylinder head. Support the head in such a way that the valves can be opened during camshaft removal.

3. Adjust the valve clearance to the maximum clearance on all rocker arms.

4. A tool set 11 1 060 and 00 1 490 or its equivalent, is used to hold the rocker arms away from the camshaft lobes. When installing the tool, move the intake rocker arms of No. 2 and 4 cylinders forward approximately ¼ inch and tighten the intake side nuts to avoid contact between the valve heads. Turn the camshaft 15 degrees clockwise to install the tool. On these engines, to avoid contact between the valve heads, first tighten the tool mounting nuts on the exhaust side to the stop and then tighten the intake side nuts slightly. Reverse this exactly during removal.

5. Remove the camshaft by rotating the camshaft so the 2 cutout areas of the camshaft flange are horizontal and remove the retaining plate bolts.

6. Carefully, remove the camshaft from the cylinder head.

7. The flange and guide plate can be removed from the camshaft by removing the lock plate and nut from the camshaft end.

To install:

8. Install the camshaft and associated components in the reverse order of removal. Swap over the guide, flange and nut from the old camshaft to the new camshaft if replacing the camshaft.

9. After installing the camshaft guide plate, the camshaft should turn easily. Measure and correct the camshaft end play. It should be 0.0012–0.0071 inch (0.03–0.18mm). Replace the guide plate if necessary to bring into range.

10. The camshaft flange must be properly aligned with the cylinder head before the sprocket is installed.

11. Install the oil tube hollow stud washer seals properly, 1 above and 1 below the oil pipe. The arrow on the oil line must face forward.

12. Install the cylinder head. Adjust the valves.

M42 & M50 Engines

▶ **See Figures 79, 80, 81, 82, 83 and 84**

1. Disconnect the negative battery cable. Remove the head.

→**Special tools are required to perform this operation. BMW tools 11 3 260, 11 3 270 and 11 3 250 or their equivalents are required for proper removal and installation of the camshafts and for retention of the valve lash compensators. Without these tools the camshafts will be damaged during removal or installation.**

2. Remove the spark plugs and attach the 11 3 260 (plus addition 11 3 270) camshaft removal fixture. Torque the hold down bolts in the spark plug bores to 17 ft. lbs. (23 Nm).

3. Apply load to the bearing caps by rotating the eccentric shaft. This relieves the tension on the bearing cap bolts. Loosen and remove the bearing cap bolts.

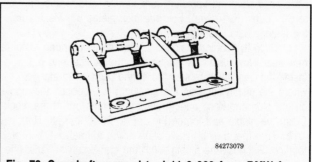

Fig. 79 Camshaft removal tool 11 3 260 from BMW for use on the M42 engine

Fig. 80 Using the camshaft removal tool to hold the camshaft bearing caps down while the bolts are removed — M42 engine shown, M50 is similar

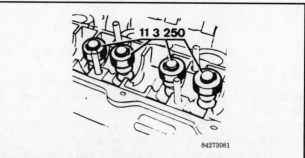

Fig. 81 Valve lash compensator holding tool 11 3 250 shown — M42 and M50 engines

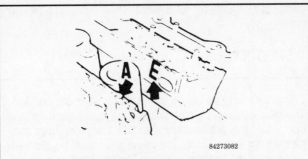

Fig. 82 The letters designate the intake (E) and exhaust sides (A) — M42 and M50 engines

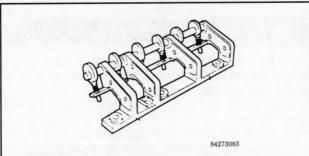

Fig. 83 Camshaft removal tools 11 3 260 and 11 3 270 from BMW for use on the M50 engine

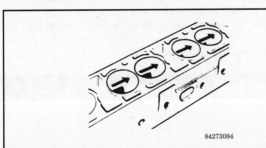

Fig. 84 Checking the bearing surfaces of the valve lash compensators for scoring and scuffing — M42 and M50 engines

4. Remove the camshaft removal fixture after releasing the tension from the eccentric shaft.

5. Remove the camshafts and the bearing caps. Note that the intake camshaft is marked 'E' and the exhaust camshaft is marked 'A'. The camshaft bearing are consecutively numbered with 'A' or 'E' to designate intake or exhaust side.

6. Hold the valve lash compensators in place using tool 11 3 250 or equivalent, and remove the bearing plate along with the valve plungers.

To install:

7. Inspect the camshafts and valve lash compensators for damage and wear and replace as necessary.

8. Install the camshafts with the cylinder number 1 intake and exhaust cam peaks pointing at each other. The flats on the sprocket ends of the camshafts should be parallel. The exhaust camshaft is marked with a notch on the flange.

9. Install the fixture. Place the bearing caps into position and press the caps down with the tool. Torque the bolts to 10-12 ft. lbs. (13-17 Nm).

10. When the camshafts have been removed and reinstalled a waiting period dependent on the ambient temperature is necessary before mounting the cylinder head on the engine. At room temperature wait 4 minutes to allow the lifters to compress fully. At temperatures down to 50° F(10° C) wait 11 minutes. At temperatures lower than 50° F(10° C) wait 30 minutes. This is to prevent contact between the valves and the piston tops.

11. The engine may not be cranked under the same conditions as above for a period of 10 minutes at room temperature; 30 minutes for temperatures down to 50° F(10° C); 75 minutes for temperatures below 50° F(10° C).

S14 & S38 Engines

➡**To perform this operation it is necessary to have a special tool 11 3 010 or equivalent. This is necessary to permit safe removal of the camshaft bearing caps and then safe release of the tension the valve springs put on the camshafts. The job also requires an adapter to keep the camshaft sprockets from turning while loosening and tightening their mounting bolts.**

1. Disconnect the negative battery cable. Remove the cylinder head cover. Remove the fan cowl and the fan.

2. Remove the mounting bolts and remove the distributor cap. Remove the mounting screws and remove the rotor. Unscrew the distributor adapter and the protective cover underneath. Inspect the O-ring that runs around the protective cover and replace it, if necessary.

3. Remove the 2 bolts and remove the protective cover from in front of the right side (intake) camshaft. Remove the bolts and remove the distributor housing from in front of the left (exhaust) side cam. Inspect the O-rings, and replace them, if necessary.

4. Remove the 6 mounting bolts from the cover at the rear end of the cylinder head and remove it. Replace the gasket. Note that on the S14 engine, 2 of these bolts are longer. These fit into the 2 holes that are sleeved.

5. Remove the 2 socket head bolts, located at the front of the head, which mount the upper timing chain guide rail. Then, remove the upper guide rail.

6. Turn the crankshaft to set the engine at No. 1 cylinder TDC. On the S14 engine, valves for No. 4 will be at overlap position — both valves just slightly open with timing marks at TDC. On the S38 engine, valves for No. 6 will be at overlap position — both valves just slightly open with timing marks at TDC.

➡**The next item to be removed is a plug which keeps the tensioner piston inside its hydraulic cylinder against considerable spring pressure. Use a socket wrench and keep pressure against the outer end of the plug, pushing inward, so spring pressure can be released very gradually once the plug's threads are free of the block.**

7. Remove the plug from the tensioner piston, and then release spring tension. Remove the spring and then the piston. Check the length of the spring. It must be 6.240-6.280 inch in

length; otherwise, replace it to maintain stable timing chain tension.

➡The timing chain should remain engaged with the crankshaft sprocket while removing the camshafts. Otherwise, it will be necessary to do additional work to restore proper timing. Keep the timing chain under slight tension by supporting it at the top while removing the camshaft sprockets.

8. Pry open the lock plates for the camshaft sprocket mounting bolts. Install an adapter to hold the sprockets still and remove the mounting bolts.

9. Using an adapter to keep the sprockets from turning and putting tension on the timing chain, loosen and remove the sprocket mounting bolts, keeping the chain supported.

10. Mount the special tool on the timing case, which mounts to the top of the head. Then, tighten the tool's shaft to the stop. This will hold both camshafts down against their lower bearings. Also, mark the camshafts as to exhaust and intake.

11. Remove the mounting bolts. Mark the camshaft bearing caps. It is possible to save time by keeping the caps in order, although they are marked for installation in the same positions.

12. Once all bolts are removed, slowly crank backwards on the tool's shaft to gradually release the tension on the camshaft bearing caps. Once all tension is released, remove the tool.

13. Carefully, remove the camshafts in such a way as to avoid nicking any bearing surfaces or cams.

To install:

14. Oil all bearing and camshaft surfaces with clean engine oil. Carefully, install the camshafts, marked E for intake and A for exhaust, to avoid nicking any wear surfaces. The camshafts should be turned so the groove between the front camshaft and sprocket mounting flange faces straight up. Install the special tool and tighten down on the shaft to seat the camshaft bearings.

15. Install all bearing caps in order or as marked. Torque the attaching bolts to 15-17 ft. lbs. (20-23 Nm). Then, release the tension provided by the tool by turning the bolt and remove the tool.

16. Install the intake sprocket (marked E), install the lock plate, and install the mounting bolts. Use the adapter to keep the sprocket from turning, and torque the bolts to 6-7 ft. lbs. (9 Nm). Do the same for the exhaust side sprocket. Make sure the timing chain stays in time.

17. Slide the timing chain tensioner piston into the opening in the cylinder in the block. Install the spring with the conically wound end facing the plug. Install the plug into the end of the sprocket and then install it over the spring. Use the socket wrench to depress the spring until the plug's threads engage with those in the block. Start the threads in carefully and then torque the plug to 27-31 ft. lbs. (37-42 Nm).

18. Crank the engine forward just 1 turn in normal direction of rotation. Now, 1 camshaft groove on each side should face toward the center of the head and 1 on each side should face the case boss on the front bearing cap. Lock the sprocket mounting bolts with the tabs on the lockplates.

19. Reverse the remaining removal procedures to complete the installation. Before final tightening of the mounting nuts for the guide rail for the top of the timing chain, go back and forth, measuring the clearance between the sprockets and the center of the guide rail to center it. Then, tighten the mounting nuts.

INSPECTION

The camshafts should be inspected for wear and damage. The most common form of wear on the camshafts is flattened cam lobes. It is not uncommon to find 1 or more lobes completely worn into a circle. The camshafts should be checked for wear on the bearing surfaces. The camshaft do not use separate bearing so the bearing surfaces in the head or camshaft housing should be checked. If any damage is found, the head or camshaft housing will need to be replaced.

Intermediate Shaft

The M20 engine uses and intermediate shaft that was used to drive the distributor in the pre-DME days. Now the shaft is used strictly to run the oil pump.

1. Disconnect the negative battery cable. Remove the front cover.

2. Remove the intermediate shaft sprocket.

3. Loosen and remove the 2 retaining screws and then remove the intermediate shaft guide plate.

4. Carefully, slide the intermediate shaft out of the block. Turn the crankshaft, if necessary, to remove it. Inspect the gear on the intermediate shaft, replacing it, if necessary.

5. Install the intermediate shaft to the block. Install the guide plate.

6. Install the front cover.

Pistons and Connecting Rods

REMOVAL

◆ See Figures 85, 86, ? and 87

While the pistons and connecting rods can be removed from the engine with the engine installed in the vehicle most of the time, it is better to remove the engine to do this procedure. With the engine removed, it is easier to inspect the engine and to manipulate the tool and parts.

Before removing the pistons and connecting rods, mark the pistons, rod bearing caps and the rods with the cylinder num-

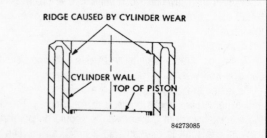

Fig. 85 There may be a cylinder bore ridge that will need to be removed before removing the pistons, if it is severe

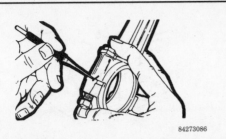

Fig. 86 Matchmark the connecting rod and the cap. The rod is shown out of the engine, but it is best to mark it before removal

Fig. 87 Push the piston out of the cylinder with a wooden rod or handle

ber and orientation. This will ensure replacement of the pistons and bearing into the correct positions.

Before removing the pistons, the top of the cylinder bore must be examined for a ridge. A ridge at the top of the bore is the result of normal cylinder wear; caused by the piston rings only traveling so far up the bore in the cause of the piston stroke.

BMW uses a very high quality material to cast the cylinder blocks and cylinder ridges tend to be slight. If the ridge can be felt by hand, it must be removed before the pistons are removed. This is to prevent the rings from breaking while the piston is pushed past the ridge.

A ridge reamer is necessary for this operation. Place the piston at the bottom of its stroke, and cover it with a rag. Cut the ridge away with the ridge reamer, using extreme care to avoid cutting too deeply. Remove the rag, and remove the cuttings that remain on the piston with a magnet and a rag soaked in clean oil. Make sure the piston top and cylinder bore are absolutely clean before moving the piston.

1. Remove the cylinder head.
2. Remove the oil pan.
3. Remove the oil pump or oil pump pickup.
4. Matchmark the connecting rod cap to the connecting rod with a scribe; each cap must be reinstalled on its proper rod in the proper direction. Remove the connecting rod bearing cap and the rod bearing. It may be necessary to rock the cap back and forth to free it. Number the top of each piston with silver paint or a felt-tip pen for later assembly.
5. Cut lengths of ⅜″ diameter rubber hose to use as rod bolt guides. Install the hose over the threads of the rod bolts,

to prevent the bolt threads from damaging the crankshaft journals and cylinder walls when the piston is removed.

6. Squirt some clean engine oil onto the cylinder wall from above until the wall is coated. Carefully push the piston and rod assembly up and out of the cylinder by tapping on the bottom of the connecting rod with a wooden hammer handle.

7. Place the rod bearing and cap back on the connecting rod, and install the nuts temporarily. Using a number stamp or punch, stamp the cylinder number on the side of the connecting rod and cap this will help keep the proper piston and rod assembly on the proper cylinder. Do not stamp in the web area of the rod.

➡On all BMW engines, the cylinders are numbered 1-4 or 1-6 from front to back.

8. Remove the remaining pistons in a similar manner.When ready for reassembly, please not the following:

a. Connecting rods/caps must be reinstalled in the same cylinder and are so marked. Make sure markings on rod and cap are on the same side when reassembling.

b. The piston pins are matched to the pistons and are not interchangeable.

c. The arrow on top of the piston must face forward (toward the timing chain). Pistons are also marked as to manufacturer and weight class + or -. All pistons must be of the same manufacturer and weight class.

d. Offset each ring gap 120 degrees from each other. Do not align any of the gaps with the piston pin bore. This reduces blowby of combustion gases.

CLEANING AND INSPECTION

Before any kind of inspection is done to the piston, cylinder or piston pin, it is imperative that they be clean. All traces of varnish, carbon or build-up be removed. Measurements will be inaccurate and signs of wear hidden on a dirty part.

Clean the piston with solvents and chip off any carbon build-up with a hardwood chisel. Do not hot tank aluminum pistons. Clean the cylinder bore with solvent, then wipe down with clean engine oil.

Inspect the piston for signs of scoring, scuffing, cracks, pitting or burning. Check the piston for mechanical damage such as valve strikes or denting due to ingested objects. Measure the piston diameter with a micrometer. Measure at points 90 degrees to the piston pin bore. Measure down from the edge of the piston skirt the proper distance from the piston skirt edge.piston diameter measuring point chart to be included in rebuilding chart

Measure the inside diameter of the cylinder at 3 points; top, middle and bottom. Measure at points which are contacted by the piston rings. If the cylinder walls are found to be tapered, scored or otherwise damaged, the cylinder will need to be honed or bored oversized.

Subtract the diameter of the piston from the diameter of the cylinder to find the piston clearance. Check that the clearance does not exceed the maximum permitted. If the clearance is too great, the cylinders will need to be bored oversized for the next available sized piston

BORING AND HONING

♦ **See Figures 88, 89, 90 and 91**

There are 2 basic machining operations that are done to a cylinder wall, boring and honing. Both procedures remove metal from the cylinder walls. The major difference is that boring removes a larger amount of metal than honing does. Boring is used to enlarge the cylinder so a larger diameter piston can be used. Honing is a finer process that gives the cylinder wall the correct machined finish for proper operation and sealing of the piston rings.

If the cylinders are out of round or tapered beyond allowable limits, the cylinders will need to be bored to the next standard oversize. Boring is done by a qualified machine shop. Provide the machine shop with the new oversized pistons. The machine shop will match the bore of the cylinder to diameter of the new piston, taking into account the piston clearance re-

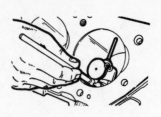

Fig. 90 Using a dial type inside micrometer to measure the inside bore of the cylinder

Fig. 91 Measure the cylinder bore in 2 directions to determine if the cylinder is out of round

quired. The machine shop will return the block and piston marked as to which piston goes to which cylinder.

Honing should be done by a machine shop to guarantee the proper cylinder wall finish. Honing can be accomplished with a hand held honing tool available from most automotive shops, but a machine shop can provide the best result. Honing is done to prepare the cylinder wall with the proper machined finish. The finish is a crosshatch pattern that catches and holds oil for the piston rings to ride on. Honing can be used without boring the cylinder when only new rings are being installed, or after the cylinder has been bored for a new piston and the proper finish is required.

PISTON PIN REPLACEMENT

♦ **See Figures 92, 93 and 94**

The piston pins are matched to the pistons and must not be interchanged. The piston pins run in bushings pressed into the small end of the connecting rod. The pins are retained by snaprings.

Remove the snaprings with a snapring removal tool. The piston pin should slide out of the bore with some finger pressure. If the pin resists being pushed out, check that varnish or carbon hasn't collected at the end of the pin bore. Clean the bore and the pin should slide freely out.

Clean the pin and connecting rod bushing. Lightly lubricate the pin and slide it into the connecting rod. The pin should slide in with only hand pressure. There should be no discernible play with the pin installed in the rod. Check the pin bushing for scoring or damage. A sign of worn bushing is a knocking sound during engine acceleration.

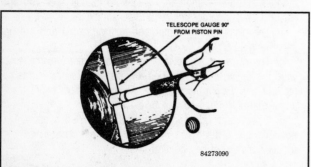

Fig. 88 Using a telescoping gauge to measure the inside bore of the cylinder

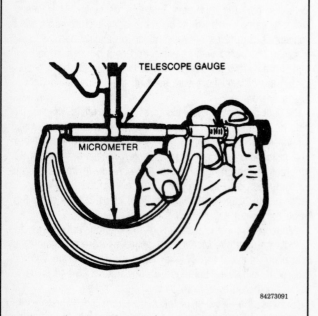

Fig. 89 Using a micrometer to measure the telescoping gauge

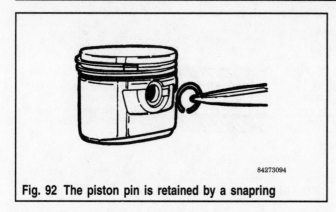

Fig. 92 The piston pin is retained by a snapring

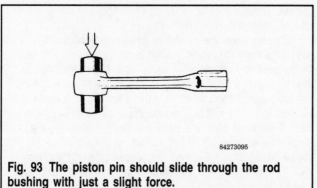

Fig. 93 The piston pin should slide through the rod bushing with just a slight force.

Have new bushing pressed into the rod if the old bushing are found to be worn or damaged. The new bushing will be drilled for the oil lubrication hole at the top of the rod.

The piston pin is installed in the piston and connecting rod, making sure the orientation of the rod and piston is correct. Check the marks previously made on the rod during removal and the arrow on the piston top. The arrow should face the timing chain or belt. Replace the snapring if the old ring was damaged, though it is a good idea to always use new snaprings. Place the gap in the snapring opposite the groove cut into the piston used for snapring removal.

PISTON RING REPLACEMENT

▶ **See Figures 95, 96, 97, 98, 99 and 100**

Piston rings provide the seal between the combustion gases and the crankcase. The rings do a tremendous job of separating the extreme pressure of the combustion chamber and the semi-vacuum of the crankcase. If the piston rings can not do

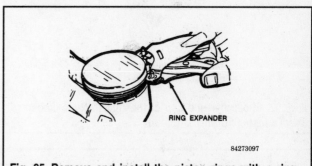

RING EXPANDER

Fig. 95 Remove and install the piston rings with a ring expanding tool to avoid breaking the rings

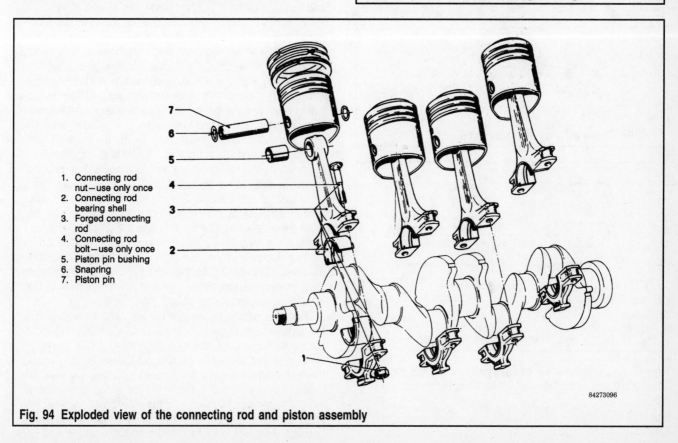

1. Connecting rod nut—use only once
2. Connecting rod bearing shell
3. Forged connecting rod
4. Connecting rod bolt—use only once
5. Piston pin bushing
6. Snapring
7. Piston pin

Fig. 94 Exploded view of the connecting rod and piston assembly

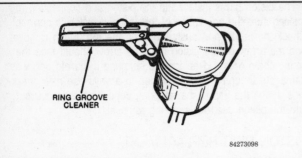

Fig. 96 Clean the ring grooves with a commercial tool or equivalent

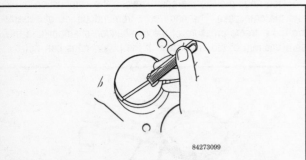

Fig. 97 Check the end gap of the ring in the cylinder before installing on the piston

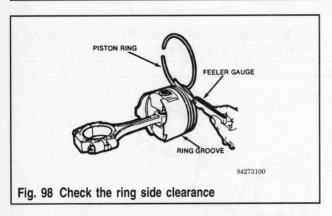

Fig. 98 Check the ring side clearance

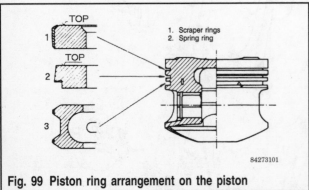

1. Scraper rings
2. Spring ring

Fig. 99 Piston ring arrangement on the piston

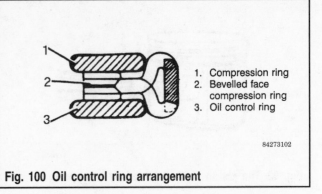

1. Compression ring
2. Bevelled face compression ring
3. Oil control ring

Fig. 100 Oil control ring arrangement

tailpipe. There will be a reduction in compression resulting in a loss of performance.

The piston rings are located in grooves, called lands, machined into the pistons. As the piston moves up and down, the rings slowly rotate in the lands. This allows the rings to seal against the cylinder wall and the piston. If the ring lands get filled with carbon or varnish, the rings will stick and not be allowed to move. This will reduce the ability of the rings to seal. If the rings stick, the rings need to be removed, the lands cleaned and the rings replaced.

The piston rings should be removed with a ring remover tool. The tool will grasp the ends of the ring at the gap and spread the ring enough to remove it from the piston. Do not use screwdrivers, pliers or any other tool not designed to do the job. The piston rings can break into sharp edged pieces of stretched too far.

With the piston rings removed, inspect the lands for carbon and varnish buildup. Clean the lands with solvent if varnish is found. Clean the lands with a mechanical cleaning tool if carbon is found. A piece of old ring can be used to remove light deposits. Check the bottom of the lands for wear. The pistons will need to be replaced if the lands are damaged or worn.

Piston ring end gap should be checked while the rings are removed from the pistons. Incorrect end gap indicates that the wrong size rings are being used; ring breakage could occur. Compress the piston rings to be used in a cylinder, one at a time, into that cylinder. Squirt clean oil into the cylinder, so that the rings and the top half of cylinder wall are coated. Using an inverted piston, press the rings approximately 1 inch below the deck of the block. Measure the ring end gap with a feeler gauge, and compare to the specifications chart in this section. Carefully pull the ring out of the cylinder and file the ends squarely with a fine file to obtain the proper clearance.

Install the rings on the piston, lowest ring first, using a piston ring expander. There is a high risk of breaking or distorting the rings, or scratching the piston, if the rings are installed by hand or other means. When installing new rings, refer to the installation diagram furnished with new parts.

Check the pistons to see that the ring grooves and oil return holes have been properly cleaned. Slide a piston ring into its groove, and check the side clearance with a feeler gauge. Make sure that you insert the gauge between the ring and its lower land (lower edge of the groove), because any wear that occurs, forms a step at the inner portion of the lower land. If the piston grooves have worn to the extent that relatively high steps exist on the lower land, the piston should be replaced, because these will interfere with the operation of the new rings and ring clearances will be excessive. Piston rings are not

the job properly, there will be leakage of oil into the combustion chamber and the resulting blue oil smoke from the

furnished in oversize widths to compensate for ring groove wear.

ROD BEARING REPLACEMENT

▶ **See Figures ? and ?**

Connecting rod bearings for the engines covered in this guide consist of 2 halves or shells which are interchangeable in the rod and cap. When the shells are placed in position, the ends extend slightly beyond the rod and cap surfaces so that when the rod bolts are torqued, the shells will be clamped tightly in place to insure positive seating and to prevent turning. A tang holds the shells in place. Place one end of the bearing into the journal and press the other end down. Squeeze the bearing shell a bit while pressing down. The bearing shell will snap into place.

➡**The ends of the bearing shells must never be filed flush with the mating surface of the rod and cap.**

If a rod bearing becomes noisy or is worn so that its clearance on the crank journal is sloppy, a new bearing of the correct size must be selected and installed since there is no provision for adjustment.

✳✳WARNING

Under no circumstances should the rod end or cap be filed to adjust the bearing clearance, nor should shims of any kind be used.

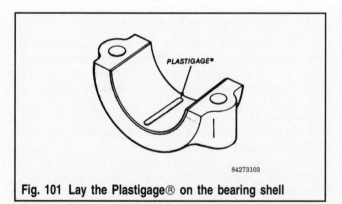

Fig. 101 Lay the Plastigage® on the bearing shell

84273103

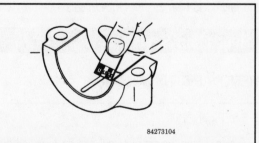

Fig. 102 Use the markings on the Plastigage® package to measure the bearing clearance after the bearing cap is torqued and removed

84273104

Inspect the rod bearings while the rod assemblies are out to the engine. If the shells are scored or show flaking, they should be replaced. If they are in good shape check for proper clearance on the crank journal (see below). Any scoring or ridges on the crank journal means the crankshaft must be replaced.

The crankshaft is surface hardened at the factory and it must not be reground without the proper surface treatment being done to the reground crankshaft. It is recommended to use a factory reground or new crankshaft if the crankshaft must be replaced. Use the proper sized undersized bearings if a reground crankshaft is used.

Connecting rod-to-crankshaft bearing clearance is checked using Plastigage® having a range of 0.0005-0.0030 inch

1. Remove the rod cap with the bearing shell. Completely clean the bearing shell and crank journal, and blow any oil from the oil hole in the crankshaft; Plastigage® is soluble in oil.

2. Place a piece of Plastigage® lengthwise along the bottom center of the lower bearing shell, then install the cap with shell and torque to specification. DO NOT turn the crankshaft with the Plastigage® in the bearing.

3. Remove the bearing cap with the shell. The flattened Plastigage® will be found sticking to either the bearing shell or crank journal. Do not remove it yet.

4. Use the scale printed on the Plastigage® envelope to measure the flattened material at its widest point. The number within the scale which most closely corresponds to the width of the Plastigage® indicates bearing clearance in thousandths of a inch.

5. Check the specifications chart in this section for the desired clearance.

➡**With the proper bearing clearance and the nuts torqued, it should be possible to move the connecting rod back and forth freely on the crank journal slightly. If the rod cannot be moved, either the rod bearing is too far undersize or the rod is misaligned.**

INSTALLATION

▶ **See Figures 103 and 104**

Before installing the pistons and rods, but after checking bearing clearances, it is recommended to replace the connecting rod bolts. BMW uses forged steel rods which are very strong and will last an extremely long time. The rod bolts should be replaced after they have been torqued and released once. It is acceptable to used the old bolts during the bearing clearance checking procedure, but they should be replaced before the final assembly and installation is completed. The bolts are pressed into the rods. A machine shop can do this for a nominal fee. The bolts have to pressed in while supporting the rod to prevent any damage to either the rod or the bolt.

Install the connecting rod to the piston, making sure piston installation notches and any marks on the rod are in proper relation to one another. Lubricate the wrist pin with clean engine oil, and install the pin into the rod and piston assembly. Install snaprings and rotate them in their grooves to make sure they are seated. Position the snaprings with the ends opposite

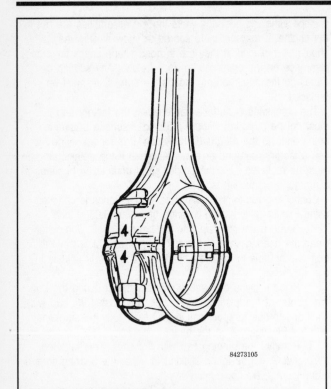

84273105

Fig. 103 Check that the markings on the rod and rod cap match before installation

84273106

Fig. 104 Use a ring compressor and tap the piston and rod assembly into the cylinder

of the removal groove. To install the piston and connecting rod assembly:

1. Make sure that the connecting rod big-ends bearings (including end cap) are of the correct size and properly installed.

2. Fit rubber hoses over the connecting rod bolts to protect the crankshaft journals, as in the 'Piston Removal' procedure. Coat the rod bearings with clean oil.

3. Using the proper ring compressor, insert the piston assembly into the cylinder so that the word **TOP** faces the front of the engine (this assumes that the dimple(s) or other markings on the connecting rods are in the correct relationship.)

4. From beneath the engine, coat each crank journal with clean oil. Pull the connecting rod, with the bearing shell in place, into position against the crank journal.

5. Remove the rubber hoses. Install the bearing cap and cap nuts and torque to the proper specifications.

➡️**If more than one rod and piston assembly is being installed, the connecting rod cap attaching nuts should only be tightened enough to keep each rod in position until all have been installed. This will ease the installation of the remaining piston assemblies as the crankshaft is rotated.**

6. Replace the oil pump if removed and the oil pan.
7. Install the cylinder head.

Freeze Plugs

The freeze plugs are the round metal disks pressed into the sides of the engine block. The freeze plugs allow access to the interior of the engine block to clean out the casting sand used during manufacture. A more proper term for freeze plugs would be core plugs. The term freeze plug came from the thought that if the coolant were to freeze and expand, the freeze plugs would be pushed out and prevent the engine block from cracking.

During the engine rebuilding process the engine block should be hot tanked or otherwise cleaned of all deposits. Before the block is cleaned, the freeze plugs should be removed allowing a greater access to the interior of the engine block.

To get access to all the freeze plugs, the engine should be removed from the vehicle and the transmission removed. All the covers should be removed from the block. It is possible to reach most of the freeze plugs with the engine still in the vehicle, but installation of the new plugs may be hindered by items in the engine compartment.

REMOVAL & INSTALLATION

1. With the coolant drained from the block, drive a punch in to the freeze plug. Do not drive the punch in more than necessary or contact may be made with the cylinders.
2. Pry the freeze plug out of the engine block.
3. Clean the bore of all deposits.

To install:

4. Coat the outside of the new freeze plug with Loctite® 270® or equivalent hardening sealer.
5. Drive the freeze plug into the engine block with the rounded side towards the interior of the block. Drive the plug in so the edge is slightly recessed.
6. Allow the sealer the proper curing time before subjecting the engine to heat or pressurized coolant.

Rear Main Seal

REMOVAL & INSTALLATION

▶ See Figure 105

The rear main bearing oil seal can be replaced after the transmission, and clutch/flywheel or the converter/flywheel has been removed from the engine.

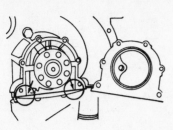

84273107

Fig. 105 Apply sealer to the joints as marked during rear main seal housing installation

Removal and installation, after the seal is exposed, is as follows.

1. Drain the engine oil and loosen the oil pan bolts. Carefully use a knife to separate the oil pan gasket from the lower surface of the end cover housing.

✳✳CAUTION

The EPA warns that prolonged contact with used engine oil may cause a number of skin disorders, including cancer. You should make every effort to minimize your exposure to used engine oil. Protective gloves should be worn when changing the oil. Wash your hands and any other exposed skin areas as soon as possible after exposure to used engine oil. Soap and water, or waterless hand cleaner should be used.

2. Remove the 2 rear oil pan bolts.
3. Remove the bolts around the outside of the cover housing and remove the end cover housing from the engine block. Remove the gasket from the block surface.
4. Remove the seal from the housing. Coat the sealing lips of the new seal with oil. Install a new seal into the end cover housing with a special seal installer BMW Tool No. 11 1 260 backed up by a mandrel, Tool No. 00 5 500 or equivalent. On M20, M30 and S38 engines, press the seal in until it is about 0.039-0.079 inch (1.00-2.00mm) deeper than the standard seal, which was installed flush.
5. While the cover is off, check the plug in the rear end of the main oil gallery. If the plug shows signs of leakage, replace it with another, coating it with Loctite® 270® or equivalent to keep it in place.
6. Coat the mating surface between the oil pan and end cover with sealer. Using a new gasket, install the end cover on the engine block and bolt it into place. Be careful to protect the lips of the seal from sharp edges while placing it over the end of the crankshaft. Torque the M6 bolts to 6-7 ft. lbs. (8-10Nm) and the M8 bolts to 15-17 ft. lbs. (20-24 Nm).
7. Reverse the removal procedure to complete the installation. If the oil pan gasket has been damaged, replace it.

Crankshaft and Main Bearings

REMOVAL

1. Drain the engine oil and remove the engine from the car. Mount the engine on a workstand in a suitable working area. Invert the engine, so the oil pan is facing up.

✳✳CAUTION

The EPA warns that prolonged contact with used engine oil may cause a number of skin disorders, including cancer! You should make every effort to minimize your exposure to used engine oil. Protective gloves should be worn when changing the oil. Wash your hands and any other exposed skin areas as soon as possible after exposure to used engine oil. Soap and water, or waterless hand cleaner should be used.

2. Remove the engine front (timing) cover.
3. Remove the timing chain/belt and gears.
4. Remove the oil pan.
5. Remove the oil pump.
6. Stamp the cylinder number on the machined surfaces of the bolt bosses of the connecting rods and caps for identification when reinstalling. If the pistons are to be removed eventually from the connecting rod, mark the cylinder number on the pistons with silver paint or felt-tip pen for proper cylinder identification and cap-to-rod location.
7. Remove the connecting rod caps. Install lengths of rubber hose on each of the connecting rod bolts, to protect the crank journals when the crank is removed.
8. Mark the main bearings caps with a number punch or punch so that they can be reinstalled in their original positions.
9. Remove all main bearing caps.
10. Carefully lift the crankshaft out of the block.

MAIN BEARING INSPECTION

Like connecting rod big-end bearings, the crankshaft main bearings are shell-type inserts that do not utilize shims and cannot be adjusted. The bearings are available in various standard sizes; if main bearing clearance is found to be too sloppy, a new bearing (both upper and lower halves) is required.

Checking Clearance

➡**Crankshaft bearing caps and bearing shells should NEVER be filed flush with the cap-to-block mating surface to adjust for wear in the old bearings. Always install new bearings.**

1. Remove the bearing cap. Wipe all oil from the crank journal and bearing cap.
2. Place a strip of Plastigage® the full width of the bearing, (parallel to the crankshaft), on the journal.

➡**Do not rotate the crankshaft while the gaging material is between the bearing and the journal.**

3. Install the bearing cap and evenly torque the cap bolts to specification.

4. Remove the bearing cap. The flattened Plastigage® will be sticking to either the bearing shell or the crank journal.

5. Use the graduated scale on the Plastigage® envelope to measure the material at its widest point.

➡**If the flattened Plastigage® tapers towards the middle or ends, there is a difference in clearance indicating the bearing or journal has a taper, low spot or other irregularity. If this is indicated, measure the crank journal with a micrometer.**

6. If bearing clearance is within specifications, the bearing insert is in good shape. Replace the insert if the clearance is not within specifications or show signs of damage. Always replace both upper and lower inserts as a unit.

7. Standard, 0.010 inch or 0.020 inch(0.025mm or 0.050mm) undersize bearing should produce the proper clearance. If these sizes still produce a sloppy fit, the crankshaft must be replaced. Recheck all clearances after installing new bearings.

8. Replace the rest of the bearings in the same manner. After all bearings have been checked, rotate the crankshaft to make sure there is no excessive drag.

INSTALLATION

◆ **See Figures 106 and 107**

If the crankshaft is being replaced with factory reground unit, it will be supplied with matching bearings. Check the bearing clearance if the original crankshaft is being reused. It is a good idea to check the bearing clearances on both new and used crankshafts.

Check the crankshaft for scoring or burn marks. The crankshaft is surface hardened at the factory and can not be reground without the surface treatment being completed.

1. Remove and inspect the crankshaft.

2. Remove the main bearings from the bearing saddles in the cylinder block and main bearing caps.

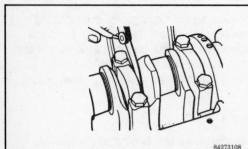

Fig. 106 Checking crankshaft end-play with a feeler gauge

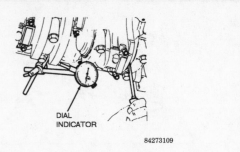

Fig. 107 Checking crankshaft end-play with a dial indicator

3. Coat the bearing surfaces of the new, correct size main bearings with clean engine oil and install them in the bearing saddles in the block and in the main bearing caps.

4. Inspect the oil spray jets in the bearing webs on the M42 and M50 engines. Install the crankshaft and bearing caps.

5. Clean and lubricate the bolts with oil. Torque the bolts on the M20 and M30 engines to 42-46 ft. lbs. (58-63 Nm). On the M42, M50, S14 and S38 engines, torque the bolts to 14-18 ft. lbs. (20-25 Nm), then turn the bolts an additional 47-53 degrees.

6. Check the end play of the crankshaft by prying in one direction, then to the other side. Insert a feeler gauge between the crankshaft and a main bearing cap to measure the play. A dial indicator can also be used to measure the end play. If the end play is not correct, loosen the thrust bearing, tap the crankshaft in both directions and retorque. Recheck the end-play.

7. Install a new pilot shaft bearing in the end of the crankshaft.

Flywheel/Flexplate and Ring Gear

REMOVAL & INSTALLATION

1. Remove the transmission. Remove the clutch cover and plate on manual transmission equipped vehicles.

2. Install a flywheel lock to hold the flywheel stationary.

3. Remove the bolts and pull the flywheel off.

To install:

4. Clean the mounting area of the crankshaft. Check the condition of the rear main seal and replace if necessary. Clean out the bolt holes.

5. Install the flywheel. Apply Loctite™270 or equivalent sealer to the new bolts.

➡**Use only new bolts when installing the flywheel. The bolts are not designed to be used more than once.**

6. Torque the bolts to 82-94 ft. lbs. (113-130 Nm).

7. Replace the clutch, if equipped and transmission.

EXHAUST SYSTEM

ENTIRE SYSTEM

The exhaust system is removed in one piece. The components of the exhaust system can be disconnected once the entire system has been removed. Allow the exhaust system to cool down completely before working on it.

REMOVAL & INSTALLATION

E30 3 Series

WITH M20 ENGINE

1. Disconnect the oxygen sensor and move the wire out of the way.
2. Remove the exhaust manifold connection nuts.
3. Remove the exhaust pipe transmission mount.
4. Remove the mount on the rear axle subframe.
5. Disconnect the rear muffler mounts and remove the exhaust system.
   To install:
6. Install the exhaust system to the car. Use new rubber mounts. Insert the rear muffler into its mounts and slide the mounts forward to preload the rubber ring 0.236 inch (6mm). Tighten the mounts. There should be a maximum torque of 10 ft. lbs. (14 Nm).
7. Loosely attach the transmission mounting point, but do not tighten.
8. Connect the rear axle subframe mount and the manifold nuts. Locate the tail pipes evenly in the opening.
9. Tighten the rear axle subframe mount to 16 ft. lbs. (22 Nm) and the manifold nuts to 36 ft. lbs. (50 Nm). Use new nuts and gaskets. Coat the studs with antisieze.
10. Tighten the transmission mount to 16 ft. lbs. (22 Nm). Check that the exhaust system does not strike any points under the car. Connect the oxygen sensor. Check for exhaust leaks.

WITH M42 ENGINE

1. Disconnect the oxygen sensor and move the wire out of the way.
2. Remove the exhaust manifold connection nuts.
3. Remove the exhaust pipe transmission mount.
4. Remove the mount on the rear axle subframe.
5. Disconnect the rear muffler mounts and remove the exhaust system.
   To install:
6. If the catalytic converter was removed, install the catalytic converter and connect the flanges. Tighten the bolts to 8-10 ft. lbs. (11-14 Nm) so the springs are flattened. Loosen the nuts 1½ turns.
7. Install the exhaust system to the car. Use new rubber mounts. Insert the rear muffler into its mounts and slide the mounts forward to preload the rubber ring 0.236 inch (6mm). Tighten the mounts. There should be a maximum torque of 10 ft. lbs. (14 Nm).
8. Loosely attach the transmission mounting point, but do not tighten.

9. Connect the rear axle subframe mount and the manifold nuts. Locate the tail pipes evenly in the opening.
10. Tighten the rear axle subframe mount to 16 ft. lbs. (22 Nm) and the manifold nuts to 36 ft. lbs. (50 Nm). Use new nuts and gaskets. Coat the studs with antisieze.
11. Tighten the transmission mount to 16 ft. lbs. (22 Nm). Check that the exhaust system does not strike any points under the car. Connect the oxygen sensor. Check for exhaust leaks.

WITH S14 ENGINE

1. Remove the exhaust manifold connection nuts.
2. Remove the rear axle subframe mounts and the rear muffler mount.
3. Lower the exhaust system.
   To install:
4. Install the exhaust system under the car. Attach the rear and subframe mounts using new rubber mounts.
5. Replace the manifold connection gasket, coat the studs with antisieze and mount the exhaust pipe to the manifold. Torque the nuts to 36 ft. lbs. (50 Nm).
6. Adjust the mounts to position the exhaust pipe in the opening at the rear of the car. Tighten the mounts to 16 ft. lbs. (22 Nm).
7. Check that the exhaust system does not strike any points under the car. Check for exhaust leaks.

E36 3 Series

WITH M42 ENGINE

1. Disconnect the oxygen sensor and remove the exhaust manifold connection nuts.
2. Remove the clamp around the exhaust pipe from the transmission bracket. Do not remove the bracket from the transmission.
3. Remove the rubber rings from the rear axle subframe and disconnect the muffler from the rear clamps. Remove the exhaust system.
   To install:
4. Install the muffler into the clamps. Preload the mounts by sliding the clamps forward 0.59 inch (15mm) and tightening to 10 ft. lbs. (14 Nm).
5. Connect the rubber rings and the manifold connection. Replace the manifold connection gasket, coat the studs with antisieze and mount the exhaust pipe to the manifold. Torque the nuts to 36 ft. lbs. (50 Nm).
6. Connect the transmission mounting point and tighten to 16 ft. lbs. (22 Nm).
7. Connect the oxygen sensor. Check the positioning of the system and adjust the mounts as necessary. Check for exhaust leaks.

WITH M50 ENGINE

1. Disconnect the oxygen sensor and remove the exhaust manifold connection nuts. Remove the transmission to engine joint crossmember on automatic transmission equipped cars. The engine and transmission will still be supported by the forward and rear mounts.

2. Remove the clamp around the exhaust pipe from the transmission bracket. Do not remove the bracket from the transmission.

3. Remove the rubber rings from the center mounting point and disconnect the muffler from the rear clamps. Remove the exhaust system.

To install:

4. Install the muffler into the clamps. Preload the mounts by sliding the clamps forward 0.59 inch (15mm) and tightening to 10 ft. lbs. (14 Nm).

5. Connect the rubber rings and the manifold connection. Replace the manifold connection gasket, coat the studs with antisieze and mount the exhaust pipe to the manifold. Torque the nuts to 22 ft. lbs. (30 Nm), then 36 ft. lbs. (50 Nm).

6. Connect the transmission mounting point and tighten to 16 ft. lbs. (22 Nm). Install the crossmember.

7. Connect the oxygen sensor. Check the positioning of the system and adjust the mounts as necessary. Check for exhaust leaks.

E34 5 Series

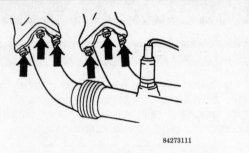

Fig. 109 Exhaust manifold connection nuts on M50 engine

▶ **See Figures 108, 109 and 110**

EXCEPT WITH S38 ENGINE

1. Disconnect the oxygen sensor and move the wire out of the way.

2. Remove the exhaust manifold connection nuts.

3. Remove the exhaust pipe transmission mount.

4. Remove the mount on the rear axle subframe.

5. Disconnect the rear muffler mounts and remove the exhaust system.

To install:

6. Install the exhaust system to the car. Use new rubber mounts. Insert the rear muffler into its mounts and slide the mounts forward to preload the rubber ring 0.275 inch (7mm). Tighten the mounts. There should be a maximum torque of 10 ft. lbs. (14 Nm).

7. Loosely attach the transmission mounting point, but do not tighten.

8. Connect the rear axle subframe mount and the manifold nuts. Locate the tail pipes evenly in the opening.

9. Tighten the rear axle subframe mount to 16 ft. lbs. (22 Nm) and the manifold nuts to 36 ft. lbs. (50 Nm). Use new nuts and gaskets. Coat the studs with antisieze.

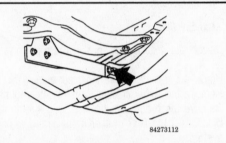

Fig. 110 Transmission mount for exhaust system. This should be the last item to be tightened when the exhaust system is installed

10. Tighten the transmission mount to 16 ft. lbs. (22 Nm). Check that the exhaust system does not strike any points under the car. Connect the oxygen sensor. Check for exhaust leaks.

WITH S38 ENGINE

1. Disconnect the oxygen sensor and move the wire out of the way. Remove the heat shield.

2. Remove the exhaust manifold connection nuts.

3. Remove the exhaust pipe transmission mount.

4. Remove the mount on the rear axle subframe.

5. Disconnect the rear muffler mounts and remove the exhaust system.

To install:

6. Install the exhaust system to the car. Use new rubber mounts. Insert the rear muffler into its mounts and slide the mounts forward to preload the rubber ring 0.197 inch (5mm). Tighten the mounts. There should be a maximum torque of 16 ft. lbs. (22 Nm).

7. Loosely attach the transmission mounting point, but do not tighten.

8. Connect the rear axle subframe mount and the manifold nuts. Locate the tail pipes evenly in the opening.

9. Tighten the rear axle subframe mount to 16 ft. lbs. (22 Nm) and the manifold nuts to 30 ft. lbs. (42 Nm). Use new nuts and gaskets. Coat the studs with antisieze.

10. Tighten the transmission mount to 16 ft. lbs. (22 Nm). Check that the exhaust system does not strike any points under the car. Connect the oxygen sensor. Check for exhaust leaks.

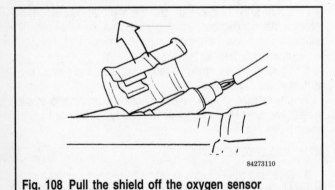

Fig. 108 Pull the shield off the oxygen sensor

M20 ENGINE REBUILDING SPECIFICATIONS CHART

Component	U.S.	Metric
Cylinder block		
Cylinder bore		
Standard size:	3.3071–3.3075 in.	84.00–84.01 mm
Intemediate size:	3.3102–3.3106 in.	84.08–84.09 mm
Overbore 1:	3.3169–3.3173 in.	84.25–84.26 mm
Overbore 2:	3.3267–3.3271 in.	84.50–84.51 mm
Maximum out-of-round:	0.0012 in.	0.03 mm
Maximum taper:	0.0008 in.	0.02 mm
Cylinder head		
Cylinder head height		
New height:	4.925 in.	125.1 mm
Minimum machined height:	4.909 in.	124.7 mm
Valve guide total length:	1.713 in.	43.5 mm
Valve guide head bore diameter		
Standard size:	0.5197 in.	13.2 mm
Overbore 1:	0.5236 in.	13.3 mm
Overbore 2:	0.5275 in.	13.4 mm
Valve guide installed inside diameter		
Standard size:	0.2756 in.	7.0 mm
Overbore 1:	0.2795 in.	7.1 mm
Overbore 2:	0.2835 in.	7.2 mm
Valve guide installing temperature		
Cylinder head:	+120°F.	+50°C.
Valve guide:	−240°F.	−150°C.
Valve guide protrusion:	0.571 in.	14.5 mm
Valve seat angle:	15/45/75 degrees	15/45/75degrees
Valve seat width		
Intake:	0.051–0.079 in.	1.3–2.0 mm
Exhaust:	0.051–0.079 in.	1.3–2.0 mm
Valve seat diameter		
Intake:	1.598 in.	40.6 mm
Exhaust:	1.362 in.	34.6 mm
Crankshaft		
Main bearing diameter		
Double classification		
Standard size		
Red:	2.358–2.357 in.	59.990–59.980 mm
Blue:	2.358–2.357 in.	59.980–59.971 mm
Undersize 1		
Red:	2.349–2.348 in.	59.740–59.730 mm
Blue:	2.348–2.347 in.	59.730–59.721 mm
Undersize 2		
Red:	2.339–2.338 in.	59.490–59.480 mm
Blue:	2.338–2.339 in.	59.480–59.471 mm
Triple classification		
Standard size		
Yellow:	2.3616–2.3618 in.	59.984–59.990 mm
Green:	2.3613–2.3615in.	59.977–59.983 mm
White:	2.3610–2.3612 in.	59.971–59.976 mm
Undersize 1, 0.25mm		
Yellow:	2.3517–2.3520 in.	59.734–59.740 mm
Green:	2.3514–2.3517 in.	59.727–59.733 mm
White:	2.3512–2.3514 in.	59.721–59.726 mm
Undersize 2, 0.50mm		
Yellow:	2.3419–2.3421 in.	59.484–59.490 mm
Green:	2.3416–2.3418 in.	59.477–59.483 mm
White:	2.3414–2.3416 in.	59.471–59.476 mm
Crankshaft main bearing clearance		
Double classification:	0.0010–0.0030 in.	0.03–0.07 mm
Triple classification:	0.0008–0.0018 in.	0.020–0.046 mm

M20 ENGINE REBUILDING SPECIFICATIONS CHART

Component	U.S.	Metric
Crankshaft thrust bearing ground size		
Standard size:	0.9842 in.	25.0 mm
Overbore 1:	0.9921 in.	25.2 mm
Overbore 2:	1.0000 in.	25.4 mm
Crankshaft end play:	0.0031–0.0064 in.	0.08–0.163mm
Connecting rod bearing journal ground size		
Standard size:	1.7707–1.7713 in.	44.975–44.991 mm
Undersize 1, 0.25mm:	1.7608–1.7614 in.	44.725–44.741 mm
Undersize 2, 0.50mm:	1.7510–1.7516 in.	44.475–44.491 mm
Connecting rod bearing clearance:	0.0008–0.0022 in.	0.020–0.055 mm
Crankshaft runout at center main:	0.006 in.	0.15 mm
Connecting rods		
Bushing diameter		
Outside:	0.9472–0.9488 in.	24.060–24.100 mm
Inside:	0.8662–0.8664 in.	22.003–22.008 mm
Maximum weight deviation in engine, without bearing shells		
Total:	± 0.14 oz.	±4g
Big end:	± 0.07 oz.	±2g
Small end:	± 0.07 oz.	±2g
Big end bore		
Red:	1.8898–1.8900 in.	48.000–48.008 mm
Blue:	1.8901–1.8904 in.	48.009–48.016 mm
Pistons		
Piston diameter		
Measured 0.354 in. (9.00mm) from bottom of the skirt with Mahle		
Measured 0.458 in. (11.65mm) from bottom of the skirt with KS		
Standard size:	3.306 in.	83.98 mm
Intemediate size:	3.309 in.	84.06 mm
Overbore 1:	3.316 in.	84.23 mm
Overbore 2:	3.326 in.	84.48 mm
Piston clearance		
New engine:	0.0004–0.0016 in.	0.01–0.04 mm
Used engine:	0.005 in.	0.12 mm
Piston rings		
Top compression		
End clearance:	0.008–0.020 in.	0.2–0.5 mm
Side clearance:	0.0016–0.0031 in.	0.04–0.08 mm
Bottom compression		
End clearance:	0.008–0.020 in.	0.2–0.5 mm
Side clearance:	0.0012–0.0027 in.	0.03–0.07 mm
Oil control		
End clearance:	0.008–0.020 in.	0.2–0.5 mm
Side clearance:	0.0008–0.0020 in.	0.02–0.05 mm
Camshaft		
End play:	0.008 in.	0.2 mm
Rocker arms		
Bushing clearance:	0.0006–0.0020 in.	0.016–0.052 mm

84273120

M20 ENGINE REBUILDING SPECIFICATIONS CHART

Component	U.S.	Metric
Valves		
Valve lash		
Cold:	0.010 in.	0.25 mm
Operating temperature:	0.012 in.	0.30 mm
Head edge thickness		
Intake:	0.051 in.	1.3 mm
Exhaust:	0.079 in.	2.0 mm
Head diameter		
Intake:	1.653 in.	42 mm
Exhaust:	1.417 in.	36 mm
Stem diameter		
Standard size:	0.275 in.	7.0 mm
Oversize 1:	0.279 in.	7.1 mm
Oversize 2:	0.283 in.	7.2 mm
Stem to guide tilt clearance:	0.031 in.	0.8 mm
Oil pump		
Pressure at idle:	7–28 psi	0.5–2.0 bar
Pressure at top speed:	57–85 psi	4.0–6.0 bar
Pressure relief valve spring length		
Bypass pressure valve:	1.732 in.	44 mm
Vibration damper		
Radial runout, maximum:	0.008 in.	0.2 mm
Axial runout, maximum:	0.012 in.	0.3 mm

84273121

M30 ENGINE REBUILDING SPECIFICATIONS CHART

Component	U.S.	Metric
Cylinder block		
Cylinder bore		
Standard size:	3.6220–3.6224 in.	92.00–92.01 mm
Intemediate size:	3.6252–3.6256 in.	92.08–92.09 mm
Overbore 1:	3.6319–3.6323 in.	92.25–92.26 mm
Overbore 2:	3.6417–3.6421 in.	92.50–92.51 mm
Maximum out-of-round:	0.0004 in.	0.01 mm
Maximum taper:	0.0004in.	0.01 mm
Cylinder head		
Cylinder head height		
New height:	5.079 in.	129.0 mm
Minimum machined height:	5.063 in.	128.6 mm
Valve guide total length:	1.988 in.	50.5 mm
Valve guide head bore diameter		
Standard size:	0.5590 in.	14.2 mm
Overbore 1:	0.5630 in.	14.3 mm
Overbore 2:	0.5669 in.	14.4 mm
Valve guide installed inside diameter		
Standard size:	0.3150 in.	8.0 mm
Overbore 1:	0.3190 in.	8.1 mm
Overbore 2:	0.3228 in.	8.2 mm
Valve guide installing temperature		
Cylinder head:	+120 °F.	+50 °C.
Valve guide:	−240 °F.	−150 °C.
Valve guide protrusion:	0.511–0.551 in.	13.0–14.0 mm
Valve seat angle:	15/45/75 degrees	15/45/75 degrees
Valve seat width		
Intake:	0.039–0.071in.	1.0–1.8 mm
Exhaust:	0.051–0.083 in.	1.3–2.1 mm
Valve seat diameter		
Intake:	1.795 in.	45.5 mm
Exhaust:	1.441 in.	36.6 mm
Crankshaft		
Main bearing diameter		
Triple classification		
Standard size		
Yellow:	2.3616–2.3618 in.	59.984–59.990 mm
Green:	2.3613–2.3615in.	59.977–59.983 mm
White:	2.3610–2.3612 in.	59.971–59.976 mm
Undersize 1, 0.25mm		
Yellow:	2.3517–2.3520 in.	59.734–59.740 mm
Green:	2.3514–2.3517 in.	59.727–59.733 mm
White:	2.3512–2.3514 in.	59.721–59.726 mm
Undersize 2, 0.50mm		
Yellow:	2.3419–2.3421 in.	59.484–59.490 mm
Green:	2.3416–2.3418 in.	59.477–59.483 mm
White:	2.3414–2.3416 in.	59.471–59.476 mm
Undersize 3, 0.75mm		
Yellow:	2.3320–2.3323 in.	59.234–59.240 mm
Green:	2.3318–2.3320 in.	59.227–59.233 mm
White:	2.3315–2.3317 in.	59.221–59.226 mm

84273122

M30 ENGINE REBUILDING SPECIFICATIONS CHART

Component	U.S.	Metric
Crankshaft main bearing clearance		
Triple classification:	0.0008–0.0018 in.	0.020–0.046 mm
Crankshaft thrust bearing ground size		
Standard size:	1.1811 in.	30.0 mm
Oversize 1:	1.1890 in.	30.2 mm
Oversize 2:	1.1968 in.	30.4 mm
Oversize 2:	1.2047 in.	30.6 mm
Crankshaft end play:	0.0033–0.0068 in.	0.085–0.174 mm
Connecting rod bearing journal ground size		
Standard size:	1.8888–1.8894 in.	47.975–47.991 mm
Undersize 1, 0.25mm:	1.8789–1.8796 in.	47.725–47.741 mm
Undersize 2, 0.50mm:	1.8691–1.8697 in.	47.475–47.491 mm
Undersize 3, 0.75mm:	1.8592–1.8599 in.	47.225–47.241 mm
Connecting rod bearing clearance:	0.0008–0.0022 in.	0.020–0.055 mm
Crankshaft runout at center main:	0.004 in.	0.1 mm
Connecting rods		
Bushing diameter		
Outside:	0.9472–0.9488 in.	24.060–24.100 mm
Inside:	0.8662–0.8664 in.	22.003–22.008 mm
Maximum weight deviation in engine, without bearing shells		
Total:	± 0.14 oz.	± 4g
Big end:	± 0.07 oz.	± 2g
Small end:	± 0.07 oz.	± 2g
Big end bore		
Red:	2.0427–2.0475 in.	52.000–52.008 mm
Blue:	2.0476–2.0479 in.	52.009–52.016 mm
Pistons		
Piston diameter		
Alcan-measured 0.531 in. (13.5mm) from bottom of skirt		
Standard size:	3.6209 in.	91.972 mm
Intemediate size:	3.6241 in.	92.052 mm
Overbore 1:	3.6308 in.	92.222 mm
Overbore 2:	3.6406 in.	92.472 mm
Mahle-measured 0.866 in. (22.0mm) from bottom of skirt		
Standard size:	3.6212 in.	91.980 mm
Intemediate size:	3.6244 in.	92.060 mm
Overbore 1:	3.6311 in.	92.230 mm
Overbore 2:	3.6409 in.	92.480 mm
Piston clearance		
New engine:	0.0008–0.0020 in.	0.02–0.05 mm
Used engine:	0.006 in.	0.15 mm
Piston rings		
Top compression		
End clearance:	0.008–0.018 in.	0.2–0.45 mm
Side clearance:	0.0016–0.0028 in.	0.04–0.072 mm
Bottom compression		
End clearance:	0.016–0.025 in.	0.4–0.65 mm
Side clearance:	0.0012–0.0024 in.	0.03–0.062 mm
Oil control		
End clearance:	0.012–0.024 in.	0.3–0.6 mm
Side clearance:	0.0008–0.0022 in.	0.02–0.055 mm
Camshaft		
End play:	0.0012–0.0071 in.	0.03–0.18 mm
Rocker arms		
Bushing clearance:	0.0006–0.0020 in.	0.016–0.052 mm

M30 ENGINE REBUILDING SPECIFICATIONS CHART

Component	U.S.	Metric
Valves		
Valve lash		
Cold:	0.012 in.	0.30 mm
Operating temperature:	0.014 in.	0.35 mm
Head edge thickness		
Intake:	0.051 in.	1.3 mm
Exhaust:	0.079 in.	2.0 mm
Head diameter		
Intake:	1.850 in.	47 mm
Exhaust:	1.496 in.	38 mm
Stem diameter		
Standard size:	0.315 in.	8.0 mm
Oversize 1:	0.319 in.	8.1 mm
Oversize 2:	0.323 in.	8.2 mm
Stem to guide tilt clearance:	0.031 in.	0.8 mm
Oil pump		
Pressure at idle:	7–28 psi	0.5–2.0 bar
Pressure at top speed:	57–85 psi	4.0–6.0 bar
Pressure relief valve spring length		
Operating pressure:	2.677 in.	68 mm
Bypass pressure:	1.732 in.	44 mm
Radial clearance between outer rotor and body:	0.004–0.006 in.	0.1–0.15 mm
Axial clearance between rotor and body:	0.0016–0.0039 in.	0.04–0.10 mm
Clearance between inner and outer rotor:	0.005–0.008 in.	0.12–0.20 mm
Distance between flange and inner rotor:	1.740–1.748 in.	44.2–44.4 mm
Vibration damper		
Radial runout, maximum:	0.008 in.	0.2 mm
Axial runout, maximum:	0.016 in.	0.4 mm

84273124

M42 ENGINE REBUILDING SPECIFICATIONS CHART

Component	U.S.	Metric
Cylinder block		
Cylinder bore		
Standard size:	3.3071–3.3077 in.	84.000–84.014 mm
Intemediate size:	3.3103–3.3109 in.	84.080–84.094 mm
Overbore 1:	3.3170–3.3176 in.	84.250–84.264 mm
Overbore 2:	3.3268–3.3274 in.	84.500–84.514 mm
Maximum out-of-round:	0.0004 in.	0.01 mm
Maximum taper:	0.0004 in.	0.01 mm
Cylinder head		
Cylinder head height		
New height:	5.512 in.	140.00 mm
Minimum machined height:	5.494 in.	139.55 mm
Valve guide total length:	1.713 in.	43.5 mm
Valve guide head bore diameter		
Standard size:	0.4922 in.	12.5 mm
Overbore 1:	0.4961 in.	12.6 mm
Overbore 2:	0.5000 in.	12.7 mm
Valve guide installed inside diameter		
Standard size:	0.2756 in.	7.0 mm
Overbore 1:	0.2796 in.	7.1 mm
Overbore 2:	0.2835 in.	7.2 mm
Valve guide installing temperature		
Cylinder head:	+68 °F.	+20 °C.
Valve guide:	−240 °F.	−150°C.
Valve guide protrusion:	0.173–0.197 in.	4.4–5.0 mm
Valve seat angle:	45/60 degrees	45/60 degrees
Valve seat width		
Intake:	0.055–0.075 in.	1.4–1.9 mm
Exhaust:	0.055–0.075 in.	1.4–1.9 mm
Valve seat diameter		
Intake:	1.244 in.	31.6 mm
Exhaust:	1.146 in.	29.1 mm
Crankshaft		
Main bearing diameter		
Triple classification		
Standard size		
Yellow:	2.3616–2.3618 in.	59.984–59.990 mm
Green:	2.3613–2.3615in.	59.977–59.983 mm
White:	2.3610–2.3612 in.	59.971–59.976 mm
Undersize 1, 0.25mm		
Yellow:	2.3517–2.3520 in.	59.734–59.740 mm
Green:	2.3514–2.3517 in.	59.727–59.733 mm
White:	2.3512–2.3514 in.	59.721–59.726 mm
Undersize 2, 0.50mm		
Yellow:	2.3419–2.3421 in.	59.484–59.490 mm
Green:	2.3416–2.3418 in.	59.477–59.483 mm
White:	2.3414–2.3416 in.	59.471–59.476 mm
Crankshaft main bearing clearance		
Triple classification:	0.0008–0.0023 in.	0.020–0.058 mm
Crankshaft thrust bearing ground size		
Standard size:	0.9842 in.	25.0 mm
Overbore 1:	0.9921 in.	25.2 mm
Overbore 2:	1.0000 in.	25.4 mm
Crankshaft end play:	0.0031–0.0064 in.	0.08–0.163mm
Connecting rod bearing journal ground size		
Standard size:	1.7721–1.7727 in.	45.009–45.025 mm
Undersize 1, 0.25mm:	1.7622–1.7628 in.	44.759–44.775 mm
Undersize 2, 0.50mm:	1.7524–1.7530 in.	44.509–44.525 mm
Connecting rod bearing clearance:	0.0008–0.0022 in.	0.020–0.055 mm
Crankshaft runout at center main:	0.006 in.	0.15 mm

84273125

M42 ENGINE REBUILDING SPECIFICATIONS CHART

Component	U.S.	Metric
Connecting rods		
Bushing diameter		
Outside:	0.9472–0.9488 in.	24.060–24.100 mm
Inside:	0.8650–0.8653 in.	22.005–22.010 mm
Maximum weight deviation in engine, without bearing shells		
Total:	± 0.14 oz.	± 4g
Big end:	± 0.07 oz.	± 2g
Small end:	± 0.07 oz.	± 2g
Big end bore		
Red:	1.8898–1.8900 in.	48.000–48.008 mm
Blue:	1.8901–1.8904 in.	48.009–48.016 mm
Pistons		
Piston diameter-measured 0.512 in. (13.00mm) from bottom of the skirt		
Standard size:	3.306 in.	83.98 mm
Intemediate size:	3.309 in.	84.06 mm
Overbore 1:	3.316 in.	84.23 mm
Overbore 2:	3.326 in.	84.48 mm
Piston clearance		
New engine:	0.0004–0.0016 in.	0.01–0.04 mm
Used engine:	0.0059 in.	0.15 mm
Piston rings		
Top compression		
End clearance:	0.008–0.016 in.	0.2–0.4 mm
Side clearance:	0.0008–0.0020 in.	0.02–0.052 mm
Bottom compression		
End clearance:	0.008–0.016 in.	0.2–0.4 mm
Side clearance:	0.0008–0.0020 in.	0.020–0.052 mm
Oil control		
End clearance:	0.008–0.018 in.	0.2–0.45 mm
Side clearance:	0.0008–0.0022 in.	0.020–0.055 mm
Camshaft		
End play:	0.006–0.013 in.	0.15–0.33 mm
Bearing clearance:	0.0008–0.0021 in.	0.020–0.54 mm
Valves		
Head diameter		
Intake:	1.299 in.	33.0 mm
Exhaust:	1.201 in.	30.5 mm
Stem diameter		
Standard size:	0.275 in.	6.975 mm
Oversize 1:	0.280 in.	7.100 mm
Oversize 2:	0.283 in.	7.200 mm
Stem to guide tilt clearance:	0.020 in.	0.5 mm
Oil pump		
Pressure at idle:	18–28 psi	1.3–2.0 bar
Pressure at top speed:	57–61 psi	4.0–4.3 bar
Pressure relief valve spring length		
Operating pressure valve:	3.311 in.	84 mm
Radial play of outer rotor to pump body:	0.0047–0.0077 in.	0.120–0.196 mm
Axial play of inner rotor:	0.0008–0.0026 in.	0.02–0.065 mm
Axial play of outer rotor:	0.0016–0.0035 in.	0.04–0.09 mm

84273126

M50 ENGINE REBUILDING SPECIFICATIONS CHART

Component	U.S.	Metric
Cylinder block		
Cylinder bore		
Standard size:	3.3071–3.3077 in.	84.000–84.014 mm
Intemediate size:	3.3103–3.3109 in.	84.080–84.094 mm
Overbore 1:	3.3170–3.3176 in.	84.250–84.264 mm
Overbore 2:	3.3268–3.3274 in.	84.500–84.514 mm
Maximum out-of-round:	0.0004 in.	0.01 mm
Maximum taper:	0.0004 in.	0.01 mm
Cylinder head		
Cylinder head height		
New height:	5.512 in.	140.00 mm
Minimum machined height:	5.494 in.	139.55 mm
Valve guide total length:	1.713 in.	43.5 mm
Valve guide head bore diameter		
Standard size:	0.4922 in.	12.5 mm
Overbore 1:	0.4961 in.	12.6 mm
Overbore 2:	0.5000 in.	12.7 mm
Valve guide installed inside diameter		
Standard size:	0.2756 in.	7.0 mm
Overbore 1:	0.2796 in.	7.1 mm
Overbore 2:	0.2835 in.	7.2 mm
Valve guide installing temperature		
Cylinder head:	+68 °F.	+20 °C.
Valve guide:	−240 °F.	−150°C.
Valve guide protrusion:	0.173–0.197 in.	4.4–5.0 mm
Valve seat angle:	45/60 degrees	45/60 degrees
Valve seat width		
Intake:	0.055–0.075 in.	1.4–1.9 mm
Exhaust:	0.055–0.075 in.	1.4–1.9 mm
Valve seat diameter		
Intake:	1.244 in.	31.6 mm
Exhaust:	1.146 in.	29.1 mm
Crankshaft		
Main bearing diameter		
Triple classification		
Standard size		
Yellow:	2.3616–2.3618 in.	59.984–59.990 mm
Green:	2.3613–2.3615in.	59.977–59.983 mm
White:	2.3610–2.3612 in.	59.971–59.976 mm
Undersize 1, 0.25mm		
Yellow:	2.3517–2.3520 in.	59.734–59.740 mm
Green:	2.3514–2.3517 in.	59.727–59.733 mm
White:	2.3512–2.3514 in.	59.721–59.726 mm
Undersize 2, 0.50mm		
Yellow:	2.3419–2.3421 in.	59.484–59.490 mm
Green:	2.3416–2.3418 in.	59.477–59.483 mm
White:	2.3414–2.3416 in.	59.471–59.476 mm
Crankshaft main bearing clearance		
Triple classification:	0.0008–0.0023 in.	0.020–0.058 mm
Crankshaft thrust bearing ground size		
Standard size:	0.9842 in.	25.0 mm
Overbore 1:	0.9921 in.	25.2 mm
Overbore 2:	1.0000 in.	25.4 mm
Crankshaft end play:	0.0031–0.0064 in.	0.08–0.163mm
Connecting rod bearing journal ground size		
Standard size:	1.7721–1.7727 in.	45.009–45.025 mm
Undersize 1, 0.25mm:	1.7622–1.7628 in.	44.759–44.775 mm
Undersize 2, 0.50mm:	1.7524–1.7530 in.	44.509–44.525 mm
Connecting rod bearing clearance:	0.0008–0.0022 in.	0.020–0.055 mm
Crankshaft runout at center main:	0.006 in.	0.15 mm

84273128

M50 ENGINE REBUILDING SPECIFICATIONS CHART

Component	U.S.	Metric
Connecting rods		
Bushing diameter		
Outside:	0.9449–0.9461 in.	24.000–24.031 mm
Inside:	0.8650–0.8653 in.	22.005–22.010 mm
Maximum weight deviation in engine, without bearing shells		
Total:	± 0.14 oz.	± 4g
Big end:	± 0.07 oz.	± 2g
Small end:	± 0.07 oz.	± 2g
Big end bore		
Red:	1.8898–1.8900 in.	48.000–48.008 mm
Blue:	1.8901–1.8904 in.	48.009–48.016 mm
Pistons		
Piston diameter-measured 0.512 in. (13.00mm) from bottom of the skirt		
Standard size:	3.306 in.	83.98 mm
Intemediate size:	3.309 in.	84.06 mm
Overbore 1:	3.316 in.	84.23 mm
Overbore 2:	3.326 in.	84.48 mm
Piston clearance		
New engine:	0.0004–0.0016 in.	0.01–0.04 mm
Used engine:	0.0059 in.	0.15 mm
Piston rings		
Top compression		
End clearance:	0.008–0.016 in.	0.2–0.4 mm
Side clearance:	0.0008–0.0020 in.	0.02–0.052 mm
Bottom compression		
End clearance:	0.008–0.016 in.	0.2–0.4 mm
Side clearance:	0.0008–0.0020 in.	0.020–0.052 mm
Oil control		
End clearance:	0.008–0.018 in.	0.2–0.45 mm
Side clearance:	0.0008–0.0022 in.	0.020–0.055 mm
Camshaft		
End play:	0.006–0.013 in.	0.15–0.33 mm
Bearing clearance:	0.0008–0.0021 in.	0.020–0.54 mm
Valves		
Head diameter		
Intake:	1.299 in.	33.0 mm
Exhaust:	1.201 in.	30.5 mm
Stem diameter		
Standard size:	0.275 in.	6.975 mm
Oversize 1:	0.280 in.	7.100 mm
Oversize 2:	0.283 in.	7.200 mm
Stem to guide tilt clearance:	0.020 in.	0.5 mm
Oil pump		
Pressure at idle:	18–28 psi	1.3–2.0 bar
Pressure at top speed:	57–61 psi	4.0–4.3 bar
Pressure relief valve spring length		
Operating pressure valve:	3.311 in.	84 mm
Radial play of outer rotor to pump body:	0.0047–0.0077 in.	0.120–0.196 mm
Axial play of inner rotor:	0.0008–0.0026 in.	0.02–0.065 mm
Axial play of outer rotor:	0.0016–0.0035 in.	0.04–0.09 mm

84273129

S14 ENGINE REBUILDING SPECIFICATIONS CHART

Component	U.S.	Metric
Cylinder block		
Cylinder bore		
Standard size:	3.6771–3.6775 in.	93.40–93.41 mm
Intemediate size:	3.6791–3.6795 in.	93.45–93.46 mm
Overbore 1:	3.6850–3.6854 in.	93.60–94.61 mm
Overbore 2:	3.6929–3.6933 in.	93.80–93.81 mm
Maximum out-of-round:	0.0002 in.	0.005 mm
Maximum taper:	0.0004 in.	0.01 mm
Cylinder head		
Cylinder head height		
New height:	3.7783–3.7707 in.	95.97–96.03 mm
Minimum machined height:	not recommended	not recommended
Valve guide total length:	1.7022–1.718 in.	43.3–43.7 mm
Valve guide head bore diameter		
Standard size:	0.4717 in.	12.0 mm
Overbore 1:	0.4796 in.	12.2 mm
Overbore 2:	0.4953 in.	12.4 mm
Valve guide installed inside diameter		
Standard size:	0.2756 in.	7.0 mm
Overbore 1:	0.2796 in.	7.1 mm
Overbore 2:	0.2835 in.	7.2 mm
Valve guide installing temperature		
Cylinder head:	+300 °F.	+150 °C.
Valve guide:	−240 °F.	−150 °C.
Valve guide protrusion:	0.5897 in.	15 mm
Valve seat angle:	35/45/60 degrees	35/45/60 degrees
Valve seat width		
Intake:	0.047–0.051 in.	1.2–1.3 mm
Exhaust:	0.055–0.059 in.	1.4–1.5 mm
Valve seat diameter		
Intake:	1.441–1.445 in.	36.6–36.7 mm
Exhaust:	1.236–1.240 in.	31.4–31.5 mm
Crankshaft		
Main bearing diameter		
Double classification		
Standard size		
Red:	2.1649–2.1645 in.	54.990–54.980 mm
Blue:	2.1645–2.1642 in.	54.980–54.971 mm
Undersize 1		
Red:	2.1551–2.1547 in.	54.740–54.730 mm
Blue:	2.1547–2.1543 in.	54.730–54.721 mm
Undersize 2		
Red:	2.1452–2.1448 in.	54.490–54.480 mm
Blue:	2.1448–2.1445 in.	54.480–54.471 mm
Undersize 3		
Red:	2.1354–2.1350 in.	54.240–54.230 mm
Blue:	2.1350–2.1346 in.	54.230–54.221 mm
Triple classification		
Standard size		
Yellow:	2.1647–2.1649 in.	54.984–54.990 mm
Green:	2.1644–2.1647 in.	54.977–54.983 mm
White:	2.1642–2.1644 in.	54.971–54.976 mm
Undersize 1, 0.25mm		
Yellow:	2.1549–2.1551 in.	54.734–54.740 mm
Green:	2.1546–2.1548 in.	54.727–54.733 mm
White:	2.1544–2.1546 in.	54.721–54.726 mm
Undersize 2, 0.50mm		
Yellow:	2.1450–2.1453 in.	54.484–54.490 mm
Green:	2.1447–2.1450 in.	54.477–54.483 mm
White:	2.1445–2.1447 in.	54.471–2.1447 mm

S14 ENGINE REBUILDING SPECIFICATIONS CHART

Component	U.S.	Metric
Undersize 3, 0.75mm		
Yellow:	2.1352–2.1354 in.	54.234–54.240 mm
Green:	2.1349–2.1351 in.	54.227–54.233 mm
White:	2.1347–2.1349 in.	54.221–54.226 mm
Crankshaft main bearing clearance		
Double classification:	0.0012–0.0027 in.	0.03–0.07 mm
Triple classification:	0.0008–0.0018 in.	0.020–0.046 mm
Crankshaft thrust bearing ground size		
Standard size:	1.1811 in.	30.0 mm
Oversize 1:	1.1890 in.	30.2 mm
Oversize 2:	1.1968 in.	30.4 mm
Oversize 3:	1.2047 in.	30.6 mm
Crankshaft end play:	0.0033–0.0068 in.	0.085–0.174 mm
Connecting rod bearing journal ground size		
Standard size:	1.8888–1.8894 in.	47.975–47.991 mm
Undersize 1, 0.25mm:	1.8789–1.8796 in.	47.725–47.741 mm
Undersize 2, 0.50mm:	1.8691–1.8697 in.	47.475–47.491 mm
Undersize 3, 0.75mm:	1.8592–1.8599 in.	47.225–47.241 mm
Connecting rod bearing clearance		
Standard classification:	0.0012–0.0027 in.	0.03–0.07 mm
Double classification:	0.0008–0.0022 in.	0.020–0.055 mm
Crankshaft runout at center main:	0.004 in.	0.1 mm
Connecting rods		
Bushing diameter		
Outside:	0.9449–0.9457 in.	24.000–24.021 mm
Inside:	0.8669–0.8671 in.	22.020–22.024 mm
Maximum weight deviation in engine, without bearing shells		
Total:	± 0.14 oz.	± 4g
Big end:	± 0.07 oz.	± 2g
Small end:	± 0.07 oz.	± 2g
Big end bore		
Red:	2.0427–2.0475 in.	52.000–52.008 mm
Blue:	2.0476–2.0479 in.	52.009–52.016 mm
Standard:	2.0472–2.0476 in.	52.000–52.010 mm
Pistons		
Piston diameter-measured 0.236 in. (6.00mm) from bottom of the skirt		
Standard size:	3.675 in.	93.35 mm
Intemediate size:	3.677 in.	93.40 mm
Overbore 1:	3.683 in.	93.55 mm
Overbore 2:	3.691 in.	93.75 mm
Piston clearance		
New engine:	0.0012–0.0024 in.	0.03–0.06 mm
Used engine:	0.006 in.	0.15 mm
Piston rings		
Top compression		
End clearance:	0.0118–0.0216 in.	0.30–0.55 mm
Side clearance:	0.0023–0.0035 in.	0.06–0.09 mm
Bottom compression		
End clearance:	0.0118–0.0216 in.	0.30–0.55 mm
Side clearance:	0.0023–0.0035 in.	0.06–0.09 mm
Oil control		
End clearance:	0.0098–0.0196 in.	0.25–0.50 mm
Side clearance:	0.0007–0.0019 in.	0.02–0.05 mm
Camshaft		
End play:	0.004–0.006 in.	0.1–0.15 mm
Bearing clearance:	0.0011–0.0021 in.	0.027–0.053 mm
Tappet bore diameter:	1.4764–1.4770 in.	37.500–37.516 mm
Tappet bore clearance:	0.0010–0.0026 in.	0.025–0.066 mm

S14 ENGINE REBUILDING SPECIFICATIONS CHART

Component	U.S.	Metric
Valves		
Valve lash		
Cold:	0.010–0.014 in.	0.26–0.35 mm
Operating temperature:	0.013–0.015 in.	0.34–0.39 mm
Head edge thickness		
Intake:	0.020 in.	0.50 mm
Exhaust:	0.037 in.	0.95 mm
Head diameter		
Intake:	1.457 in.	37 mm
Exhaust:	1.260 in.	32 mm
Stem diameter		
Standard size:	0.275 in.	7.0 mm
Oversize 1:	0.279 in.	7.1 mm
Oversize 2:	0.283 in.	7.2 mm
Stem to guide tilt clearance		
Intake:	0.025 in.	0.65 mm
Exhaust:	0.031 in.	0.80 mm
Oil pump		
Pressure at idle:	7–28 psi	0.5–2.0 bar
Pressure at top speed:	57–85 psi	4.0–6.0 bar
Pressure relief valve spring length		
Operating pressure valve:	2.677 in.	68.0 mm
Bypass pressure valve:	1.732 in.	44 mm
Vibration damper		
Radial runout, maximum:	0.012 in.	0.3 mm
Axial runout, maximum:	0.012 in.	0.3 mm

84273133

S38 ENGINE REBUILDING SPECIFICATIONS CHART

Component	U.S.	Metric
Cylinder block		
Cylinder bore		
Standard size:	3.6771–3.6775 in.	93.40–93.41 mm
Intemediate size:	3.6791–3.6795 in.	93.45–93.46 mm
Overbore 1:	3.6850–3.6854 in.	93.60–94.61 mm
Overbore 2:	3.6929–3.6933 in.	93.80–93.81 mm
Maximum out-of-round:	0.0002 in.	0.005 mm
Maximum taper:	0.0004 in.	0.01 mm
Cylinder head		
Cylinder head height		
New height:	3.7767–3.7822 in.	95.93–96.07 mm
Minimum machined height:	not recommended	not recommended
Valve guide total length:	1.7022–1.718 in.	43.3–43.7 mm
Valve guide head bore diameter		
Standard size:	0.4717 in.	12.0 mm
Overbore 1:	0.4796 in.	12.2 mm
Overbore 2:	0.4953 in.	12.4 mm
Valve guide installed inside diameter		
Standard size:	0.2756 in.	7.0 mm
Overbore 1:	0.2796 in.	7.1 mm
Overbore 2:	0.2835 in.	7.2 mm
Valve guide installing temperature		
Cylinder head:	+300 °F.	+150 °C.
Valve guide:	−240 °F.	−150°C.
Valve guide protrusion:	0.5897 in.	15 mm
Valve seat angle:	35/45/60 degrees	35/45/60 degrees
Valve seat width		
Intake:	0.047–0.051 in.	1.2–1.3 mm
Exhaust:	0.055–0.059 in.	1.4–1.5 mm
Valve seat diameter		
Intake:	1.441–1.445 in.	36.6–36.7 mm
Exhaust:	1.236–1.240 in.	31.4–31.5 mm
Crankshaft		
Main bearing diameter		
Double classification		
Standard size		
Standard size		
Red:	2.358–2.357 in.	59.990–59.980 mm
Blue:	2.358–2.357 in.	59.980–59.971 mm
Undersize 1		
Red:	2.349–2.348 in.	59.740–59.730 mm
Blue:	2.348–2.347 in.	59.730–59.721 mm
Undersize 2		
Red:	2.339–2.338 in.	59.490–59.480 mm
Blue:	2.338–2.339 in.	59.480–59.471 mm
Undersize 3		
Red:	2.3313–2.3309 in.	59.240–59.230 mm
Blue:	2.3319–2.3316 in.	59.230–59.221 mm
Triple classification		
Standard size		
Yellow:	2.3616–2.3618 in.	59.984–59.990 mm
Green:	2.3613–2.3615in.	59.977–59.983 mm
White:	2.3610–2.3612 in.	59.971–59.976 mm
Undersize 1, 0.25mm		
Yellow:	2.3517–2.3520 in.	59.734–59.740 mm
Green:	2.3514–2.3517 in.	59.727–59.733 mm
White:	2.3512–2.3514 in.	59.721–59.726 mm
Undersize 2, 0.50mm		
Yellow:	2.3419–2.3421 in.	59.484–59.490 mm
Green:	2.3416–2.3418 in.	59.477–59.483 mm
White:	2.3414–2.3416 in.	59.471–59.476 mm

S38 ENGINE REBUILDING SPECIFICATIONS CHART

Component	U.S.	Metric
Undersize 3, 0.75mm		
Yellow:	2.3320–2.3323 in.	59.234–59.240 mm
Green:	2.3318–2.3320 in.	59.227–59.233 mm
White:	2.3315–2.3317 in.	59.221–59.226 mm
Crankshaft main bearing clearance		
Double classification:	0.0012–0.0027 in.	0.03–0.07 mm
Triple classification:	0.0008–0.0018 in.	0.020–0.046 mm
Crankshaft thrust bearing ground size		
Standard size:	1.1811 in.	30.0 mm
Oversize 1:	1.1890 in.	30.2 mm
Oversize 2:	1.1968 in.	30.4 mm
Oversize 3:	1.2047 in.	30.6 mm
Crankshaft end play:	0.0033–0.0068 in.	0.085–0.174 mm
Connecting rod bearing journal ground size		
Standard size:	1.8888–1.8894 in.	47.975–47.991 mm
Undersize 1, 0.25mm:	1.8789–1.8796 in.	47.725–47.741 mm
Undersize 2, 0.50mm:	1.8691–1.8697 in.	47.475–47.491 mm
Undersize 3, 0.75mm:	1.8592–1.8599 in.	47.225–47.241 mm
Connecting rod bearing clearance		
Standard classification:	0.0012–0.0027 in.	0.03–0.07 mm
Double classification:	0.0008–0.0022 in.	0.020–0.055 mm
Crankshaft runout at center main:	0.004 in.	0.1 mm
Connecting rods		
Bushing diameter		
Outside:	0.9449–0.9457 in.	24.000–24.021 mm
Inside:	0.8669–0.8671 in.	22.020–22.024 mm
Maximum weight deviation in engine, without bearing shells		
Total:	± 0.14 oz.	± 4g
Big end:	± 0.07 oz.	± 2g
Small end:	± 0.07 oz.	± 2g
Big end bore		
Red:	2.0427–2.0475 in.	52.000–52.008 mm
Blue:	2.0476–2.0479 in.	52.009–52.016 mm
Standard:	2.0472–2.0476 in.	52.000–52.010 mm
Pistons		
Piston diameter-measured 0.236 in. (6.00mm) from bottom of the skirt		
Standard size:	3.675 in.	93.35 mm
Intemediate size:	3.677 in.	93.40 mm
Overbore 1:	3.683 in.	93.55 mm
Overbore 2:	3.691 in.	93.75 mm
Piston clearance		
New engine:	0.0012–0.0024 in.	0.03–0.06 mm
Used engine:	0.006 in.	0.15 mm
Piston rings		
Top compression		
End clearance:	0.0118–0.0216 in.	0.30–0.55 mm
Side clearance:	0.0023–0.0035 in.	0.06–0.09 mm
Bottom compression		
End clearance:	0.0118–0.0216 in.	0.30–0.55 mm
Side clearance:	0.0023–0.0035 in.	0.06–0.09 mm
Oil control		
End clearance:	0.0098–0.0196 in.	0.25–0.50 mm
Side clearance:	0.0007–0.0019 in.	0.02–0.05 mm
Camshaft		
End play:	0.004–0.006 in.	0.1–0.15 mm
Bearing clearance:	0.0011–0.0021 in.	0.027–0.053 mm
Tappet bore diameter:	1.4764–1.4770 in.	37.500–37.516 mm
Tappet bore clearance:	0.0010–0.0026 in.	0.025–0.066 mm

84273135

S38 ENGINE REBUILDING SPECIFICATIONS CHART

Component	U.S.	Metric
Valves		
Valve lash		
Cold:	0.011–0.013 in.	0.28–0.33 mm
Head edge thickness		
Intake:	0.020 in.	0.50 mm
Exhaust:	0.037 in.	0.95 mm
Head diameter		
Intake:	1.457 in.	37 mm
Exhaust:	1.260 in.	32 mm
Stem diameter		
Standard size:	0.275 in.	7.0 mm
Oversize 1:	0.279 in.	7.1 mm
Oversize 2:	0.283 in.	7.2 mm
Stem to guide tilt clearance		
Intake:	0.025 in.	0.65 mm
Exhaust:	0.031 in.	0.80 mm
Oil pump		
Pressure at idle:	7–28 psi	0.5–2.0 bar
Pressure at top speed:	43–57 psi	3.0–4.0 bar
Pressure relief valve spring length		
Operating pressure valve:	2.677 in.	68.0 mm
Bypass pressure valve:	1.732 in.	44 mm
Vibration damper		
Radial runout, maximum:	0.008 in.	0.2 mm
Axial runout, maximum:	0.016 in.	0.4 mm

84273136

TORQUE SPECIFICATIONS

Component	U.S.	Metric
Air injection check valve to hose		
S38 engine:	19–23 ft. lbs.	26–32 Nm
Automatic transmission cooling lines		
Adapter connection to transmission:	25–27 ft. lbs.	35–38 Nm
Coupling nut connection to radiator:	13–15 ft. lbs.	18–21 Nm
Coupling nut connection to transmission:	13–15 ft. lbs.	18–21 Nm
Hollow bolt connection to transmission:	25–27 ft. lbs.	35–38 Nm
Hollow bolt connection to oil cooler:	18–21 ft. lbs.	25–28 Nm
Camshaft bearing cap bolts		
M42 engine:	10–12 ft. lbs.	13–17 Nm
M50 engine:	10–12 ft. lbs.	13–17 Nm
S14 engine:	15–17 ft. lbs.	20–23 Nm
S38 engine:	15–17 ft. lbs.	20–23 Nm
Camshaft flange bolts		
M30 engine:	99–107 ft. lbs.	137–147 Nm
Camshaft oiling rail hollow bolt		
M20 engine:	4–6 ft. lbs.	6–8 Nm
M30 engine:	8–9 ft. lbs.	11–13 Nm
Camshaft sprocket bolt		
M20 engine:	47–51 ft. lbs.	65–70 Nm
M30 engine:	5 ft. lbs.	7 Nm
M42 engine:	10–12 ft. lbs.	13–17 Nm
M50 engine:	16 ft. lbs.	22 Nm
S14 engine:	6–7 ft. lbs.	9–10 Nm
S38 engine:	6–7 ft. lbs.	9–10 Nm
Connecting rod bearing caps		
M20 engine		
Bolts		
Step 1:	17 ft. lbs.	23 Nm
Step 2:	+ 70 degrees turn	+ 70 degrees turn
M30 engine		
Bolts:	38–41 ft. lbs.	51–57 Nm
M42 engine		
Bolts		
Step 1:	17 ft. lbs.	23 Nm
Step 2:	+ 70 degrees turn	+ 70 degrees turn
M50 engine		
Bolts		
Step 1:	17 ft. lbs.	23 Nm
Step 2:	+ 70 degrees turn	+ 70 degrees turn
S14 engine		
Bolts		
Step 1:	7 ft. lbs.	9.5 Nm
Step 2:	22 ft. lbs.	30 Nm
Step 3:	+ 60–62 degrees turn	+ 60–62 degrees turn
S38 engine		
Bolts		
Step 1:	7 ft. lbs.	9.5 Nm
Step 2:	22 ft. lbs.	30 Nm
Step 3:	+ 60–62 degrees turn	+ 60–62 degrees turn
Coolant pipe to cylinder head		
S14 and S38 engines:	8.0–8.5 ft. lbs.	11–12 Nm
Coolant pipe plug-rear		
S38 engines:	21–29 ft. lbs.	30–40 Nm
Crankcase coolant drain plug		
All	36–40 ft. lbs.	50–56 Nm

84273137

TORQUE SPECIFICATIONS

Component	U.S.	Metric
Crankshaft hub bolt		
M20 engine:	281–309 ft. lbs.	390–430 Nm
M30 engine:	311–325 ft. lbs.	430–450 Nm
M42 engine:	217–231 ft. lbs.	300–320 Nm
M50 engine:	281–309 ft. lbs.	390–430 Nm
S14 engine:	311–325 ft. lbs.	430–450 Nm
S38 engine		
Step 1:	43 ft. lbs.	58 Nm
Step 2:	+ 60 degree turn	+ 60 degree turn
Step 3:	+ 60 degree turn	+ 60 degree turn
Step 4:	+ 30 degree turn	+ 30 degree turn
Cylinder head bolts		
M42 engine		
Step 1:	22–25 ft. lbs.	30–35 Nm
Step 2:	+ 90–95 degree turn	+ 90–95 degree turn
Step 3:	+ 90–95 degree turn	+ 90–95 degree turn
M50 engine		
Step 1:	22–25 ft. lbs.	30–35 Nm
Step 2:	+ 90–95 degree turn	+ 90–95 degree turn
Step 3:	+ 90–95 degree turn	+ 90–95 degree turn
Torx M6:	7.2 ft. lbs.	9.9 Nm
S14 engine		
Step 1:	35–37 ft. lbs.	48–52 Nm
Step 2:	57–59 ft.	78–82 Nm
Step 3:	wait 15 minutes	wait 15 minutes
Step 4:	71–73 ft. lbs.	98–102 Nm
M20 engine		
Hex head bolts		
Step 1:	29–33 ft. lbs.	40–45 Nm
Step 2:	wait 15 minutes	wait 15 minutes
Step 3:	43–47 ft. lbs.	55–65 Nm
Step 4:	run engine 25 minutes	run engine 25 minutes
Step 5:	+ 25–30 degree turn	+ 25–30 degree turn
Torx head bolts		
Step 1:	22 ft. lbs.	30 Nm
Step 2:	+ 90 degrees turn	+ 90 degrees turn
Step 3:	+ 90 degrees turn	+ 90 degrees turn
M30 engine		
Step 1:	42–44 ft. lbs.	58–62 Nm
Step 2:	wait 20 minutes	wait 20 minutes
Step 3:	57–59 ft. lbs.	78–82 Nm
Step 4:	run engine 25 minutes	run engine 25 minutes
Step 5:	+ 30–40 degrees turn	+ 30–40 degrees turn
S38 engine		
Step 1:	35–37 ft. lbs.	48–52 Nm
Step 2:	57–59 ft.	78–82 Nm
Step 3:	wait 15 minutes	wait 15 minutes
Step 4:	71–73 ft. lbs.	98–102 Nm
Damper to crankshaft hub		
All:	16.5–17.5 ft. lbs.	22–24 Nm
Distributor rotor to rotor adapter	1.9–2.1 ft. lbs.	2.6–3.0 Nm
Distributor rotor adapter to camshaft		
Except M20 engine:	16.5–17.5 ft. lbs.	22–24 Nm
M20 engine:	39–47 ft. lbs.	55–65 Nm
Engine mounts to axle carrier		
M8 bolts:	16 ft. lbs.	22 Nm
M10 bolts:	30 ft. lbs.	42 Nm
Engine mounts to engine block		
M8 bolts:	16 ft. lbs.	22 Nm
M10 bolts:	30 ft. lbs.	42 Nm

TORQUE SPECIFICATIONS

Component	U.S.	Metric
Exhaust manifold		
M20 engine		
Step 1:	coat threads with sealer	coat threads with sealer
Step 2:	16–18 ft. lbs.	22–25 Nm
M30 engine		
Step 1:	coat threads with sealer	coat threads with sealer
Step 2:	16–18 ft. lbs.	22–25 Nm
M42 engine:	16–18 ft. lbs.	22–24 Nm
M50 engine:	14 ft. lbs.	19 Nm
S14 engine:	6.5–8.0 ft. lbs.	9–11 Nm
S38 engine		
M6 bolts:	6.5–8.0 ft. lbs.	9–11 Nm
M8 bolts:	14–17 ft. lbs.	19–23 Nm
Exhaust system		
Bracket to rear subframe:	17 ft. lbs.	24 Nm
Clamp to exhaust carrier:	16–17 ft. lbs.	22–24 Nm
Clamp to catalytic converter:	16–17 ft. lbs.	22–24 Nm
Exhaust pipe to manifold:		
With spring:		
Initial torque to compress spring:	5.5–8.5 ft. lbs.	8–12 Nm
Final step:	loosen 1½ turns	loosen 1½ turns
Without spring:		
Initial torque:	25 ft. lbs.	35 Nm
Final torque:	40 ft. lbs.	55 Nm
Rear muffler clamp:	10 ft. lbs.	14 Nm
Transmission carrier:	16–17 ft. lbs.	22–24 Nm
Triangular flange:	15–17 ft. lbs.	20–24 Nm
Fan coupling-left hand threads		
All:	29–36 ft. lbs.	40–50 Nm
Fan to clutch		
All:	6–7 ft. lbs.	8–10 Nm
Front cover (not timing cover)		
M6 bolts:	6.5–8.0 ft. lbs.	9–11 Nm
M8 bolts:	13–15 ft. lbs.	18–22 Nm
Flywheel-to-crankshaft		
All	82–94 ft. lbs.	113–130 Nm
Intake manifold		
M20 engine:	16–18 ft. lbs.	22–25 Nm
M30 engine:	16–18 ft. lbs.	22–25 Nm
M42 engine:	10–12 ft. lbs.	13–17 Nm
M50 engine:	10–12 ft. lbs.	13–17 Nm
S14 engine:	6.5–8.0 ft. lbs.	9–11 Nm
S38 engine		
M6 bolts:	6.5–8.0 ft. lbs.	9–11 Nm
M8 bolts:	14–17 ft. lbs.	20–24 Nm
Intake manifold support		
All:	15–17 ft. lbs.	20–24 Nm
Intermediate shaft sprocket bolts		
M20 engine:	39–47 ft. lbs.	55–65 Nm

TORQUE SPECIFICATIONS

Component	U.S.	Metric
Main bearing cap		
M20 engine:	42–46 ft. lbs.	58–63 Nm
M30 engine:	42–46 ft. lbs.	58–63 Nm
M42 engine		
Step 1:	14–18 ft. lbs.	20–25 Nm
Step 2:	+ 47–53 degrees turn	+ 47–53 degrees turn
M50 engine		
Step 1:	14–18 ft. lbs.	20–25 Nm
Step 2:	+ 47–53 degrees turn	+ 47–53 degrees turn
S14 engine		
Step 1:	14–18 ft. lbs.	20–25 Nm
Step 2:	+ 47–53 degrees turn	+ 47–53 degrees turn
S38 engine		
Step 1:	14–18 ft. lbs.	20–25 Nm
Step 2:	+ 47–53 degrees turn	+ 47–53 degrees turn
Oil cooler		
Lines to filter housing connections:	22–29 ft. lbs.	30–40 Nm
Lines to oil cooler connections:	18.0–21.5 ft. lbs.	25–30 Nm
Line holder bolt:	3.5–4.0 ft. lbs.	5–6 Nm
Mounting bolts	9–11 ft. lbs.	12–15 Nm
Oil drain plug		
Wrench size 17mm:	24–26 ft. lbs.	33–36 Nm
Wrench size 19mm:	43–46 ft. lbs.	59–64 Nm
Oil filter cover retaining bolt-full flow		
All	20–24 ft. lbs.	27–33 Nm
Oil filter-spin on		
M20 engine	hand tighten	hand tighten
S14 engine	hand tighten	hand tighten
Oil filter housing		
M20 engine	25–33 ft. lbs.	35–45 Nm
M30 engine	14–17 ft. lbs.	20–24 Nm
M50 engine	14–17 ft. lbs.	20–24 Nm
S38 engine	14–17 ft. lbs.	20–24 Nm
Oil filter plug		
S38 engine	12–16 ft. lbs.	17–23 Nm
Oil pan		
M6 bolts:	6.5–8.0 ft. lbs.	9–11 Nm
M8 bolts:	13–15 ft. lbs.	18–22 Nm
Oil pressure bore plug		
S14 engine:	16–20 ft. lbs.	22–28 Nm
S38 engine:	23–25 ft. lbs.	31–35 Nm
Oil pressure switch		
M20 engine	22–29 ft. lbs.	30–40 Nm
M30 engine	22–29 ft. lbs.	30–40 Nm
M42 engine	17–22 ft. lbs.	24–31 Nm
M50 engine	12–17 ft. lbs.	17–23 Nm
S14 engine	12–17 ft. lbs.	17–23 Nm
S38 engine	12–17 ft. lbs.	17–23 Nm
Oil pump cover retaining bolts		
All	6–7 ft. lbs.	8–10 Nm
Oil pump high pressure relief valve		
M20 engine	18–22 ft. lbs.	25–30 Nm
M30 engine	25–29 ft. lbs.	35–40 Nm
Oil pump retaining bolts		
All	15–17 ft. lbs.	20–22 Nm

TORQUE SPECIFICATIONS

Component	U.S.	Metric
Oil pump sprocket retaining bolts		
M30 engine-M6 bolts	6–7 ft. lbs.	8–10 Nm
M30 engine-M10 bolt	18–22 ft. lbs.	25–30 Nm
M50 engine-M6 bolt	18 ft. lbs.	25 Nm
S14 engine-M10 bolt	18–22 ft. lbs.	25–30 Nm
S38 engine-M10 bolt	18–22 ft. lbs.	25–30 Nm
Oxygen sensor		
All:	36–44 ft. lbs.	50–60 Nm
Pulley to crankshaft hub		
All:	16.5–17.5 ft. lbs.	22–24 Nm
Radiator		
Drain plug	1.1–1.9 ft. lbs.	1.5–3 Nm
Expansion tank to radiator	6.0–6.5 ft. lbs.	8–9 Nm
Self tapping mounting screw	6.0–6.5 ft. lbs.	8–9 Nm
Mounting bolt	6.5–7.0 ft. lbs.	9–10 Nm
Rear main seal housing		
M6 bolts:	6.5–8.0 ft. lbs.	9–11 Nm
M8 bolts:	13–15 ft. lbs.	18–22 Nm
Reversing wheel to cover		
M20 engine:	15–17 ft. lbs.	20–22 Nm
Starter		
Mounting bolts	34–36 ft. lbs.	47–50 Nm
Battery terminal connection		
Plastic	0.7–1.1 ft. lbs.	1.0–1.5 Nm
Metal	3.6–4.4 ft. lbs.	5.0–6.0 Nm
Temperature sensors and switches		
Radiator temperature switch:	9.5–10.0 ft. lbs.	13–14 Nm
Expansion tank level switch:	2.2–2.5 ft. lbs.	3.0–3.5 Nm
Except above:	12.5–13.5 ft. lbs.	17–19 Nm
Tensioner wheel holder to block		
M20 engine:	15–17 ft. lbs.	20–22 Nm
Timing case to cylinder head bolts		
S14 and S38 engines:		
M7 bolts:	10–12 ft. lbs.	13–17 Nm
M8 bolts:	14.5–15.5 ft. lbs.	20–22 Nm
Timing chain housing bolts		
All		
M6 bolts:	6.5–8.0 ft. lbs.	9–11 Nm
M8 bolts:	15–17 ft. lbs.	20–24 Nm
Timing chain tensioner piston housing		
M50 engine:	35–37 ft. lbs.	48–52 Nm
S14 engine:	35–37 ft. lbs.	48–52 Nm
S38 engine:	35–37 ft. lbs.	48–52 Nm
Timing chain tensioner piston plug		
M30 engine:	21–29 ft. lbs.	30–40 Nm
M42 engine:	17–19 ft. lbs.	23–27 Nm
M50 engine:	28–30 ft. lbs.	38–42 Nm
S14 engine:	28–30 ft. lbs.	38–42 Nm
S38 engine:	28–30 ft. lbs.	38–42 Nm
Thermostat housing		
All:	6–7 ft. lbs.	8–10 Nm
Thermostat housing bleeder screw		
All:	4–7 ft. lbs.	6–10 Nm
Valve cover		
All:	6.5–7.5 ft. lbs.	8–10 Nm
Valve lash adjusting eccentric nut		
All:	6.5–7.5 ft. lbs.	8–10 Nm

TORQUE SPECIFICATIONS

Component	U.S.	Metric
Water pump-to-block		
All		
M6 bolts:	6–7 ft. lbs.	8–10 Nm
M8 bolts:	15–17 ft. lbs.	20–24 Nm
Water pump pulley to water pump		
All		
M6 bolts:	6–7 ft. lbs.	8–10 Nm

84273142

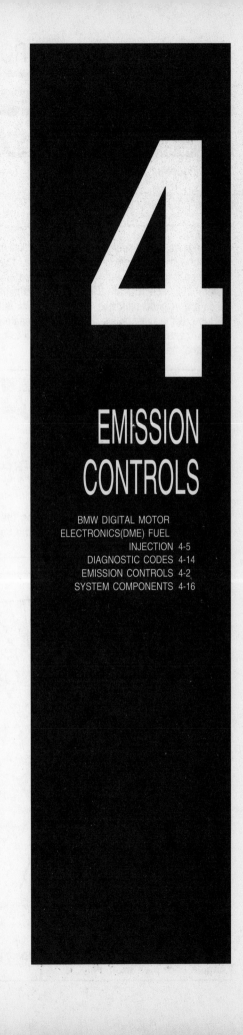

4

EMISSION CONTROLS

EMISSION CONTROLS

Crankcase Ventilation System

◆ **See Figures 1 and 2**

OPERATION

All engines use a sealed crankcase ventilation system that does not allow fresh air into the crankcase. This means the crankcase is under vacuum at all times and any leak in the system is a vacuum leak. It is important to make sure all hoses are in good condition and the dipstick is firmly sealed in the tube. If the dipstick tube is not firmly seated, a vacuum leak will occur which may cause engine oil to be drawn into the intake manifold.

The crankcase ventilation system draws the crankcase vapors a connection on the valve cover. The vapors are drawn into the intake air stream and burned with the air and fuel mixture. This reduces the emission of hydrocarbons into the atmosphere.

SERVICE

◆ **See Figures 3 and 4**

The crankcase ventilation system is essentially maintenance free. There are no mechanical portions that need to be adjusted, nor are there any parts that need to be replaced on a scheduled basis.

84274001

Fig. 1 View of the M42 engine showing the crankcase ventilation breather hose connecting the valve cover to the intake manifold

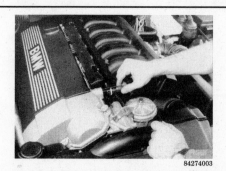

84274003

Fig. 3 Crankcase ventilation connector — M50 engine

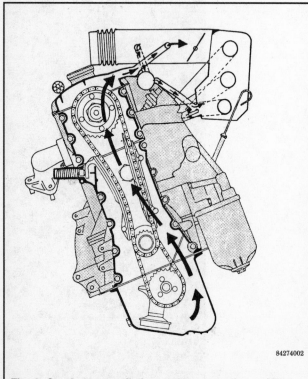

84274002

Fig. 2 Crankcase ventilation system operation — M30 engine shown as example

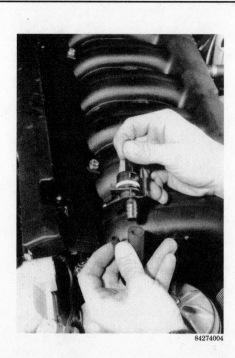

84274004

Fig. 4 Unplug the hoses and check for blockages and cracked hoses — M50 engine

The only checks that can be made to the system is for plugged or cracked hoses and faulty connections. Pull the hoses off the connections and check for plugging. Inspect the hoses for cracking. Check that the hoses are fully seated on the connection points.

Evaporative Emission Controls

OPERATION

▶ **See Figure 5**

The evaporative emission control system consists of the fuel tank, expansion tank, carbon canister, fuel filler cap, solenoid-activated purge valve and connecting lines or hoses. The filler cap is a check valve that allows air into the tank but does not allow vapors out.

With the engine off, gasoline vapors are collected in the expansion tank, while liquid fuel is condensed and flows back to the fuel tank. Vapors are routed to the carbon canister where they are stored until the engine is started. They are drawn from the carbon canister by engine vacuum. When the ignition switch is **ON**, the purge valve receives 12 volts from the main DME relay. The control unit will complete the circuit by providing ground and the valve will close.

As the appropriate conditions are met, the control unit will provide or deny ground to cycle the valve open and closed. When the valve is open, manifold vacuum pulls fresh air into the canister and the air/vapor mixture is drawn into the intake manifold or throttle body. This air flow is not measured by the air mass meter but the duty cycle of the valve is accounted for by the control unit. If the hose is leaking between the valve the intake manifold, there will be a vacuum leak.

The purge valve can also be referred to as the venting valve. The carbon canister is also known as a charcoal canister. These terms can be used interchangeably.

➡**On vehicles equipped with the M20 engine, the molded hose that connects the purge valve to the intake manifold can crack and cause a rough idle. Check the small end of the hose where it is connected to the intake manifold for damage caused by the clamp and replace if necessary.**

Testing

SOLENOID PURGE VALVE

▶ **See Figure 6**

1. Unplug the purge valve electrical connector. The valve located under the air intake hose or intake manifold. It has 1 electrical connector and 2 vacuum lines, 1 leading to manifold vacuum and the other to the carbon canister.
2. The coil resistance should be 25-65 ohms.
3. Attach a hand vacuum pump and gauge to the intake manifold side of the valve. Supply 12 volts to the valve to hold the valve closed. Apply 15-21 in. Hg. (500-700 mbar) of vacuum to the valve.
4. Wait 20 seconds and check the gauge to determine if a vacuum has been lost. If a drop of more than 1.5 in. Hg. (50 mbar) occurs, the valve must be replaced.
5. If the valve is good, but the system is still suspect, reinstall the valve, then start and warm the engine to normal operating temperature.
6. When the engine has reached normal operating temperature and the system should be normally operating, carefully

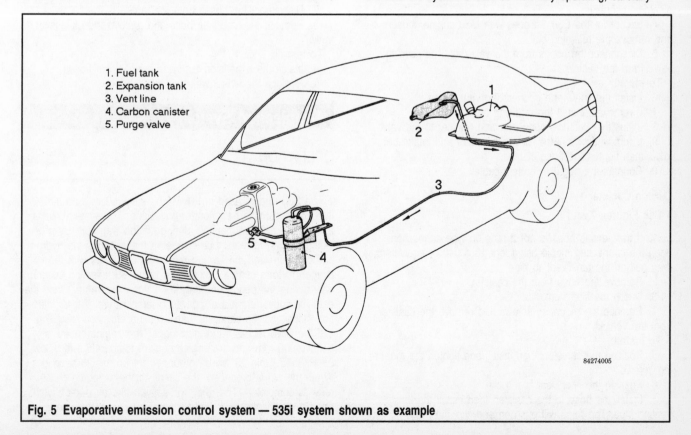

1. Fuel tank
2. Expansion tank
3. Vent line
4. Carbon canister
5. Purge valve

84274005

Fig. 5 Evaporative emission control system — 535i system shown as example

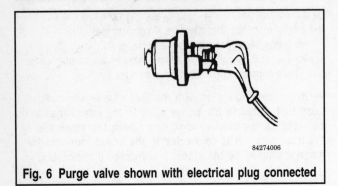

Fig. 6 Purge valve shown with electrical plug connected

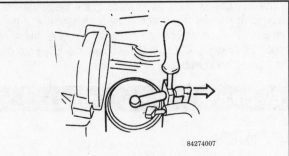

Fig. 7 Disconnecting the venting hose using tool 16 1 040 or equivalent, from the carbon canister

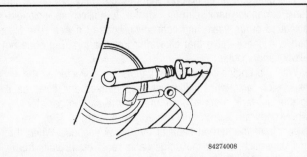

Fig. 8 Venting lines shown disconnected from the carbon canister

unplug the electrical connector from the valve. Connect a voltmeter to the connector terminals; the meter should cycle between 0-12 volts as the control unit supplies and denies ground.

7. If there is no voltage, check the wiring between the valve, DME relay and the control unit for continuity. If the wiring is good, the control unit is faulty.

8. If the voltage is **ON** continuously, turn the ignition switch **OFF** and check for a short in the wiring or short to ground.

REMOVAL & INSTALLATION

Solenoid Purge Valve

1. Disconnect the negative battery cable.
2. For the E36 3 Series with M50 engine, open the hose clamps, then remove the intake bellows and air mass sensor to provide access.
3. Lift off or compress the retainer, then unplug the valve electrical connector.
4. Except for the E36 3 Series with M50 engine, loosen and remove the retaining bolt.
5. Disconnect the hoses from the valve, then remove the valve from the vehicle.

To install:
6. Install the valve and connect the vent hoses.
7. If removed, install the retaining bolt.
8. Install the electrical connector and retainer to the valve.
9. If removed, install the air mass sensor and intake bellows, then tighten the hose clamps.
10. Connect the negative battery cable.

Carbon Canister
▶ **See Figures 7 and 8**

1. If the venting hose is not a slide-on type connection, open the connecting nipple using tool 16 1 040 or equivalent, then pull off the tank venting pipe.
2. Remove the hose from the canister.
3. Unclip the filter vent.
4. Remove the mounting screws and remove the canister from the vehicle.

To install:
5. Position the canister, then install and tighten the mounting screws.
6. Position the filter vent in the clip.
7. Install the hose to the canister, then install the tank venting pipe. The hose will push on and clip into place.

Expansion Tank
▶ **See Figure 9**

1. Remove the right rear wheel. Remove the wheel well rear trim.
2. Disconnect the hoses from the tank.
3. Remove the mounting bolts and remove the expansion tank.

To install:
4. Install the expansion tank and connect the hoses.
5. Replace the wheel well trim and the wheel.

Air Injection System

OPERATION

The S38 engine used in the M5 is equipped with an air injection system to help control emissions. The system injects air into the exhaust manifold during engine warm-up. By providing oxygen to the unburned fuel in the exhaust, the hydrocarbons burn and the carbon monoxide combines with the oxygen to form carbon dioxide and water. Air injection occurs only during the period of catalytic converter warm-up. Once the catalytic converters are at operating temperature, the air injection stops and the catalysts take over the emission reduction.

If the DME receives the start signal, the engine speed is below 4600 rpm and the engine coolant temperature is below 86°F.(30°C.), pin 23 will be grounded for up to 125 seconds. When the pin is grounded, the circuit to the air pump clutch relay is completed. The relay will activate the air pump clutch and an electrically controlled vacuum valve. The vacuum valve

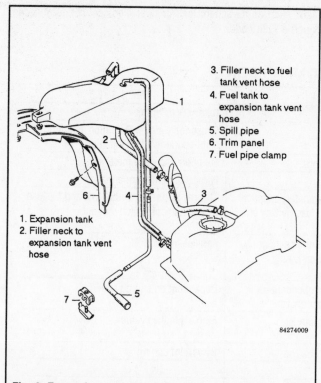

3. Filler neck to fuel tank vent hose
4. Fuel tank to expansion tank vent hose
5. Spill pipe
6. Trim panel
7. Fuel pipe clamp

1. Expansion tank
2. Filler neck to expansion tank vent hose

84274009

Fig. 9 Expansion tank mounting and connections — E34 5 Series

will allow vacuum to pass to a vacuum controlled air valve and the valve will open. Air from the pump will pass through the valve, through a check valve and into the injection manifold.

The vacuum controlled valve, when closed, will force the air to be released into the atmosphere via the pressure control valve. The valve also prevents air from being drawn into the manifold when it is not needed. The check valve prevents exhaust gases from reversing into the system.

The air pump clutch relay is located in the ... the engine compartment along with the DME uni... pump is located on the engine and is driven by a b... electrically controlled vacuum valve is next to the idle c... valve, below the intake runners for cylinders 1 and 2. The vacuum controlled air valve is on the front right side of the engine near the check valve. the pressure control valve is located in the same line bolted to the block.

REMOVAL & INSTALLATION

Air Injection Manifold

1. Disconnect the negative battery cable. Remove the exhaust system. Drain the coolant below the level of the head. Disconnect the right side engine mount and ground strap.

2. Disconnect the air injection pipe at the check valve and the heat shield. Remove the fan cowl and coolant expansion tank. Remove the air pump air filter housing.

3. Lift the right side of the engine as far as possible without damaging any connections.

4. Remove the heat shield holder and the air injection pipe. It may be necessary to use an universal joint on an extension. There is a mounting tab at cylinder number 1.

   To install:

5. Clean the manifold mounting surfaces. Replace the air injection pipe gaskets and the air injection pipe. Torque to 25-33 ft. lbs. (35-45 Nm).

6. Install the heat shield. Lower the engine. Install the air pump filter, coolant expansion tank and the fan cowl. Connect the air injection pipe and tighten to 25-33 ft. lbs. (35-45 Nm). Install the heat shield holder.

7. Connect the ground strap and the engine mount. Torque to 30 ft. lbs. (42 Nm). Install the exhaust system and fill the cooling system. Connect the negative battery terminal.

BMW DIGITAL MOTOR ELECTRONICS (DME) FUEL INJECTION

General Information

▶ **See Figure 10**

All vehicles covered in this book are equipped with the Bosch Digital Motor Electronics (DME) system. The DME system operates the ignition and fuel injection systems with a single control unit. The DME is a very sophisticated computerized engine management system that works as well on a racing engine as it does on a street car.

➡ **For removal and installation procedures for the components of the DME system, refer to Section 5. This section contains the description and testing procedures for the DME system.**

The DME control unit accepts input signals from the intake air flow or air mass sensor, crankshaft pulse sensor, cylinder identifying sensor, coolant and air temperature sensors, an exhaust oxygen sensor, a throttle position switch and if so equipped, the automatic transmission control unit. Optimum fuel quantity and spark timing requirements are calculated based on sensor inputs and internal programs and are adjusted as required for each engine revolution. Output signals operate the idle control valve, fuel pump relay, fuel injectors and the ignition system. Fuel injectors are operated semi sequentially or sequentially depending on the engine. The air/fuel ratio, ignition timing and idle speed are not adjustable.

Most items of the DME system can be tested with a volt/ohm meter, however some in depth testing procedures that utilize the full power of the DME system can only be performed using the BMW Diagnostic Tester that only a dealer or specialty shop would own. This does not preclude the average person from working on the fuel injection as most problem can be diagnosed and solved using common tools and testing methods. A variety of test connectors is also required but some of these can be easily made up as needed. The control unit includes a self diagnostic program that will store fault codes.

The first step in repair or service to engine management systems is to gain as much information as possible, especially regarding intermittent problems. Also check any service records which may be available. Before checking fault codes, it is

...vious mechanical faults ...only indicates which ...blem. Simple mechanical faults such as a vacuum leak or poor electrical connection can cause a fault code.

DME SYSTEM COMPARISON

	DME 3.1	DME 1.1–1.3
	Direct, solid state	Rotary Distributor
	Camshaft sensor	Sensor on cylinder 6 ignition lead for semi-sequential fuel injection
Load sensing	Hot wire air mass metering	Volumetric air flow metering
Type of fuel injection	Fully sequential	Parallel or semi-sequential
Throttle position sensing	Throttle butterfly potentiometer; adaptive idle setting; part and full load by way of resistance value	Throttle butterfly switch, idle and full load by mechanical switch contact
Starting	Advance fuel pump run and injection; double spark (max. 250 ms); fully sequential injection	Parallel injection
Full load ignition timing	Altitude compensation; dependent on engine speed and cylinder charge	Dependent on engine speed
Idling control	Adaptive value with/without air conditioning	Single adaptive value
Model application identification	By mapped characteristic	By variant coding
Self-diagnostics	Extended	
Emergency running	Improved from DME 1.1–1.3	
Memory board	40 Kb	32 Kb
Plug pins	88	55
Electromagnetic compatibility	4X multilayer technique	Additional suppression

84274037

DME VERSION ENGINE APPLICATION

Year	Model	Engine Displacement Liters (cc)	Engine Series Identification	Fuel System ①	No. of Cylinders	Engine Type
1989	325i	2.5 (2494)	M20B25	M1.3	6	OHC
	325iC	2.5 (2494)	M20B25	M1.3	6	OHC
	325iX	2.5 (2494)	M20B25	M1.3	6	OHC
	M3	2.3 (2302)	S14B23	M1.2②	4	16V DOHC
	525i	2.5 (2494)	M20B25	M1.3	6	OHC
	535i	3.5 (3430)	M30B35	M1.3	6	OHC
1990	325i	2.5 (2494)	M20B25	M1.3	6	OHC
	325iC	2.5 (2494)	M20B25	M1.3	6	OHC
	325iX	2.5 (2494)	M20B25	M1.3	6	OHC
	M3	2.3 (2302)	S14B23	M1.2②	4	16V DOHC
	525i	2.5 (2494)	M20B25	M1.3	6	OHC
	535i	3.5 (3430)	M30B35	M1.3	6	OHC
1991	318i	1.8 (1796)	M42B18	M1.7	4	16V DOHC
	318iC	1.8 (1796)	M42B18	M1.7	4	16V DOHC
	318iS	1.8 (1796)	M42B18	M1.7	4	16V DOHC
	325i	2.5 (2494)	M20B25	M1.3	6	OHC
	325iC	2.5 (2494)	M20B25	M1.3	6	OHC
	325iX	2.5 (2494)	M20B25	M1.3	6	OHC
	M3	2.3 (2302)	S14B23	M1.2②	4	16V DOHC
	525i	2.5 (2494)	M20B25	M3.1	6	24V DOHC
	535i	3.5 (3430)	M30B35	M1.3	6	OHC
	M5	3.6 (3535)	S38B36	M1.2②	6	24V DOHC
1992-93	318i	1.8 (1796)	M42B18	M1.7	4	16V DOHC
	318iS	1.8 (1796)	M42B18	M1.7	4	16V DOHC
	318iC	1.8 (1796)	M42B18	M1.7	4	16V DOHC
	325i	2.5 (2494)	M50B25	M3.1	6	24V DOHC
	325iS	2.5 (2494)	M50B25	M3.1	6	24V DOHC
	325iC	2.5 (2494)	M20B25	M1.3	6	OHC
	525i	2.5 (2494)	M50B25	M3.1	6	24V DOHC
	525iT	2.5 (2494)	M50B25	M3.1	6	24V DOHC
	535i	3.5 (3430)	M30B35	M1.3	6	OHC
	M5	3.6 (3535)	S38B36	M1.2②	6	24V DOHC

OHC—Overhead Camshaft
DOHC—Double Overhead Camshaft
① Digital Motor Electronic
② Motorsport Motronics

84274038

➡**Never disconnect any wiring with the ignition switch ON. Always turn the ignition switch OFF when using an ohmmeter. Any time the battery or main power terminal is disconnected, the control unit fault memory will be erased. Make sure all codes have been retrieved before disconnecting the battery or removing the control unit connector.**

DME CONTROL UNIT AND RELAY

E30 3 Series

M20 ENGINE

The DME unit is located above the glove compartment. The fuel pump relay is mounted on a bracket on the left inner fender in front of the shock tower. There is a grouping of 3 relays. The forward relay is the main DME relay. The middle relay is the fuel pump relay. The rear most relay is the oxygen sensor heater relay.

M42 ENGINE

The DME unit is located above the glove compartment. The relays are mounted on the firewall above and to the right of the brake booster. The relay on the right is the main DME relay. The middle relay is the fuel pump relay. The leftmost relay is the oxygen sensor heater relay.

S14 ENGINE

The DME unit is located above the glove compartment. The relays are located on the far right of the firewall. The relay on the right is the evaporative purge relay. The middle relay is the main DME relay. The leftmost relay is for both the oxygen sensor heater and the fuel pump.

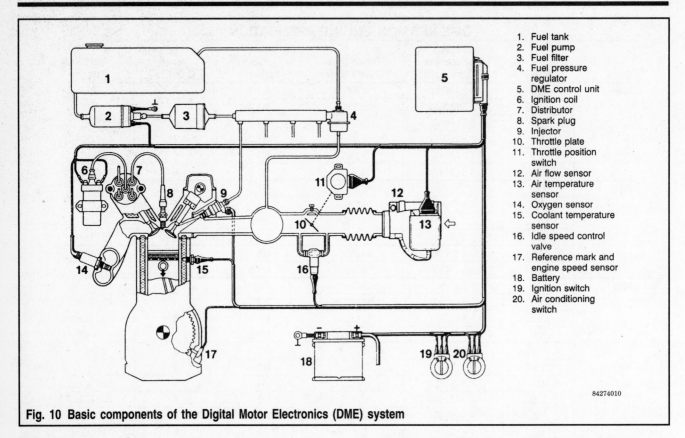

1. Fuel tank
2. Fuel pump
3. Fuel filter
4. Fuel pressure regulator
5. DME control unit
6. Ignition coil
7. Distributor
8. Spark plug
9. Injector
10. Throttle plate
11. Throttle position switch
12. Air flow sensor
13. Air temperature sensor
14. Oxygen sensor
15. Coolant temperature sensor
16. Idle speed control valve
17. Reference mark and engine speed sensor
18. Battery
19. Ignition switch
20. Air conditioning switch

84274010

Fig. 10 Basic components of the Digital Motor Electronics (DME) system

E36 3 Series

The DME unit is located behind a cover on the right side of the engine compartment firewall. The relays are located in the relay and fuse box on the left side of the engine compartment. The relays will be marked on the cover of the relay and fuse box. If the cover is not available, the relays are in the row of relays closest to the engine. The forward relay is the fuel pump relay. The middle relay is the main DME relay. The rear most relay is the oxygen sensor heater relay.

E34 5 Series

The DME control unit is mounted in the electronic control box under the hood, on the right side of the firewall. With the cover removed, the DME control unit is closest to the firewall. The box also contains the cruise control module, the automatic transmission control module, the main DME relay, the fuel pump relay, a main power connection and the oxygen sensor heater relay. Some models have a fan below the DME control unit that runs when ever the ignition switch is on.

The main DME relay coil receives 12 volts at all times on terminal 86 and the control unit supplies ground to terminal 85 to operate the relay. When the relay is closed, voltage is supplied to the fuel injectors, idle speed actuator, carbon canister purge valve, air mass sensor, ABS control unit, ignition system and the fuel pump relay. On vehicles equipped with the factory installed anti-theft system, the control unit will not operate the relay when the system is armed.

M20 ENGINE

The relays are located in the electronics box at the right, rear of the engine compartment. With the lid of the electronics box removed, visible is a group of 3 relays centered in the box. The relay on the left is the main DME relay. The center relay is the fuel pump relay. The right relay is the oxygen sensor heater relay.

Some vehicles may only have the main DME relay and the fuel pump relay in the electronics box. In this case the relay on the left is the main DME relay and the right relay is the fuel pump relay.

M30 ENGINE

The relays are located in the electronics box at the right, rear of the engine compartment. With the lid of the electronics box removed, visible is a group of 3 relays centered in the box. The relay on the left is the main DME relay. The center relay is the fuel pump relay. The right relay is the oxygen sensor heater relay.

M50 ENGINE

The relays are located in the electronics box at the right, rear of the engine compartment. With the lid of the electronics box removed, visible is a group of 3 relays centered in the box. The relay on the left is the main DME relay. The center relay is the fuel pump relay. The right relay is the oxygen sensor heater relay.

S38 ENGINE

The relays are located in the electronics box at the right, rear of the engine compartment. With the lid of the electronics box removed, visible is a group of 3 relays centered in the box. The center relay is the fuel pump relay. In 1991, the relay on the left is the air pump relay and the right relay is the main DME relay. In 1992 and later, the left and right relay positions are reversed.

DATA SENSORS

Air Flow Sensor
▶ See Figure 11

Two types of air flow sensor are used, an electronic air mass sensor and an electro-mechanical vane type air flow meter. On the vane type, when air enters the housing and moves the air vane, the vane moves a potentiometer. The control unit sends a voltage to the potentiometer and the return signal to the control unit is calculated as air flow. The air flow meter housing also contains a temperature sensor at the inlet side. If either the flow meter or the sensor fails, the control unit will substitute pre-programmed values to allow 'limp home' operation of the engine. On previous models, the CO and idle speed adjustments were on the air flow meter. These adjustments have been eliminated, CO and idle speed can no longer be adjusted. The air flow meter and temperature sensor cannot be repaired.

Air Mass Sensor
▶ See Figures 12 and 13

This unit is a fully electronic hot wire air mass sensor with no moving parts. It consists of a platinum resistor wire that is part of a bridge circuit that includes a measuring resistor. An amplifier mounted on the side of the housing controls and monitors this circuit. The temperature of the wire is maintained at a constant 311°F (155°C). As air flow changes, the current required to maintain the temperature changes. As the circuit adjusts the current, the measuring resistor reports the change in voltage to the control unit, which then calculates the mass of air flowing through the sensor housing. This type of air

Fig. 12 The air mass sensor is mounted on the air cleaner assembly — S38 engine

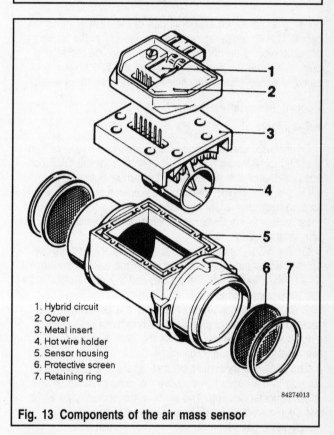

1. Hybrid circuit
2. Cover
3. Metal insert
4. Hot wire holder
5. Sensor housing
6. Protective screen
7. Retaining ring

84274013

Fig. 13 Components of the air mass sensor

measurement system automatically compensates for changes in air temperature, humidity and altitude. When the engine is stopped and after a delay of approximately 4 seconds, the bridge circuit is altered for approximately 1 second. The hot wire is heated to a temperature of approximately 1832°F (1000°C) to burn free any deposits which could influence the resistance or mea suring results.

When testing or removing the air mass meter, do not touch the hot wire element or any other electronic parts inside. Protect the element from dirt and fluids. The screen in front of the element can be cleaned or replaced but there are no other serviceable parts.

Intake Air Temperature Sensor
▶ See Figure 14

On engines with a vane type air flow sensor, the M20, M30, M42 and S14 engines, the air temperature sensor is inside the

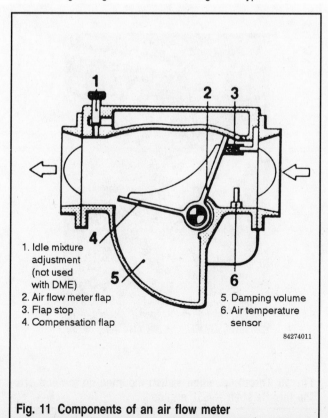

1. Idle mixture adjustment (not used with DME)
2. Air flow meter flap
3. Flap stop
4. Compensation flap
5. Damping volume
6. Air temperature sensor

84274011

Fig. 11 Components of an air flow meter

84274014

Fig. 14 The air temperature sensor is located next to the throttle body on the intake manifold — M50 engine

housing and must be tested as part of the air flow meter circuit. The air temperature sensor is located in the intake manifold next to the throttle body and switch on the M50 engine. The air temperature sensor on the S38 engine is located in the air cleaner housing next to the air mass sensor.

Coolant Temperature Sensor

▶ **See Figure 15**

On the M20 and M30 engines, 2 sensors are mounted on the thermostat housing. The blue sensor is for the DME control unit, the brown sensor is for the temperature gauge.

On the M42 engine, the coolant temperature sensors are located under the intake manifold on the engine. The forward most sensor is the DME sensor and the rear sensor is for the temperature gauge.

On the M50 engine, the coolant temperature sensors are located under the intake manifold near the front of the engine. The forward sensor is for the DME and the rear sensor is for the temperature gauge.

The coolant temperature sensors on the S14 engine are located in the coolant pipe above the exhaust side of the engine. The rear sensor services the DME and the forward services the temperature gauge.

The coolant temperature sensors on the S38 engine are located in the coolant pipe above the exhaust manifold and in the thermostat housing. The senor in the coolant pipe is for the DME and the sensor in the thermostat housing is for the temperature gauge.

The sensors are an NTC (negative temperature coefficient) type, meaning as the temperature increases, electrical resistance of the sensor decreases. The control unit reads the voltage change in the circuit as temperature. They are the

same type as the air temperature sensors and can be tested the same way using the same temperature/resistance chart.

Throttle Position Switches

▶ **See Figure 16**

The throttle position switches are used to tell the control unit when the throttle is fully closed or fully open. They are mounted in a single housing on the end of the throttle assembly. If either switch fails, the control unit will use air meter signals to calculate idle and full load control and a fault code will be set in memory.

Accelerator Pedal Sensor

▶ **See Figure 17**

The E34 5 Series with the M30 engine and traction control is equipped with the EML (throttle by wire) throttle control system. A pedal sensor is used to send pedal position and speed of movement to the EML control unit. This unit is mounted in the box with the DME control unit and has its own diagnostic program and fault codes. The sensor is attached to a bracket above the accelerator pedal and mechanically connected to the pedal. When the sensor is removed or replaced, it must be adjusted and tested for correct output signal. Any time the EML system is worked on, the external safety path check must be made.

Speed/Position Reference Sensor

▶ **See Figures 18 and 19**

Engine rpm and crankshaft position are detected with a sensor mounted on the front of the engine. If this sensor fails, the engine will not run. A special wheel is mounted on the vibra-

84274015

Fig. 15 The connector visible directly below the engine lifting bracket is for the DME coolant temperature sensor — M42 engine

84274016

Fig. 16 Throttle position switch mounted on the end of the throttle shaft — S38 engine

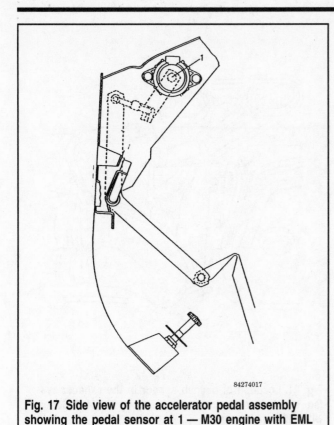

84274017

Fig. 17 Side view of the accelerator pedal assembly showing the pedal sensor at 1 — M30 engine with EML

84274018

Fig. 18 Location of the speed and position reference sensor — M50 engine

tion on the front of the crankshaft. As the teeth in the wheel pass the sensor, a magnetic pulse is generated and sent to the control unit, which reads the pulse frequency as engine

rpm. A wide gap in the teeth indicates TDC of number 1 cylinder but the gap will not be at the same place on the wheel as the 0/T timing mark stamped on the wheel used to manually set the engine to TDC.

The sensor is a magnetic pick-up mounted in a bracket that holds the gap between the sensor and the wheel. Power to the sensor and the sensor resistance can be checked with a volt/ohm meter. Sensor function can only be checked with an oscilloscope, though a resistance measurement can be made as a quick test.

Cylinder Identifying Sender
▶ **See Figure 20**

This is an inductive pulse sensor similar to the crankshaft sensor. It consists of a coil attached to an ignition wire, supplied with 5 volts from the control unit or camshaft sensor similar to the crankshaft sensor. When that spark plug is fired, the fluctuation in the return signal is used as a real time reference for sequential fuel injection and ignition control functions. If the sender fails while the engine is running, the engine will be operated in parallel fuel injection control instead of sequential.

There are 2 types of sensors. One type of sensor is attached to spark plug wire No. 6 near the distributor. The sender can be replaced by cutting the distributor end off the ignition wire and sliding the sender off the end. The other type of sensor reads off the camshaft and is similar to the speed reference sensor. It is bolted into the cam cover and is used on the M42 and M50 engines.

Oxygen Sensor
▶ **See Figures 21 and 22**

The oxygen sensor consists of a ceramic tube coated with a thin layer of platinum. The closed end of the tube is in the exhaust stream and the reference end is open to the air. When the sensor is at operating temperature, oxygen in the exhaust will cause the unit to generate a voltage. The control unit reads the signal and adjusts the fuel injection to control the amount of oxygen in the exhaust. This is called 'Closed Loop' control strategy. Under normal conditions, the control unit will constantly oscillate between rich and lean to create an average ideal air/fuel ratio. This means the output of the oxygen sensor also oscillates between 0 and 1 volt.

The sensor is equipped with an internal resistance heater to bring it to operating temperature quickly. Power for the heater comes from a separate relay mounted near the control unit. If the heater fails, the engine will take longer to switch into Closed Loop operation. If the sensor fails completely, the engine will be operated in Open Loop control and slightly lean to protect the catalytic converter from overheating.

CONTROLLED OUTPUTS

Throttle Motors

Vehicles with traction control utilize the EML system and do not have a throttle cable or idle speed actuator. The throttle is operated with a motor and controlled by the accelerator pedal sender and the EML control unit. Inputs are accepted from the accelerator pedal sensor, vehicle speed sensor, coolant tem-

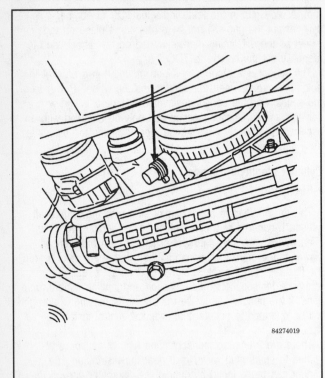

84274019

Fig. 19 Location of the speed and position reference sensor — M42 engine

84274020

Fig. 20 Cylinder identification sensor mounted in the timing cover. It is also called the camshaft sensor in this application — M42 engine

perature sensor, throttle motor feedback potentiometers, air conditioner relay, the clutch switch on manual transmissions and the control units for anti-lock braking, anti-skid, traction control, door locks, body and instrument control units and the automatic transmission control unit. Output signals are sent to all of the control units as well as to the throttle motors.

The motors are a single winding DC type that is driven in both directions. The motor unit includes a position feedback potentiometer to tell the control unit throttle position and speed of movement. This potentiometer also includes the throttle position switches whose state (open or closed) is compared with the state of the switches in the pedal sensor. If the information provided from the switches does not match the information provided by the potentiometer, the engine will be operated at reduced power and a warning light is displayed on the instrument panel. If this condition exists, check the pedal sensor adjustment first.

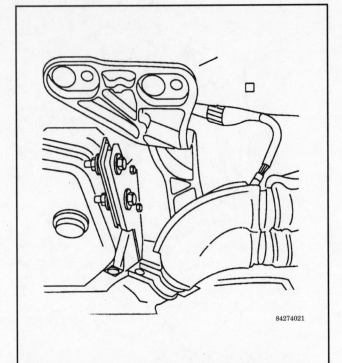

84274021

Fig. 21 Location of oxygen sensor in the exhaust system and the connector under the body — E36 3 Series with M50 engine shown

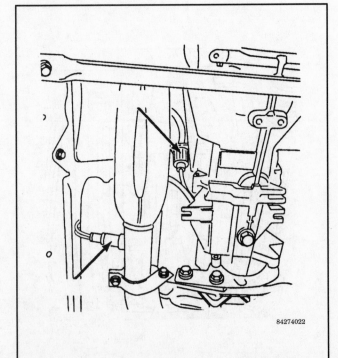

84274022

Fig. 22 Location of oxygen sensor in the exhaust system and the connector under the body — E36 3 Series with M42 engine shown

A feature of the EML system is a fail-safe mode that will cut the fuel to the injectors. The EML control unit is constantly monitoring the operation of the system and if a situation occurs that denotes a fault, the fail-safe mode will activated. As an example, if the system sees a steady throttle position that would be typical of a stretch of steady speed driving, the EML unit will see this a typical. A steady throttle position can also indicate a stuck throttle and if the brake pedal is applied while the EML unit is seeing a steady state throttle position, the fail-safe will activate and reduce power.

If a fault occurs that could affect the engine speed, the EML will reduce the throttle opening to 20 degrees or to idle position. If the throttle plate is sensed not to move, the EML control unit sends a signal to the DME to reduce power by adjusting the fuel injection.

Since this system communicates with so many of the other control units in the vehicle, the complete cannot be tested without the BMW Diagnostic Tester or equivalent. Some basic tests and position adjustments can be made, but complete testing should be left to a qualified BMW technician.

As this system relies strictly on computer controls, with no direct mechanical control of the throttle plates, the integrity of the system is of utmost importance. Any time any work has been performed on the EML system, a check of the safety system incorporated into the system has to be made. This will examine the safety controls of the EML system. This is called the external safety path.

❊❊CAUTION

The throttle motors are strong enough to cause injury if the throttle closes on a finger. Use caution when working around the throttles.

Idle Speed Actuator
▶ **See Figure 23**

On vehicles with a throttle cable, idle speed is controlled with a motor operated rotary valve. The motor is double wound and can be driven in both directions. Power is supplied from the main DME relay anytime the ignition switch is **ON**. The control unit selects which of 2 ground circuits to complete to open or close the valve as required to maintain the programmed idle speed. Further idle speed control is accomplished with very fine ignition timing adjustments. This allows very fast idle speed control so that turning on the air conditioner compressor at idle will produce almost no momentary drop in idle speed.

Idle speed and idle CO cannot be adjusted or changed. If the either is incorrect and the valve works properly, look for a vacuum leak, ignition or fuel injection problems.

Diagnosis and Testing

SERVICE PRECAUTIONS

BMW offers the following cautions that should be observed to protect the DME system and components:
- Always disconnect the battery, the DME control unit and the ignition coils when using an electric welder on the vehicle or when charging the battery or when the vehicle is placed in a paint drying oven.
- Remove the main DME relay to disable both the fu ignition systems when checking the compression. Never c the engine after removing the distributor cap or disconnectin the high tension wire on the ignition coil.
- Never apply more than standard battery voltage to the electrical system. This includes 24 volt jump starters or battery chargers.
- Never disconnect the battery or wires on the alternator, starter or spark plugs when the engine is running.
- Never connect a test lamp on terminal 1 of the ignition coil.
- Never connect terminal 1 of the ignition coil with ground or B+. This means if installing a burglar alarm, terminal 1 should not be used for starter interlocking.
- Whenever performing work on the EML throttle by wire system, a check of the external safety path must be made. This is to check the proper operation of the EML safeguards.
- When working with the EML throttle by wire systems do not place hands or fingers in or near the throttle plates. The throttle motors can close the throttle plates with considerable force.

EXTERNAL SAFETY PATH (EML)

Checking

The external safety path must be checked anytime a component of the EML throttle by wire system is removed or adjusted.

1. Read all fault codes from the EML memory before checking the external safety path. This will require the BMW Diagnostic tester or equivalent.
2. Turn the ignition switch to **OFF**. Unplug the EML connector. The EML connector is grouped with the DME engine connector and the diagnostic connector on the left side of engine compartment near the fuse box.
3. Install the EML testing adapter 12 7 010 or equivalent to the EML connector inline. Make sure all connections are tight.
4. Turn the knob on the tester to the left position and start the engine. Adjust the engine speed to 2500 rpm with the tester knob.
5. Depress the brake pedal. The engine speed should drop immediately due to the overrun shutoff provision.
6. If the engine speed does not drop immediately, check the EML system for faults. If the speed does drop immediately, the EML external safety path is functioning.
7. Shut off the engine and remove the tester. Reconnect the EML connector and erase any fault codes from the EML control unit.

D.M.E. Version	M1.2/M1.3/M1.7	M3.1
Malfunction	**MCU Code**	**MCU Code**
Engine control module function	1211	1211
Mass air flow/volume air flow sensor	1215	1215
Throttle potentiometer	1216	1216
Oxygen sensor	1221	1221
Oxygen sensor 1 control range limit	1222	1222
Coolant temperature	1223	1223
Air intake temperature	1224	1224
Battery voltage	1231	1231
Throttle position sensor (idle)	1232	—
Throttle position sensor (full load)	1233	—
Fuel injection valves (group 1)	1251	
Fuel injection valves (group 2)	1252	
Fuel injection valve cyl. 1	—	1251
Fuel injection valve cyl. 2	—	1252
Fuel injection valve cyl. 3	—	1253
Fuel injection valve cyl. 4	—	1254
Fuel injection valve cyl. 5	—	1255
Fuel injection valve cyl. 6	—	1256
Fuel pump relay	1261	1261
Idle speed control valve	1262	1262
Purge valve	1263	1263
Oxygen sensor heating relay	1264	1264
Undefined fuel injection valve	—	1283
No failure	1444	1444

84274039

Reading Codes

The DME control unit is equipped with a self diagnostic program that will detect emissions related malfunctions and turn the CHECK ENGINE light **ON** while the engine is running. Emissions related fault codes stored in the DME control unit can be read by activating the program and counting the flashes of the CHECK ENGINE light on the instrument panel. Fault codes stored in all other control units are only accessible with the BMW Service Tester that connects to the diagnostic connector in the engine compartment. The tester is menu driven and will provide operation instructions on the screen.

In the DME control unit, fault codes provide information about which circuit or component is malfunctioning at the time of the test. Intermittent malfunctions are also stored as an existing fault. As useful as these codes are, the first step in repair or service to engine management systems is to gain as much information as possible about the vehicle, especially regarding intermittent problems. Also check any service records which may be available. Before repairing any reported faults, it is absolutely essential to check for any obvious mechanical faults or failures. Remember, a fault code only indicates which sensor or circuit is effected by the problem. Simple mechanical faults such as a vacuum leak, bad battery or poor electrical connection can cause a fault code.

The fault code memory will be erased anytime the battery or DME control unit is disconnected. Fault codes will also be erased after the engine is started 60 times with no additional failures.

1. All DME codes are 4 digits. The first digit will always be **1**.

2. With the ignition switch **ON** and the engine not running, press the accelerator pedal to the floor 5 times in less than 5 seconds. This will close the full load switch to activate the diagnostic program. If the program will not activate, the full load switch on the throttle body or accelerator pedal sensor is not working.

3. The CHECK ENGINE light will stay **ON** for 5 seconds, then flash once, then begin flashing the first fault code.

4. The light will flash once for **1**; twice for **2**, etc. Each digit will be flashed with about 2.5 seconds between digits. When the whole code has been displayed, the light will stay **ON** for 2.5 seconds, then start on the next code, if existent. Count the flashes and write the numbers down.

5. If the first code is 1444, no faults are stored in memory.

Clearing Codes

1. The fault codes will be cleared after 60 engine starts without an additional failures.

2. The codes will be cleared if the battery is disconnected. If this method is used, make sure the ignition is **OFF**.

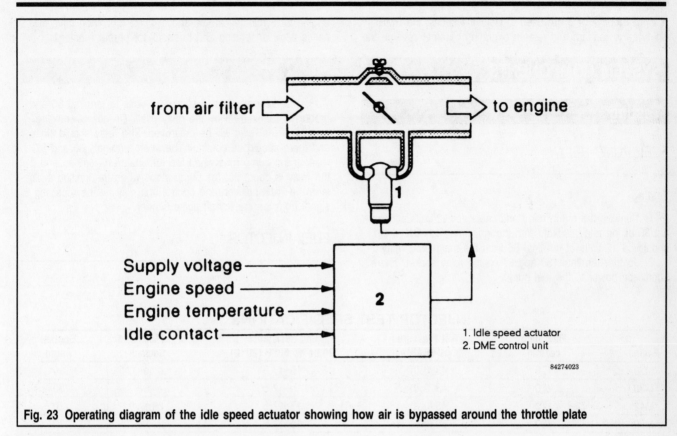

Supply voltage
Engine speed
Engine temperature
Idle contact

1. Idle speed actuator
2. DME control unit

84274023

Fig. 23 Operating diagram of the idle speed actuator showing how air is bypassed around the throttle plate

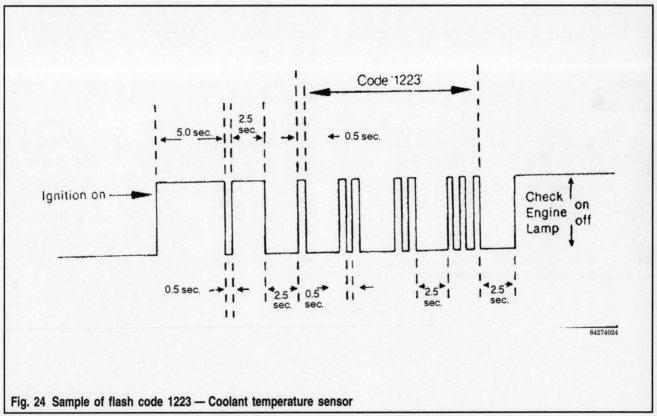

84274024

Fig. 24 Sample of flash code 1223 — Coolant temperature sensor

3. Alternately the DME unit can be unplugged to remove power from the memory circuits. If this method is used, make sure the ignition is **OFF**.

4. The codes can also be cleared using the BMW Diagnostic Tester or equivalent.

5. If Steps 2 or 3 are used to clear the codes, the DME will need to readapt and relearn operating parameters. Run the engine for 5 minutes at idle and at 2002 rpm, then drive the car to allow adaptation and to check for proper running.

SYSTEM COMPONENTS

Testing

FUEL PUMP RELAY

Testing

1. Remove the pump relay and check for 12 volts at terminal 30 of the relay socket. With the ignition switch **ON**, there should be 12 volts at terminal 86 from the main DME relay.

2. Jumper terminals 30 and 87 on the relay socket. There should be power to the fuel pump.

3. Use jumper wires to supply 12 volts to terminal 86 and ground to terminal 85 on the relay itself. Do not reverse the polarity or the relay will be destroyed. The relay should close and there should be continuity between terminals 30 and 87.

4. If the pump runs when the terminals are jumped and if the relay is good, but the pump stops when the ignition switch is in the **RUN** position, the control unit may not be receiving a signal from the crankshaft pulse sender.

FUEL INJECTOR

INJECTOR TEST SPECIFICATIONS

Engine	Flow Rate cc/min	Test Pressure psi (BAR)	Coil Resistance Ohms @ 68°F (20°C)	Plug Color	Ejection Angle
M20	170	43 (3.0)	15–17.5	blue	30
M30	220	43 (3.0)	15–17.5	yellow	30
M42	170	43 (3.0)	15–17.5	blue	30
M50	180	50 (3.5)	15–17.5	green	20
S14	236	43 (3.0)	2–3	gray	30
S38	270	43 (3.0)	15–17.5	ivory	30

84274040

Testing

ELECTRICAL

1. Unplug the injector connectors and check the resistance across the injector terminals. On the S14 engines, resistance should be 2-3 ohms, on all other engines it should be 15.0-17.5 ohms.

2. With the ignition switch **ON**, check for 12 volts at the red/white wire terminal on the injector connectors. This power comes from the DME relay.

3. To check the signal from the control unit, connect an oscilloscope between the brown wire terminal on an injector and ground and operate the starter. If there is no signal from a single injector, that injectors wiring is faulty. If there is no signal from any connector, the control unit may not be receiving an rpm signal or the control unit is faulty.

FUEL LEAK

1. Remove the injector wiring harness and remove the injectors and supply rail as an assembly. Make sure all hose clamps and injector holder clips are secure.

2. Examine the nozzle tips for signs of damage or leaking and wipe them clean.

3. Remove the fuel pump relay and jumper socket terminals 30 and 87 to run the pump. If fuel drips from the tip of the nozzle faster than about 1 drip per minute at the correct system pressure, replace the injector. Be sure to use new O-rings.

AIR FLOW METER

Testing

M20, M30 AND S14 ENGINES

▶ **See Figure 25**

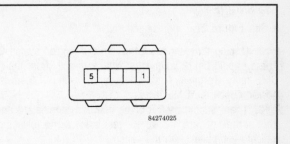

Fig. 25 Pinout of the air flow sensor — M20, M30 and S14 engines

AIR AND COOLANT TEMPERATURE SENSOR RESISTANCES

°F (°C)	kilo-ohms
14 ± 2 (−10 ± 1)	8.2–10.5
68 ± 2 (+20 ± 1)	2.2–2.7
176 ± 2 (+80 ± 1)	0.3–0.36

1. Unplug the sensor connector and connect a voltmeter to terminal **3** of the connector. With the ignition switch **ON**, there should be about 5 volts to the sensor.

2. Turn the ignition **OFF**. Remove the air flow meter. Connect an ohmmeter across terminals 2 and 3 of the meter.

3. Use a non-metal tool to reach into the housing and move the vane. The vane should move smoothly and the resistance should change smoothly. If there are jumps or dead spots in the vane movement or resistance changes, replace the air flow meter.

4. To check the temperature sensor, connect the ohmmeter to terminals 1 and 4 and make sure the air vane is fully closed. Measure the air temperature and check the chart to determine the correct sensor resistance. Ohmmeter readings should be within 10 percent of specification.

M42 ENGINE

▶ **See Figure 26**

1. Unplug the sensor connector and connect a voltmeter to terminal **1** of the connector. With the ignition switch **ON**, there should be about 5 volts to the sensor.

2. Turn the ignition **OFF**. Remove the air flow meter. Connect an ohmmeter across terminals 1 and 2 of the meter.

3. Use a non-metal tool to reach into the housing and move the vane. The vane should move smoothly and the resistance should change smoothly. If there are jumps or dead spots in the vane movement or resistance changes, replace the air flow meter.

4. To check the temperature sensor, connect the ohmmeter to terminals 4 and 5 and make sure the air vane is fully

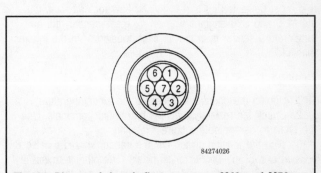

Fig. 26 Pinout of the air flow sensor — M42 and M50 engines

closed. Measure the air temperature and check the chart to determine the correct sensor resistance. Ohmmeter readings should be within 10 percent of specification.

M50 ENGINE

▶ **See Figure 26**

1. Disconnect the air flow meter plug. Check for battery voltage between terminals 2 and 4 on the wiring harness side of the connector. If battery voltage is not present, check the main DME relay and related wiring.

2. Check the resistances at the air flow meter connector. There should be 3-4 ohms between terminals 5 and 6. There should be 16.3 ohms between terminals 1 and 5.

3. If the air flow meter does not meet the above specifications, replace the unit.

S38 ENGINE

▶ **See Figure 27**

1. Unplug the connector and turn the ignition switch **ON**. There should be 12 volts at terminal 2 directly from the main DME relay. Terminal 4 goes directly to ground. If there is no power, check the DME relay.

2. There should be 3-5 ohms between terminals 3 and 5. This is the hot wire and infinite resistance or no resistance will indicate a problem with the sensor.

3. If the voltages are not correct, check the wiring between the air mass sensor, DME relay and the control unit. If the wiring is good and the DME relay is functioning, the control unit is faulty. If the voltages are correct but the fault code remains in memory, the air mass sensor may not be burning itself clean.

4. To test the burn-off function, connect all wiring but leave the air duct off to look into the sensor. Run the engine up to operating temperature, raise the speed above 2000 rpm, then turn the ignition switch **OFF** and watch the sensor. After a delay of about 4 seconds, there should be 3.5 volts between terminals 3 and 5. If it does not, the control unit is faulty.

INTAKE AIR TEMPERATURE SENSOR

On M20, M30, M42 and S14 engines with a vane type air flow sensor, the air temperature sensor is inside the housing and must be tested as part of the air flow meter circuit. On the M50 and S38 engines with an air mass sensor, the air temperature sensor is in the air filter housing or in the intake manifold.

Testing

1. Unplug the connector. Measure the air temperature.

2. Check the resistance across the sensor terminals. Use the chart to determine the correct reading.

3. With the ignition switch **ON** the sensor should receive 5 volts at one of the connector terminals. The other terminal is the return signal to the control unit, do not use it for voltmeter ground.

COOLANT TEMPERATURE SENSOR

On the M20 and M30 engines, 2 sensors are mounted on the thermostat housing. The blue sensor is for the DME control unit, the brown sensor is for the temperature gauge.

On the M42 engine, the coolant temperature sensors are located under the intake manifold on the engine. The forward most sensor is the DME sensor and the rear sensor is for the temperature gauge.

On the M50 engine, the coolant temperature sensors are located under the intake manifold near the front of the engine. The forward sensor is for the DME and the rear sensor is for the temperature gauge.

The coolant temperature sensors on the S14 engine are located in the coolant pipe above the exhaust side of the engine. The rear sensor services the DME and the forward services the temperature gauge.

The coolant temperature sensors on the S38 engine are located in the coolant pipe above the exhaust manifold and in the thermostat housing. The senor in the coolant pipe is for the DME and the sensor in the thermostat housing is for the temperature gauge.

The sensors are an NTC (negative temperature coefficient) type, meaning as the temperature increases, electrical resistance of the sensor decreases. The control unit reads the voltage change in the circuit as temperature. They are the same type as the air temperature sensors and can be tested the same way using the same temperature/resistance chart.

Testing

1. Unplug the sensor. Measure the coolant temperature as close as possible to the location of the sensor.

2. Measure the resistance between the terminals of the sensor. Compare the results to the chart.

3. With the ignition switch **ON** the sensor should receive 5 volts at one of the connector terminals. The other terminal is the return signal to the control unit, do not use it for voltmeter ground.

THROTTLE POSITION SWITCH

Testing

M20, M30, S14 & S38 ENGINES

▶ **See Figures 28, 29 and 30**

1. Unplug the switch connector and use a continuity tester or ohmmeter for this test.

2. There should be continuity between terminals 4 and 6 (automatic transmission and S38 engine) or 2 and 18 (manual transmission, except S38 engine) when the throttle is closed (idle).

3. There should be continuity between terminals 4 and 5 (automatic transmission and S38 engine) or 3 and 18 (manual transmission, except S38 engine) when the throttle is fully open.

4. Loosen the screws on the side of the housing to adjust the switch. If the switch cannot be correctly adjusted for both test results, replace the switch.

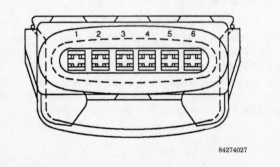

84274027

Fig. 27 Pinout of the air flow sensor — S38 engine

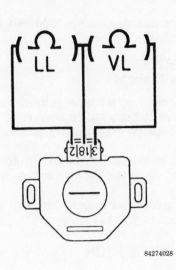

84274028

Fig. 28 Throttle position switch pinout. LL is the idle position and VI is the full load position — M20, M30 and S14 engines with manual transmissions

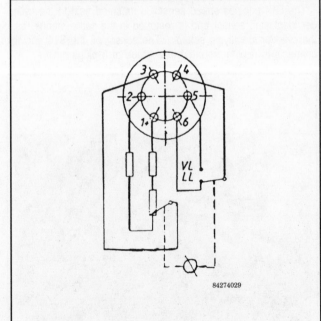

84274029

Fig. 29 Throttle position switch pinout. LL is the idle position and VI is the full load position — M20 and M30 engines with automatic transmissions and S38 engine

84274030

Fig. 30 Throttle position switch mounted on the end of the throttle shaft — S38 engine

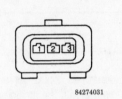

84274031

Fig. 31 Throttle position potentiometer pinout shown from the wiring harness side of the connector — M42 and M50 engines

84274032

Fig. 32 Disconnecting the throttle position potentiometer — M42 engine

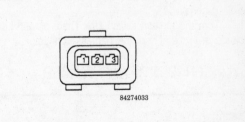

84274033

Fig. 33 Cylinder identifying and engine speed sensor pinouts

M42 AND M50 ENGINES

▶ **See Figures 31 and 32**

1. With the ignition switch **ON** the potentiometer should receive 5 volts at connector terminal 1.

2. With the ignition switch **OFF**, disconnect the potentiometer connection. There should be 4.6 kilo-ohms between terminals 1 and 3 of potentiometer.

3. Connect the ohmmeter to terminals 1 and 2 of the potentiometer. Move the throttle throughout the range of movement. The resistance must change smoothly without any jumps, skips or breaks. The resistance should range from 0.8-1.2 ohms to 3.2-4.8 ohms.

IDLE SPEED ACTUATOR

Testing

3-PIN CONNECTOR

1. Unplug the idle speed control valve connector and check for 12 volts at terminal 2 with the ignition switch **ON**. Power comes from terminal 87 of the main DME relay.

2. To check the motor resistance, connect an ohmmeter to terminals 2 and 3 of the actuator. It should read about 20 ohms. Terminals 2 and 1 should also read 20 ohms. Resistance across terminals 1 and 3 should be about 40 ohms. The terminal numbers will be imprinted on the connector body with terminal 2 in the middle position. Terminals 1 and 3 are the outer terminals and the exact positions are not critical to this test.

3. If voltage and resistance readings are correct, remove the actuator and use a tool to carefully push the rotary valve sideways to the fully open position. With the wiring connected and the ignition switch **ON**, the valve should move to about the 50 percent position and remain stable.

2-PIN CONNECTOR

1. With the ignition switch in the **OFF** position, unplug the idle speed control valve. Pin 1 is on the same side of the valve as the side hose connection.

2. Check the resistance of the idle speed control valve. Measure across the 2 pins of the valve. The resistance should be 6-10 ohms.

3. Turn the ignition switch **ON**. There should be battery voltage at terminal 2 of the harness connector.

CYLINDER IDENTIFYING SENDER

Testing

M20, M30, S14 & S38 ENGINES

▶ **See Figure 33**

The cylinder identifying sender is mounted on the ignition lead for cylinder 6 on the M20, M30 and S38 engines. The sender on the S14 engine is mounted in the bellhousing flange and connects to a gray colored plug mounted in the center of a group of 3 plugs on the engine compartment rear wall, next to the engine harness connector and diagnosis socket.

1. Turn the ignition switch to the **OFF** position.

2. Trace the sensor lead back to the connector and disconnect. The S38 engine might require the fan and shroud be removed and the water pipe be moved out of the way to access the plug.

3. Check the resistance between terminals 1 and 2. The resistance should be 0.2-1.0 ohms.

M42 & M50 ENGINES

▶ **See Figures 33 and 34**

The cylinder identifying sender, or camshaft sender as it is sometimes called, is located on the timing cover. The connector is located below the intake manifold, towards the front of the engine.

1. Turn the ignition switch to the **OFF** position.

2. Trace the sensor lead back to the connector and disconnect.

3. Check the resistance between terminals 1 and 2. The resistance should be 1.15-1.41 kilo-ohms.

ENGINE SPEED SENSOR

Testing

▶ **See Figures 33 and 34**

The engine speed sensor provides the DME unit with engine speed information. The sensor reads the information from a tooth wheel mounted on the crankshaft hub except on the S14 engine. It can also be called the crankshaft sensor.

The S14 engines speed sensor is mounted next to the cylinder identifying sensor and is removed in the same manner as the cylinder identifying sensor. The sensor on the S14 engine connects to a plug mounted in a group of 3 plugs on the

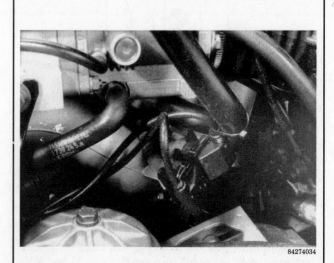

84274034

Fig. 34 The upper connector is for the cylinder identifying sender and the lower is for the speed sensor (DME) — M42 engine shown, M50 has similar arrangement

engine compartment rear wall, next to the engine harness connector and diagnosis socket. It is the connector on the right side.

1. Turn the ignition switch to the **OFF** position.

2. Trace the sensor lead back to the connector and disconnect.

3. Check the resistance between terminals 1 and 2. The resistance should be 490-590 ohms.

OXYGEN SENSOR

Testing

Testing the oxygen sensor requires the use of a CO tester. These can be borrowed or rented from a automotive tool supply or rental store.

1. With the engine not running, unscrew the exhaust tap on the exhaust manifold or downpipe. Insert the CO tester probe into the tap.

2. Disconnect the oxygen sensor plug and squeeze shut the vacuum line to the fuel pressure regulator.

3. Start the engine and note the CO level. Connect the oxygen sensor. The CO level should go down.

DIAGNOSTIC CONNECTOR

▶ **See Figures 35 and 36**

The diagnostic connector is used to connect the BMW Diagnostic Tester or equivalent, or the Service Interval Indicator reset tool. Keep the connector closed while not using it. Do not run the engine with the connector open.

84274035

Fig. 35 Diagnostic connector location — E34 chassis with S38 engine shown

84274036

Fig. 36 Diagnostic connector location — E36 chassis with M50 engine shown

PIN NUMBER	TERMINAL NUMBER	TERMINAL DESCRIPTION		WIRE COLOR
1	1	IGNITION COIL		SW
2	–	NOT OCCUPIED		
3	–	NOT OCCUPIED		
4	FT	VOLTAGE: TEMPERATURE SENSOR	M5	BR/VI
5	–	NOT OCCUPIED		
6	–	NOT OCCUPIED		
7	SI	SERVICE INTERVAL RESET		WS/GN
8	–	NOT OCCUPIED		
9	–	NOT OCCUPIED		
10	–	NOT OCCUPIED		
11	50	VOLTAGE: IGNITION SWITCH IN START		SW/GE
12	61(D+)	ALTERNATOR CHARGE INDICATOR		BL
13	–	NOT OCCUPIED		
14	30	VOLTAGE: HOT AT ALL TIMES		RT
15	RXD	RECEIVE		WS/GE
16	15S	VOLTAGE: IGNITION SWITCH IN RUN		GN/WS
17	–	NOT OCCUPIED		
18	PGSP	DME-PROGRAMING		GN/BL
19	31	GROUND		BR
20	TXD	TRANSMIT		WS/VI

84274042

Fig. 37 Diagnostic connector terminal identification

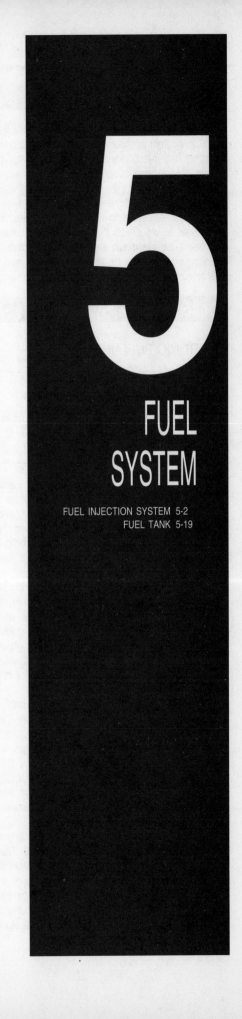

5

FUEL
SYSTEM

FUEL INJECTION SYSTEM

This section covers the removal and installation of the fuel injection system components. Complete diagnosis of the Motronic fuel injection system is covered in Section 4.

This section also covers the testing, removal and installation of the fuel delivery system. This includes the fuel pump, fuel tank, fuel pressure regulator, fuel rail and fuel injectors.

Fuel injection systems contain components that can be hazardous to work with due to the inflammable nature of gasoline. The electronic and mechanical parts of the fuel injection system tend to be expensive so care must be exercised not to damage them.

Description of Systems

MOTRONIC FUEL INJECTION

For a complete description of the operation of the Motronic fuel injection system, refer to Section 4.

FUEL DELIVERY SYSTEM

The fuel pump provides fuel to the fuel injection system at a high pressure and at a high enough flow rate to supply the demands of the fuel injectors. The pump provides enough fuel pressure that the pressure must be reduced by a fuel pressure regulator. The fuel flow provided by the pump is beyond the needs of the fuel injectors and most of the fuel flow is returned to the fuel tank.

The pump is a roller-cell design and is electrically powered. The fuel pump is mounted in the tank and can be reached through a panel in the floor of the trunk. On the top of the pump is a pressure damper and a check valve that can be replaced. Wiring for the pump and gauge unit are on the same connector. The pump can be tested separately for delivery quantity but the pressure test is for the whole fuel system.

The flow from the fuel pump is sent through a fuel filter that prevents dirt and contaminants from fouling the fuel injectors. After the fuel passes through the filter, it goes to a fuel pressure regulator that controls the pressure at the injectors. The fuel pressure regulator is controlled by the manifold vacuum and maintains the pressure differential between the manifold vacuum and fuel pressure. As the vacuum drops due to larger throttle openings, the fuel pressure is increased. The excess fuel is returned to the fuel tank.

The fuel at the correct pressure for the given moment in engine operation is queued in the fuel rail. The fuel injectors are mounted in the intake manifold and have the fuel rail mounted across the inlets. The fuel injectors are electrically controlled pintle valves. As the injector receives the signal to open from the Motronic control unit, the current flows into the solenoid winding and pulls open the pintle valve approximately

0.05mm. The fuel sprays out of the tiny opening at the front of the injector in a finely atomized mist. The extremely small droplets ensure complete combustion and efficient operation of the engine.

Precautions

The following cautions should be observed to protect the DME system and components:

• Always disconnect the battery, the DME control unit and the ignition coils when using an electric welder on the vehicle or when charging the battery or when the vehicle is placed in a paint drying oven.

• Relieve the fuel system pressure before disconnecting any component of the fuel injection system that contains fuel.

• Remove the main DME relay to disable both the fuel and ignition systems when checking the compression. Never crank the engine after removing the distributor cap or disconnecting the high tension wire on the ignition coil.

• Never disconnect the battery or wires on the alternator, starter or spark plugs when the engine is running.

• Never connect a test lamp on terminal 1 of the ignition coil.

• Never connect terminal 1 of the ignition coil with ground or B+. This means if installing a burglar alarm, terminal 1 should not be used for starter interlocking.

• Whenever performing work on the EML throttle by wire system, a check of the external safety path must be made. This is to check the proper operation of the EML safeguards.

• When working with the EML throttle by wire systems do not place hands or fingers in or near the throttle plates. The throttle motors can close the throttle plates with considerable force.

Relieving the Fuel System Pressure

✳✳CAUTION

Anytime the fuel system is serviced the generation of spilled fuel and fuel vapor expose the technician to possibility of flash fire or explosion. All work should be performed in a well ventilated area with easy access to a fire extinguisher. All spilled fuel must be removed immediately. Wear protective eyewear. Failure to observe these precautions may result in personal injury.

1. Clean the fuel rail inlet connection. Wrap a shop towel around the fuel rail inlet connection. Be prepared with a suitable container to catch fuel spilling out of the connection.

2. Slowly loosen the hose clamp on the fuel inlet connection.

3. Remove the connection and drain the fuel into the container. Cap the line and connection to prevent contaminants from entering the system.

Fuel Pump, Oxygen Sensor and Main Relays

LOCATION

E30 3 Series

M20 ENGINE

The fuel pump relay is mounted on a bracket on the left inner fender in front of the shock tower. There is a grouping of 3 relays. The forward relay is the main DME relay. The middle relay is the fuel pump relay. The rear most relay is the oxygen sensor heater relay.

M42 ENGINE

The relays are mounted on the firewall above and to the right of the brake booster. The relay on the right is the main DME relay. The middle relay is the fuel pump relay. The leftmost relay is the oxygen sensor heater relay.

S14 ENGINE

The relays are located on the far right of the firewall. The relay on the right is the evaporative purge relay. The middle relay is the main DME relay. The leftmost relay is for both the oxygen sensor heater and the fuel pump.

E36 3 Series

▶ See Figure 1

The relays are located in the relay and fuse box on the left side of the engine compartment. The relays will be marked on the cover of the relay and fuse box. If the cover is not available, the relays are in the row of relays closest to the engine. The forward relay is the fuel pump relay. The middle relay is the main DME relay. The rear most relay is the oxygen sensor heater relay.

E34 5 Series

M20 ENGINE

The relays are located in the electronics box at the right, rear of the engine compartment. With the lid of the electronics box removed, visible is a group of 3 relays centered in the box. The relay on the left is the main DME relay. The center relay is the fuel pump relay. The right relay is the oxygen sensor heater relay.

Some vehicles may only have the main DME relay and the fuel pump relay in the electronics box. In this case the relay on the left is the main DME relay and the right relay is the fuel pump relay.

M30 ENGINE

The relays are located in the electronics box at the right, rear of the engine compartment. With the lid of the electronics box removed, visible is a group of 3 relays centered in the box. The relay on the left is the main DME relay. The center relay is the fuel pump relay. The right relay is the oxygen sensor heater relay.

M50 ENGINE

The relays are located in the electronics box at the right, rear of the engine compartment. With the lid of the electronics box removed, visible is a group of 3 relays centered in the box. The relay on the left is the main DME relay. The center relay is the fuel pump relay. The right relay is the oxygen sensor heater relay.

S38 ENGINE

The relays are located in the electronics box at the right, rear of the engine compartment. With the lid of the electronics box removed, visible is a group of 3 relays centered in the box. The center relay is the fuel pump relay. In 1991, the relay on the left is the air pump relay and the right relay is the main DME relay. In 1992 and later, the left and right relay positions are reversed.

Fuel Pump

TESTING

Electrical
▶ See Figure 2

When the ignition switch is first turned to **START**, the control unit will complete the ground circuit for the pump relay coil and the relay closes to run the pump. When the control unit receives a signal from the crankshaft pulse sensor, it will continue to operate the pump relay with the ignition switch in the **RUN** position. If the engine is not running, the pump will not run. The pump relay terminals can be jumped to test the electrical system and to run the pump for fuel system pressure testing.

1. If a fuel supply problem is suspected, remove the pump relay and check for 12 volts at terminal 30 of the relay socket. With the ignition switch **ON**, there should be 12 volts at terminal 86 from the main DME relay.

2. Jumper terminals 30 and 87 on the relay socket. There should be power to the pump through fuse 23 (and fuse 24 if applicable) even if the ignition is **OFF**.

3. Use jumper wires to supply 12 volts to terminal 86 and ground to terminal 85 on the relay itself. Do not reverse the polarity or the relay will be destroyed. The relay should close and there should be continuity between terminals 30 and 87.

4. If the pump runs when the terminals are jumped and the relay is good, but the pump stops when the ignition switch is in the **RUN** position, the control unit may not be receiving a signal from the crankshaft pulse sensor.

FLOW AND PRESSURE TESTING

✳✳CAUTION

The following procedure will produce fuel vapors. Make sure there is proper ventilation and take the appropriate fire safety precautions otherwise personal injury may occur.

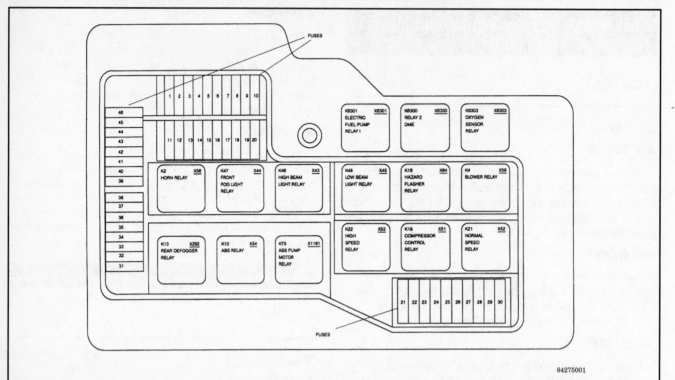

Fig. 1 Relay and fuse box containing the fuel pump relay, oxygen sensor heater relay and the main DME relay — E36 3 Series

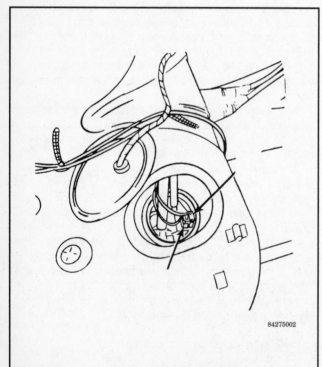

Fig. 2 The fuel pump is located in the fuel tank and is accessible once the rear seat cushion is removed — E36 3 Series

1. Make sure the battery is in good condition and the fuel pump wiring and ground connections are good. It is important the pump receive a full 12 volts.

2. Disconnect the fuel supply hose. Install a 13 3 60 or an equivalent 100 psi pressure gauge with a tee fitting.

3. Disconnect the fuel return hose and securely install a long hose to the return fitting. Place the other end into a 4 quart or 4000 cc measuring container.

4. Remove the fuel pump relay and connect a jumper wire with a switch to relay socket terminals 30 and 87. The pump will run whenever the terminals are connected, so be sure to use a jumper with a switch.

5. Run the pump for 30 seconds and time the run carefully. Except with the M42 and M50 engines , the pump should flow 29.6 oz. (875 cc) in 30 seconds and the pressure should be about 43 psi (3.0 bar). On the M42 and M50 engines, the pump should flow 34.8 oz. (1030 cc) in 30 seconds and the pressure should be about 58 psi (4.0 bar). When the pump is stopped, the pressure should stay above 38 psi (2.6 BAR) for 20 minutes.

6. If the flow is low, the pump is faulty or the filter is clogged.

7. If the flow is correct but the pressure is low or does not hold, clamp the return hose and run the pump again briefly to read the pressure. If the pressure is now correct and holds, the pressure regulator at the front of the supply rail is faulty.

8. If the pressure is still low or does not hold, there is a leak in the system, possibly an injector or the fuel pump check valve. The pressure will be lower if the engine is running because the pressure regulator will be supplied with engine vacuum.

REMOVAL & INSTALLATION

Follow all precautions when working with gasoline and the resulting gasoline vapors. Relieve the fuel pressure before performing any work on the fuel system.

✳✳CAUTION

This procedure will generate gasoline fumes. Absolutely no flame or sparks should be in the area of the work being done. Gasoline fumes are heavier than air and will travel on the floor towards possible sources of ignition. Work in a well ventilated area and wipe up any gasoline spills. Gasoline will irritate skin; avoid contact with gasoline. Failure to follow these precautions may result in personal injury.

E30 3 Series

EXCEPT WITH S14 ENGINE

1. If the tank is full, remove some fuel to lower the level.
2. Remove the rear seat cushion and peel back the insulating sheet to access the right side cover.
3. Remove the screws from the cover and lift the cover off. Pull of the electrical plug and disconnect the fuel lines. Catch any spilled fuel.
4. Remove the 4 screws from the sender portion of pickup assembly. Slowly remove the sender to allow the fuel to drain into the tank.
5. Rotate the pickup assembly counterclockwise and pull out slowly. Allow the fuel to drain back into the tank.

   To install:
6. Replace the gasket and lower the pickup assembly into the fuel tank. Rotate the assembly clockwise to lock into place.
7. Replace the gasket and lower the fuel level sender into the pickup assembly. Replace the screws.
8. Connect the fuel lines and electrical connector. Replace the cover and the insulating sheet. Install the rear seat cushion.

WITH S14 ENGINE
▶ **See Figure 3**

The M3 is equipped with 2 fuel pumps. The main pump is located outside the fuel tank and is removed using the procedure below. The M3 also uses a pre-pump or transfer pump mounted in the fuel tank. The procedure to remove the tank mounted fuel pump is as listed in the previous procedure.

1. Make sure the ignition switch is in the **OFF** position.
2. Use fuel line block-off clamps on the inlet and outlet lines of the fuel pump to prevent fuel from leaking out once the fuel pump has been removed.
3. Pull back the electrical connection covers and remove the wires. Loosen the hose connections and remove the hoses.
4. Remove the nuts holding the fuel pump and remove the assembly. Disconnect the hose from the pump and remove the pump from the bracket.

To install:
5. Install the pump in the bracket and connect the hose. Install the pump and bracket onto the car. Replace the rubber isolators if necessary.
6. Connect the hoses and the electrical connections. Remove the block off clamps.

E36 3 Series
▶ **See Figure 4**

1. Drain the fuel from the fuel tank if the level is high. It is best to do this procedure with little fuel in the tank.
2. Remove the rear seat cushion and pull off the cover on the right side to expose the top of the fuel pickup assembly.
3. Disconnect the plugs on the top of the assembly. The black connector is for the fuel pump. The white connector is for the fuel level sender.
4. Mark and disconnect the fuel lines. Using tool 16 1 020 or equivalent, rotate the mounting ring and remove the assembly. Press the level arm in slightly to make clearance when removing.

   To install:
5. The entire unit must be replaced. The individual parts are not serviceable.
6. Using a new seal and mounting ring, install the pump assembly. Move the unit from side to side to make sure the level sender is free and in the correct location. There is a rib on the flange that should align with a mark on the fuel tank.
7. Using tool 16 1 020 or equivalent, torque the mounting ring to 27-31 ft. lbs. (37-43 Nm).
8. Connect the fuel lines and the electrical connectors. Install the cover and rear seat.

E34 5 Series
▶ **See Figures 5 and 6**

1. Drain the fuel from the fuel tank if the level is high. It is best to do this procedure with little fuel in the tank.
2. Remove the trunk panels to expose the tank access cover on the right side, front corner. Remove the screws holding the cover.
3. Mark the fuel lines and disconnect them. Disconnect the electrical connection.
4. The models with M20, M30 and M50 engines are equipped with a large mounting ring that holds the fuel pump and level sender assembly. The mounting ring is removed using tool 16 1 020 or equivalent. The tool grips the edge of the mounting ring and allows the use of a breaker bar or socket wrench to remove the ring.
5. The M5 with the S38 engine has the fuel pump and level sender assembly retained with 8 screws or nuts around the perimeter. Remove the screws to remove the assembly.
6. Remove the assembly from the tank slowly to avoid spilling any fuel. The level sender with come out first. Compress the mounting hooks and remove the fuel pump.
7. Remove the hoses from the fuel pump and disconnect the wires. Unscrew the pressure damper and the check valve from the fuel pump and pull the pump out of the holder. Remove the fuel filter mounting screw and the fuel filter.

   To install:
8. Install the fuel filter to the bottom of the fuel pump and install the pump into the holder. Install the pressure damper

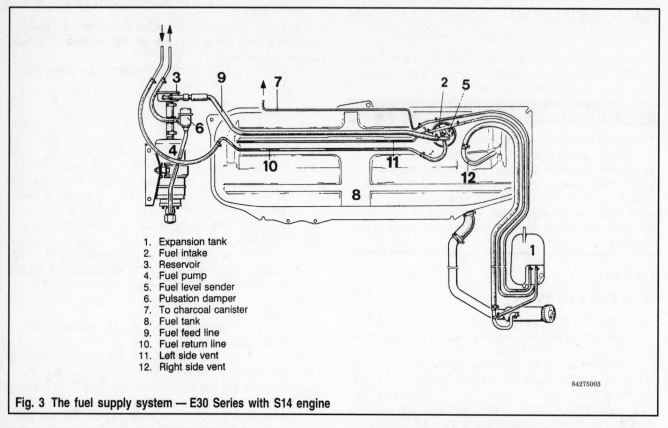

1. Expansion tank
2. Fuel intake
3. Reservoir
4. Fuel pump
5. Fuel level sender
6. Pulsation damper
7. To charcoal canister
8. Fuel tank
9. Fuel feed line
10. Fuel return line
11. Left side vent
12. Right side vent

84275003

Fig. 3 The fuel supply system — E30 Series with S14 engine

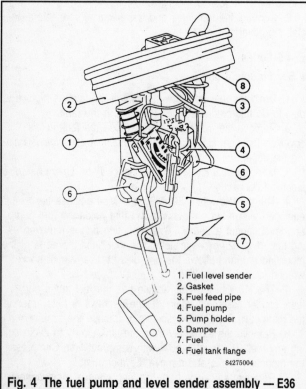

1. Fuel level sender
2. Gasket
3. Fuel feed pipe
4. Fuel pump
5. Pump holder
6. Damper
7. Fuel
8. Fuel tank flange

84275004

Fig. 4 The fuel pump and level sender assembly — E36 3 Series

and the check valve. Connect the fuel lines and wires. The wires should be wire-tied to the fuel hose at the midway point.

9. Install the fuel pump into the tank and make sure the mounting hooks are secure on the fuel pump.

10. Replace the gasket and install the fuel level sender. Tighten the nuts or screws on the M5. On the mounting ring type units, using tool 16 1 020 or equivalent, torque the mounting ring to 27-31 ft. lbs. (37-43 Nm).

11. Connect the wires and the fuel lines. Replace the cover and the trunk trim.

Throttle Body

The throttle body contains the throttle plates which controls the amount of air flowing into the engine. The throttle plate is connected to the accelerator pedal via a cable on all models except the 5 Series with traction control. The 5 Series cars that have traction control have a system called EML, translated into English is Electronic Motor Load regulation.

EML is a system that controls the throttle not by cable, but by an electric servo motor. A sensor on the accelerator pedal feeds information about throttle position to the EML controller. The EML controller tells the servo motor on the throttle body how far to open the throttle plate. Because of the electronic control, there is no need for a separate cruise control actuator, for a transmission control cable or for a throttle cable. The

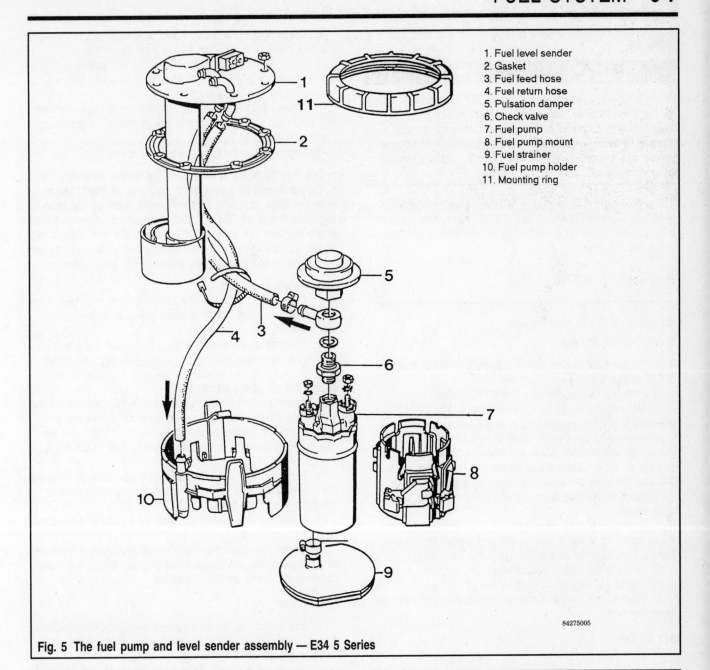

1. Fuel level sender
2. Gasket
3. Fuel feed hose
4. Fuel return hose
5. Pulsation damper
6. Check valve
7. Fuel pump
8. Fuel pump mount
9. Fuel strainer
10. Fuel pump holder
11. Mounting ring

84275005

Fig. 5 The fuel pump and level sender assembly — E34 5 Series

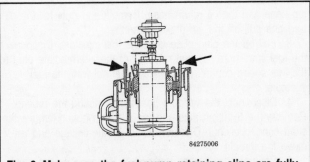

84275006

Fig. 6 Make sure the fuel pump retaining clips are fully engaged when installing — E34 5 Series

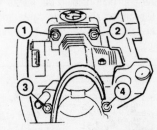

84275007

Fig. 7 Nuts 1 through 4 retain the throttle body — M42 engine

only connection to the throttle body is a multi-pin electrical connector.

❄❄CAUTION

When ever work is performed on an EML component, such as the throttle body, the external safety check must be made. This is to make sure that the electronic throttle system is working properly. If the electronic throttle system is not working properly, the car may behave erratically causing personal injury or death.

The procedure to perform the external safety path check requires a special BMW tool 12 7 010 or equivalent. Do not attempt any repairs on an EML related part without having access to the tool.

REMOVAL & INSTALLATION

M20, M30, M42 and M50 Engines

▶ See Figures 7 and 8

1. On the M20 engine drain the coolant to below the level of the throttle body.
2. Turn the ignition switch to the **OFF** position.
3. Remove the intake air duct from the throttle body. If equipped with EML, remove the multi-pin connector.
4. Disconnect the throttle cable, the transmission cable and the cruise control cable. Mark and disconnect the vacuum lines and the air hoses. Move the idle speed control valve out of the way. Disconnect the coolant hoses on the M20 engine.
5. Remove the mounting nuts and remove the throttle body.
To install:
6. Clean the mating surfaces of the throttle body and the intake manifold. Install a new gasket and the throttle body. Torque the mounting nuts to 6.5-8.0 ft. lbs. (9-11 Nm).
7. Connect the hoses, vacuum lines and air hoses to the throttle body. Replace the idle speed control valve.
8. Connect the throttle cables or EML connector. Install the intake air duct.

S14 Engine

1. Turn the ignition switch to the **OFF** position.
2. Remove the cap nuts holding the intake manifold to the throttle bodies. Disconnect the throttle cable and the air hoses. The crankcase breather hose will have to be cut off. Remove the intake manifold.

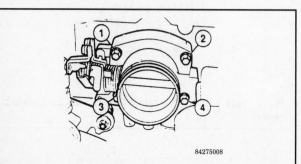

84275008

Fig. 8 Nuts 1 through 4 retain the throttle body — M50 engine

3. Disconnect the harness from the throttle switch. Remove the fuel injector electrical plug plate from the injectors.
4. Remove the vacuum hose from the fuel pressure regulator. Remove the 2 mounting bolts and remove the fuel rail complete with the fuel injectors.
5. Disconnect the nut holding the throttle linkage. Remove the Torx nuts holding the throttle bodies to the cylinder head. Remove the throttle bodies.
6. Separate the throttle bodies if necessary.

➡**The throttle shaft is supported by needle bearings. Do not draw the shaft through the bearings without making sure the shaft is clean. Dirt will cause damage the bearings and the shaft. Do not use any tools on the shaft that could damage the surface of the shaft. Do not disturb any of the adjustments on the throttle bodies. The settings are optimized at the factory and marked with paint dots.**

To install:
7. If any components on the throttle bodies or linkage have been disturbed, they will have to be adjusted for proper operation.
8. The throttle body gaskets may be reused if there is no damage to the ridge around the gasket opening. Use a thin bead of silicon sealer around the opening ridge. Replace the gasket if there is any damage.
9. Attach the throttle bodies and check the condition of the connecting pipe O-ring for damage. Replace if necessary.
10. Install the throttle bodies to the cylinder head with the new or used gasket. Torque the mounting nuts to 6.5-8.0 ft. lbs. (9-11 Nm).
11. Connect the throttle linkage with a new locknut. Replace the fuel injectors and fuel rail. Torque the mounting nuts to 6.5-8.0 ft. lbs. (9-11 Nm).
12. Install the fuel injector electrical plug plate and the throttle switch connector.
13. Check the intake manifold O-rings and replace if necessary. Install a new crankcase breather hose. Install the intake manifold, air hoses and throttle cable.

S38 Engine

1. Disconnect the negative battery terminal. Disconnect the throttle cable. Remove the air intake hose. Remove the screws on each throttle valve assembly.
2. Disconnect the hose for the idle speed control, the venting hose and the oil return hose. Remove the nuts for the oil trap and pull off the air intake assembly.
3. Pull off the plug plate from the fuel injectors. Disconnect the fuel lines from the fuel rail. Pull of the intermediate plug for the idle speed control. Remove the fuel rail with the fuel injectors.
4. Disconnect the vacuum hoses after noting the routing. Remove the 6 10mm nuts and the 9 13mm nuts. Remove the shaft connection nut. Disconnect the throttle linkage and remove the throttle bodies.
5. Separate the throttle bodies by disconnecting the connecting pipes. Check the O-rings on the pipe. Clean the throttle shafts before pulling out of the bores and do not use tools on the shaft or it may be damaged.
To install:
6. Install the throttle bodies together using new O-rings on the connecting pipes. Install the throttle bodies on the engine

using new gaskets. Tighten the 10mm nuts to 6.5-8.0 ft. lbs. (9-11 Nm) and the 13mm nuts to 14-17 ft. lbs. (20-24 Nm).

7. Route and connect the vacuum hoses. Install the shaft connection nut and the throttle linkage. Install the fuel rail and the fuel connections. Connect the intermediate plug and the injector plug plate.

8. Check the O-rings on the air intake assembly and attach the pins at the bottom of the assembly. Install the air intake assembly.

9. Connect the oil return hose, the idle speed hose and the venting hose. Install the air intake duct and install the screws at each throttle. Connect the negative battery terminal.

ADJUSTMENTS

The only throttle body adjustments that can or should be done are on the S14 and S38 engines. The other engines are equipped with throttle bodies that need no adjustments. The S14 and S38 engine throttle body adjustments should be performed only if the throttle bodies were disassembled or damage occurred.

Special tools needed for these procedures include feeler gauges, dial indicators, dial indicator mounts, and vernier calipers. The settings are very precise and require familiarity with the tools being used.

Idle Speed Stop

1. Loosen the idle speed adjustment stop lock nut and loosen the screw 1/10 of a turn in the counterclockwise direction.

2. Close the throttle plates and press the throttle lever against the stop screw. Tighten the nut.

3. Install a dial indicator on the throttle body with the tip on the deepest point of the throttle plate. Preload the tip and zero the dial.

4. Loosen the nut and turn in the screw to move the throttle plate 0.004-0.006 inch (0.10-0.15mm). This will be approximately 1/10 of a turn. Tighten the locknut and mark with a paint dot.

Axial Clearance

1. The measurements used in this procedure are based on the ambient temperature being 68°F. (20°C.).

2. Close the throttle plates. Check that the throttles move easily.

3. Check that a 0.008 inch (0.2mm) feeler gauge can fit between throttle body housing and the snapring or throttle lever.

4. Check for damage or warpage if the feeler gauge does not fit.

Full Load Stop

1. Open the throttle plates to the full open position.

2. Measure the distance from the top edge of the throttle plate to the top of the throttle bore. The measurement should be 0.854 inch (21.7mm).

3. If the measurement is not correct, loosen the locknut on the screw mounted in the middle of each throttle housing, between the throttle bores. Move the screw to achieve the correct measurement. Do not change the length of the throttle linkages.

4. If there is any deviation from the measurement, it should be evenly shared by each of the throttle housing.

Throttle Lever

S14 ENGINE

1. The throttle lever pushrods must be check and adjusted for length. On the S14 engine, the pushrod for cylinders 1 and 2 should be 3.937 inch (100mm) and the pushrod for cylinders 3 and 4 should be 3.822-3.854 inch (97.1-97.9mm).

2. Install the pushrods and align the levers. Loosen and move the clamps to obtain alignment.

3. Install a dial indicator on cylinder 3 and 4 throttle lever. Adjust the cylinders 1 and 2 pushrod until movement is noted on the dial indicator. The throttle levers are adjusted when they evenly hit the idle speed stop.

S38 ENGINE

1. The throttle lever pushrods must be check and adjusted for length. On the S38 engine, the pushrods for cylinder pairs 1 and 2, 3 and 4 should be 3.858 inch (98mm) and the pushrod for cylinders 5 and 6 should be 3.822-3.854 inch (97.1-97.9mm).

2. Install the pushrods and align the levers. Loosen and move the clamps to obtain alignment.

3. Install a dial indicator on cylinder 5 and 6 throttle lever. Evenly adjust the cylinder 1 and 2, and 3 and 4 pushrods until movement is noted on the dial indicator. The throttle levers are adjusted when they evenly hit the idle speed stop.

CHECKING EXTERNAL SAFETY PATH

This procedure must be completed anytime a component of the EML throttle by wire system is removed or disconnected. It requires tool 12 7 010 or equivalent. Do not work on any EML component without having access to this tool.

1. Turn the ignition switch to **OFF**. Unplug the EML connector. The EML connector is grouped with the DME engine connectors. The EML connector is next to the engine diagnostic connector, centered in the group of 3 circular connectors.

2. Install the EML testing adapter 12 7 010 or equivalent to the EML connector inline. Make sure all connections are tight.

3. Turn the knob on the tester to the left position and start the engine. Adjust the engine speed to 2500 rpm with the tester knob.

4. Depress the brake pedal. The engine speed should drop immediately due to the overrun shutoff provision.

5. If the engine speed does not drop immediately, check the EML system for faults. If the speed does drop immediately, the EML external safety path is functioning.

6. Shut off the engine and remove the tester.

Fuel Injectors

REMOVAL & INSTALLATION

▶ **See Figure 9**

Replace fuel injectors with like units. Different manufacturers where used for the fuel injectors, Bosch being the predominant supplier. In March 1991 Lucas fuel injectors where installed in the M30 engines. They function and test the same way as the Bosch units, but the 2 manufacturers injectors should not be mixed on the same engine.

M20 Engine

1. Remove the intake manifold support from the manifold and valve cover.
2. Disconnect the fuel injector electrical plug plate lead under the intake manifold.
3. Disconnect the 2 coolant temperature sensors. Pull up and remove the fuel injector electrical plug plate.
4. Remove the 4 mounting bolts and pull the fuel rail up and out of the intake manifold. Remove the fuel injectors from the fuel rail.

To install:

5. Check the O-rings on the injector and replace if necessary. Check that all the injectors are of like types. Lightly grease the O-rings with petroleum jelly and install on the fuel rail.
6. Install the fuel rail on the manifold and tighten the bolts to 6.5-8.0 ft. lbs. (9-11 Nm). Install the electrical plate and connectors.
7. Connect the temperature sensors and the fuel injector electrical plate. Install the intake manifold support and tighten the bolts to 15-17 ft. lbs. (20-24 Nm).

M30 Engine

1. Remove the air intake hose passing over the fuel rail. Remove the plastic caps from the fuel rail cover.
2. Remove the 2 5mm setscrews from the fuel injector electrical plug plate. Pull up on the plug plate to remove.
3. Remove the 3 fuel rail bolts and pull up on the fuel rail. Disconnect the plugs from the injectors. Remove the retainers and the fuel injectors from the fuel rail.

To install:

4. Check the O-rings on the injector and replace if necessary. Check that all the injectors are of like types. Lightly

grease the O-rings with petroleum jelly and install on the fuel rail. Connect the electrical plugs.

5. Install the fuel rail on the manifold and tighten the bolts to 6.5-8.0 ft. lbs. (9-11 Nm). Install the electrical plug plate and the 2 5mm setscrews.
6. Install the fuel rail cover and the plastic plugs. Install the air intake hose.

M42 Engine

▶ **See Figures 10, 11 and 12**

1. Remove the upper section of the intake manifold.
2. Remove the electrical plug plate from the injectors. Disconnect the fuel lines from the fuel rail.
3. Remove the fuel rail mounting bolts and pull the fuel rail with injectors up and off. Remove the retainers and the injectors from the fuel rail.

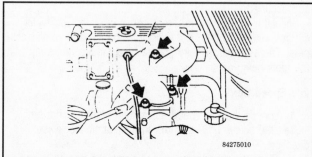

Fig. 10 Upper manifold retaining nuts and vacuum line — M42 engine

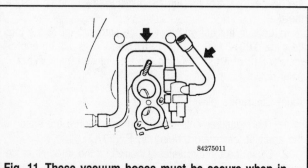

Fig. 11 These vacuum hoses must be secure when installing the manifold — M42 engine

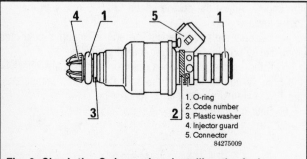

1. O-ring
2. Code number
3. Plastic washer
4. Injector guard
5. Connector

Fig. 9 Check the O-rings when installing the fuel injector

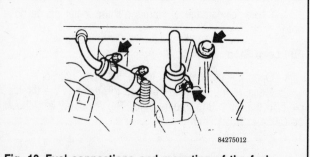

Fig. 12 Fuel connections and mounting of the fuel rail — M42 engine

To install:

4. Check the O-rings on the injector and replace if necessary. Check that all the injectors are of like types. Lightly grease the O-rings with petroleum jelly and install on the fuel rail.

5. Install the fuel rail on the lower manifold and tighten the bolts to 6.5-8.0 ft. lbs. (9-11 Nm). Connect the fuel lines. Install the electrical plug plate and the upper intake manifold.

M50 Engine

▶ **See Figures 13 and 14**

1. On the E36 3 Series with this engine, remove the DME module housing cover screws on the right side of the firewall.

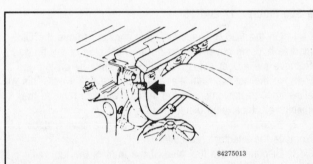

Fig. 13 Fuel feed hose connection to the fuel rail — M50 engine

Fig. 14 The fuel rail is on the right and the injector plug plate on the left is shown with the cover loosened to show the interior wiring. It is not necessary to uncover the wiring when removing the plug plate — M50 engine

Remove the rubber strips along the wire duct by pulling up. Remove the screws from the wire duct and pull it out. This will allow enough movement in the injector wires to remove the injector electrical plug plate.

2. Remove the oil filler cap and the valve cover cladding. Remove the injector area cover.

3. Disconnect the fuel feed at the front of the fuel rail. Remove the 2 screws holding the injector electrical plug plate. Pull up and remove from the injectors.

4. Disconnect the fuel return line. Remove the 2 bolts holding the fuel rail and remove the fuel rail by pulling off with the injectors. Remove the injectors from the fuel rail.

To install:

5. Check the O-rings on the injector and replace if necessary. Check that all the injectors are of like types. Lightly grease the O-rings with petroleum jelly and install on the fuel rail.

6. Install the fuel rail and tighten the bolts to 6.5-8.0 ft. lbs. (9-11 Nm). Connect the fuel lines. Install the electrical plug plate.

7. Install the fuel rail cover and the valve cover cladding with the oil filler cap. Install the wire duct and the rubber stripping.

S14 Engine

1. Remove the bolts from the fuel rail. Disconnect the throttle switch electrical plug.

2. Disconnect the fuel lines and pressure regulator vacuum hose.

3. Pull the fuel rail up and out of the intake manifold. Remove the fuel injector electrical plug clips and plug plate from the fuel rail. Remove the injectors from the fuel rail.

To install:

4. Check the O-rings on the injector and replace if necessary. Check that all the injectors are of like types. Lightly grease the O-rings with petroleum jelly and install on the fuel rail.

5. Install the fuel rail on the manifold and tighten the bolts to 6.5-8.0 ft. lbs. (9-11 Nm). Install the electrical plate and connectors.

S38 Engine

1. Remove the bolts from the fuel rail. Disconnect the idle speed control valve electrical plug.

2. Pull up and remove the fuel injector electrical plug plate.

3. Disconnect the fuel lines and pressure regulator vacuum hose.

4. Pull the fuel rail up and out of the intake manifold. Remove the fuel injectors from the fuel rail.

To install:

5. Check the O-rings on the injector and replace if necessary. Check that all the injectors are of like types. Lightly grease the O-rings with petroleum jelly and install on the fuel rail.

6. Install the fuel rail on the manifold and tighten the bolts to 6.5-8.0 ft. lbs. (9-11 Nm). Install the electrical plate and connectors.

Fuel Pressure Regulator

REMOVAL & INSTALLATION

M20 AND M30 Engines

1. The fuel pressure regulator is mounted on the end of the fuel rail and has a vacuum line and a fuel line leading to it.
2. Relieve the fuel pressure. Disconnect the fuel hose and the vacuum hose.
3. Remove the 2 bolts holding the regulator to the fuel rail. Pull the regulator off the fuel rail.
   To install:
4. Inspect the O-ring on the fuel rail inlet of the regulator. Install the regulator on the fuel rail and tighten the bolts.
5. Connect the fuel hose and vacuum hose.

M42 Engine

MOUNTED IN E30 CHASSIS

1. Remove the front intake manifold support brace.
2. Disconnect the vacuum hose from the regulator. Loosen the mounting clamp bolt and remove the clamp.
3. Be ready to catch the fuel that will leak out of the fuel rail. Pull the regulator down and out of the fuel rail.
   To install:
4. Inspect the O-ring on the fuel rail inlet of the regulator. Install the regulator on the fuel rail and mount the clamp. Tighten the bolts.
5. Connect the fuel hose and vacuum hose. Install the front manifold brace.

MOUNTED IN E36 CHASSIS

▶ See Figures 15 and 16

1. Remove the front intake manifold support brace.
2. Disconnect the vacuum hose from the regulator. Loosen the mounting bracket bolt and remove the bracket.
3. Be ready to catch the fuel that will leak out of the fuel rail. Pull the regulator out of the fuel rail.
   To install:
4. Inspect the O-ring on the fuel rail inlet of the regulator. Install the regulator on the fuel rail and mount the bracket. Tighten the bolt.
5. Connect the fuel hose and vacuum hose. Install the front manifold brace.

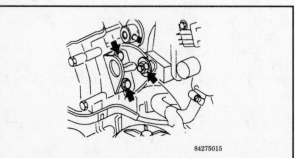

Fig. 15 Remove the front brace to access the fuel pressure regulator — M42 engine

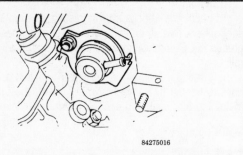

Fig. 16 Remove the bolt to remove the fuel pressure regulator — M42 engine

M50 Engine

▶ See Figures 17 and 18

1. On the E36 3 Series with this engine, remove the DME module housing cover screws on the right side of the firewall. Remove the rubber strips along the wire duct by pulling up. Remove the screws from the wire duct and pull it out. This will allow enough movement in the injector wires to remove the injector electrical plug plate.
2. Remove the oil filler cap and the valve cover cladding. Remove the injector area cover.
3. Disconnect the fuel feed at the front of the fuel rail. Remove the 2 screws holding the injector electrical plug plate. Pull up and remove from the injectors.
4. Disconnect the fuel return line. Remove the 2 bolts holding the fuel rail and remove the fuel rail by pulling off with the injectors. Remove the clamp holding the regulator and remove from the fuel rail.

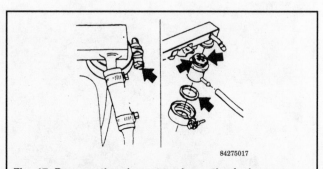

Fig. 17 Remove the clamp to release the fuel pressure regulator — M50 engine

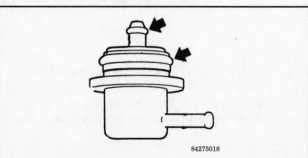

Fig. 18 Check the condition of the fuel pressure regulator O-rings before installation

To install:

5. Check the O-rings on the regulator and replace if necessary. Install on the fuel rail.

6. Install the fuel rail and tighten the bolts to 6.5-8.0 ft. lbs. (9-11 Nm). Connect the fuel lines. Install the electrical plug plate. Connect the vacuum hose to the regulator.

7. Install the fuel rail cover and the valve cover cladding with the oil filler cap. Install the wire duct and the rubber stripping.

S14 Engines

1. The fuel pressure regulator is mounted on the end of the fuel rail and has a vacuum line and a fuel line leading to it.

2. Relieve the fuel pressure. Disconnect the fuel hose and the vacuum hose.

3. Remove the 2 bolts holding the regulator to the fuel rail. Pull the regulator off the fuel rail.

To install:

4. Inspect the O-ring on the fuel rail inlet of the regulator. Install the regulator on the fuel rail and tighten the bolts.

5. Connect the fuel hose and vacuum hose.

S38 Engines

1. The fuel pressure regulator is mounted on the end of the fuel rail and has a vacuum line and a fuel line leading to it.

2. Relieve the fuel pressure. Disconnect the fuel hose and the vacuum hose.

3. Remove the clamp bolt holding the regulator to the fuel rail. Remove the clamp and pull the regulator off the fuel rail.

To install:

4. Inspect the O-ring on the fuel rail inlet of the regulator. Install the regulator with clamp on the fuel rail and tighten the bolt.

5. Connect the fuel hose and vacuum hose.

Intake Manifold Resonance Flap Control System

▶ See Figure 19

As a measure to boost torque and engine performance on the S38 engine, BMW developed a system that features electronically controlled ram air induction. The BMW ram air induction system uses the energy in the intake pulses to help draw more air into the cylinders. This a non-mechanical form of supercharging; more air is forced into the cylinders using this system than the piston alone could draw.

84275019

Fig. 19 Intake manifold resonance flap actuator — S38 engine

The intake manifold is designed with a vacuum actuated flap that divides the interior. The flap will open and close depending on engine speed and throttle position. The two positions form a long path and a short path for the air to flow before it is drawn into the intake runners for each cylinder. By changing the effective length of the intake manifold, the intake pulses of air will resonate at differing frequencies. By varying the resonant frequencies as the engine speed varies, a greater ram effect can be achieved.

For the flap to actuate, two conditions must be met. The throttle must be at full open, with the full throttle switch closed, and the engine speed must be less than 4120 rpm or greater than 6720 rpm. If these conditions are not met, the flap will not actuate. When these conditions are met, the resonance flap control unit will signal an electric vacuum switch to open allowing vacuum to operate the flap. A tolerance of 60 rpm in each direction for the engine speed switching points prevents constant motion of the flap if the engine is operated at exactly either of those speeds.

On cold engine start-up, the resonance flap control unit does a self-check. The flap will be actuated and can be watched as the linkage moves. The electric vacuum valve has battery voltage applied to one terminal and the other terminal goes to the control unit. The control unit will ground the terminal allowing the circuit to be completed.

The resonance flap control unit is located under the relays in the electronics box mounted in the engine compartment. The electric vacuum valve is located under the intake manifold next to the oil trap. The flap actuator is attached to the intake manifold at the top and has a link connecting to the flap inside the manifold.

The vacuum source for the system is a vacuum reservoir mounted below the intake runner for cylinder 5. The vacuum tank is necessary since there would not be enough manifold vacuum to operate the flap at wide throttle positions. A check valve prevents loss of vacuum from the tank while the manifold vacuum is low or when the engine is not running. The tank provides enough vacuum for 6 operations of the flap without manifold vacuum.

TESTING

Resonance Flap Control Unit

1. Start the engine and watch the linkage from the vacuum actuator. The linkage should move the flap each time the engine is started.

2. If the flap linkage doesn't move, move the linkage by hand to check is the linkage is stiff or frozen.

3. Check the vacuum hose for cracks or breaks.

4. Check the actuator and the electric vacuum valve.

5. If these checks do not indicate a problem, replace the control unit.

Actuator

1. Disconnect the vacuum hose from the actuator.

2. Connect a hand held vacuum pump to the actuator.

3. Apply vacuum to the actuator. Replace the actuator if found faulty.

Electric Vacuum Valve

1. Check for battery voltage to one of the terminals on the valve when the ignition switch is **ON**. If there is no voltage, check the wire going to the control unit in the electronics box.

2. If there is voltage to the terminal, ground the other terminal. This will simulate the operation of the control unit and the valve should operate.

3. Replace the valve is found defective.

Idle Speed Control Valve

The idle speed control valve controls the idle speed as directed by the DME unit. The idle speed control valve is an electrically controlled valve that controls the amount of air that bypasses the throttle plate. Physically the valve has 2 hoses, one connected to the intake manifold and the other to the air intake after the air filter.

REMOVAL & INSTALLATION

M20 Engine

1. The idle speed control valve is mounted on the air intake hose near the throttle body. The ignition switch must be in the **OFF** position.

2. Disconnect the electrical plug from the back of the valve.

3. Remove the strap from around the valve body.

4. Pull the valve from the connection hose and the intake duct.

To install:

5. Install the valve on the intake duct and connect the hose.

6. Install the strap around the valve body and connect the electrical plug.

M30 Engine

1. The idle speed control valve is mounted on the air intake hose near the air flow meter. The ignition switch must be in the **OFF** position.

2. Disconnect the electrical plug from the back of the valve.

3. Remove the strap from around the valve body.

4. Pull the valve from the connection hose and the intake duct.

To install:

5. Install the valve on the intake duct and connect the hose.

6. Install the strap around the valve body and connect the electrical plug.

M42 Engine

E30 CHASSIS

1. The idle speed control valve is mounted on the intake manifold attached by a bracket. The ignition switch must be in the **OFF** position.

2. Disconnect the electrical plug from the back of the valve.

3. Remove the nuts holding the valve bracket.

4. Pull the valve from the connection hoses.

To install:

5. Install the valve on the intake manifold and connect the hoses.

6. Connect the electrical plug.

E36 CHASSIS
▶ See Figure 20

1. The idle speed control valve is mounted on the intake manifold attached by a strap. The ignition switch must be in the **OFF** position.

2. Disconnect the electrical plug from the back of the valve.

3. Pull the valve out with the rubber holder.

4. Pull the valve from the connection hoses.

To install:

5. Connect the hoses and install the valve on the intake manifold.

6. Connect the electrical plug.

M50 Engine
▶ See Figure 21

1. The idle speed control valve is mounted under the intake manifold. The ignition switch must be in the **OFF** position.

2. Remove the air intake duct from the intake manifold and disconnect the hoses.

3. Disconnect the electrical plug from the back of the valve.

4. Disconnect the coolant hose and move out of the way. Disconnect the hoses from the valve.

5. Disconnect the vacuum hose and pull the valve from the retainer.

To install:

6. Install the valve in the retainer and connect the hoses.

7. Install the coolant hose and connect the electrical plug.

8. Install the air intake duct and hoses.

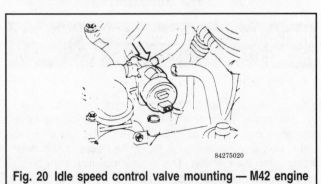

84275020

Fig. 20 Idle speed control valve mounting — M42 engine

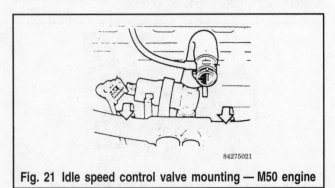

84275021

Fig. 21 Idle speed control valve mounting — M50 engine

S14 & S38 Engines

1. The idle speed control valve is mounted below the intake manifold. The intake manifold must be removed up to the point of the throttle bodies. It is not necessary to remove the throttle bodies. The ignition switch must be in the **OFF** position.
2. Disconnect the electrical plug from the valve.
3. Loosen the hose clamps at the valve and remove the valve.

To install:
4. Install the valve on the hoses and tighten the clamps.
5. Connect the electrical plug.
6. Install the intake manifold. Check the condition of the O-rings and replace as necessary.

Cylinder Identifying Sender

The cylinder identifying sender provides the DME unit information on engine position. A signal is produced that the DME can interpret and use to control the fuel injection and ignition.

There are 3 types of senders. The M20, M30 and S38 engines mount on ignition lead for cylinder 6. The M42 and M50 engines mount on the timing cover and can be called the camshaft sensor. The S14 engines mount on the bellhousing. The sensor on the S14 engine connects to a gray colored plug mounted in the center of a group of 3 plugs on the engine compartment rear wall, next to the engine harness connector and diagnosis socket.

REMOVAL & INSTALLATION

M20, M30 & S38 Engines

1. The ignition switch must be in the **OFF** position.
2. Remove the distributor cap cover to expose the ignition leads. The sensor will be mounted on the ignition lead for cylinder 6. Disconnect cylinder 6 ignition lead from the distributor cap.
3. Trace the sensor lead back to the connector and disconnect. The S38 engine might require the fan and shroud be removed and the water pipe be moved out of the way to access the plug.
4. Cut the distributor connector off the lead and slide the sensor off. Alternately, the entire ignition lead may be replaced if the entire assembly is available as a single unit.

To install:
5. Slide the new sensor onto the ignition lead.
6. Strip off 1/4 in. (5mm) of insulation from the ignition lead end. Place a new coupling on the lead. Crimp the new coupling on the wire end first, then crimp the insulation end.
7. Remove the cut off wire from the distributor connector. Use tool 12 1 096 or equivalent to install the lead into the distributor connector.
8. Install the ignition lead and the distributor cover. Install the fan, shroud and water pipe on the S38 engine, if removed.

M42 & M50 Engines

1. The ignition switch must be in the **OFF** position.
2. The cylinder identifying connector is mounted on the timing cover with a bolt.

3. Remove the bolt and pull the sensor out of the timing cover.
4. Unplug the connector at the mounting bracket.

To install:
5. Check the o-ring around the sensor and install in the timing cover.
6. Tighten the mounting bolt to 4.5-5.5 ft. lbs. (6-8 Nm).
7. Plug in the connector and route the wire.

S14 Engine

1. The ignition switch must be in the **OFF** position.
2. The cylinder identifying connector is mounted on the left side of the bell housing. There is a shield mounted over the sensor with 2 bolts.
3. Remove the bolts and pull the sensor out of the bell housing.
4. Unplug the connector at the mounting bracket.

To install:
5. Install in the bell housing with the shield.
6. Tighten the mounting bolts to 4.5-5.5 ft. lbs. (6-8 Nm).
7. Plug in the connector and route the wire.

Engine Speed Sensor

The engine speed sensor provides the DME unit with engine speed information. The sensor reads the information from a tooth wheel mounted on the crankshaft hub except on the S14 engine. It can also be called the crankshaft sensor.

The S14 engines speed sensor is mounted next to the cylinder identifying sensor and is removed in the same manner as the cylinder identifying sensor. The sensor on the S14 engine connects to a plug mounted in a group of 3 plugs on the engine compartment rear wall, next to the engine harness connector and diagnosis socket. It is the connector on the right side.

REMOVAL & INSTALLATION

▶ See Figure 22

1. Turn the ignition switch **OFF**.
2. Unplug the connector.
3. Unscrew the bolt holding the sender to the engine. Withdraw the sender from the holder.
4. Unclip the lead from the lead guide and remove sender from the vehicle.

To install:
5. Replace the sender and check that it is properly seated. Tighten the mounting bolts to 4.5-5.5 ft. lbs. (6-8 Nm).
6. Replace the lead in the lead guide and plug in the connector. Make sure that the lead can not rub on the drive belt.

Knock Sensor

The knock sensors provide information to the DME to determine whether knocking is taking place. The sensors are mounted to the engine block under the intake manifold. The sensor are used on M42 engines.

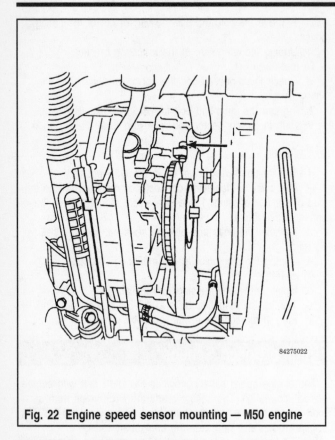

Fig. 22 Engine speed sensor mounting — M50 engine

REMOVAL & INSTALLATION

1. Turn the ignition switch **OFF**.
2. Disconnect the injector plug plate from the injectors and place to the side.
3. Remove the upper intake manifold and disconnect the wire duct from the lower intake manifold.
4. The knock sensors are plugged into the holder with the upper plug for cylinder 1 and 2 knock sensor. The lower plug is for cylinder 3 and 4 knock sensor. Mark the locations of the plugs and disconnect.
5. Note the routing of the leads and the angle the sensors are mounted. Disconnect the water pipe crossing past the knock sensors. Remove the sensors from the engine block.
To install:
6. Install the cylinder 1 and 2 knock sensor with the lead pointing toward the back of the engine. The lead should make a 70 degree angle from vertical to avoid interference with other engine components.
7. Install the cylinder 3 and 4 knock sensor with the lead point to the front of the engine, parallel with the centerline of the crankshaft.
8. Install the water pipe and connect the knock sensor plugs. Install the wire duct and upper intake manifold. Install the injector plug plate.

Throttle Position Switch

The throttle position switch provides the DME unit information regarding when the throttle is wide open and when it is at idle position. The switch is adjustable except on the M42 and M50 engines.

REMOVAL & INSTALLATION

▶ **See Figures 23 and 24**

1. Turn the ignition switch **OFF**.
2. Unplug the connector from the switch body.
3. Remove the 2 screws from the switch body and pull the switch off the throttle body. It may be necessary to remove the throttle body on the M42 engine.
4. Replace the switch and tighten the 2 screws. Connect the electrical connector. Adjust the switch. It is not necessary to adjust the switch on the M42 and M50 engine.

ADJUSTMENT

▶ **See Figures 25 and 26**

1. Unplug the switch connector and use a continuity tester or ohmmeter for this adjustment.
2. There should be continuity between terminals 4 and 6 (automatic transmission) or 2 and 18 (manual transmission) when the throttle is closed (idle).
3. There should be continuity between terminals 4 and 5 (automatic transmission) or 3 and 18 (manual transmission) when the throttle is fully open.
4. Loosen the screws on the side of the housing to adjust the switch. If the switch cannot be correctly adjusted for both test results, replace the switch.

Fig. 23 Disconnecting the throttle position switch — M42 engine

Fig. 24 Location of the throttle position switch — S38 engine, S14 is similar

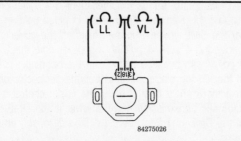

Fig. 25 Throttle position switch connector pinout for manual transmission equipped models. LL is the idle position and VL is the full throttle position

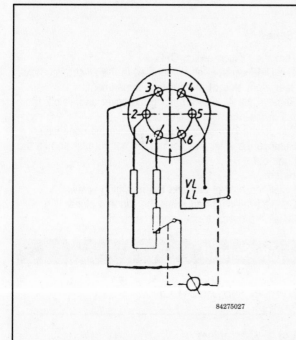

Fig. 26 Throttle position switch connector pinout for automatic transmission equipped models. LL is the idle position and VL is the full throttle position

Accelerator Pedal Sender

The accelerator pedal sender is used on EML equipped vehicles. This is the sensor that tells the EML unit how far the accelerator pedal has been depressed. This takes the place of the throttle cable.

➡**Anytime the accelerator pedal sender is adjusted or replaced, the external safety path check must be made. Be sure to have the tester tool 12 7 010 or equivalent, is available for use before starting these procedures.**

REMOVAL & INSTALLATION

1. Turn the ignition switch **OFF**.
2. Remove the lower dash trim from around the accelerator pedal location.

3. Unscrew the nut from the sender shaft and pull off the pedal lever.
4. Remove the 2 bolts from the sender and disconnect the electrical connector. Note the positions of the spacers, if equipped, for installation.
5. Rotate the sender until the eye can pass through the opening, then rotate until the other mounting eye can pass through the opening. Tilt the sender so the clips can pass through the opening. Turn the sender so the eyes align with the mounting holes and remove completely.
   To install:
6. Align the eyes with the mounting holes and tilt up to pass the clips through the opening. Insert the sender and rotate so both eyes pass through the opening.
7. Tighten the bolts to 3.25-3.50 ft. lbs. (4.5-5.0 Nm). Connect the electrical connector.
8. Install the pedal lever on the sensor shaft and tighten the nut to 4.3 ft. lbs. (6 Nm).
9. Adjust the sensor. Run the external safety path check.

ADJUSTMENT

▶ **See Figure 27**

1. Install the sensor to the mounting bracket and connect the linkage. Snug the mounting screws and loosen the linkage nut on the end of the sensor.
2. Move the linkage to produce a gap between the idle stop and pedal lever. Secure a 0.118 inch (3.0mm) feeler gauge in place to maintain the gap. Support the linkage and tighten the nut to 4.3 ft. lbs. (6 Nm).

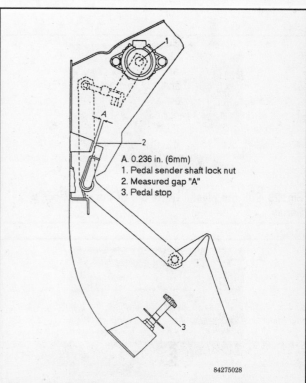

A. 0.236 in. (6mm)
1. Pedal sender shaft lock nut
2. Measured gap "A"
3. Pedal stop

Fig. 27 Accelerator pedal sender — M30 engine with EML and traction control

3. If equipped with a manual transmission, move the pedal to the kickdown detent. Turn the pedal stop knurled nut to touch the pedal and tighten the locknut.

4. If equipped with an automatic transmission, move the pedal to the kickdown detent. Turn the pedal stop knurled nut to produce a gap of 0.236 inch (6mm) between the stop and the pedal and tighten the locknut.

5. Perform the external safety path check.

DME Control Unit

REMOVAL & INSTALLATION

E30 3 Series

1. Turn the ignition switch **OFF**.
2. Open the glove compartment and remove the pins from the straps so the door drops down.
3. Remove the upper trim piece to access the DME unit.
4. Push the plug retainer back and remove the plug. Remove the 4 bolts and remove the DME unit.

To install:

5. Install the DME unit and the 4 bolts.
6. Install the plug onto the DME unit and snap the retainer into place.
7. Replace the trim and the glove compartment door.

E36 3 Series

▶ See Figures 28, 29, 30 and 31

1. Turn the ignition switch **OFF**.

Fig. 28 Pull the plastic rivets out of the cover — E36 3 Series

Fig. 29 Pull back the rubber cover to expose the DME compartment cover — E36 3 Series

2. The DME control unit is mounted behind a panel on the firewall at the right. Remove the 3 press in plugs holding the shield over the DME cover. Pull the shield off the cover.

3. Remove the 4 screws holding the cover onto the firewall. Move the cover with the wire away from the opening.

4. Pull the locking clamp out and pull the connector off the DME unit. If there are 2 control units, the upper control unit is for the automatic transmission and the lower is the DME.

5. Pull the DME unit from the clips. Do not loosen any of the bolts.

To install:

6. Install the DME unit and connect the plug. Lock the connector down.

7. Install both covers. Check the routing of the wiring harness.

E34 5 Series

1. Turn the ignition switch **OFF**.
2. The DME control unit is mounted in the electronics box at the rear, right side of the engine compartment.
3. Remove the 4 screws holding the cover and lift off. the DME unit is the rearmost control unit.
4. Pull up the connector clip and remove the connector.
5. Remove the 2 screws holding the control unit and lift the control unit out.

To install:

6. Install the control unit and the mounting screws.
7. Connect the plug and press the clip into place.
8. Install the cover on the electronics box.

Air Flow Sensor

REMOVAL & INSTALLATION

M20, M42 & S14 Engines

1. Turn the ignition switch **OFF**.
2. Loosen the hose clamp securing the air duct to the body of the air flow meter. Pull off the duct.
3. Disconnect the electrical connector from the side of the air flow meter. On the M42 engine rotate the connector and remove with a screwdriver.
4. Loosen the air cleaner mounting nuts and remove the air cleaner assembly from the vehicle. There may be a wire tie holding the harness in place; cut the tie if necessary. On the 525i and M3, only the upper portion of the air cleaner housing must be removed.
5. Separate the air cleaner housing halves and remove the air flow meter mounting nuts and screw.

To install:

6. Replace the air flow meter and secure the mounting nuts and screw. Assemble the air cleaner housing and replace into the vehicle.

7. Use a new wire tie to hold the harness, if originally equipped. Check the mounting bushings and replace the mounting nuts. Attach the electrical connector and replace the air duct and hose clamp.

M30 Engine

1. Turn the ignition switch **OFF**.

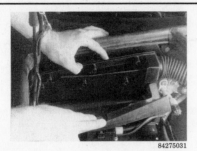

Fig. 30 Remove the DME compartment cover screws — E36 3 series

Fig. 31 DME is visible after pulling back the wiring harness and cover — E36 3 Series

2. Disconnect the electrical connector from the air flow meter. Loosen the hose clamps holding the air ducts to the air flow meter. Remove the ducts from the meter body.

3. Pull off the 3 fasteners holding the air flow meter body. Remove the air flow meter.

To install:

4. Check the rubber mounts and replace the air flow meter.

5. Press the fasteners back into position and connect the air ducting and electrical connector.

FUEL TANK

General Description

The fuel tank is mounted below the vehicle under the trunk area or rear seat area. The tanks on the E30 and E36 3 Series are divided into 2 sections, bisected by the driveshaft. Fuel is transferred from one side to the fuel pump side by a jet action pump. Fuel being returned by the fuel pressure regulator draws the fuel from the left side of the tank through an orifice, using a venturi effect so no mechanical pump is necessary. The fuel is directed to the right side tank and is picked up by the electrical fuel pump.

M50 and S38 Engines

1. Turn the ignition switch **OFF**.
2. Disconnect the air mass sensor electrical connector.
3. Loosen the air duct clamp and remove the air duct.
4. Remove the air cleaner assembly and unscrew the air mass sensor mounting bolts.
5. Remove the air mass sensor.

To install:

6. Install the air mass sensor with the web side towards the air cleaner. The web must be in perfect condition. On the M5 make sure that the intake neck is spaced with equal clearance around its perimeter.

7. Install the air cleaner and connect the air duct and electrical connector.

Oxygen Sensor

REMOVAL & INSTALLATION

1. Turn the ignition switch **OFF**.
2. The exhaust system on the M30 engine equipped vehicles may have to be disconnected at the exhaust manifolds to gain enough working room.
3. Remove the heat shield from the oxygen sensor body and disconnect the electrical connector.
4. Unscrew the oxygen sensor from the exhaust system.

To install:

5. Coat the threads of the oxygen sensor with anti-seize. Do not clean or lubricate the sensor portion of the unit. Do not cover the oxygen sensor connector when undercoating.

6. Check the inside threads of the oxygen sensor port. Clean any carbon build-up.

7. Thread in the oxygen sensor by hand. Torque the unit to 40 ft. lbs. (55 Nm).

8. Connect the oxygen sensor electrical connector.

REMOVAL & INSTALLATION

✳✳CAUTION

Gasoline is extremely flammable and the vapors can be explosive. Work in a well ventilated area away from any sources of ignition. Keep a fire extinguisher of the type for liquid fueled fires within reach during the handling of gasoline. Personal injury or death can result from mishandling gasoline.

E30 3 Series

1. Turn the ignition switch to the **OFF** position. Remove the fuel from the tank by draining or siphoning.

2. Remove the rear seat bottom cushion and pull back the plastic sheet.

3. Remove the covers on both sides to expose the fuel pickups and level senders. Mark and disconnect the hoses and electrical plugs.

4. Remove the fuel level senders from both sides of the tank as equipped. Siphon out any remaining fuel from the tank from the openings.

5. Remove the rear muffler, heat shield and the connecting pipe. Remove the driveshaft.

6. Disconnect the fuel pipes and hoses from the tank. Remove the stone guards on both sides.

7. Support the fuel tank. Remove the fastening hardware and tilt the tank down to remove.

To install:

8. Tilt the tank into place and torque the nuts to 18-20 ft. lbs. (25-28 Nm). Torque the bolts to 16-17 ft. lbs. (22-24 Nm).

9. Install the stone guards and connect the hoses and pipes to the tank. Install the driveshaft. Install the connecting pipe and torque to 17-19 ft. lbs. (23-27 Nm).

10. Install the heat shield and torque to 6.0-6.5 ft. lbs. (8-9 Nm). Install the rear muffler.

11. Install the fuel level senders in the tank. Connect the electrical plugs and the hoses.

12. Install the covers and the plastic sheet. Install the rear seat cushion. Torque the drain plug to 16-18 ft. lbs. (21-25 Nm). Fill the tank with gasoline before operating the fuel pumps.

E36 3 Series

▶ See Figures 32, 33 and 34

1. Turn the ignition switch to the **OFF** position. Remove the fuel from the tank by draining or siphoning.

2. Remove the rear seat bottom cushion and pull back the plastic sheet.

3. Remove the covers on both sides to expose the fuel pickups and level senders. Mark and disconnect the hoses and electrical plugs.

4. From under the vehicle, use fuel line block-off clamps on the fuel feed and return lines. This will prevent fuel from running out of the lines once disconnected. Loosen the hose clamps at the connections and disconnect the lines.

5. Remove the 6 screws holding the heat shield. Remove from the vehicle. Remove the driveshaft.

6. Disconnect the parking brake cables from the parking brake lever. Push the cables out from the clamps and pull out of the holder.

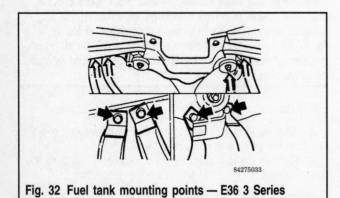

Fig. 32 Fuel tank mounting points — E36 3 Series

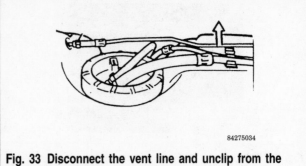

Fig. 33 Disconnect the vent line and unclip from the tank — E36 3 Series

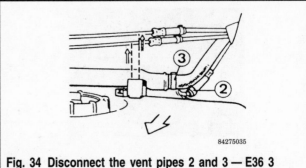

Fig. 34 Disconnect the vent pipes 2 and 3 — E36 3 Series

7. Disconnect the filler hose from the fuel tank. Support the fuel tank from below. Remove the mounting bolts and lower the tank.

8. Disconnect the tank vent line at the tank. Unclip the lines and remove the fuel tank.

To install:

9. Place the tank into position and connect the vent line. Replace the vent lines into position. Install the tank mounting bolts and torque to 16-17 ft. lbs. (22-24 Nm).

10. Connect the filler hose. Install the parking brake cables by passing through the holders and into the clamps. Connect at the parking brake lever.

11. Install the driveshaft and the heat shield. Connect the fuel feed and return lines. Remove the block-off clamps. Connect the fuel lines and the electrical connectors at the fuel pickups and level senders.

12. Install the rear seat cushion. Fill the tank with gasoline before operating the fuel pumps.

E34 5 Series

▶ See Figure 35

1. Turn the ignition switch to the **OFF** position. Remove the fuel from the tank by draining or siphoning.

2. Remove the trunk trim panels to expose the cover at the right, front of the trunk.

3. Remove the cover to expose the fuel pickup and level sender. Mark and disconnect the hoses and electrical plugs.

4. Open the fuel filler door and remove the rubber bellows. Remove the right, rear wheel and remove the wheelwell trim to expose the expansion tank. Disconnect the vent hoses.

5. Support the tank. Remove the heat shield. Remove the strap bolts and remove the tank.

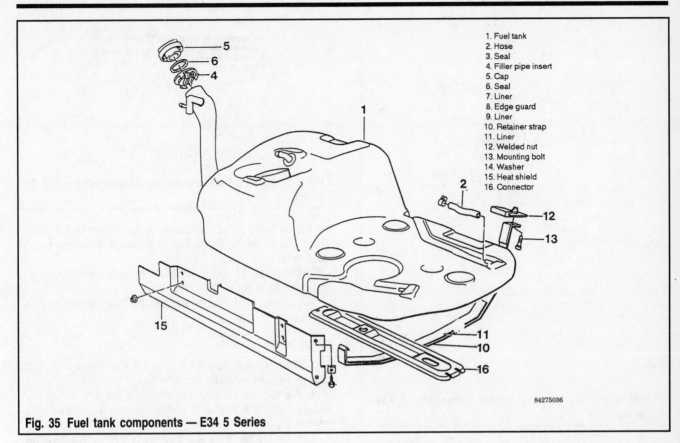

1. Fuel tank
2. Hose
3. Seal
4. Filler pipe insert
5. Cap
6. Seal
7. Liner
8. Edge guard
9. Liner
10. Retainer strap
11. Liner
12. Welded nut
13. Mounting bolt
14. Washer
15. Heat shield
16. Connector

84275036

Fig. 35 Fuel tank components — E34 5 Series

To install:

6. Install the fuel tank, replacing the strap liners and tank pads as necessary. Torque the strap bolts to 6.0-6.5 ft. lbs. (8-9 Nm).

7. Install the heat shield. Connect the vent lines and install the wheel well trim. Install the fuel filler opening rubber bellows.

8. Connect the fuel hoses and electrical plugs. Install the cover in the trunk and the trunk trim panels.

9. Fill the tank with gasoline before operating the fuel pumps.

Fuel Level Sender

E30 3 Series

1. If the tank is full, remove some fuel to lower the level.

2. Remove the rear seat cushion and peel back the insulating sheet to access both covers.

3. Remove the screws from the covers and lift off. Pull of the electrical plug and disconnect the fuel lines. Catch any spilled fuel.

4. If equipped with a level sender held by 4 screws, remove the 4 screws from the sender portion of pickup assembly on the right side. Slowly remove the sender to allow the fuel to drain into the tank. If there are no screws, rotate the assembly counterclockwise and remove.

5. Rotate the left side sender assembly counterclockwise and pull out slowly. Allow the fuel to drain back into the tank.

To install:

6. Replace the gasket and lower the left side sender assembly into the fuel tank. Rotate the assembly clockwise to lock into place.

7. Replace the gasket and lower the fuel level sender into the pickup assembly, if equipped. Replace the screws.

8. Connect the fuel lines and electrical connector. Replace the covers and the insulating sheet. Install the rear seat cushion.

E36 3 Series

RIGHT SIDE

▶ See Figure 36

1. Drain the fuel from the fuel tank if the level is high. It is best to do this procedure with little fuel in the tank.

2. Remove the rear seat cushion and pull off the cover on the right side to expose the top of the fuel pickup assembly.

3. Disconnect the plugs on the top of the assembly. The black connector is for the fuel pump. The white connector is for the fuel level sender.

4. Mark and disconnect the fuel lines. Using tool 16 1 020 or equivalent, rotate the mounting ring and remove the assembly. Press the level arm in slightly to make clearance when removing.

To install:

5. The entire unit must be replaced. The individual parts are not serviceable.

6. Using a new seal and mounting ring, install the assembly. Move the unit from side to side to make sure the level sender is free and in the correct location. There is a rib on the flange that should align with a mark on the fuel tank.

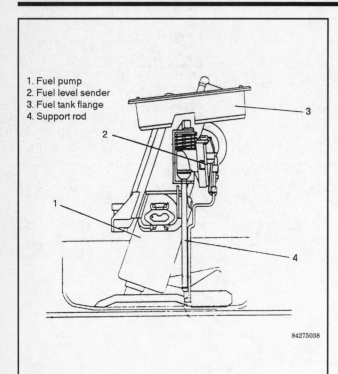

Fig. 36 Right side fuel level sender components — E36 3 Series

84275038

7. Using tool 16 1 020 or equivalent, torque the mounting ring to 27-31 ft. lbs. (37-43 Nm).

8. Connect the fuel lines and the electrical connectors. Install the cover and rear seat.

LEFT SIDE

▶ See Figure 37

1. Drain the fuel from the fuel tank if the level is high. It is best to do this procedure with little fuel in the tank.

2. Remove the rear seat cushion and pull off the cover on the left side to expose the top of the fuel pickup assembly.

3. Disconnect the plugs on the top of the assembly.

4. Mark and disconnect the fuel lines. Using tool 16 1 020 or equivalent, rotate the mounting ring and remove the assembly. Press the level arm in slightly to make clearance when removing.

To install:

5. The entire unit must be replaced. The individual parts are not serviceable.

6. Using a new seal and mounting ring, install the assembly. Insert the fuel pickup and float into the tank. Press the center rod upwards and in the direction of the pickup. Release

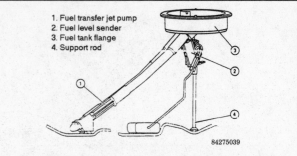

Fig. 37 Left side fuel level sender components — E36 3 Series

84275039

the rod so it sits in the depression on the bottom of the tank. There is a rib on the flange that should align with a mark on the fuel tank.

7. Using tool 16 1 020 or equivalent, torque the mounting ring to 27-31 ft. lbs. (37-43 Nm).

8. Connect the fuel lines and the electrical connector. Install the cover and rear seat.

E34 5 Series

1. Drain the fuel from the fuel tank if the level is high. It is best to do this procedure with little fuel in the tank.

2. Remove the trunk panels to expose the tank access cover on the right side, front corner. Remove the screws holding the cover.

3. Mark the fuel lines and disconnect them. Disconnect the electrical connection.

4. The models with M20, M30 and M50 engines are equipped with a large mounting ring that holds the fuel pump and level sender assembly. The mounting ring is removed using tool 16 1 020 or equivalent. The tool grips the edge of the mounting ring and allows the use of a breaker bar or socket wrench to remove the ring.

5. The M5 with the S38 engine has the fuel pump and level sender assembly retained with 8 screws or nuts around the perimeter. Remove the screws to remove the assembly.

6. Remove the assembly from the tank slowly to avoid spilling any fuel. The level sender with come out first. Compress the mounting hooks and remove the fuel pump.

To install:

7. Install the fuel pump into the tank and make sure the mounting hooks are secure on the fuel pump.

8. Replace the gasket and install the fuel level sender. Tighten the nuts or screws on the M5. On the mounting ring type units, using tool 16 1 020 or equivalent, torque the mounting ring to 27-31 ft. lbs. (37-43 Nm).

9. Connect the wires and the fuel lines. Replace the cover and the trunk trim.

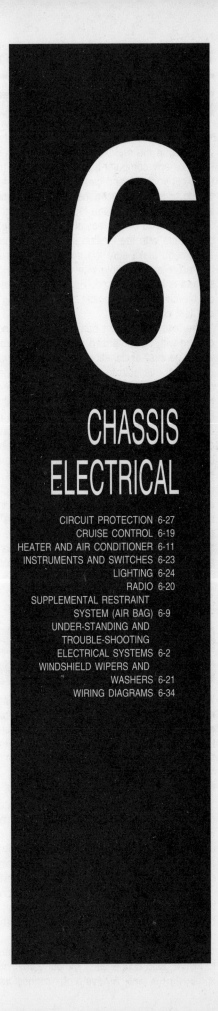

6

CHASSIS
ELECTRICAL

UNDER-STANDING AND TROUBLE-SHOOTING ELECTRICAL SYSTEMS

While it is true that electronic components should never wear out, in the real world malfunctions do occur. It is also true that any computer-based system is extremely sensitive to electrical voltages and cannot tolerate careless or haphazard testing or service procedures. An inexperienced individual can literally do major damage looking for a minor problem by using the wrong kind of test equipment or connecting test leads or connectors with the ignition switch ON. When selecting test equipment, make sure the manufacturers instructions state that the tester is compatible with whatever type of electronic control system is being serviced. Read all instructions carefully and double check all test points before installing probes or making any test connections.

The following section outlines basic diagnosis techniques for dealing with computerized automotive control systems. Along with a general explanation of the various types of test equipment available to aid in servicing modern electronic automotive systems, basic repair techniques for wiring harnesses and connectors is given. Read the basic information before attempting any repairs or testing on any computerized system, to provide the background of information necessary to avoid the most common and obvious mistakes that can cost both time and money. Although the replacement and testing procedures are simple in themselves, the systems are not, and unless one has a thorough understanding of all components and their function within a particular computerized control system, the logical test sequence these systems demand cannot be followed. Minor malfunctions can make a big difference, so it is important to know how each component affects the operation of the overall electronic system to find the ultimat e cause of a problem without replacing good components unnecessarily. It is not enough to use the correct test equipment; the test equipment must be used correctly.

Safety Precautions

✳✳CAUTION

Whenever working on or around any computer based microprocessor control system, always observe these general precautions to prevent the possibility of personal injury or damage to electronic components.

• Never install or remove battery cables with the key ON or the engine running.

• Jumper cables should be connected with the key OFF to avoid power surges that can damage electronic control units. Engines equipped with computer controlled systems should avoid both giving and getting jump starts due to the possibility of serious damage to components from arcing in the engine compartment when connections are made with the ignition ON.

• Always remove the battery cables before charging the battery. Never use a high output charger on an installed battery or attempt to use any type of 'hot shot' (24 volt) starting aid.

• Exercise care when inserting test probes into connectors to insure good connections without damaging the connector or spreading the pins. Always probe connectors from the rear

(wire) side, NOT the pin side, to avoid accidental shorting of terminals during test procedures.

• Never remove or attach wiring harness connectors with the ignition switch ON, especially to an electronic control unit.

• Do not drop any components during service procedures and never apply 12 volts directly to any component (like a solenoid or relay) unless instructed specifically to do so. Some component electrical windings are designed to safely handle only 4 or 5 volts and can be destroyed in seconds if 12 volts are applied directly to the connector.

• Remove the electronic control unit if the vehicle is to be placed in an environment where temperatures exceed approximately 176°F (80°C), such as a paint spray booth or when arc or gas welding near the control unit location in the car.

ORGANIZED TROUBLESHOOTING

When diagnosing a specific problem, organized troubleshooting is a must. The complexity of a modern automobile demands that you approach any problem in a logical, organized manner. There are certain troubleshooting techniques that are standard:

1. Establish when the problem occurs. Does the problem appear only under certain conditions? Were there any noises, odors, or other unusual symptoms?

2. Isolate the problem area. To do this, make some simple tests and observations; then eliminate the systems that are working properly. Check for obvious problems such as broken wires, dirty connections or split or disconnected vacuum hoses. Always check the obvious before assuming something complicated is the cause.

3. Test for problems systematically to determine the cause once the problem area is isolated. Are all the components functioning properly? Is there power going to electrical switches and motors? Is there vacuum at vacuum switches and/or actuators? Is there a mechanical problem such as bent linkage or loose mounting screws? Doing careful, systematic checks will often turn up most causes on the first inspection without wasting time checking components that have little or no relationship to the problem.

4. Test all repairs after the work is done to make sure that the problem is fixed. Some causes can be traced to more than one component, so a careful verification of repair work is important to pick up additional malfunctions that may cause a problem to reappear or a different problem to arise. A blown fuse, for example, is a simple problem that may require more than another fuse to repair. If you don't look for a problem that caused a fuse to blow, for example, a shorted wire may go undetected.

Experience has shown that most problems tend to be the result of a fairly simple and obvious cause, such as loose or corroded connectors or air leaks in the intake system; making careful inspection of components during testing essential to quick and accurate troubleshooting. Special, hand held computerized testers designed specifically for diagnosing the system are available from a variety of aftermarket sources, as well as from the vehicle manufacturer, but care should be taken that any test equipment being used is designed to diagnose that particular computer controlled system accurately without damaging the control unit (ECU) or components being tested.

➡️**Pinpointing the exact cause of trouble in an electrical system can sometimes only be accomplished by the use of special test equipment. The following describes commonly used test equipment and explains how to put it to best use in diagnosis. In addition to the information covered below, the manufacturer's instructions booklet provided with the tester should be read and clearly understood before attempting any test procedures.**

TEST EQUIPMENT

Jumper Wires

Jumper wires are simple, yet extremely valuable, pieces of test equipment. Jumper wires are merely wires that are used to bypass sections of a circuit. The simplest type of jumper wire is merely a length of multistrand wire with an inline fuse and alligator clips on the ends. Jumper wires are usually fabricated from lengths of standard automotive wire and whatever type of connector (alligator clip, spade connector or pin connector) that is required for the particular vehicle being tested. The well equipped tool box will have several different styles of jumper wires in several different lengths. Some jumper wires are made with three or more terminals coming from a common splice for special purpose testing. In cramped, hard-to-reach areas it is advisable to have insulated boots over the jumper wire terminals in order to prevent accidental grounding, sparks, and possible fire, especially when testing fuel system components. Any and all jumper wires must be fused.

Jumper wires are used primarily to locate open electrical circuits, on either the ground (-) side of the circuit or on the hot (+) side. If an electrical component fails to operate, connect the jumper wire between the component and a good ground. If the component operates only with the jumper installed, the ground circuit is open. If the ground circuit is good, but the component does not operate, the circuit between the power feed and component is open. You can sometimes connect the jumper wire directly from the battery to the hot terminal of the component, but first make sure the component uses 12 volts in operation. Some electrical components, such as fuel injectors, are designed to operate on about 4 volts and running 12 volts directly to the injector terminals can burn out the wiring. By inserting an inline fuseholder between a set of test leads, a fused jumper wire can be used for bypassing open circuits. Use a 5 amp fuse to provide protection against voltage spikes. When in doubt, use a voltmeter to check the voltage input to the component and measure how much voltage is being applied normally. By moving the jumper wire successively back from the lamp toward the power source, you can isolate the area of the circuit where the open is located. When the component stops functioning, or the power is cut off,

the open is in the segment of wire between the jumper and the point previously tested.

✳✳CAUTION

Never use jumpers made from wire that is of lighter gauge than used in the circuit under test. If the jumper wire is of too small gauge, it may overheat and possibly melt. Never use jumpers to bypass high resistance loads (such as motors) in a circuit. Bypassing resistances, in effect, creates a short circuit which may, in turn, cause damage and fire. Never use a jumper for anything other than temporary bypassing of components in a circuit.

Test Light

The most basic of electrical testing tools, the test light, has been brought into the computer age. For working on vehicles with computer controlled systems as all BMW's are, the old fashioned incandescent bulb test light is not appropriate. Use a LED type test light on your BMW. An incandescent test light can load a circuit enough to cause damage to the ECU or other electronic components.

LED type test lights are available at most auto supply stores or tool houses.

Continuity Testing

In the same way that the incandescent bulb test light should not be used computer controlled circuits, self-powered test lights should not be used to perform continuity testing. Use a digital multimeter to perform these tests. Digital multimeters are inexpensive and easily obtained at any electronics or automotive supply shop. A basic multimeter will test voltage, resistance, current and also have a continuity function. The continuity function will often offer a audible tone feature allowing testing without having to look at the multimeter.

If the multimeter does not have a continuity test feature, place the unit into the resistance mode and test the circuit. A circuit with continuity will show 0-5 ohms resistance. If the resistance is much higher, there is a component inline with the wire being tested, or there is bad connection at some point. If the multimeter shows infinite resistance, there is a no continuity and there is most likely a break in the wire or a switch in the **OFF** position.

Voltmeter

A voltmeter is used to measure voltage at any point in a circuit, or to measure the voltage drop across any part of a circuit. It can also be used to check continuity in a wire or circuit by indicating current flow from one end to the other. Voltmeters usually have various scales on the meter dial and a selector switch to allow the selection of different voltages. The voltmeter has a positive and a negative lead. To avoid damage to the meter, always connect the negative lead to the negative (-) side of circuit (to ground or nearest the ground side of the circuit) and connect the positive lead to the positive (+) side of the circuit (to the power source or the nearest power source). Note that the negative voltmeter lead will always be black and that the positive voltmeter will always be some color other than black (usually red). Depending on how the voltmeter is connected into the circuit, it has several uses.

A voltmeter can be connected either in parallel or in series with a circuit and it has a very high resistance to current flow. When connected in parallel, only a small amount of current will flow through the voltmeter current path; the rest will flow through the normal circuit current path and the circuit will work normally. When the voltmeter is connected in series with a circuit, only a small amount of current can flow through the circuit. The circuit will not work properly, but the voltmeter reading will show if the circuit is complete or not.

Available Voltage Measurement

Set the voltmeter selector switch to the 20V position and connect the meter negative lead to the negative post of the battery. Connect the positive meter lead to the positive post of the battery and turn the ignition switch ON to provide a load. Read the voltage on the meter or digital display. A well charged battery should register over 12 volts. If the meter reads below 11.5 volts, the battery power may be insufficient to operate the electrical system properly. This test determines voltage available from the battery and should be the first step in any electrical trouble diagnosis procedure. Many electrical problems, especially on computer controlled systems, can be caused by a low state of charge in the battery. Excessive corrosion at the battery cable terminals can cause a poor contact that will prevent proper charging and full battery current flow.

Normal battery voltage is 12 volts when fully charged. When the battery is supplying current to one or more circuits it is said to be 'under load'. When everything is off the electrical system is under a 'no-load' condition. A fully charged battery may show about 12.5 volts at no load; will drop to 12 volts under medium load; and will drop even lower under heavy load. If the battery is partially discharged the voltage decrease under heavy load may be excessive, even though the battery shows 12 volts or more at no load. When allowed to discharge further, the battery's available voltage under load will decrease more severely. For this reason, it is important that the battery be fully charged during all testing procedures to avoid errors in diagnosis and incorrect test results.

Voltage Drop

When current flows through a resistance, the voltage beyond the resistance is reduced (the larger the current, the greater the reduction in voltage). When no current is flowing, there is no voltage drop because there is no current flow. All points in the circuit which are connected to the power source are at the same voltage as the power source. The total voltage drop always equals the total source voltage. In a long circuit with many connectors, a series of small, unwanted voltage drops due to corrosion at the connectors can add up to a total loss of voltage which impairs the operation of the normal loads in the circuit.

Ohmmeter

The ohmmeter is designed to read resistance (ohms) in a circuit or component. Although there are several different styles of ohmmeters, all will usually have a selector switch which permits the measurement of different ranges of resistance (usually the selector switch allows the multiplication of the meter reading by 10, 100, 1000, and 10,000). A calibration knob allows the meter to be set at zero for accurate

measurement. Since all ohmmeters are powered by an internal battery (usually 9 volts), the ohmmeter can be used as a self-powered test light. When the ohmmeter is connected, current from the ohmmeter flows through the circuit or component being tested. Since the ohmmeter's internal resistance and voltage are known values, the amount of current flow through the meter depends on the resistance of the circuit or component being tested.

The ohmmeter can be used to perform continuity test for opens or shorts (either by observation of the meter needle or as a self-powered test light), and to read actual resistance in a circuit. It should be noted that the ohmmeter is used to check the resistance of a component or wire while there is no voltage applied to the circuit. Current flow from an outside voltage source (such as the vehicle battery) can damage the ohmmeter, so the circuit or component should be isolated from the vehicle electrical system before any testing is done. Since the ohmmeter uses its own voltage source, either lead can be connected to any test point.

➡**When checking diodes or other solid state components, the ohmmeter leads can only be connected one way in order to measure current flow in a single direction. Make sure the positive (+) and negative (-) terminal connections are as described in the test procedures to verify the one-way diode operation.**

In using the meter for making continuity checks, do not be concerned with the actual resistance readings. Zero resistance, or any resistance readings, indicate continuity in the circuit. Infinite resistance indicates an open in the circuit. A high resistance reading where there should be none indicates a problem in the circuit. Checks for short circuits are made in the same manner as checks for open circuits except that the circuit must be isolated from both power and normal ground. Infinite resistance indicates no continuity to ground, while zero resistance indicates a dead short to ground.

RESISTANCE MEASUREMENT

The batteries in an ohmmeter will weaken with age and temperature, so the ohmmeter must be calibrated or 'zeroed' before taking measurements. To zero the meter, place the selector switch in its lowest range and touch the two ohmmeter leads together. Turn the calibration knob until the meter needle is exactly on zero.

➡**All analog (needle) type ohmmeters must be zeroed before use, but some digital ohmmeter models are automatically calibrated when the switch is turned on. Self-calibrating digital ohmmeters do not have an adjusting knob, but its a good idea to check for a zero readout before use by touching the leads together. All computer controlled systems require the use of a digital ohmmeter with at least 10 megohms impedance for testing. Before any test procedures are attempted, make sure the ohmmeter used is compatible with the electrical system or damage to the on-board computer could result.**

To measure resistance, first isolate the circuit from the vehicle power source by disconnecting the battery cables or the harness connector. Make sure the key is OFF when disconnecting any components or the battery. Where necessary, also isolate at least one side of the circuit to be checked to avoid reading parallel resistances. Parallel circuit resistances will always give a lower reading than the actual resistance of either of the branches. When measuring the resistance of parallel circuits, the total resistance will always be lower than the smallest resistance in the circuit. Connect the meter leads to both sides of the circuit (wire or component) and read the actual measured ohms on the meter scale. Make sure the selector switch is set to the proper ohm scale for the circuit being tested to avoid misreading the ohmmeter test value.

✳✳CAUTION

Never use an ohmmeter with power applied to the circuit. Like the self-powered test light, the ohmmeter is designed to operate on its own power supply. The normal 12 volt automotive electrical system current could damage the meter.

Ammeters

An ammeter measures the amount of current flowing through a circuit in units called amperes or amps. Amperes are units of electron flow which indicate how fast the electrons are flowing through the circuit. Since Ohms Law dictates that current flow in a circuit is equal to the circuit voltage divided by the total circuit resistance, increasing voltage also increases the current level (amps). Likewise, any decrease in resistance will increase the amount of amps in a circuit. At normal operating voltage, most circuits have a characteristic amount of amperes, called 'current draw' which can be measured using an ammeter. By referring to a specified current draw rating, measuring the amperes, and comparing the two values, one can determine what is happening within the circuit to aid in diagnosis. An open circuit, for example, will not allow any current to flow so the ammeter reading will be zero. More current flows through a heavily loaded circuit or when the charging system is operating.

An ammeter is always connected in series with the circuit being tested. All of the current that normally flows through the circuit must also flow through the ammeter; if there is any other path for the current to follow, the ammeter reading will not be accurate. The ammeter itself has very little resistance to current flow and therefore will not affect the circuit, but it will measure current draw only when the circuit is closed and electricity is flowing. Excessive current draw can blow fuses and drain the battery, while a reduced current draw can cause motors to run slowly, lights to dim and other components to not operate properly. The ammeter can help diagnose these conditions by locating the cause of the high or low reading.

Multimeters

Different combinations of test meters can be built into a single unit designed for specific tests. Some of the more common combination test devices are known as Volt/Amp testers, Tach/Dwell meters, or Digital Multimeters. The Volt/Amp tester is used for charging system, starting system or battery tests and consists of a voltmeter, an ammeter and a variable resistance carbon pile. The voltmeter will usually have at least two ranges for use with 6, 12 and 24 volt systems. The ammeter also has more than one range for testing various levels of battery loads and starter current draw and the carbon

pile can be adjusted to offer different amounts of resistance. The Volt/Amp tester has heavy leads to carry large amounts of current and many later models have an inductive ammeter pickup that clamps around the wire to simplify test connections. On some models, the ammeter also has a zero-center scale to allow testing of charging and starting systems without switching leads or polarity. A digital multimeter i s a voltmeter, ammeter and ohmmeter combined in an instrument which gives a digital readout. These are often used when testing solid state circuits because of their high input impedance (usually 10 megohms or more).

The tach/dwell meter combines a tachometer and a dwell (cam angle) meter and is a specialized kind of voltmeter. The tachometer scale is marked to show engine speed in rpm and the dwell scale is marked to show degrees of distributor shaft rotation. In most electronic ignition systems, dwell is determined by the control unit, but the dwell meter can also be used to check the duty cycle (operation) of some electronic engine control systems. Some tach/dwell meters are powered by an internal battery, while others take their power from the car battery in use. The battery powered testers usually require calibration much like an ohmmeter before testing.

Special Test Equipment

A variety of diagnostic tools are available to help troubleshoot and repair computerized engine control systems. The most sophisticated of these devices are the console type engine analyzers that usually occupy a garage service bay, but there are several types of aftermarket electronic testers available that will allow quick circuit tests of the engine control system by plugging directly into a special connector located in the engine compartment or under the dashboard. Several tool and equipment manufacturers offer simple, hand held testers that measure various circuit voltage levels on command to check all system components for proper operation. Although these testers usually cost about $300-$500, consider that the average computer control unit (or ECM) can cost just as much and the money saved by not replacing perfectly good sensors or components in an attempt to correct a problem could justify the purchase price of a special diagnostic tester the first time it's used.

These computerized testers can allow quick and easy test measurements while the engine is operating or while the car is being driven. In addition, the on-board computer memory can be read to access any stored trouble codes; in effect allowing the computer to tell you where it hurts and aid trouble diagnosis by pinpointing exactly which circuit or component is malfunctioning. In the same manner, repairs can be tested to make sure the problem has been corrected. The biggest advantage these special testers have is their relatively easy hookups that minimize or eliminate the chances of making the wrong connections and getting false voltage readings or damaging the computer accidentally.

➡**It should be remembered that these testers check voltage levels in circuits; they don't detect mechanical problems or failed components if the circuit voltage falls within the preprogrammed limits stored in the tester PROM unit. Also, most of the hand held testers are designed to work only on one or two systems made by a specific manufacturer. Check for availability of a tester for your system.**

A variety of aftermarket testers are available to help diagnose different computerized control systems. Owatonna Tool Company (OTC), for example, markets a device called the OTC Monitor which plugs directly into the diagnostic port. The OTC tester makes diagnosis a simple matter of pressing the correct buttons and, by changing the internal PROM or inserting a different diagnosis cartridge, it will work on any model from full size to subcompact, over a wide range of years. An adapter is supplied with the tester to allow connection to all types of diagnostic ports, regardless of the number of pin terminals used. By inserting an updated PROM into the OTC tester, it can be easily updated to diagnose any new modifications of computerized control systems.

Wiring Harnesses

The average automobile contains about ½ mile of wiring, with hundreds of individual connections. To protect the many wires from damage and to keep them from becoming a confusing tangle, they are organized into bundles, enclosed in plastic or taped together and called wire harnesses. Different wiring harnesses serve different parts of the vehicle. Individual wires are color coded to help trace them through a harness where sections are hidden from view.

A loose or corroded connection or a replacement wire that is too small for the circuit will add extra resistance and an additional voltage drop to the circuit. A ten percent voltage drop can result in slow or erratic motor operation, for example, even though the circuit is complete. Automotive wiring or circuit conductors can be in any one of three forms:
1. Single strand wire
2. Multistrand wire
3. Printed circuitry

Single strand wire has a solid metal core and is usually used inside such components as alternators, motors, relays and other devices. Multistrand wire has a core made of many small strands of wire twisted together into a single conductor. Most of the wiring in an automotive electrical system is made up of multistrand wire, either as a single conductor or grouped together in a harness. All wiring is color coded on the insulator, either as a solid color or as a colored wire with an identification stripe. A printed circuit is a thin film of copper or other conductor that is printed on an insulator backing. Occasionally, a printed circuit is sandwiched between two sheets of plastic for more protection and flexibility. A complete printed circuit, consisting of conductors, insulating material and connectors for lamps or other components is called a printed circuit board. Printed circuitry is used in place of individual wires or harnesses in places where space is limited, such as behind instrument panel s.

Wire Gauge

Since computer controlled automotive electrical systems are very sensitive to changes in resistance, the selection of properly sized wires is critical when systems are repaired. The wire gauge number is an expression of the cross section area of the conductor. The most common system for expressing wire size is the American Wire Gauge (AWG) system.

Wire cross section area is measured in circular mils. A mil is 1/1000″ (0.001″); a circular mil is the area of a circle one mil in diameter. For example, a conductor ¼″ in diameter is 0.250 in. or 250 mils. The circular mil cross section area of the wire is 250 squared (250^2)or 62,500 circular mils. Imported car models usually use metric wire gauge designations, which is simply the cross section area of the conductor in square millimeters (mm^2).

Gauge numbers are assigned to conductors of various cross section areas. As gauge number increases, area decreases and the conductor becomes smaller. A 5 gauge conductor is smaller than a 1 gauge conductor and a 10 gauge is smaller than a 5 gauge. As the cross section area of a conductor decreases, resistance increases and so does the gauge number. A conductor with a higher gauge number will carry less current than a conductor with a lower gauge number.

➡**Gauge wire size refers to the size of the conductor, not the size of the complete wire. It is possible to have two wires of the same gauge with different diameters because one may have thicker insulation than the other.**

12 volt automotive electrical systems generally use 10, 12, 14, 16 and 18 gauge wire. Main power distribution circuits and larger accessories usually use 10 and 12 gauge wire. Battery cables are usually 4 or 6 gauge, although 1 and 2 gauge wires are occasionally used. Wire length must also be considered when making repairs to a circuit. As conductor length increases, so does resistance. An 18 gauge wire, for example, can carry a 10 amp load for 10 feet without excessive voltage drop; however if a 15 foot wire is required for the same 10 amp load, it must be a 16 gauge wire.

An electrical schematic shows the electrical current paths when a circuit is operating properly. It is essential to understand how a circuit works before trying to figure out why it doesn't. Schematics break the entire electrical system down into individual circuits and show only one particular circuit. In a schematic, no attempt is made to represent wiring and components as they physically appear on the vehicle; switches and other components are shown as simply as possible. Face views of harness connectors show the cavity or terminal locations in all multi-pin connectors to help locate test points.

If you need to backprobe a connector while it is on the component, the order of the terminals must be mentally reversed. The wire color code can help in this situation, as well as a keyway, lock tab or other reference mark.

WIRING REPAIR

Soldering is a quick, efficient method of joining metals permanently. Everyone who has the occasion to make wiring repairs should know how to solder. Electrical connections that are soldered are far less likely to come apart and will conduct electricity much better than connections that are only 'pig-tailed' together. The most popular (and preferred) method of soldering is with an electrical soldering gun. Soldering irons are available in many sizes and wattage ratings. Irons with higher wattage ratings deliver higher temperatures and recover lost heat faster. A small soldering iron rated for no more than 50 watts is recommended, especially on electrical systems where excess heat can damage the components being soldered.

➡ It is recommended that a butane or battery powered cordless soldering iron be used. Certain types of 120 volt AC power soldering irons have voltage present on the heated tips and this could damage an ECU if the voltage found its way into the ECU.

There are three ingredients necessary for successful soldering; proper flux, good solder and sufficient heat. A soldering flux is necessary to clean the metal of tarnish, prepare it for soldering and to enable the solder to spread into tiny crevices. When soldering, always use a resin flux or resin core solder which is non-corrosive and will not attract moisture once the job is finished. Other types of flux (acid core) will leave a residue that will attract moisture and cause the wires to corrode. Tin is a unique metal with a low melting point. In a molten state, it dissolves and alloys easily with many metals. Solder is made by mixing tin with lead. The most common proportions are 40/60, 50/50 and 60/40, with the percentage of tin listed first. Low priced solders usually contain less tin, making them very difficult for a beginner to use because more heat is required to melt the solder. A common solder is 40/60 which is well suited for all-around general use, but 60/40 melts easier, has more tin for a better joint and is preferred for electrical work.

Soldering Techniques

Successful soldering requires that the metals to be joined be heated to a temperature that will melt the solder — usually 360-460°F (182-238°C). Contrary to popular belief, the purpose of the soldering iron is not to melt the solder itself, but to heat the parts being soldered to a temperature high enough to melt the solder when it is touched to the work. Melting flux-cored solder on the soldering iron will usually destroy the effectiveness of the flux.

➡ Soldering tips are made of copper for good heat conductivity, but must be 'tinned' regularly for quick transference of heat to the project and to prevent the solder from sticking to the iron. To 'tin' the iron, simply heat it and touch the flux-cored solder to the tip; the solder will flow over the hot tip. Wipe the excess off with a clean rag, but be careful as the iron will be hot.

After some use, the tip may become pitted. If so, simply dress the tip smooth with a smooth file and 'tin' the tip again. An old saying holds that 'metals well cleaned are half soldered.' Flux-cored solder will remove oxides but rust, bits of insulation and oil or grease must be removed with a wire brush or emery cloth. For maximum strength in soldered parts, the joint must start off clean and tight. Weak joints will result in gaps too wide for the solder to bridge.

If a separate soldering flux is used, it should be brushed or swabbed on only those areas that are to be soldered. Most solders contain a core of flux and separate fluxing is unnecessary. Hold the work to be soldered firmly. It is best to solder on a wooden board, because a metal vise will only rob the piece to be soldered of heat and make it difficult to melt the solder. Hold the soldering tip with the broadest face against the work to be soldered. Apply solder under the tip close to the work, using enough solder to give a heavy film

between the iron and the piece being soldered, while moving slowly and making sure the solder melts properly. Keep the work level or the solder will run to the lowest part and favor the thicker parts, because these require more heat to melt the solder. If the soldering tip overheats (the solder coating on the face of the tip burns up), it should be retinned. Once the soldering is completed, let the soldered joint stand until cool. Tape and seal all soldered wire splices after the repair has cooled.

Wire Harness and Connectors

The on-board computer (ECM) wire harness electrically connects the control unit to the various solenoids, switches and sensors used by the control system. Most connectors in the engine compartment or otherwise exposed to the elements are protected against moisture and dirt which could create oxidation and deposits on the terminals. This protection is important because of the very low voltage and current levels used by the computer and sensors. All connectors have a lock which secures the male and female terminals together, with a secondary lock holding the seal and terminal into the connector. Both terminal locks must be released when disconnecting ECM connectors.

These special connectors are weather-proof and all repairs require the use of a special terminal and the tool required to service it. This tool is used to remove the pin and sleeve terminals. If removal is attempted with an ordinary pick, there is a good chance that the terminal will be bent or deformed. Unlike standard blade type terminals, these terminals cannot be straightened once they are bent. Make certain that the connectors are properly seated and all of the sealing rings in place when connecting leads. On some models, a hinge-type flap provides a backup or secondary locking feature for the terminals. Most secondary locks are used to improve the connector reliability by retaining the terminals if the small terminal lock tangs are not positioned properly.

Molded-on connectors require complete replacement of the connection. This means splicing a new connector assembly into the harness. All splices in on-board computer systems should be soldered to insure proper contact. Use care when probing the connections or replacing terminals in them as it is possible to short between opposite terminals. If this happens to the wrong terminal pair, it is possible to damage certain components. Always use jumper wires between connectors for circuit checking and never probe through weatherproof seals.

Open circuits are often difficult to locate by sight because corrosion or terminal misalignment are hidden by the connectors. Merely wiggling a connector on a sensor or in the wiring harness may correct the open circuit condition. This should always be considered when an open circuit or a failed sensor is indicated. Intermittent problems may also be caused by oxidized or loose connections. When using a circuit tester for diagnosis, always probe connections from the wire side. Be careful not to damage sealed connectors with test probes.

All wiring harnesses should be replaced with identical parts, using the same gauge wire and connectors. When signal wires are spliced into a harness, use wire with high temperature insulation only. With the low voltage and current levels found in the system, it is important that the best possible connection at all wire splices be made by soldering the splices together. It is seldom necessary to replace a complete harness. If replacement is necessary, pay close attention to insure proper harness routing. Secure the harness with suitable plastic wire clamps to prevent vibrations from causing the harness to wear in spots or contact any hot components.

➡**Weatherproof connectors cannot be replaced with standard connectors. Instructions are provided with replacement connector and terminal packages. Some wire harnesses have mounting indicators (usually pieces of colored tape) to mark where the harness is to be secured.**

In making wiring repairs, it's important that you always replace damaged wires with wires that are the same gauge as the wire being replaced. The heavier the wire, the smaller the gauge number. Wires are color-coded to aid in identification and whenever possible the same color coded wire should be used for replacement. A wire stripping and crimping tool is necessary to install solderless terminal connectors. Test all crimps by pulling on the wires; it should not be possible to pull the wires out of a good crimp.

Wires which are open, exposed or otherwise damaged are repaired by simple splicing. Where possible, if the wiring harness is accessible and the damaged place in the wire can be located, it is best to open the harness and check for all possible damage. In an inaccessible harness, the wire must be bypassed with a new insert, usually taped to the outside of the old harness.

When replacing fusible links, be sure to use fusible link wire, NOT ordinary automotive wire. Make sure the fusible segment is of the same gauge and construction as the one being replaced and double the stripped end when crimping the terminal connector for a good contact. The melted (open) fusible link segment of the wiring harness should be cut off as close to the harness as possible, then a new segment spliced in as described. In the case of a damaged fusible link that feeds two harness wires, the harness connections should be replaced with two fusible link wires so that each circuit will have its own separate protection.

➡**Most of the problems caused in the wiring harness are due to bad ground connections. Always check all vehicle ground connections for corrosion or looseness before performing any power feed checks to eliminate the chance of a bad ground affecting the circuit.**

Repairing Hard Shell Connectors

Unlike molded connectors, the terminal contacts in hard shell connectors can be replaced. Weatherproof hard-shell connectors with the leads molded into the shell have non-replaceable terminal ends. Replacement usually involves the use of a special terminal removal tool that depress the locking tangs (barbs) on the connector terminal and allow the connector to be removed from the rear of the shell. The connector shell should be replaced if it shows any evidence of burning, melting, cracks, or breaks. Replace individual terminals that are burnt, corroded, distorted or loose.

➡**The insulation crimp must be tight to prevent the insulation from sliding back on the wire when the wire is pulled. The insulation must be visibly compressed under the crimp tabs, and the ends of the crimp should be turned in for a firm grip on the insulation.**

The wire crimp must be made with all wire strands inside the crimp. The terminal must be fully compressed on the wire strands with the ends of the crimp tabs turned in to make a firm grip on the wire. Check all connections with an ohmmeter to insure a good contact. There should be no measurable resistance between the wire and the terminal when connected.

Mechanical Test Equipment

VACUUM GAUGE

Most gauges are graduated in inches of mercury (in.Hg), although a device called a manometer reads vacuum in inches of water (in. H_2O). The normal vacuum reading usually varies between 18 and 22 in.Hg at sea level. To test engine vacuum, the vacuum gauge must be connected to a source of manifold vacuum. Many engines have a plug in the intake manifold which can be removed and replaced with an adapter fitting. Connect the vacuum gauge to the fitting with a suitable rubber hose or, if no manifold plug is available, connect the vacuum gauge to any device using manifold vacuum. The vacuum gauge can be used to determine if enough vacuum is reaching a component to allow its actuation.

HAND VACUUM PUMP

Small, hand-held vacuum pumps come in a variety of designs. Most have a built-in vacuum gauge and allow the component to be tested without removing it from the vehicle. Operate the pump lever or plunger to apply the correct amount of vacuum required for the test specified in the diagnosis routines. The level of vacuum in inches of Mercury (in.Hg) is indicated on the pump gauge. For some testing, an additional vacuum gauge may be necessary.

Intake manifold vacuum is used to operate various systems and devices. To correctly diagnose and solve problems in vacuum control systems, a vacuum source is necessary for testing. In some cases, vacuum can be taken from the intake manifold when the engine is running, but vacuum is normally provided by a hand vacuum pump. These hand vacuum pumps have a built-in vacuum gauge that allow testing while the device is still attached to the component. For some tests, an additional vacuum gauge may be necessary.

SUPPLEMENTAL RESTRAINT SYSTEM (AIR BAG)

General Information

BMW provides a Supplemental Restraint System (SRS) for the protection of the driver. An air bag is used in conjunction with the standard seatbelt to lessen the possibility of injury in case of a frontal, or near frontal, collision. The E36 3 Series and the E34 5 Series also provide an automatic belt tensioner system to take up slack from the seatbelt at the same time as air bag deployment.

➡ **The SRS can only be of use when used in conjunction with the standard seatbelt. This is why it is considered supplemental. Use of the standard seatbelt is mandatory for the best possible protection from all the safety devices built into a BMW vehicle.**

SYSTEM OPERATION

▶ **See Figure 1**

In the case of a frontal collision, as defined by an area 30 degrees left and right of the centerline of the vehicle and traveling at least 12 mph (20 km/h), the air bag will deploy and if equipped, the seatbelt tensioner will operate. This will provide a cushion for the upper body of the driver and will draw the seatbelts tight providing additional restraint.

The system consists of crash sensors, an air bag in the steering wheel, a control unit, steering wheel contact ring and seatbelt tensioners on vehicles so equipped. All the components and wiring are colored orange to indicate the component being part of the SRS.

When either of the sensors are activated by a collision with a solid object and the safing sensor is also activated, the control unit sends current to the air bag and the seatbelt retractors. The current sets off the ignitors within the air bag and seatbelt retractors. The solid fuel burns, generating a harmless gas that fills the air bag extremely quickly. The solid fuel in the seatbelt retractor burns and the resulting gas pushes a piston down, taking the slack out of the seatbelt.

The air bag deploys from the center pad of the steering wheel. It fills with gas to full inflation within 30 milliseconds. The deployment sound is that of a loud bang. The inflation rate is so quick, that by the time the occupant strikes the air

bag, the air bag is already deflating. This allows a controlled release of energy, preventing injury to the occupant. The occupant will only realize that the air bag deployed after the air bag is fully deflated and has done its job.

Some common misconceptions about air bags have crept into the common knowledge and should be corrected. The air bag will not suffocate the occupant, nor will it block the view of the occupant; the inflation and deflation times are too quick for this to occur. The dust produced after the air bag is deployed is not harmful; it is a combination of the burnt fuel and the talc powder that some air bags are packed in to facilitate smooth deployment. A parking lot tap will not deploy the air bag, unless it is a frontal collision above 12 mph (20 km/h). An air bag is not to be used in lieu of a seatbelt; it must be used in conjunction with a seatbelt. Being rear ended will not deploy the air bag. The air bag can not protect the occupant in a side impact, only the seatbelt can provide any measure of restraint.

➡ **Always wear your seatbelt! If it is good enough for use by every racecar driver, it should be good enough for you.**

When the ignition switch is activated, the SRS light will illuminate for 6 seconds and extinguish. This indicates normal operation. If the light does not illuminate, illuminates after the 6 second period or flashes for 5 minutes during driving then stays lit, there is a problem with the SRS. Have the system checked by a qualified BMW technician. The SRS does not lend itself to being serviced by a non qualified person. If the SRS is activated, the system must be replaced, as it can only be used once.

SYSTEM COMPONENTS

Control Module

The control module is located under the left side of the dashboard on the E30 3 Series and the E34 5 Series. The control module on the E36 3 Series is located behind the glove compartment.

The control module monitors the entire SRS and will warn the driver of malfunctions by illuminating the SRS lamp on the dashboard. The control module monitors the operation of the crash sensors and will activate the air bag and seatbelt retractors.

Crash Sensors
▶ **See Figures 2 and 3**

The crash sensors are mounted on the left and right inner fenders. The sensors will complete a circuit to the control module if the impact is great enough. The sensors must be mounted with the arrows facing forward. they should not be tampered with or disassembled.

The control unit a safing sensor built into it. The safing sensor only allow deployment in cases where all criteria for deployment are met. As a result, during an accident, the safing sensor and at least one of the inner fender mounted sensors must be activated.

30°   30°

84276001

Fig. 1 The air bag will only deploy in a frontal collision within 30 degrees of center

Fig. 2 Left side SRS crash sensor between the shock tower and the cruise control actuator — E36 3 Series shown

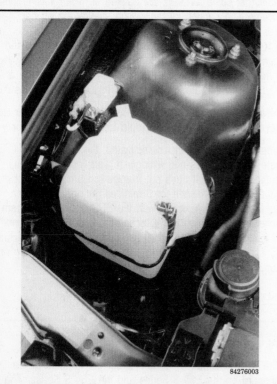

Fig. 3 Right side SRS crash sensor above the washer reservoir

Air Bag

The air bag is packed in the center pad of the steering wheel assembly. There is an ignitor and solid fuel that produces the gas to fill the air bag. As the fuel starts to burn and the air bag begins to expand, the air bag breaks through the outer skin of the steering wheel center pad. The air bag unfolds and fills to full expansion. Two vents on the back side allow the gases to exit the air bag and release energy.

The air bag is fully deployed within 30 milliseconds and is deflating by the time the occupant strikes the bag. This is to control the levels of forces that the occupant is subjected to and to provide the best possible level of occupant protection.

Seat Belt Tensioners

The are 2 styles of seatbelt tensioners. The E34 5 Series uses a pyrotechnic style ignitor and solid fuel, similar to the air bag. The E36 3 Series uses a mechanical system that oper-

ates independently of the air bag. The seatbelt tensioners operate on both the drivers and passenger seatbelts.

On the E34 5 Series, at the same time the air bag is deployed, the ignitor and solid fuel of the seatbelt tensioner is deployed. The gases produced by the burning fuel in the seatbelt tensioner force a piston down, pulling a steel cable that is attached to the seatbelt reel. The seatbelt is pulled taut, providing a more positive restraint for the occupant

The mechanical system on the E36 3 Series is similar in operation to the pyrotechnic system of the E34 5 Series, except the solid fuel and ignitor is replaced by a spring and inertia lock. If the force of the accident is great enough, the inertia lock built into the seatbelt reel assembly, will release the spring, pulling the seatbelt taut.

Steering Wheel Contact Ring

The purpose of the steering wheel contact ring is to provide a continuous electrical path to the ignitor in the air bag. The contact ring allows rotation of the steering wheel while providing the electrical path in an uninterrupted fashion.

SERVICE PRECAUTIONS

✳✳CAUTION

The service precautions must be adhered to, to prevent personal injury. Unintended deployment of the air bag or seatbelt tensioner can cause injury

- Before servicing, disarm the air bag system by turning the ignition switch to the **OFF** position, disconnect the negative battery cable and the air bag connector under the steering column.
- Sensors must be installed with their arrows pointing toward the front of the vehicle.
- Always make sure the steering wheel contact ring has been aligned to the center position before installing. Do not turn the steering wheel with the steering gear disconnected.
- Always replace the air bag system fasteners with new ones. Do not reuse the old fasteners.
- Do not disassemble any air bag system components.
- Always carry an air bag with the trim cover pointed away.
- Always place an air bag on the workbench with the pad side facing upward, away from loose objects.
- After deployment, the air bag surface may contain sodium hydroxide dust. Always wear gloves and safety glasses when handling the assembly. Wash hands afterwards.
- Always inspect the air bag sensors and steering wheel pad after the vehicle has been involved in a collision (even in cases of minor collision) where the air bag did not deploy.
- Never disconnect any electrical connection with the ignition switch ON.
- Before disconnecting the negative battery cable, make a record of the contents memorized by each memory system like the clock, audio, etc. When service or repairs are completed make certain to reset these memory systems.
- Avoid touching module connector pins.
- Always touch a vehicle ground after sliding across a vehicle seat or walking across vinyl or carpeted floors to avoid static charge damage.

- All sensors are specifically calibrated to a particular vehicle. Do not interchange. The sensors, mounting brackets and wiring harness must never be modified from original design.
- Never strike or jar a sensor, or deployment could happen.
- The air bag must be deployed before it is scrapped. Return the air bag to a dealer for disposal.
- Any visible damage to sensors requires component replacement.
- Never bake dry paint on vehicle or subject the vehicle to temperatures exceeding 200°F (93°C), without disabling the air bag system and removing the air bag, sensors, SRS control module and the steering wheel contact ring.
- Never allow welding cables to lay on, near or across any vehicle electrical wiring.
- Caution labels are important when servicing the air bag system in the field. If they are dirty or damaged, replace them with new ones.
- If the crash sensors or the control unit has been dropped 1.5 ft. (0.5 m) or more, they must be replaced.
- Do not subject the air bag to extreme temperatures above 212° F. (100° C.)

DISARMING THE SYSTEM

1. Place the ignition switch in the **OFF** position.

HEATER AND AIR CONDITIONER

➡ **All the procedures needing the air conditioner refrigerant lines to be disconnected require that the system be discharged and the refrigerant recovered by a qualified and properly equipped shop. Do not discharge the refrigerant into the atmosphere. See Section 1 for more information regarding air conditioner refrigerant systems, discharging and charging.**

Heater Blower Motor

REMOVAL & INSTALLATION

E30 3 Series

The blower is accessible by removing the cover at the top of the firewall in the engine compartment.

1. Disconnect the negative battery cable. To remove the motor cover, pull off the rubber weatherstrip, cut off wire ties holding the wire that runs diagonally across the cover, unscrew and remove the bolts, and pull the cover aside.
2. Release the retaining straps, move them to the side, and then remove the blower cover.
3. Pull off both electrical connectors. Disengage the clamp that fastens the assembly in place by pulling the bottom. Lift out the motor/fan assembly, being careful not to damage the flap underneath.
   To install:
4. The fan and motor assembly is balanced at the factory. Do not disturb the orientation of the fan and motor during

2. Disconnect the negative battery terminal and cover the battery terminal to prevent accidental contact.
3. Disconnect the crash sensors in the engine compartment.
4. Remove the lower cover of the steering column and disconnect the orange connector. The E30 3 Series has a small panel on the bottom of the steering column that when pulled down, holds the connector.
5. On the E34 5 Series, disconnect the seatbelt tensioner connectors.

ENABLING THE SYSTEM

1. Place the ignition switch in the **OFF** position.
2. Connect the sensors, the steering column connector and the seatbelt tensioner connectors.
3. Connect the negative battery terminal.
4. Place the ignition switch in the **ON** position. Check that the SRS light illuminates for 6 seconds and extinguishes. If it illuminates in any other pattern, there is a problem that needs to be rectified by a qualified BMW technician.

installation. Place the fan and motor into the heater and install the clamp.
5. Connect the wires and install the fan cover. Attach the straps.
6. Install the outside cover and install the 4 bolts. Install new wire ties on the diagonal wire and replace the weatherstripping. Connect the negative battery cable.

E36 3 Series
▶ **See Figures 4, 5, 6 and 7**

1. Turn the ignition switch to the **OFF** position. Remove the air intake cowl weather-stripping. Remove the grill by gently prying out.
2. Remove the 2 screws inside the air intake cowl holding the electrical duct.
3. Remove the 2 screws holding the right side of the air intake cowl and remove the screw holding the left side. Pull

84276004

Fig. 4 Remove the electrical duct screws from inside the air intake cowl — E36 3 Series

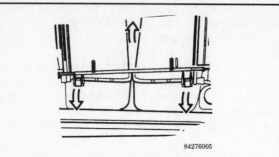

Fig. 5 Release the clips to remove the blower cover — E36 3 Series

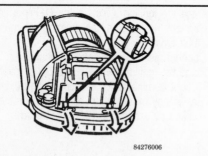

Fig. 6 Release the clips from the left flap upper section to gain access to the blower — E36 3 Series

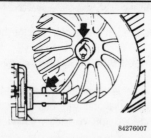

Fig. 7 Match the color dots and indents with the shaft when installing the fans on the motor shaft — E36 3 Series

the cowl out from above. It may be very hard to remove, but it will come out.

4. On M50 equipped vehicles, remove the injector cover plate and the valve cover cladding from the engine.

5. On M50 equipped vehicles, remove the cover from the control unit housing on the right side of the firewall and disconnect the control units plugs. Remove the screws from the injector plug plate and place the plate off to the side. Disconnect the control cable inside the housing.

6. Unclip the heater blower cover. Disconnect the wiring from the motor.

7. Undo the left flap upper section clips and remove. Disconnect the blower from the brace and remove.

To install:

8. If the blower fans are removed, install them so the drive pins fit into the correct indents and the color dots match.

9. Install the fan into the brace and connect the wires. Clip the blower cover into place.

10. On M50 equipped vehicles, connect the control cable, install the injector plug plate, connect the control unit plugs and install the control unit housing cover. Install the valve cover cladding and the injector cover.

11. Install the air intake cowl and screws. Replace the electrical duct screws and the intake grill. Install the weather-stripping.

E34 5 Series

1. Disconnect the negative battery cable.

2. Remove the rubber insulator from the cowl. Remove the mounting bolts and the radiator expansion tank located under the windshield on vehicles equipped. Remove the intensive washing fluid reservoir, if necessary.

3. Remove the wire ties holding the cable to the cover. Remove the screws holding the housing cover and remove the cover. Remove the cable and release the clips to remove the blower cover.

4. Disconnect the electrical connector for the motor. Unclip the retaining strap for the motor and remove the motor and blower wheels.

To install:

5. Replace the motor and blower wheels as an assembly (prebalanced). The motor will fit into the housing only one way. The flat surface on the inlet cowls face the body.

6. Install the blower cover and clip into place. Install the housing cover and replace the screws. Replace the cable wire ties.

7. Install the intensive washing fluid reservoir or the expansion tank, as equipped. Install the weather-stripping.

Heater Core

REMOVAL & INSTALLATION

E30 3 Series

1. Disconnect the negative battery terminal. Remove the center console and the drivers side instrument panel trim next to the steering column. Drain the coolant.

2. Loosen the coolant pipe clamp near the heater connection.

3. Remove the duct from the heater to the rear heating duct.

4. Place some rags or a small container under the heater connection to catch any spilled coolant. Remove the bolts from the heater connection and separate the joint.

5. Remove the heater core bolts and remove from the heater housing.

To install:

6. Replace the heater core into the heater housing and replace the bolts. Replace the O-rings on the heater pipe joint. Connect the pipe to the heater core and install the bolts.

7. Install the rear heating duct connection and the pipe holding clamp. Install the instrument panel trim and the center console. Fill the cooling system and bleed. Connect the negative battery terminal.

E36 3 Series

▶ **See Figures 8, 9, 10, 11 and 12**

1. Turn the ignition switch to the **OFF** position. Remove the air intake cowl weather-stripping. Remove the grill by gently prying out.

2. Remove the 2 screws inside the air intake cowl holding the electrical duct.

3. Remove the 2 screws holding the right side of the air intake cowl and remove the screw holding the left side. Pull the cowl out from above. It may be very hard to remove, but it will come out.

4. Remove the nut from the heater connection and pull off the connection. Blow air into the intake hose to force the coolant out of the heater core. This will prevent coolant from dripping onto the carpeting.

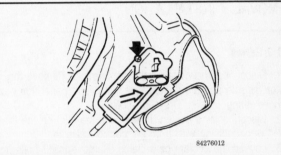

Fig. 11 Remove the bolt to disconnect the flange at the heater core — E36 3 Series

Fig. 12 Remove the screw to withdraw the heater core — E36 3 Series

5. Remove the nut from the connection in the engine compartment. Remove the screws from the left, lower instrument trim panel and pry off.

6. Remove the screw from the pipe connection at the heater core. Remove the heater core mounting nut and remove the heater core.

To install:

7. Replace the heater core and the mounting screw. Replace the O-rings on the pipe connection and install the mounting bolts.

8. Install the trim panel and screws. Install the nut on the engine compartment side of the pipe connection.

9. Replace the O-rings on the connection and install the flange and nut.

10. Install the air intake cowl and screws. Replace the electrical duct screws and the intake grill. Install the weatherstripping.

E34 5 Series

1. Remove the center console and the glove compartment.

2. Disconnect the coolant hoses from the heater. The upper hose is the return line, the middle hose the water feed for the right side and the bottom is the feed for the left side. Blow air into the return connection to remove the remaining coolant from the core.

3. Remove the screws from the holder. Remove the screws from the right holder and remove the holder.

4. Remove the motor for the front vents and disconnect the inside temperature sensor.

5. Disconnect the screws, straps and clips holding the heater cover. Remove the cover to expose the internal coolant pipes.

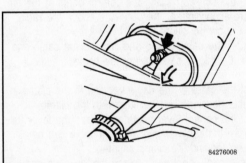

Fig. 8 Remove the nut to disconnect the water flange — E36 3 Series

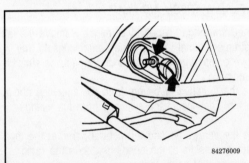

Fig. 9 Remove the nut and the O-rings from the flange — E36 3 Series

Fig. 10 Remove the trim screws before disconnecting the lower trim — E36 3 Series

6. Remove the mounting screws from the coolant pipes and lift out. The heater core remove from the right.

To install:

7. Install the heater core and the coolant pipes with new O-rings. Install the cover and connect the clips, straps and screws.

8. Install the vent motor and connect the inside temperature sensor. Install the holders and screws.

9. Connect the coolant hoses. Install the center console and glove compartment. Fill and bleed the cooling system.

Heater Water Control Valve

REMOVAL & INSTALLATION

E30 3 Series

1. Disconnect the negative battery terminal. Remove the center console and the drivers side instrument panel trim next to the steering column. Drain the coolant.

2. Disconnect the coolant hoses from the inlet on the firewall. Disconnect the wire from the control valve.

3. Loosen the coolant pipe clamp. Remove the 2 bolts from the pipe connection at the control valve and the 3 bolts from the heater connection.

To install:

4. With power applied to the control valve, it will close. With power removed, it will be open. Replace the O-rings at the connections.

5. Replace the bolts in the connections and attach the pipe clamp. Connect the wire to the control valve.

6. Connect the coolant hose at the firewall. Install the center console and the instrument panel trim. Fill and bleed the cooling system. Connect the negative battery terminal.

E36 3 Series

1. Disconnect the electrical plug from the heater control valve located to the left of the hose connections on the firewall.

2. Drain the coolant and remove the hose connections from the valve. Note where the hoses are connected.

3. Pull the valve assembly from the bottom to disconnect it from the rubber mount. Lift the valve from the upper mount.

To install:

4. Place the upper portion of the valve into the mount and press the bottom part into the mount.

5. Connect the coolant hoses in the original locations sand connect the electrical plug. Fill and bleed the coolant system.

E34 5 Series

1. Drain the cooling system. Disconnect the heater hoses from the control valve and the feed hose to the electric water pump, if equipped.

2. Disconnect the electrical plug from the top of the valve. Remove the screws and the clamp.

3. Remove the valve by lifting out.

To install:

4. The valve can be checked by applying battery voltage to the top of the pyramid of terminals and alternately grounding the bottom pins. The valve will actuate.

5. Install the valve, bolts and electrical connector. Connect the coolant hoses. Fill and bleed the cooling system.

Control Cables

REMOVAL & INSTALLATION

E30 3 Series

FOOTWELL FLAP

1. Disconnect the negative battery terminal. Remove the left side lower instrument panel trim and the center console tray. Remove the radio.

2. Remove the switches or covers from the openings above the radio opening. Disconnect the switches from the wiring harness.

3. Remove the screws holding the control panel at the top. The screws are accessible at the openings above the radio opening. Pull the control panel forward.

4. Disconnect the cable clamp and remove the cable end from the lever. Do this at each end of the cable.

To install:

5. Connect the cable at the flap lever and fit the clamp in place. The cable housing must be flush with the clamp.

6. Connect the control lever cable and move the lever fully to the right. Turn the cable sleeve until the cable can be placed in the holder and the clamp secured.

7. Affix the control panel and replace the switches and covers. Install the radio, console tray and the trim panel. Connect the negative battery terminal.

DEFOGGER FLAP & FRESH AIR FLAP

1. Disconnect the negative battery terminal. Remove the left side lower instrument panel trim and the center console tray. Lower the glove compartment door and disconnect the straps. Remove the radio.

2. Remove the switches or covers from the openings above the radio opening. Disconnect the switches from the wiring harness.

3. Remove the screws holding the control panel at the top. The screws are accessible at the openings above the radio opening. Pull the control panel forward.

4. Disconnect the cable clamp and remove the cable end from the lever. Do this at each end of the cable.

To install:

5. Connect the cable at the flap lever and fit the clamp in place. The cable housing must be flush with the clamp.

6. Connect the control lever cable and move the lever fully to the right. Turn the cable sleeve until the cable can be placed in the holder and the clamp secured.

7. Affix the control panel and replace the switches and covers. Install the radio, console tray, glove compartment door straps and the trim panel. Connect the negative battery terminal.

MIXING FLAP

1. Disconnect the negative battery terminal. Remove the left side lower instrument panel trim and the center console tray.

Lower the glove compartment door and disconnect the straps. Remove the radio.

2. Remove the switches or covers from the openings above the radio opening. Disconnect the switches from the wiring harness.

3. Remove the screws holding the control panel at the top. The screws are accessible at the openings above the radio opening. Pull the control panel forward.

4. Disconnect the cable clamp and remove the cable end from the lever. Do this at each end of the cable.

To install:

5. Connect the cable at the flap lever and fit the clamp in place.

6. Connect the temperature selector wheel cable end and move the wheel to the **WARM** position. Turn the cable knurl nut so the flap moves to the **WARM** position. Adjust the nut so the cable can be placed in the holder and the clamp secured.

7. Affix the control panel and replace the switches and covers. Install the radio, console tray, glove compartment door straps and the trim panel. Connect the negative battery terminal.

E36 3 Series

FRESH AIR FLAP

1. Insert a feeler gauge blade between the bottom of the trip computer display and the frame at the right side. Move the blade towards the right to release the display. Disconnect the wiring from the display and remove.

2. Remove the ashtray or lower console bin, as equipped, by pulling out.

3. Remove the knobs from the heater control panel. Remove the panel mounting screws in the depressions for the knobs and pull the panel out.

4. Push the controls back and guide downwards to be able to disconnect the wiring, shaft and cable.

5. Place the vents above the glove compartment straight forward and remove from the dashboard.

6. Remove the 6 screws holding the glove compartment and remove the unit.

7. Disconnect the cable from the retainer and squeeze the tabs together to remove the cable from the holder.

To install:

8. Connect the wiring, cable and shaft to the control panel. Install the panel and knobs. Install the ashtray or bin and the trip computer display.

9. Install the cable into the holder and the retainer.

10. Turn the blower control to **4** and press the control lever towards the holder. This will adjust the cable.

11. Install the glove compartment and vents.

E34 5 Series

1. Remove the radio and the heater control panel.

2. Remove the desired cable by squeezing the clip and releasing from the holder.

3. Remove the glove compartment and the lower trim panel. Remove the desired cable by squeezing the clip and releasing from the holder.

To install:

4. The control cables and the levers are color coded. Install the cable on the control and clip into place.

5. Install the cable to the control lever and install the panel in the dashboard. The cables will be automatically adjusted by moving the levers fully in both directions.

6. Install the glove compartment and the lower trim panel. Install the radio.

Control Panel

REMOVAL & INSTALLATION

E30 3 Series

1. Disconnect the negative battery terminal. Remove the left side lower instrument panel trim and the center console tray. Remove the radio.

2. Remove the switches or covers from the openings above the radio opening. Disconnect the switches from the wiring harness.

3. Remove the screws holding the control panel at the top. The screws are accessible at the openings above the radio opening. Pull the control panel forward.

4. Disconnect the cable clamps and remove the cable ends from the levers.

To install:

5. Connect the cables. Install the panel into the dashboard and replace the screws.

6. Install the switches and the radio. Install the center console tray and the trim panel. Connect the negative battery terminal.

E36 3 Series

1. Insert a feeler gauge blade between the bottom of the trip computer display and the frame at the right side. Move the blade towards the right to release the display. Disconnect the wiring from the display and remove.

2. Remove the ashtray or lower console bin, as equipped, by pulling out.

3. Remove the knobs from the heater control panel. Remove the panel mounting screws in the depressions for the knobs and pull the panel out.

4. Push the controls back and guide downwards to be able to disconnect the wiring, shaft and cable.

To install:

5. Connect the shaft, wiring and cable to the control panel.

6. Guide the panel into place and install the mounting screws. Replace the knobs.

7. Install the ashtray or bin by pressing into place. Connect the wiring to the trip computer display and press into place.

E34 5 Series

STANDARD CONTROLS

1. Remove the radio from the opening.
2. Press the clip on the left and pull out the control panel.
3. Unclip the cables and disconnect the electrical plug.
4. Install in reverse order.

AUTOMATIC CONTROLS

1. Remove the cover from the rear defogger switch.

2. Use a tool to press the clip accessible from the defogger switch opening.

3. Pull the control unit out and disconnect the plugs.

4. Install in reverse order.

Microfilter

BMW uses a microfilter to clean the air being passed to the passenger compartment. The unit cleans pollen, dust and other particles from the air to allow better driving comfort. A reduced flow of air from the vents is an indication of a clogged microfilter.

REMOVAL & INSTALLATION

E30 3 Series

1. Open the glove compartment door and remove the inside trim at the heater side.

2. Remove the glove compartment door straps and the hinge mounting nuts. Remove the door.

3. Remove the 4 screws holding the cover on the side of the heater unit. Remove the microfilter from under this cover.

4. Install the filter, cover and glove compartment door.

E36 3 Series

Canadian versions not equipped with air conditioning use microfilters attached to the blower housing. These filters are removed by accessing the blower housing through the engine compartment. The other vehicles have the microfilter in the heater and air conditioning unit within the vehicle. This procedure covers the internal microfilter removal and installation.

1. Place the vents above the glove compartment straight forward and remove from the dashboard.

2. Remove the 6 screws holding the glove compartment and remove the unit complete with the lower trim panel.

3. Remove the footwell duct for the heater. Remove the screws holding the control unit bracket and tilt down.

4. Turn the lock and remove the cover. Pull the filter out of the housing.\
   To install:

5. Install the new filter and replace the cover. Turn the cover lock.

6. Install the control unit holder and the heater duct.

7. Install the glove compartment, trim and the vents.

E34 5 Series

1. Remove the glove compartment and pull the trim panel out from the rear clip.

2. Remove the cover by disconnecting the clip and pulling out. Remove the air duct screws and lift out.

3. Disconnect the wires from the control unit. Remove the stage from the filter cover.

4. Remove the cover screw and turn the holder. Remove the cover and the filter.
   To install:

5. Install the filter, cover and stage. Connect the control unit.

6. Install the air duct and the cover. Install the trim panel and the glove compartment.

Compressor

REMOVAL & INSTALLATION

E30 3 Series

1. Have the air conditioning system discharged and the refrigerant recovered by a properly equipped shop.

2. Remove the air cleaner assembly. Disconnect the electrical leads from the compressor. Loosen and remove the belt.

3. Disconnect the refrigerant lines from the body of the compressor and plug the opening immediately.

4. Remove the compressor mounting bolts and remove the compressor. On the M42 engine, use tool 64 5 070 or equivalent to pull out the pivot sleeve. This tool acts as a spacer allowing the use of the mounting bolt to pull the sleeve out of the bracket.
   To install:

5. Install the compressor and torque the mounting bolts. Tighten all M8 bolts to 16-17 ft. lbs. (23-24 Nm) and all M10 bolts to 31-35 ft. lbs. (47-48 Nm).

6. Connect the refrigerant lines. Tighten the $5/8$ in. line to 14.5 ft. lbs. (20 Nm), the $3/4$ in. line to 28 ft. lbs. (39 Nm), the $7/8$ lines to 30 ft. lbs. (42 Nm) and the $11/16$ in. lines to 35 ft. lbs. (48 Nm).

7. Connect the electrical wiring and install the belt. Tighten the belt. Install the air cleaner assembly.

8. Have the system charged and the proper amount of oil added.

E36 3 Series

1. Have the air conditioning system discharged and the refrigerant recovered by a properly equipped shop.

2. Disconnect the electrical leads from the compressor. Loosen and remove the belt.

3. Disconnect the refrigerant lines from the body of the compressor and plug the openings immediately.

4. Remove the compressor mounting bolts and remove the compressor. On the M42 engine, use tool 64 5 070 or equivalent to pull out the pivot sleeve. This tool acts as a spacer allowing the use of the mounting bolt to pull the sleeve out of the bracket.
   To install:

5. Install the compressor and torque the mounting bolts. Tighten all M8 bolts to 17 ft. lbs. (24 Nm) and all M10 bolts to 35 ft. lbs. (48 Nm).

6. Connect the refrigerant lines. Tighten the $5/8$ in. line to 14.5 ft. lbs. (20 Nm), the $3/4$ in. line to 28 ft. lbs. (39 Nm), the $7/8$ lines to 30 ft. lbs. (42 Nm) and the $11/16$ in. lines to 35 ft. lbs. (48 Nm).

7. Connect the electrical wiring and install the belt. Tension the belt.

8. Have the system charged and the proper amount of oil added.

E34 5 Series

1. Have the air conditioning system discharged and the refrigerant recovered by a properly equipped shop.

2. Disconnect the electrical leads from the compressor. Loosen and remove the belt.

3. Disconnect the refrigerant lines from the body of the compressor and plug the openings immediately.

4. Remove the compressor mounting bolts and remove the compressor. On the M42 engine, use tool 64 5 070 or equivalent to pull out the pivot sleeve. This tool acts as a spacer allowing the use of the mounting bolt to pull the sleeve out of the bracket.

To install:

5. Install the compressor and torque the mounting bolts. Tighten all M8 bolts to 17 ft. lbs. (24 Nm) and all M10 bolts to 35 ft. lbs. (48 Nm).

6. Connect the refrigerant lines. Tighten the ⅝ in. line to 14.5 ft. lbs. (20 Nm), the ¾ in. line to 28 ft. lbs. (39 Nm), the ⅞ lines to 30 ft. lbs. (42 Nm) and the ¹¹/₁₆ in. lines to 35 ft. lbs. (48 Nm).

7. Connect the electrical wiring and install the belt. Tension the belt.

8. Have the system charged and the proper amount of oil added.

Condenser

REMOVAL & INSTALLATION

1. Disconnect the negative battery cable.

2. Have the air conditioning system properly discharged by a qualified shop.

3. Drain the cooling system. Remove the radiator and fan from the vehicle.

4. Remove the bolts retaining the right and center grille, remove the grilles.

5. Disconnect and plug the refrigerant lines at the condenser, through the right side grille opening.

6. Disconnect the auxiliary cooling fan connector. Remove the cooling fan from the condenser.

7. Remove the condenser mounting bolts and remove the condenser upward.

To install:

8. Install the condenser in position and install the mounting bolts.

9. Install the auxiliary cooling fan.

10. Reconnect the refrigerant lines at the condenser, using new gaskets. Tighten the ⅝ in. line to 14.5 ft. lbs. (20 Nm), the ¾ in. line to 28 ft. lbs. (39 Nm), the ⅞ lines to 30 ft. lbs. (42 Nm) and the ¹¹/₁₆ in. lines to 35 ft. lbs. (48 Nm).

11. Install the radiator into the vehicle. Install the grille pieces.

12. Refill the cooling system and properly recharge the air conditioning system.

13. Reconnect the negative battery cable. Bleed the cooling system.

Evaporator Core & Expansion Valve

REMOVAL & INSTALLATION

E30 3 Series

1. Have the air conditioning system discharged by a qualified shop.

2. Disconnect the negative battery terminal. Remove the center console and the left side lower instrument panel trim next to the steering column.

3. Remove the glove compartment door and the inside trim.

4. Use a wrench to hold the expansion valve while removing the refrigerant lines from the evaporator core. Remove the 4 screws holding the cover panel. Remove the cover panel and the foam rubber.

5. Disconnect the wires and remove the bolts. Remove the temperature switch with the sensor without bending the sensor.

6. Pull the evaporator from the housing and disconnect the lines from the expansion valve using a wrench to hold the expansion valve.

To install:

7. Install the expansion valve on the evaporator core. Tighten the ⅝ in. line to 14.5 ft. lbs. (20 Nm), the ¾ in. line to 28 ft. lbs. (39 Nm), the ⅞ lines to 30 ft. lbs. (42 Nm) and the ¹¹/₁₆ in. lines to 35 ft. lbs. (48 Nm).

8. Install the evaporator core in the housing and replace the temperature switch. Install the bolts and connect the wires. Install the foam rubber and the cover.

9. Connect the lines to the expansion valve. Tighten the ⅝ in. line to 14.5 ft. lbs. (20 Nm), the ¾ in. line to 28 ft. lbs. (39 Nm), the ⅞ lines to 30 ft. lbs. (42 Nm) and the ¹¹/₁₆ in. lines to 35 ft. lbs. (48 Nm).

10. Install the glove compartment and trim panels. Install the center console and connect the negative battery terminal. Have the system charged by a qualified shop.

E36 3 Series

1. Have the air conditioning system discharged by a qualified shop.

2. Turn the ignition switch to the **OFF** position. Remove the air intake cowl weather-stripping. Remove the grill by gently prying out.

3. Remove the 2 screws inside the air intake cowl holding the electrical duct.

4. Remove the 2 screws holding the right side of the air intake cowl and remove the screw holding the left side. Pull the cowl out from above. It may be very hard to remove, but it will come out.

5. Remove the nut from the heater connection and pull off the connection. Blow air into the intake hose to force the coolant out of the heater core. This will prevent coolant from dripping onto the carpeting.

6. Remove the nut from the connection in the engine compartment.

7. Remove the braces on both sides of the unit. Remove the nut holding the refrigerant line flange to the evaporator core.

8. Place the dashboard vent grills above the glove compartment in the forward position and pull out. Remove the 6 screws holding the glove compartment and pull out.

9. Remove both A-pillar trim pieces by unclipping. Remove the lower dashboard trim piece at the right side. Remove the trim panel screw at the bottom left and pry the panel off.

10. Unbolt and lower the steering column. Remove the screws holding the instrument cluster and pull out. Disconnect the instrument cluster wiring.

11. Remove the hazard flasher switch directly behind the shifter opening and remove the screw. Remove the rear ashtray from the console and remove the screws. Remove the parking brake console. Remove the screws and the center console.

12. Remove the screws on both sides and remove the dashboard. Remove the control unit upwards and disconnect the plug. Remove the steering column reinforcement. Disconnect the wires and ducts. Remove the screws and the heater unit with the evaporator.

13. Remove the nuts and the evaporator core. Remove the nut and stud holding the expansion valve.

To install:

14. Install new O-rings on the expansion valve and flange. Attach the expansion valve to the evaporator core. Install the evaporator core. Install the heater unit and connect the wiring, ducts and steering column reinforcement. Install the control unit and the dashboard.

15. Install the center and brake handle consoles. Install the instrument cluster and the steering column.

16. Install the trim panels and the glove compartment. Install the vent grills. Connect the line flange with new O-rings. Install the bolts in the braces.

17. Install the heater line flange with new O-rings. Install the air intake cowl and connect the electrical duct. Install the grill in the cowl.

18. Have the system recharged by a qualified shop.

E34 5 Series

1. Disconnect the negative battery cable.

2. Remove the rubber insulator from the cowl. Remove the mounting bolts and the radiator expansion tank located under the windshield on vehicles equipped. Remove the intensive washing fluid reservoir, if necessary.

3. Remove the wire ties holding the cable to the cover. Remove the screws holding the housing cover and remove the cover.

4. Remove the nut and stud holding the refrigerant line flange. The nut is held with threadlocker and may need to be heated with a hot air gun before removal.

5. Remove the glove compartment and the inside trim. Remove the side trim panel. Remove the air duct.

6. Disconnect the electrical harness and set to the side. Remove the evaporator cover panel.

7. Remove the bolt and disconnect the line flange. Remove the screws and the expansion valve. Pull the evaporator core out from the housing.

To install:

8. Install the evaporator core. Install new O-rings on the flange and expansion valve. Install the expansion valve and the flange. Install the cover and connect the electrical harness.

9. Install the air duct, trim panels and the glove compartment.

10. Install new O-rings on the refrigerant line flange sand connect the flange. Use Loctite® 270 or equivalent threadlocker.

11. Install the blower cover and clip into place. Install the housing cover and replace the screws. Replace the cable wire ties.

12. Install the intensive washing fluid reservoir or the expansion tank, as equipped. Install the weather-stripping.

Drier Unit

REMOVAL & INSTALLATION

E30 3 Series

1. Have the air conditioning system discharged by a qualified shop.

2. Remove the washer fluid tank and the lower trim.

3. Use a backup wrench and disconnect the refrigerant lines. Disconnect the switches. Plug the lines. Remove the bolts holding the unit and the drier.

To install:

4. Install the drier and bolts. Connect the switches and the refrigerant lines.

5. Tighten the ⅝ inch line to 14.5 ft. lbs. (20 Nm), the ¾ inch line to 28 ft. lbs. (39 Nm), the ⅞ lines to 30 ft. lbs. (42 Nm) and the ¹¹/₁₆ inch lines to 35 ft. lbs. (48 Nm).

6. Install the trim panel and the washer tank. Have the system recharged by a qualified shop.

E36 3 Series

1. Have the air conditioning system discharged by a qualified shop.

2. Use a backup wrench and disconnect the refrigerant lines. Disconnect the switches. Plug the lines. Remove the bolts holding the unit and the drier.

To install:

3. Install the drier and bolts. Connect the switches and the refrigerant lines.

4. Tighten the ⅝ inch line to 14.5 ft. lbs. (20 Nm), the ¾ inch line to 28 ft. lbs. (39 Nm), the ⅞ lines to 30 ft. lbs. (42 Nm) and the ¹¹/₁₆ inch lines to 35 ft. lbs. (48 Nm).

5. Have the system recharged by a qualified shop.

E34 5 Series

1. Have the air conditioning system discharged by a qualified shop.

2. Remove the washer tank.

3. Use a backup wrench and disconnect the refrigerant lines. Disconnect the switches. Plug the lines. Remove the bolts holding the unit and the drier.

To install:

4. Install the drier and bolts. Connect the switches and the refrigerant lines.

5. Tighten the ⅝ inch line to 14.5 ft. lbs. (20 Nm), the ¾ inch line to 28 ft. lbs. (39 Nm), the ⅞ lines to 30 ft. lbs. (42 Nm) and the ¹¹/₁₆ inch lines to 35 ft. lbs. (48 Nm).

6. Install the washer tank. Have the system recharged by a qualified shop.

CRUISE CONTROL

Control Switch

REMOVAL & INSTALLATION

E30 3 Series

1. Disconnect the negative battery terminal. Remove the steering wheel.
2. Remove the trim panel at the bottom left of the instrument panel and the lower steering column casing.
3. Remove the screws holding the switch. Remove the switch and disconnect the plug.
   To install:
4. Install the switch and connect the plug. The ground wire must be connected and the retainers must fit into the holes.
5. Install the trim panels and steering wheel. Connect the negative battery terminal.

E36 3 Series

1. Remove the lower dashboard trim panel at the left. Remove the lower section of the steering column casing.
2. Remove the steering wheel and compress the clip to release the switch. Disconnect the plug.
3. Install the switch and connect the plug. Install the steering wheel and trim panels.

E34 5 Series

1. Remove the lower dashboard trim panel at the left. Remove the lower section of the steering column casing.
2. Remove the steering wheel and compress the clip to release the switch. Disconnect the plug.
3. Install the switch and connect the plug. Install the steering wheel and trim panels.

Cruise Control Module

REMOVAL & INSTALLATION

E30 3 Series

1. Disconnect the negative battery terminal.
2. Open the glove compartment door and remove the upper trim.
3. Remove the DME control unit. The cruise control module is mounted above the DME. Remove the cruise control module.
4. Install the modules and trim. Connect the negative battery terminal.

E36 3 Series
▶ See Figure 13

1. Place the vents above the glove compartment straight forward and remove from the dashboard.
2. Remove the 6 screws holding the glove compartment and remove the unit.
3. Disconnect the plug from the control unit and dismount the control unit.
4. Connect the plug, mount the control unit and install the glove compartment with vents.

E34 5 Series

This procedure is for vehicles not equipped with the throttle by wire EML system; vehicles equipped with traction control. The cruise control function is combined with the EML control unit on these vehicles.

1. Remove the cover from the electronics box at the rear, right side of engine compartment.
2. Turn the ignition switch **OFF**.
3. The control module is between the DME unit at the back of the electronics box and the row of relays. Disconnect the module and remove.
4. Install the module and install the electronics box cover.

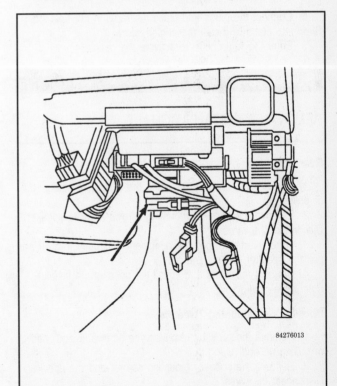

84276013

Fig. 13 Location of the cruise control module behind the glove compartment — E36 3 Series

ACTUATOR

REMOVAL & INSTALLATION

1. Turn the ignition switch to the **OFF** position.

RADIO

Radio Receiver Unit

REMOVAL & INSTALLATION

Make note of the radio code supplied on a tag with the owners information. As an antitheft feature the code must be entered into the radio once power has been removed.

1. Turn the ignition switch to the **OFF** position.
2. Insert radio removal hooks into the holes at the sides of the radio chassis. Seat the hooks and pull the radio out. Disconnect the plugs.
3. If not equipped with holes at the sides of the chassis, pull the knob off and insert the hooks at the holes at the cassette opening and pull out.
4. If equipped with screws at the edges of the chassis mounted at an angle, remove the screws and pull the chassis out.
5. Connect the plugs and place the radio in the opening. Snap into place or install the angled screws.
6. Enter the radio code to activate the radio.

Speakers

REMOVAL & INSTALLATION

Rear Speakers

1. Remove the grills by removing the screws, if equipped, or pulling up.
2. Remove the speaker mounting screws and the speakers. Disconnect the wires.
3. On convertibles, pull the door handle release trim off and pull the speaker grill up and off.
4. Connect the wires and install the speakers in the cutouts. Install the screws and grills.

Door & Dash Mounted Tweeters

1. Remove the grills by removing the screws, if equipped, or pulling up and prying out.
2. Remove the speaker mounting screws and the speakers. Disconnect the wires.

2. Disconnect the electrical connections from the actuator.
3. Disconnect the actuator cable from the throttle linkage and remove the nuts holding the actuator.
4. Install the actuator and connect the wiring and cable.

3. Connect the wires and install the speakers in the cutouts. Install the screws and grills.

Front Speakers

1. Remove the hood release lever on the left side and remove the kick panel trim. On E34 5 Series, remove the door seal and turn the screws 90 degrees. Pull the panel out and to the rear to remove.
2. Remove the screws and wires from the speakers and remove.
3. Connect the wires and install the speakers in the cutouts. Install the screws and kick panels.

Power Antenna Mast

REMOVAL & INSTALLATION

1. Turn the radio **ON** to extend the mast as far as it will go.
2. Remove the nut at the base of the mast. Pull the mast out of the antenna assembly. A firm pull may be necessary.
3. Install the new mast cable end into the opening and turn the radio **OFF** to draw the mast into the housing. Guide the mast and cable into the housing.
4. Install the nut and operate the antenna several times to check the operation.

Power Antenna

REMOVAL & INSTALLATION

1. Remove the trim panel at the antenna location. The rear light cover may need to be removed.
2. Disconnect the antenna mounting bracket. Unplug the wiring.
3. Loosen and remove the mounting nut at the body hole, if equipped. Pull the antenna out of the opening.
4. Install the antenna and the mounting nut at the body hole. Install the mounting bracket and connect the wiring. Install the trim panel.

WINDSHIELD WIPERS AND WASHERS

Windshield Wiper Blades & Arms

REMOVAL & INSTALLATION

▶ See Figures 14, 15, 16 and 17

1. Lift the cover off the arm mounting nut. Note the position of the arm to return it to the original position.
2. Loosen the nut and pull the arm off the shaft.
3. Install the arm on the shaft and press down to fully seat. Install the nut and cover.

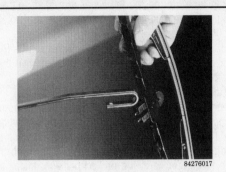
Fig. 17 Pull the arm out of the blade

Fig. 14 Remove the cover to access to the wiper arm mounting nut

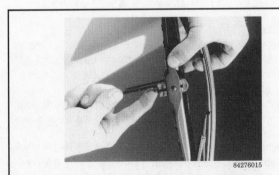
Fig. 15 Pull the clip back to release the blade

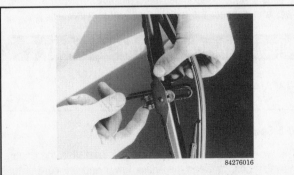
Fig. 16 Push the arm down over the clip

Windshield Wiper Motor & Linkage

REMOVAL & INSTALLATION

E30 3 Series

1. Remove the heater blower motor and the bracket under the wiper motor.
2. Disconnect the motor wiring. If only removing the motor, remove the shaft nut and the 3 mounting nuts. Pull the motor out.
3. Release the clips on the blower plate and disconnect the flaps to remove the blower plate.
4. Remove the wiper arms and the grill. Disconnect the links on the mount for the left pivot.
5. Remove the shaft covers and remove the nut. Remove the washer and pull the linkage out of the opening.
   To install:
6. Install the linkage, washer and nuts. Install the shaft covers and connect the left pivot links. Install the grill and the wiper arms.
7. Install the blower plate and clip into place. Install the motor and link on the shaft.
8. Connect the wires, install the mount and the blower motor.

E36 3 Series

4 DOOR

1. Return the wipers to the parked position and remove the fuse. Remove the wiper arms. Disconnect the negative battery terminal.

➡**Do not operate the wipers while the hood is open. With the hood open the wiper arms could damage the hood and windshield.**

2. Remove the intake air cowl grill cover. Remove the bolts at the ends of the cowl and from the inside holding the electrical duct. Pull the cowl out from the left.
3. On M50 equipped vehicles, remove the injector cover and the valve cover cladding.
4. Protect the inside and edges of the cowl area to prevent scratching. Loosen and remove the wiper arm shaft nuts. Re-

move the brace holding the linkage and disconnect the wiring plug.

5. Wrap tape around the left wiper arm shaft to prevent scratching. Pull the linkage down on the right and rotate the linkage out of the cowl.

6. Pull of the linkage rods from the motor crank. Remove the motor crank nut and pull off the crank. Remove the 3 mounting bolts and remove the motor.

To install:

7. Connect the wiper motor to the electrical plug and actuate the motor to return the motor to the parked position, if necessary. Install the motor on the linkage and press on the crank arm. The arm should make a straight line with the right side drive linkage while in the parked position. Install the nut on the motor shaft. Press on the linkage arms.

8. Install the linkage starting with the left side. Rotate the linkage into place and pass the wiper arm shafts through the openings.

9. Install the wiper arm shaft nuts, then the brace to motor bolt and then the brace to the body bolt. Check the rubber bushings on the wiring at the electrical ducts are secure to prevent water from entering. Connect the wiper plug.

10. On M50 equipped vehicles, install the injector cover and the valve cover cladding.

11. Install the air intake cowl. Connect the electrical duct and install the grill.

12. Connect the negative battery terminal and the wiper fuse. Cycle the wiper motor and install the wiper arms. Close the hood before operating the wipers again.

2 DOOR

1. Return the wipers to the parked position and remove the fuse. Remove the wiper arms. Disconnect the negative battery terminal.

2. Open the hood and remove the bolts from both sides. Pull the hood towards the front and remove the cowl trim piece.

3. Remove the intake air cowl grill cover. Remove the bolts at the ends of the cowl and from the inside holding the electrical duct. Pull the cowl out from the left.

4. Remove the 4 linkage mounting bolts along the cowl starting at the right side near the center of the vehicle and working to the left. Remove the 2 bolts holding the motor brace and disconnect the motor electrical plug. To be able to remove the linkage from the cowl, unscrew the connector from the firewall, but do not push it into the opening.

5. Protect the inside and edges of the cowl area to prevent scratching. Loosen and remove the wiper arm shaft nuts.

6. Wrap tape around the left wiper arm shaft to prevent scratching. Pull the linkage down on the right and rotate the linkage out of the cowl.

7. Pull of the linkage rods from the motor crank. Remove the motor crank nut and pull off the crank. Remove the 3 mounting bolts and remove the motor.

To install:

8. Connect the wiper motor to the electrical plug and actuate the motor to return the motor to the parked position, if necessary. Install the motor on the linkage and press on the crank arm. The arm should make a straight line with the right

side drive linkage while in the parked position. Install the nut on the motor shaft. Press on the linkage arms.

9. Install the linkage starting with the left side. Rotate the linkage into place and pass the wiper arm shafts through the openings. Install the connector and connect the plug. Attach the wire to the holder with a wire tie.

10. Install and tighten the 4 linkage mounting bolts to finger tight. To prevent body damage, tighten the bolts starting with the leftmost bolt near the hood hinge, then the bolt nearest the center of the vehicle. Tighten the bolt next to that one and then the last bolt.

11. Install the wiper arm shaft nuts, then the brace to motor bolt and then the brace to the body bolt. Check the rubber bushings on the wiring at the electrical ducts are secure to prevent water from entering.

12. Install the air intake cowl. Connect the electrical duct and install the grill.

13. Connect the negative battery terminal and the wiper fuse. Cycle the wiper motor and install the wiper arms.

E34 5 Series

1. Cycle the wipers to return to parked position. Turn the heater blower control to 0 and turn the ignition switch **ON** and **OFF** to close the heater box ventilation flaps. Remove the heater blower and remove the heater linkage cover.

2. Disconnect the negative battery terminal and disconnect the heater linkage. Pull out the temperature sensor. Remove the retainers to pull the inlet cowls out and remove the cover.

3. Disconnect the motor mounting brace. Remove the wiper arms. Remove the cowl cover retainers and the cover.

4. Loosen and remove the wiper arm shaft nuts. Disconnect the wiring plug. Pull the linkage out of the cowl.

5. Mark the relationship of the crank arm to the motor shaft and remove. Remove the 3 mounting bolts to remove the motor.

To install:

6. Install the motor to the linkage. If the position of the motor has been changed or a new motor is being installed, connect the motor to the electrical plug and cycle the motor once to return it to the parked position.

7. Install the crank arm to the original position as marked. If it is a new motor, align the crank arm with the linkage arm so they form a straight line.

8. Install the linkage in the cowl. Connect the motor electrical plug and install the wiper arm shaft nuts. Install the cowl cover and the wiper arms. Install the motor brace.

9. Install the inlet cowls and the cover. Install the temperature sensor and connect the heater linkage. Install the heater blower and connect the negative battery terminal.

Wiper & Washer Control Unit/Relay

REMOVAL & INSTALLATION

E30 3 Series

The wiper and washer control relay is located in the under hood relay box, between the shock tower and the cowl. The relay the rightmost, rear unit and pull out of the socket.

E36 3 Series

The control module for the wiper and washer is located under the left kick panel near the footrest and hood release lever. Disconnect the multi-pin connector to remove.

E34 5 Series

The control module for the wiper and washer is located under the left, rear seat. Disconnect the negative battery terminal and remove the rear seat cushion. Remove the screws and the cover. Use tool 00 5 590 or equivalent to pull the units out. The unit on the outside is the control module and the inside unit is the control relay.

INSTRUMENTS AND SWITCHES

Instrument Cluster

REMOVAL & INSTALLATION

E30 3 Series

1. Turn the ignition switch to **OFF**.
2. Turn the screws 90 degrees and remove the lower dashboard trim. Remove the mounting nuts for the lower instrument panel trim from behind the panel.
3. Remove the 4 screws from the bottom of the instrument cluster, noting the lengths and positions for installation. Remove the upper 4 screws. Pull the instrument panel forward.
4. Pull the sliding lock out on the combination plug and remove the plug. Remove the other electrical connections and remove the cluster.
5. Connect the plugs and install the cluster. Replace the screws in the original positions. Install the trim panels.

E36 3 Series

The instrument cluster will need to be recoded after it has been removed. A BMW dealer or qualified shop will be able to perform this function. Check on the availability of this service before disconnecting the instrument cluster.

1. Turn the ignition switch to **OFF**.
2. Remove the steering wheel and the instrument cluster mounting screws.
3. Protect the top of the steering column and tilt the instrument cluster down. Pull the cluster out.
4. Push the levers forward to disconnect the plugs. Remove the instrument cluster.
5. With the levers out, connect the plugs and lock into place. Install the instrument cluster and the steering wheel.

E34 5 Series

1. Turn the ignition switch to **OFF**.
2. Remove the steering wheel and the instrument cluster mounting screws.
3. Protect the top of the steering column and tilt the instrument cluster down. Pull the cluster out.
4. Push the levers forward to disconnect the plugs. Remove the instrument cluster.
5. With the levers out, connect the plugs and lock into place. Install the instrument cluster and the steering wheel.

Gauges

REMOVAL & INSTALLATION

E30 3 Series

1. Remove the instrument cluster.
2. Remove the 9 screws from the back of the cluster; 8 arranged around the perimeter and 1 in the center.
3. Pull the housing off the cluster.
4. Remove the gauge mounting screws and pull the gauge off.
5. Install the gauge and the mounting screws. Mount the housing on the cluster and affix the screws.
6. Install the cluster in the dashboard.

E36 3 Series

The instrument cluster is replaced as a unit. Do not disassemble the instrument cluster.

E34 5 Series

1. Remove the instrument cluster.
2. Rotate the toggle screws 90 degrees to the left and turn up the housing with the printed circuit board. Pull the housing off. Pull off the knobs.
3. Remove the 6 screws from the carrier section and slide off. Note the position of the spacers on the bottom screws and prevent the LCD display from falling out.
4. Pull the instrument off the board to remove.
5. Insert the instrument and assemble the housing. Install the instrument panel.

Service Interval Assembly

The Service Interval (SI) display circuit board is removable on the E30 3 Series. Other vehicles have the Service Interval assembly as an integral part of the instrument panel.

Most problems with the SI stem from bad connections, faulty grounds, relays replaced with nonstandard non diode relays, or bad batteries. The circuit board can be exchanged or have the batteries replaced by soldering new tab batteries in place.

REMOVAL & ASSEMBLY

E30 3 Series

1. Remove the instrument cluster.

2. Disassemble the instrument cluster to separate the carrier from the instruments.

3. Remove the screw holding the light guide at the center of the carrier assembly. Slide the Service Interval circuit board out.

Speed Sender

The vehicle speed is determined via a sensor mounted on the back cover of the rear differential. No speedometer cable is used.

REMOVAL & INSTALLATION

1. Raise and safely support the rear of the vehicle.
2. Turn the ignition switch **OFF**.
3. Squeeze the connector of the electrical plug and disconnect the plug on the rear axle cover.
4. Remove the 2 bolts holding the sensor in place. Catch any lubricant that leaks out.
5. Install a new O-ring on the sender and install in the rear axle. Install the electrical connector.

Windshield Wiper Switch

REMOVAL & INSTALLATION

E30 3 Series

1. Disconnect the negative battery terminal. Remove the steering wheel.
2. Remove the trim panel at the bottom left of the instrument panel and the lower steering column casing.
3. Remove the screws holding the switch. Remove the switch and disconnect the plug.
   To install:
4. Install the switch and connect the plug. The ground wire must be connected and the retainers must fit into the holes.
5. Install the trim panels and steering wheel. Connect the negative battery terminal.

E36 3 Series

1. Remove the lower dashboard trim panel at the left. Remove the lower section of the steering column casing.

2. Remove the steering wheel and compress the clip to release the switch. Disconnect the plug.

3. Install the switch and connect the plug. Install the steering wheel and trim panels.

E34 5 Series

1. Remove the lower dashboard trim panel at the left. Remove the lower section of the steering column casing.
2. Remove the steering wheel and compress the clip to release the switch. Disconnect the plug.
3. Install the switch and connect the plug. Install the steering wheel and trim panels.

Headlight Switch

REMOVAL & INSTALLATION

E30 3 Series

1. Disconnect the negative battery terminal. Remove the lower left dashboard trim below the light switch.
2. Unscrew the light switch knob. Disconnect the electrical connector and pull off the light switch.
3. Install the switch, connector and knob.

E36 3 Series

1. Disconnect the negative battery terminal. Remove the screws for the lower left dashboard trim below the light switch. Remove the panel.
2. Pull the light switch knob off the shaft. Remove the switch shaft mounting nut.
3. Disconnect the electrical plug and remove the switch from the back of the dashboard.
4. Install the switch with the notch matching the retainer in the dashboard. Install the nut and knob. Connect the wiring.

E34 5 Series

1. Disconnect the negative battery terminal.
2. Push the switch to the right and slide a feeler gauge blade into the gap to unlock and remove the switch trim.
3. Pull the plug off the switch and press the switch out of the opening.
4. Install the switch and connect the wiring. Use the feeler gauge blade to depress the locks and install the switch trim.

LIGHTING

Headlights

The headlights must be aimed correctly for best function. Properly aimed headlights make driving at night easier and more enjoyable. Have the headlights aimed by a shop with the correct aiming equipment.

While it takes special equipment to aim the headlights, a burned out headlight bulb is simple and easy to replace. It is a good idea to carry a spare low beam bulb in the car.

REMOVAL & INSTALLATION

▶ See Figures 18 and 19

1. Disconnect the negative battery terminal.
2. Open the hood and remove the plastic cover over the headlight assemblies, if equipped.
3. Disconnect the wiring from the bulb.

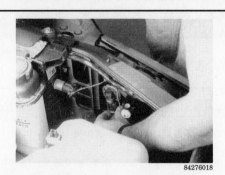

Fig. 18 Disconnect the wiring from the bulb

Fig. 19 Rotate the bulb and pull out of the headlight assembly

4. Rotate the bulb at the rear of the headlight assembly and pull out.

➡**Do not touch the glass portion of the bulb. This will shorten the life of the bulb. Allow the bulb to cool before removing from the headlight assembly.**

5. Install the new bulb and rotate into position. Connect the wiring and replace the plastic cover. Connect the negative battery terminal.

Signal & Marker Lights

REMOVAL & INSTALLATION

Front Turn Signals & Parking Lights

E30 3 SERIES

1. Remove the 2 screws holding the lens. Remove the lens.
2. Gently press the bulb in and rotate counterclockwise.
3. Pull the bulb out of the socket. Inspect the socket for corrosion.
4. Install the new bulb. Press in and rotate clockwise. Install the lens and screws.

E36 3 SERIES

1. Open the hood. From behind the turn signal, release the clip.

2. Pull the light forward and unlock the bulb socket.
3. Gently press the bulb in and rotate counterclockwise.
4. Pull the bulb out of the socket. Inspect the socket for corrosion.
5. Install the new bulb. Press in and rotate clockwise. Install the socket and lens. The lens will snap into place.

E34 5 SERIES

1. Open the hood. From behind the turn signal, remove the cover.
2. Pull the bulb socket forward.
3. Gently press the bulb in and rotate counterclockwise.
4. Pull the bulb out of the socket. Inspect the socket for corrosion.
5. Install the new bulb. Press in and rotate clockwise. Install the socket and cover.

Side Marker Lights

The side market lights on the E30 3 Series and the E34 5 Series are held in by clips and are removed by prying out. The E36 3 Series side marker lights are integrated with the front and rear turn signals and are replaced in the same fashion as the turn signals.

Rear Turn Signals, Brake & Parking Lights

▶ **See Figures 20, 21 and 22**

1. Remove the light assembly cover from inside the trunk.
2. On the E30 3 Series, the bulbs will be exposed when the cover is removed. On the E36 3 Series and E34 5 Series, rotate the bulb holders to expose the bulbs.
3. Press the bulb in and rotate counterclockwise to remove
4. Install the bulb holder and cover.

High Mount (Third) Brake Light

1. From inside the trunk remove the bulb holder directly beneath the brake light. On convertibles, remove the 4 screws under the light on the trunk lid and remove the cover. On the M3, pull the cover back and down.
2. Remove the bulb from the socket.
3. Check the socket for corrosion and replace the bulb. Replace the socket or cover.

License Plate Lights

1. Remove the screws from the light and pull out to the side.
2. Remove the bulb from the assembly.
3. Check the contacts for corrosion and secure fit against the bulb when replaced.
4. Install the new bulb and the assembly into the body. Install the screws.

Interior Lights

1. Pull the housing down from the headliner.
2. Remove the bulb from the assembly.
3. Check the contacts for corrosion and secure fit against the bulb when replaced.
4. Install the new bulb and the assembly into the body.

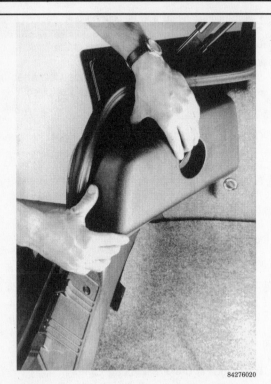

Fig. 20 Remove the rear cover by rotating the handle — E36 3 Series shown

Fig. 21 Rotate the bulb holder to remove

Fig. 22 Press the bulb in and rotate counterclockwise to remove

Fog/Driving Lights

REMOVAL & INSTALLATION

E30 3 Series

1. Remove the plugs over the screws and remove the screws.
2. Pull the assembly forward and remove the cover over the bulb.
3. Compress the clip holding the bulb and remove the bulb. Disconnect the wiring from the bulb.
4. Connect the wiring and replace the bulb. Install the cover and the light. Replace the screws.

E36 3 Series

1. Press the clip in accessible from the upper opening next to the light assembly.
2. Remove the bulb cover by turning to the left. Release the bulb spring and remove the bulb.
3. Install the new bulb and replace the clip and cover.
4. Press the assembly into the opening. The unit will seat into place with a click.

E34 5 Series

1. Flip down the cover for the towing eye. Remove the screw for the light and pull out.
2. Remove the bulb cover by turning to the left. Release the bulb spring and remove the bulb.
3. Install the new bulb and replace the clip and cover.
4. Install the assembly and the screw. Replace the towing eye cover.

CIRCUIT PROTECTION

Fuses & Fusible Links

The fuses are easily checked by visual inspection. With the ignition switch **OFF** pull the fuse out of the holder. Check the fuse filament. It should be continuous and not broken. If the filament is broken, replace the fuse with one of the same amperage rating.

The fuse and relay box on the E30 3 Series, E36 3 Series is located in the engine compartment. The E36 3 Series has relay boxes located under the left side of the dashboard. The E36 3 Series has a usable link inline with the positive battery lead.

The front fuse and relay box on the E34 5 Series is located in the engine compartment. The auxiliary relay box on the E34 5 Series is located in the engine compartment in front of the left shock tower. The rear fuse and relay box is located under the rear seat cushion on the left side. Fusible links are located under the rear seat cushion on the left side, inline with the battery lead and attached to the right shock tower inline with the battery lead.

Relays, Sensors, Modules, Switches, and Computer Locations

E30 3 SERIES

- **A/C 150 Degree Compressor Oil Temperature Switch** is located in the lower right side of the engine compartment, on the compressor.
- **A/C Refrigerant Pressure Switch** — is behind the right headlight, on the receiver/dryer.
- **ABS Electronic Control Unit** — is below the left side of the instrument panel, above the hood release.
- **ABS Hydraulic Unit** — is in the left corner of the engine compartment.
- **ABS Wheel Speed Sensors** — is on the strut assembly at the hub.
- **Active Check Control Unit** — is located above the rear view mirror.
- **Air Bag** — see SRS.
- **Air Flow Meter** — is located in the left of the engine compartment, behind the air cleaner.
- **Automatic Transmission Range Switch** — is at the base of the gear shift lever.
- **Auxiliary Fan Normal Speed Blower Resistor** — is in front of the radiator, left side of the auxiliary fan.
- **Auxiliary Fan** — is located in front of the radiator.
- **Auxiliary Fuel Pump (S14 engine)** — is below the right side of the rear seat, in the fuel tank, below the access panel.
- **Back-Up Light Switch** — is on the top right side of the transmission.
- **Battery Junction Block (M42 engine)** — is at the positive terminal of the battery.
- **Battery Junction Block (except M42 engine)** — is in the right rear of the engine compartment, on the bulkhead.

- **Battery** — is in the right rear corner of the trunk.
- **Blower Motor** — is inside the fresh air intake cowl.
- **Blower Resistors** — is inside the fresh air intake cowl, inside the blower motor housing.
- **Brake Fluid Level Switch** — is on the brake fluid reservoir.
- **Brake Switch** — is below the left side of the instrument panel, on the brake pedal support.
- **Brake Wear Sensors** — is on the left front and right rear brake pads.
- **Central Locking Control Unit** — is inside the left kick panel, below the left front speaker.
- **Chime Module** — is mounted on the left dash hush panel.
- **Clutch Switch** — is below the left side of the instrument panel, on the clutch pedal support.
- **Compressor Clutch Diode** — is on the lower right side of the engine, on the compressor.
- **Compressor Control Unit** — is behind the center of the instrument panel, on the right side of the evaporator housing.
- **Convertible Switch 1** — is in the trunk, behind the right side of the center trim panel.
- **Convertible Switch 2** — is in the trunk, behind the right side of the center trim panel.
- **Convertible Top Control Unit** — is in the trunk, behind the center trim panel.
- **Convertible Top Cover Motor** — is in the trunk, behind the center of the center trim panel.
- **Convertible Top Motor** — is in the trunk, behind the right side of the center trim panel.
- **Convertible Top Position Sensor** — is in the left side of the soft top stowage compartment.
- **Cover Micro Switch Close** — is in the trunk, behind the center of the center trim panel.
- **Cover Micro Switch Open** — is in the trunk, behind the center of the center trim panel.
- **Crankshaft Sensor** — see TDC Sensor.
- **Cruise Control Actuator** — is in the left front corner of the engine compartment.
- **Cruise Control Unit** — is behind the right side of the instrument panel, above the glove box.
- **Dead Point Micro Switch** — is on the right side of the windshield header.
- **Dual Temperature Switch (M42 engine)** — is on the lower right front corner of the engine compartment.
- **Dual Temperature Switch (S14 engine and M20 engine)** — is on the top of the right side of the radiator.
- **Engine Coolant Level Switch (M42 engine and M20 engine)** — is in the coolant reservoir, in front of the left wheel well.
- **Engine Coolant Level Switch (S14 engine)** — is in the coolant reservoir, rear of the right front wheel well.
- **Engine Coolant Temperature Sender (M42 engine)** — is on the top left side of the engine, below the intake manifold.
- **Engine Coolant Temperature Sender (S14 engine)** — is on the lower right front side of the engine, on the coolant manifold.
- **Engine Coolant Temperature Sender (M20 engine)** — is on the top front of the engine, on top of the thermostat housing.

- **Engine Coolant Temperature Sensor (M42 engine)** — is on the top left side of the engine, below the intake manifold.
- **Engine Coolant Temperature Sensor (S14 engine)** — is on the lower right side of the engine, on the coolant manifold.
- **Engine Coolant Temperature Sensor (M20 engine)** — is on the top front of the engine, on top of the thermostat housing.
- **Evaporative Purge Valve (M20 engine)** — is below the left side of the throttle body.
- **Evaporative Purge Valve Relay** — is in the right rear corner of the engine compartment, on the bulkhead.
- **Evaporative Purge Valve** — is on the lower left side of the engine, forward of the shock tower.
- **Evaporator Temperature Regulator** — is on the left side of the evaporator housing.
- **Evaporator Temperature Sensor** — is on the left side of the evaporator housing.
- **Flasher** — is on the upper part of the steering column.
- **Fresh Recirculating Air Relays** — is behind the A/C face plate.
- **Fresh/Recirculating Air Flap Door Motors** — is behind the A/C face plate, on either side of the evaporator housing.
- **Fuel Pump Relay (S14 engine)** — is in the center rear of the engine compartment, on the bracket.
- **Fuel Pump Relay** — is on the front of the left front shock tower, on the bracket.
- **Fuel Tank Sender** — is below the right side of the rear seat, in the fuel tank.
- **Gas Filler Lock Motor** — is in the right side of the trunk, behind the right wheel well.
- **Heated Oxygen Sensor Relay** — is in the center rear of the engine compartment, on the bracket.
- **Heated Oxygen Sensor** — is under the center of the vehicle on the left exhaust pipe.
- **Hot Water Cut-Out Switch** — is behind the center of the instrument panel, near the rotary temperature control.
- **Ignition Coil(s)** — is on the right front wheel well, forward of the shock tower.
- **Ignition Switch** — is on the top right side of the steering column.
- **Interior Light Timer Control** — is inside the left kick panel, below the left front speaker.
- **Lights Check Relay (rear, M42 engine)** — is in the right front corner of the engine compartment.
- **Lights Check Relay (rear, S14 engine and M20 engine)** — is on the inside front of the left rear quarter panel, behind the trim panel.
- **Lock Heater Control Unit** — is in the top of the left front door.
- **Main Fuel Pump (M42 engine)** — is below the left rear of the vehicle, in front of the rear wheel.
- **Main Fuel Pump (S14 engine and M20 engine)** — is below the right side of the rear seat, in the fuel tank.
- **Main Relay (M42 engine and M20 engine)** — is on the front left front shock tower, on the bracket.
- **Main Relay (M42 engine)** — is in the right rear corner of the engine compartment, on the bulkhead.
- **Main Relay (S14 engine)** — is in the center of the rear engine compartment, on the bracket.
- **Oil Level Sensor** — is in the top left side of the oil pan.
- **Oil Pressure Switch (M42 engine and S14 engine)** — is on the lower left front of the engine, below the oil filter.

- **Oil Pressure Switch (M20 engine)** — is on the lower right side of the engine, below the oil filter.
- **Oil Temperature Sensor** — is on the lower left front of the engine.
- **On-Board Computer Horn Diode (S14 engine)** — is on the on-board computer horn.
- **On-Board Computer Horn** — is behind the left corner of the front bumper.
- **On-Board Computer Module** — is in the center of the instrument panel, on right side of the radio.
- **On-Board Computer Relay Box** — is below the left side of the instrument panel, behind the ABS electronic control unit.
- **Outside Temperature Sensor** — is inside the air intake, near the left fog light.
- **Oxygen Sensor Heater Relay (M20 engine)** — is on the front left shock tower, on the bracket.
- **Oxygen Sensor/Fuel Pump Relay (S14 engine)** — is in the right rear corner of the engine compartment, on the bulkhead.
- **Oxygen Sensor** — is in the lower right rear of the engine compartment, on the exhaust manifold.
- **Park Brake Switch** — is at the base of the parking brake.
- **Power Distribution Box** — is in the left rear corner of the engine compartment.
- **Rear Window Blower Relay** — is on the rear window blower.
- **Rear Window Blower** — is behind the center of the rear seat back.
- **Seat Belt and SRS Warning Module** — is in the center of the windshield header.
- **Seat Belt Tension Generator (convertible and M3)** — is on the right side of the rear seat, behind the trim panel.
- **Seat Belt Tension Generator (except convertible and M3)** — is in the right B-pillar, part of the seat belt assembly.
- **Seat Belt Warning Timer (M42 engine and M20 engine)** — is behind the left side of the instrument panel, on the electrical bracket.
- **Seat Belt Warning Timer (S14 engine)** — is behind the left side of the instrument panel, on the kick panel.
- **SRS Crash Sensors** — is in the left and right sides of the engine compartment, in front of the shock towers.
- **SRS Diagnostic Module** — is behind the left side of the instrument panel, above the ABS electronic control unit.
- **SRS Gas Generator** — is located in the center of the steering wheel.
- **Starter Relay** — is behind the left side of the instrument panel, on the accessory connector bracket.
- **Starter Solenoid** — is on the lower left side of the engine, on the starter.
- **Supplemental Restraint System** — see SRS.
- **TDC Sensor** — is on the lower left rear of the engine.
- **Throttle Switch** — is on the left side of the engine, below the throttle body.
- **Unlock Inhibit Switch** — is in the top rear of the left door.
- **Vehicle Speed Sensor** — is on the rear of the rear differential.
- **Washer Fluid Level Switch** — is behind the right headlight, in the washer fluid reservoir.
- **Washer Pump** — is ahead of the right front wheel well, on the washer fluid reservoir.

- **Water Shut-Off Solenoid** — is on the left side of the evaporator housing.
- **Wiper Motor** — is inside the left side of the fresh air intake cowl.

E36 3 SERIES

- **ABS Electronic Control Unit** — is in the right side of the instrument panel, behind the glove box.
- **ABS Hydraulic Unit** — is in the rear left side of the engine compartment, near the brake master cylinder, top of the brake fluid reservoir.
- **ABS Pedal Travel Sensor** — is on the rear left side of the engine fire wall, near the master cylinder.
- **ABS Relay** — is in the rear left side of the engine compartment, in the front power distribution box.
- **ABS Speed Sensor (left front)** — is on the left front wheel, above the brake caliper.
- **ABS Speed Sensor (left rear)** — is on the left rear wheel, above the brake caliper.
- **ABS Speed Sensor (right front)** — is on the right front wheel, above the brake caliper.
- **ABS Speed Sensor (right rear)** — is on the right rear wheel, above the brake caliper.
- **Air Bag** — see SRS.
- **Air Mass Meter** — is in the front left side of the engine compartment, right of the left shock tower.
- **Antenna Amplifier** — is in the upper left C-pillar.
- **Anti-Theft Horn** — is in the rear right side of the engine compartment, back of the right side shock tower.
- **Anti-Theft Module (Alpine)** — is in the right side of the instrument panel, behind the glove box.
- **Automatic Transmission Kick Down Switch** — is on the left footwell, on the gas pedal support bracket.
- **Back-Up Switch** — is under the front of vehicle, on the left side of transmission.
- **Blower Motor** — is in the rear of the engine compartment, behind the right fresh air cowl.
- **Blower Relay** — is in the rear left side of the engine compartment, in the front power distribution box.
- **Blower Resistors** — is behind the center of the instrument panel, right side of the IHKR plenum.
- **Brake Light Switch** — is in the left footwell, on the brake pedal support bracket behind the left footwell trim.
- **Brake Pad Sensor (left front)** — is behind the left front wheel, on the brake caliper.
- **Brake Pad sensor (right rear)** — is behind the right rear wheel, on the brake caliper.
- **CD Changer** — is in the right of the rear luggage compartment.
- **Central Locking Module** — is in the right side of the instrument panel, behind the glove box.
- **Changeover Valve 1** — is in the rear left side of the engine compartment.
- **Check Control Module** — is below the left side of the instrument panel.
- **Chime Module** — is below the left side of the instrument panel.
- **Clutch Switch** — is in the left footwell on the clutch pedal support bracket behind the left footwell trim panel.

- **Comfort Relay** — is below the left side of the instrument panel.
- **Compressor Control Relay** — is in the rear left side of the engine compartment in the front power distribution box.
- **Contact Ring** — is on the top of the steering column.
- **Crankshaft Sensor (M42 engine)** — is under the front of the vehicle, near the vibration damper.
- **Cruise Control Actuator (Tempomat)** — is in the front left of engine compartment.
- **Cruise Control Module (Tempomat)** — is in the right side of the instrument panel, behind the glove box.
- **Dash Vent Mixing Flap Motor** — is below the left side of the instrument panel, right side of the steering column.
- **Daytime Running Lights Coding Diode** — is in the left side of the instrument panel.
- **Diagnosis Module (SRS)** — is in the right side of the instrument panel, behind the glove box.
- **Diagnostic Connector** — is in the rear right of engine compartment, front of the battery.
- **DME Control Unit** — is in the right rear of the engine compartment, in the E-Box.
- **DME Relay** — is in the rear left of the engine compartment, in the front power distribution box.
- **Driver's Seat Belt Switch** — is in the left front seat buckle.
- **Driver's Seat Cushion Tilt Motor** — is under the left front seat.
- **Driver's Seat Height Motor** — is under the left front seat.
- **Driver's Seat Movement Motor** — is under the left front seat.
- **Driver's Seatback Recliner Motor** — is under the left front seat.
- **EGS Control Unit** — is in the rear right of the engine compartment, in the E-Box.
- **Electric Fuel Pump Relay 1** — is in the rear left of engine compartment, in the front power distribution box.
- **Engine Coolant Temperature Sensor** — is on the right front of the engine, below the intake manifold.
- **Engine Intake Air Temperature Sensor** — is on the left side of the engine, near the oil level stick.
- **Evaporative Purge Valve** — is in the front left of the engine compartment, right of the left shock tower.
- **Evaporator Temperature Sensor** — is on the right side of the left footwell, left side of the IHKR plenum.
- **Fog Light Relay, Front** — is in the rear left of the engine compartment, in the front power distribution box.
- **Fresh Air Flap Motor** — is below the right side of the instrument panel, near the center console.
- **Front Power Distribution Box** — is in the rear left of engine compartment.
- **Fuel Pump** — is below the right side of the rear seat.
- **Fuel Tank Sensor 2** — is below the right side of the rear seat.
- **Fuel Tank Sensor** — is below the left side of the rear seat.
- **Gas Filler Lock Motor** — is in the right rear of the luggage compartment.
- **Hazard Flasher Relay** — is in the rear left of the engine compartment, in the front power distribution box.
- **Headlight/Fog Light Cleaning Module (SRA)** — is below the left side of the instrument panel.

- **Heat Exchanger Temperature Sensor left** — is the center console.
- **Heat Exchanger Temperature Sensor right** — is the center console.
- **HIFI Amplifier** — is in the left forward side of the luggage compartment.
- **High Beam Light Relay** — is in the rear left side of the engine compartment, in the front power distribution box.
- **High Speed Relay** — is in the rear left side of the engine compartment, in the front power distribution box.
- **Horn Relay** — is in the rear left of the engine compartment, in the front power distribution box.
- **Idle Speed Actuator (M42 engine)** — is in the left of the engine compartment, near the oil level dipstick.
- **Idle Speed Actuator (M50 engine)** — is on the right front of the engine, below the intake manifold.
- **Ignition Switch** — is in the left side of the instrument panel, top of the steering column.
- **Inertia Switch** — is in the lower right A-pillar.
- **Integrated Climate Regulation Control Unit** — is above the center console.
- **Knock Sensor** — are located on the left side of the engine, in the block between the freeze plugs, below the intake manifold.
- **Low Beam Light Relay** — is in the rear left side of the engine compartment, in the front power distribution box.
- **Normal Speed Relay** — is in the rear left of the engine compartment, in the front power distribution box.
- **Oil Pressure Switch (M42 engine)** — is in the left side of the engine compartment, near the oil level stick.
- **Oil Pressure Switch (M50 engine)** — is on the right front of the engine, below the intake manifold.
- **On-Board Computer Horn Relay** — is in the right side of the instrument panel, behind the glove box.
- **On-Board Computer Temperature Sensor** — is in the front right of the engine compartment.
- **On-Board Computer** — is in the center console.
- **Outside Temperature Sensor** — is in the rear of the engine compartment, behind the fresh air cowl.
- **Park Heating/Ventilation Relay Box** — is below the left side of the instrument panel.
- **Park Light/License Plate Light Relays (right and left)** — are in the right side of the instrument panel, behind the glove box.
- **Parking Brake Switch** — is in the center console on the rear of the parking brake lever.
- **Power Window Module (left)** — is in the lower part of the left front door, behind the trim panel.
- **Power Window Module (right)** — is in the lower right door, behind the trim panel.
- **Pressure Switch** — is near the right headlight assembly.
- **Rear Defogger Relay** — is in the rear left side of the engine compartment, in the front power distribution box.
- **Recirculation Flap Motor** — is below the left side of the instrument panel, right side of the steering column.
- **SRS Air Bag Generator** — is behind the steering wheel.
- **SRS Crash Control Unit** — is below the left side of the instrument panel.
- **SRS Left Front Crash Sensor** — is in the left side of the engine compartment.
- **SRS Right Front Crash Sensor** — is in the right side of the engine compartment.

- **Starter Relay** — is below the left side of the instrument panel.
- **Starter** — is in the rear left of the engine compartment.
- **Supplemental Restraint System** — see SRS.
- **Suppression Filter** — is in the upper right C-pillar.
- **Telephone Transceiver** — is in the front left side of the luggage compartment.
- **Temperature Switch** — is in the front right of the engine compartment, right top of the radiator.
- **Throttle Potentiometer** — is on the left side of the engine.
- **Twin Relay Module** — is below the left side of the instrument panel.
- **Unloader Relay, Terminal 15** — is below the left side of the instrument panel.
- **Unloader Relay, Terminal R** — is below the left side of the instrument panel.
- **Vehicle Speed Sensor** — is under the rear of the vehicle on the differential.
- **Washer Fluid Level Switch** — is in the front right of the engine compartment, on the washer fluid reservoir.
- **Washer Pump** — is in the front right of the engine compartment, on the washer fluid reservoir.
- **Water Valve Assembly** — is in the rear left of the engine compartment, near the brake master cylinder, top of the brake fluid reservoir.
- **Wiper Motor** — is in the rear of the engine compartment, below the center of the cowl.
- **Wiper Relay** — is below the left side of the instrument panel.
- **Wiper/Washer Module** — is on the left side of the left footwell, under the footrest.

E34 5 SERIES

- **A/C Compressor Control Unit** — is inside the left kick panel.
- **A/C Relay** — is in the left side of the engine compartment, in the auxiliary relay box.
- **ABS Electronic Control Unit** — is behind the right front shock tower, in the E-Box.
- **ABS Hydraulic Unit** — is in the left side of the engine compartment, near the shock tower.
- **ABS Relay** — is in the left rear of the engine compartment.
- **ABS Wheel Speed Sensor (left front)** — is behind the left front wheel.
- **ABS Wheel Speed Sensor (left rear)** — is behind the left rear wheel.
- **ABS Wheel Speed Sensor (right front)** — is behind the right front wheel.
- **ABS Wheel Speed Sensor (right rear)** — is behind the right rear wheel.
- **ABS/ASC Electronic Control Unit** — is behind the left side of the instrument panel.
- **Air Bag** — see SRS.
- **Air Mass Meter** — is in the left front of the engine compartment, in front of the left shock tower.
- **Air Pump Relay** — is behind the right front shock tower, in the E-Box.

- **Air Quantity Meter** — is on the top center of the engine, ahead of the oil fill cap.
- **Air-Intake Control Unit** — is behind the right front shock tower, in the E-Box.
- **Antenna Amplifier** — is in the left C-pillar.
- **Anti-Theft Horn** — is behind the right fresh air cowl.
- **Anti-Theft Module** — is under the left side of the rear seat.
- **Audible Turn Signal Relay** — is below the steering column.
- **Automatic Air Recalculation Control Unit** — is inside the left kick panel.
- **Automatic Transmission Range Switch** — is below the center console, at the base of the gear shift lever.
- **Auxiliary Fan Motor** — is in the center front of the engine compartment, behind the bumper.
- **Auxiliary Relay Box** — is in the left front of the engine compartment, ahead of the left shock tower.
- **Auxiliary Water Pump Relay** — is in the left rear of the engine compartment, in the front power distribution box.
- **Back-Up Switch** — is on the top right side of the transmission.
- **Battery Switch** — is under the right side of the rear seat, near the battery.
- **Blower Motor** — is behind the center of the fresh air cowl panel.
- **Blower Relay** — is in the left rear of the engine compartment, in the front power distribution box.
- **Blower Resistors** — is below the left side of the instrument panel, on the left rear of plenum.
- **Brake Fluid Level Switch** — is in the left rear of the engine compartment, top of the brake fluid reservoir.
- **Brake Light Switch** — is below the left side of the instrument panel, on the brake pedal support bracket.
- **Brake Pad Sensor (left front)** — is behind the left front wheel, on the brake pad.
- **Brake Pad Sensor (right rear)** — is behind the right rear wheel, on the brake pad.
- **CD Changer** — is in the front left side of the luggage compartment.
- **Central Locking Lift Gate Motor Relay** — is on the right side of the luggage compartment, behind the side panel.
- **Changeover Valve 1** — is on the left side of the engine, near the oil level stick.
- **Changeover Valve 2** — is on the left front of the engine.
- **Charging Plug** — is in the left side of the glove box.
- **Check Control Module** — is in the left rear of the engine compartment, in the front power distribution box.
- **Chime Module** — is below the left side of the instrument panel, mounted in the hush panel.
- **Clutch Switch** — is behind the left side of the instrument panel, on the clutch pedal support bracket.
- **Combination Switch** — is inside the top of the steering column.
- **Compressor Clutch** — is on the lower right side of the engine.
- **Compressor Control Relay (M50 engine and M30 engine)** — is in the left side of the engine compartment, in the auxiliary relay box.
- **Compressor Control Relay (S38 engine)** — is inside the left kick panel.
- **Contact Ring** — is inside the steering wheel.

- **Cruise Control Actuator** — is in the left front of the engine compartment, ahead of the left shock tower.
- **Cruise Control Module** — is inside the right kick panel.
- **Cylinder Identification Sensor (M50 engine)** — is on the left front of the engine.
- **Cylinder Identification Sensor (M30 engine)** — is on the right front of the engine, near the distributor.
- **Cylinder Identification Sensor (S38 engine)** — is on the front of the engine, near the distributor.
- **Dash Vent Mixing Flap Motor** — is below the right side of the instrument panel, on the right side of plenum .
- **Daytime Running Lights Coding Diodes (Canada)** — is behind the left side of the instrument panel.
- **Defogger Control Unit** — is behind the center of the instrument panel, right side of the plenum.
- **Defogger Coupler** — is in the right C-pillar.
- **Defroster Flap Motor** — is behind the left side of the instrument panel, on the lower left side of the plenum.
- **Diagnostic Connector** — is in the left rear of the engine compartment, right side of the shock tower.
- **DME Control Unit** — is behind the right front shock tower, in the E-Box.
- **Door Lock Heater** — is in the door, at the key lock assembly.
- **Door Lock Motor (left rear)** — is on the top of the rear of the left rear door.
- **Door Lock Motor (right rear)** — is the top rear of the right rear door.
- **Double Panel Power Sunroof Control Unit (DDSHD)** — is in the rear of the roof, behind the top trim panel.
- **Double Panel Power Sunroof Sensor 1** — is in the center of windshield header, behind the top trim panel.
- **Double Panel Power Sunroof Sensor 2** — is in the rear of the roof, behind the top trim panel.
- **Driver's Door Lock Motor** — is in the top rear of the driver's door.
- **Driver's Headrest Motor** — is in the top right corner of the driver's seatback.
- **Driver's Seat Belt Switch** — is in the driver's side seat buckle.
- **Driver's Seat Cushion Tilt Motor** — is under the left side of the driver's seat.
- **Driver's Seat Heater Relay** — is below the driver's seat.
- **Driver's Seat Heater** — is in the driver's seat.
- **Driver's Seat Height Motor** — is under the front of the driver's seat.
- **Driver's Seat Movement Motor** — is under the right side of the driver's seat.
- **Driver's Seatback Heater** — is in the back of the driver's seat.
- **Driver's Seatback Recliner Motor** — is under the front of the driver's seat.
- **Driver's Thigh Support Motor** — is in the right front corner of the driver's seat.
- **E-Box Fan** — is in the E-Box, below the modules.
- **E-Box** — is on the right rear of the engine, behind the right front shock tower.
- **EGS Control Unit** — is inside the right kick panel.
- **EGS RPM Sensor** — is below the front of the vehicle.
- **Electric Fuel Pump Relay 1** — is in the rear of the engine compartment.

- **Electric Power Protection Relay** — is below the left side of the rear seat, on the rear power distribution box.
- **Electro-Hydraulic Convertor** — is in the lower left of the engine compartment, behind the left front wheel.
- **Electro-Hydraulic Lock Relay (EH)** — is in the right rear side of the engine compartment, in the front power distribution box.
- **Electronic Transmission Control Unit (AEGS)** — is inside the right kick panel.
- **EML Control Unit** — is behind the right front shock tower, in the E-Box.
- **Engine Coolant Level Switch (M30 engine)** — is in the center rear of the engine compartment, top of the coolant reservoir.
- **Engine Coolant Level Switch (S38 engine)** — is in the right side of the engine compartment, on the coolant reservoir.
- **Engine Coolant Temperature Sender (M30 engine)** — is on the coolant inlet, near the right valve cover.
- **Engine Coolant Temperature Sender (S38 engine)** — is on the right side of the engine, on the coolant inlet.
- **Engine Coolant Temperature Sensor (M30 engine and S38 engine)** — is right side of engine, on coolant inlet.
- **Engine Intake Air Temperature Sensor** — is in the left front of the engine compartment, in front of the left shock tower.
- **Engine Speed/Reference Point Sensor (M50 engine)** — is on the left front of the engine.
- **Engine Speed/Reference Point Sensor (M30 engine)** — is on the front of the engine, below the distributor.
- **Engine Speed/Reference Point Sensor (S38 engine)** — is on the front of the engine, below the distributor.
- **Evaporative Purge Valve (M50 engine)** — is the left side of the engine compartment.
- **Evaporative Purge Valve (M30 engine)** — is on the left side of the engine, right side of the oil filter.
- **Evaporative Purge Valve (S38 engine)** — is on the left side of the engine, near the oil level dipstick.
- **Evaporator Temperature Sensor** — is below the left side of the instrument panel, on the lower left side of the plenum.
- **Final Stage Unit** — is in the left side of the right footwell, ahead of the plenum.
- **Footwell Flap Motor** — is below the left side of the instrument panel, on the left side of the plenum .
- **Fresh Air Flap Motor** — is below the left side of the instrument panel, on the left side of the plenum.
- **Front Power Distribution Box** — is in the left rear side of the engine compartment.
- **Fuel Injectors (M50 engine)** — are on the top right side of the engine.
- **Fuel Injectors (M30 engine and S38 engine)** — are on the top of the engine, on the intake manifold.
- **Fuel Pump Relay** — is behind the right front shock tower, in the E-Box.
- **Fuel Pump** — is below the trunk, right side of the spare tire.
- **Fuel Tank Sensor** — is below the right side of the trunk, through the maintenance cover, right side of the spare tire.
- **Full Load Cut-Off Relay** — is below the right side of the instrument panel.
- **Fuse 3amp** — is on the left front of the trunk.
- **Fuse 5amp** — is on the right front of the trunk, near the telephone transceiver.

- **Fuse 100ma** — is on the right front of the trunk, near the telephone transceiver.
- **Gas filler Lock Motor** — is on the right side of the trunk, behind the wheel well.
- **General Module** — is below the left side of the rear seat, in the rear power distribution box.
- **Hazard Flasher Relay** — is on the left rear of the engine compartment, in the front power distribution box.
- **Headlight/Fog Light Module** — is on the left side of the engine compartment.
- **Headlight/Fog Light Washer Pump** — is on the left front of the engine compartment.
- **Heat Exchanger Temperature Sensor (IHKA/F3)(right)** — is below the right side of the instrument panel, in the right side of the plenum.
- **Heat Exchanger Temperature Sensor (left)** — is below the left side of the instrument panel, on the left side of the plenum.
- **HIFI Amplifier** — is on the left side of the trunk, on the brace.
- **High Speed Relay** — is on the left side of the engine compartment, in the auxiliary relay box.
- **Horn Relay** — is on the left rear of the engine compartment, in the front power distribution box.
- **Horns (left and right)** — are in the front of vehicle, behind the grille.
- **Idle Speed Actuator (M50 engine)** — is on the top center of the engine.
- **Idle Speed Actuator (M30 engine)** — is on the top of the engine, center rear on the throttle body.
- **Idle Speed Actuator (S38 engine)** — is on the top of the engine.
- **Ignition Coil** — is on the right side of the engine compartment, at the strut tower.
- **Ignition Coils** — are on the top right side of the engine.
- **Ignition Switch** — is on the top right side of the steering column.
- **Inertia Switch** — is below the center of the rear seat, right side of the rear power distribution box.
- **Integrated Climate Regulation 2 Switching Unit** — is behind the center console.
- **Integrated Climate Regulation Control Unit 3** — is below the center of the instrument panel, ahead of the plenum.
- **Jumper Plug for Horn/Telephone** — is on the left rear of the engine compartment, in the front power distribution box.
- **Jumper Plug** — is on the left rear of the engine compartment, in the front power distribution box.
- **Lamp Control Module** — is on the left rear of the engine compartment, in the front power distribution box.
- **Lift Gate Motor** — is on the rear side of the luggage compartment.
- **Lift Gate Open Warning Relay** — is below the left side of the rear seat, on the rear power distribution box.
- **Main Relay** — is behind the right front shock tower, in the E-Box.
- **Memory Seat/Mirrors Control Unit** — is below the left side of the instrument panel.
- **Motronic Control Unit (DME)** — is behind the right front shock tower, in the E-Box.
- **Normal Speed Relay** — is on the left side of the engine compartment, in the auxiliary relay box.

- **Oil Level Sensor (M30 engine and S38 engine)** — is on the lower left front of the engine, on the bottom of the oil pan.
- **Oil Pressure Switch (M50 engine)** — is on the left side of the engine.
- **Oil Pressure Switch (M30 engine)** — is on the top rear of the engine, rear of the cylinder head.
- **Oil Pressure Switch (S38 engine)** — is on the left front of the engine.
- **On-Board Computer Anti-Theft Horn** — is behind the center of the fresh air cowl panel.
- **On-Board Computer Relay** — is on the right side of the luggage compartment, behind the side panel.
- **On-Board Computer Temperature Sensor** — is under the right side of the front bumper.
- **On-Board Computer** — is on the center of the instrument panel, right side of the radio.
- **Outside Temperature Sensor** — is behind the center of the fresh air cowl panel, on the right side of blower motor.
- **Oxygen Sensor (M50 engine)** — is on the lower left rear of the engine, in the exhaust pipe.
- **Oxygen Sensor (M30 engine)** — is in the top of the catalytic converter, near the rear of the transmission.
- **Oxygen Sensor (S38 engine)** — is below the center of the catalytic converter.
- **Oxygen Sensor Relay** — is behind the right front shock tower, in the E-Box.
- **Park Brake Switch** — is below the center console, on the rear of the park brake lever.
- **Park Heating Unit** — is on the right rear of the engine compartment.
- **Park Light/License Plate Light Relay (right)** — is below the left side of the instrument panel.
- **Park Lights Relay (left)** — is below the left side of the instrument panel.
- **Park/Heating Ventilation Box** — is inside the right kick panel.
- **Passenger's Headrest Motor** — is in the top right corner of the passenger's seatback.
- **Passenger's Seat Cushion Tilt Motor** — is under the left side of the passenger's seat.
- **Passenger's Seat Heater Relay** — is below the passenger's seat.
- **Passenger's Seat Heater** — is in the passenger's seat.
- **Passenger's Seat Height Motor** — is under the front of the passenger's seat.
- **Passenger's Seat Movement Motor** — is under the right side of the passenger's seat.
- **Passenger's Seatback Heater** — is in the back of the passenger's seat.
- **Passenger's Seatback Recliner Motor** — is under the front of the passenger's seat.
- **Passenger's Thigh Support Motor** — is in the right front corner of the passenger's seat.
- **Pressure Switch** — is in the right front of the engine compartment.
- **Program Switch** — is on the middle console, left side of the gear shift selector.
- **Rear Defogger Relay** — is below the left side of the rear seat, on the rear power distribution box.
- **Rear Power Distribution Box** — is below the left side of the rear seat.

- **Rear Window Lock Motor Relay** — is on the right side of the luggage compartment, behind the side panel.
- **Rear Window Lock Motor** — is on the rear side of the luggage compartment.
- **Rear Window Washer Motor** — is on the rear side of the luggage compartment.
- **Rear Window Washer Pump** — is on the right side of the luggage compartment, behind the side panel.
- **Rear Window Washer Relay** — is on the right side of the luggage compartment, behind the side panel.
- **Rear Window Wiper Relay 1** — is on the right side of the luggage compartment, behind the side panel.
- **Rear Window Wiper Relay 2** — is on the right side of the luggage compartment, behind the side panel.
- **Rear Wiper/Washer Fluid Level Switch** — is on the right rear of the luggage compartment, behind the side panel.
- **Rear Wiper/Washer Interval Control Unit** — is on the right side of the luggage compartment, behind the side panel.
- **Relay Module** — is in the rear power distribution box.
- **Safety Switch** — is on the left side of the engine compartment, near the left front crash sensor.
- **Seat Heating Relay (rear)** — is below the left side of the rear seat.
- **Seat Switch (rear)** — is under the right side of the rear seat, right of the battery.
- **SRS Air Bag Generator** — is inside the center of the steering wheel.
- **SRS Crash Control Unit** — is in the left rear of the engine compartment, in the front power distribution box.
- **SRS Crash Sensor (left front)** — is ahead of the left shock tower.
- **SRS Crash Sensor (right front)** — is ahead of the right shock tower.
- **SRS Diagnostic Module** — is below the left side of the instrument panel, left side of the steering column.
- **Starter (M30 engine)** — is on the left rear side of the engine, below the intake manifold.
- **Starter (S38 engine)** — is on the lower left side of the engine, below the intake manifold.
- **Starter Relay** — is on the left rear of the engine compartment, in the front power distribution box.
- **Sunroof Motor** — is in the center of the windshield header, near the rear view mirror.
- **Supplemental Restraint System** — see SRS.
- **Telephone Interface (USA)** — is on the front right side of the luggage compartment.
- **Telephone Transceiver** — is in the luggage compartment.
- **Temperature Distribution Potentiometer** — is behind the center of the instrument panel, above the radio.
- **Temperature Switch** — is behind the right front shock tower, in the E-Box.
- **Temperature Switch** — is on the top right side of the radiator.
- **Throttle Switch (M50 engine)** — is on the left rear of the engine.
- **Throttle Switch (M30 engine)** — is on the top of the engine, on the throttle body.
- **Throttle Switch (S38 engine)** — is on the top front of the engine, on the throttle body.
- **Throttle Switch (EGS)** — is on the left side of the engine compartment.

- **Transmission Gear Shift** — is below the center of the vehicle, near the transmission.
- **Transmission Kick Down Switch** — is below the left side of the instrument panel, underneath the accelerator pedal.
- **Trunk Lock Motor** — is in the trunk lid, on the right side of the lid lock assembly.
- **Uncoupling Diode KL61** — is below the male side of the engine harness connector.
- **Unloader Relay KL61** — is on the left rear of the engine compartment, in the front power distribution box.
- **Unloader Relay, KLR** — is on the left rear of the engine compartment, in the front power distribution box.
- **Unloader Relay, Terminal 15** — is on the left rear of the engine compartment, in the front power distribution box.
- **Vehicle Speed Sensor** — is below the rear of the vehicle, on the rear differential.
- **Washer Fluid Level Switch** — is on the right side of the engine compartment, on the right side of the windshield washer fluid reservoir.
- **Washer Pump Relay** — is on the left rear of the engine compartment, in the front power distribution box.
- **Washer Pump** — is on the right front of the engine compartment, on the windshield washer fluid reservoir.

- **Water Pump** — is on the left rear of the engine compartment, on the engine bulkhead.
- **Water Temperature Sensor** — is on the left front of the engine.
- **Water Valve Assembly** — is on the left rear of the engine compartment, on the engine bulkhead.
- **Wheel Camber Control Unit** — is below the right rear of the vehicle, near the rear differential.
- **Window Motor (left rear)** — is on the lower front of the left rear door.
- **Window Motor (right rear)** — is on the lower front of the right rear door.
- **Windshield Washer Jet Heater (left)** — is on the left rear of the engine compartment hood, under the cover.
- **Windshield Washer Jet Heater (right)** — is in the right rear of the engine compartment, under the cover.
- **Wiper Motor** — is behind the left side of the fresh air cowl panel.
- **Wiper Pressure Control Motor** — is behind the left side of the fresh air cowl.
- **Wiper Pressure Control Relay** — is below the left side of the rear seat, on the rear power distribution box.
- **Wiper Relay** — is below the left side of the rear seat, on the rear power distribution box.

WIRING DIAGRAMS

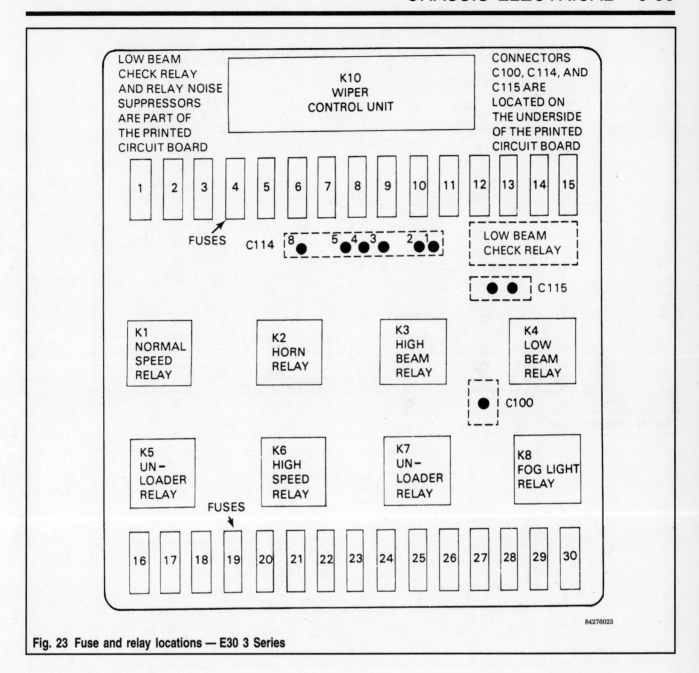

Fig. 23 Fuse and relay locations — E30 3 Series

84276023

FUSE NO.	SIZE	CIRCUIT NAME
1	7.5A	Headlights (also fuses 2, 13, 14); High Beam Indicator.
2	7.5A	Headlights (also fuses 1, 13, 14).
3	15A	Auxiliary Fan (also fuses 18, 19, 20).
4	15A	Lights: Turn/Hazard Warning (also fuse 24); Active Check Control (also fuses 6, 10, 21, 22, 23); Glove Box Light; Electro-Mechanical Convertible Top (also fuse 21, 25).
5	30A	Wiper/Washer.
6	7.5A	Stop Lights; Active Check Control (also fuses 4, 10, 21, 22, 23); Antilock Braking System; Cruise Control (also fuse 10); Map Reading Light.
7	15A	Horn.
8	30A	Rear Defogger (also fuse 23).
9	15A	Injection Electronics (also fuses 10, 11, 21).
10	7.5A	Ignition Key Warning/Seatbelt Warning (also Fuse 21); Service Interval Indicator (also fuse 21); Tachometer/Fuel Economy Gauges (also fuse 21); Gauges/Indicators; Brake Warning System; Back Up Lights; On-Board Computer (also fuses 12, 21, 27); Start; Injection Electronics (also fuses 9, 11, 21); Active Check Control (also fuses 4, 6, 21, 22, 23); Cruise Control (also fuse 6).
11	7.5A	Injection Electronics (also fuses 9, 10, 21).
12	7.5A	Radio/Antenna (also fuses 21, 27, 28); Speedometer/Indicators; On-Board Computer (also fuses 10, 21, 27).
13	7.5A	Headlights (also fuses 1, 2, 14).
14	7.5A	Headlights (also fuses 1, 2, 13).
15		Not Used.
16	15A	Heated Seats.
17	30A	Power Windows.
18	30A	Auxiliary Fan (also fuses 3, 19, 20).

FUSE NO.	SIZE	CIRCUIT NAME
19	7.5A	Auxiliary Fan (also fuses 3, 18, 20); Interior Lights (also fuses 21, 27); Power Mirrors.
20	30A	Heater/Air Conditioning; Auxiliary Fan (also fuses 3, 18, 19).
21	7.5A	Auto-Charging Flashlight; Ignition Key Warning/Seatbelt Warning (also fuse 10); Injection Electronics (also fuses 9, 10, 11); Interior Lights (also fuses 19, 27); Radio/Antenna (also fuses 12, 27, 28); Trunk Light; Active Check Control (also fuses 4, 6, 10, 22, 23); Service Interval Indicator (also fuse 10); On-Board Computer (also fuses 10, 12, 23, 27); Tachometer/Fuel Economy Gauge (also fuse 10); Electro-Mechanical Convertible Top (also fuse 4, 25).
22	7.5A	Active Check Control (also fuses 4, 6, 10, 21, 23); Lights: Front Park/Tail (also fuse 23); Lights: Front Side Marker (also fuse 23).
23	7.5A	Lights: Dash; Lights: Front Park/Tail (also fuse 22); Lights: Front Side Marker (also fuse 22); Lights: Rear Marker/License; Active Check Control (also fuses 4, 6, 10, 21 & 22); Rear Defogger (also fuse 8).
24	15A	Lights: Turn/Hazard Warning (also fuse 4).
25	30A	Electro-Mechanical Covertible Top (also fuse 4, 21).
26		Not Used.
27	30A	Interior Lights (also fuses 19, 21); Central Locking; Radio/Antenna (also fuses 12, 21, 28); On-Board Computer (also fuses 10, 12, 21).
28	30A	Cigar Lighter; Radio/Antenna (also fuses 12, 21, 27).
29	7.5A	Fog Lights (also fuse 30), Fog Light Indicator.
30	7.5A	Fog Lights (also fuse 29).
POWER WINDOW CIRCUIT BREAKER	15A	Power Windows.

84276024

Fig. 24 Fuse applications — E30 3 Series

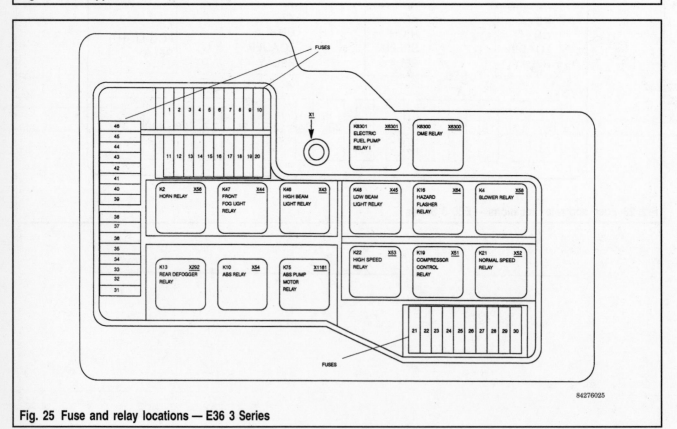

84276025

Fig. 25 Fuse and relay locations — E36 3 Series

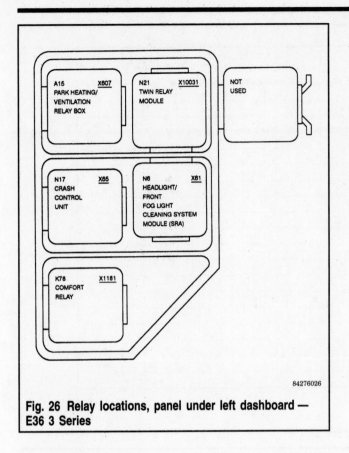

**Fig. 26 Relay locations, panel under left dashboard —
E36 3 Series**

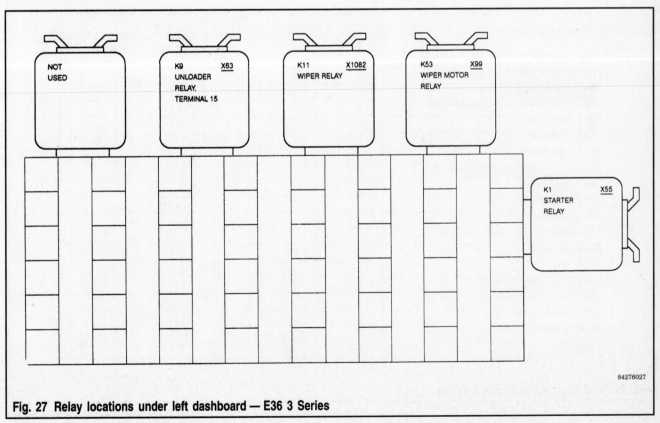

Fig. 27 Relay locations under left dashboard — E36 3 Series

FUSE NUMBER

Code	Application	1	2	3	4	5	6	7	8	9	10	11	12	13	14	15	16	17	18	19	20	21	22	23	24	25	26	27	28	29
		30A		30A	15A	30A	20A	5A	15A	20A	30A	7.5A	7.5A		30A	5A	5A		15A	15A	30A	5A	5A	5A	10A	5A	15A	5A	5A	7.5A
1210.7	DIGITAL ENGINE ELECTRONICS (DME M3.1, 6-CYLINDER M50)																●		●										●	
1210.9	DIGITAL ENGINE ELECTRONICS (DME M1.7, 4-CYLINDER M42)																		●											
1230.0	CHARGING SYSTEM																													
1240.0	START																												●	
2460.2	ELECTRONIC TRANSMISSION CONTROL (EGS A4S 310R)																								●		●			
3234.0	SUPPLEMENTAL RESTRAINT SYSTEM (AIR BAG)																													
3450.0	ANTILOCK BRAKE SYSTEM (ABS)											●									●						●			
5116.0	POWER MIRRORS																							●						
5126.2	CENTRAL LOCKING MODULE II (ZVM II)						●																							
5133.1	POWER WINDOWS (FH)													●																
5200.0	POWER SEATS					●																								
5203.0	HEATED SEATS				●																			●						
5410.1	POWER SUN ROOF (SHD)	●																												
6133.0	HORN								●																					
6160.1	WIPER/ WASHER MODULE (WWM)																													
6167.1	HEADLIGHT WASHER (SRA)			●																										
6211.0	INSTRUMENT CLUSTER																						●				●			
6213.2	MULTI-FUNCTION CLOCK																						●				●			
6300.0	LIGHT SWITCH DETAILS																					●			●					

84276028

Fig. 28 Fuse applications — E36 3 Series

FUSE NUMBER

Code	Application	1	2	3	4	5	6	7	8	9	10	11	12	13	14	15	16	17	18	19	20	21	22	23	24	25	26	27	28	29
		30A		30A	15A	30A	20A	5A	15A	20A	30A	7.5A	7.5A		30A	15A	5A		15A	15A	30A	5A	5A	5A	10A	5A	15A	5A	5A	7.5A
6312.0	HEADLIGHTS/ FOG LIGHTS											●	●			●							●	●		●				●
6313.0	TURN/HAZARD LIGHTS																							●						
6314.0	PARK/TAIL LIGHTS																						●							
6320.0	LICENSE PLATE/ LUGGAGE COMPARTMENT LIGHTS																													
6322.0	BACK UP LIGHTS																										●			
6325.0	BRAKE LIGHTS																													
6330.3	INTERIOR LIGHTS																													
6332.1	GLOVE BOX LIGHT/CASSETTE BOX/ASHTRAY LIGHT/ CHARGING SOCKET/CIGAR LIGHTER																													
6350.0	CRASH CONTROL UNIT											●	●													●				●
6412.5	PARK VENTILATION WITH IHKR																			●	●									
6424.0	REAR WINDOW DEFOGGER						●																	●						
6450.4	INTEGRATED CLIMATE REGULATION (IHKR E36)																●				●			●						
6510.0	RADIO/STEREO									●																				
6510.1	RADIO/HIFI									●																				
6561.0	CELLULAR TELEPHONE (PROVISIONS)																													
6571.0	CRUISE CONTROL (TEMPOMAT)																												●	
6575.2	ANTITHEFT SYSTEM (ALPINE)																													
6581.2	ON-BOARD COMPUTER (BC V)											●	●											●		●				

84276029

Fig. 29 Fuse applications — E36 3 Series

	FUSE NUMBER																
	30	31	32	33	34	35	36	37	38	39	40	41	42	43	44	45	46
	7.5A	5A	30A	10A	15A	25A	30A	10A	30A	7.5A	30A	30A		5A	15A	7.5A	15A
1210.7 DIGITAL ENGINE ELECTRONICS (DME M3.1, 6-CYLINDER M50)																	
1210.9 DIGITAL ENGINE ELECTRONICS (DME M1.7, 4-CYLINDER M42)																	
1230.0 CHARGING SYSTEM																	
1240.0 START																	
2460.2 ELECTRONIC TRANSMISSION CONTROL (EGS A4S 310R)															●		
3234.0 SUPPLEMENTAL RESTRAINT SYSTEM (AIR BAG)																	
3450.0 ANTILOCK BRAKE SYSTEM (ABS)								●							●		
5116.0 POWER MIRRORS																	
5126.2 CENTRAL LOCKING MODULE II (ZVM II)							●						●				
5133.1 POWER WINDOWS (FH)																	
5200.0 POWER SEATS										●							
5203.0 HEATED SEATS																	
5410.1 POWER SUN ROOF (SHD)																	
6133.0 HORN																	
6160.1 WIPER/ WASHER MODULE (WWM)							●	●						●	●		
6167.1 HEADLIGHT WASHER (SRA)																	
6211.0 INSTRUMENT CLUSTER		●														●	
6213.2 MULTI-FUNCTION CLOCK		●													●	●	
6300.0 LIGHT SWITCH DETAILS			●					●									

Fig. 30 Fuse applications — E36 3 Series

84276030

	FUSE NUMBER																
	30	31	32	33	34	35	36	37	38	39	40	41	42	43	44	45	46
	7.5A	5A	30A	10A	15A	25A	30A	10A	30A	7.5A	30A	30A		5A	15A	7.5A	15A
6312.0 HEADLIGHTS/ FOG LIGHTS	●																
6313.0 TURN/HAZARD LIGHTS					●												
6314.0 PARK/TAIL LIGHTS				●				●									
6320.0 LICENSE PLATE/ LUGGAGE COMPARTMENT LIGHTS																	
6322.0 BACK UP LIGHTS																	
6325.0 BRAKE LIGHTS																●	
6330.3 INTERIOR LIGHTS				●									●				
6332.1 GLOVE BOX LIGHT/CASSETTE BOX/ASHTRAY LIGHT/ CHARGING SOCKET/CIGAR LIGHTER			●	●				●					●				
6350.0 CRASH CONTROL UNIT						●											
6412.5 PARK VENTILATION WITH IHKR																	
6424.0 REAR WINDOW DEFOGGER																	
6450.4 INTEGRATED CLIMATE REGULATION (IHKR E36)	●								●	●	●						
6510.0 RADIO/STEREO														●			
6510.1 RADIO/HIFI														●			
6561.0 CELLULAR TELEPHONE (PROVISIONS)				●									●				
6571.0 CRUISE CONTROL (TEMPOMAT)																●	
6575.2 ANTITHEFT SYSTEM (ALPINE)				●									●				
6581.2 ON-BOARD COMPUTER (BC V)	●			●				●								●	●

Fig. 31 Fuse applications — E36 3 Series

84276031

COMPONENTS IN FRONT POWER DISTRIBUTION		
NUMBER	CONNECTOR	DESCRIPTION
A3	X12	LAMP CONTROL MODULE
A4	X18, X19	CHECK CONTROL MODULE
K1	X55	STARTER RELAY
B900	X55	JUMPER PLUG (MANUAL)
K2	X56	HORN RELAY
K3	X57	UNLOADER RELAY, KLR
K4	X58	BLOWER RELAY
	X62	NOT IN U.S.
K9	X63	UNLOADER RELAY, KL 15
K16	X64	HAZARD FLASHER RELAY
K50	X47	WATER PUMP RELAY
K51	X941	PHONE ALERT RELAY
K61	X1021	UNLOADER RELAY KL61
N17	X65	CRASH CONTROL UNIT

84276032

Fig. 32 Fuse and relay locations — 1989-90 E34 5 Series

COMPONENTS IN REAR POWER DISTRIBUTION		
NUMBER	CONNECTOR	DESCRIPTION
A1	X253, X254 X255, X332	GENERAL MODULE
A5	X258, X259	RELAY MODULE
K11	X293	WIPER RELAY
K13	X292	REAR DEFOGGER RELAY
K15	X294	ELECTRIC POWER PROTECTION RELAY
	X297	NOT IN U.S.

84276033

Fig. 33 Fuse and relay locations — 1989-90 E34 5 Series

FUSE	CIRCUIT PROTECTED	
F1 15A	3450.0	ABS Antilock Brake System (Also Fuse 17)
	6200.0	Instrument Cluster Check Control (K/CC) (Also Fuses 17, 20, 29)
	6301.0	Lamp Monitor (LKM) (Also Fuses 2, 3, 4, 5, 7, 10, 11, 13, 14, 15)
	6325.0	Brake Lights (Also Fuse 15)
	6571.0	Cruise Control (Tempomat) (Also Fuse 17)
	6581.0	On-Board Computer (BCIV) (Also Fuses 17, 20)
F2 7.5A	6300.0	Light Switch Details (Also Fuses 3, 4, 5)
	6301.0	Lamp Monitor (LKM) (Also Fuses 1, 3, 4, 5, 7, 10, 11, 13, 14, 15)
	6312.0	Headlights/Fog Lights (Also Fuses 3, 5, 7, 10, 11, 13, 14)
	6313.0	Turn/Hazard Lights (Also Fuses 3, 6, 13, 14)
F3 7.5A	6100.0	Central Body Electronics (ZKE) (Also Fuses 5, 17, 30, 44, 47)
	6300.0	Light Switch Details (Also Fuses 2, 4, 5)
	6301.0	Lamp Monitor (LKM) (Also Fuses 1, 2, 4, 5, 7, 10, 11, 13, 14, 15)
	6312.0	Headlights/Fog Lights (Also Fuses 2, 5, 7, 10, 11, 13, 14)
	6313.0	Turn/Hazard Lights (Also Fuses 2, 6, 13, 14)
F4 7.5A	6300.0	Light Switch Details (Also Fuses 2, 3, 5)
	6301.0	Lamp Monitor (LKM) (Also Fuses 1, 2, 3, 5, 7, 10, 11, 13, 14, 15)
	6314.0	Park/Tail/Underhood Lights (Also Fuses 5, 15, 20)
F5 10A	6100.0	Central Body Electronics (ZKE) (Also Fuses 3, 17, 30, 44, 47)
	6300.0	Light Switch Details (Also Fuses 2, 3, 4)
	6301.0	Lamp Monitor (LKM) (Also Fuses 1, 2, 3, 4, 7, 10, 11, 13, 14, 15)
	6312.0	Headlights/Fog Lights (Also Fuses 2, 3, 7, 10, 11, 13, 14)
	6314.0	Park/Tail/Underhood Lights (Also Fuses 4, 15, 20)
	6320.0	License/Trunk Lights (Also Fuses 15, 21)
	6330.0	ZKE Interior Lights (Also Fuses 17, 18, 21, 30, 44)
	6332.0	Glove Box Light/Cigar Lighter/Charging Plug (Also Fuses 18, 21, 26)
F6 15A	6313.0	Turn/Hazard Lights (Also Fuses 2, 3, 13, 14)
F7 15A	6301.0	Lamp Monitor (LKM) (Also Fuses 1, 2, 3, 4, 5, 10, 11, 13, 14, 15)
	6312.0	Headlights/Fog Lights (Also Fuses 2, 3, 5, 10, 11, 13, 14)

84276034

Fig. 34 Fuse applications — 1989-90 E34 5 Series

FUSE	CIRCUIT PROTECTED	
F9 15A	6133.0	Horn
	6450.1	Integrated Climate Regulation (IHKR) (Also Fuses 19, 20, 27, 29, 46)
	6561.0	Cellular Telephone (Provisions) (Also Fuses 18, 31)
F10 7.5A	6301.0	Lamp Monitor (LKM) (Also Fuses 1, 2, 3, 4, 5, 7, 11, 13, 14, 15)
	6312.0	Headlights/Fog Lights (Also Fuses 2, 3, 5, 7, 11, 13, 14)
F11 7.5A	6301.0	Lamp Monitor (LKM) (Also Fuses 1, 2, 3, 4, 5, 7, 10, 13, 14, 15)
	6312.0	Headlights/Fog Lights (Also Fuses 2, 3, 5, 7, 10, 13, 14)
F12 15A	5116.0	Power Mirrors
	6169.0	Windshield Washer Jet Heaters
	6322.0	Back Up Lights
F13 7.5A	6301.0	Lamp Monitor (LKM) (Also Fuses 1, 2, 3, 4, 5, 7, 10, 11, 14, 15)
	6312.0	Headlights/Fog Lights (Also Fuses 2, 3, 5, 7, 10, 11, 14)
	6313.0	Turn/Hazard Lights (Also Fuses 2, 3, 6, 14)
F14 7.5A	6301.0	Lamp Monitor (LKM) (Also Fuses 1, 2, 3, 4, 5, 7, 10, 11, 13, 15)
	6312.0	Headlights/Fog Lights (Also Fuses 2, 3, 5, 7, 10, 11, 13)
	6313.0	Turn/Hazard Lights (Also Fuses 2, 3, 6, 13)
F15 7.5A	6301.0	Lamp Monitor (LKM) (Also Fuses 1, 2, 3, 4, 5, 7, 10, 11, 13, 14)
	6314.0	Park/Tail/Underhood Lights (Also Fuses 4, 5, 20)
	6320.0	License/Trunk Lights (Also Fuses 5, 21)
	6325.0	Brake Lights (Also Fuse 1)
F16 30A	5203.0	Heated Seats

84276035

Fig. 35 Fuse applications — 1989-90 E34 5 Series

FUSE	CIRCUIT PROTECTED	
F17 7.5A	1210.2	Injection Electronics (DME 1.3) (Also Fuse 23)
	1230.0	Charging System (Also Fuse 28)
	1240.0	Start
	1290.0	E-Box Fan (Also Fuse 28)
	2460.0	Electronic Transmission Control (AEGS)
	3450.0	Antilock Brake System (ABS) (Also Fuse 1)
	5120.0	ZKE Door Lock Heating (TSH) (Also Fuse 30)
	5133.0	ZKE Power Windows (FH) (Also Fuses 30, 31, 47)
	5410.0	ZKE Sunroof (SHD) (Also Fuses 30, 31, 47)
	6100.0	Central Body Electronics (ZKE) (Also Fuses 3, 5, 30, 44, 47)
	6200.0	Instrument Cluster/Check Control (K/CC) (Also Fuses 1, 20, 29)
	6330.0	ZKE Interior Lights (IB) (Also Fuses 5, 18, 21, 30, 44)
	6571.0	Cruise Control (Tempomat) (Also Fuse 1)
	6581.0	On Board Computer (BCIV) (Also Fuses 1, 20)
F18 15A	6330.0	ZKE Interior Lights (IB) (Also Fuses 5, 17, 21, 30, 44)
	6332.0	Glove Box Light/Cigar Lighter/Charging Plug (Also Fuses 5, 21, 26)
	6510.0	Radio/CD Player (Provisions) (Also Fuse 41)
	6561.0	Cellular Telephone (Provisions) (Also Fuses 9, 31)
F19 30A	6450.1	Integrated Climate Regulation (IHKR) (Also Fuses 9, 20, 27, 29, 46)
F20 7.5A	6200.0	Instrument Cluster/Check Control (K/CC) (Also Fuses 1, 17, 29)
	6314.0	Park/Tail/Underhood Lights (Also Fuses 4, 5, 15)
	6450.1	(Also fuses 9, 19, 27, 29, 46)
	6581.0	On Board Computer (BCIV) (Also Fuses 1, 17)
F21 10A	6320.0	License/Trunk Lights (Also Fuses 5, 15)
	6330.0	ZKE Interior Lights (IB) (Also Fuses 5, 17, 18, 30, 44)
	6332.0	Glove Box Light/Cigar Lighter/Charging Plug (Also Fuses 5, 18, 26)
F22 30A	NOT USED	

84276036

Fig. 36 Fuse applications — 1989-90 E34 5 Series

FUSE	CIRCUIT PROTECTED	
F23 7.5A	1210.2	Injection Electronics (DME 1.3) (Also Fuse 17)
F24 7.5A	6160.0	ZKE Windshield Wiper Control (SWS) (Also Fuse 44)
F25 30A	6454.0	Auxiliary Fan (Also Fuse 29)
F26 30A	6332.0	Glove Box Light/Cigar Lighter/Charging Plug (Also Fuses 5, 18, 21)
F27 7.5A	6450.1	Integrated Climate Regulation (IHKR) (Also Fuses 9, 19, 20, 29, 46)
F28 15A	1230.0 1290.0 3240.0	Charging System (Also Fuse 17) E-Box Fan (Also Fuse 17) Power Assist Steering (Servotronic)
F29 7.5A	6200.0 6450.1 6454.0	Instrument Cluster/Check Control (K/CC) (Also Fuses 1, 17, 20) Integrated Climate Regulation (IHKR) (Also Fuses 9, 19, 20, 27, 46) Auxiliary Fan (Also Fuse 25)
F30 7.5A	5120.0 5126.0 5133.0 5410.0 6100.0 6330.0	ZKE Door Lock Heating (TSH) (Also Fuse 17) ZKE Central Locking (ZV) (Also Fuses 31, 47) ZKE Power Windows (FH) (Also Fuses 17, 31, 47) ZKE Sunroof (SHD) (Also Fuses 17, 31, 47) Central Body Electronics (ZKE) (Also Fuses 3, 5, 17, 44, 47) ZKE Interior Lights (Also Fuses 5, 17, 18, 21, 44)
F31 7.5A	5126.0 5133.0 5410.0 6561.0	ZKE Central Locking (ZV) (Also Fuses 30, 47) ZKE Power Windows (FH) (Also Fuses 17, 30, 47) ZKE Sunroof (SHD) (Also Fuses 17, 30, 47) Cellular Telephone (Provisions) (Also Fuses 9, 18)
F32 7.5A	NOT USED	
F40 15A	NOT USED	
F41 30A	6510.0	Radio/CD Player (Provisions) (Also Fuse 18)
F42 30A	5200.0	Power Seats (Also Fuse 43)
F43 30A	5200.0	Power Seats (Also Fuse 42)

84276037

Fig. 37 Fuse applications — 1989-90 E34 5 Series

FUSE	CIRCUIT PROTECTED	
F44 30A	6100.0	Central Body Electronics (ZKE) (Also Fuses 3, 5, 17, 30, 47)
	6160.0	ZKE Windshield Wiper Control (SWS) (Also Fuse 24)
	6330.0	ZKE Interior Lights (IB) (Also Fuses 5, 17, 18, 21, 30)
F46 30A	6450.1	Integrated Climate Regulation (IHKR) (Also Fuses 9, 19, 20, 27, 29)
F47 30A	5126.0	ZKE Central Locking (ZV) (Also Fuses 30, 31)
	5133.0	ZKE Power Windows (FH) (Also Fuses 17, 30, 31)
	5410.0	ZKE Sunroof (SHD) (Also Fuses 17, 30, 31)
	6100.0	Central Body Electronics (ZKE) (Also Fuses 3, 5, 17, 30, 44)
F48 15A	NOT USED	
F49	NOT USED	

84276038

Fig. 38 Fuse applications — 1989-90 E34 5 Series

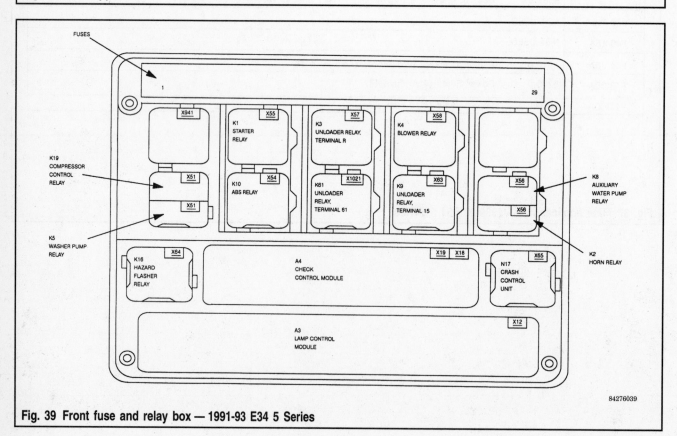

84276039

Fig. 39 Front fuse and relay box — 1991-93 E34 5 Series

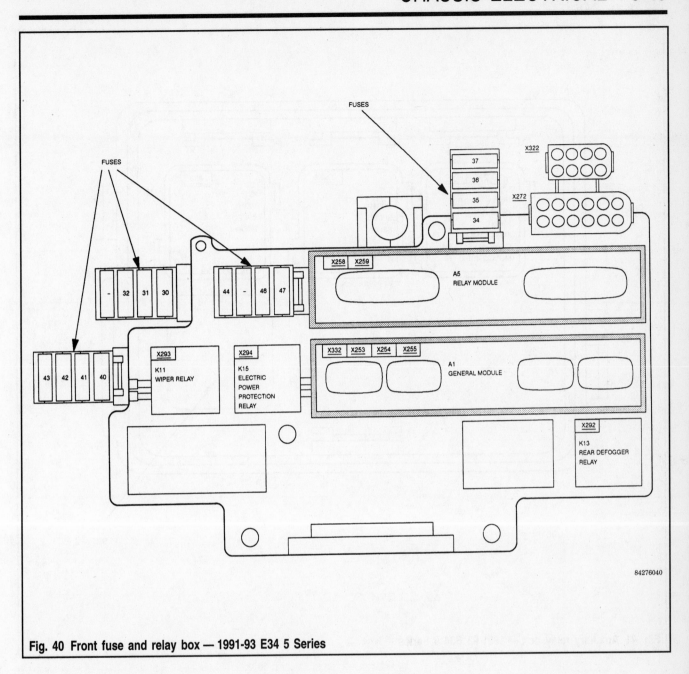

Fig. 40 Front fuse and relay box — 1991-93 E34 5 Series

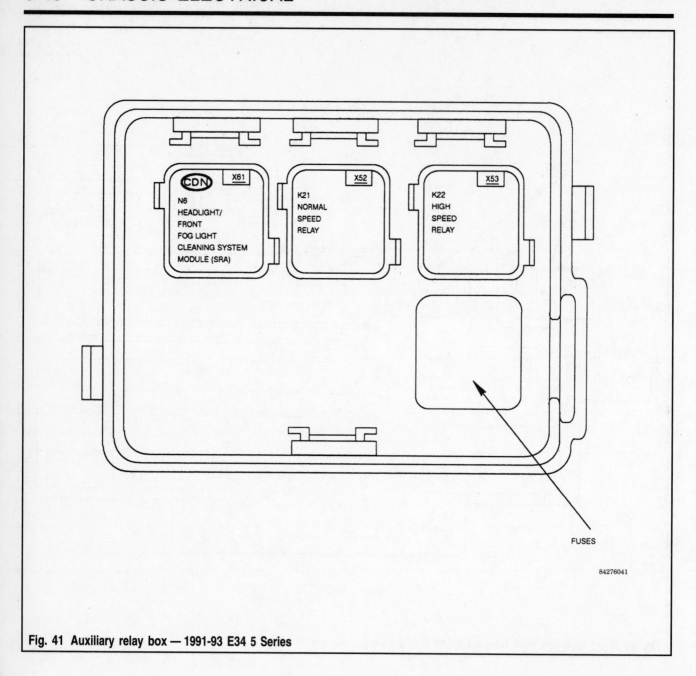

Fig. 41 Auxiliary relay box — 1991-93 E34 5 Series

		FUSE NUMBER																												
		1	2	3	4	5	6	7	8	9	10	11	12	13	14	15	16	17	18	19	20	21	22	23	24	25	26	27	28	29
		15A	7.5A	7.5A	7.5A	10A	15A	15A					15A	7.5A	7.5A	15A	7.5A	30A	7.5A	15A	10A	10A	30A	15A	10A	30A	30A	7.5A	15A	7.5A
1210.1	DIGITAL ENGINE ELECTRONICS (DME M1.3, 6-CYLINDER M30 WITH EML)																	•						•						
1210.2	DIGITAL ENGINE ELECTRONICS (DME M1.3, 6-CYLINDER M30)																	•						•						
1210.4	DIGITAL ENGINE ELECTRONICS (DME M1.2, 6-CYLINDER S38)																							•						
1210.7	DIGITAL ENGINE ELECTRONICS (DME M3.1, 6-CYLINDER M50)																	•						•						
1230.0	CHARGING SYSTEM																	•										•		
1240.0	START																	•												
1270.0	ELECTRONIC THROTTLE CONTROL (EML 6-CYLINDER)	•																•		•										
1290.0	E-BOX FAN																	•										•		
2460.0	ELECTRONIC TRANSMISSION CONTROL (EGS 4HP-22)	•																•												
2460.2	ELECTRONIC TRANSMISSION CONTROL (EGS A4S 310R)	•																•												
3231.0	ELECTRIC STEERING COLUMN ADJUSTMENT																													
3240.0	POWER ASSIST STEERING (SERVOTRONIC)																											•		
3450.0	ANTILOCK BRAKE SYSTEM (ABS)	•																•												
3450.1	AUTOMATIC STABILITY CONTROL (ASC)	•																•												•
5116.0	POWER MIRRORS				•	•							•																	
5120.0	ZKE DOOR LOCK HEATING (TSH)																	•												
5126.0	ZKE CENTRAL LOCKING (ZV)																													
5133.0	ZKE POWER WINDOWS (FH)																	•												
5200.0	POWER SEATS																													

84276042

Fig. 42 Fuse 1 through 29 applications — 1991-93 E34 5 Series

		FUSE NUMBER																												
		1	2	3	4	5	6	7	8	9	10	11	12	13	14	15	16	17	18	19	20	21	22	23	24	25	26	27	28	29
		15A	7.5A	7.5A	7.5A	10A	15A	15A					15A	7.5A	7.5A	15A	7.5A	30A	7.5A	15A	10A	10A	30A	15A	10A	30A	30A	7.5A	15A	7.5A
5200.1	MEMORY SEATS/ MIRRORS (SM/SPM)												•					•		•										
5203.0	HEATED SEATS																	•												
5410.0	ZKE SUNROOF (SHD)																	•												
5410.2	DOUBLE PANEL POWER SUNROOF (ZKE)																													
6100.0	CENTRAL BODY ELECTRONICS (ZKE)				•	•	•											•						•						
6133.0	HORN										•																			
6160.0	ZKE WIPER/WASHER CONTROL	•																												
6162.0	REAR WINDOW WIPER/WASHER CONTROL																													
6167.0	ZKE HEADLIGHT WASHER (SRA)				•	•	•											•				•								
6169.0	WINDSHIELD WASHER JET HEATERS														•															
6200.0	INSTRUMENT CLUSTER/ CHECK CONTROL (K/CC)	•																•			•									•
6213.2	MULTI-FUNCTION CLOCK	•																			•									
6300.0	LIGHT SWITCH DETAILS			•	•	•	•																							
6301.0	LAMP MONITOR (LKM)	•	•	•	•	•	•		•				•	•		•	•	•												
6312.0	HEADLIGHTS/ FOG LIGHTS			•	•		•		•				•	•		•	•													
6313.0	TURN/HAZARD LIGHTS			•	•			•								•	•													
6314.0	PARK/TAIL/ UNDERHOOD LIGHTS						•	•									•				•									
6320.0	LICENSE PLATE/ LUGGAGE COMPARTMENT LIGHTS							•									•						•							
6322.0	BACK UP LIGHTS												•																	

84276043

Fig. 43 Fuse 1 through 29 applications — 1991-93 E34 5 Series

										FUSE NUMBER																		
1	2	3	4	5	6	7	8	9	10	11	12	13	14	15	16	17	18	19	20	21	22	23	24	25	26	27	28	29
15A	7.5A	7.5A	7.5A	10A	15A	15A		15A	7.5A	7.5A	15A	7.5A	7.5A	7.5A	30A	7.5A	15A	30A	10A	10A	30A	15A	10A	30A	30A	7.5A	15A	7.5A

Code	Description	Fuses
6325.0	BRAKE LIGHTS	1, 16
6330.0	ZKE INTERIOR LIGHTS CONTROL (IB)	5, 18, 20, 21
6332.0	GLOVE BOX LIGHT/CIGAR LIGHTER/ CHARGING SOCKET	5, 18, 21, 26
6350.0	CRASH CONTROL UNIT	2, 6, 10, 11
6412.19	PARK VENTILATION WITH IHKR/F3	19, 20
6424.0	REAR WINDOW DEFOGGER	
6450.5	INTEGRATED CLIMATE REGULATION WITH FILTER (IHKR/F3)	9, 19, 20, 27, 29
6454.0	AUXILIARY FAN	9, 25, 29
6510.1	RADIO/HIFI	18
6510.2	RADIO PROVISIONS	18
6561.0	CELLULAR TELEPHONE (PROVISIONS)	9, 18
6571.0	CRUISE CONTROL (TEMPOMAT)	1, 15
6575.2	ANTITHEFT SYSTEM (ALPINE)	18, 21
6581.0	ON-BOARD COMPUTER (BCIV)	1, 15, 19

84276044

Fig. 44 Fuse 1 through 29 applications — 1991-93 E34 5 Series

								FUSE NUMBER											
30	31	32	33	34	35	36	37	38	39	40	41	42	43	44	45	46	47	48	49
7.5A	7.5A			20A		30A	20A				30A	30A	30A	30A		30A	30A		

Code	Description	Fuses
1210.1	DIGITAL ENGINE ELECTRONICS (DME M1.3, 6-CYLINDER M30 WITH EML)	
1210.2	DIGITAL ENGINE ELECTRONICS (DME M1.3, 6-CYLINDER M30)	
1210.4	DIGITAL ENGINE ELECTRONICS (DME M1.2, 6-CYLINDER S38)	
1210.7	DIGITAL ENGINE ELECTRONICS (DME M3.1, 6-CYLINDER M50)	
1230.0	CHARGING SYSTEM	
1240.0	START	
1270.0	ELECTRONIC THROTTLE CONTROL (EML 6-CYLINDER)	
1290.0	E-BOX FAN	
2460.0	ELECTRONIC TRANSMISSION CONTROL (EGS 4HP-22/24)	
2460.2	ELECTRONIC TRANSMISSION CONTROL (EGS A4S 310R)	
3231.0	ELECTRIC STEERING COLUMN ADJUSTMENT	34
3240.0	POWER ASSIST STEERING (SERVOTRONIC)	
3450.0	ANTILOCK BRAKE SYSTEM (ABS)	
3450.1	AUTOMATIC STABILITY CONTROL (ASC)	
5116.0	POWER MIRRORS	
5120.0	ZKE DOOR LOCK HEATING (TSH)	30
5126.0	ZKE CENTRAL LOCKING (ZV)	30, 31, 37, 46
5133.0	ZKE POWER WINDOWS (FH)	30, 31, 46
5200.0	POWER SEATS	41, 42

84276045

Fig. 45 Fuse 30 through 49 applications — 1991-93 E34 5 Series

			FUSE NUMBER																		
			30	31	32	33	34	35	36	37	38	39	40	41	42	43	44	45	46	47	48	49
			7.5A	7.5A			20A			30A	20A			30A	30A	30A	30A		30A	30A		
5200.1	MEMORY SEATS/ MIRRORS (SM/SPM)																					
5203.0	HEATED SEATS																					
5410.0	ZKE SUNROOF (SHD)		●	●																●		
5410.2	DOUBLE PANEL POWER SUNROOF (ZKE)		●																			
6100.0	CENTRAL BODY ELECTRONICS (ZKE)		●																	●		
6133.0	HORN																					
6160.0	ZKE WIPER/WASHER CONTROL															●						
6162.0	REAR WINDOW WIPER/WASHER CONTROL									●												
6167.0	ZKE HEADLIGHT WASHER (SRA)																					
6169.0	WINDSHIELD WASHER JET HEATERS																					
6200.0	INSTRUMENT CLUSTER/ CHECK CONTROL (K/CC)																					
6213.2	MULTI-FUNCTION CLOCK																					
6300.0	LIGHT SWITCH DETAILS																					
6301.0	LAMP MONITOR (LKM)																					
6312.0	HEADLIGHTS/ FOG LIGHTS																					
6313.0	TURN/HAZARD LIGHTS																					
6314.0	PARK/TAIL/ UNDERHOOD LIGHTS																					
6320.0	LICENSE PLATE/ LUGGAGE COMPARTMENT LIGHTS																					
6322.0	BACK UP LIGHTS																					

84276046

Fig. 46 Fuse 30 through 49 applications — 1991-93 E34 5 Series

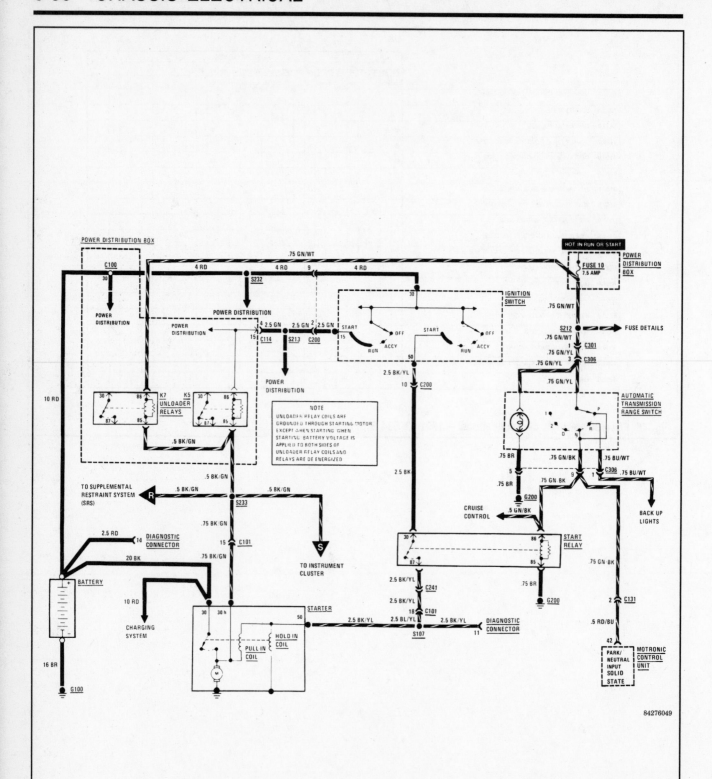

Fig. 49 Starting circuit, automatic transmission — E30 3 Series

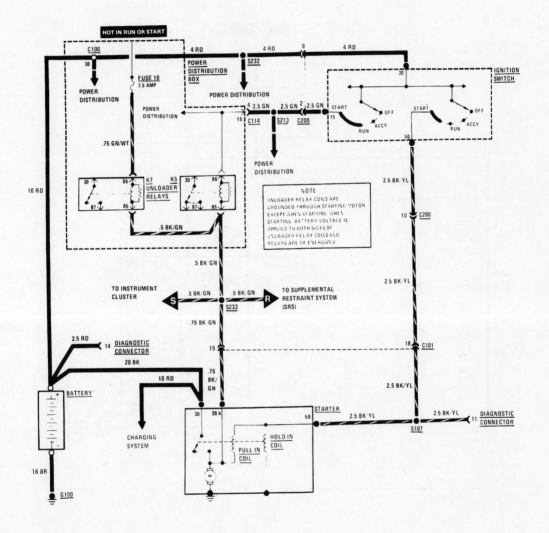

Fig. 50 Starting circuit, manual transmission — E30 3 Series

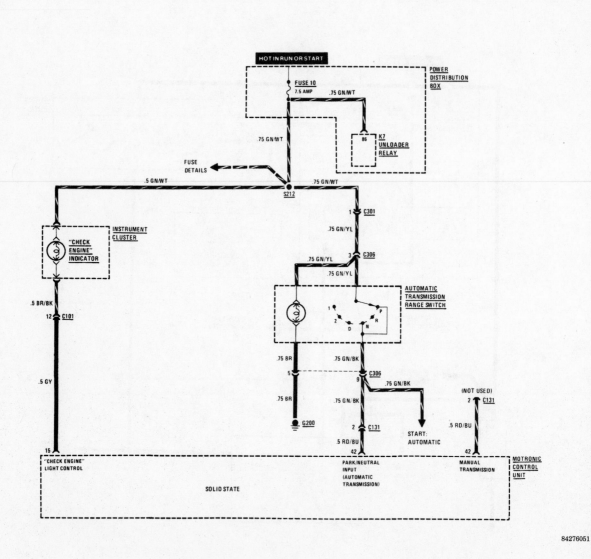

Fig. 51 Fuel injection circuit with M20 engine — E30 3 Series

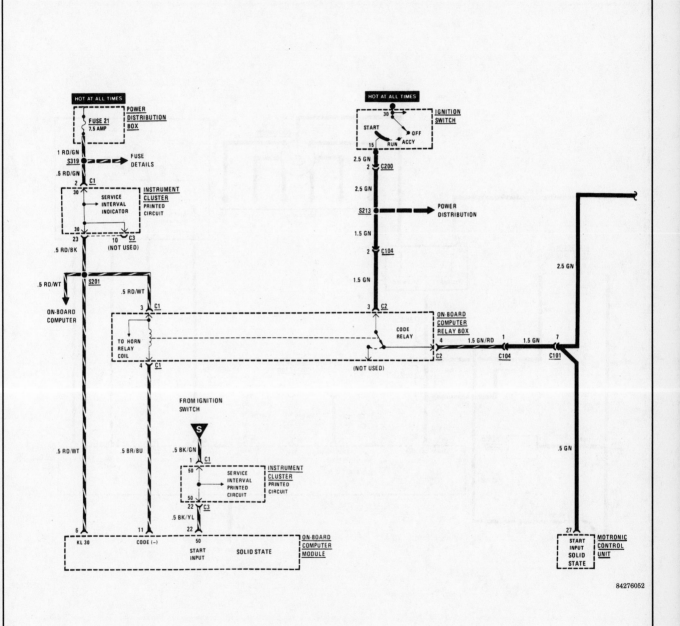

Fig. 52 Fuel injection circuit with M20 engine — E30 3 Series

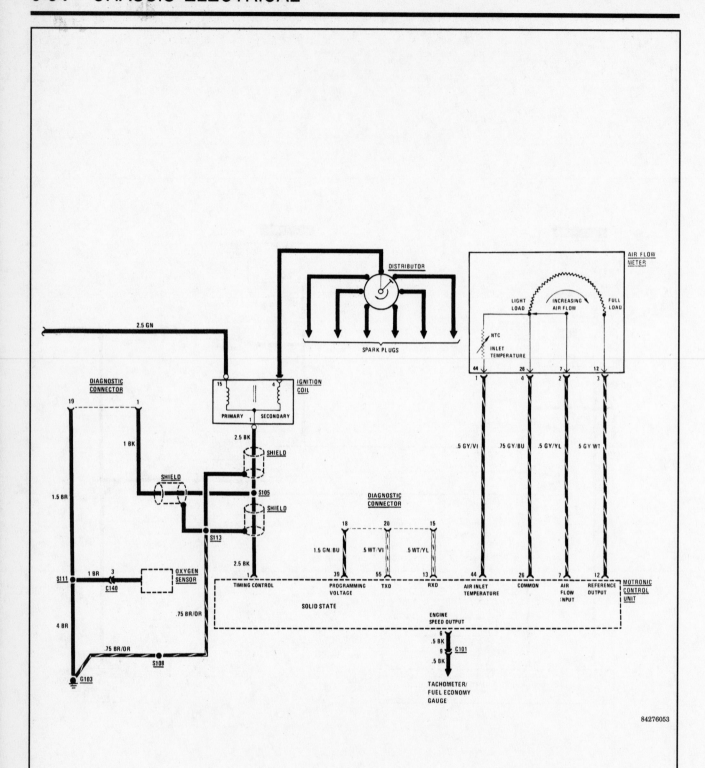

Fig. 53 Fuel injection circuit with M20 engine — E30 3 Series

84276053

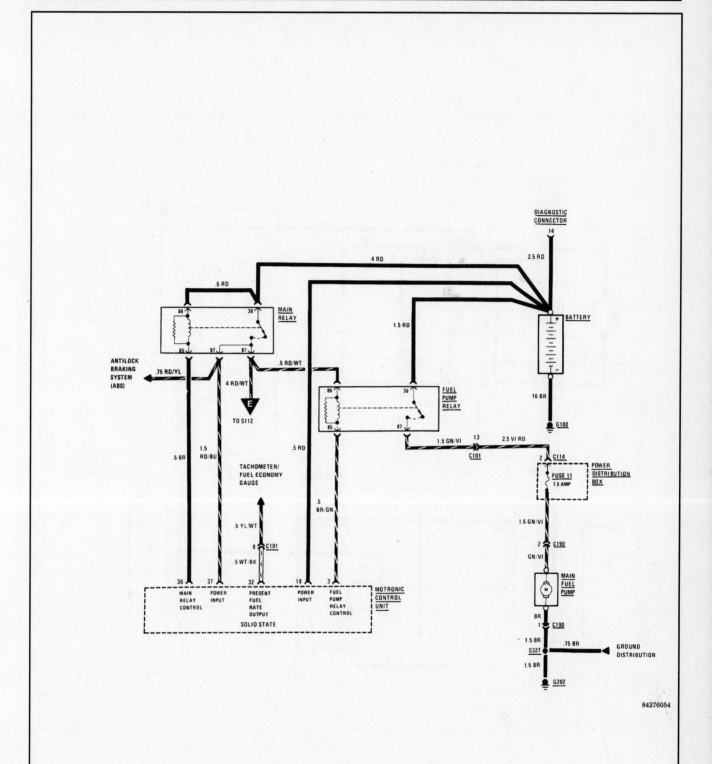

Fig. 54 Fuel injection circuit with M20 engine — E30 3 Series

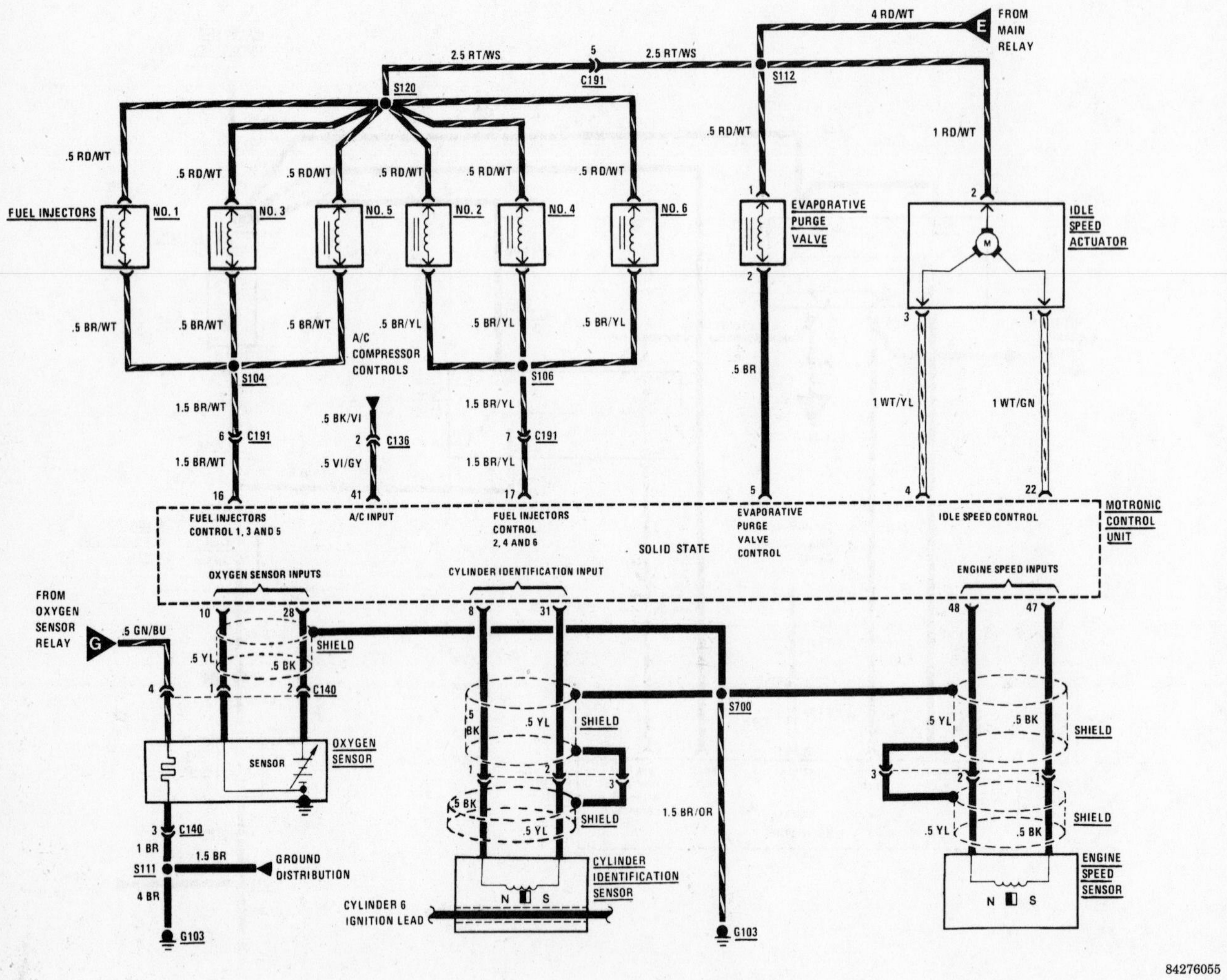

Fig. 55 Fuel injection circuit with M20 engine — E30 3 Series

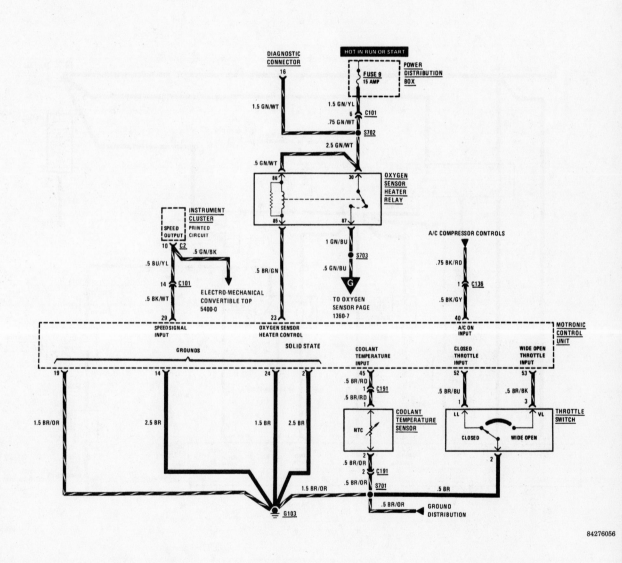

Fig. 56 Fuel injection circuit with M20 engine — E30 3 Series

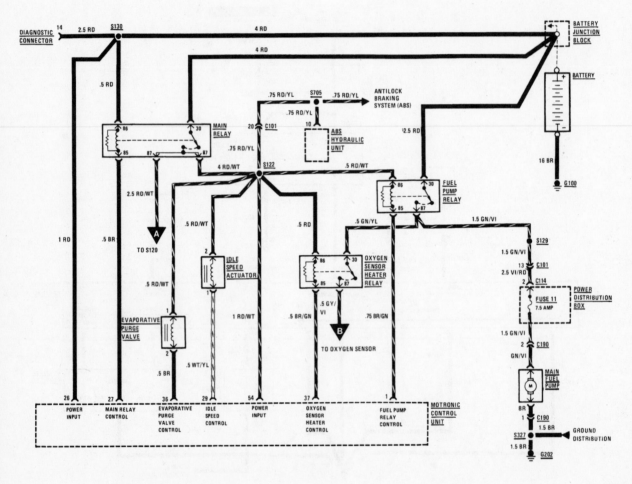

Fig. 57 Fuel injection circuit with M42 engine — E30 3 Series

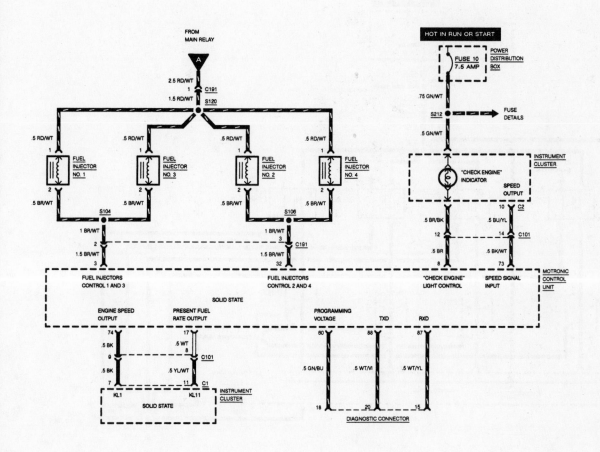

Fig. 58 Fuel injection circuit with M42 engine — E30 3 Series

84276058

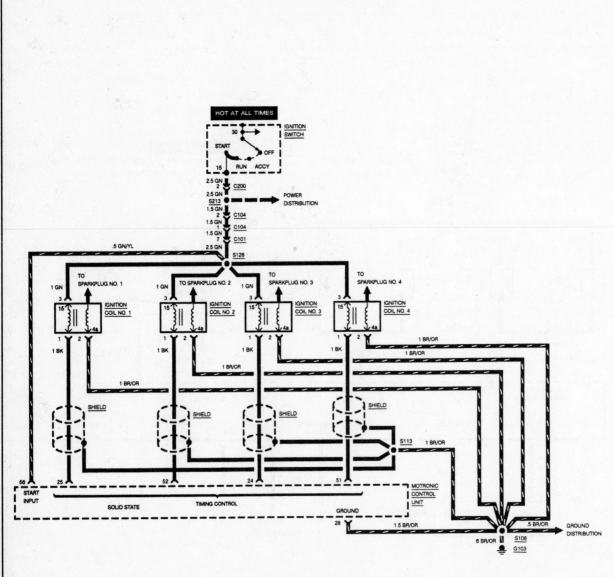

Fig. 59 Fuel injection circuit with M42 engine — E30 3 Series

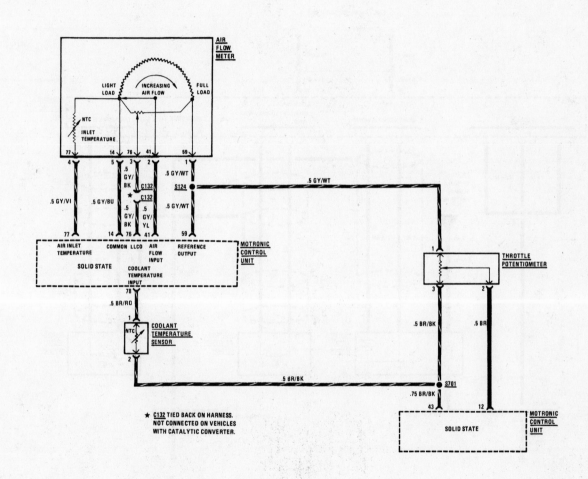

Fig. 60 Fuel injection circuit with M42 engine — E30 3 Series

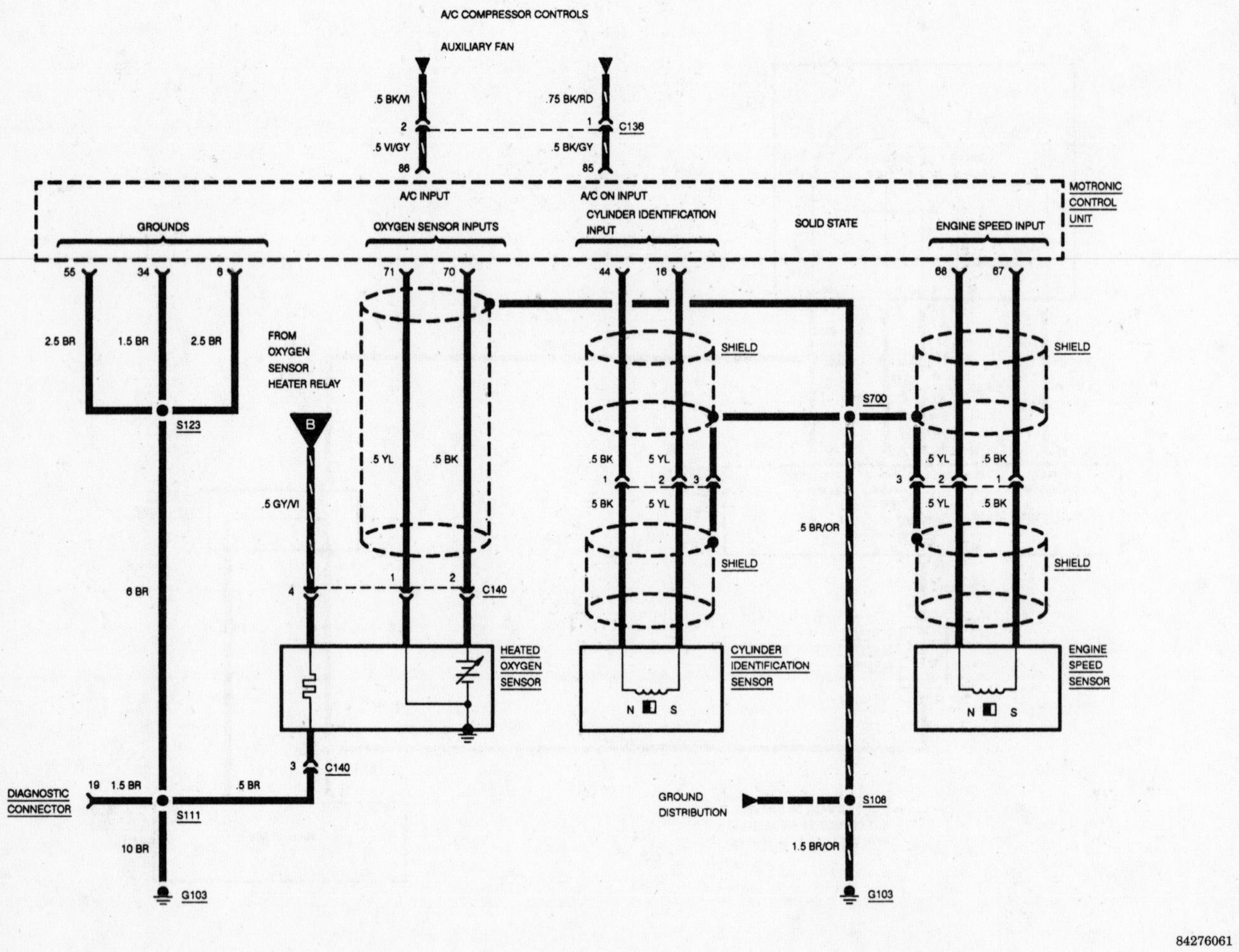

A/C COMPRESSOR CONTROLS

AUXILIARY FAN

.5 BK/VI   .75 BK/RD

2   1   C136

.5 VI/GY   .5 BK/GY

86   85

A/C INPUT   A/C ON INPUT

MOTRONIC
CONTROL
UNIT

GROUNDS   OXYGEN SENSOR INPUTS   CYLINDER IDENTIFICATION INPUT   SOLID STATE   ENGINE SPEED INPUT

55   34   6   71   70   44   16   68   87

2.5 BR   1.5 BR   2.5 BR

FROM
OXYGEN
SENSOR
HEATER RELAY

SHIELD   SHIELD

S700

S123

B

.5 GY/VI

.5 YL   .5 BK   .5 BK   .5 YL   .5 YL   .5 BK

1   2   3   3   2   1

5 BK   5 YL   .5 YL   .5 BK

6 BR

.5 BR/OR

SHIELD   SHIELD

4   1   2   C140

HEATED
OXYGEN
SENSOR

CYLINDER
IDENTIFICATION
SENSOR

ENGINE
SPEED
SENSOR

N   S   N   S

3   C140

DIAGNOSTIC   19   1.5 BR   .5 BR
CONNECTOR

GROUND   S108
DISTRIBUTION

S111

10 BR   1.5 BR/OR

G103   G103

84276061

Fig. 61 Fuel injection circuit with M42 engine — E30 3 Series

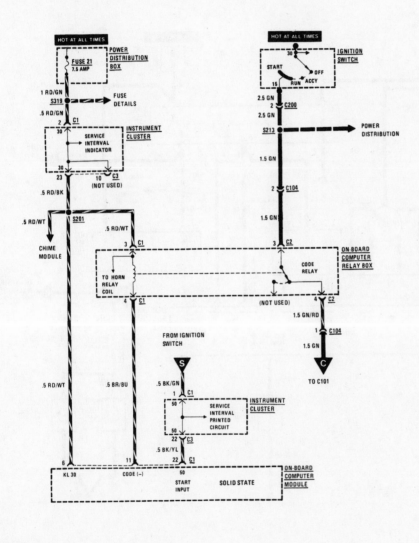

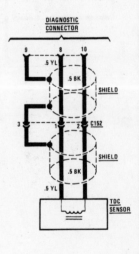

84276062

Fig. 62 Fuel injection circuit with S14 engine — E30 3 Series

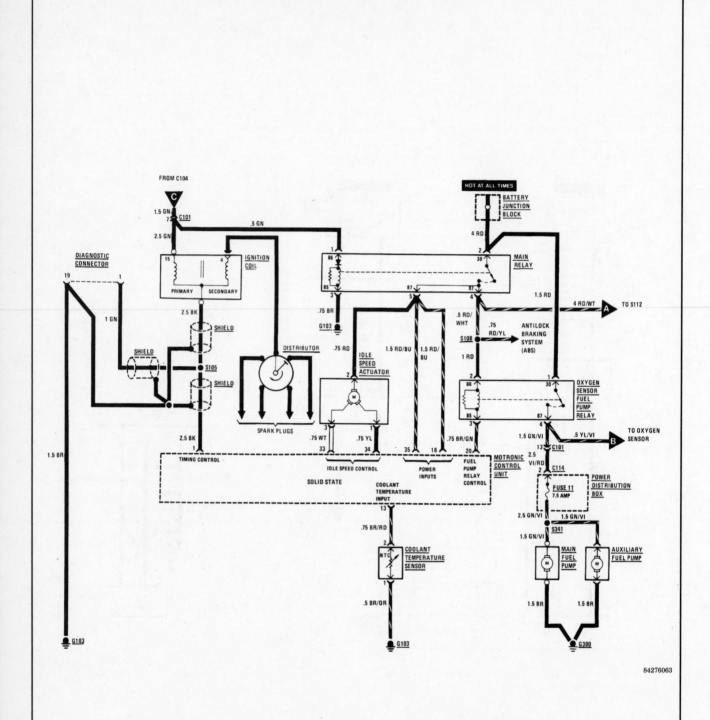

Fig. 63 Fuel injection circuit with S14 engine — E30 3 Series

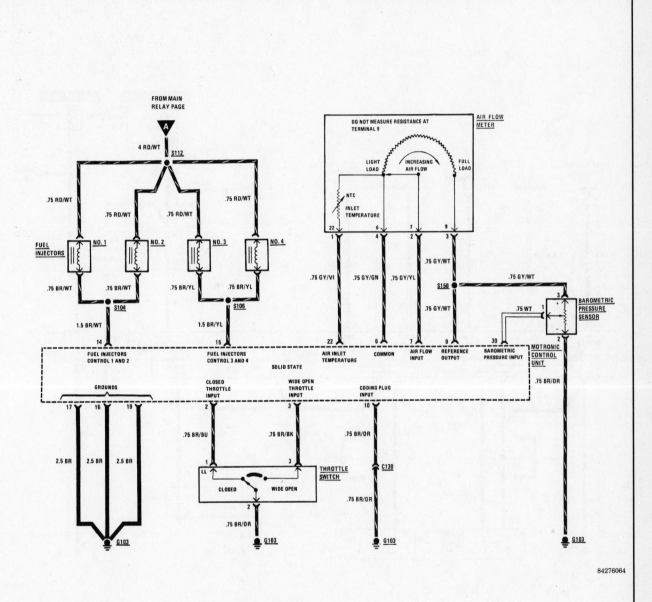

Fig. 64 Fuel injection circuit with S14 engine — E30 3 Series

84276064

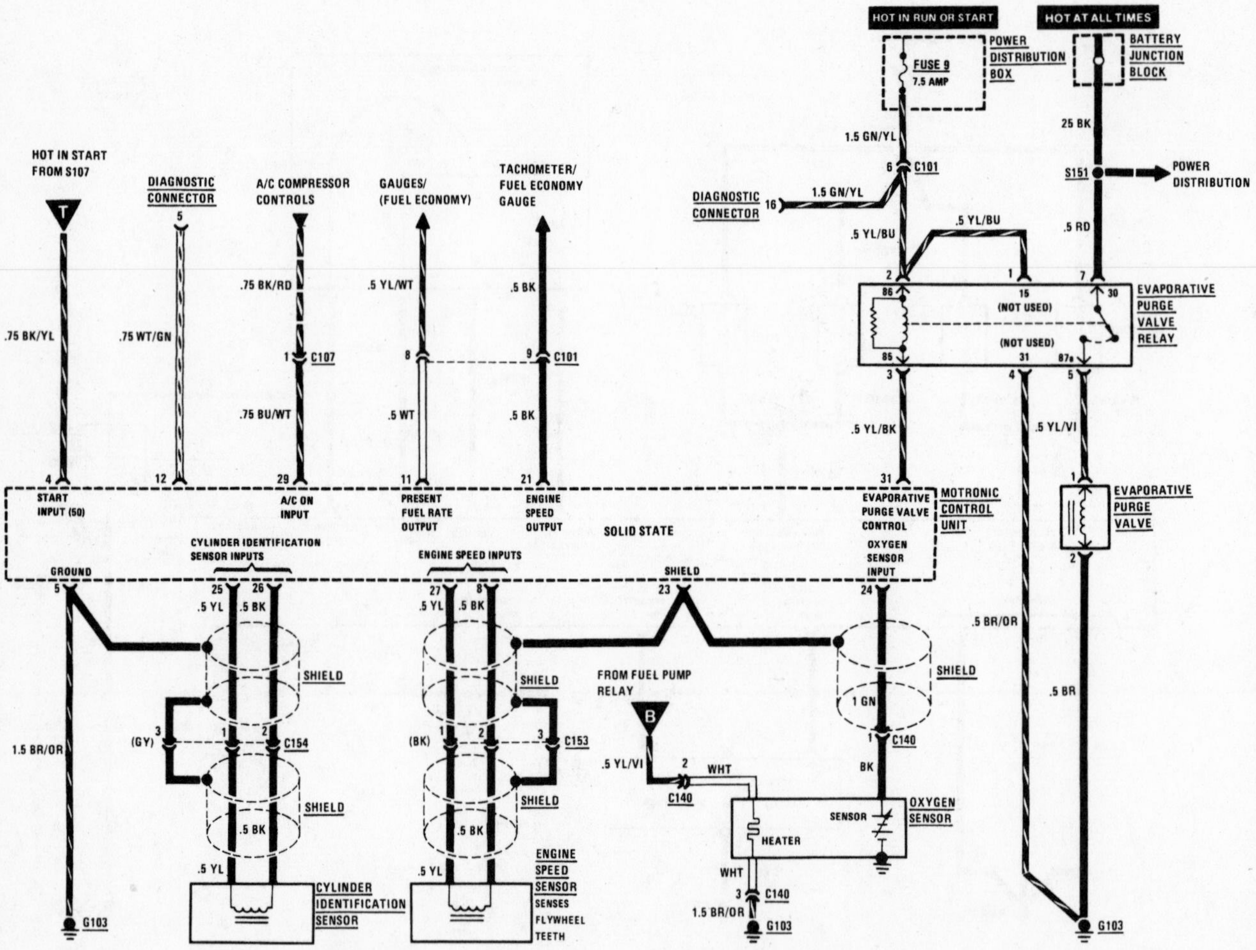

Fig. 65 Fuel injection circuit with S14 engine — E30 3 Series

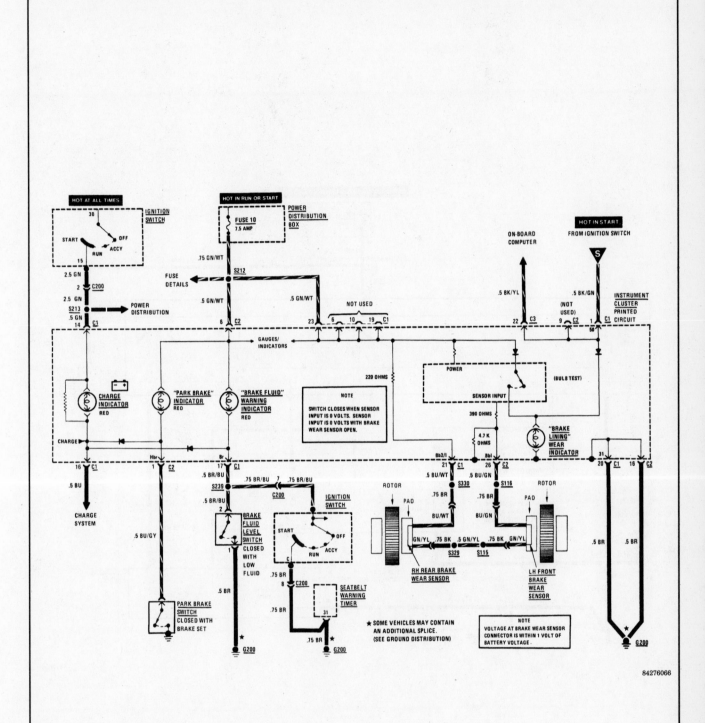

Fig. 66 Brake warning system circuit — E30 3 Series

84276066

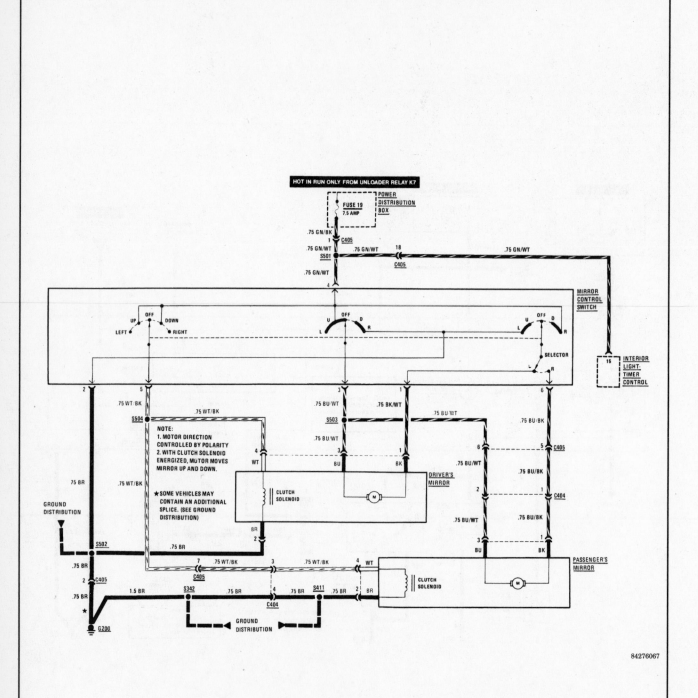

Fig. 67 Power mirror circuit — E30 3 Series

84276067

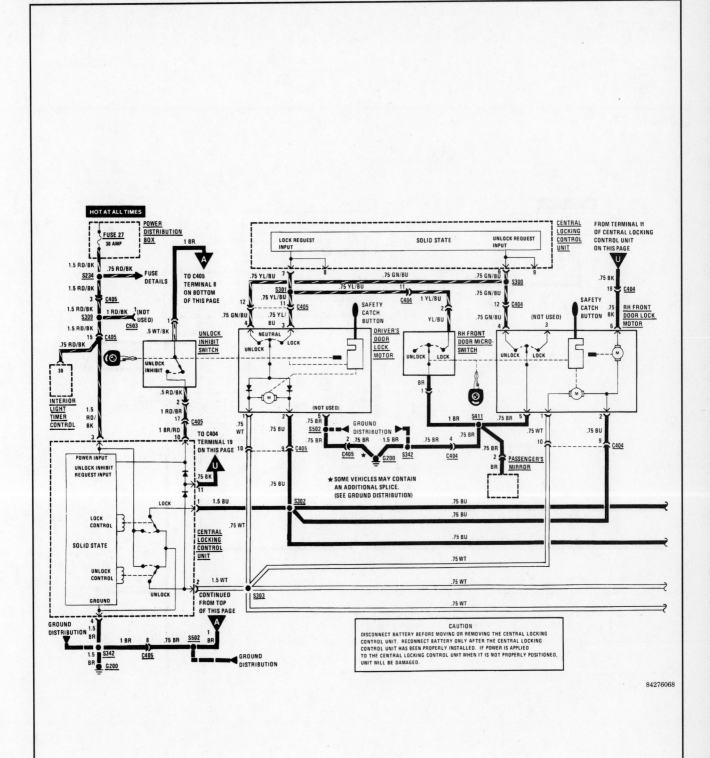

Fig. 68 Central locking system wiring — E30 3 Series convertible

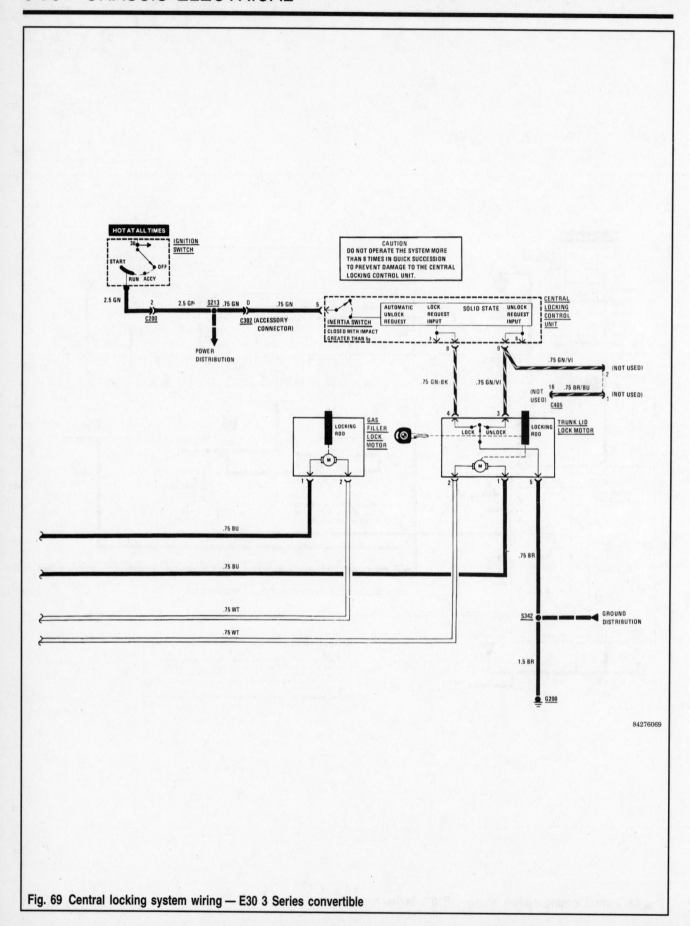

Fig. 69 Central locking system wiring — E30 3 Series convertible

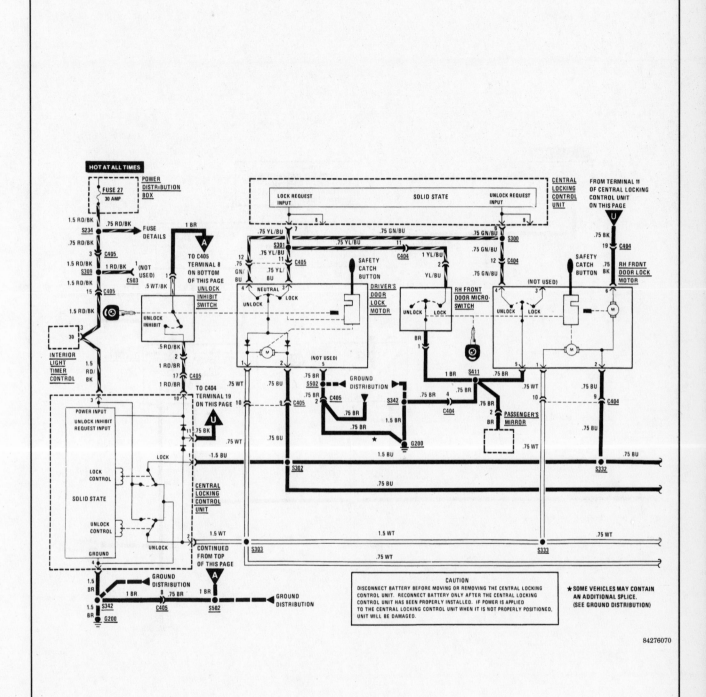

Fig. 70 Central locking system wiring — E30 3 Series 2 door

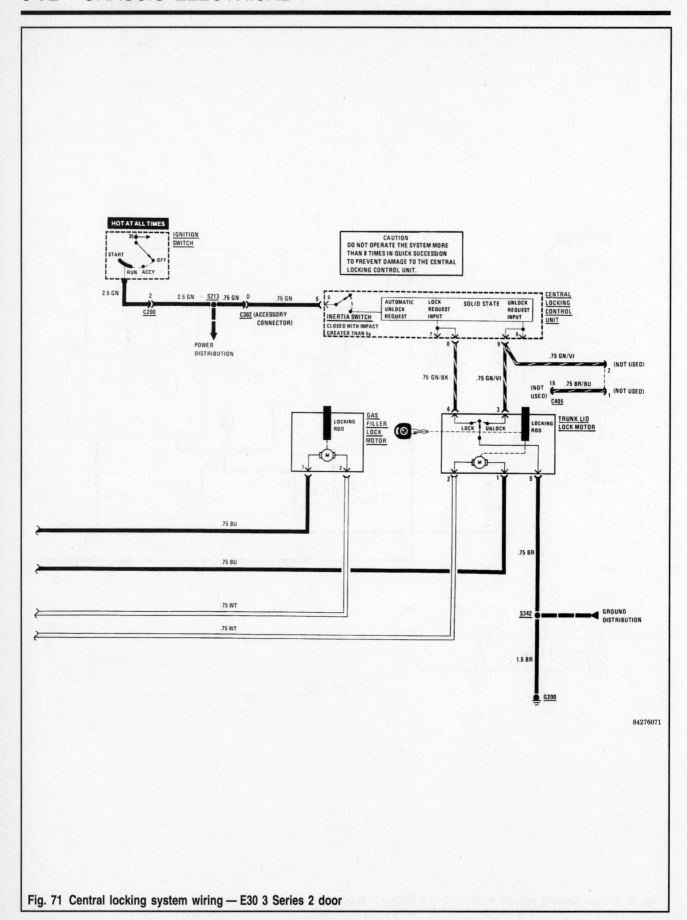

Fig. 71 Central locking system wiring — E30 3 Series 2 door

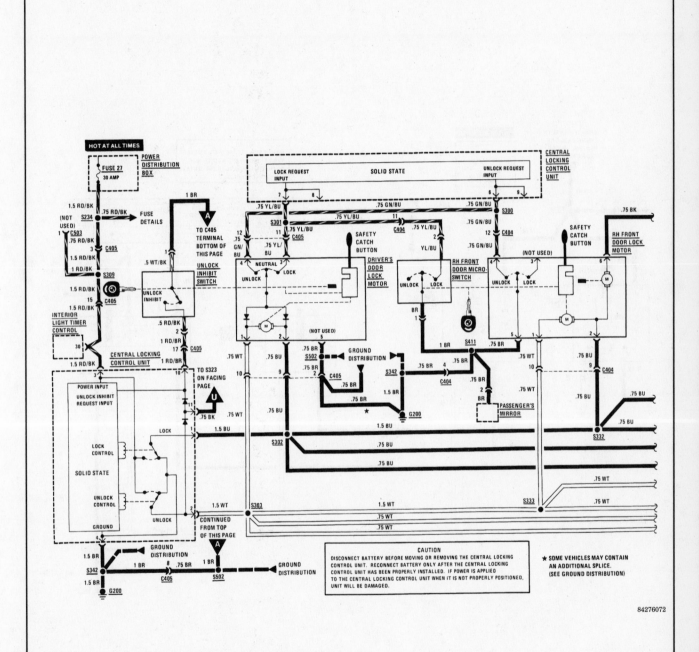

Fig. 72 Central locking system wiring — E30 3 Series 4 door

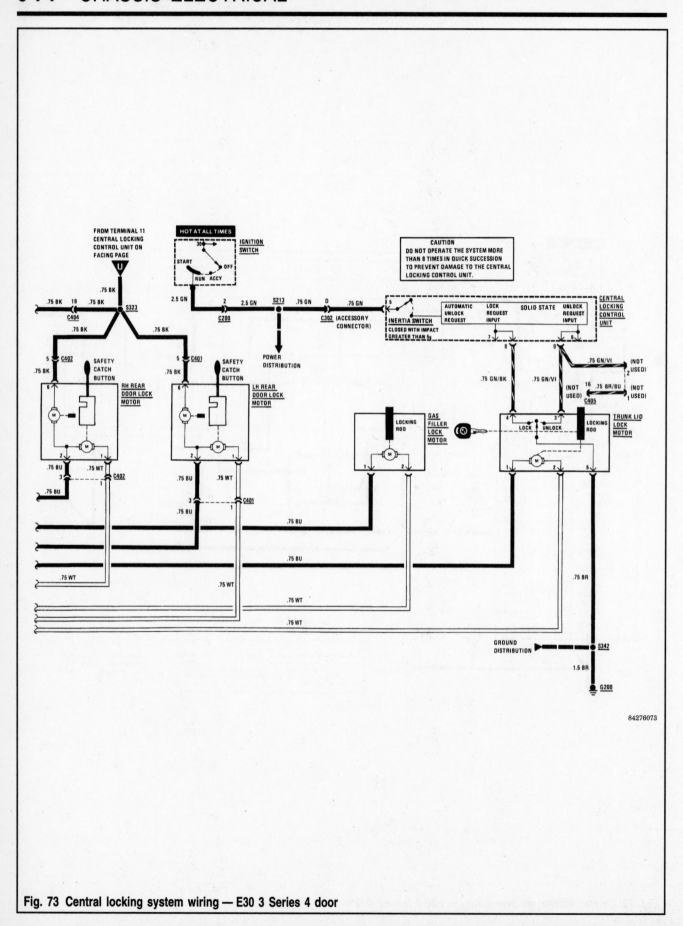

Fig. 73 Central locking system wiring — E30 3 Series 4 door

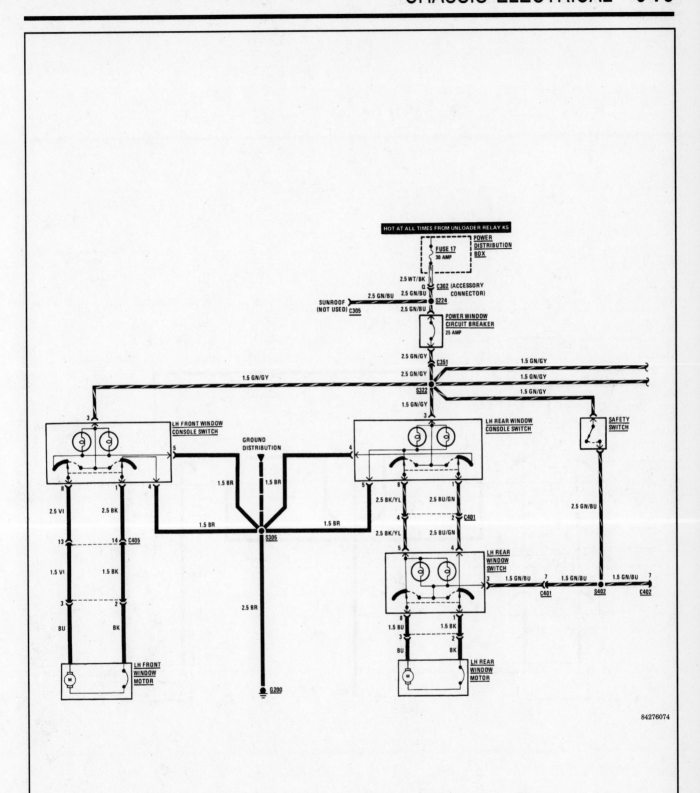

Fig. 74 Power window system wiring — E30 3 Series 4 door

84276074

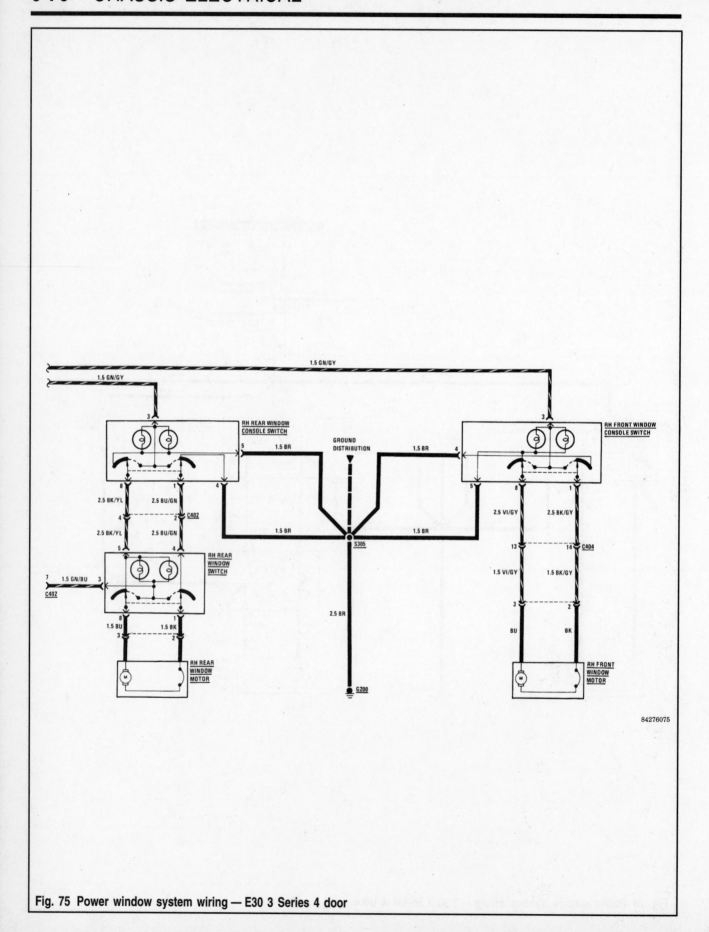

Fig. 75 Power window system wiring — E30 3 Series 4 door

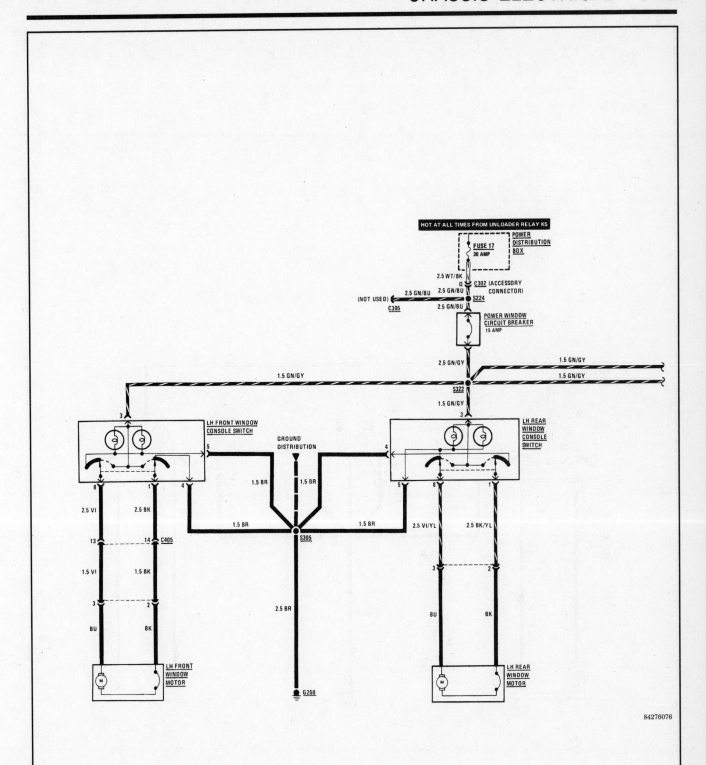

Fig. 76 Power window system wiring — E30 3 Series 2 door

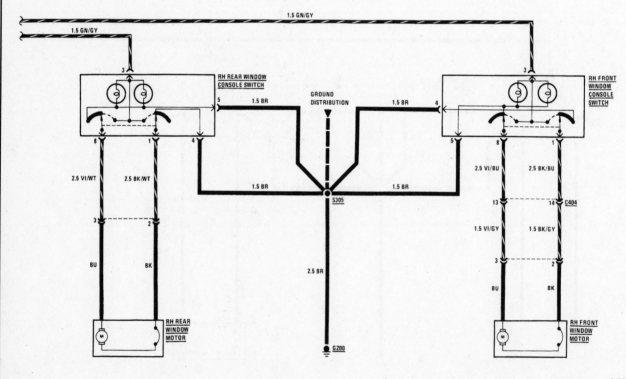

Fig. 77 Power window system wiring — E30 3 Series convertible

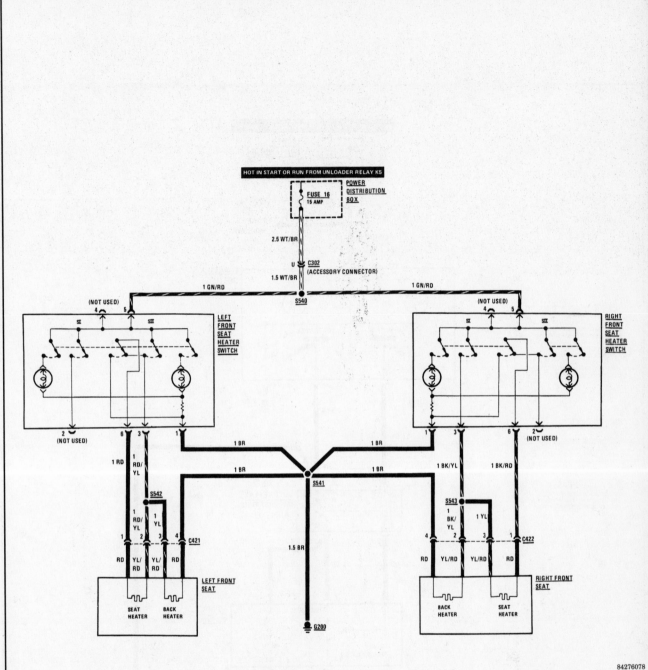

Fig. 78 Power window system wiring — E30 3 Series convertible

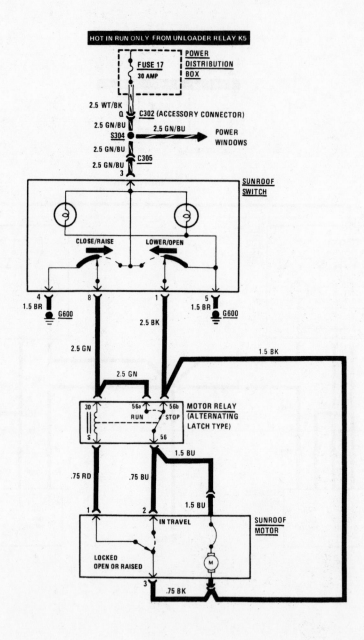

HOT IN RUN ONLY FROM UNLOADER RELAY K5

POWER DISTRIBUTION BOX

FUSE 17 30 AMP

2.5 WT/BK

C302 (ACCESSORY CONNECTOR)

2.5 GN/BU   2.5 GN/BU → POWER WINDOWS

S304

2.5 GN/BU

2.5 GN/BU   C305

3

SUNROOF SWITCH

CLOSE/RAISE   LOWER/OPEN

4   8   1   5
1.5 BR   1.5 BR
G600   G600

2.5 BK

2.5 GN

2.5 GN   1.5 BK

MOTOR RELAY (ALTERNATING LATCH TYPE)

30   56a   56b
S   RUN   STOP
                              56

1.5 BU

.75 RD   .75 BU   1.5 BU

1   2   1.5 BU   SUNROOF MOTOR

IN TRAVEL

LOCKED OPEN OR RAISED   M

3   .75 BK

84276079

Fig. 79 Sunroof circuit — E30 3 Series

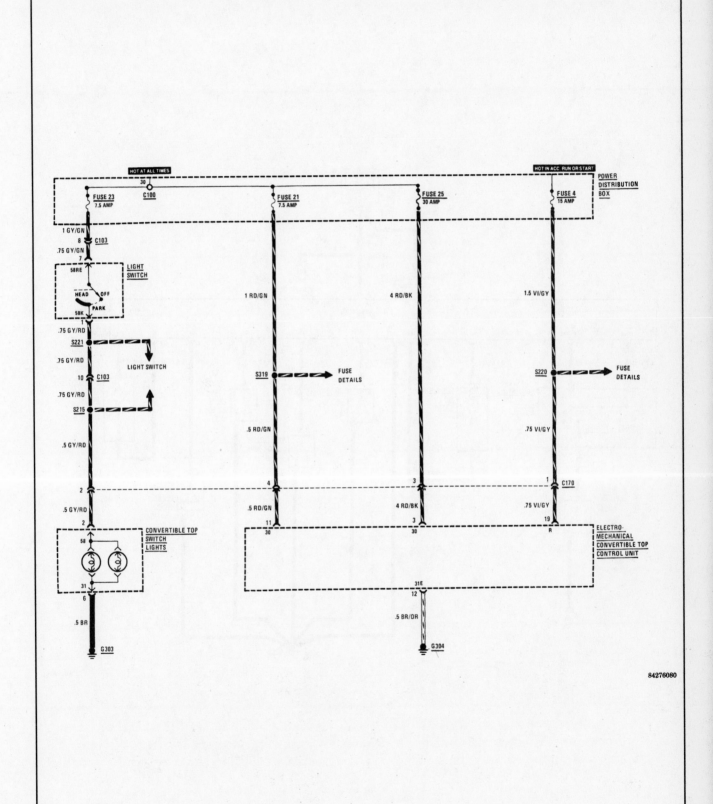

Fig. 80 Power convertible top circuit — E30 3 Series

84276080

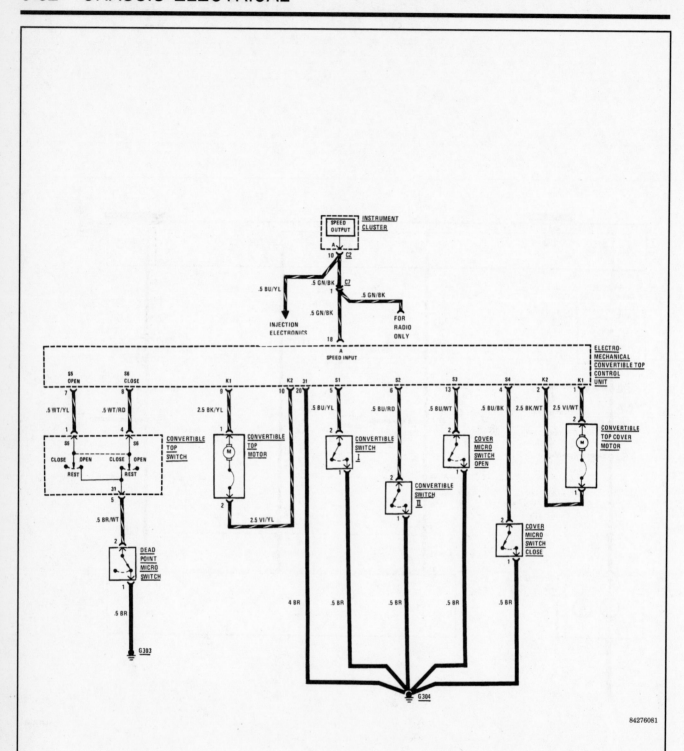

84276081

Fig. 81 Power convertible top circuit — E30 3 Series

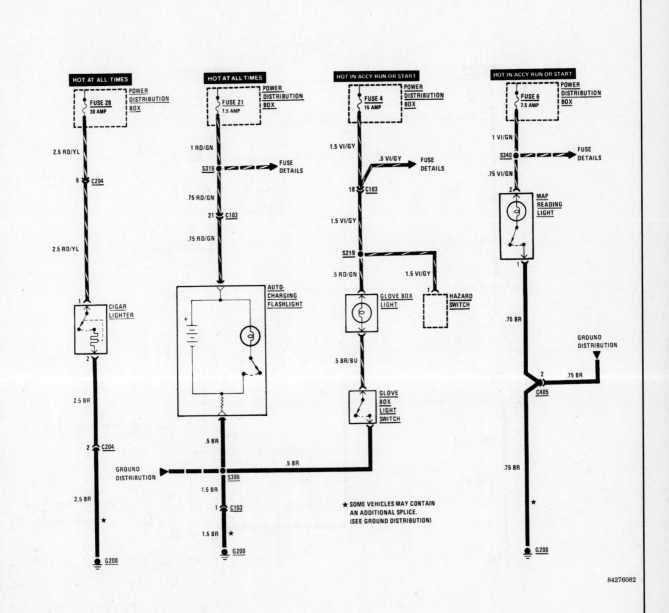

Fig. 82 Lighter, glove compartment light circuits — E30 3 Series

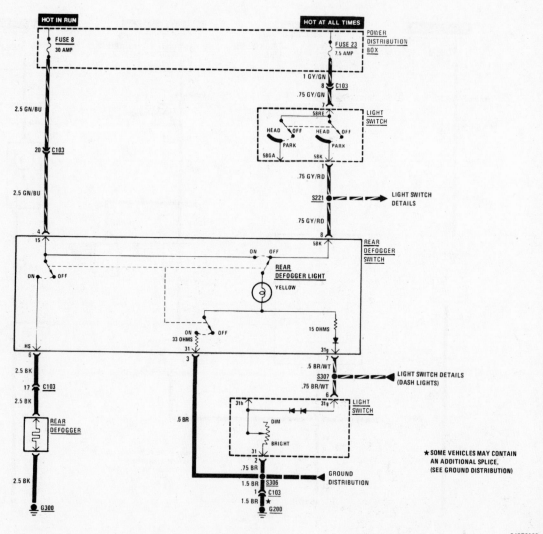

Fig. 83 Rear defogger circuit — E30 3 Series except convertible

84276083

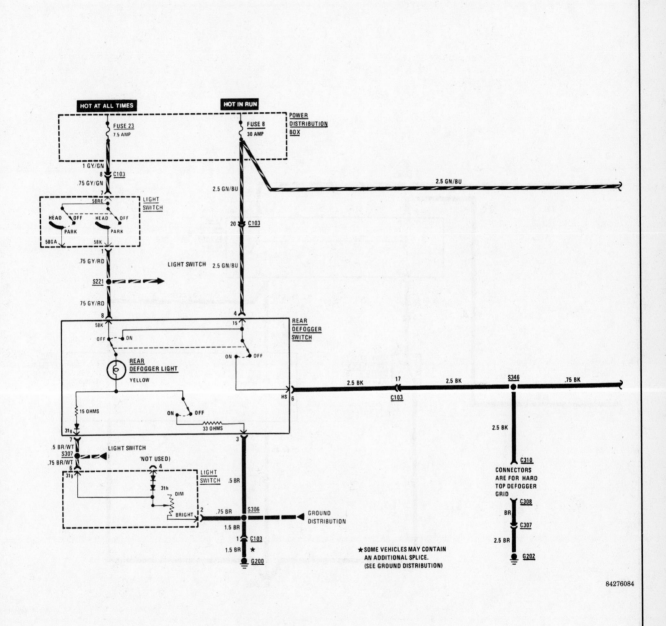

Fig. 84 Rear defogger circuit — E30 3 Series convertible

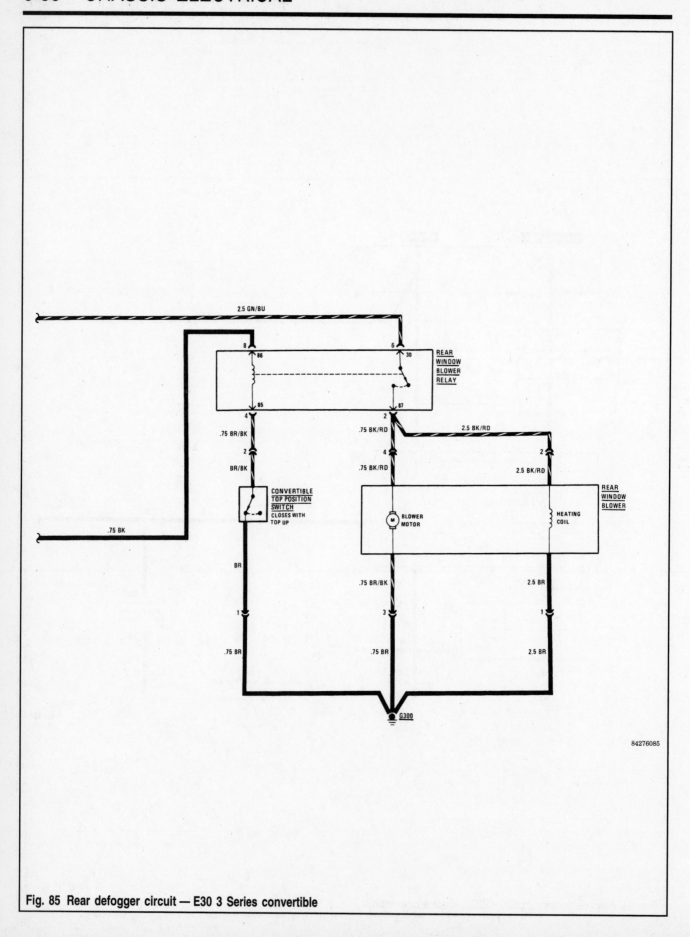

Fig. 85 Rear defogger circuit — E30 3 Series convertible

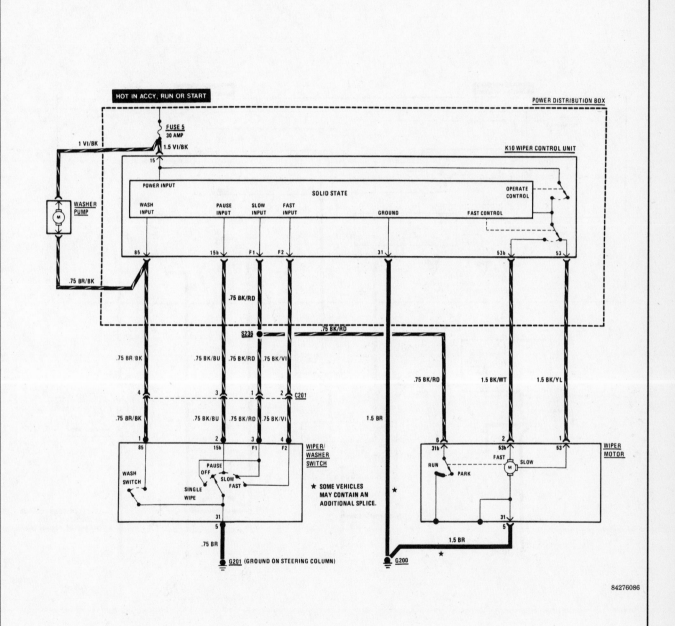

Fig. 86 Windshield wiper circuit — E30 3 Series

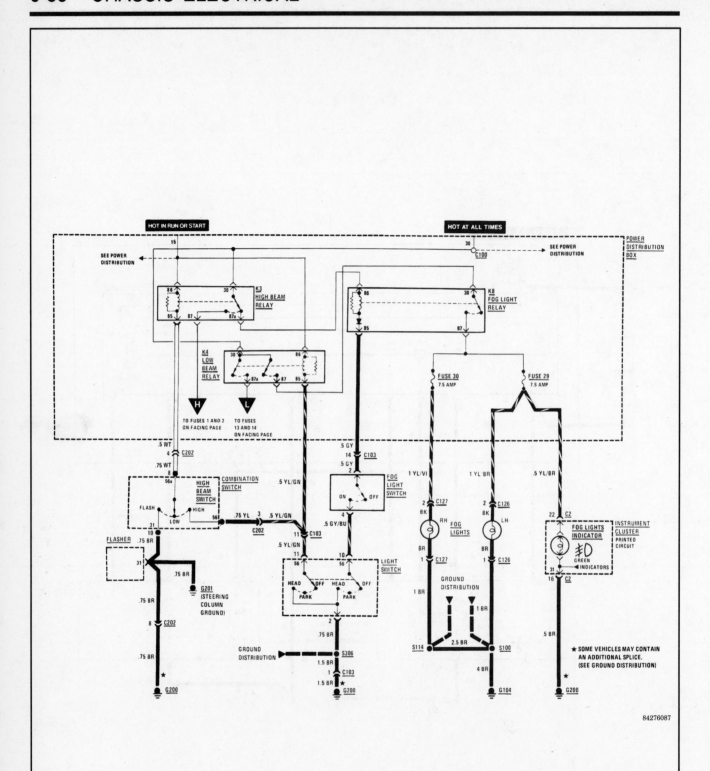

Fig. 87 Headlight and foglight circuit — E30 3 Series

84276087

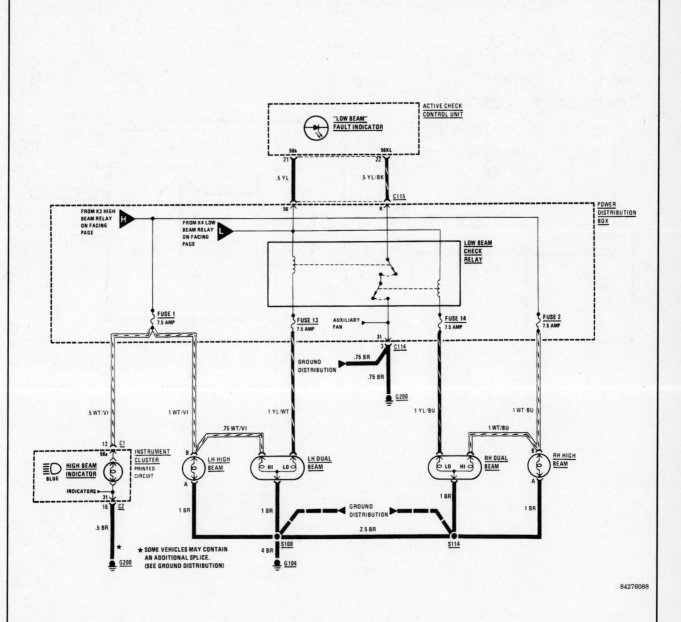

Fig. 88 Headlight and foglight circuit — E30 3 Series

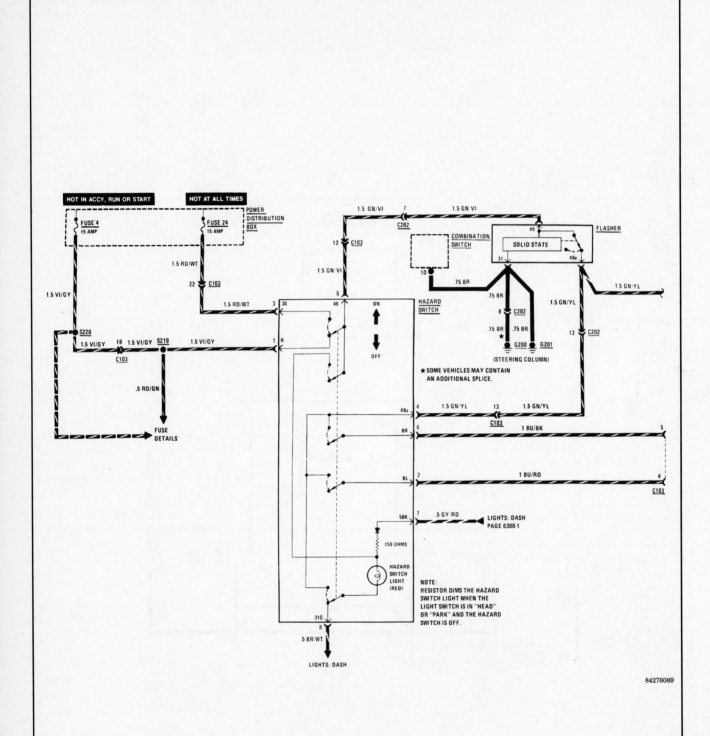

Fig. 89 Turn signal and hazard light circuit — E30 3 Series

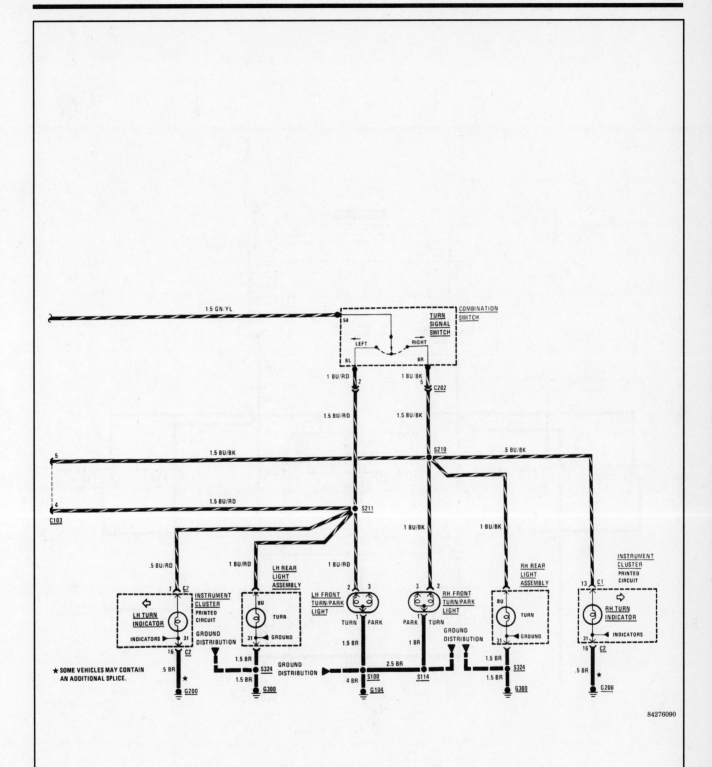

Fig. 90 Turn signal and hazard light circuit — E30 3 Series

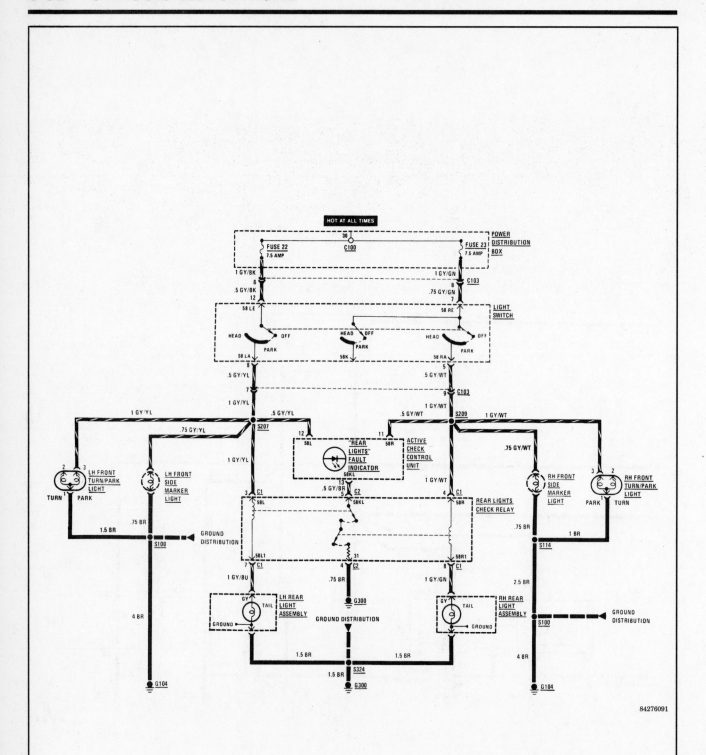

Fig. 91 Parking, tail and front marker light circuit — E30 3 Series

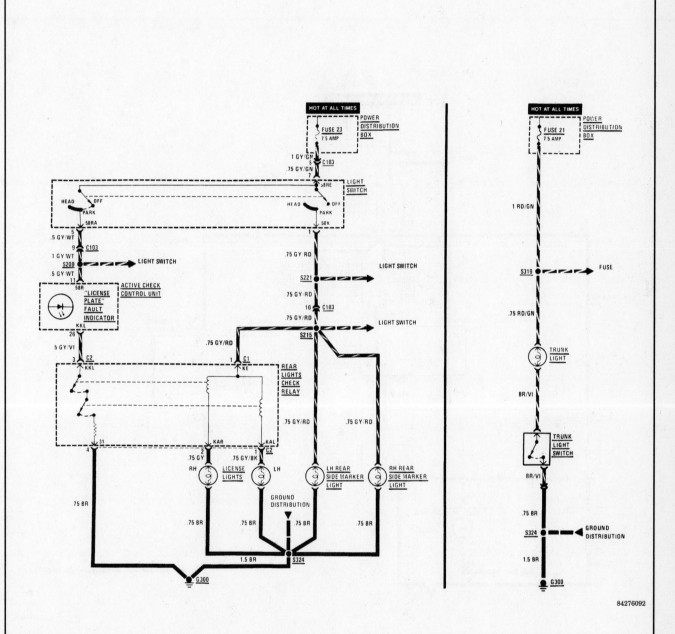

Fig. 92 Rear marker, license and trunk light circuit — E30 3 Series

84276092

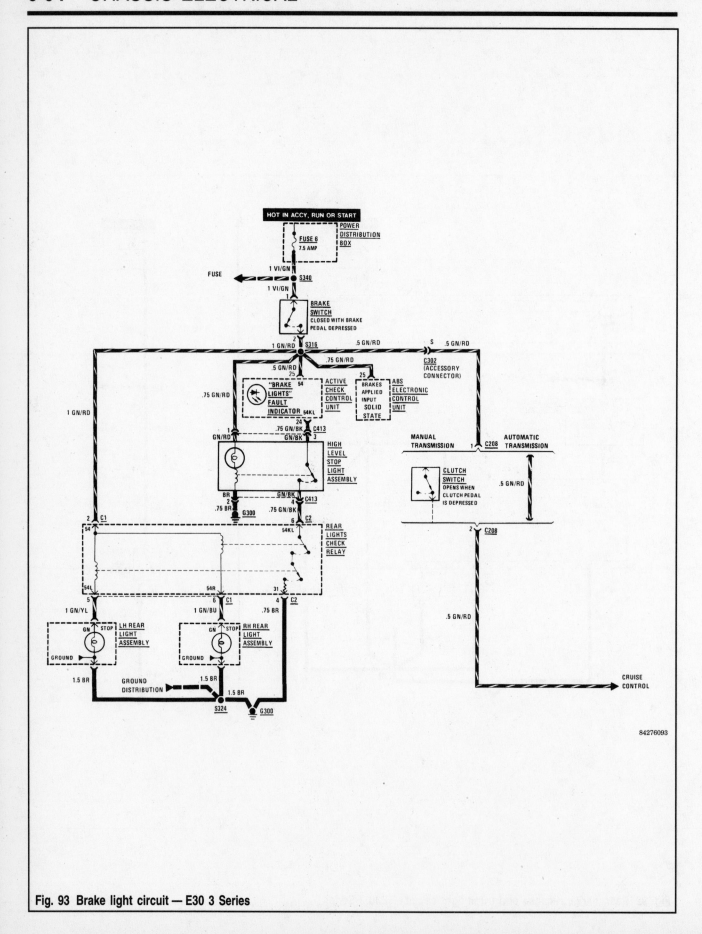

Fig. 93 Brake light circuit — E30 3 Series

84276093

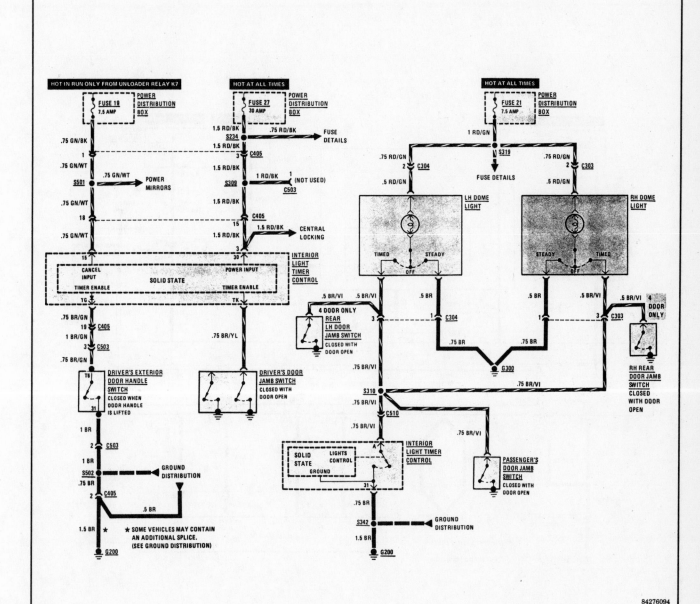

Fig. 94 Interior light circuit — E30 3 Series (Note: convertibles do not use the timer circuit)

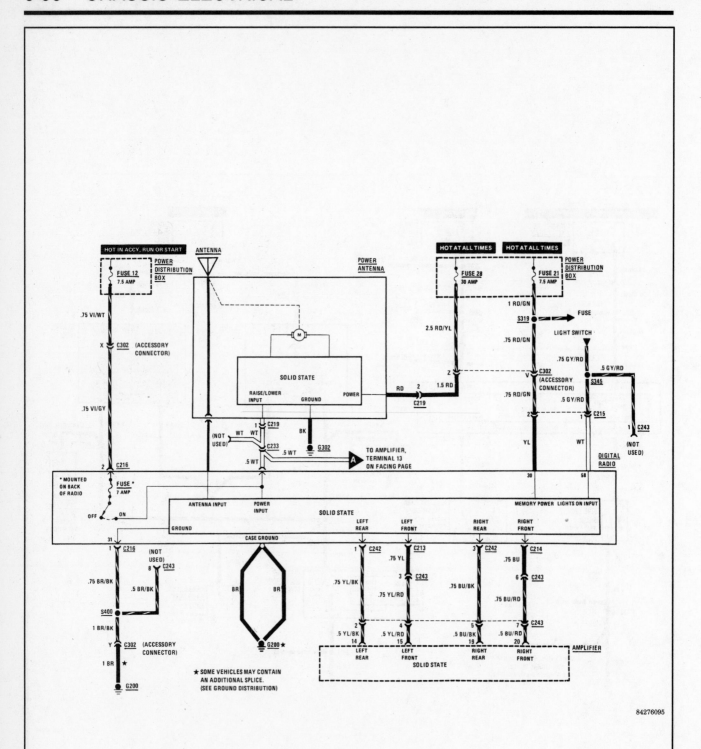

Fig. 95 Radio circuit — E30 3 Series

84276095

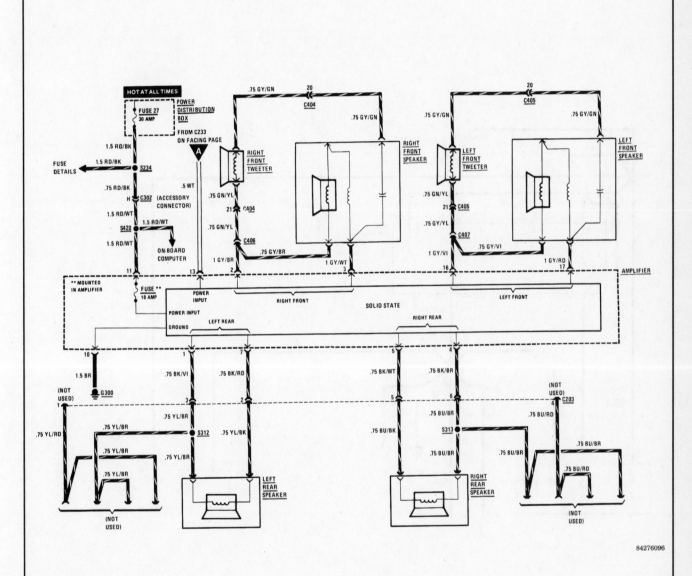

Fig. 96 Radio circuit — E30 3 Series

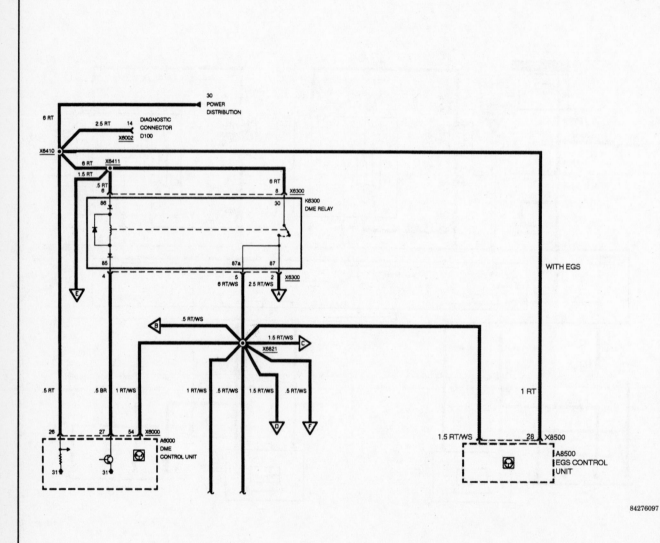

Fig. 97 Fuel injection circuit with M50 engine — E36 3 Series

84276097

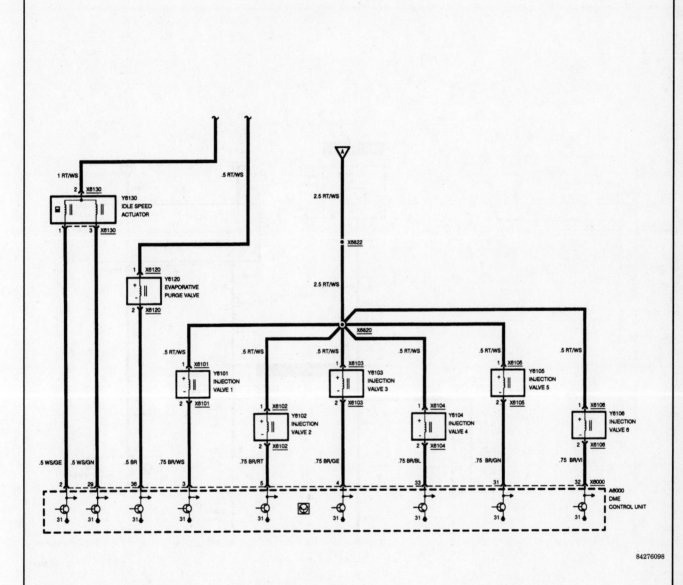

Fig. 98 Fuel injection circuit with M50 engine — E36 3 Series

84276098

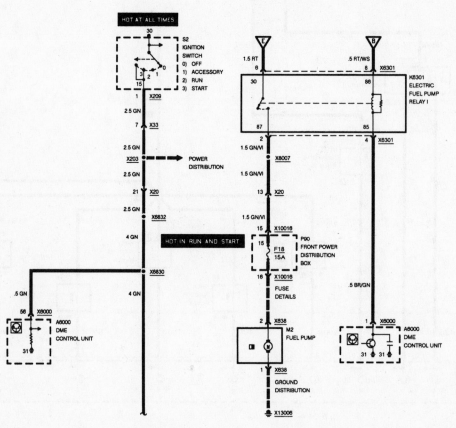

Fig. 99 Fuel injection circuit with M50 engine — E36 3 Series

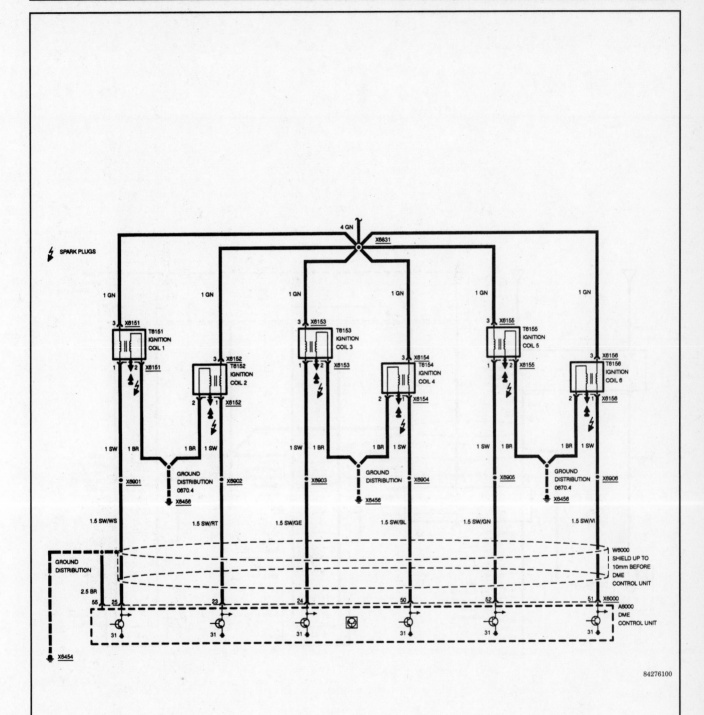

Fig. 100 Fuel injection circuit with M50 engine — E36 3 Series

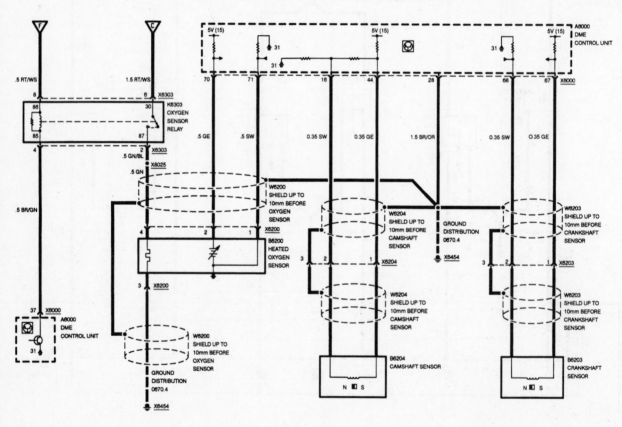

Fig. 101 Fuel injection circuit with M50 engine — E36 3 Series

84276101

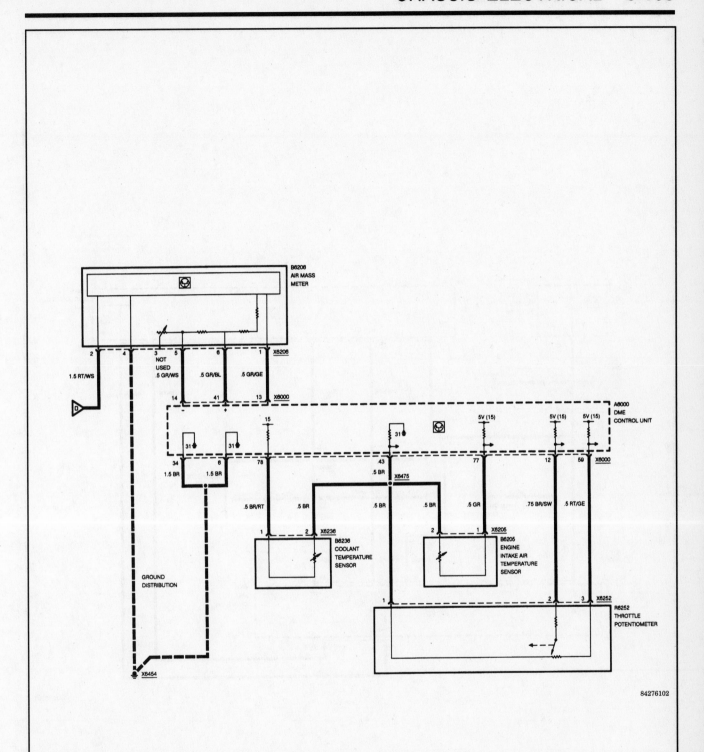

Fig. 102 Fuel injection circuit with M50 engine — E36 3 Series

84276102

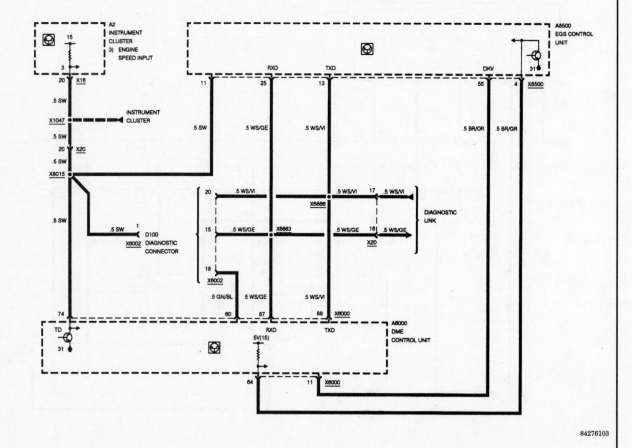

Fig. 103 Fuel injection circuit with M50 engine — E36 3 Series

84276103

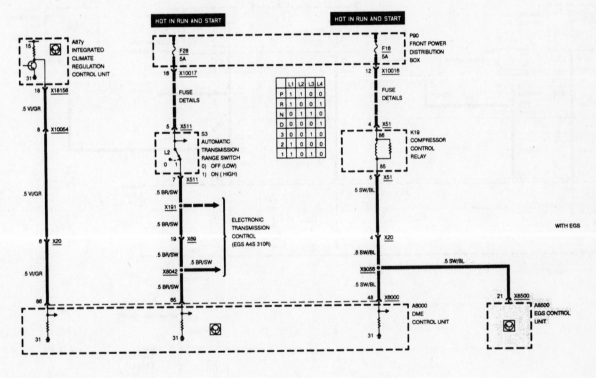

Fig. 104 Fuel injection circuit with M50 engine — E36 3 Series

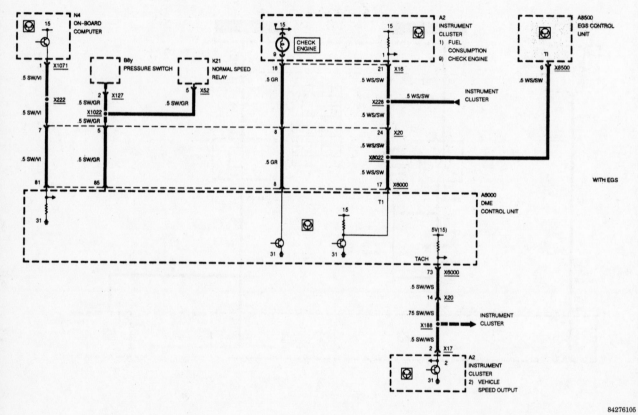

Fig. 105 Fuel injection circuit with M50 engine — E36 3 Series

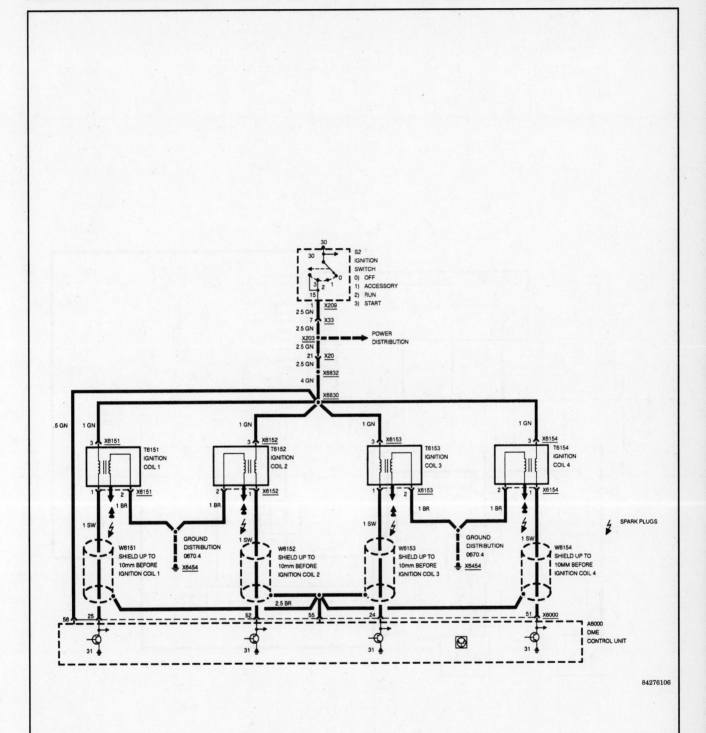

Fig. 106 Fuel injection circuit with M42 engine — E36 3 Series

84276106

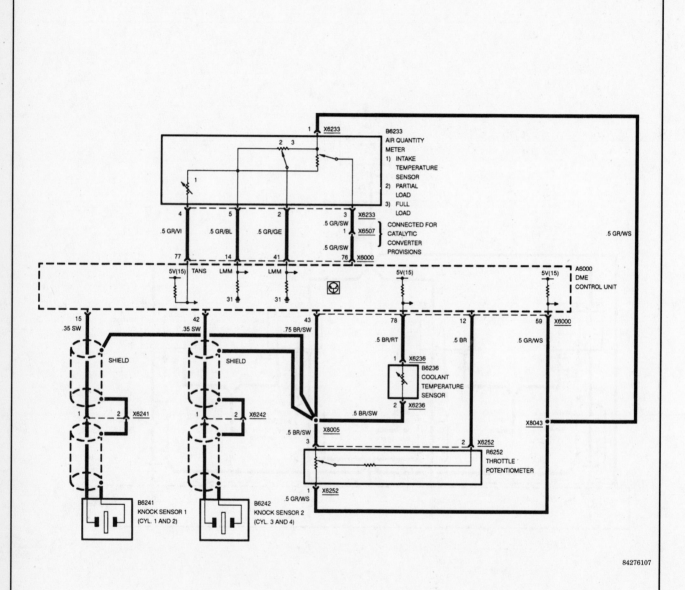

Fig. 107 Fuel injection circuit with M42 engine — E36 3 Series

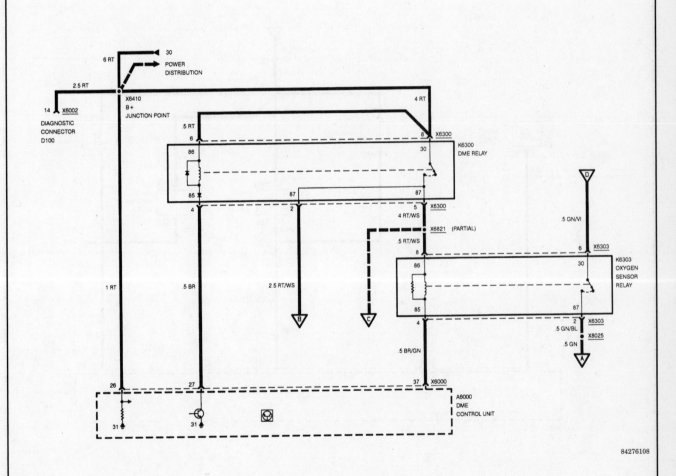

Fig. 108 Fuel injection circuit with M42 engine — E36 3 Series

84276108

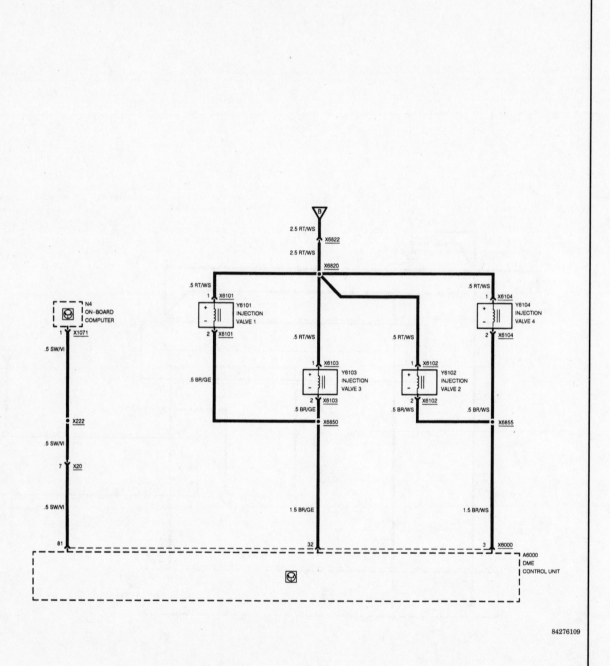

84276109

Fig. 109 Fuel injection circuit with M42 engine — E36 3 Series

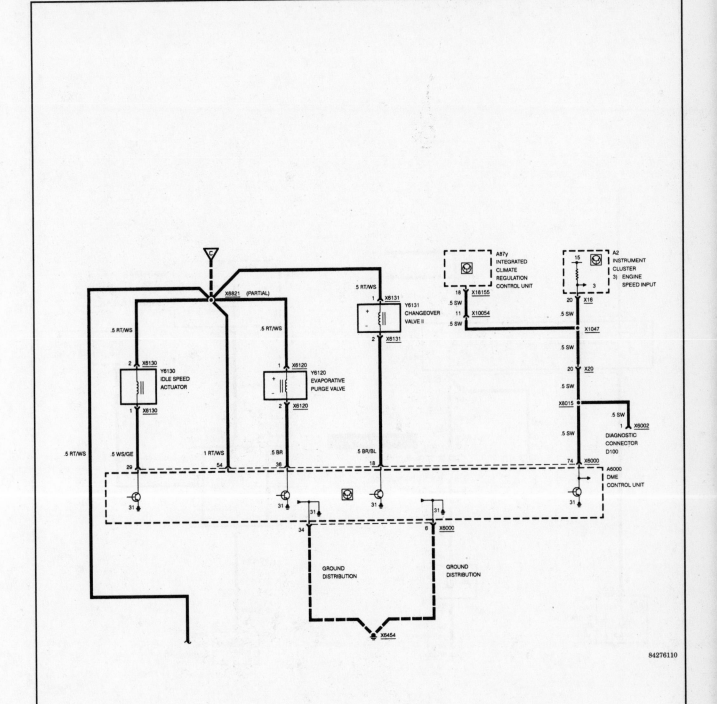

Fig. 110 Fuel injection circuit with M42 engine — E36 3 Series

84276110

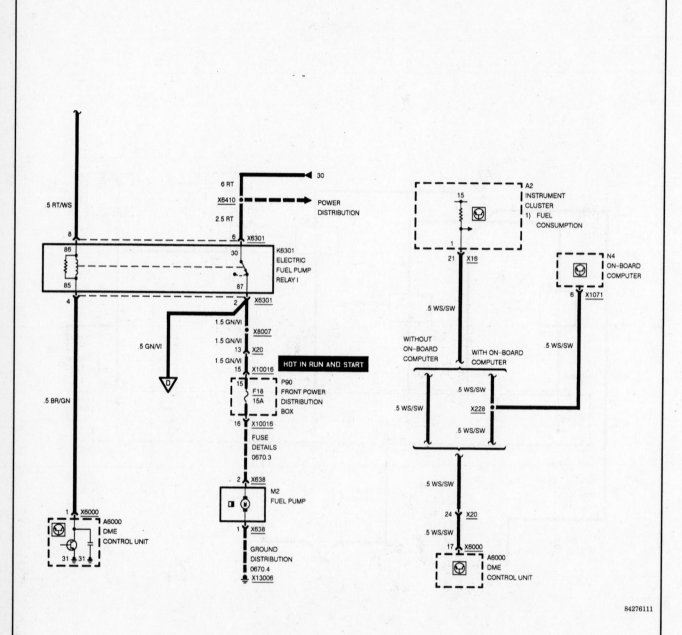

Fig. 111 Fuel injection circuit with M42 engine — E36 3 Series

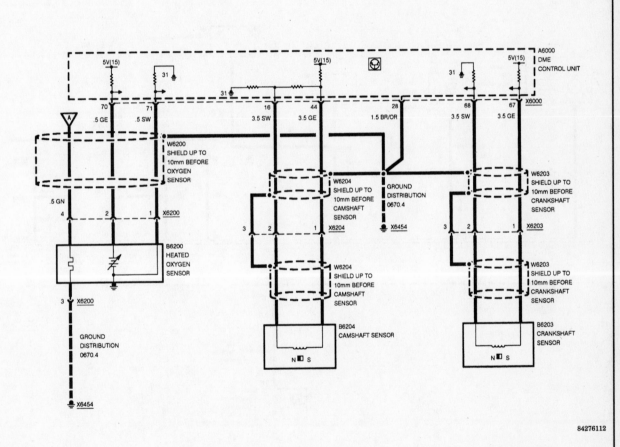

Fig. 112 Fuel injection circuit with M42 engine — E36 3 Series

84276112

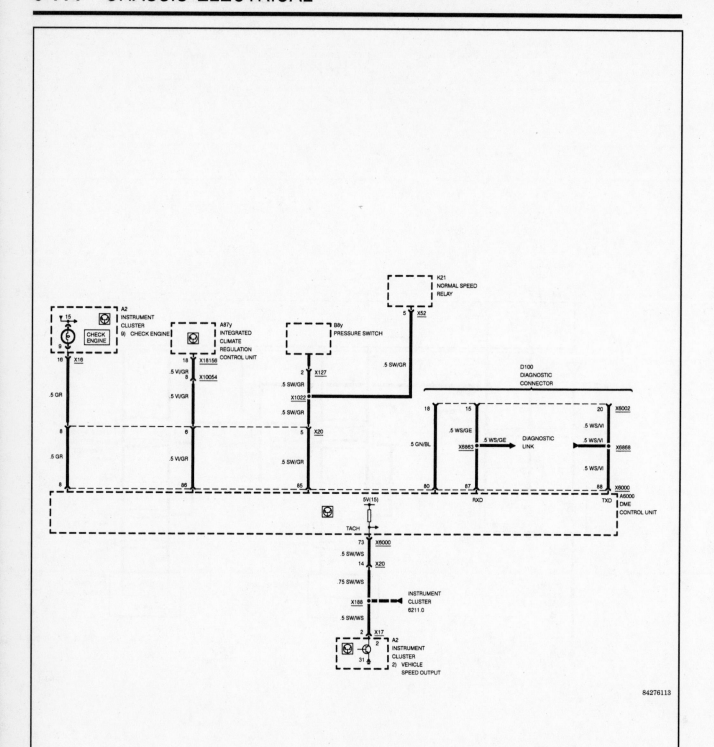

Fig. 113 Fuel injection circuit with M42 engine — E36 3 Series

84276113

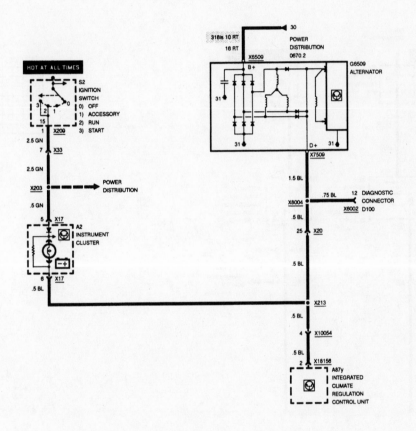

Fig. 114 Charging system circuit — E36 3 Series

84276114

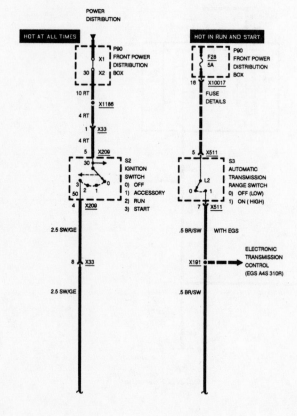

	L1	L2	L3	L4
P	1	1	0	0
R	1	0	0	1
N	0	1	1	0
D	0	0	0	1
3	0	0	1	0
2	1	0	0	0
1	1	0	1	0

Fig. 115 Starter circuit — E36 3 Series

84276115

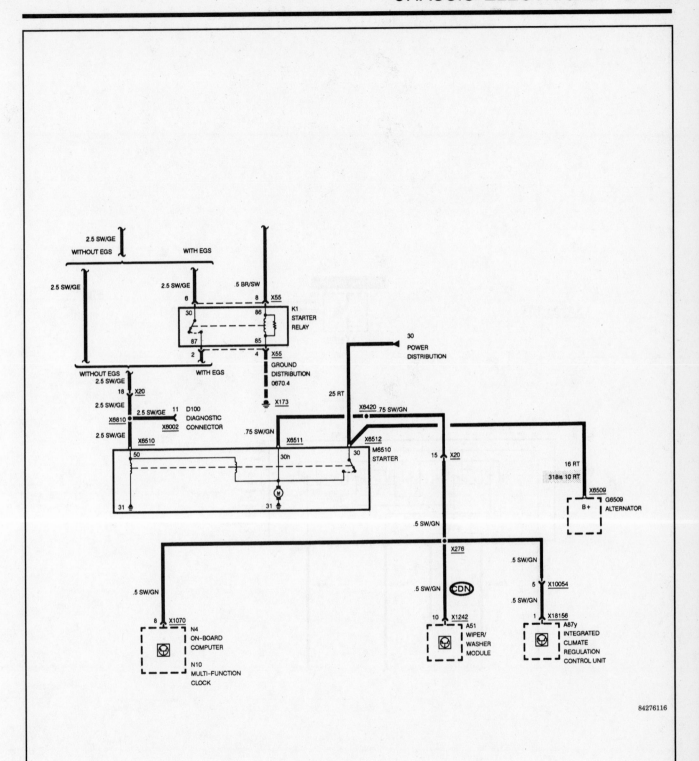

Fig. 116 Starter circuit — E36 3 Series

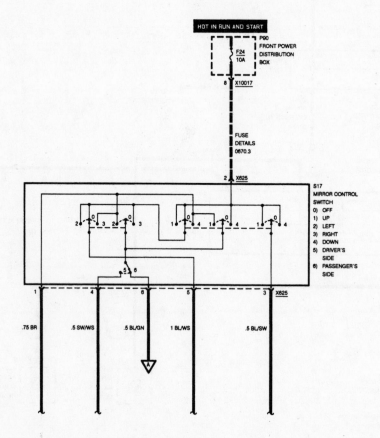

HOT IN RUN AND START

P90
FRONT POWER
DISTRIBUTION
BOX

F24
10A

8 X10017

FUSE
DETAILS
0670.3

2 X625

S17
MIRROR CONTROL
SWITCH
0) OFF
1) UP
2) LEFT
3) RIGHT
4) DOWN
5) DRIVER'S
   SIDE
6) PASSENGER'S
   SIDE

X625

1   4   6   5   3

.75 BR   .5 SW/WS   .5 BL/GN   1 BL/WS   .5 BL/SW

84276117

Fig. 117 Power mirror circuit — E36 3 Series

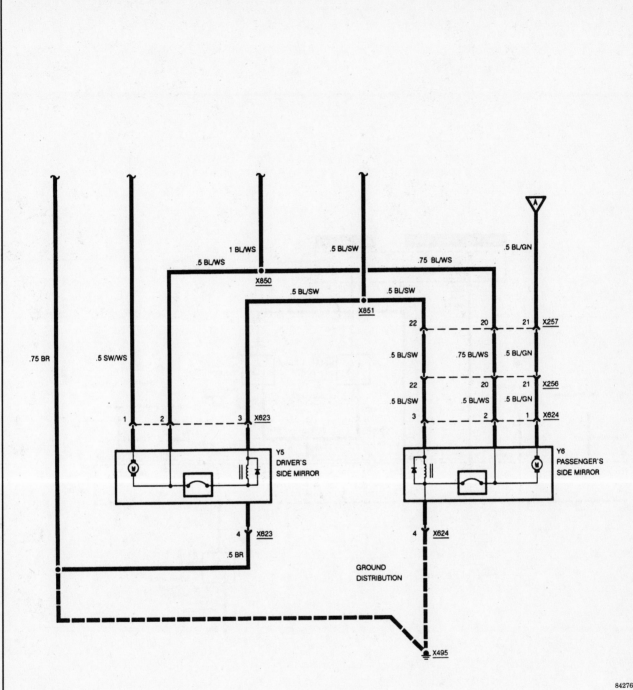

Fig. 118 Power mirror circuit — E36 3 Series

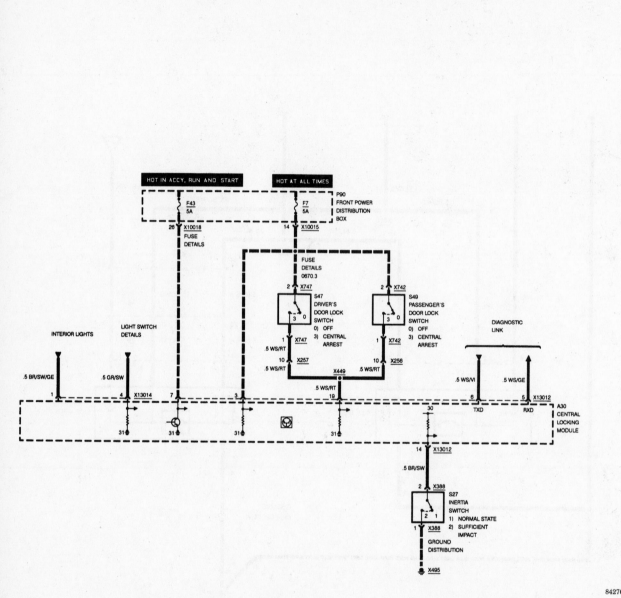

Fig. 119 Central locking circuit — E36 3 Series

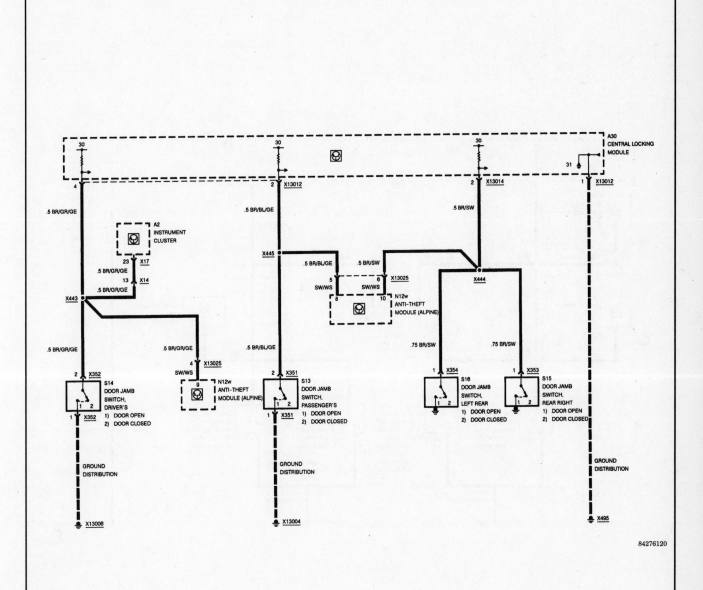

Fig. 120 Central locking circuit — E36 3 Series

84276120

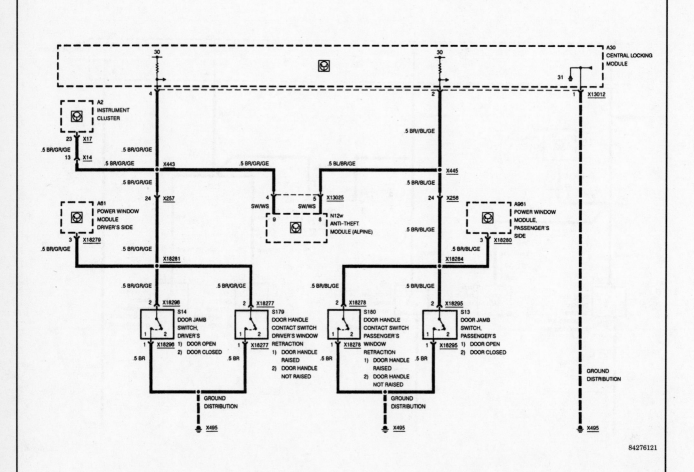

Fig. 121 Central locking circuit — E36 3 Series

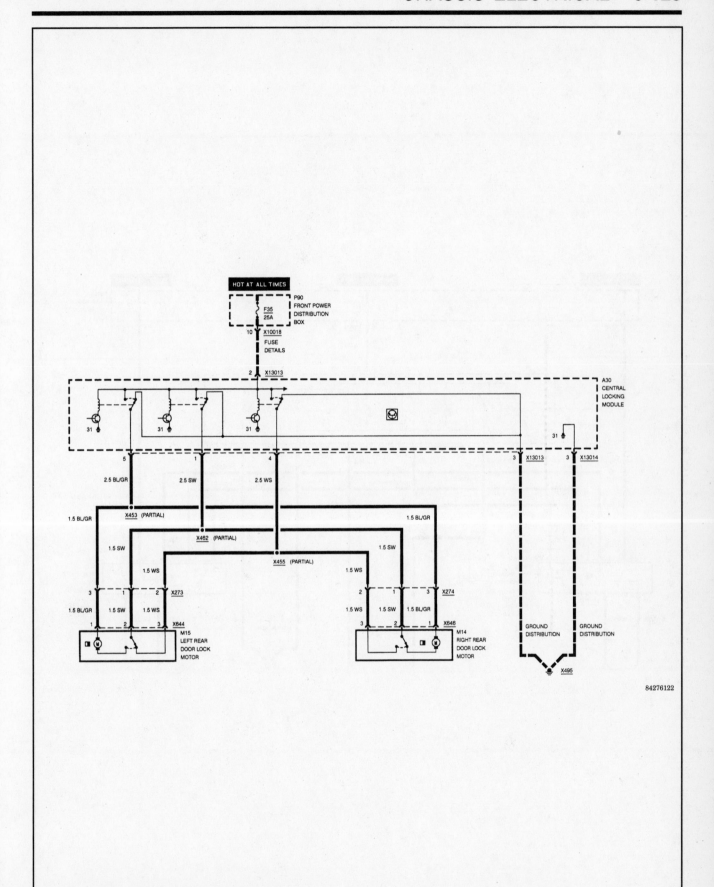

Fig. 122 Central locking circuit — E36 3 Series

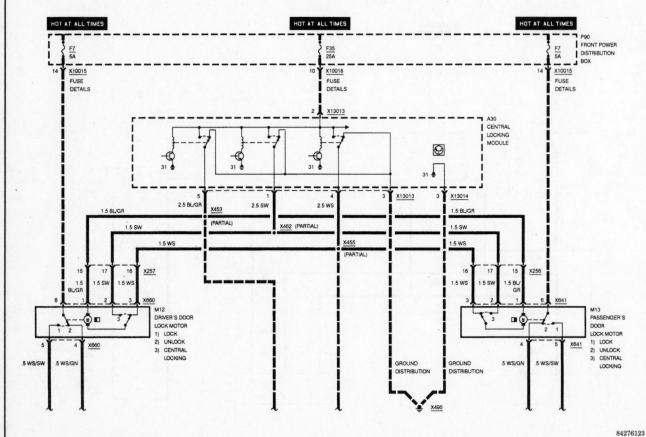

Fig. 123 Central locking circuit — E36 3 Series

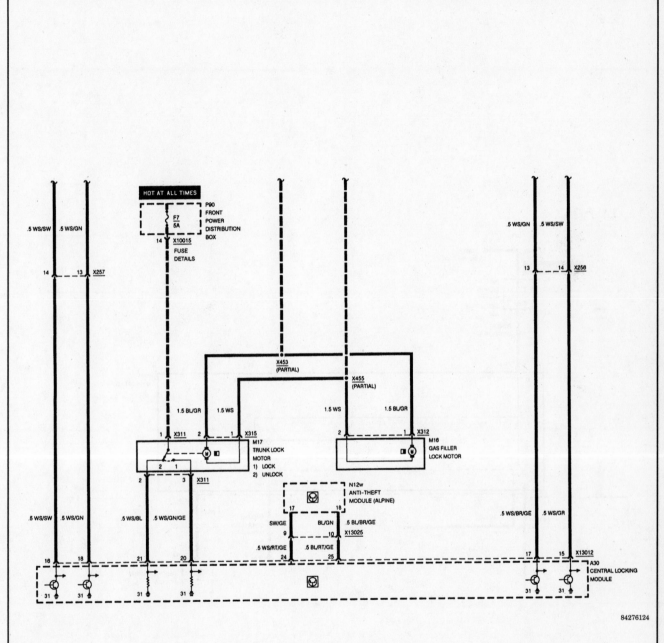

Fig. 124 Central locking circuit — E36 3 Series

84276124

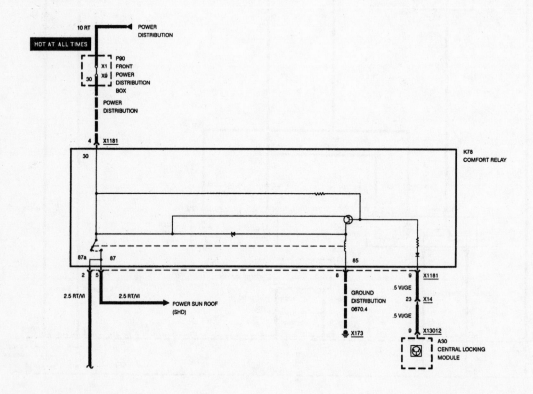

Fig. 125 Power window circuit — E36 3 Series 4 door

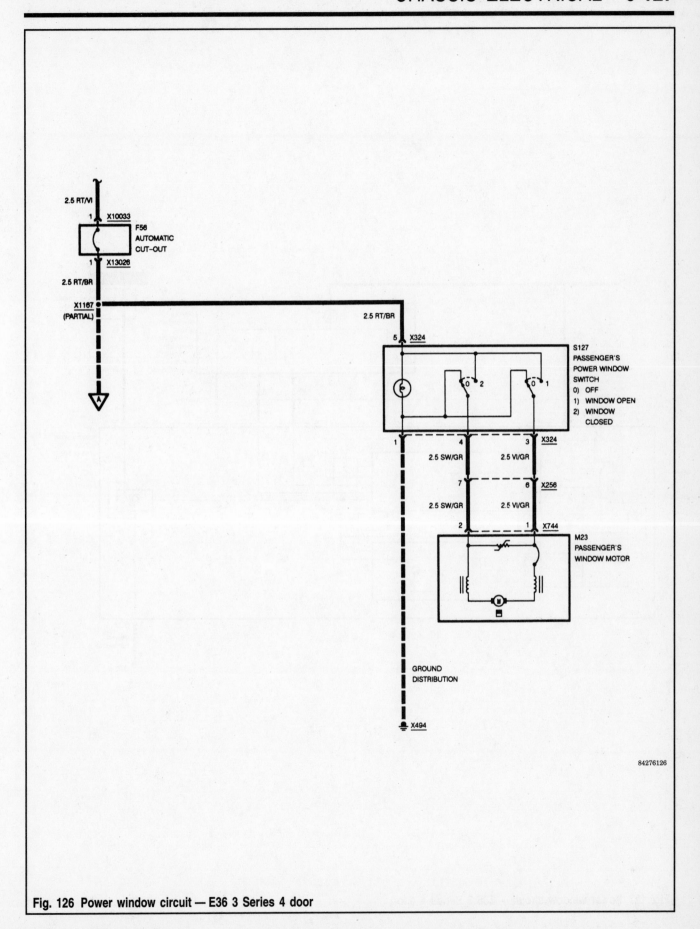

Fig. 126 Power window circuit — E36 3 Series 4 door

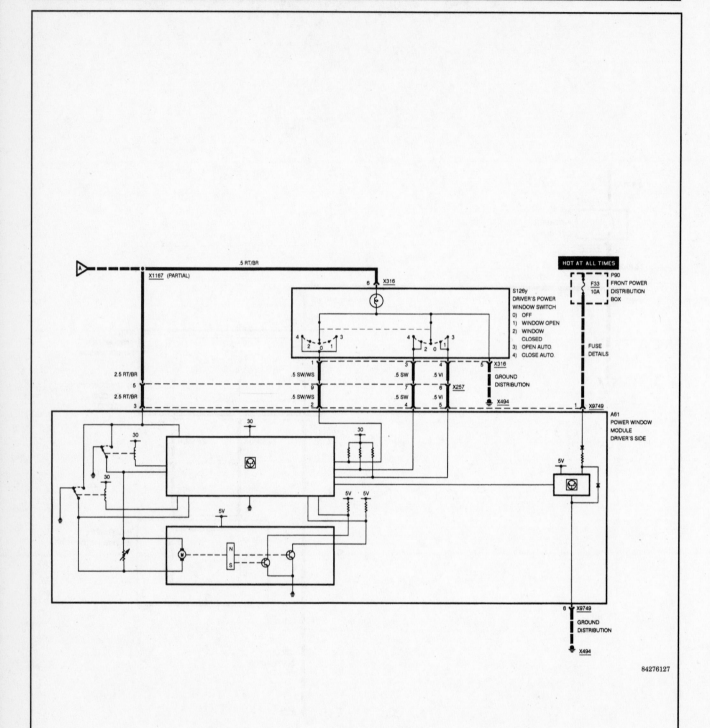

Fig. 127 Power window circuit — E36 3 Series 4 door

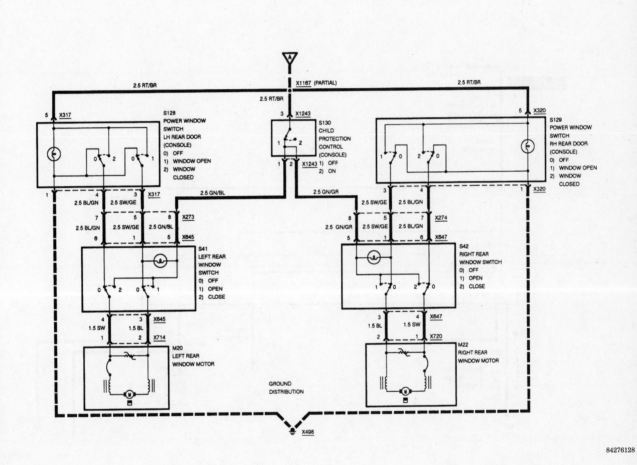

Fig. 128 Power window circuit — E36 3 Series 4 door

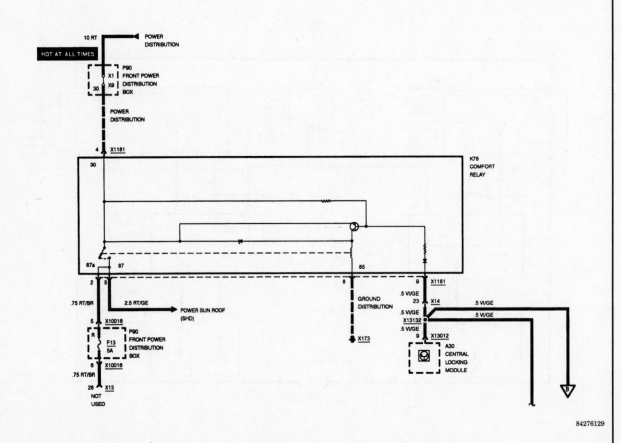

Fig. 129 Power window circuit — E36 3 Series 2 door

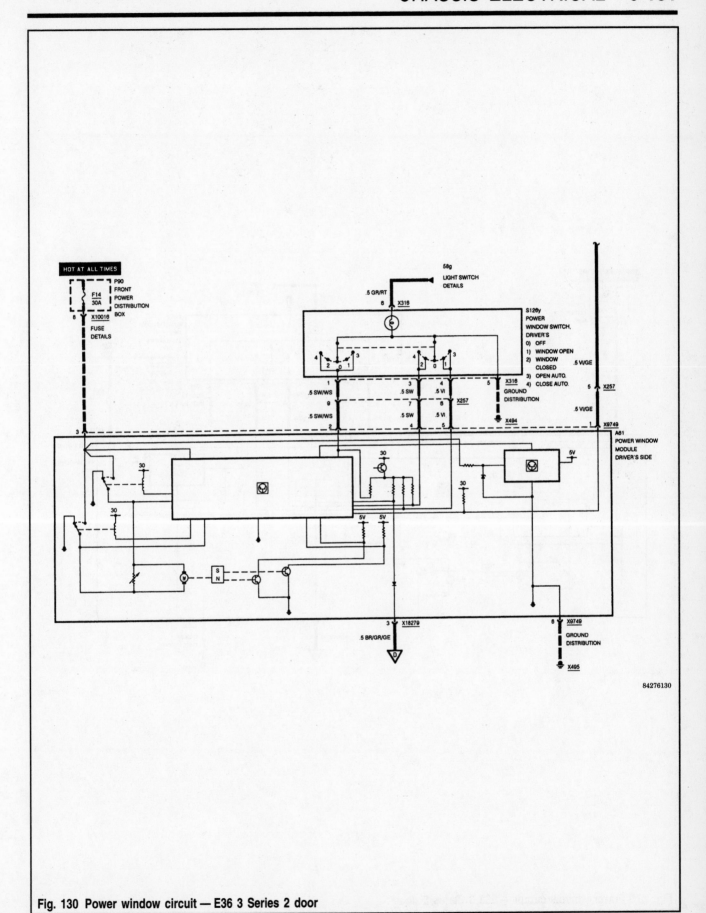

Fig. 130 Power window circuit — E36 3 Series 2 door

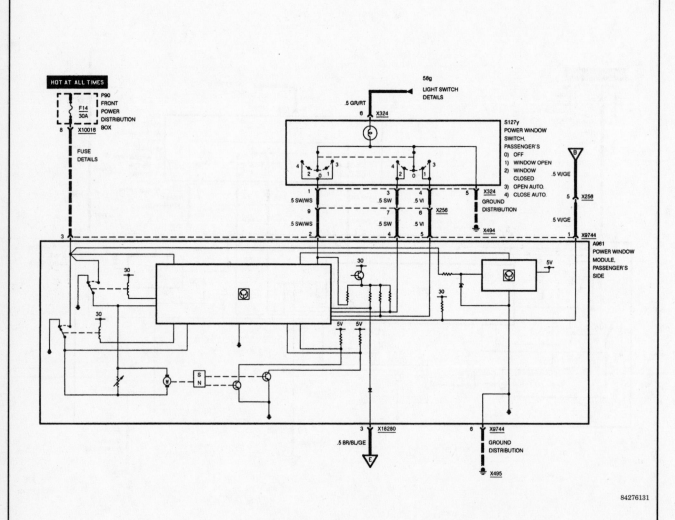

Fig. 131 Power window circuit — E36 3 Series 2 door

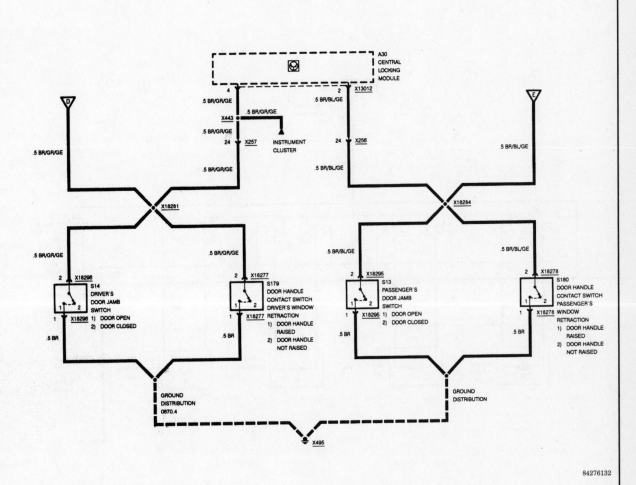

Fig. 132 Power window circuit — E36 3 Series 2 door

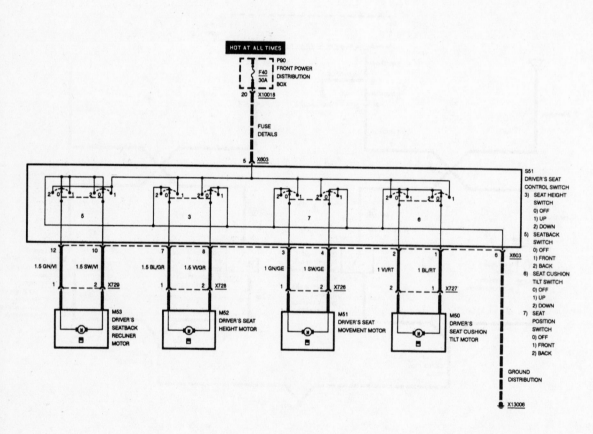

HOT AT ALL TIMES

P90
FRONT POWER
DISTRIBUTION
BOX

F40
30A

20 X10018

FUSE
DETAILS

5 X603

S51
DRIVER'S SEAT
CONTROL SWITCH
3) SEAT HEIGHT
SWITCH
0) OFF
1) UP
2) DOWN
5) SEATBACK
SWITCH
0) OFF
1) FRONT
2) BACK
6) SEAT CUSHION
TILT SWITCH
0) OFF
1) UP
2) DOWN
7) SEAT
POSITION
SWITCH
0) OFF
1) FRONT
2) BACK

12   10   7   8   3   4   2   1   6   X603

1.5 GN/VI 1.5 SW/VI   1.5 BL/GR 1.5 VI/GR   1 GN/GE 1 SW/GE   1 VI/RT 1 BL/RT

1   2 X729   1   2 X728   1   2 X726   1   2 X727

M53
DRIVER'S
SEATBACK
RECLINER
MOTOR

M52
DRIVER'S SEAT
HEIGHT MOTOR

M51
DRIVER'S SEAT
MOVEMENT MOTOR

M50
DRIVER'S
SEAT CUSHION
TILT MOTOR

GROUND
DISTRIBUTION

X13006

84276133

Fig. 133 Power seat circuit — E36 3 Series

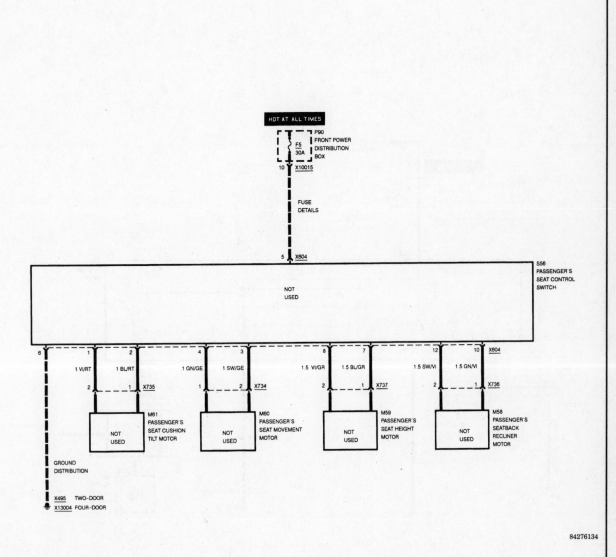

HOT AT ALL TIMES

P90
FRONT POWER
DISTRIBUTION
BOX

F5
30A

10   X10015

FUSE
DETAILS

5   X604

S56
PASSENGER'S
SEAT CONTROL
SWITCH

NOT
USED

6   1   2   4   3   8   7   12   10   X604

1 VI/RT 1 BL/RT   1 GN/GE 1 SW/GE   1.5 VI/GR 1.5 BL/GR   1.5 SW/VI 1.5 GN/VI

2   1   X735   1   2   X734   2   1   X737   2   1   X736

NOT   M61   NOT   M60   NOT   M59   NOT   M58
USED   PASSENGER'S   USED   PASSENGER'S   USED   PASSENGER'S   USED   PASSENGER'S
        SEAT CUSHION   SEAT MOVEMENT   SEAT HEIGHT   SEATBACK
        TILT MOTOR   MOTOR   MOTOR   RECLINER
                                                                            MOTOR

GROUND
DISTRIBUTION

X495   TWO-DOOR
X13004   FOUR-DOOR

84276134

Fig. 134 Power seat circuit — E36 3 Series

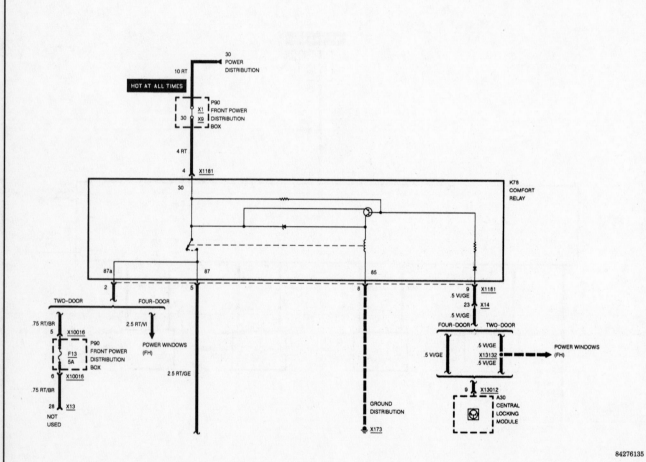

Fig. 135 Power sunroof circuit — E36 3 Series

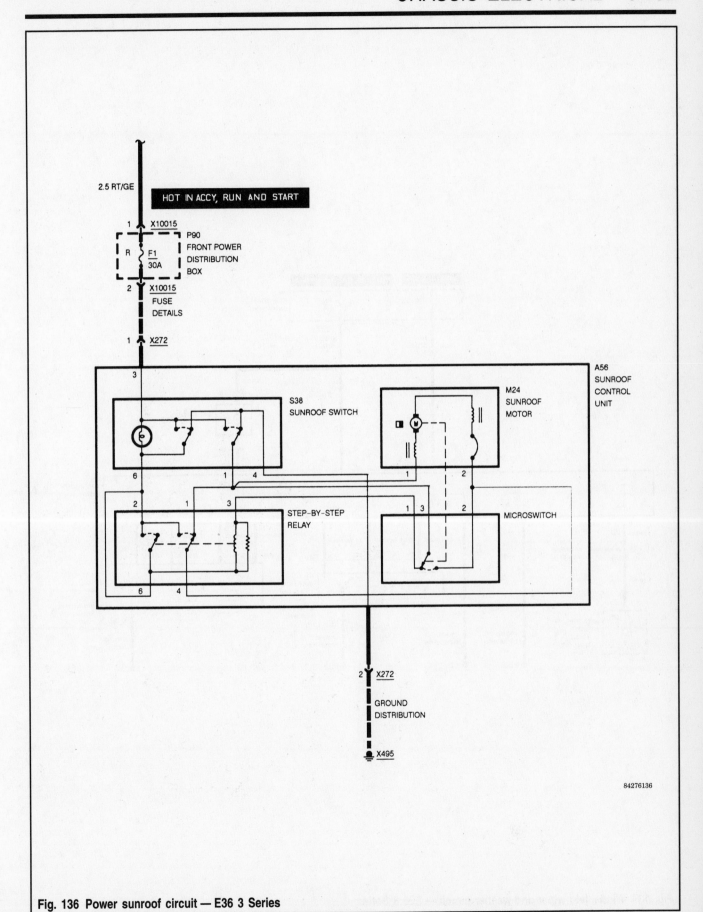

Fig. 136 Power sunroof circuit — E36 3 Series

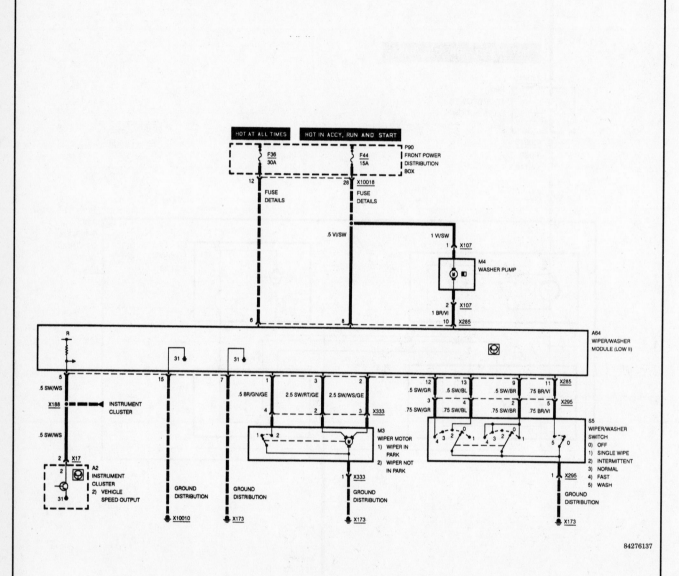

Fig. 137 Windshield wiper and washer circuit — E36 3 Series

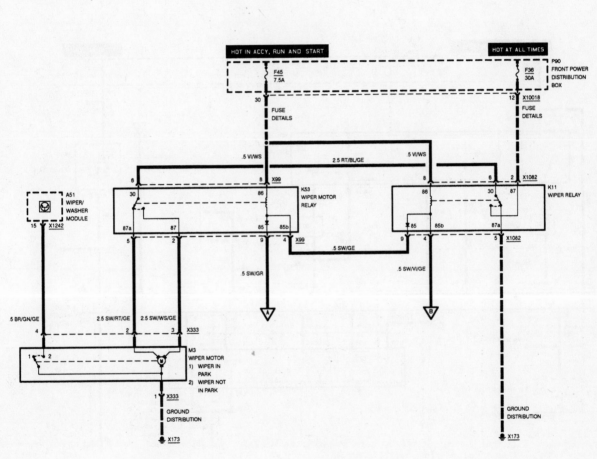

Fig. 138 Windshield wiper and washer circuit — E36 3 Series

84276138

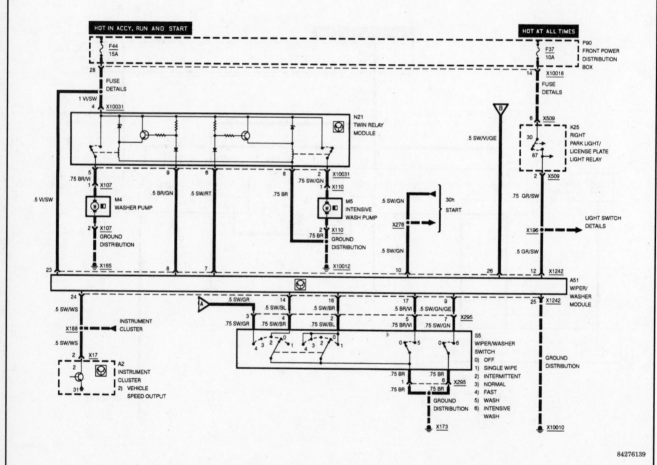

Fig. 139 Windshield wiper and washer circuit — E36 3 Series

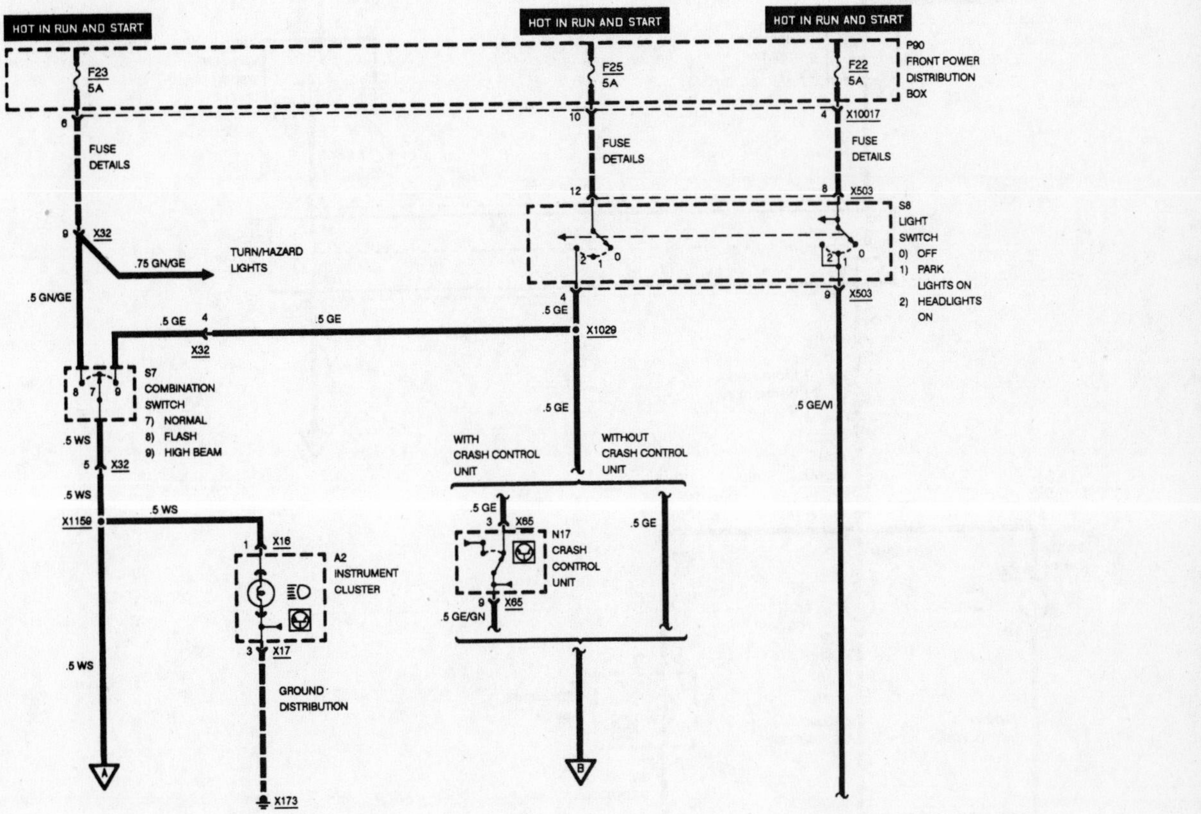

Fig. 140 Headlight and foglight circuit — E36 3 Series USA

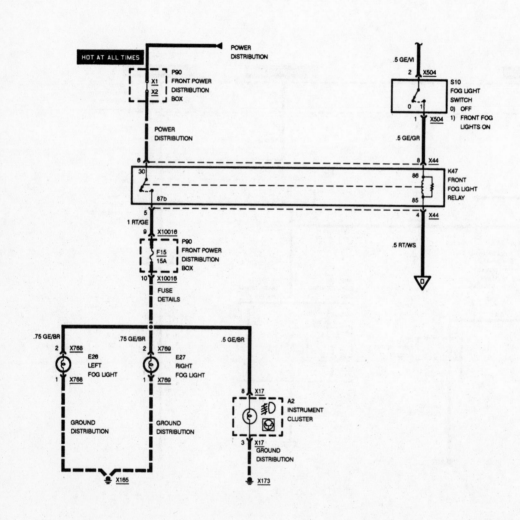

Fig. 141 Headlight and foglight circuit — E36 3 Series USA

84276141

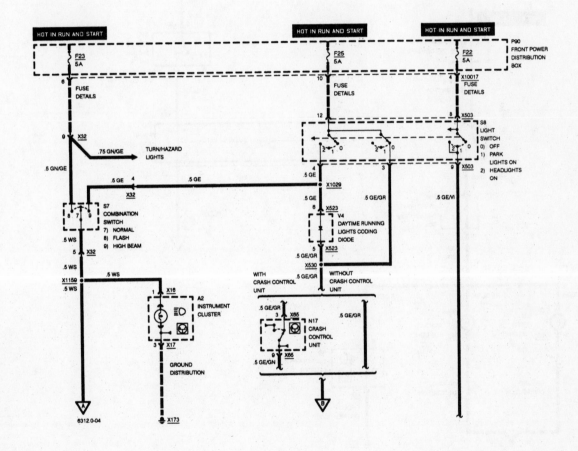

Fig. 142 Headlight and foglight circuit — E36 3 Series Canada

84276142

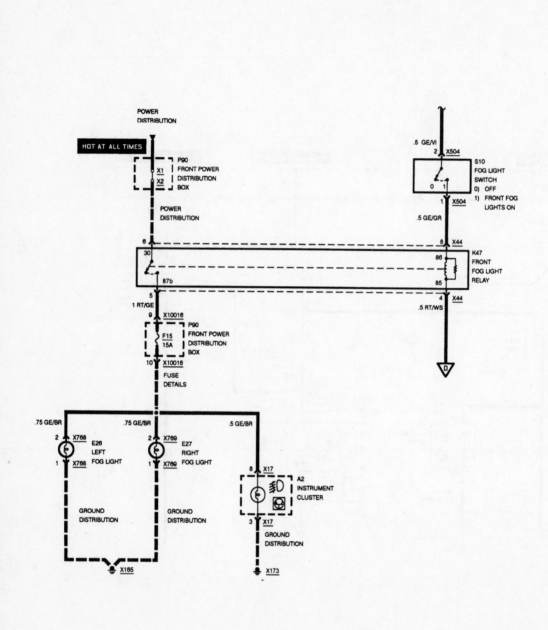

POWER
DISTRIBUTION

HOT AT ALL TIMES

P90
X1   FRONT POWER
      DISTRIBUTION
X2   BOX

POWER
DISTRIBUTION

.5 GE/VI

2   X504
          S10
          FOG LIGHT
          SWITCH
0   1   0) OFF
1   X504 1) FRONT FOG
               LIGHTS ON

.5 GE/GR

6   8   X44
30   86   K47
                                    FRONT
                                    FOG LIGHT
                                    RELAY
87b   85

5   4   X44
1 RT/GE   .5 RT/WS

9   X10016

P90
F15   FRONT POWER
15A   DISTRIBUTION
      BOX

10   X10016

FUSE
DETAILS

.75 GE/BR   .75 GE/BR   .5 GE/BR

2   X768   2   X769   8   X17
     E26   E27   A2
     LEFT   RIGHT   INSTRUMENT
1   X768   FOG 1   X769   FOG   CLUSTER
     LIGHT   LIGHT   3   X17

GROUND   GROUND   GROUND
DISTRIBUTION   DISTRIBUTION   DISTRIBUTION

X165   X173

84276143

Fig. 143 Headlight and foglight circuit — E36 3 Series Canada

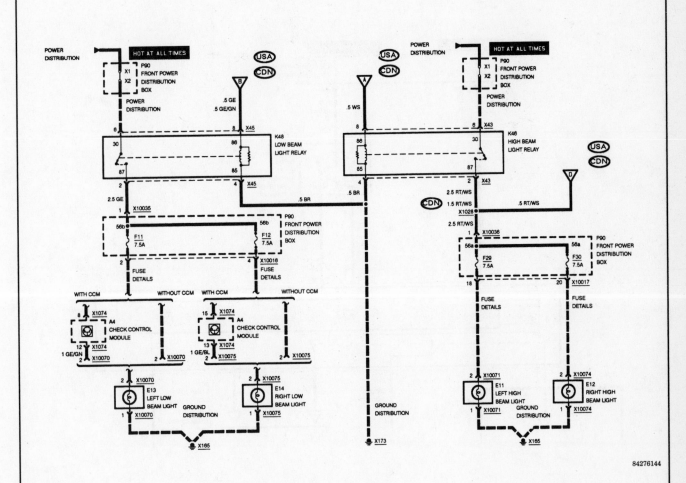

Fig. 144 Headlight and foglight circuit — E36 3 Series

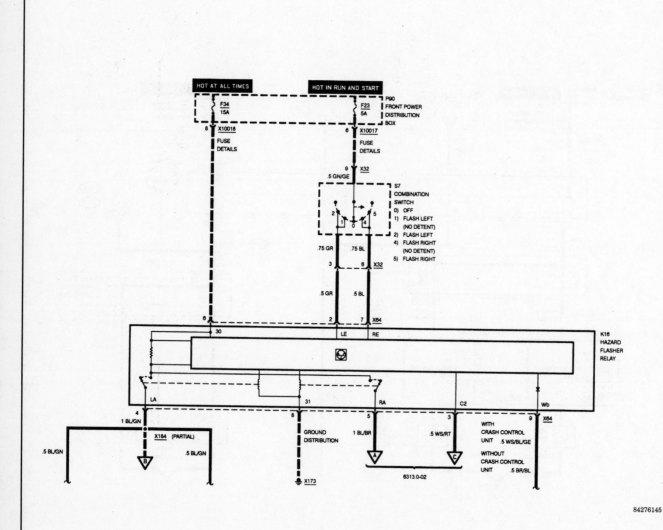

Fig. 145 Turn signal and hazard light circuit — E36 3 Series

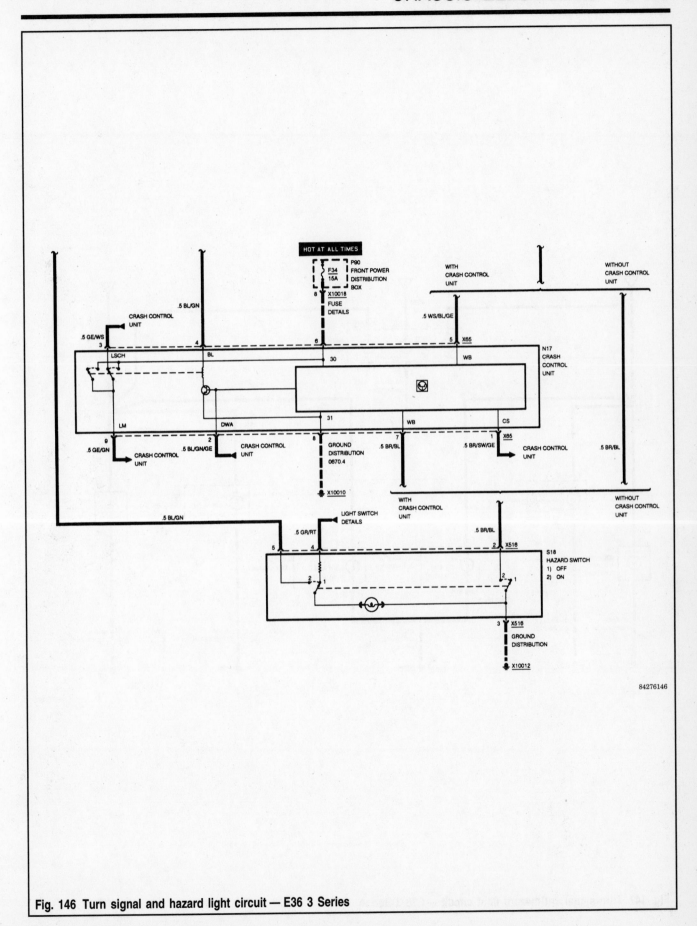

Fig. 146 Turn signal and hazard light circuit — E36 3 Series

84276146

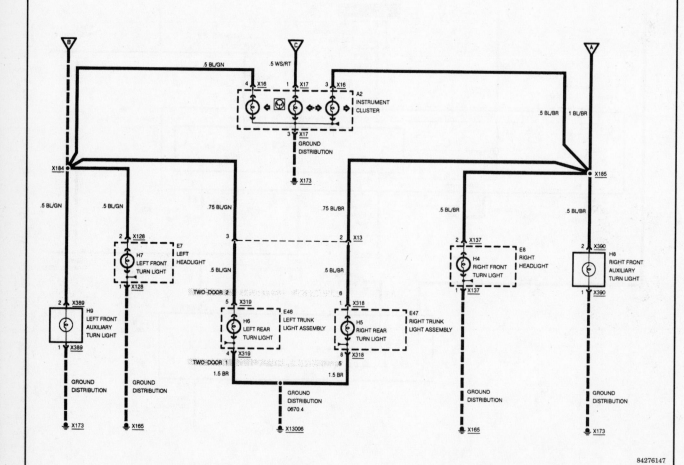

Fig. 147 Turn signal and hazard light circuit — E36 3 Series

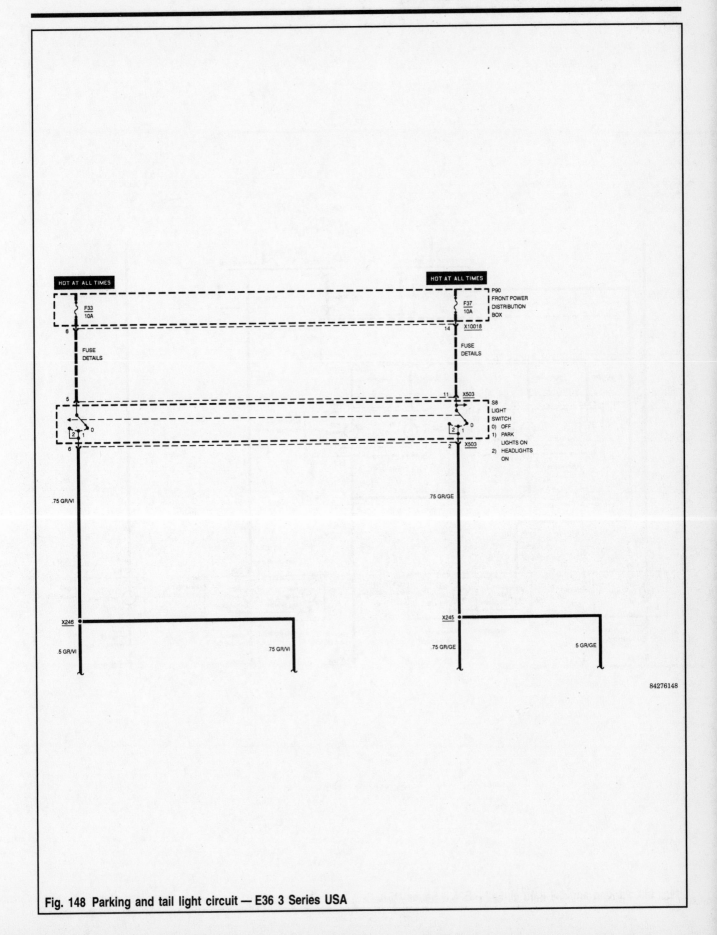

Fig. 148 Parking and tail light circuit — E36 3 Series USA

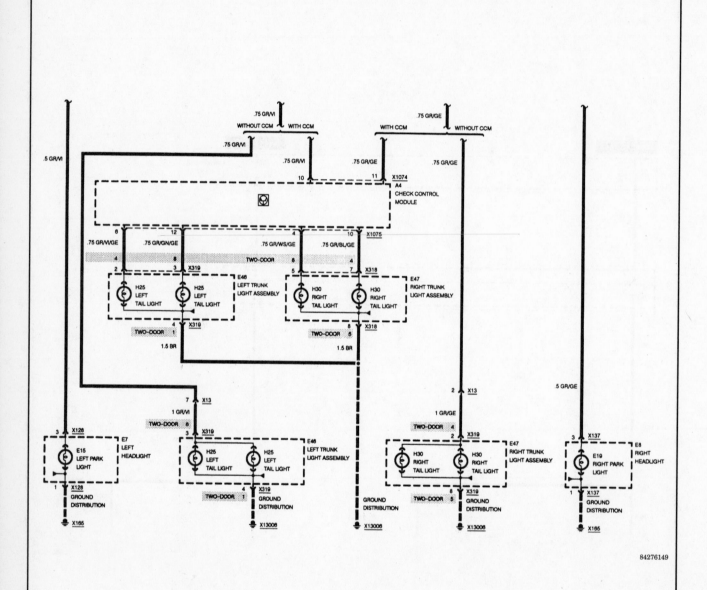

Fig. 149 Parking and tail light circuit — E36 3 Series USA

84276149

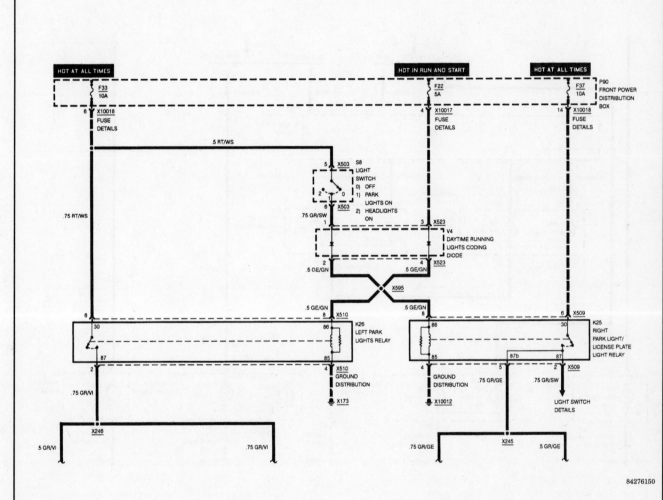

Fig. 150 Parking and tail light circuit — E36 3 Series Canada

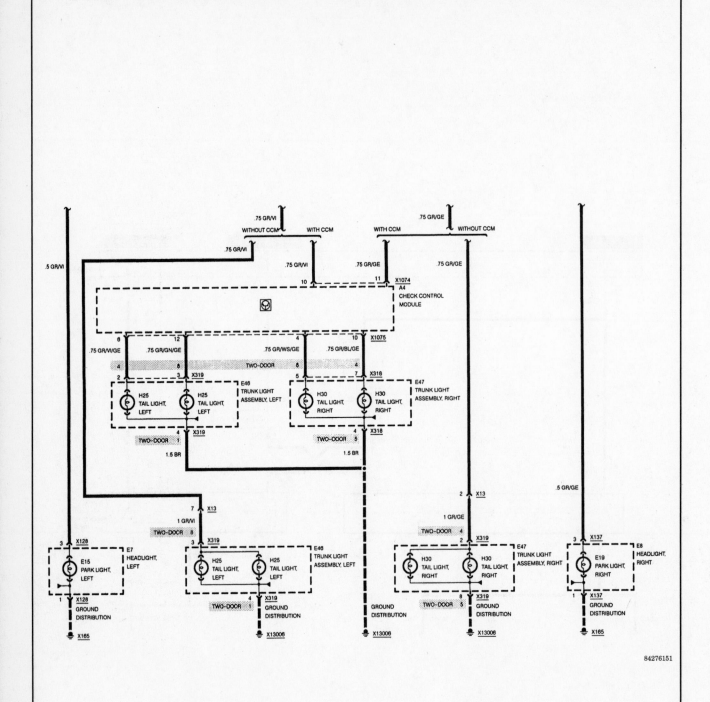

Fig. 151 Parking and tail light circuit — E36 3 Series Canada

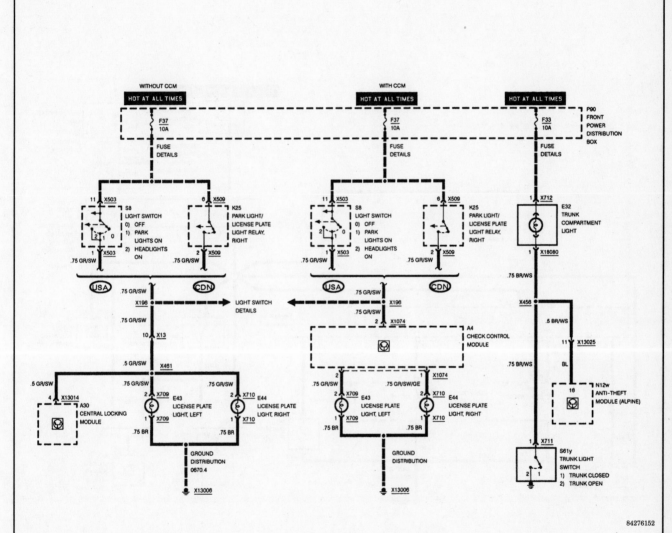

Fig. 152 License plate and trunk light circuit — E36 3 Series

84276152

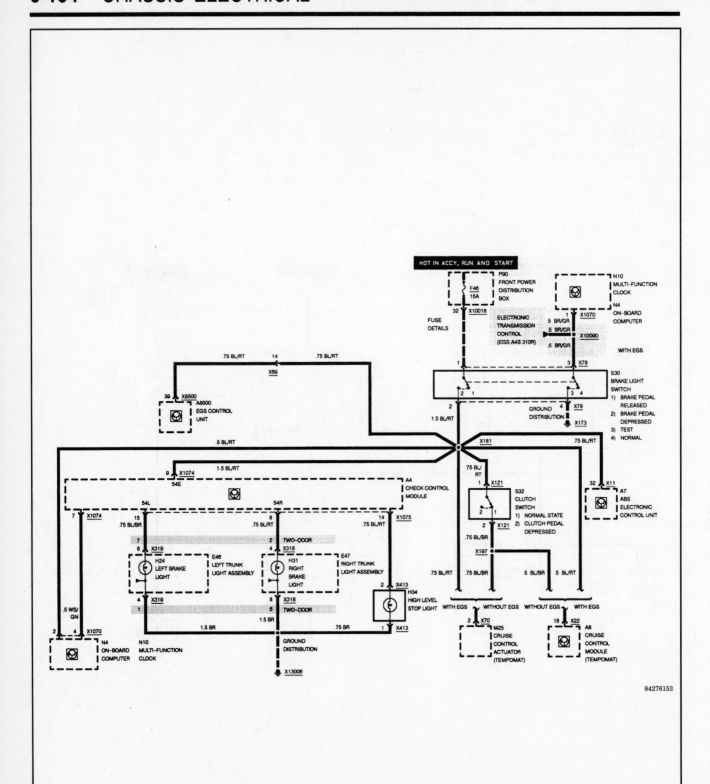

Fig. 153 Brake light circuit with check control module — E36 3 Series

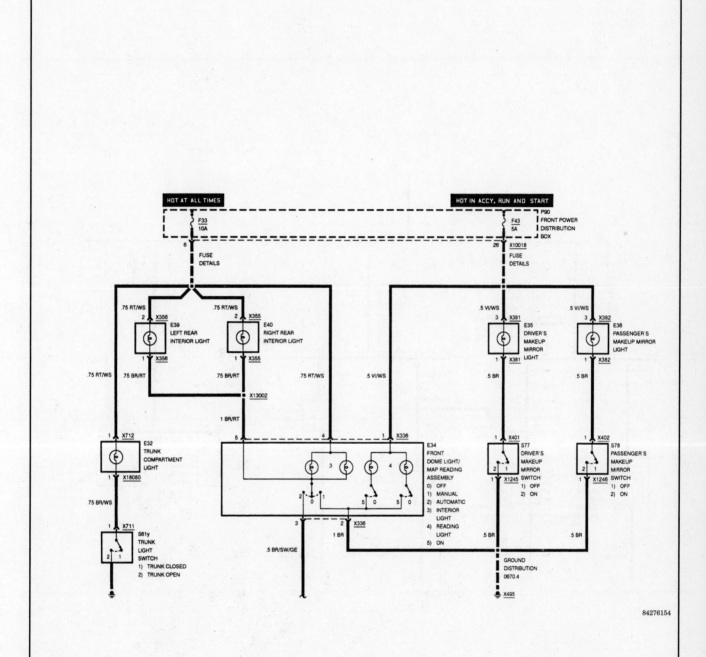

Fig. 154 Interior light circuit — E36 3 Series

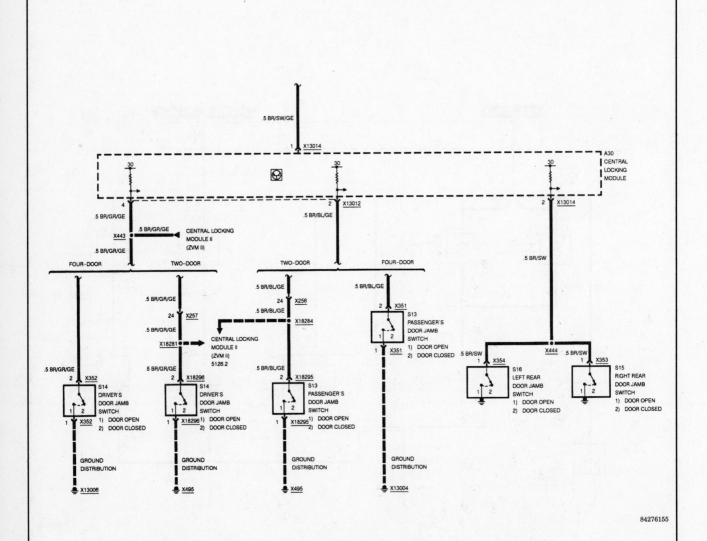

Fig. 155 Interior light circuit — E36 3 Series

84276155

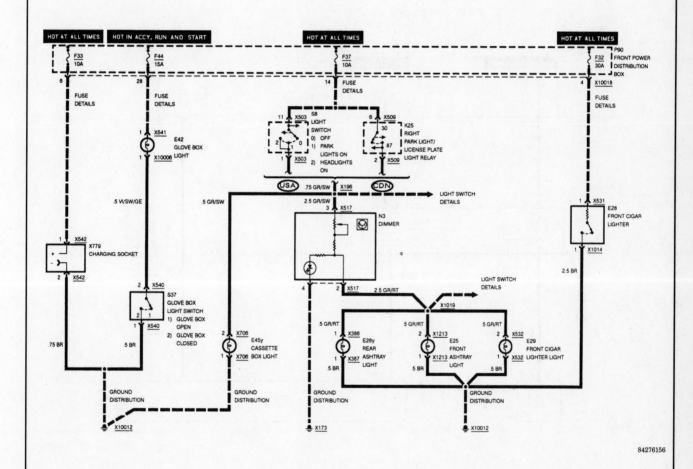

Fig. 156 Glove compartment, lighter, ashtray light circuit — E36 3 Series

84276156

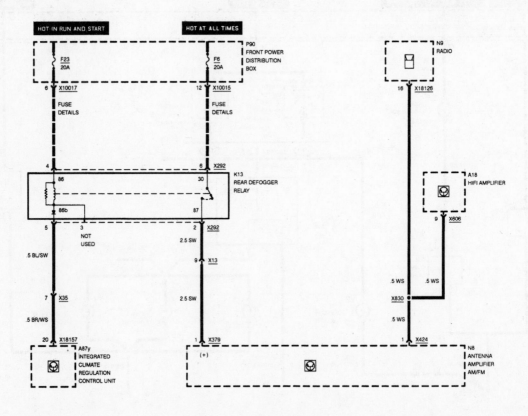

Fig. 157 Rear window defogger circuit — E36 3 Series

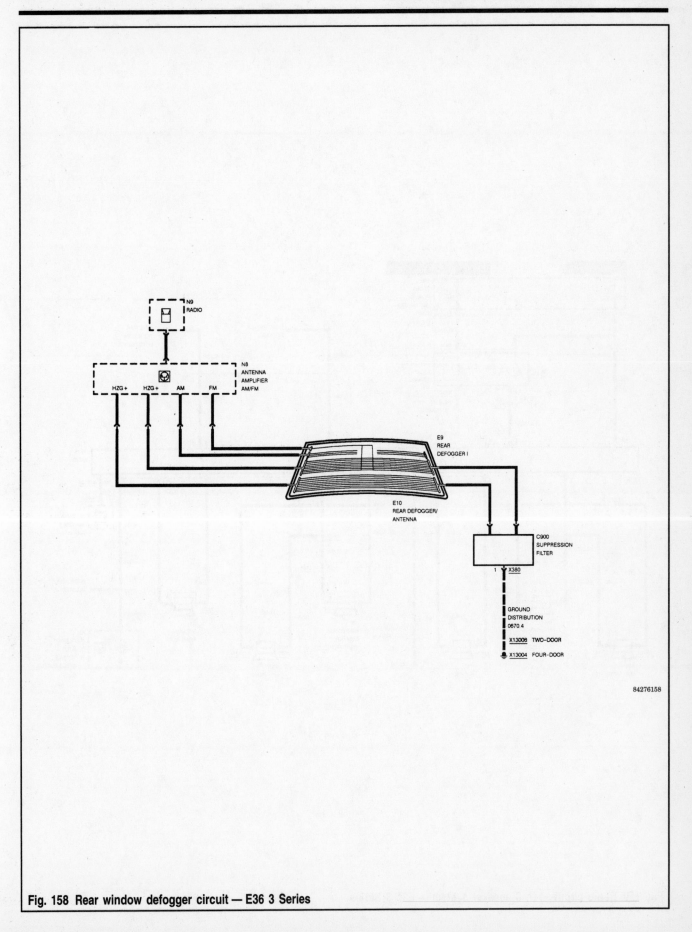

Fig. 158 Rear window defogger circuit — E36 3 Series

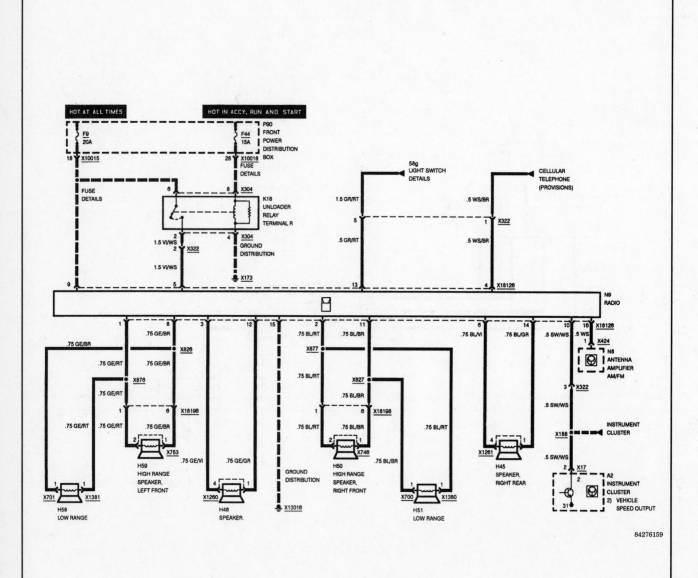

Fig. 159 Radio circuit with 6 speaker system — E36 3 Series

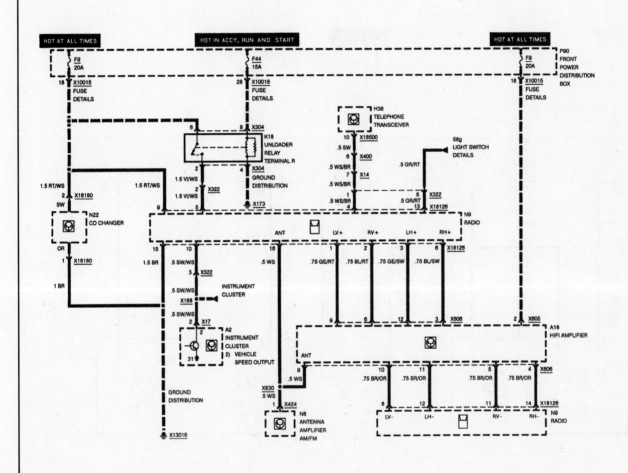

Fig. 160 Radio circuit with 10 speaker system — E36 3 Series

84276160

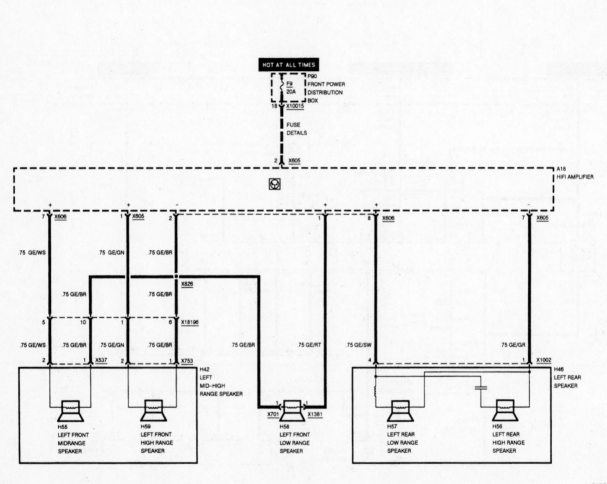

Fig. 161 Radio circuit with 10 speaker system — E36 3 Series

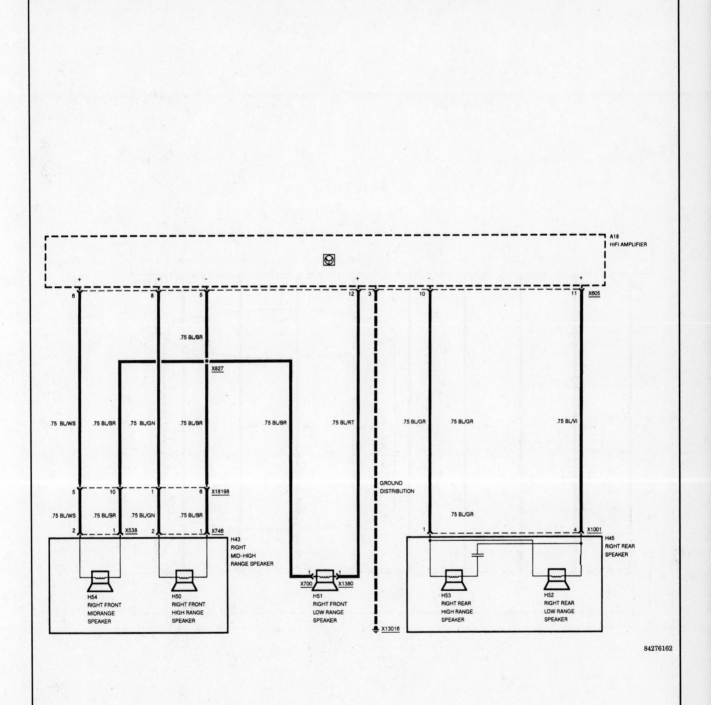

Fig. 162 Radio circuit with 10 speaker system — E36 3 Series

84276162

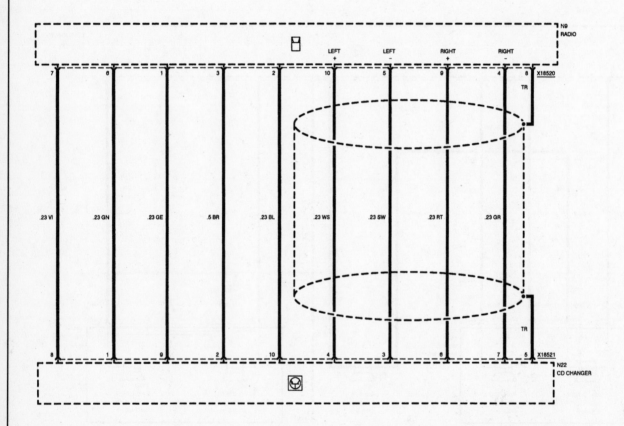

Fig. 163 Radio circuit with CD player and 10 speaker system — E36 3 Series

84276163

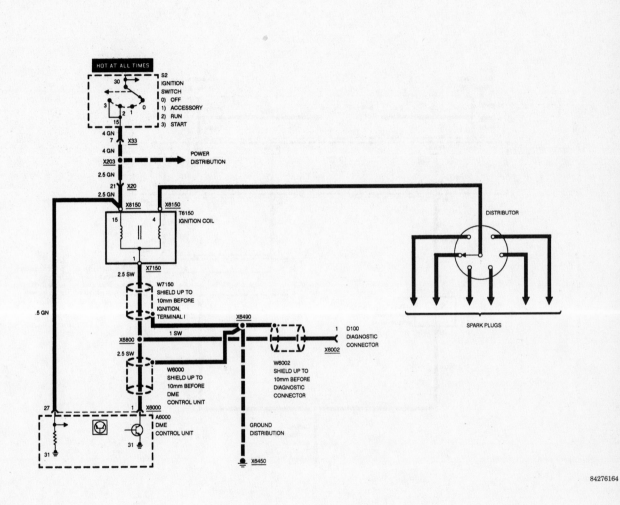

Fig. 164 Fuel injection circuit with M20 or M30 engine — E34 5 Series

84276164

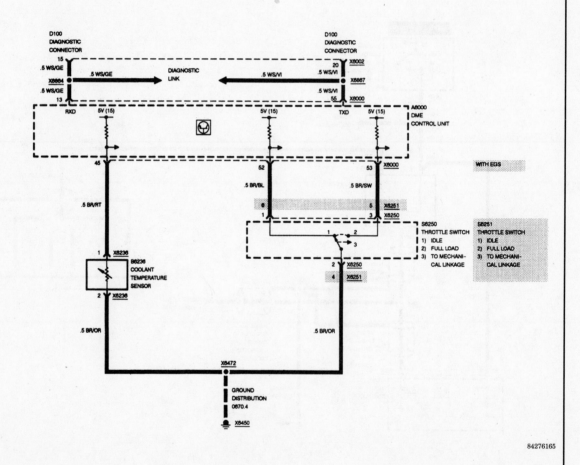

Fig. 165 Fuel injection circuit with M20 or M30 engine — E34 5 Series

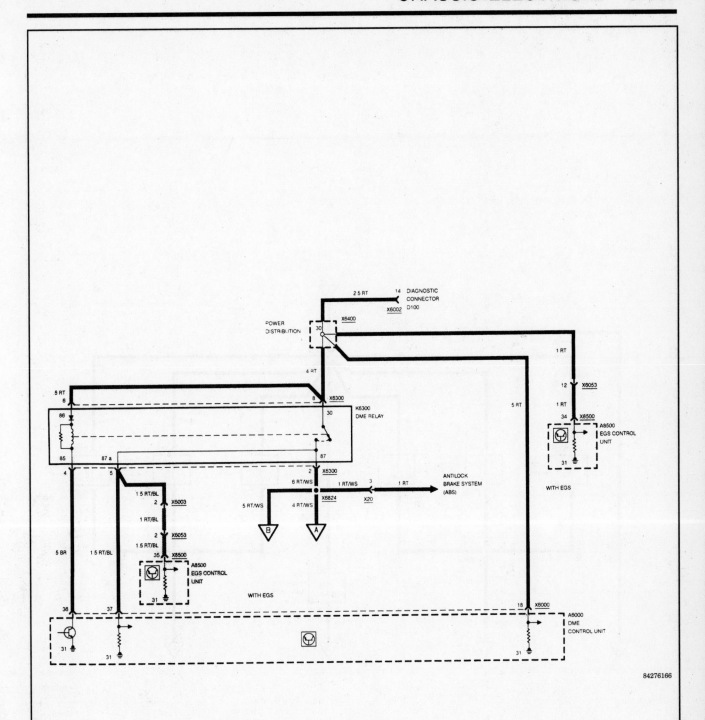

Fig. 166 Fuel injection circuit with M20 or M30 engine — E34 5 Series

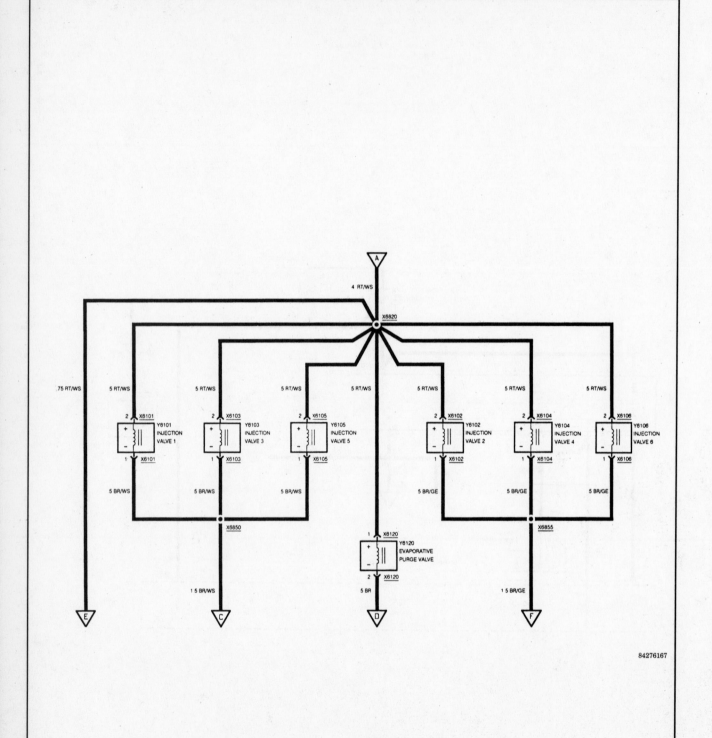

Fig. 167 Fuel injection circuit with M20 or M30 engine — E34 5 Series

84276167

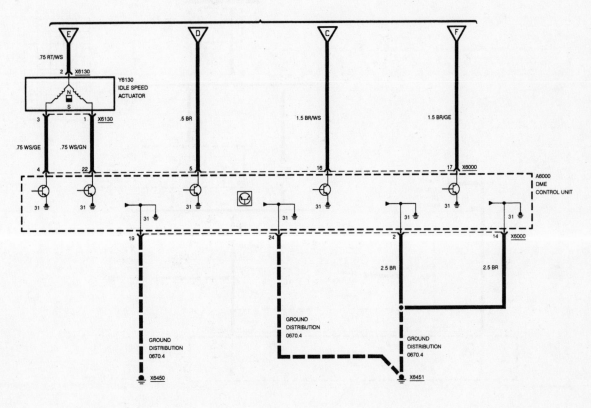

Fig. 168 Fuel injection circuit with M20 or M30 engine — E34 5 Series

84276168

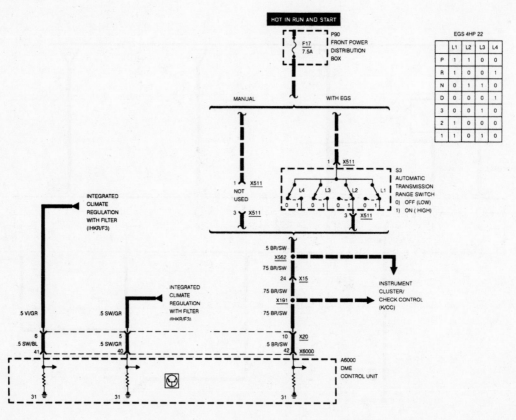

Fig. 169 Fuel injection circuit with M20 or M30 engine — E34 5 Series

84276169

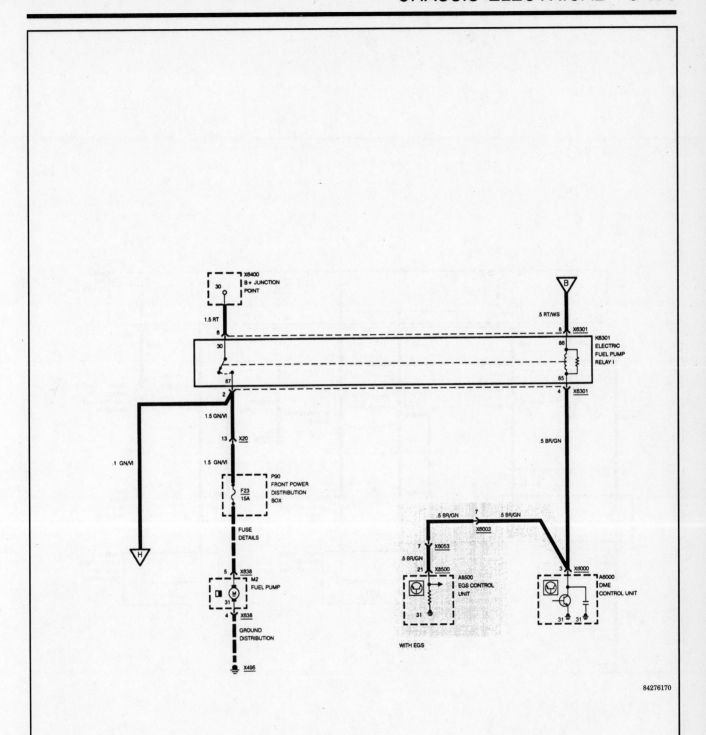

Fig. 170 Fuel injection circuit with M20 or M30 engine — E34 5 Series

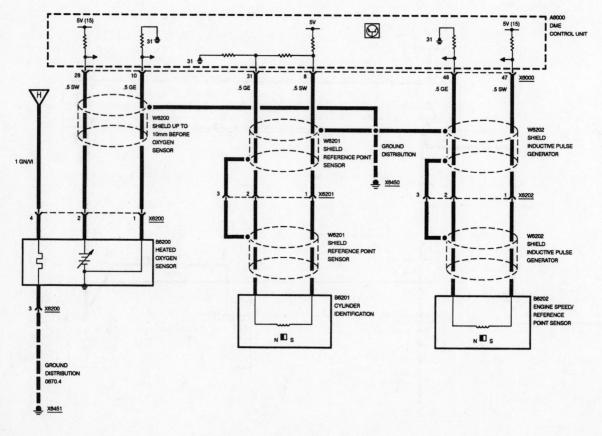

Fig. 171 Fuel injection circuit with M20 or M30 engine — E34 5 Series

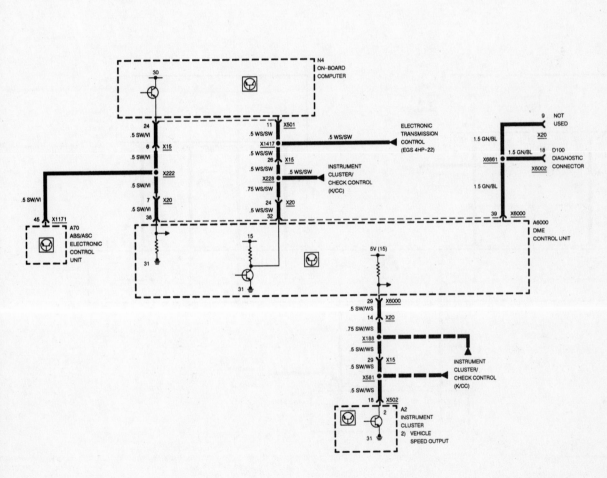

Fig. 172 Fuel injection circuit with M20 or M30 engine — E34 5 Series

84276172

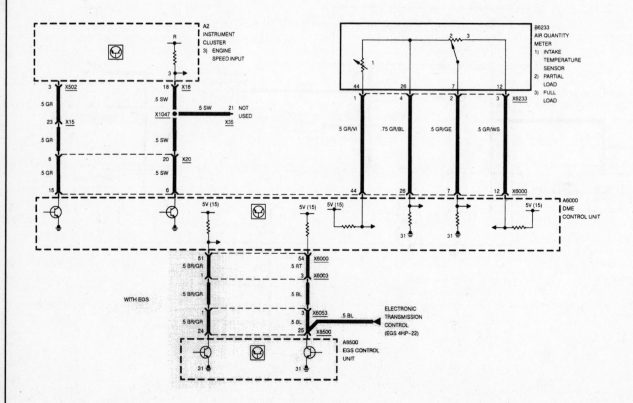

84276173

Fig. 173 Fuel injection circuit with M20 or M30 engine — E34 5 Series

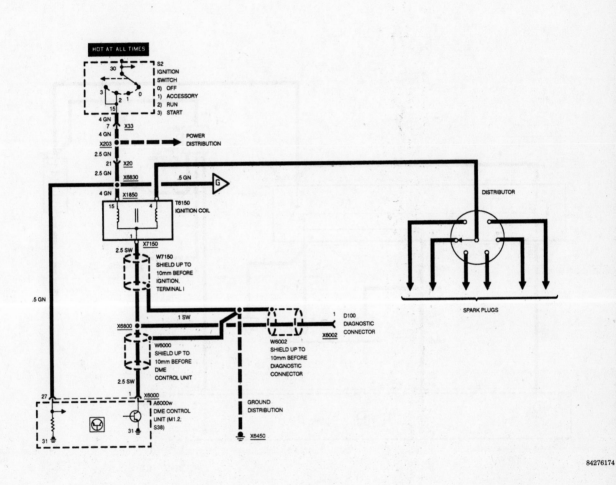

Fig. 174 Fuel injection circuit with S38 engine — E34 5 Series

84276174

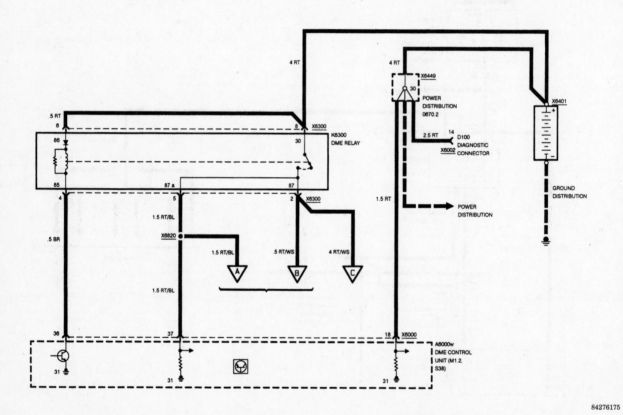

Fig. 175 Fuel injection circuit with S38 engine — E34 5 Series

84276175

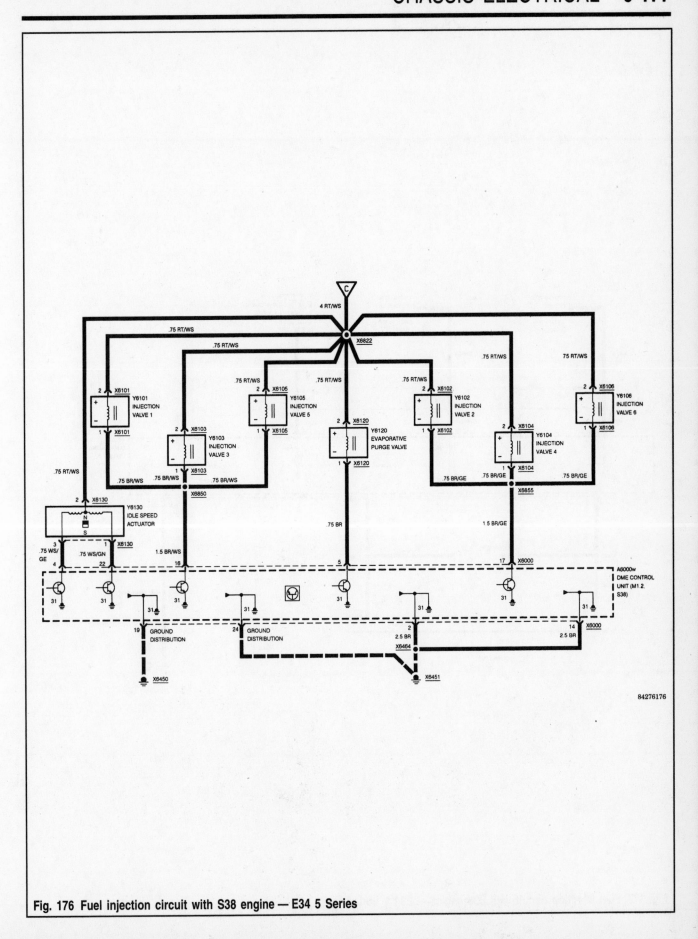

Fig. 176 Fuel injection circuit with S38 engine — E34 5 Series

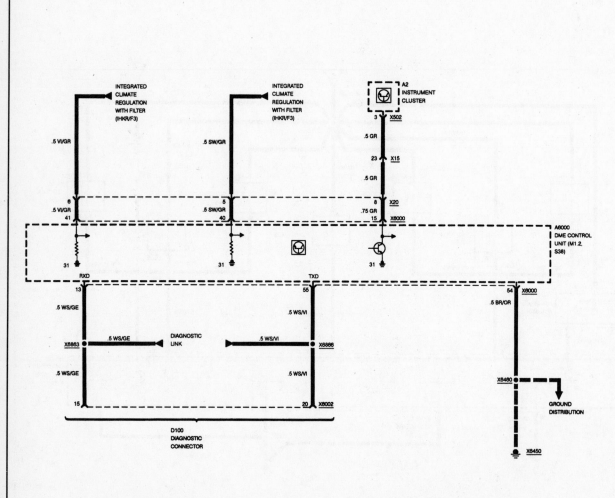

Fig. 177 Fuel injection circuit with S38 engine — E34 5 Series

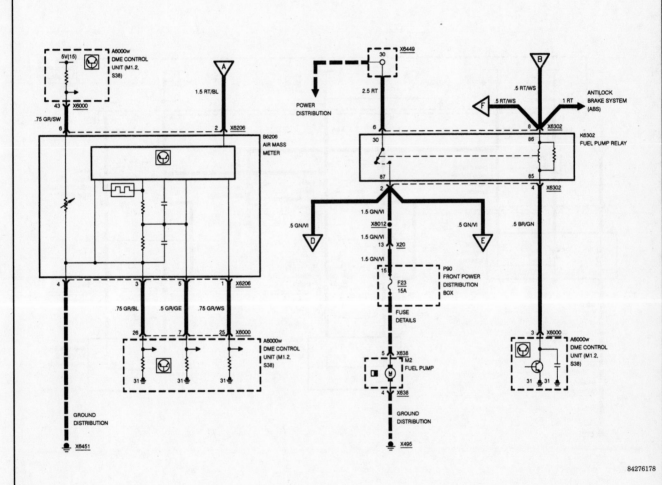

Fig. 178 Fuel injection circuit with S38 engine — E34 5 Series

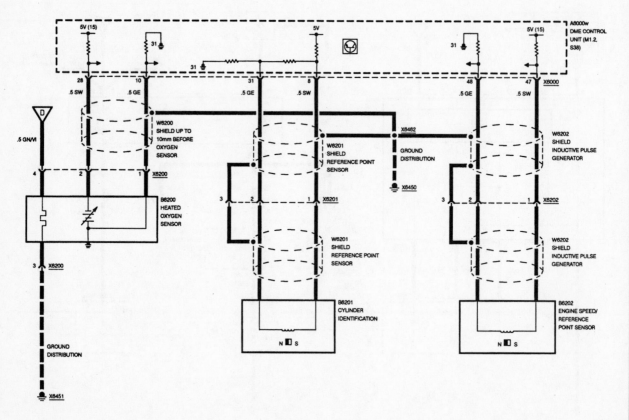

Fig. 179 Fuel injection circuit with S38 engine — E34 5 Series

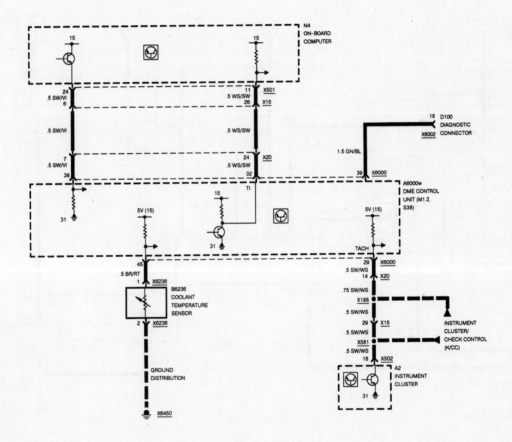

Fig. 180 Fuel injection circuit with S38 engine — E34 5 Series

84276180

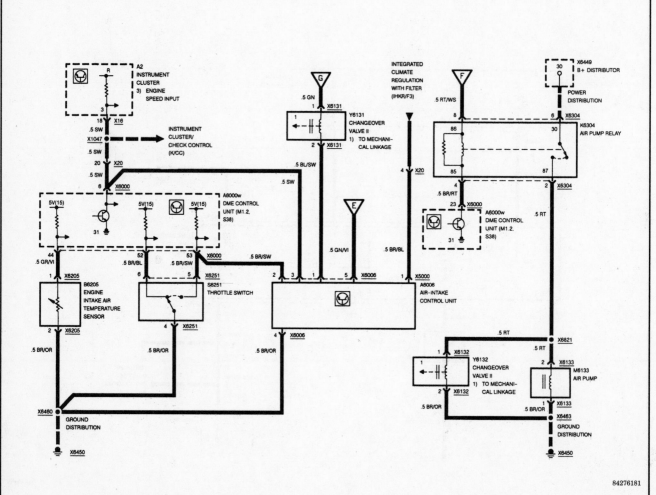

Fig. 181 Fuel injection circuit with S38 engine — E34 5 Series

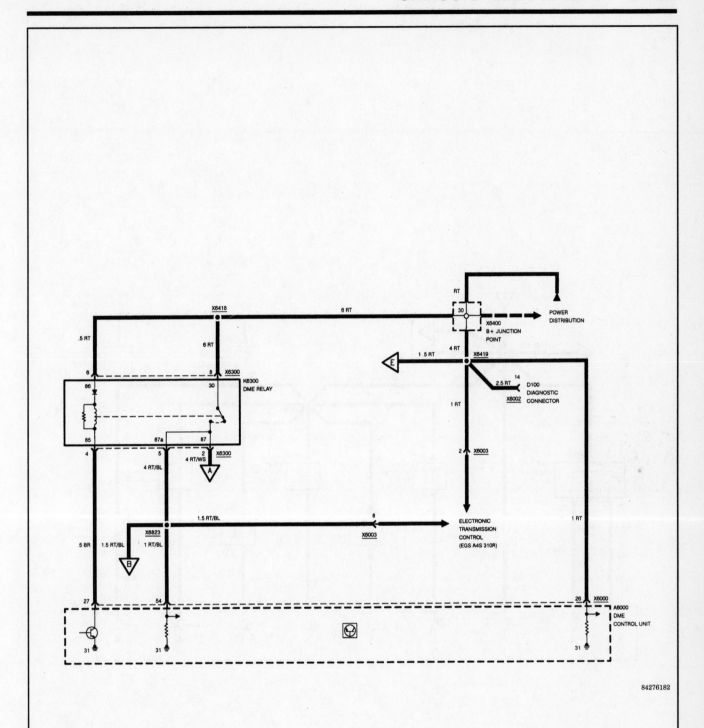

Fig. 182 Fuel injection circuit with M50 engine — E34 5 Series

84276182

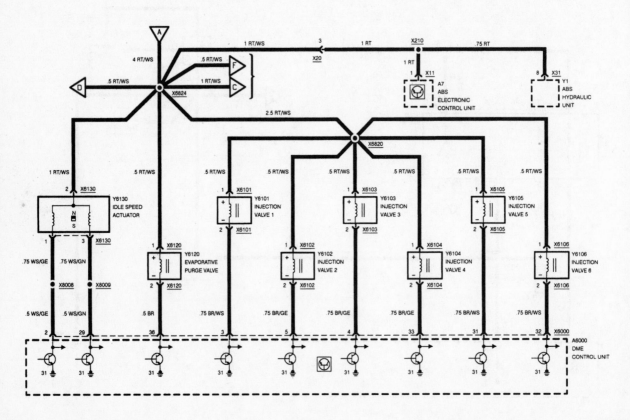

84276183

Fig. 183 Fuel injection circuit with M50 engine — E34 5 Series

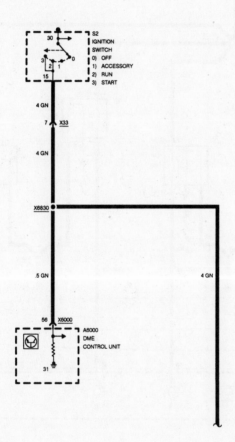

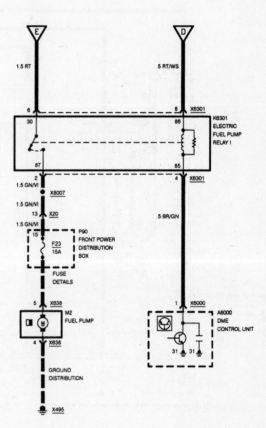

84276184

Fig. 184 Fuel injection circuit with M50 engine — E34 5 Series

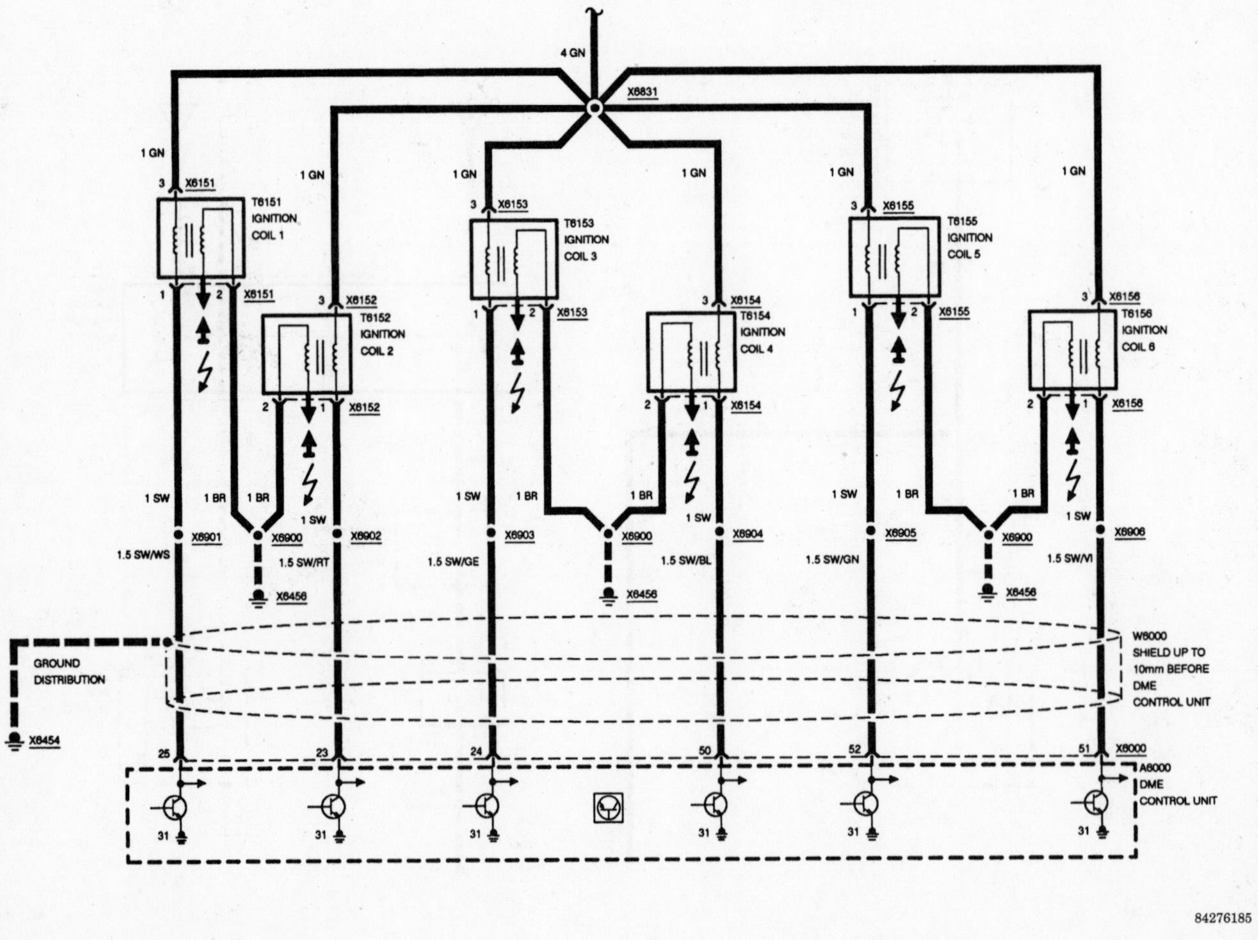

Fig. 185 Fuel injection circuit with M50 engine — E34 5 Series

84276185

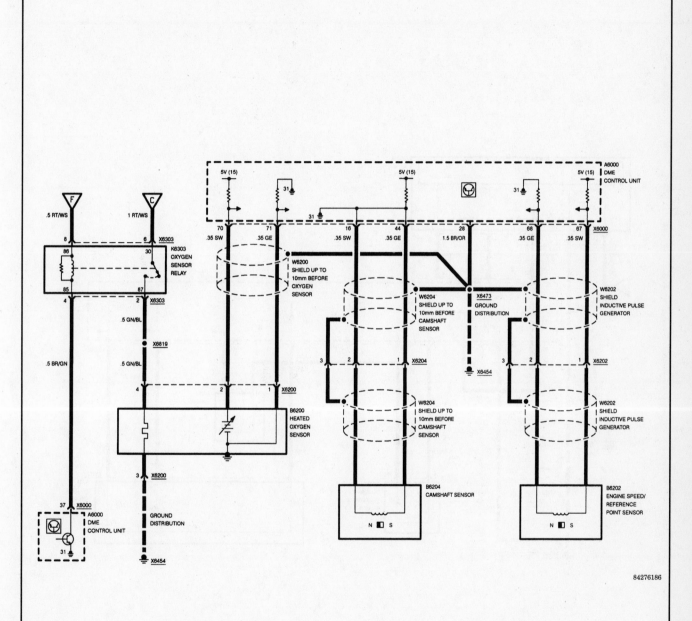

Fig. 186 Fuel injection circuit with M50 engine — E34 5 Series

84276186

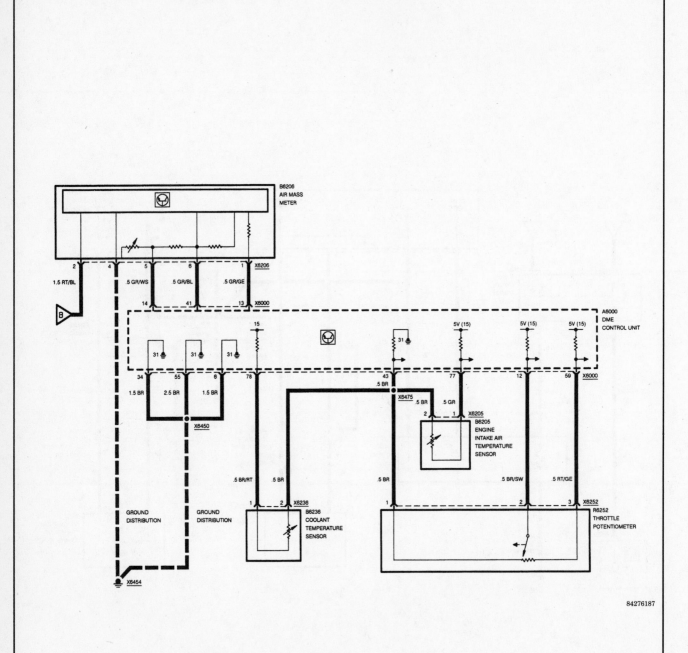

Fig. 187 Fuel injection circuit with M50 engine — E34 5 Series

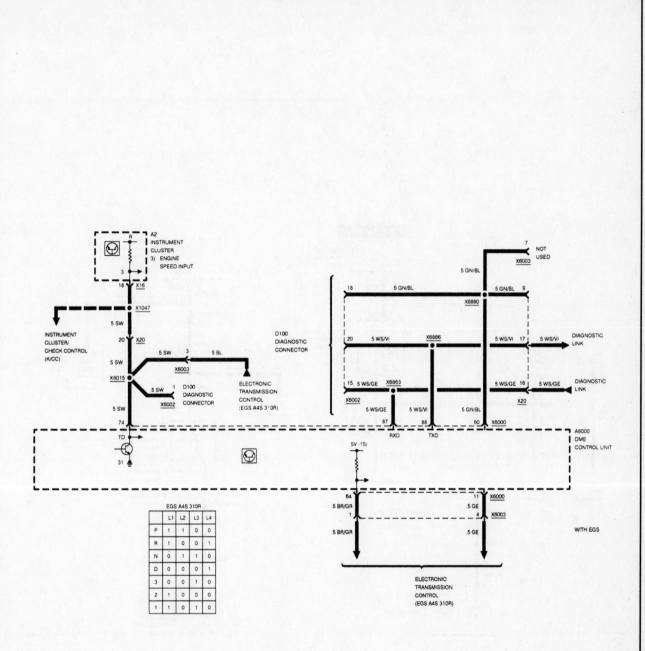

Fig. 188 Fuel injection circuit with M50 engine — E34 5 Series

84276188

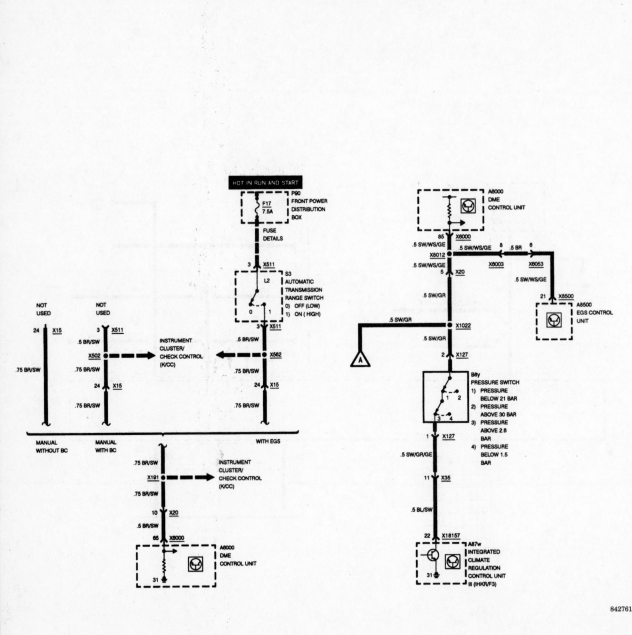

Fig. 189 Fuel injection circuit with M50 engine — E34 5 Series

84276189

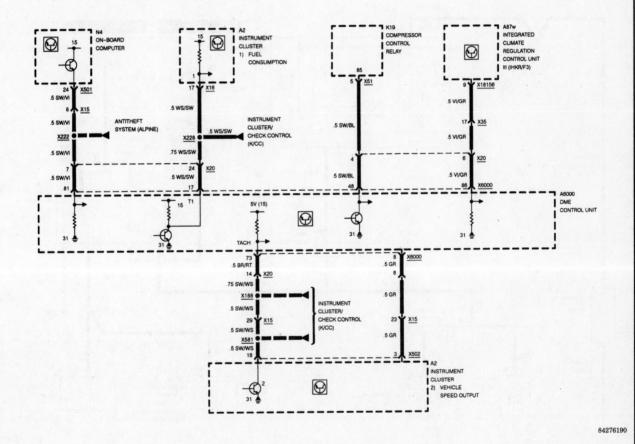

Fig. 190 Fuel injection circuit with M50 engine — E34 5 Series

84276190

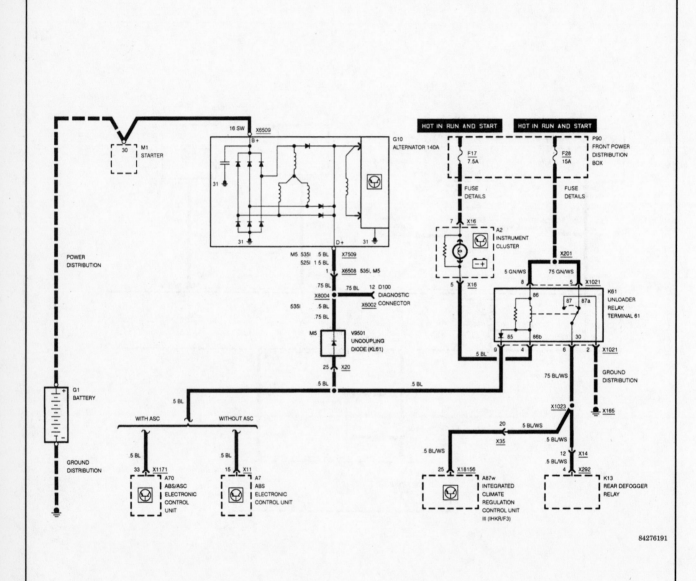

Fig. 191 Charging system circuit — E34 5 Series

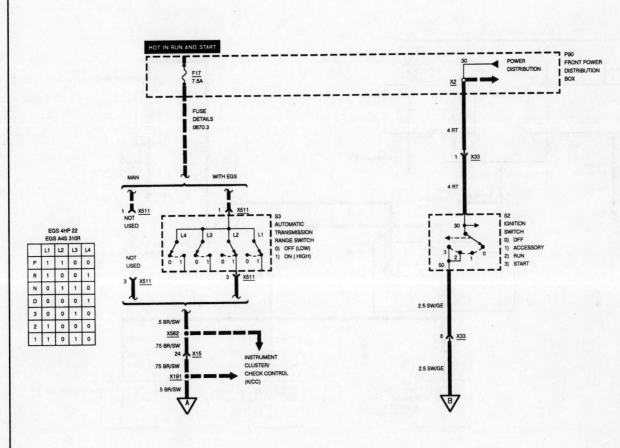

Fig. 192 Starting system circuit — E34 5 Series

84276192

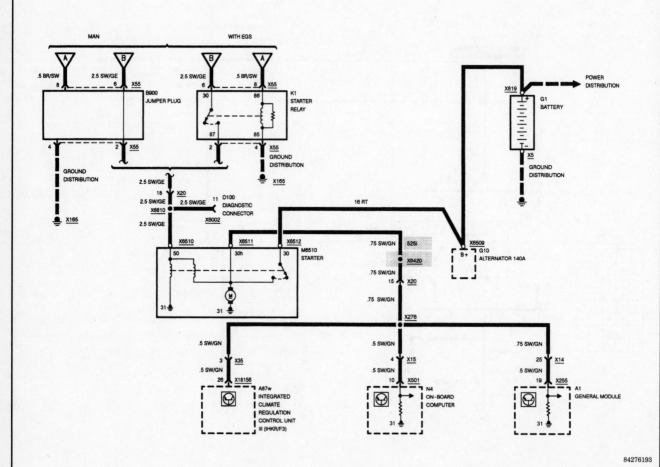

Fig. 193 Starting system circuit — E34 5 Series

84276193

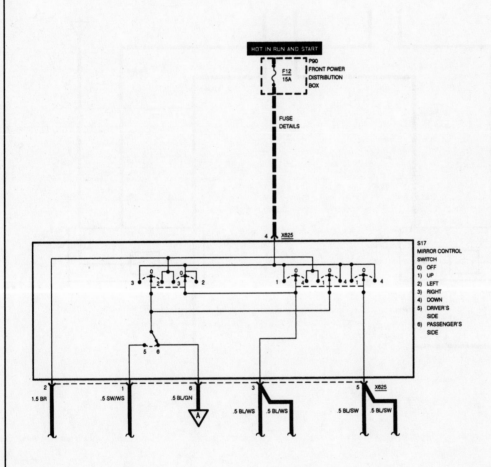

HOT IN RUN AND START

P90
FRONT POWER
DISTRIBUTION
BOX

F12
15A

FUSE
DETAILS

4 X625

S17
MIRROR CONTROL
SWITCH
0) OFF
1) UP
2) LEFT
3) RIGHT
4) DOWN
5) DRIVER'S
   SIDE
6) PASSENGER'S
   SIDE

5 6

2   1   6   3   5   X625
1.5 BR   .5 SW/WS   .5 BL/GN   .5 BL/WS .5 BL/WS   .5 BL/SW .5 BL/SW

A

84276194

Fig. 194 Power mirror circuit — E34 5 Series

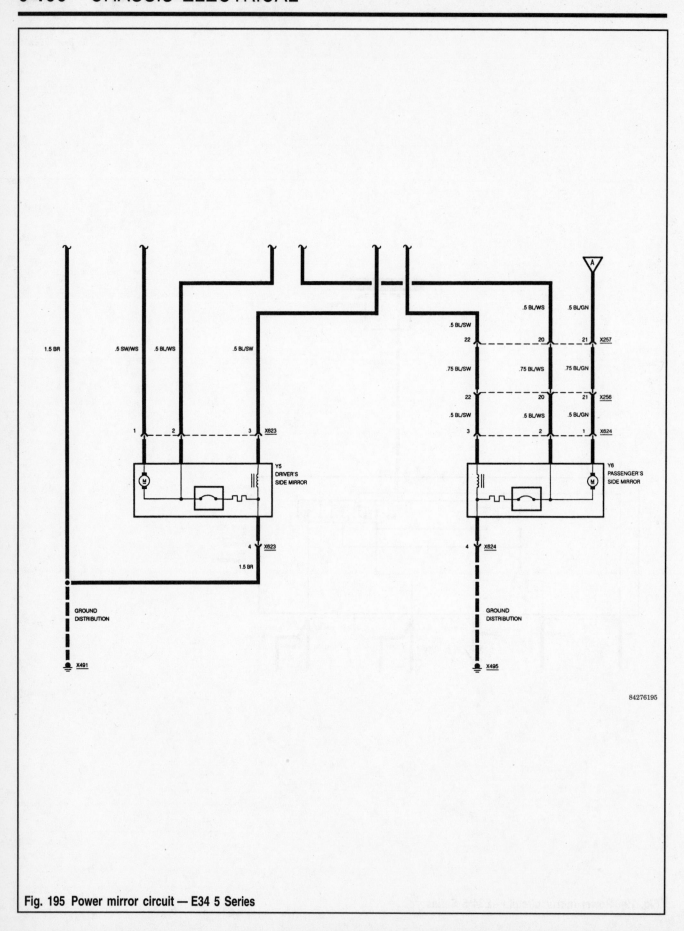

Fig. 195 Power mirror circuit — E34 5 Series

84276195

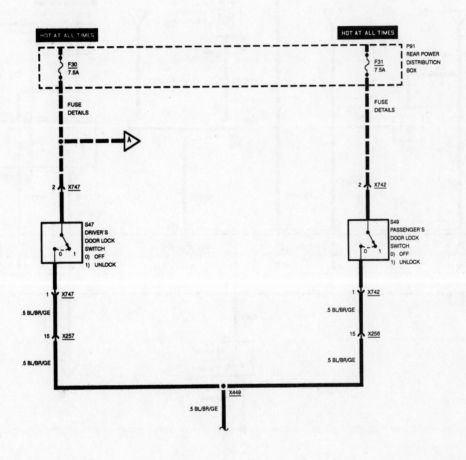

Fig. 196 Power door lock circuit — E34 5 Series

84276196

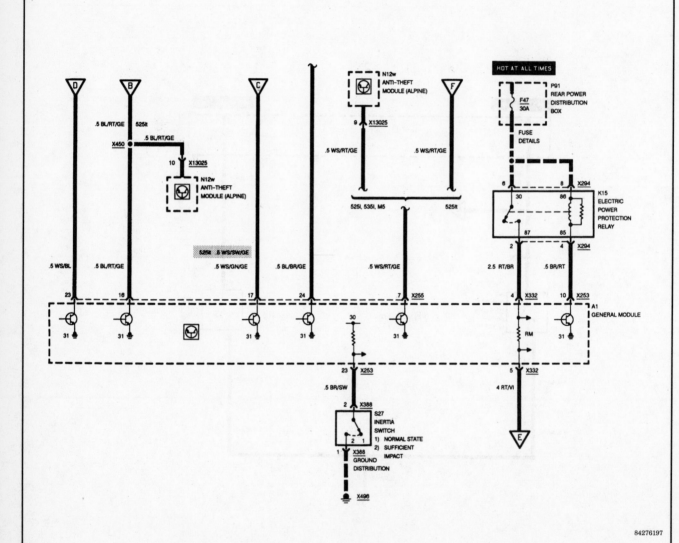

Fig. 197 Power door lock circuit — E34 5 Series

84276197

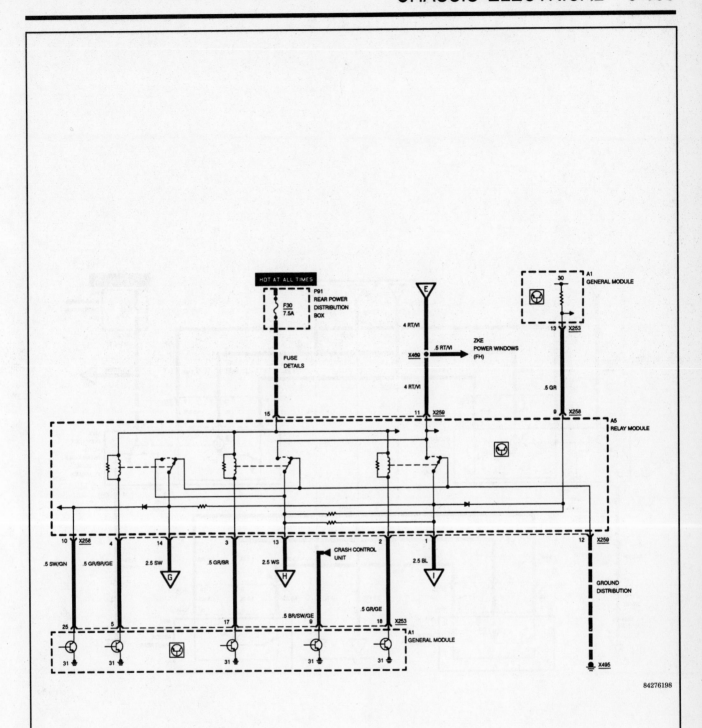

Fig. 198 Power door lock circuit — E34 5 Series

84276198

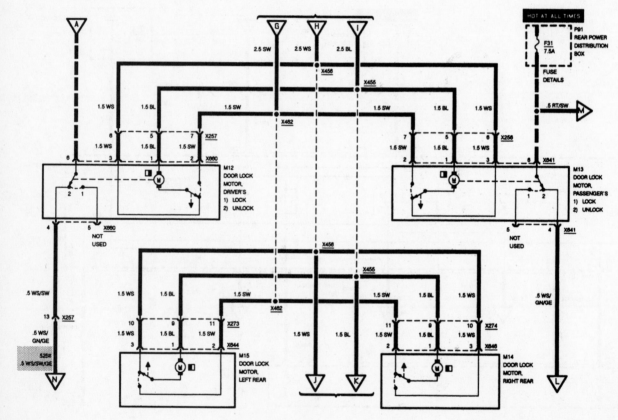

Fig. 199 Power door lock circuit — E34 5 Series

84276199

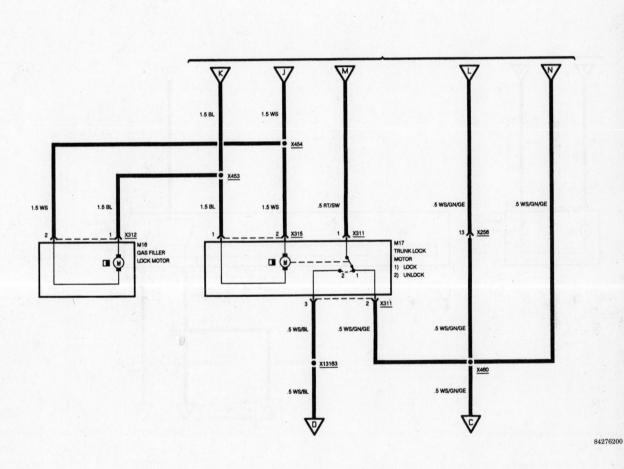

Fig. 200 Power door lock circuit — E34 5 Series

84276200

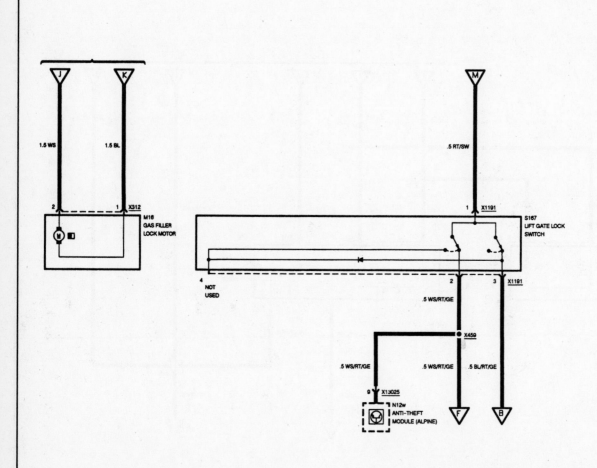

Fig. 201 Power door lock circuit — E34 5 Series

84276201

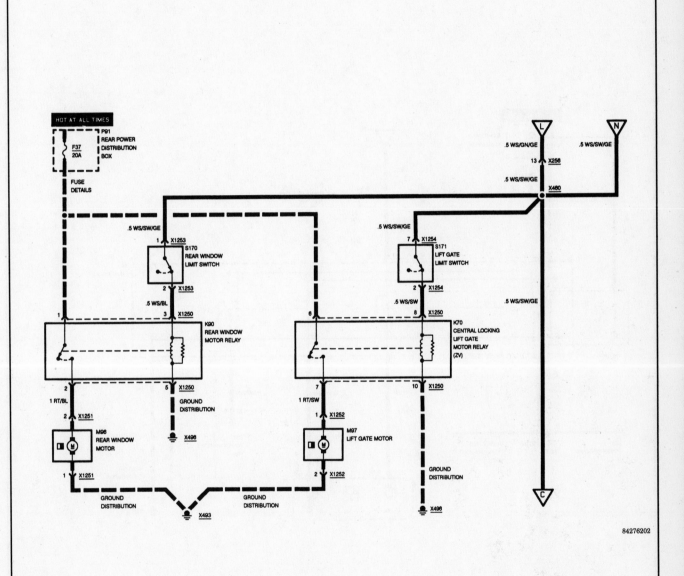

Fig. 202 Power door lock circuit — E34 5 Series

84276202

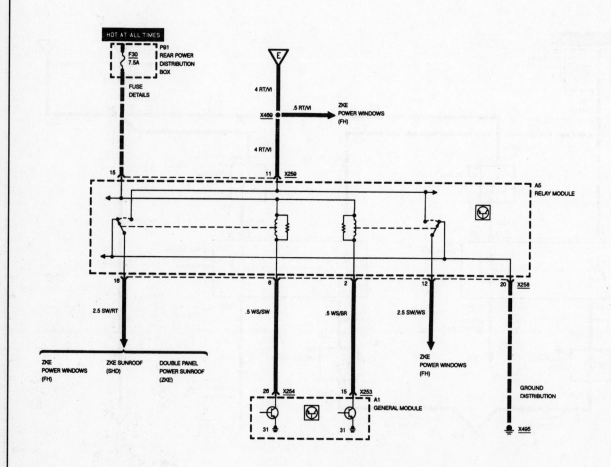

Fig. 203 Power door lock circuit — E34 5 Series

84276203

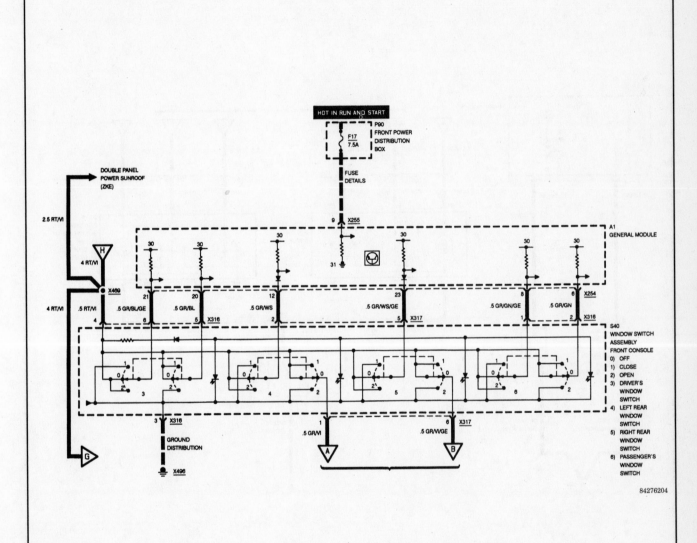

Fig. 204 Power window circuit — E34 5 Series

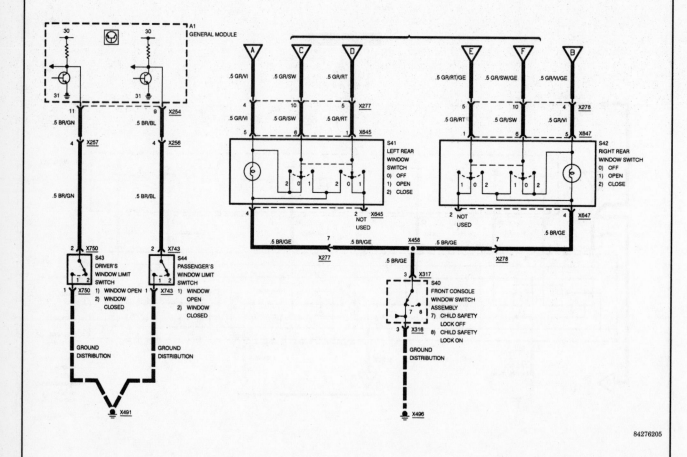

Fig. 205 Power window circuit — E34 5 Series

84276205

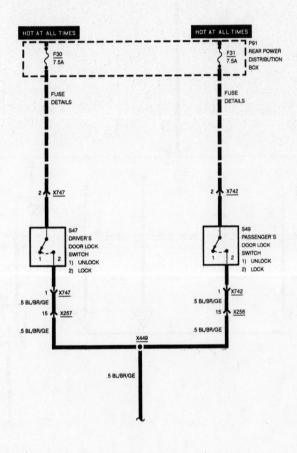

Fig. 206 Power window circuit — E34 5 Series

84276206

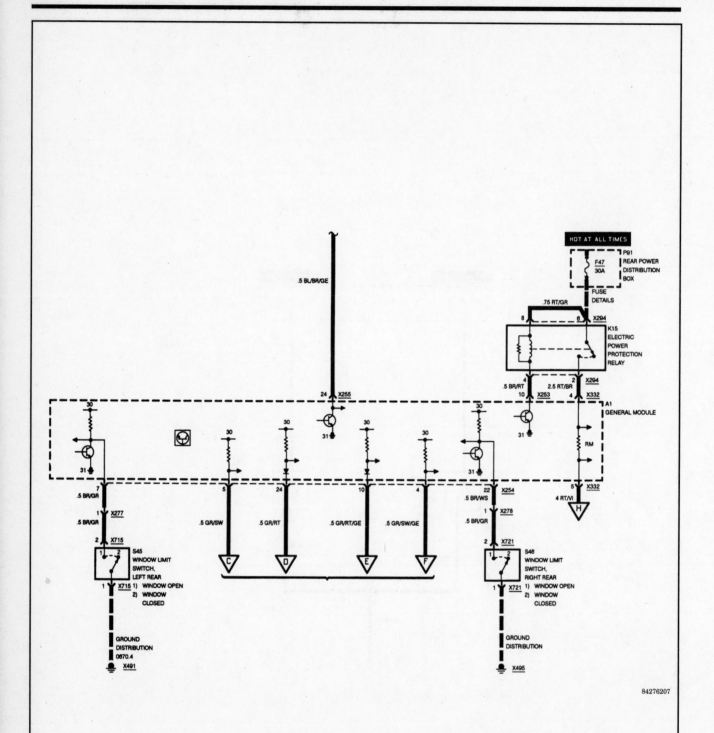

Fig. 207 Power window circuit — E34 5 Series

84276207

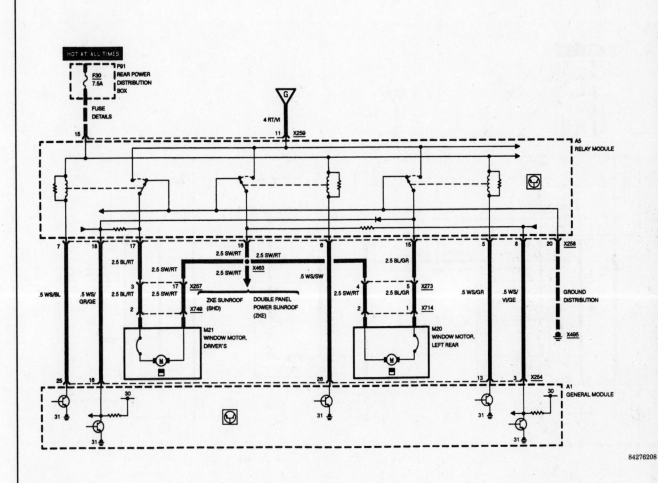

Fig. 208 Power window circuit — E34 5 Series

84276208

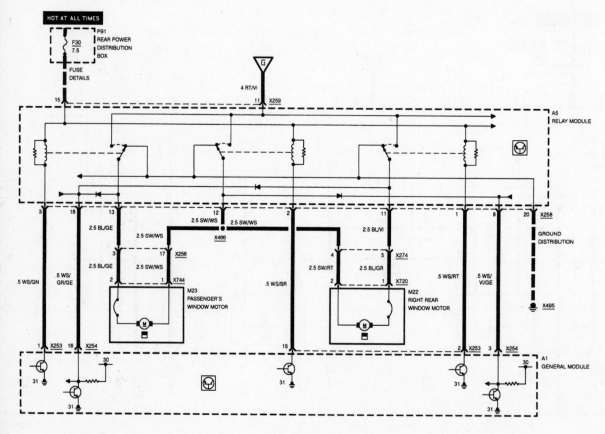

Fig. 209 Power window circuit — E34 5 Series

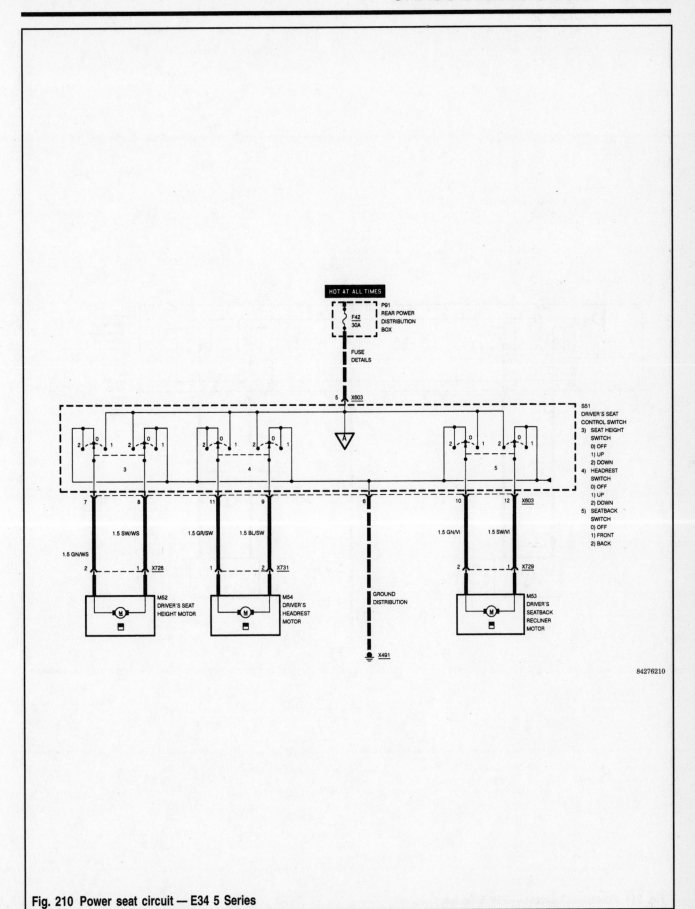

Fig. 210 Power seat circuit — E34 5 Series

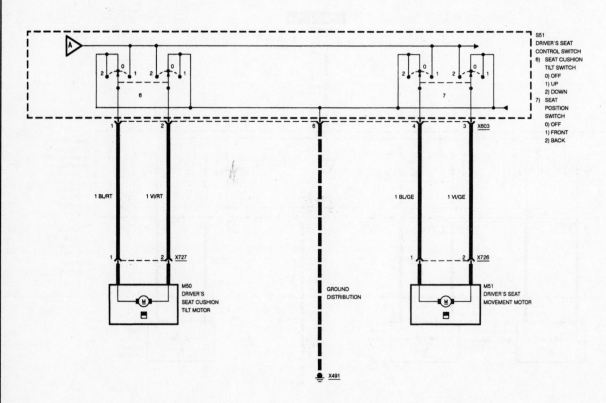

Fig. 211 Power seat circuit — E34 5 Series

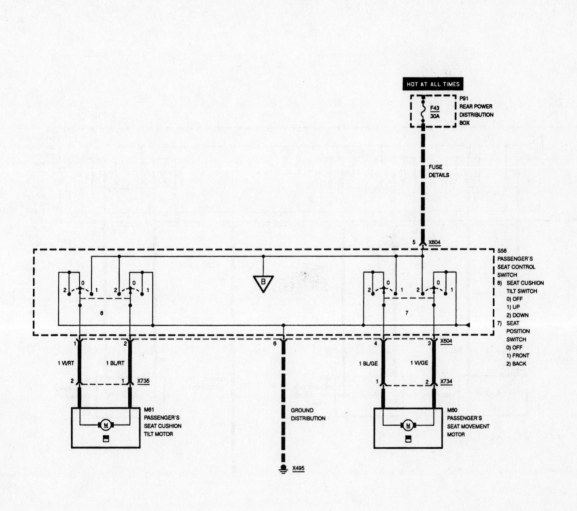

Fig. 212 Power seat circuit — E34 5 Series

84276212

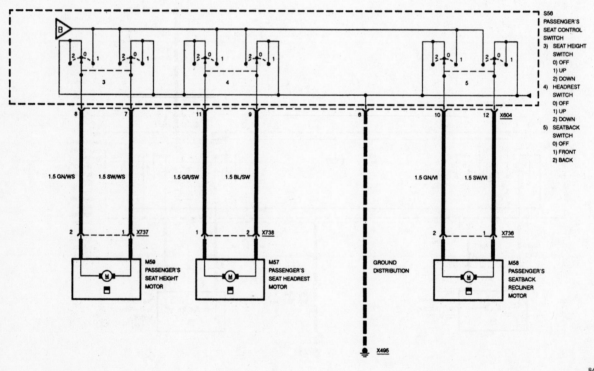

Fig. 213 Power seat circuit — E34 5 Series

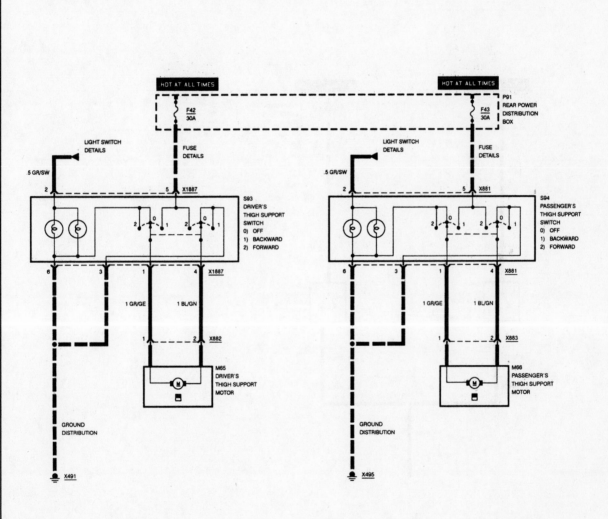

Fig. 214 Power seat circuit — E34 5 Series

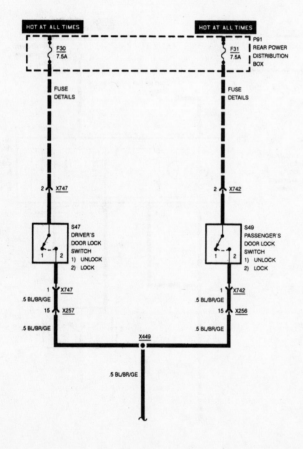

HOT AT ALL TIMES		HOT AT ALL TIMES	P91

F30
7.5A

F31
7.5A

REAR POWER
DISTRIBUTION
BOX

FUSE
DETAILS

FUSE
DETAILS

2 X747

2 X742

S47
DRIVER'S
DOOR LOCK
SWITCH
1) UNLOCK
2) LOCK

S49
PASSENGER'S
DOOR LOCK
SWITCH
1) UNLOCK
2) LOCK

1 X747

1 X742

.5 BL/BR/GE

.5 BL/BR/GE

15 X257

15 X256

.5 BL/BR/GE

.5 BL/BR/GE

X449

.5 BL/BR/GE

84276215

Fig. 215 Power sunroof circuit — E34 5 Series

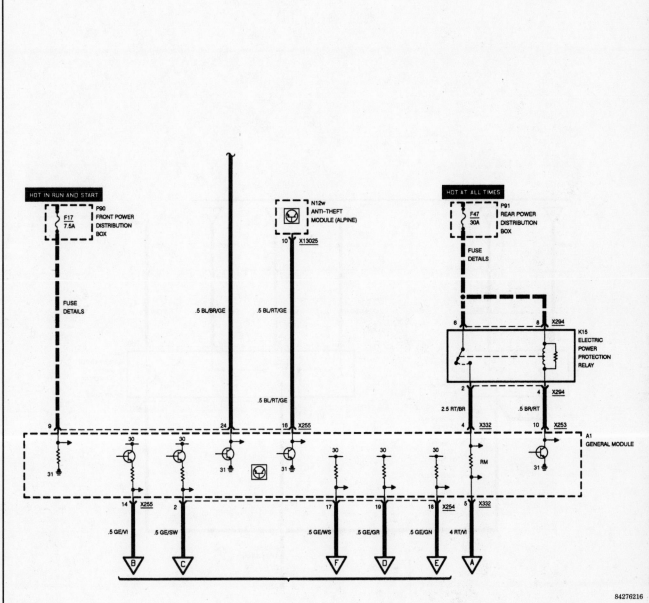

Fig. 216 Power sunroof circuit — E34 5 Series

84276216

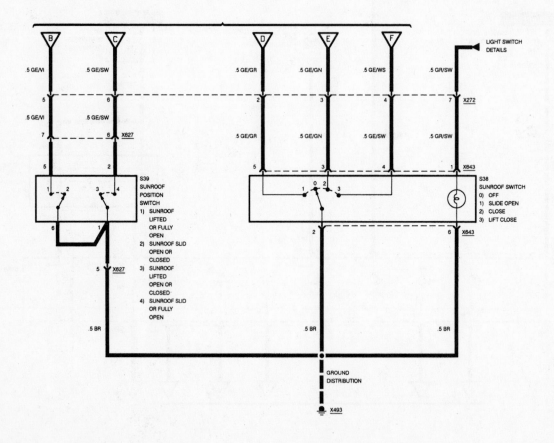

Fig. 217 Power sunroof circuit — E34 5 Series

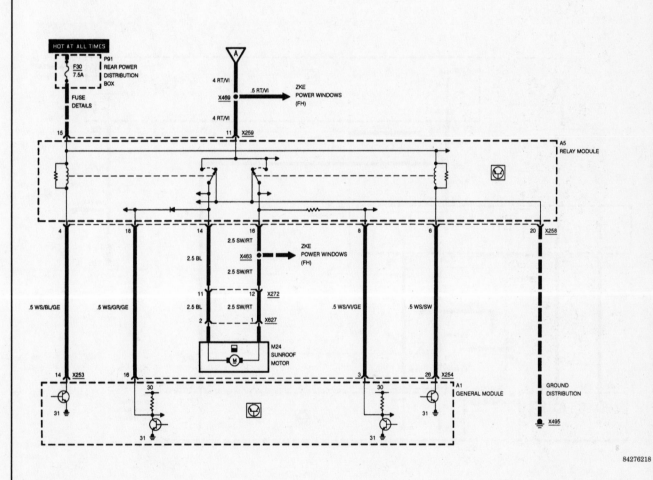

Fig. 218 Power sunroof circuit — E34 5 Series

84276218

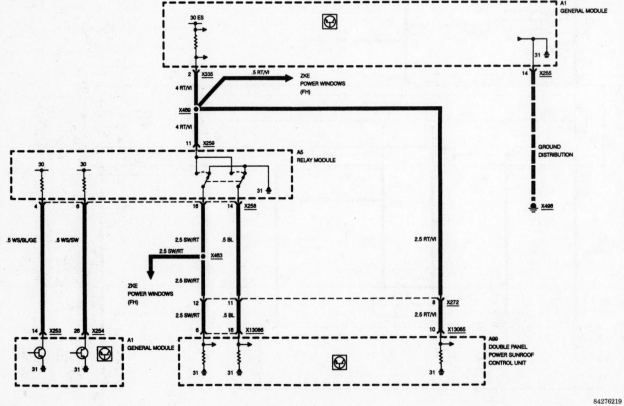

Fig. 219 Double panel power sunroof circuit — E34 5 Series touring

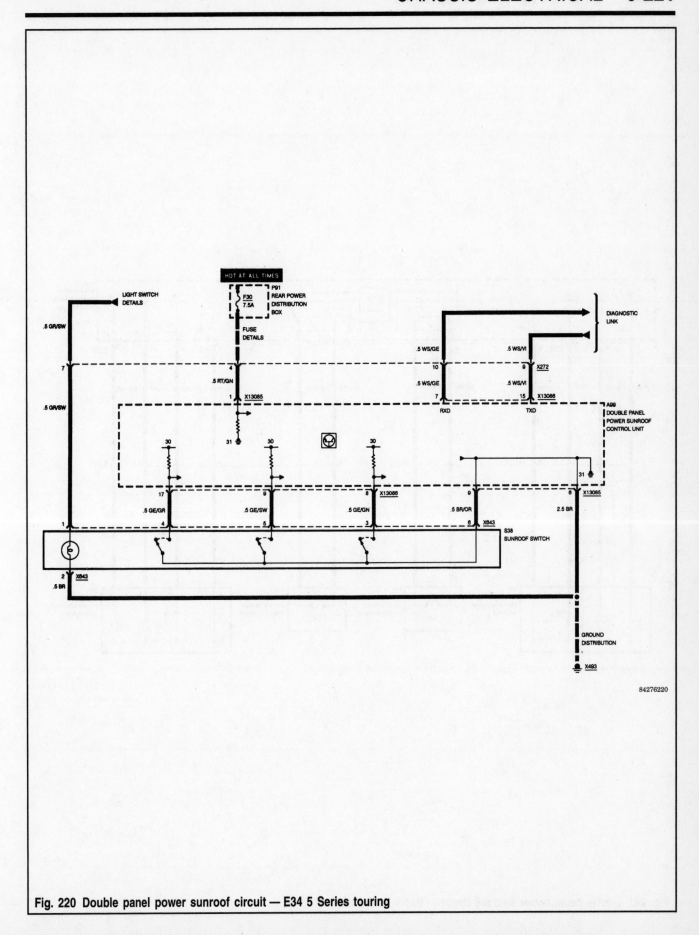

Fig. 220 Double panel power sunroof circuit — E34 5 Series touring

84276220

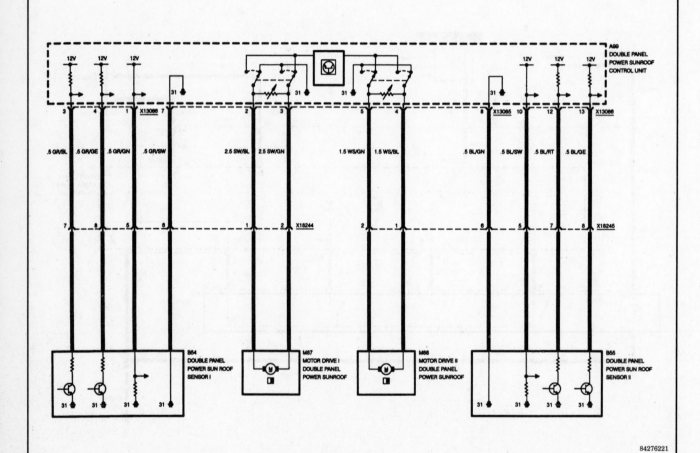

Fig. 221 Double panel power sunroof circuit — E34 5 Series touring

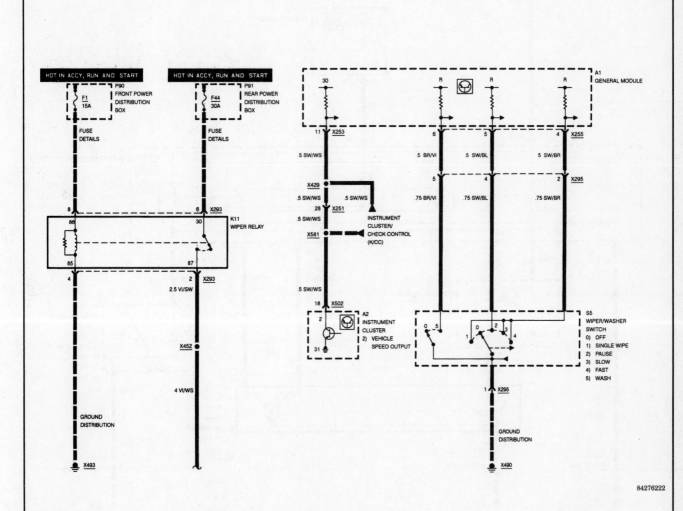

Fig. 222 Windshield wiper and washer circuit — E34 5 Series

84276222

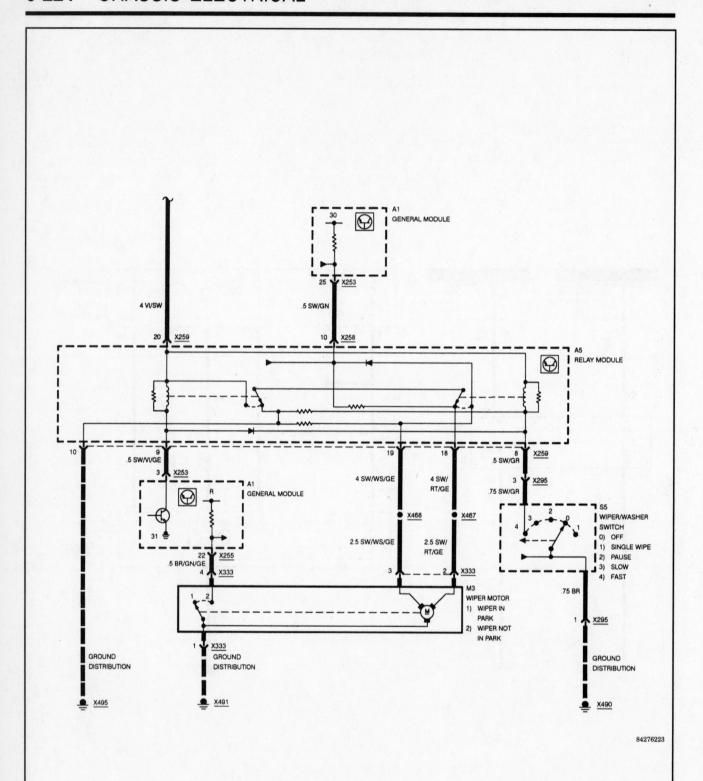

Fig. 223 Windshield wiper and washer circuit — E34 5 Series

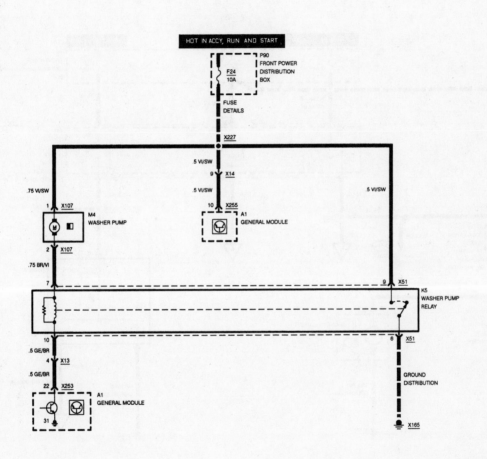

Fig. 224 Windshield wiper and washer circuit — E34 5 Series

84276224

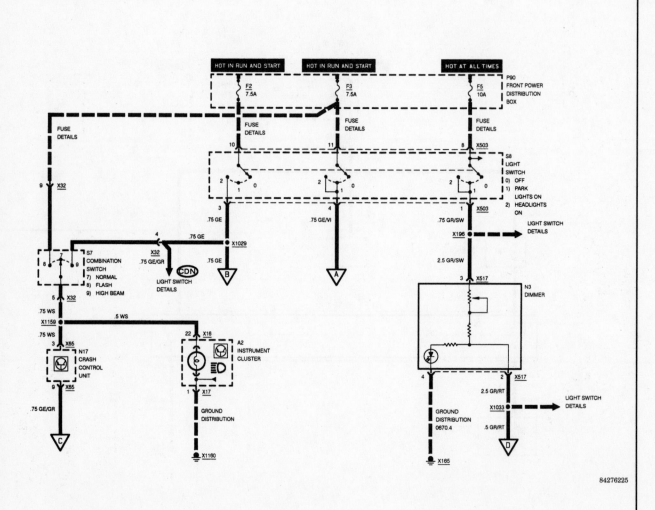

Fig. 225 Headlight and fog light circuit — E34 5 Series

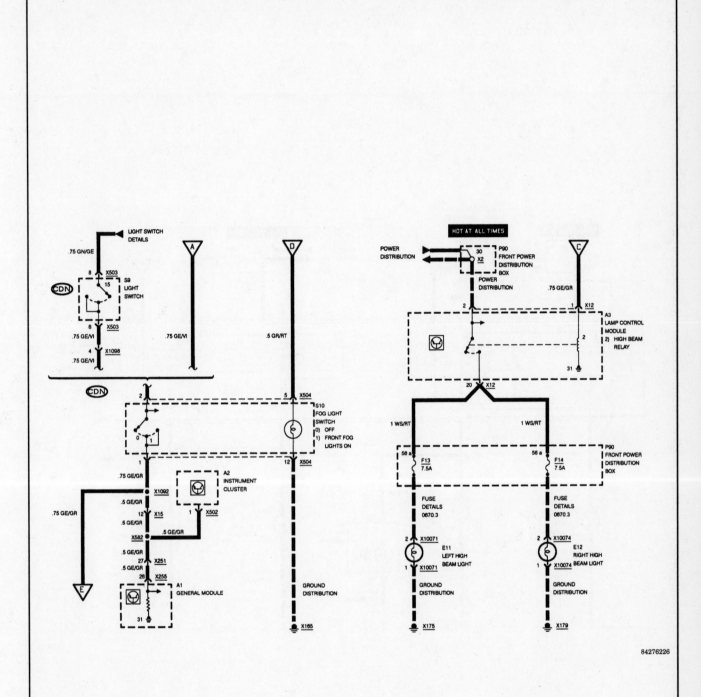

Fig. 226 Headlight and fog light circuit — E34 5 Series

84276226

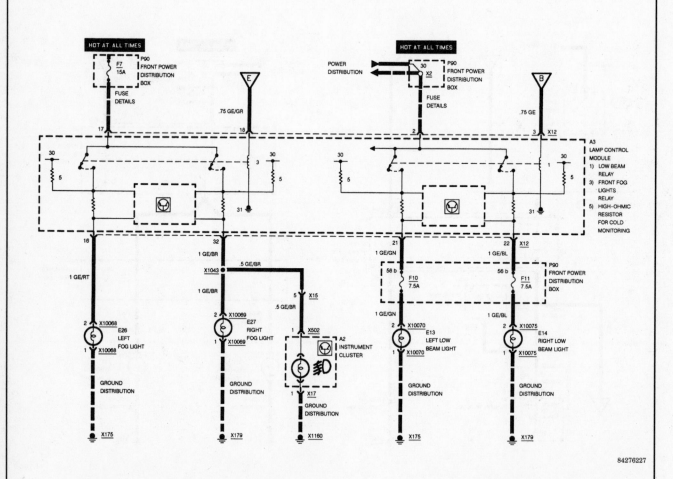

Fig. 227 Headlight and fog light circuit — E34 5 Series

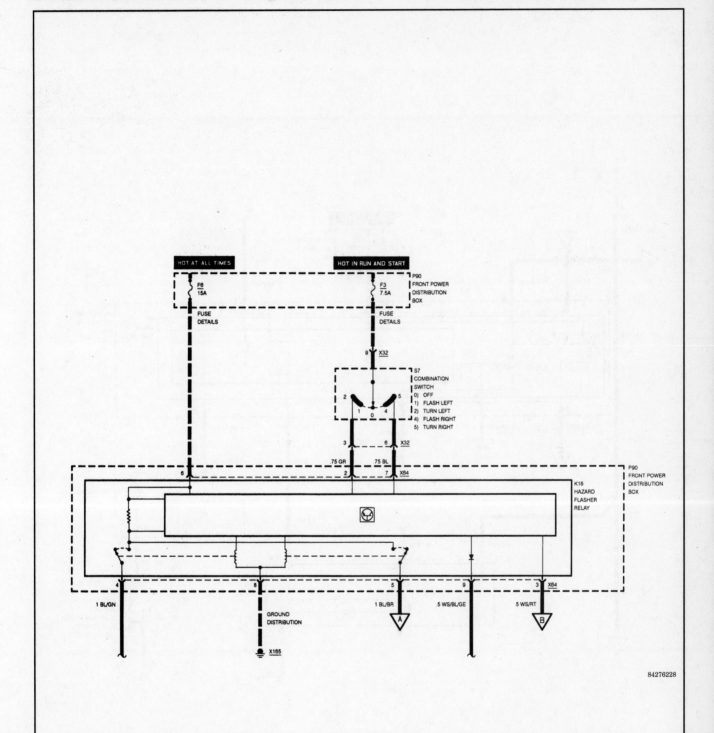

Fig. 228 Turn signal and hazard circuit — E34 5 Series

84276228

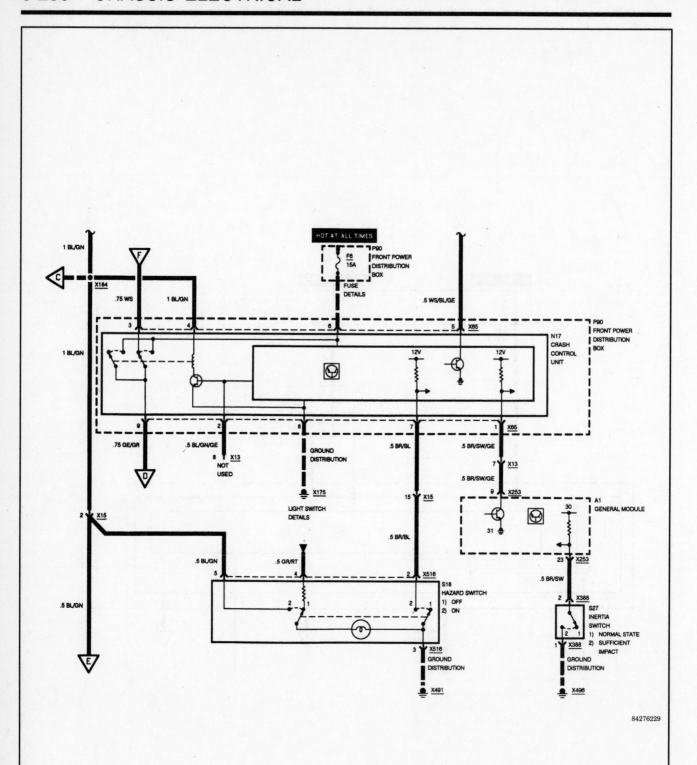

Fig. 229 Turn signal and hazard circuit — E34 5 Series

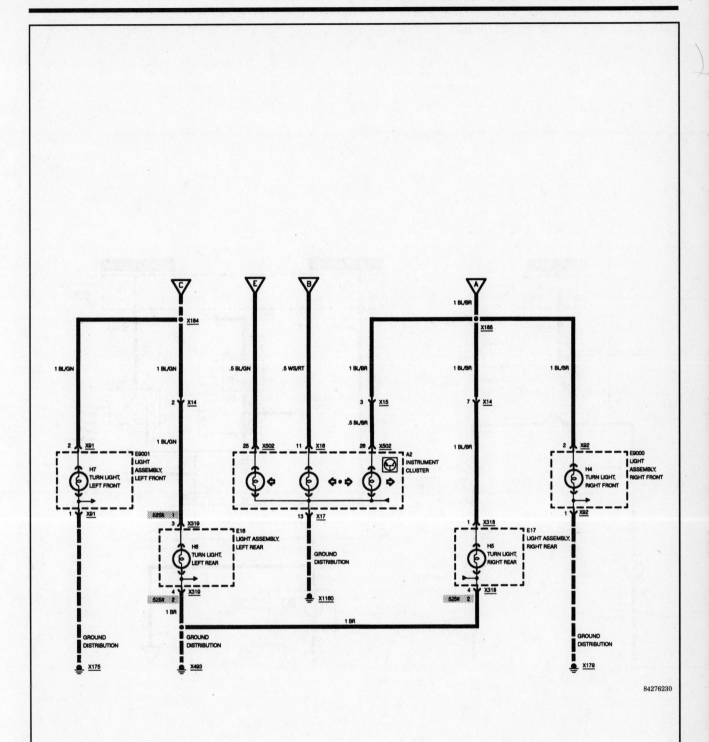

Fig. 230 Turn signal and hazard circuit — E34 5 Series

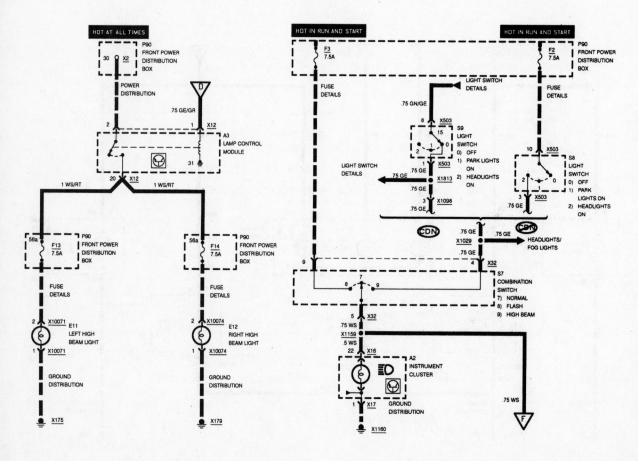

Fig. 231 Turn signal and hazard circuit — E34 5 Series

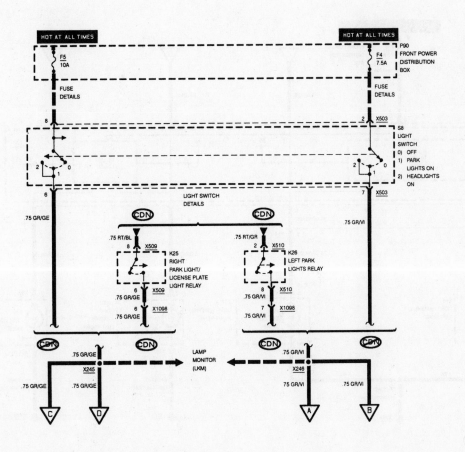

Fig. 232 Parking and tail light circuit — E34 5 Series

84276232

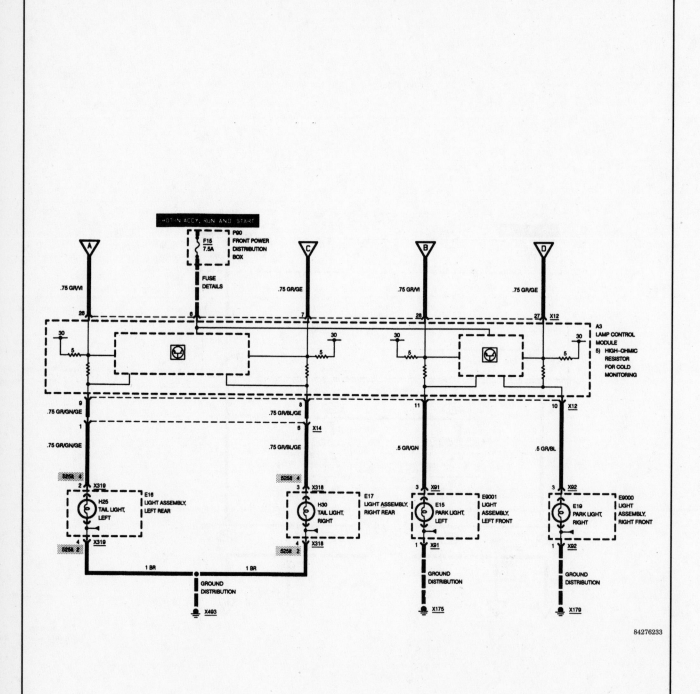

Fig. 233 Parking and tail light circuit — E34 5 Series

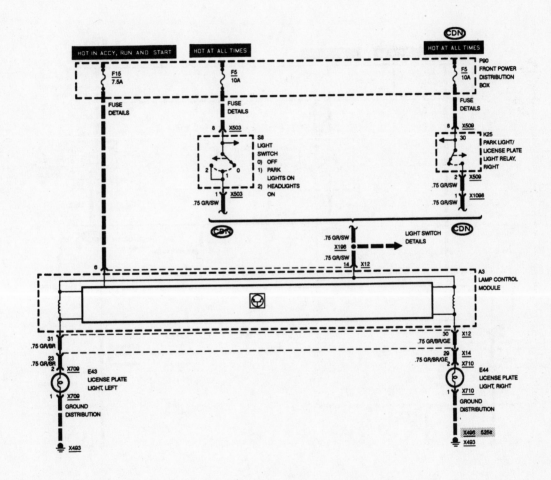

Fig. 234 License plate and luggage compartment light circuit — E34 5 Series

84276234

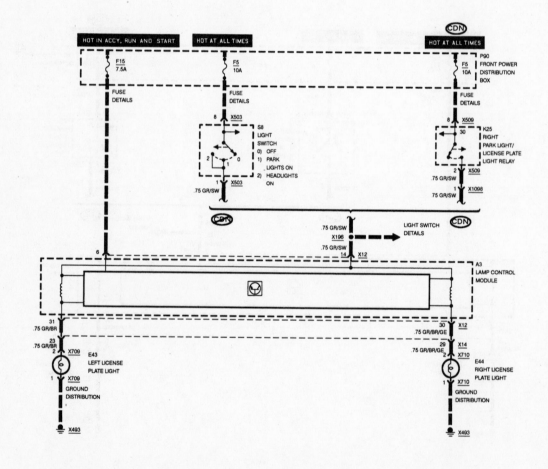

Fig. 235 License plate and luggage compartment light circuit — E34 5 Series

84276235

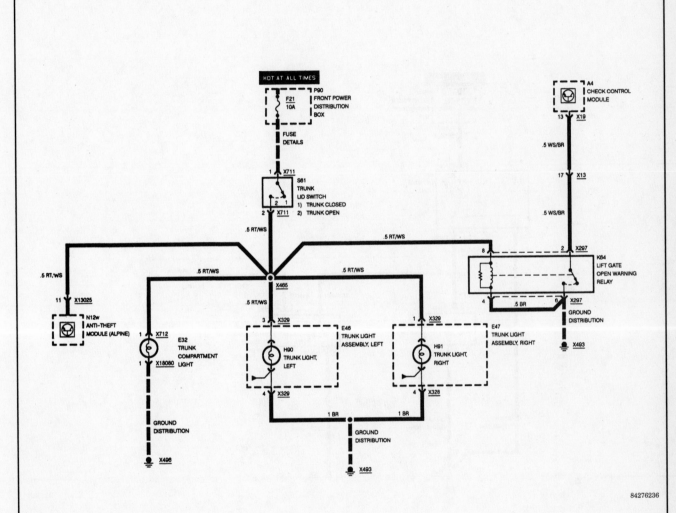

Fig. 236 License plate and luggage compartment light circuit — E34 5 Series

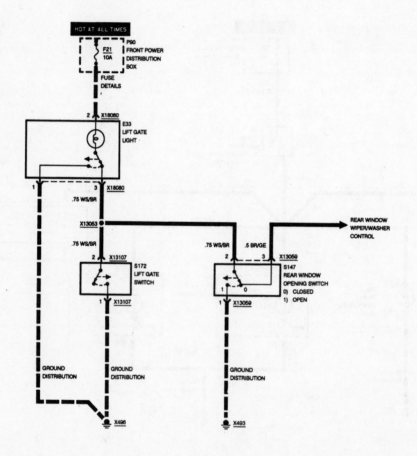

HOT AT ALL TIMES

P90
FRONT POWER
DISTRIBUTION
BOX

F21
10A

FUSE
DETAILS

2 X18080

E33
LIFT GATE
LIGHT

1   3 X18080

.75 WS/BR

X13053

REAR WINDOW
WIPER/WASHER
CONTROL

.75 WS/BR   .75 WS/BR   .5 BR/GE

2 X13107   2   3 X13059

S172
LIFT GATE
SWITCH

S147
REAR WINDOW
OPENING SWITCH
0) CLOSED
1) OPEN

1   0

1 X13107   1 X13059

GROUND
DISTRIBUTION

GROUND
DISTRIBUTION

GROUND
DISTRIBUTION

X496   X493

84276237

Fig. 237 License plate and luggage compartment light circuit — E34 5 Series

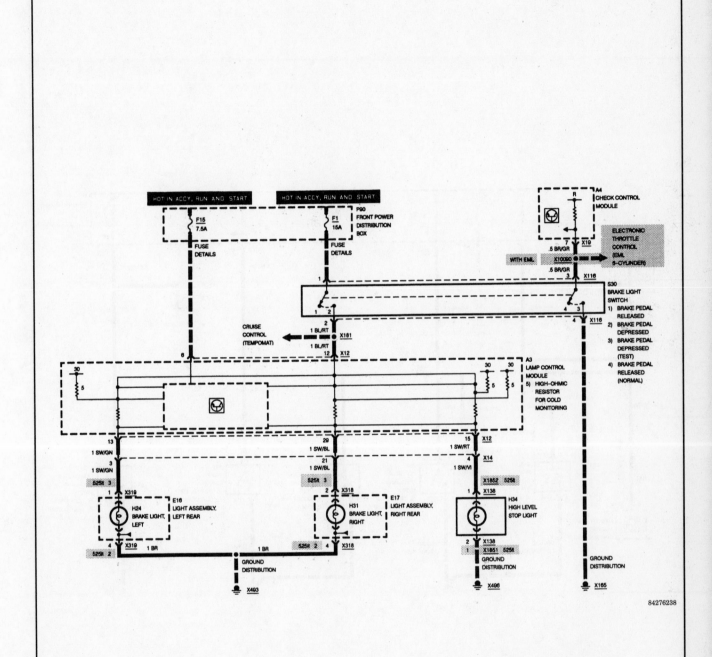

Fig. 238 Brake light circuit — E34 5 Series

84276238

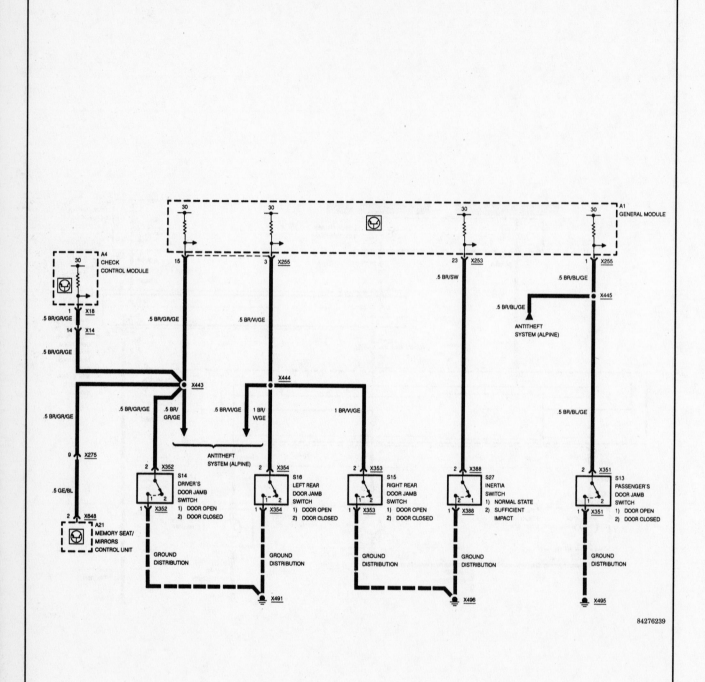

Fig. 239 Interior light circuit — E34 5 Series

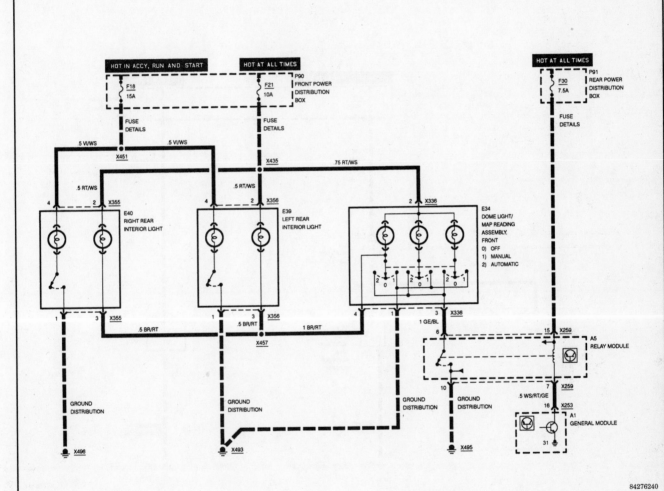

Fig. 240 Interior light circuit — E34 5 Series

84276240

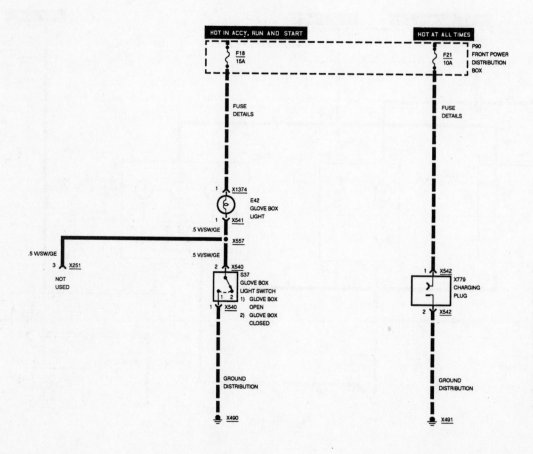

HOT IN ACCY, RUN AND START	HOT AT ALL TIMES	P90 FRONT POWER DISTRIBUTION BOX

F18 15A

F21 10A

FUSE DETAILS

FUSE DETAILS

1 X1374

E42 GLOVE BOX LIGHT

1 X541

.5 VI/SW/GE

X557

.5 VI/SW/GE

.5 VI/SW/GE

3 X251

NOT USED

2 X540

S37 GLOVE BOX LIGHT SWITCH
1) GLOVE BOX OPEN
2) GLOVE BOX CLOSED

1 2

1 X540

1 X542

X779 CHARGING PLUG

2 X542

GROUND DISTRIBUTION

GROUND DISTRIBUTION

X490

X491

84276241

Fig. 241 Glove compartment and lighter circuit — E34 5 Series

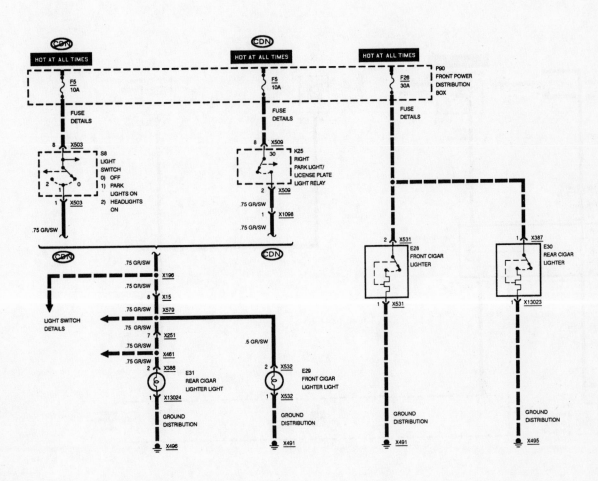

Fig. 242 Glove compartment and lighter circuit — E34 5 Series

84276242

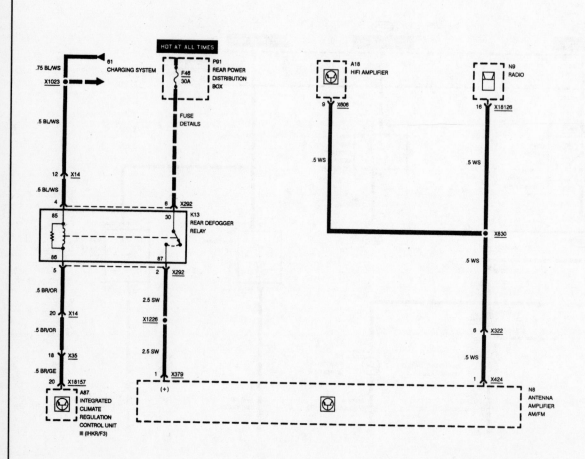

Fig. 243 Rear window defogger circuit — E34 5 Series

84276243

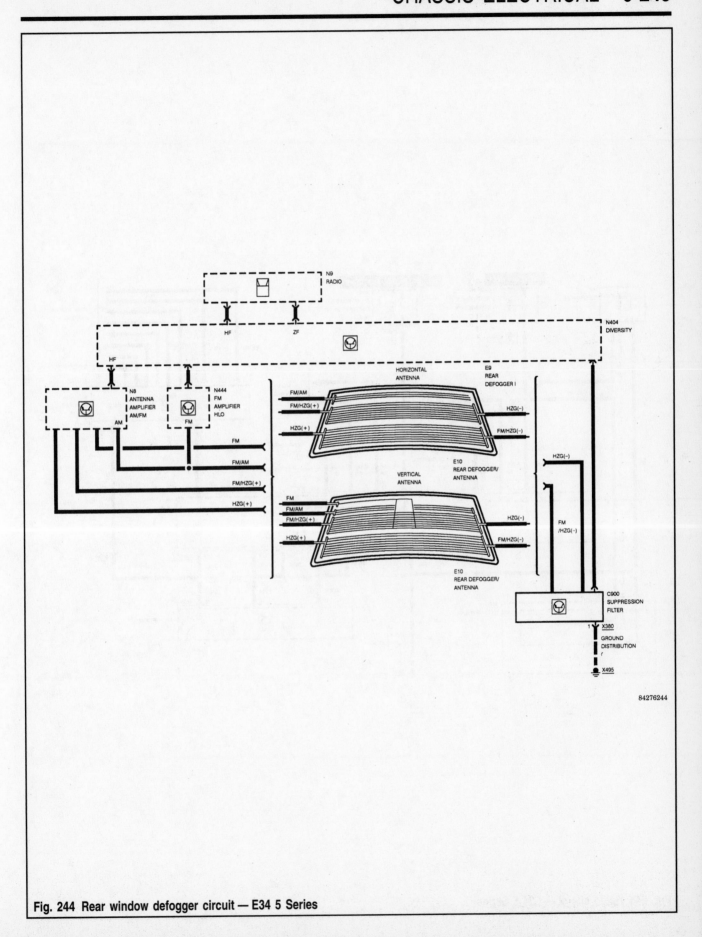

Fig. 244 Rear window defogger circuit — E34 5 Series

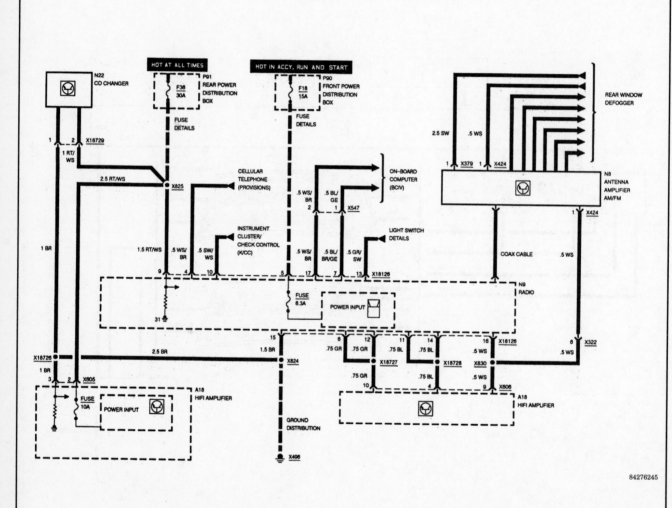

Fig. 245 Radio circuit — E34 5 Series

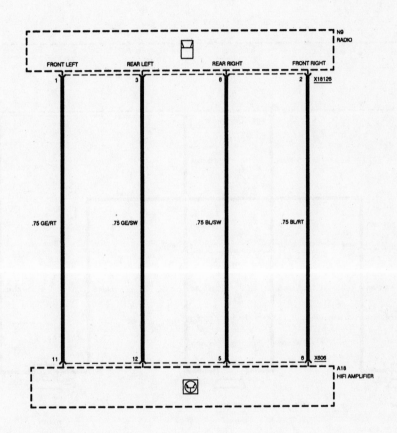

Fig. 246 Radio circuit — E34 5 Series

84276246

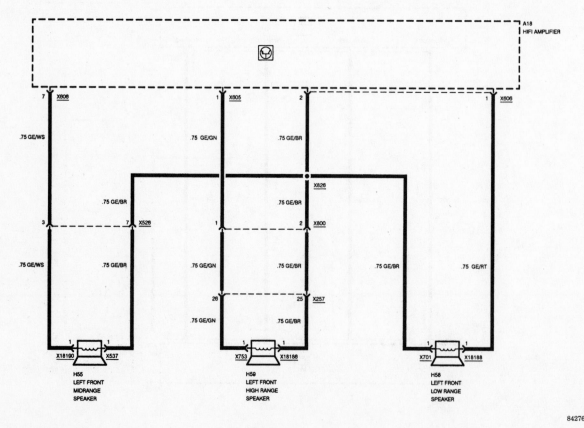

84276247

Fig. 247 Radio circuit — E34 5 Series

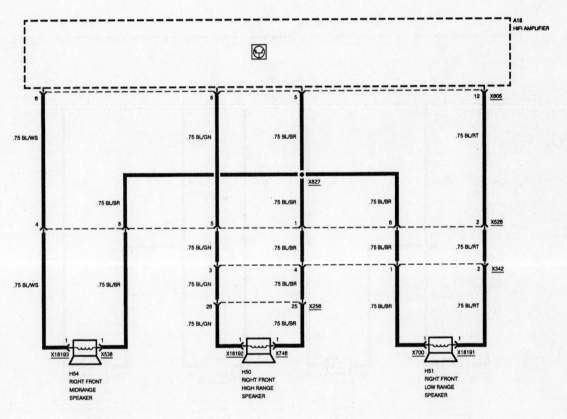

Fig. 248 Radio circuit — E34 5 Series

84276248

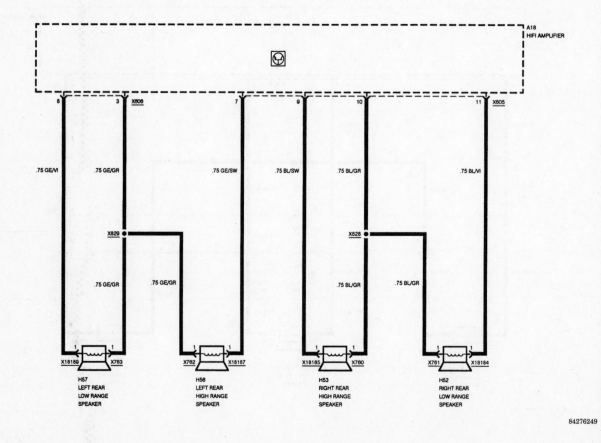

Fig. 249 Radio circuit — E34 5 Series

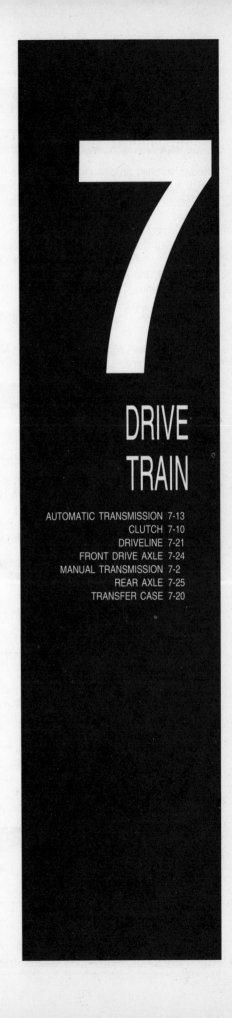

7

DRIVE TRAIN

MANUAL TRANSMISSION

Identification

Known for their precise shifting and short throws, BMW manual transmissions have been targets for other manufactures to match. All the transmissions covered are fully synchronized, 5 speed units. The transmissions are primarily built by Getrag to BMW specifications.

A variety of transmissions are used, usage being determined by the chassis and engine combination. By chassis and engine, this is the application:

- E30 3 Series M20 engine — 260/5 M42 engine — 240/5 S14 engine — 265/6
- S14 3 Series M42 engine — S5D 200G M50 engine — S5D 250G
- E34 5 Series M20 engine — 260/5 M30 engine — 260/6 M50 engine — S5D 310Z S38 engine — 280/5

Shifter Knob

REMOVAL & INSTALLATION

1. Pull up the leather boot from the console.
2. Disconnect the shift knob illumination harness, if equipped.
3. The shift knob either unscrews from the shaft or pull off.
4. Install in reverse order and align the knob.

Shift Linkage

▶ See Figures 1 and 2

REMOVAL & INSTALLATION

1. Remove the shifter knob and boot.
2. Remove the rubber cover from the shifter pivot. Remove the snapring, if equipped. Remove the shifter pivot.
3. Remove the snaprings holding the shift rod and pull the rod off.
4. Remove the bolts holding the shift arm or pry up the clip holding the shift arm. Remove the shift arm. The entire shifter assembly will come out.
5. Install the shifter arm and linkage. Replace the snaprings, pivot and rubber cover. Install the shifter and boot.

Transmission

REMOVAL & INSTALLATION

E30 3 Series

1. Disconnect the negative battery cable. Raise and safely support the vehicle. Remove the exhaust system. Remove the cross brace and heat shield. On the 325iX, remove the transfer case.

2. Hold the nuts on the front with one wrench, and remove bolts from the rear with another to disconnect the flexible coupling at the front of the driveshaft. Some vehicles have a vibration damper at this point in the drivetrain. This damper is mounted on the transmission output flange with bolts that are pressed into the damper. On these vehicles, unscrew and remove the nuts located behind the damper.

3. Loosen the threaded sleeve on the driveshaft. Get a special tool to hold the splined portion of the shaft while turning the sleeve.

4. Remove its mounting bolts and remove the center driveshaft mount. Then, bend the driveshaft down at the center and pull it off the transmission output flange. Keep the sections of the driveshaft from pulling apart and suspend it from the vehicle with wire.

5. Remove the retainer and washer, and pull out the shift selector rod.

6. Use a hex-head wrench to remove the self-locking bolts that retain the shift rod bracket at the rear of the transmission and then remove the bracket. If the vehicle has a shift arm, use a screwdriver to pry the spring clip up off the boss on the transmission case and swing it upward. Then, pull out the shift shaft pin.

7. Unscrew and remove the clutch slave cylinder and support it so the hydraulic line can remain connected.

8. The transmission may incorporate sending units for flywheel rotating speed and position. Remove the heat shield that protects these from exhaust heat and then remove the retaining bolt for each sending unit. Note that the speed sending unit, which has no identifying ring goes in the bore on the right, and that the reference mark sending unit, which has a marking ring, goes in the bore on the left. If the sending units are installed in reverse positions, the engine will not run at all. Pull these units out of the flywheel housing.

9. Disconnect the wiring connector going to the backup light switch and pull the wires out of the harness.

10. Support the transmission from underneath in a secure manner. Remove mounting bolts and remove the crossmember holding the rear of the transmission to the body. Then, lower the transmission onto the front axle carrier.

11. Using the proper tool, remove the bolts holding the transmission flywheel housing to the engine at the front. If there is a separate clutch bellhousing, remove the transmission to bellhousing bolts. Make sure to retain the washers with the bolts. Pull the transmission rearward to slide the input shaft out of the clutch disc and then lower the transmission and remove from the vehicle.

To install:

12. Install the transmission in position under the vehicle. Align the input shaft and install the transmission, note the following points:

a. Coat the input shaft splines and flywheel housing guide pins with a light coating of suitable grease. Coat the release bearing interior groove with grease.

b. Make sure the front mounting bolts are installed with their washers. For hex head bolts, torque the M8 bolts to 16-19.5 ft. lbs. (22-27 Nm), torque the M10 bolts to 34-37 ft.

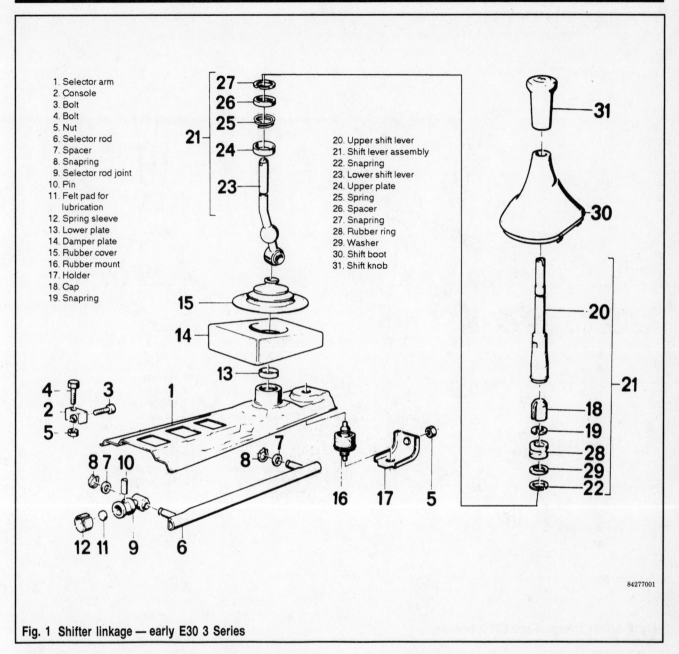

1. Selector arm
2. Console
3. Bolt
4. Bolt
5. Nut
6. Selector rod
7. Spacer
8. Snapring
9. Selector rod joint
10. Pin
11. Felt pad for lubrication
12. Spring sleeve
13. Lower plate
14. Damper plate
15. Rubber cover
16. Rubber mount
17. Holder
18. Cap
19. Snapring
20. Upper shift lever
21. Shift lever assembly
22. Snapring
23. Lower shift lever
24. Upper plate
25. Spring
26. Spacer
27. Snapring
28. Rubber ring
29. Washer
30. Shift boot
31. Shift knob

84277001

Fig. 1 Shifter linkage — early E30 3 Series

lbs. (47-51 Nm), torque the M12 bolts to 48-59 ft. lbs. (66-82 Nm). For Torx® head bolts, torque the M8 bolts to 14.5-17 ft. lbs. (20-24 Nm), torque the M10 bolts to 27.5-34 ft. lbs. (38-47 Nm), torque the M12 bolts to 52-58 ft. lbs. (70-80 Nm).

c. Before reinstalling the sending units for flywheel position and speed, make sure their faces are free of either grease or dirt and then coat them with a light coating of a suitable lubricant. Inspect the O-rings and replace them if they are cut, cracked, crushed, or stretched.

d. When installing the shift rod bracket at the rear of the transmission, use new self-locking bolts and make sure the bracket is level before tightening them. Torque the shift rod bracket bolts to 16.5 ft. lbs. (22 Nm) except with the S14 engine, which uses an aluminum bracket. With the S14 engine, torque these bolts to 8 ft. lbs. (12 Nm).

e. Install the clutch slave cylinder.

f. When installing the driveshaft center bearing, preload it forward 0.157-0.236 inch Check the driveshaft alignment with an appropriate tool such. Replace the nuts and then torque the center mount bolts to 16-17 ft. lbs. (21-23 Nm).

g. Torque the M10-8.8 flexible coupling bolts to 35 ft. lbs. (48 Nm). Torque the M10-10.9 flexible coupling bolts to 52 ft. lbs. (72 Nm).

h. Torque the driveshaft threaded sleeve to 12 ft. lbs. (17 Nm) after it complete installation.

i. Fill the transmission with proper lubricant.

E36 3 Series

1. Disconnect the negative battery cable. Raise and safely support the vehicle. Remove the exhaust system. Remove the cross brace and heat shield.

2. Hold the nuts on the front with one wrench, and remove bolts from the rear with another to disconnect the flexible coupling at the front of the driveshaft. Some vehicles have a

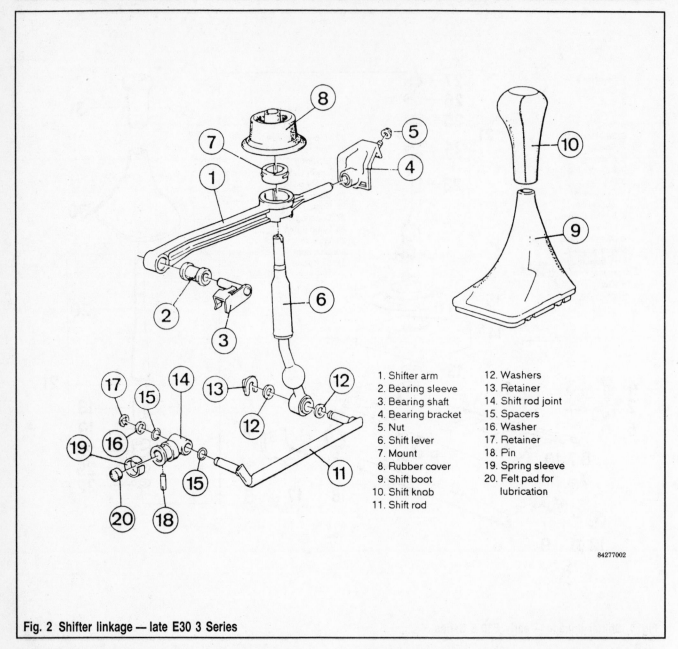

1. Shifter arm
2. Bearing sleeve
3. Bearing shaft
4. Bearing bracket
5. Nut
6. Shift lever
7. Mount
8. Rubber cover
9. Shift boot
10. Shift knob
11. Shift rod
12. Washers
13. Retainer
14. Shift rod joint
15. Spacers
16. Washer
17. Retainer
18. Pin
19. Spring sleeve
20. Felt pad for lubrication

84277002

Fig. 2 Shifter linkage — late E30 3 Series

vibration damper at this point in the drivetrain. This damper is mounted on the transmission output flange with bolts that are pressed into the damper. On these vehicles, unscrew and remove the nuts located behind the damper.

3. Loosen the threaded sleeve on the driveshaft. Get a special tool to hold the splined portion of the shaft while turning the sleeve.

4. Remove its mounting bolts and remove the center driveshaft mount. Then, bend the driveshaft down at the center and pull it off the transmission output flange. Keep the sections of the driveshaft from pulling apart and suspend it from the vehicle with wire.

5. Remove the retainer and washer, and pull out the shift selector rod.

6. Unscrew and remove the clutch slave cylinder and support it so the hydraulic line can remain connected.

7. Disconnect the wiring connector going to the backup light switch and pull the wires out of the harness.

8. Support the rear of the engine to prevent it from falling down at the rear.

9. Support the transmission from underneath in a secure manner. Remove mounting bolts and remove the crossmember holding the rear of the transmission to the body. Then, lower the transmission onto the front axle carrier.

10. Use a screwdriver to pry the shift arm spring clip up off the boss on the transmission case and swing it upward. Then, pull out the shift shaft pin.

11. Using the proper tool, remove the bolts holding the transmission flywheel housing to the engine at the front. If there is a separate clutch bellhousing, remove the transmission to bellhousing bolts. Make sure to retain the washers with the bolts. Pull the transmission rearward to slide the input shaft out of the clutch disc and then lower the transmission and remove from the vehicle.

To install:

12. Install the transmission in position under the vehicle. Align the input shaft and install the transmission, note the following points:

a. Coat the input shaft splines and flywheel housing guide pins with a light coating of suitable grease. Coat the release bearing interior groove with grease.

b. Make sure the front mounting bolts are installed with their washers. For hex head bolts, torque the M8 bolts to 16-19.5 ft. lbs. (22-27 Nm), torque the M10 bolts to 34-37 ft. lbs. (47-51 Nm), torque the M12 bolts to 48-59 ft. lbs. (66-82 Nm). For Torx® head bolts, torque the M8 bolts to 14.5-17 ft. lbs. (20-24 Nm), torque the M10 bolts to 27.5-34 ft. lbs. (38-47 Nm), torque the M12 bolts to 52-58 ft. lbs. (70-80 Nm).

c. Replace the shift arm and press the spring clip into place.

d. Install the clutch slave cylinder.

e. When installing the driveshaft center bearing, preload it forward 0.157-0.236 inch Check the driveshaft alignment with an appropriate tool such. Replace the nuts and then torque the center mount bolts to 16-17 ft. lbs. (21-23 Nm).

f. Torque the M10-8.8 flexible coupling bolts to 35 ft. lbs. (48 Nm). Torque the M10-10.9 flexible coupling bolts to 52 ft. lbs. (72 Nm).

g. Torque the driveshaft threaded sleeve to 12 ft. lbs. (17 Nm) after it complete installation.

h. Fill the transmission with proper lubricant.

E34 5 Series

1. Disconnect the negative battery cable. Raise and safely support the vehicle. Remove the exhaust system. Remove the attaching bolts and remove the heat shield mounted just to the rear of the transmission on the floorpan.

2. Support the transmission securely from underneath. Then, remove the crossmember that supports it at the rear from the body by removing the mounting bolts on both sides.

3. Using wrenches on both the bolt heads and on the nuts, remove the bolts passing through the vibration damper and front universal joint at the front of the driveshaft.

4. Remove its mounting bolts and remove the center driveshaft mount. Then, bend the driveshaft down at the center and pull it off the transmission output flange. Keep the sections of the driveshaft from pulling apart and suspend it from the vehicle with wire.

5. Pull out the circlip, slide off the washer, and then pull the shift selector rod off the transmission shift shaft. Disconnect the backup light switch.

6. Lower the transmission slightly for access. Then, use a small prybar to lift the spring out of the holder on the bracket and then raise the arm. Pull out the shift shaft bolt.

7. Remove the upper and lower attaching nuts and remove the clutch slave cylinder, supporting it so the hydraulic line need not be disconnected.

8. Unscrew the bolts fastening the transmission to the bell housing. Use a Torx® wrench to remove the bolts. Make sure to retain the washer with each bolt to ensure that they can be readily removed later, if necessary. Pull the transmission rearward until the input shaft has disengaged from the clutch disc and then lower and remove the transmission.

To install:

9. Install the transmission in position under the vehicle. Align the input shaft and install the transmission. Follow these procedures:

a. Coat the input shaft splines and flywheel housing guide pins with a light coating of suitable grease. Coat the release bearing interior groove with grease.

b. Make sure the front mounting bolts are installed with their washers. For hex head bolts, torque the M8 bolts to 16-19.5 ft. lbs. (22-27 Nm), torque the M10 bolts to 34-37 ft. lbs. (47-51 Nm), torque the M12 bolts to 48-59 ft. lbs. (66-82 Nm). For Torx® head bolts, torque the M8 bolts to 14.5-17 ft. lbs. (20-24 Nm), torque the M10 bolts to 27.5-34 ft. lbs. (38-47 Nm), torque the M12 bolts to 52-58 ft. lbs. (70-80 Nm).

c. Replace the shift arm and press the spring clip into place.

d. Install the clutch slave cylinder.

e. When installing the driveshaft center bearing, preload it forward 0.157-0.236 inch Check the driveshaft alignment with an appropriate tool such. Replace the nuts and then torque the center mount bolts to 16-17 ft. lbs. (21-23 Nm).

f. Torque the M10-8.8 flexible coupling bolts to 35 ft. lbs. (48 Nm). Torque the M10-10.9 flexible coupling bolts to 52 ft. lbs. (72 Nm).

g. Torque the driveshaft threaded sleeve to 12 ft. lbs. (17 Nm) after it complete installation.

h. Fill the transmission with proper lubricant.

CASE REMOVAL

260 Series Transmissions

▶ See Figures 3, 4 and 5

1. Remove the drain plug and drain the fluid from the transmission. Remove the transmission.

2. Disconnect the spring and remove the release bearing and arm.

3. Remove the bolts holding the release bearing sleeve to the transmission case. Save the shims for replacement.

4. Remove the reverse light switch from the side of the transmission. Remove the plug located forward of the reverse light switch and pull out the lockpin and spring. Note the position of the lockpin when removing.

5. Remove the snapring and washer from around the input shaft. Remove the bolt from the left side of the transmission case at the rear.

6. Drive out the pins from the rear housing joint. Remove the bolts noting the locations. The top, right bolt is 8x60mm.

7. Pull the front case off the transmission using tool 23 1 460 and 33 1 301 or equivalent. Do not hammer on the sides of the case to remove. The tools mount a plate to the release bearing sleeve threaded holes and use a slide hammer to evenly tap the front case off the rear housing.

To install:

8. Place the roller bearing on the lay shaft with the small end facing out. Coat the rollers with grease to facilitate assembly.

9. Clean the area in the front case where the reverse gear shaft mounts. Coat the area with sealing compound.

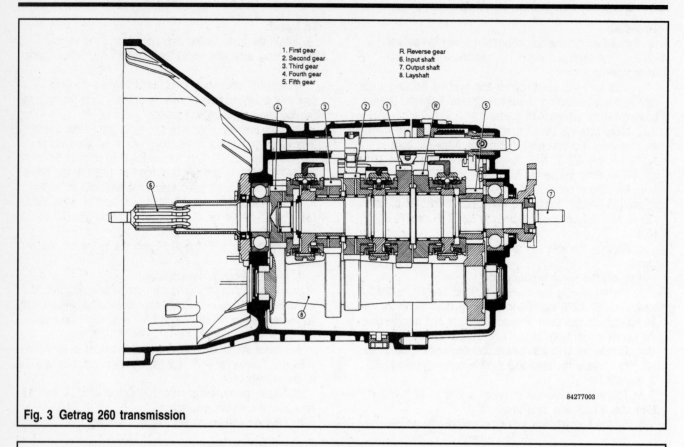

1. First gear
2. Second gear
3. Third gear
4. Fourth gear
5. Fifth gear

R. Reverse gear
6. Input shaft
7. Output shaft
8. Layshaft

84277003

Fig. 3 Getrag 260 transmission

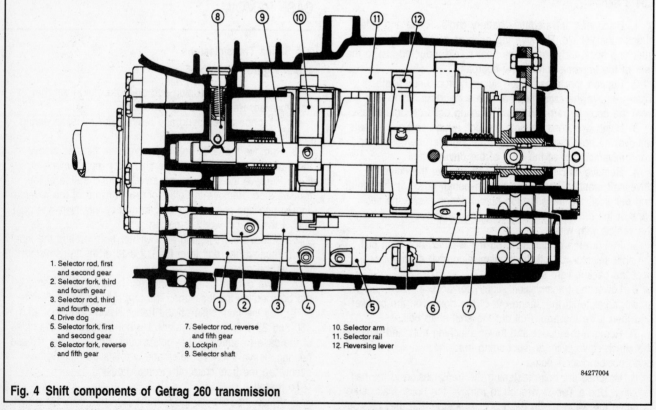

1. Selector rod, first and second gear
2. Selector fork, third and fourth gear
3. Selector rod, third and fourth gear
4. Drive dog
5. Selector fork, first and second gear
6. Selector fork, reverse and fifth gear

7. Selector rod, reverse and fifth gear
8. Lockpin
9. Selector shaft

10. Selector arm
11. Selector rail
12. Reversing lever

84277004

Fig. 4 Shift components of Getrag 260 transmission

10. Remove the input shaft bearing. Clean the mating faces and coat with a sealing compound.

11. Except with M30 engine, place the front case over the transmission. Align the intermediate shaft with the bearing race using the drain plug hole for access. Press on the input shaft

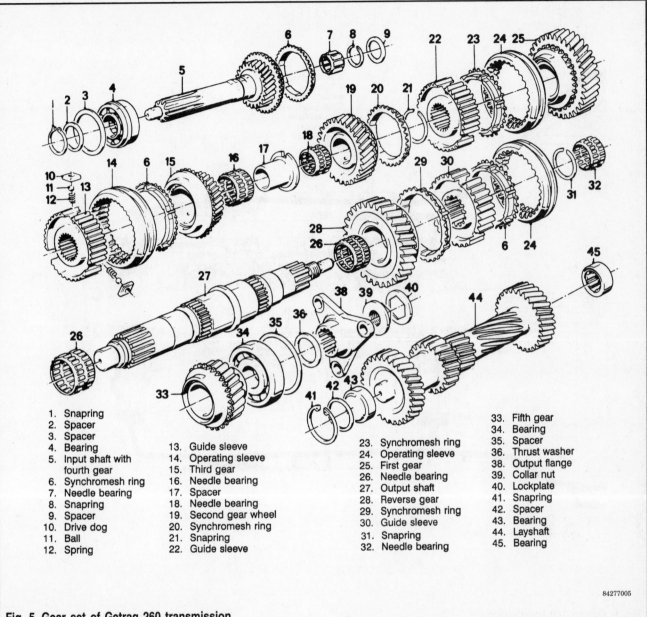

Fig. 5 Gear set of Getrag 260 transmission

1. Snapring
2. Spacer
3. Spacer
4. Bearing
5. Input shaft with fourth gear
6. Synchromesh ring
7. Needle bearing
8. Snapring
9. Spacer
10. Drive dog
11. Ball
12. Spring

13. Guide sleeve
14. Operating sleeve
15. Third gear
16. Needle bearing
17. Spacer
18. Needle bearing
19. Second gear wheel
20. Synchromesh ring
21. Snapring
22. Guide sleeve

23. Synchromesh ring
24. Operating sleeve
25. First gear
26. Needle bearing
27. Output shaft
28. Reverse gear
29. Synchromesh ring
30. Guide sleeve
31. Snapring
32. Needle bearing

33. Fifth gear
34. Bearing
35. Spacer
36. Thrust washer
38. Output flange
39. Collar nut
40. Lockplate
41. Snapring
42. Spacer
43. Bearing
44. Layshaft
45. Bearing

84277005

bearing with the protruding inner race side towards the gearset.

12. With M30 engine, install the input shaft bearing in the front case with the protruding side of the inner race towards the gearset. Heat the inner bearing race with a heat gun to 175°F. (80°C.), being careful of the plastic bearing cage. Slide the front case over the input shaft, aligning the intermediate shaft in the bearing race.

13. Torque the case mounting bolts to 16 ft. lbs. (22 Nm). Install the lock pin, spring and plug. Install the reverse light switch. Install the dowel pin in the case. Install the bolt in the side of the transmission case.

14. Install the shim(s) between the input shaft snapring and the bearing. Install the shims so the play is 0.0000-0.0035 inch (0.00-0.09mm).

15. Install the release bearing sleeve with the oil groove mounted in line with the oil bore in the transmission case. Measure the distance from the outer bearing race to the flange on the sleeve and adjust the play with shims to 0.0000-0.0035 inch (0.00-0.09mm). Torque the M6 bolts to 7 ft. lbs. (10 Nm), the M8x22 bolts to 13 ft. lbs. (18 Nm) and the M8x30 bolts to 18 ft. lbs. (25 Nm).

16. Fill the groove inside the release bearing with moly grease, except with the dual mass flywheel which uses Microlube® 261 or equivalent. Apply the same grease to the release arm pivot points. Install the release shaft and bearing.

240 Series Transmissions
▶ **See Figures 6 and 7**

1. Remove the drain plug and drain the fluid from the transmission. Remove the transmission.

2. Disconnect the spring and remove the release bearing and arm.

3. Remove the bolts holding the release bearing sleeve to the transmission case. Save the shims for replacement.

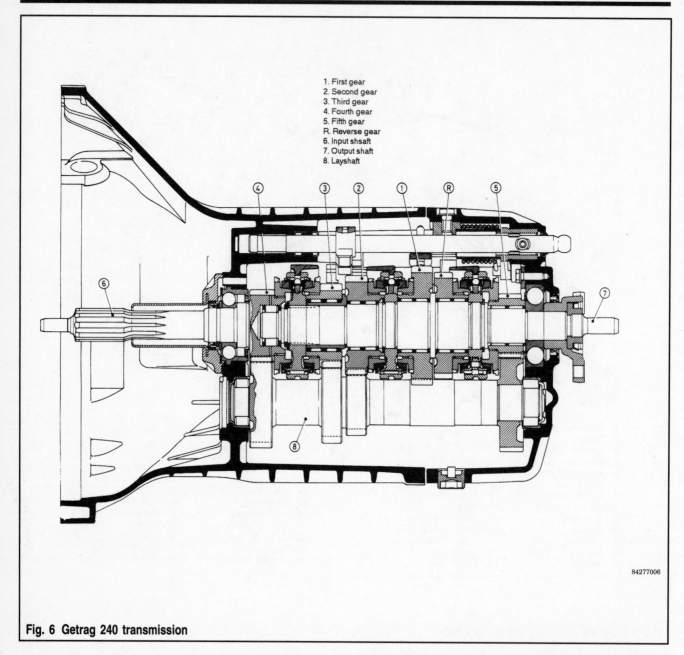

1. First gear
2. Second gear
3. Third gear
4. Fourth gear
5. Fifth gear
R. Reverse gear
6. Input shsaft
7. Output shaft
8. Layshaft

84277006

Fig. 6 Getrag 240 transmission

4. Remove the plug and pull out the lockpin and spring. Note the position of the lockpin when removing.

5. Remove the snapring and washer from around the input shaft. Use a bearing puller and pull the input shaft bearing from the case.

6. Drive out the pins from the rear housing joint. Remove the bolts noting the locations.

7. Pull the front case off the transmission. Do not hammer on the sides of the case to remove.

To install:

8. Clean the mating faces and coat with a sealing compound. Place the front case over the transmission. Heat the inner bearing race with a heat gun to 175°F. (80°C.), being careful of the plastic bearing cage. Press on the input shaft bearing until it seats.

9. Torque the case mounting bolts to 16 ft. lbs. (22 Nm). Install the lock pin, spring tand plug. Install the dowel pin in the case.

10. Install the release bearing sleeve with the oil groove mounted in line with the oil bore in the transmission case. Measure the distance from the outer bearing race to the flange on the sleeve and adjust the play with shims to 0.0000-0.0035 inch (0.00-0.09mm). Torque the M6 bolts to 7 ft. lbs. (10 Nm), the M8x22 bolts to 13 ft. lbs. (18 Nm) and the M8x30 bolts to 18 ft. lbs. (25 Nm). Use sealer on the flange.

11. Fill the groove inside the release bearing with moly grease, except with the dual mass flywheel which uses Microlube® 261 or equivalent. Apply the same grease to the release arm pivot points. Install the release shaft and bearing.

265 Series Transmissions

1. Remove the drain plug and drain the fluid from the transmission. Remove the transmission.

2. Place the shifter shaft into 3rd gear position and remove the shift coupling from the shaft by driving out the pin. Disconnect the spring and remove the release bearing and arm.

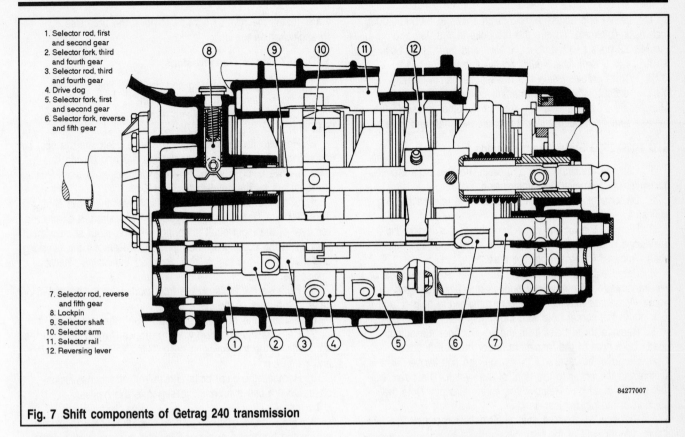

1. Selector rod, first and second gear
2. Selector fork, third and fourth gear
3. Selector rod, third and fourth gear
4. Drive dog
5. Selector fork, first and second gear
6. Selector fork, reverse and fifth gear

7. Selector rod, reverse and fifth gear
8. Lockpin
9. Selector shaft
10. Selector arm
11. Selector rail
12. Reversing lever

84277007

Fig. 7 Shift components of Getrag 240 transmission

3. Remove the bolts holding the release bearing sleeve to the transmission case. Save the shims for replacement.

4. Remove the reverse light switch. Remove the plug and pull out the lockpin and spring. Note the position of the lockpin when removing.

5. Remove the snapring and washer from around the input shaft.

6. Drive out the pins from the rear housing joint. Remove the bolts noting the locations.

7. Pull the front case off the transmission. Do not hammer on the sides of the case to remove.

To install:

8. Clean the mating faces and coat with a sealing compound. Place the front case over the transmission. Heat the inner bearing race with a heat gun to 175°F. (80°C.), being careful of the plastic bearing cage. Draw up the input shaft to seat the bearing.

9. Torque the case mounting bolts to 16 ft. lbs. (22 Nm). Install the lock pin, spring and plug. Install the dowel pin in the case. Install the reverse light switch.

10. Install the release bearing sleeve with the oil groove mounted in line with the oil bore in the transmission case. Measure the distance from the outer bearing race to the flange on the sleeve and adjust the play with shims to 0.0000-0.0035 inch (0.00-0.09mm). Torque the M6 bolts to 7 ft. lbs. (10 Nm), the M8x22 bolts to 13 ft. lbs. (18 Nm) and the M8x30 bolts to 18 ft. lbs. (25 Nm). Use sealer on the flange.

11. Fill the groove inside the release bearing with moly grease, except with the dual mass flywheel which uses Microlube® 261 or equivalent. Apply the same grease to the release arm pivot points. Install the release shaft and bearing.

280 Series Transmissions

1. Remove the drain plug and drain the fluid from the transmission. Remove the transmission.

2. Disconnect the spring and remove the release bearing and arm.

3. Remove the bolts holding the release bearing sleeve to the transmission case. Save the shims for replacement.

4. Remove the snapring and washer from around the input shaft. Remove the bolts from the cover under the input shaft. Pry out the cover and remove the shim. Engage 4th gear and hold the output flange. Remove the bolt from under the cover.

5. Remove the reverse light switch. Remove the plug and pull out the lockpin and spring. Note the position of the lockpin when removing.

6. Drive out the pins from the rear housing joint. Remove the bolts noting the locations.

7. Pull the front case off the transmission. Do not hammer on the sides of the case to remove.

To install:

8. Clean the mating faces and coat with a sealing compound. Place the front case over the transmission. Heat the inner bearing race with a heat gun to 175°F. (80°C.), being careful of the plastic bearing cage. Draw up the input shaft to seat the bearing.

9. Torque the case mounting bolts to 16 ft. lbs. (22 Nm). Install the lock pin, spring and plug. Install the dowel pin in the case. Install the reverse light switch.

10. Install the bolt in the end of the shaft with thread sealer. Install the shim and sealing cover.

11. Install the release bearing sleeve with the oil groove mounted in line with the oil bore in the transmission case. Measure the distance from the outer bearing race to the flange

on the sleeve and adjust the play with shims to 0.0000-0.0035 inch (0.00-0.09mm). Torque the M6 bolts to 7 ft. lbs. (10 Nm), the M8x22 bolts to 13 ft. lbs. (18 Nm) and the M8x30 bolts to 18 ft. lbs. (25 Nm). Use sealer on the flange.

12. Fill the groove inside the release bearing with moly grease, except with the dual mass flywheel which uses Microlube® 261 or equivalent. Apply the same grease to the release arm pivot points. Install the release shaft and bearing.

S5D 200G/250G Series Transmissions

1. Remove the drain plug and drain the fluid from the transmission. Remove the transmission.

2. Disconnect the spring and remove the release bearing and arm.

3. Remove the locking plate from the output flange. Hold the flange and remove the nut. Pull the flange off the output shaft. Remove the seal from the bore.

4. Remove the 2 bolts holding the cover at the rear top of the transmission. Remove the springs and balls from the bores. A magnet may be needed to remove the balls. Place a lock pin in the center hole with the transmission in 2nd gear.

5. Remove the 4 bolts from the cover under the output shaft. Take note of the insulators under the bolt heads.

6. Remove the reverse light switch, the bolt above the switch and the cover to the right of the switch. The cover will need to be pried out. Remove the spring and pin. Note the position of the pin for installation.

7. Remove the reverse gear shaft bolts located on the slave cylinder side of the transmission.

8. Loosen the case mounting bolts and press out the dowel pins. Pull off the rear transmission housing.

To install:

9. Clean the mating surfaces of the cases and slide the case together. Install bolts and new seals to the cover under the output shaft. Drive in the dowel pins. Install the case bolts and torque to 16 ft. lbs. (22 Nm).

10. Install the reverse gear shaft bolts with threadlocker. Install new seals for the shifter rod and the output shaft. Install the output flange and nut. Torque to 123 ft. lbs. (170 Nm), loosen, then torque to 87 ft. lbs. (120 Nm). Install the lock plate.

11. Install the Locking balls and the springs. Install the springs and dowels. Install the cover plate with the bolts and threadlocker.

12. Install the catch pin with the roller horizontal. Install the spring and end cap.

13. Install the reverse light switch and the bolt. Use threadlocker on the bolt.

S5D 310Z Series Transmissions

1. Remove the drain plug and drain the fluid from the transmission. Remove the transmission.

2. Disconnect the spring and remove the release bearing and arm.

3. Remove the release bearing sleeve. Remove the seal by punching holes where the indentations are and driving one side in while using a screw to press out the other side. Pull the seal out by the screw.

4. Slide tool 23 2 380 or equivalent over the input shaft. This tool is a sleeve that fits over the input shaft. It allows the removal of the input shaft snapring over the input shaft without scratching the coating on the input shaft. Remove the snapring and place it on the tool sleeve. Remove the sleeve. Remove the spacer.

5. Remove the bolts on the front portion of the transmission case in the area of the slave cylinder.

6. Remove the reverse light switch and the bolt above it.

7. Remove the snapring from the forward most bore on the right side of the transmission case. Remove the cover, spring and catch pin.

8. Remove the case bolts and pull off the transmission case. Do not use a hammer to separate the halves.

To install:

9. Use a piece of string to hold the 5th/reverse gear shift arm in the horizontal position. Slide the case on to the dowel pins. Use 2 bolts to center the case. Use too 23 2 293 and 23 2 290 or equivalent, to draw the case together only enough so the string can still be removed.

10. Install the 5th/reverse gear shift arm bolt hand tight. Remove the string and draw the case together. Install the case bolts and torque to 16 ft. lbs. (22 Nm).

11. Install the side bolts with sealer and tighten.

12. Install the catch pin, spring, cover and snapring. Install the reverse light switch.

13. Install the input shaft spacer and snapring. Use the shaft protection tool used in the removal of the snapring. Install a new seal lubricated with ATF. Install the release bearing sleeve and torque the M6 bolts to 7 ft. lbs. (10 Nm), the M8x22 bolts to 13 ft. lbs. (18 Nm) and the M8x30 bolts to 18 ft. lbs. (25 Nm).

CLUTCH

❋❋CAUTION

The clutch disk contains asbestos, which causes some forms of lung disease and may be a cancer causing agent. Do not clean the clutch or housing with compressed air. Use a damp rag to wipe off surfaces and throw away the rag. Use commercial available brake cleaners if a solvent is necessary. Avoid inhaling any dust from the clutch surfaces.

Clutch Pedal

HEIGHT ADJUSTMENT

E30 3 Series
◗ See Figure 8

1. Measure from the clutch pedal to the firewall should be 9.96-10.39 inch (253-264 mm).

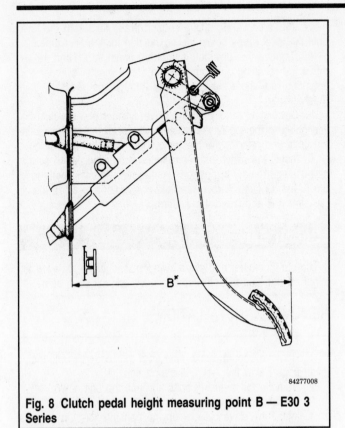

Fig. 8 Clutch pedal height measuring point B — E30 3 Series

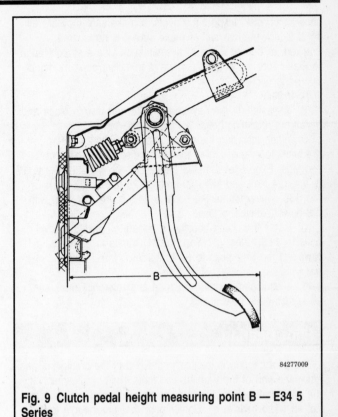

Fig. 9 Clutch pedal height measuring point B — E34 5 Series

2. If the measurement is not correct, rotate the eccentric bolt at the master cylinder pushrod connection point. The dot on the bolt must be in line with the pushrod.

3. If the eccentric bolt cannot bring the pedal height to specification, there is a damaged part that needs replacing.

E36 3 Series

There is no provision for pedal height adjustment. If the pedal height is incorrect, there is a damaged part that needs replacement. The height from the pedal to the firewall should be 10.23-10.63 inch (260-270 mm).

E34 5 Series
◆ See Figure 9

1. Measure from the clutch pedal to the firewall should be 10.43-10.83 inch (265-275 mm).

2. If the measurement is not correct, rotate the eccentric bolt at the master cylinder pushrod connection point. The dot on the bolt must be in line with the pushrod.

3. If the eccentric bolt cannot bring the pedal height to specification, there is a damaged part that needs replacing.

REMOVAL & INSTALLATION

1. Remove the lower trim from the dash panel.
2. Disconnect the clutch return spring.
3. Disconnect the master cylinder connection eccentric bolt.
4. Remove the shaft mounting nut and slide the pedal off the shaft.

5. Install the pedal and connect the master cylinder, return spring and the shaft nut. The dot on the eccentric bolts must align with master cylinder pushrod. Check the pedal height.

6. Torque the shaft nut to 20 ft. lbs. (27 Nm). Torque the eccentric bolt nut to 16 ft. lbs. (22 Nm).

Clutch Assembly

REMOVAL & INSTALLATION

1. Disconnect the negative battery cable. Raise and safely support the vehicle. Remove the heat shield and then the mounting bolts. Disconnect the speed and reference mark sensors at the flywheel housing. Mark the plugs for reinstallation.

2. Remove the transmission.

3. If equipped with a 265/6 transmission (without an integral clutch housing), remove the clutch housing. A Torx® socket is required.

4. Prevent the flywheel from turning, using a locking tool.

5. Loosen the mounting bolts one after another gradually, 1-1½ turns at a time, to relieve tension from the clutch.

6. Remove the mounting bolts, clutch, and drive plate. Note the mounted direction of the drive plate for installation. Coat the splines of the transmission input shaft with Molykote® Long-term 2 for standard flywheels, or Microlube® GL 261 for dual mass flywheels, or equivalent. Make sure the clutch pilot bearing, located in the center of the crankshaft, turns easily. Replace the pilot bearing, if necessary.

7. Check the clutch driven disc for excess wear or cracks. Check the integral torsional damping springs, used with standard flywheels only, for tight fit. Dual mass flywheels use a

solid clutch disk. Inspect the rivets to make sure they are all tight. Check the flywheel to make sure it is not scored, cracked, or burned, even at a small spot. Use a straight edge to make sure the contact surface is true. Replace any defective parts.

To install:

8. To install, fit the new clutch plate and disc in place and install the mounting bolts.

9. When installing the clutch retaining bolts turn them in gradually to evenly tighten the clutch disc and to prevent warpage. Except for the S38 engine, torque M8-8.8 bolts to 17 ft. lbs. (24 Nm) and M8-10.9 bolts to 25 ft. lbs. (35 Nm). On the S38 engine torque the bolts to 24.5 ft. lbs. (34 Nm) with the dowel sleeves installed.

10. Install the clutch housing, if separate. Torque the M8 bolts to 19.5 ft. lbs. (27 Nm), the M10 bolts to 37 ft. lbs. (51 Nm) and the M12 bolts to 62 ft. lbs. (86 Nm). Install the transmission.

11. If equipped, install the speed and reference mark sensors. Install the heat shield.

Pilot Bearing

The pilot bearing is located in the end of the crankshaft and holds the end of the transmission input shaft in alignment. If the pilot shaft seizes, the transmission will grind into gear on not shift into gear at all. Sometimes what are thought to be transmission problems can be cured with a new pilot bearing, if found to be stuck or sticking. It is always a good idea to replace the pilot bearing along with the clutch and release bearing.

REMOVAL & INSTALLATION

1. Remove the transmission and clutch.
2. Use a small bore bearing puller to remove the bearing from the end of the crankshaft. Note the order of washers and spacers when removing.
3. Clean the bore in the crankshaft of the old grease.
4. Lubricate the new bearing with 1 gram of grease and drive into the crankshaft bore.
5. Install the washers and spacers onto the crankshaft. Clean any excess grease from the surrounding area.
6. Install the clutch and transmission.

Clutch Master Cylinder

The clutch master and slave cylinders should be replaced as a pair. If one unit fails, the other usually will fail soon after.

REMOVAL & INSTALLATION

1. Remove the necessary trim panel or carpet.
2. Disconnect the pushrod at the clutch pedal.
3. Remove the cap on the reservoir tank. On some vehicles, there is a clutch master cylinder reservoir, while on others there is a common reservoir shared with the brake master cylinder. Remove the float container, if equipped. Re-

move the screen and remove enough brake fluid from the tank until the level drops below the connection for the filler pipe.

4. Remove the lower/left instrument panel trim. Then, remove the retaining nut from the end of the master cylinder actuating rod where the bolt passes through the pedal mechanism.

5. Disconnect the line to the slave cylinder and the fluid fill line going to the top of the master cylinder. Remove the retaining bolts and remove the master cylinder from the firewall.

6. Install the clutch master cylinder in position. Make sure all bushings remain in position. Torque the mounting bolts to 6.5 ft. lbs. (9 Nm). Torque the fluid connections to 12 ft. lbs. (16 Nm). Fill and bleed the system.

Clutch Slave Cylinder

The clutch master and slave cylinders should be replaced as a pair. If one unit fails, the other usually will fail soon after.

REMOVAL & INSTALLATION

1. Remove enough brake fluid from the reservoir until the level drops below the refill line connection.
2. Remove the retaining bolts and pull the unit down.
3. Disconnect the line and remove the slave cylinder.
4. Install the slave cylinder on the transmission. On engines equipped with the dual mass flywheel, make sure a larger cylinder with a diameter of 0.874 inch (22.2 mm) is used instead of the usual cylinder, diameter 0.812 inch (20.64 mm). Torque the bolts to 17 ft. lbs. (24 Nm). Torque the fluid connections to 12 ft. lbs. (16 Nm).
5. Make sure to install the cylinder with the bleed screw facing down. When installing the front pushrod, coat it with the proper anti-seize compound. Bleed the system.

Clutch Hydraulic System

BLEEDING

1. Fill the reservoir.
2. Connect a bleeder hose from the bleeder screw to a container filled with brake fluid so air cannot be drawn in during bleeding procedures.
3. Pump the clutch pedal about 10 times and then hold it down.
4. Open the bleeder screw and watch the stream of escaping fluid. When no more bubbles escape, close the bleeder screw and tighten it.
5. Release the clutch pedal and repeat the above procedure until no more bubbles can be seen when the screw is opened.
6. If this procedure fails to produce a bubble-free stream:
   a. Pull the slave cylinder off the transmission without disconnecting the fluid line.

➡**Do not depress the clutch pedal while the slave cylinder is dismounted.**

b. Depress the pushrod in the cylinder until it hits the internal stop and release. This will force any trapped air up into the reservoir. Then, reinstall the cylinder and bleed again.

AUTOMATIC TRANSMISSION

Identification

▶ See Figure 10

Most of the automatic transmissions used by BMW are manufactured by ZF. They are 4 speed overdrive units with torque converter lockup and electronic controls. They can be identified by a single oil sump.

All of the M50 engine and some of the M42 engine equipped vehicles are supplied with transmissions manufactured by Hydra-Matic. The Turbo-Hydra-Matic units also feature 4 speeds with a lockup torque converter and electronic controls. They can be identified by a dual oil sump.

A variety of transmissions are used, usage being determined by the chassis and engine combination. By chassis and engine, this is the application:

• E30 3 Series   M20 engine — 4HP 22   M42 engine — 4HP 22   S14 engine — not available
• E36 3 Series   M42 engine — THM-R1   M50 engine — THM-R1
• E34 5 Series   M20 engine — 4HP 22   M30 engine — 4HP 22   M50 engine — THM-R1   S38 engine — not available

7. Check the level of the fluid in the reservoir and fill to the line.

FLUID PAN

REMOVAL & INSTALLATION

▶ See Figure 11

On the THM-R1 transmission remove both sumps and replace both gaskets. This will more completely drain the system.

1. Raise and safely support the vehicle in a level plane. Place a drain pan under the transmission sump. Remove the dipstick on vehicles so equipped. On vehicles with locking dipsticks, tilt the top of the dipstick to unlock.

2. Loosen and remove the oil filler tube from the sump pan if not equipped with a drain plug. Be ready to catch fluid as it drains.

3. Remove the sump pan drain plug and catch the draining fluid.

4. Note the positions of the pan holder at each bolt and loosen and remove the bolts.

5. Remove the pan and gasket. Remove the screws from the filter. Note their positions. Check that the O-ring from the filter did not stick to the transmission valve body.

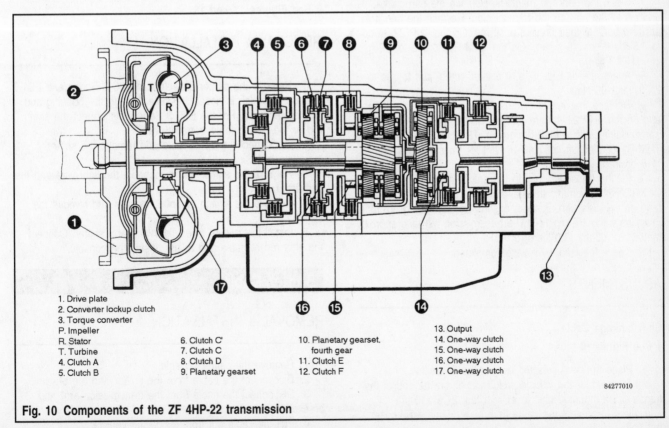

1. Drive plate
2. Converter lockup clutch
3. Torque converter
P. Impeller
R. Stator
T. Turbine
4. Clutch A
5. Clutch B
6. Clutch C'
7. Clutch C
8. Clutch D
9. Planetary gearset
10. Planetary gearset, fourth gear
11. Clutch E
12. Clutch F
13. Output
14. One-way clutch
15. One-way clutch
16. One-way clutch
17. One-way clutch

84277010

Fig. 10 Components of the ZF 4HP-22 transmission

84277011

Fig. 11 Both pans should be removed on the THM-R1

6. Install the new filter and O-ring. Replace the screws in their original positions. On the 4HP 22, torque to 6 ft. lbs. (8 Nm). On the THM-R1, torque to 13-15 ft. lbs. (18-21 Nm).

7. Clean the pan and magnets. Replace the pan gasket and install the pan on the transmission. Replace the pan holders and bolts at their original positions. On the 4HP 22, torque to 4.5-5.0 ft. lbs. (6-7 Nm). On the THM-R1, torque to 7-9 ft. lbs. (10-13 Nm).

8. Attach the oil filler tube, if disconnected, and torque to 71 ft. lbs. (98 Nm).

9. Replace the gasket or crush washer on the drain plug and on the 4HP 22, torque to 11-12 ft. lbs. (15-17 Nm) for transmissions with a M10 drain plug, 18 ft. lbs. (25 Nm) on the THM-R1 or 29-33 ft. lbs. (40-46 Nm) for transmissions with a M18 drain plug.

10. Fill the transmission with the proper amount of DEXRON®II automatic transmission fluid through the dipstick tube on vehicles with dipsticks or through the fill plug on transmissions without a dipstick. The transmission will take approximately 3.2 quarts (3.0 liters) of ATF.

11. Check the fluid level once completed.

ADJUSTMENTS

Shift Linkage Cable

▶ **See Figure 12**

1. Place the gear selector lever in the **P** position.
2. From under the vehicle, hold the bolt on the end of the transmission mounted shift lever with tool 24 5 210 or equivalent to prevent the cable from being damaged. Loosen the bolt.

3. Push the transmission mounted shift lever forward while pushing the cable rearwards.
4. Torque the shift lever bolt to 7 — 9 ft. lbs. (10 — 12 Nm).

Shift Linkage Rod

▶ **See Figure 13**

1. Disconnect the shift rod from the shifter lever
2. Place the shifter into neutral and the tranmission lever into neutral.
3. Press the shifter forward against the neutral gate lockout and adjust the shifter rod to fit into the shifter lever.
4. Shorten the shift rod effective length by screwing in the shift rod pin 1-2 turns. Attach the pin to the lever.

Throttle Linkage

▶ **See Figures 14, 15 and 16**

1. On the injection system throttle body, loosen the 2 locknuts at the end of the throttle cable and adjust the cable until there is a play of 0.010-0.030 inches.
2. Loosen the locknut and lower the kickdown stop under the accelerator pedal. Have someone depress the accelerator pedal until the transmission detent can be felt. Then, back the kickdown stop back out until it just touches the pedal.
3. Check that the distance from the seal at the throttle body end of the cable housing is at least 1.732 inch from the rear end of the threaded sleeve. If this dimension checks out, tighten all the locknuts.

Shifter Switch

▶ **See Figures 17 and 18**

REMOVAL & INSTALLATION

1. Remove the center console. On E36 3 Series and E34 5 Series the switch is now accessible through the opening and can be removed. For the E30 3 Series, disconnect the shaft rod or the shifter cable from the lever.
2. Disconnect the switch plug and remove the shifter mounting bolts.
3. Remove the shifter and disconnect the light wire and the shift lever.
4. Remove the switch mounting screws and remove the switch.
5. Install the switch, lever, light wire and shifter. Connect the shift rod or cable and adjust. Install the console.

Shifter Cable

REMOVAL & INSTALLATION

1. Remove the center console.
2. Disconnect the cable from the shifter and the bracket.
3. Disconnect the cable from the transmission arm and bracket.
4. Pull the cable out from inside the vehicle.

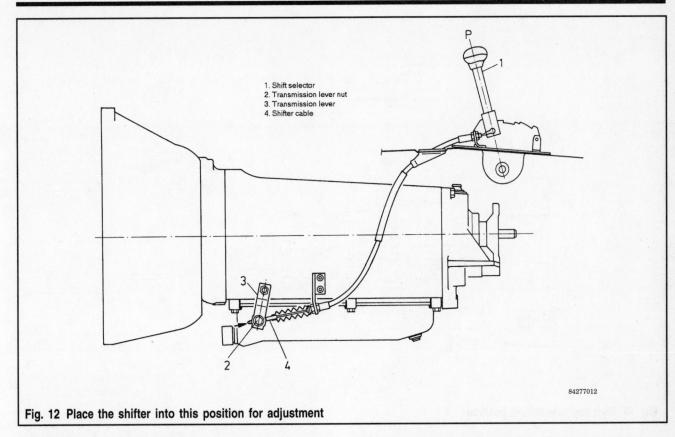

1. Shift selector
2. Transmission lever nut
3. Transmission lever
4. Shifter cable

84277012

Fig. 12 Place the shifter into this position for adjustment

5. Install the cable and adjust.

Rear Output Seal

REMOVAL & INSTALLATION

1. Disconnect the driveshaft from the output flange and support with wire.
2. Counterhold the output flange and remove the nut. Pull off the output flange.
3. Use a seal puller to remove the seal.
4. Install the new seal with the lip facing in. Use a seal driver to install.
5. Install the output flange and torque the nut to 72 ft. lbs. (100 Nm). Install the driveshaft.

Transmission

REMOVAL & INSTALLATION

E30 3 Series

➡To perform this operation, a support for the transmission, BMW tool 24 0 120 and 00 2 020 or equivalent and a tool for tightening the driveshaft locking ring, BMW tool 26 1 040 or equivalent, are required.

1. Disconnect the battery ground cable. Loosen the throttle cable adjusting nuts, release the cable tension, and disconnect the cable at the throttle lever. Then, remove (and retain) the nuts, and pull the cable housing out of the bracket.
2. Disconnect the exhaust system at the manifold and hangers and lower it aside. Remove the hanger that runs across under the driveshaft. Remove the exhaust heat shield from under the center of the vehicle.
3. On the 325iX, remove the transfer case from the rear of the transmission.
4. Drain the transmission oil and discard it. Remove the oil filler neck. Disconnect the oil cooler lines at the transmission by unscrewing the flare nuts and plug the open connections.
5. Support the transmission with the proper tools. Separate the torque converter housing from the transmission by removing the Torx® bolts with the proper tool from behind and the regular bolts from underneath. Retain the washers used with the Torx® bolts.
6. On the 325iX, disconnect the front driveshaft.
7. Remove bolts attaching the torque converter housing to the engine, making sure to retain the spacer used behind one of the bolts. Then, loosen the mounting bolts for the oil level switch just enough so the plate can be removed while pushing the switch mounting bracket to one side.
8. Remove the bolts attaching the torque converter to the drive plate. Turn the flywheel as necessary to gain access to each of the bolts, which are spaced at equal intervals around it. Make sure to re-use the same bolts and retain the washers.
9. To remove the speed and reference mark sensors, remove the attaching bolt for each and remove each sensor. Keep the sensors clean.
10. Turn the bayonet type electrical connector counterclockwise and then pull the plug out of the socket. Then, lift the wiring harness out of the harness bails.

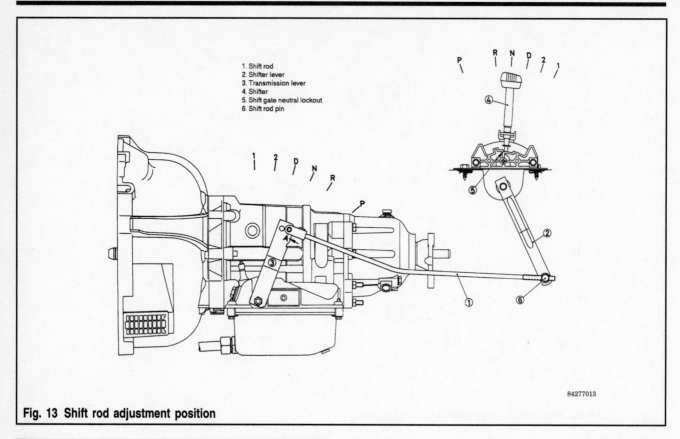

1. Shift rod
2. Shifter lever
3. Transmission lever
4. Shifter
5. Shift gate neutral lockout
6. Shift rod pin

84277013

Fig. 13 Shift rod adjustment position

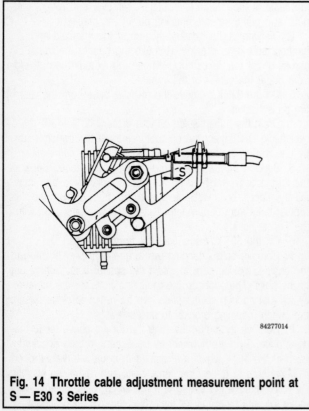

84277014

Fig. 14 Throttle cable adjustment measurement point at S — E30 3 Series

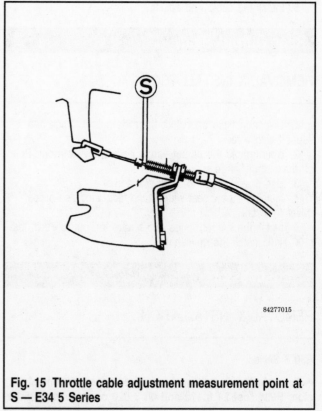

84277015

Fig. 15 Throttle cable adjustment measurement point at S — E34 5 Series

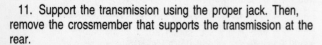

11. Support the transmission using the proper jack. Then, remove the crossmember that supports the transmission at the rear.

12. Disconnect the transmission shift rod. Then, remove the nuts and then the through bolts from the damper-type U-joint at the front of the transmission.

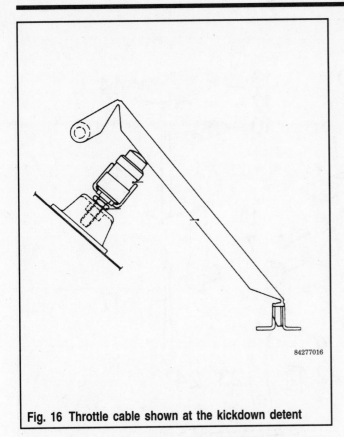

84277016

Fig. 16 Throttle cable shown at the kickdown detent

13. Unscrew the driveshaft spline locking ring at the center mount, if equipped, using the special tool designed for this purpose. Then, remove the bolts and remove the center mount. Bend the driveshaft downward and pull it off the centering pin. Suspend it with wire from the underside of the vehicle.

14. Lower the transmission as far as possible. Then, remove all the Torx® or standard type bolts attaching the transmission to the engine.

15. Remove the small grill from the bottom of the transmission. Then press the converter off with a large prybar passing through this opening while sliding the transmission out.

To install:

16. Install the transmission in position under the vehicle and raise it into position. Observe the following points:

a. Make sure the converter is fully installed onto the transmission — so the ring on the front is inside the edge of the case. Only use M10x16mm bolts as originally equipped or damage will occur.

b. When reinstalling the driveshaft, tighten the lockring with the proper tool.

c. Make sure to replace the self-locking nuts on the driveshaft flexible joint and to hold the bolts still while tightening the nuts to keep from distorting it.

d. When installing the center mount, preload it forward from its most natural position 0.157-0.236 inches.

e. When reconnecting the bayonet type electrical connector, make sure the alignment marks are aligned after the plug it twisted into its final position.

f. When reinstalling the speed and reference mark sensors, inspect the O-rings used on the sensors and install new ones, if necessary. Make sure to install the speed sen-

sor into the bore marked D and the reference mark sensor, which is marked with a ring, into the bore marked B.

g. Torque the crossmember mounting bolts to 16-17 ft. lbs. (21-23 Nm).

h. If O-rings are used with the transmission oil cooler connections, replace them.

i. Adjust the throttle cables.

E36 3 Series

1. Disconnect the negative battery terminal. Drain the transmission fluid and discard. Do not reuse the old oil. Remove the exhaust system.

2. Mark the mounted position of the crossmember under the driveshaft, the remove.

3. Disconnect the driveshaft from the output flange of the transmission. Loosen the driveshaft spline lockring and remove the center support from the floorpan. Position the driveshaft out of the way and support with wire.

4. Disconnect the shifter cable from the transmission and bracket. Disconnect the connectors from the transmission and the speed sender.

5. Pull out the access plug from the side of the case to reach the torque converter mounting bolts. Use tool 24 1 110 or equivalent to remove the bolts.

6. Place a transmission jack under the transmission and support. Disconnect the oxygen sensor cable and remove the transmission crossmember. Disconnect the oil cooler lines and clamps.

7. Remove the bolts from the transmission to engine joint. Pull the transmission back with the torque converter and lower.

To install:

8. Check the condition of the dowel sleeves and flexplate.

9. Align the torque converter and the flexplate. Place the transmission into position and bolt to the engine. With hexhead bolts, torque the M8 bolts to 17 ft. lbs. (24 Nm), the M10 bolts to 33 ft. lbs. (45 Nm) and the M12 bolts to 57 — 62 ft. lbs. (78 — 86 Nm). With Torx® bolts, torque the M8 bolts to 15 ft. lbs. (21 Nm), the M12 bolts to 52 ft. lbs. (72 Nm).

10. Torque the M10x16mm toque converter bolts to 33 ft. lbs. (45 Nm) with tool 24 1 110 or equivalent.

11. Install the oil cooler lines after checking the condition of the O-rings. Install the crossmember and wiring connections.

12. Connect the shifter cable and adjust. Install the driveshaft. Preload the center bearing 0.157 — 0.236 in (4 — 6 mm) forward. Torque the flange bolts to 59 ft. lbs. (81 Nm). After completing the installation, torque the spline locking ring to 12 ft. lbs. (17 Nm).

13. Install the crossmember over the driveshaft in the original mounting position. Install the exhaust system and splashguards. Fill the transmission and check the level. Connect the negative battery terminal.

E34 5 Series

4HP 22

1. Disconnect the battery ground cable. Loosen the throttle cable adjusting nuts, release the cable tension, and disconnect the cable at the throttle lever. Then, remove (and retain) the nuts, and pull the cable housing out of the bracket.

2. Disconnect the exhaust system at the manifold and hangers and lower it aside. Remove the hanger that runs

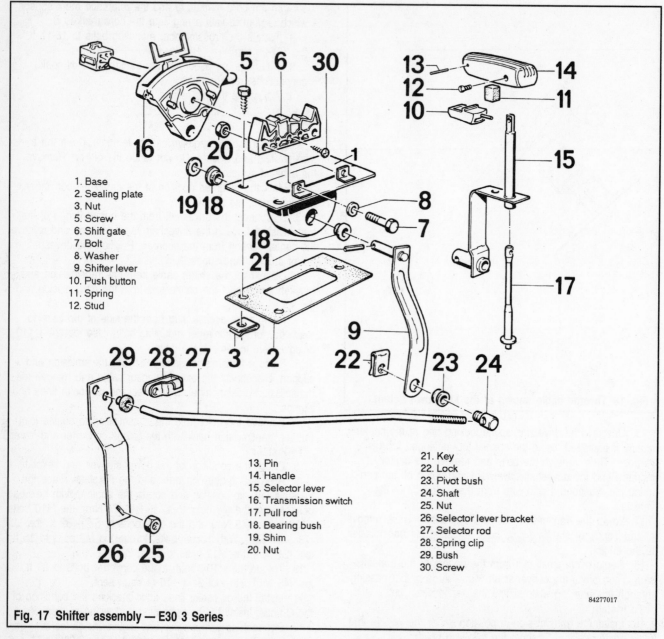

1. Base
2. Sealing plate
3. Nut
5. Screw
6. Shift gate
7. Bolt
8. Washer
9. Shifter lever
10. Push button
11. Spring
12. Stud

13. Pin
14. Handle
15. Selector lever
16. Transmission switch
17. Pull rod
18. Bearing bush
19. Shim
20. Nut

21. Key
22. Lock
23. Pivot bush
24. Shaft
25. Nut
26. Selector lever bracket
27. Selector rod
28. Spring clip
29. Bush
30. Screw

84277017

Fig. 17 Shifter assembly — E30 3 Series

across under the driveshaft. Remove the exhaust heat shield from under the center of the vehicle.

3. Drain the transmission oil and discard it. Remove the oil filler neck. Disconnect the oil cooler lines at the transmission by unscrewing the flare nuts and plug the open connections.

4. Support the transmission with the proper tools. Separate the torque converter housing from the transmission by removing the Torx® bolts with the proper tool from behind and the regular bolts from underneath. Retain the washers used with the Torx® bolts.

5. Remove bolts attaching the torque converter housing to the engine, making sure to retain the spacer used behind one of the bolts. Then, loosen the mounting bolts for the oil level switch just enough so the plate can be removed while pushing the switch mounting bracket to one side.

6. Remove the bolts attaching the torque converter to the drive plate. Turn the flywheel as necessary to gain access to

each of the bolts, which are spaced at equal intervals around it. Make sure to re-use the same bolts and retain the washers.

7. To remove the speed and reference mark sensors, remove the attaching bolt for each and remove each sensor. Keep the sensors clean.

8. Turn the bayonet type electrical connector counterclockwise and then pull the plug out of the socket. Then, lift the wiring harness out of the harness bails.

9. Support the transmission using the proper jack. Then, remove the crossmember that supports the transmission at the rear.

10. Disconnect the transmission shift rod. Then, remove the nuts and then the through bolts from the damper-type U-joint at the front of the transmission.

11. Unscrew the driveshaft spline locking ring at the center mount, if equipped, using the special tool designed for this purpose. Then, remove the bolts and remove the center mount. Bend the driveshaft downward and pull it off the cen-

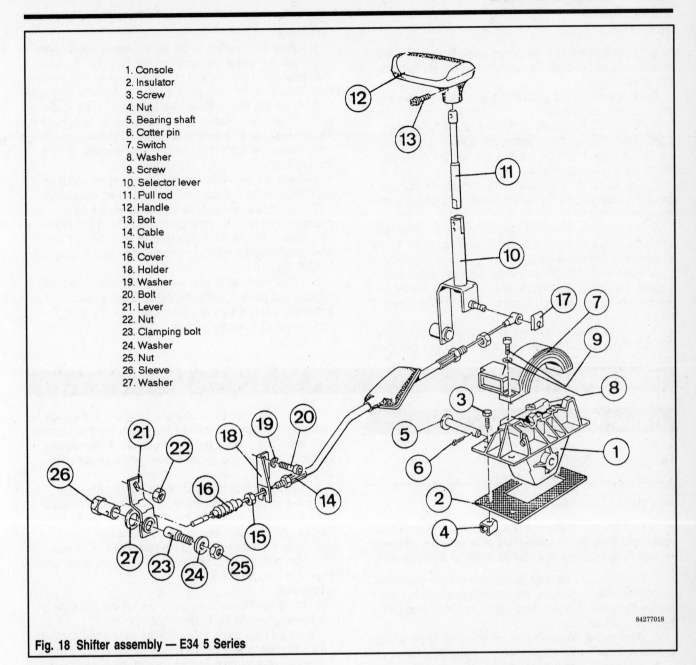

1. Console
2. Insulator
3. Screw
4. Nut
5. Bearing shaft
6. Cotter pin
7. Switch
8. Washer
9. Screw
10. Selector lever
11. Pull rod
12. Handle
13. Bolt
14. Cable
15. Nut
16. Cover
18. Holder
19. Washer
20. Bolt
21. Lever
22. Nut
23. Clamping bolt
24. Washer
25. Nut
26. Sleeve
27. Washer

84277018

Fig. 18 Shifter assembly — E34 5 Series

tering pin. Suspend it with wire from the underside of the vehicle.

12. Lower the transmission as far as possible. Then, remove all the Torx® or standard type bolts attaching the transmission to the engine.

13. Remove the small grill from the bottom of the transmission. Then press the converter off with a large prybar passing through this opening while sliding the transmission out.

To install:

14. Install the transmission in position under the vehicle and raise it into position. Observe the following points:

a. Make sure the converter is fully installed onto the transmission — so the ring on the front is inside the edge of the case. Only use M10x16mm bolts as originally equipped or damage will occur.

b. When reinstalling the driveshaft, tighten the lockring with the proper tool.

c. Make sure to replace the self-locking nuts on the driveshaft flexible joint and to hold the bolts still while tightening the nuts to keep from distorting it.

d. When installing the center mount, preload it forward from its most natural position 0.157-0.236 inches.

e. When reconnecting the bayonet type electrical connector, make sure the alignment marks are aligned after the plug it twisted into its final position.

f. When reinstalling the speed and reference mark sensors, inspect the O-rings used on the sensors and install new ones, if necessary. Make sure to install the speed sensor into the bore marked D and the reference mark sensor, which is marked with a ring, into the bore marked B.

g. Torque the crossmember mounting bolts to 16-17 ft. lbs. (21-23 Nm).

h. If O-rings are used with the transmission oil cooler connections, replace them.

i. Adjust the throttle cables.

THM-R1

1. Disconnect the negative battery terminal. Drain the transmission fluid and discard. Do not reuse the old oil. Remove the exhaust system.

2. Mark the mounted position of the crossmember under the driveshaft, the remove.

3. Disconnect the driveshaft from the output flange of the transmission. Loosen the driveshaft spline lockring and remove the center support from the floorpan. Position the driveshaft out of the way and support with wire.

4. Disconnect the shifter cable from the transmission and bracket. Disconnect the connectors from the transmission and the speed sender.

5. Pull out the access plug from the side of the case to reach the torque converter mounting bolts. Use tool 24 1 110 or equivalent to remove the bolts.

6. Place a transmission jack under the transmission and support. Disconnect the oxygen sensor cable and remove the transmission crossmember. Disconnect the oil cooler lines and clamps.

7. Remove the bolts from the transmission to engine joint. Pull the transmission back with the torque converter and lower.

To install:

8. Check the condition of the dowel sleeves and flexplate.

9. Align the torque converter and the flexplate. Place the transmission into position and bolt to the engine. With hexhead bolts, torque the M8 bolts to 17 ft. lbs. (24 Nm), the M10 bolts to 33 ft. lbs. (45 Nm) and the M12 bolts to 57 — 62 ft. lbs. (78 — 86 Nm). With Torx® bolts, torque the M8 bolts to 15 ft. lbs. (21 Nm), the M12 bolts to 52 ft. lbs. (72 Nm).

10. Torque the M10x16mm torque converter bolts to 33 ft. lbs. (45 Nm) with tool 24 1 110 or equivalent.

11. Install the oil cooler lines after checking the condition of the O-rings. Install the crossmember and wiring connections.

12. Connect the shifter cable and adjust. Install the driveshaft. Preload the center bearing 0.157 — 0.236 in (4 — 6 mm) forward. Torque the flange bolts to 59 ft. lbs. (81 Nm). After completing the installation, torque the spline locking ring to 12 ft. lbs. (17 Nm).

13. Install the crossmember over the driveshaft in the original mounting position. Install the exhaust system and splashguards. Fill the transmission and check the level. Connect the negative battery terminal.

TRANSFER CASE

Transfer Case Assembly

REMOVAL & INSTALLATION

With Manual Transmission

➡**To perform this procedure, a special, large wrench that locks onto flats on alternate sides of a section of the rear driveshaft is required. Use tool 26 1 060 or an equivalent.**

1. Disconnect the negative battery cable. Raise and safely support the vehicle. Remove the exhaust system. Unbolt and remove the exhaust system heat shields located behind and below the transfer case.

2. Unscrew the rear section of the driveshaft at the sliding joint located behind the output flange of the transfer case.

3. Hold the through-bolts stationary and remove the self-locking nuts from in front of the flexible coupling at the transfer case output flange. Discard all the self-locking nuts and replace them.

➡**During the next step, be careful not to let the driveshaft rest on the metal fuel line that crosses under it or the line could be damaged.**

4. Slide the sections of the driveshaft together at the sliding joint and then pull the front of the driveshaft off the centering pin at the transmission output shaft.

5. Remove the nuts and through bolts from the flexible coupling linking the transmission output flange with the short driveshaft linking the transmission and the transfer case.

6. Support the transmission from underneath in a secure manner. Then, mark each of the 4 bolts fastening the crossmember that supports the transmission at the rear to the body, bolts are of different lengths. Remove the crossmember.

7. Lower the transmission/transfer case unit just enough to gain access to the bolts linking the 2 boxes together. Remove the 2 lower and 2 upper bolts. It is possible to gain access to the upper bolts using a socket wrench with a U-joint and extension.

8. There is a protective cap on the forward driveshaft where it links up with the transfer case. The cap is made of a brittle material, so it must be handled carefully. Gently slide the cap forward until is free of the transfer case.

9. Slide the transfer case to the rear so it can be separated from both the transmission and the forward driveshaft. When it is free, remove it.

To install:

10. Install the transfer case under the vehicle and raise it into position, bearing the following points in mind:

   a. Inspect the dowel holes locating the transfer case with the transmission and the guide hole for the output shaft where it slides into the transfer case to make sure these parts will be properly located. Lubricate the guide pin and the splines of the front driveshaft section with grease.

   b. When fitting the transfer case onto the transmission, check to make sure the output flange of the transmission is properly aligned with the flexible coupling. Put the through-bolts through the flexible coupling and then install and torque the nuts to 65 ft. lbs. (88 Nm) while holding the bolts stationary, rather than turning them.

   c. When reconnecting the transfer case to the gearbox, torque the bolts to 30 ft. lbs. (41 Nm).

   d. Before fitting the driveshaft back onto the rear of the transmission, retain the seal in the protective cap by applying grease to it.

   e. Torque the transmission crossmember bolts to 17 ft. lbs. (23 Nm).

   f. Check the fluid level and fill with the recommended lubricant.

With Automatic Transmission

➡To perform this procedure, a special, large wrench that locks onto flats on alternate sides of a section of the rear driveshaft is required. Use tool 26 1 060 or an equivalent.

1. Disconnect the negative battery cable. Raise and safely support the vehicle. Remove the exhaust system. Unbolt and remove the exhaust system heat shields located behind and below the transfer case.

2. Unscrew the rear section of the driveshaft at the sliding joint located behind the output flange of the transfer case.

3. Hold the through-bolts stationary and remove the self-locking nuts from in front of the flexible coupling at the transfer case output flange. Discard all the self-locking nuts and replace them.

➡During the next step, be careful not to let the driveshaft rest on the metal fuel line that crosses under it or the line could be damaged.

4. Slide the sections of the driveshaft together at the sliding joint and then pull the front of the driveshaft off the centering pin at the transmission output shaft.

5. Remove the nuts and through bolts from the flexible coupling linking the transmission output flange with the short driveshaft linking the transmission and the transfer case.

6. Note the locations of all the washers and then loosen the retaining nut and disconnect the range selector lever cable at the transmission by pulling out the pin. Be careful not to bend the cable in doing this. Then, loosen the nuts that position the cable housing onto the transmission and slide the cable housing backward so it can be separated from the bracket on the transmission housing.

7. There is a protective cap on the forward driveshaft where it links up with the transfer case. The cap is made of a brittle material, so it must be handled carefully. Gently slide the cap forward until is free of the transfer case.

8. Remove the drain plug in the bottom of the pan and drain the transmission fluid.

9. Support the transmission from underneath in a secure manner. Then, mark each of the 4 bolts fastening the crossmember that supports the transmission at the rear to the body, bolts are of different lengths. Remove the crossmember.

10. Remove the 9 nuts fastening the transfer case to the transmission housing. Note the location of the wiring holder so it will be possible to reinstall it on the same bolt.

11. Slide the transfer case to the rear and off the transmission.

To install:

12. Install the transfer case under the vehicle and raise it into position, bearing the following points in mind:

a. Inspect the sealing surfaces as well as the dowel holes in the transfer case to make sure they will seal and locate properly. Clean the sealing surfaces and replace the gasket.

b. When sliding the transfer case back onto the transmission, turn the front driveshaft section slightly to help make the splines mesh.

c. When reconnecting the shift cable, inspect the rubber mounts and replace any that are cut, crushed, or cracked. Adjust the shift cable.

d. Before fitting the driveshaft back onto the rear of the transmission, retain the seal in the protective cap by applying grease to it.

e. When fitting the transfer case onto the transmission, check to make sure the output flange of the transmission is properly aligned with the flexible coupling. Put the through-bolts through the flexible coupling and then install and torque the nuts to 65 ft. lbs. (88 Nm) while holding the bolts stationary, rather than turning them.

f. Torque the bolts holding the transfer case to the transmission to 65 ft. lbs. (88 Nm).

g. Torque the transmission crossmember bolts to 17 ft. lbs. (23 Nm).

h. Check the fluid level and fill with the recommended lubricant.

DRIVELINE

Front Driveshaft

REMOVAL & INSTALLATION

1. Remove the 6 bolts from the flex coupling at the front differential.

2. Push the driveshaft back, then pull down and out of the transfer case.

3. Plug the opening in the transfer case.

4. Check the condition of the transfer case seal and the dust cap. Replace if necessary.

5. Install the driveshaft into the transfer case. Install a new flex coupling at the front differential. The arrows must face the arms of the flanges.

6. Install the bolts and torque the M10-8.8 bolts to 35 ft. lbs. (48 Nm) and the M10-10.9 bolts to 52 ft. lbs. (72 Nm). Hold the nut or bolt at the flex coupling side and turn of the flange side. This prevents stressing the flex coupling.

7. Slide the dust cap into position.

Rear Driveshaft

REMOVAL & INSTALLATION

E30 3 Series

2 WHEEL DRIVE

1. Remove the exhaust system. Remove the crossbrace under the driveshaft. Remove the heatshields. Mark the relationship of the driveshaft flanges to the differential flange and the transmission output flange for installation.

2. Use tool 26 1 040 or equivalent to loosen the spline locking ring behind the center bearing.

3. Support the transmission and remove the transmission crossmember. Remove the bolts holding the flex coupling to

the transmission output flange. If equipped with a vibration damper, rotate the damper and pull off with the flex coupling.

4. Remove the bolts at the driveshaft to differential flange.

5. Remove the center bearing bolts and pull the driveshaft down and out. Avoid catching the fuel tank connector pipe at the rear. Avoid severe angles at the joints.

To install:

6. Install the driveshaft and loosely install the center bearing to the body. Connect the rear joint to the differential. If equipped with U-joints, torque to 52 ft. lbs. (72 Nm). If equipped with a constant velocity joint, torque the M8 bolts to 23 ft. lbs. (32 Nm) and the M10 bolts to 46 ft. lbs. (64 Nm).

7. Install the front flex coupling and vibration damper. Torque the M10-8.8 bolts to 35 ft. lbs. (48 Nm) and the M10-10.9 bolts to 52 ft. lbs. (72 Nm).

8. Install the transmission crossmember. Preload the center bearing forward 0.157-0.236 inch (4-6 mm) and tighten. Torque the spline locking ring to 12 ft. lbs. (17 Nm).

9. Install the heatshields and crossmember. Install the exhaust system.

4 WHEEL DRIVE

1. Remove the exhaust system. Remove the crossbrace under the driveshaft. Remove the heatshields.

2. Use tool 26 1 040 or equivalent to loosen the spline locking ring at the rear of the shaft.

3. Remove the bolts holding the flex coupling to the transmission output flange. If equipped with a vibration damper, rotate the damper and pull off with the flex coupling.

4. Remove the bolts at the driveshaft to differential flange.

5. Remove the center bearing bolts and pull the driveshaft down and out. Avoid catching the fuel tank connector pipe at the rear. Avoid severe angles at the joints.

To install:

6. Install the driveshaft and loosely install the center bearing to the body. Connect the rear joint to the differential. If equipped with U-joints, torque to 52 ft. lbs. (72 Nm). If equipped with a constant velocity joint, torque the M8 bolts to 23 ft. lbs. (32 Nm) and the M10 bolts to 46 ft. lbs. (64 Nm).

7. Install the front flex coupling and vibration damper. Torque the M10-8.8 bolts to 35 ft. lbs. (48 Nm) and the M10-10.9 bolts to 52 ft. lbs. (72 Nm).

8. Preload the center bearing forward 0.157-0.236 inch (4-6 mm) and tighten. Torque the spline locking ring to 16 ft. lbs. (22 Nm).

9. Install the heatshields and crossmember. Install the exhaust system.

E36 3 Series

1. Remove the exhaust system. Remove the cross brace under the driveshaft. Remove the heatshields. Mark the relationship of the driveshaft flanges to the differential flange and the transmission output flange for installation.

2. Use tool 26 1 040 or equivalent to loosen the spline locking ring behind the center bearing.

3. Remove the bolts holding the flex coupling to the transmission output flange. If equipped with a vibration damper, rotate the damper and pull off with the flex coupling.

4. Remove the bolts at the driveshaft to differential flange.

5. Remove the center bearing bolts and pull the driveshaft down and out. Avoid catching the fuel tank connector pipe at the rear. Avoid severe angles at the joints.

To install:

6. Install the driveshaft and loosely install the center bearing to the body. Connect the rear joint to the differential. If equipped with U-joints, torque to 52 ft. lbs. (72 Nm). If equipped with a constant velocity joint, torque the M8 bolts to 23 ft. lbs. (32 Nm) and the M10 bolts to 46 ft. lbs. (64 Nm).

7. Install the front flex coupling and vibration damper. Torque the M10-8.8 bolts to 35 ft. lbs. (48 Nm) and the M10-10.9 bolts to 52 ft. lbs. (72 Nm).

8. Preload the center bearing forward 0.157-0.236 inch (4-6 mm) and tighten. Torque the spline locking ring to 12 ft. lbs. (17 Nm).

9. Install the heatshields and crossmember. Install the exhaust system.

E34 5 Series

1. Remove the exhaust system. Remove the crossbrace under the driveshaft. Remove the heatshields. Mark the relationship of the driveshaft flanges to the differential flange and the transmission output flange for installation.

2. Use tool 26 1 040 or equivalent to loosen the spline locking ring behind the center bearing.

3. Support the transmission and remove the transmission crossmember. Remove the bolts holding the flex coupling to the transmission output flange. If equipped with a vibration damper, rotate the damper and pull off with the flex coupling.

4. Remove the bolts at the driveshaft to differential flange.

5. Remove the center bearing bolts and pull the driveshaft down and out. Avoid catching the fuel tank connector pipe at the rear. Avoid severe angles at the joints.

To install:

6. Install the driveshaft and loosely install the center bearing to the body. Connect the rear joint to the differential. If equipped with U-joints, torque to 52 ft. lbs. (72 Nm). If equipped with a constant velocity joint, torque the M8 bolts to 23 ft. lbs. (32 Nm) and the M10 bolts to 46 ft. lbs. (64 Nm).

7. Install the front flex coupling and vibration damper. Torque the M10-8.8 bolts to 35 ft. lbs. (48 Nm) and the M10-10.9 bolts to 52 ft. lbs. (72 Nm).

8. Install the transmission crossmember. Preload the center bearing forward 0.157-0.236 inch (4-6 mm) and tighten. Torque the spline locking ring to 12 ft. lbs. (17 Nm).

9. Install the heatshields and crossmember. Install the exhaust system.

Center Bearing

REMOVAL & INSTALLATION

1. Mark the driveshaft at the flanges and at the center bearing for installation back into its original orientation. It is critical for balance that the 2 halves of the driveshaft be replaced into their original relationship.

2. Remove the driveshaft.

3. Loosen the spline locking sleeve at the center bearing and separate the front section from the rear section.

4. Remove the snapring at the splines.

5. Use a puller or press to remove the center bearing from the shaft. Note the location of the dust shields.

To install:

6. Press the new center bearing onto the driveshaft. The dust shield should be flush with the center mount.

7. Clean the splines and coat with moly lubricant. Install the front half to the rear half in the same position as it was removed.

8. Install the driveshaft and torque the spline locking sleeve to 12 ft. lbs. (17 Nm), except for 4 wheel drive which is 16 ft. lbs. (22 Nm). If not equipped with splines, use a threadlocking compound and torque to 70 ft. lbs. (97 Nm).

Flex Coupling (Guibo Disk)

REMOVAL & INSTALLATION

1. Remove the exhaust system. Remove the crossbrace under the driveshaft. Remove the heatshields. Mark the relationship of the driveshaft flange to the transmission output flange for installation.

2. Use tool 26 1 040 or equivalent to loosen the spline locking ring behind the center bearing.

3. Support the transmission and remove the transmission crossmember, if blocking the access to the coupling. Remove the bolts holding the flex coupling to the transmission output flange and the driveshaft. If equipped with a vibration damper, rotate the damper and pull off with the flex coupling.

To install:

4. Install the front flex coupling and vibration damper. The arrows must face the flange arms. Torque the M10-8.8 bolts to 35 ft. lbs. (48 Nm) and the M10-10.9 bolts to 52 ft. lbs. (72 Nm).

5. Install the transmission crossmember. Torque the spline locking ring to 12 ft. lbs. (17 Nm) for 2 wheel drive and 16 ft. lbs. (22 Nm) for 4 wheel drive.

6. Install the heatshields and crossmember. Install the exhaust system.

Driveshaft End Bearing

REMOVAL & INSTALLATION

▶ **See Figure 19**

1. Remove the exhaust system. Remove the crossbrace under the driveshaft. Remove the heatshields. Mark the relationship of the driveshaft flange to the transmission output flange for installation.

2. Use tool 26 1 040 or equivalent to loosen the spline locking ring behind the center bearing.

3. Support the transmission and remove the transmission crossmember, if blocking the access to the coupling. Remove the bolts holding the flex coupling to the transmission output flange. If equipped with a vibration damper, rotate the damper and pull off with the flex coupling.

4. Fill the opening of the bearing with grease. Use a tool the same diameter as the bore in the bearing and drive in. The hydraulic force developed will drive the bearing out from the back side.

To install:

5. Clean the grease from the bore and fill with 2 grams of moly lubricant grease. Drive the new bearing in until so it protrudes 0.177 inch (4.5 mm).

6. Install the front flex coupling and vibration damper. The arrows must face the flange arms. Torque the M10-8.8 bolts to 35 ft. lbs. (48 Nm) and the M10-10.9 bolts to 52 ft. lbs. (72 Nm).

7. Install the transmission crossmember. Torque the spline locking ring to 12 ft. lbs. (17 Nm) for 2 wheel drive and 16 ft. lbs. (22 Nm) for 4 wheel drive.

8. Install the heatshields and crossmember. Install the exhaust system.

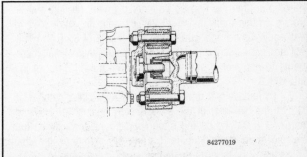

84277019

Fig. 19 Check the condition of the end bearing at the flex coupling

FRONT DRIVE AXLE

Half Shafts

REMOVAL & INSTALLATION

➡️**A number of special tools are required to perform this operation. Use the BMW factory numbers given to shop for these from factory sources, or to cross-reference similar tools that may be available in the aftermarket. Use 33 4 050 and 00 5 500 to drive in a new lockplate for the brake disc. The tie rod must be pressed off with 342 2 070. Control arms are pressed off with 31 2 160. Use 33 2 112 and 33 2 113 to press the output shafts out of the brake discs and 33 2 112, 33 2 124 and 33 4 042 to press them back in. On the left side, the output shaft is pulled out of the drive axle with 31 5 011 and 30 31 581. On the right side, 31 5 011 and 31 5 012 are used to pull the output shaft out of the axle.**

1. Raise the car and support it securely. Remove the front wheels. Remove the drain plug and drain the lube oil from the front axle.

2. Lift out the lockplate in the center of the brake disc with a screwdriver. Then, unscrew the collar nut.

3. Remove the attaching nut from each tie rod and then press the rod off the steering knuckle with 33 2 070.

4. Remove the retaining nut and then press the control arm off the steering knuckle on either side.

5. Mount 33 2 112 and 33 2 113 to the brake disc with 2 wheel bolts. Press the output shaft out of the center of the steering knuckle on that side. Repeat on the other side.

6. To remove the drive axle from the differential on the left side: Install special tool 31 5 011 by bolting it together around the axle so that the ring on its inner diameter fits into the groove on the shaft. Install 30 31 581 onto the shaft so it will rest against the housing and the bolt heads of 31 5 011 will rest against it. Screw the 2 bolts in alternately in small increments to get even pressure on the shaft, pulling it out of the differential.

7. To remove the drive axle on the right side: Install 31 5 012 on the diameter of the shaft directly against the housing. Install 31 5 011 by bolting it together around the axle so that the ring on its inner diameter fits into the groove on the shaft. Screw the 2 bolts in alternately in small increments to get even pressure on the shaft, pulling it out of the differential.

To install:

8. Install the halfshafts, bearing the following points in mind:

a. Install the shafts into the housing until the snapring inside engages in the groove of the shaft. It may be necessary to install the removal tool and tap against it with a plastic-headed hammer to drive the shaft far enough into the housing.

b. Before installing the shafts into the steering knuckle, coat the spline with light oil.

c. When installing the control arms onto the steering knuckle, torque the nut to 61.5 ft. lbs. and use a new cotter pin. When installing the tie rod onto the steering knuckle, torque to 61.5 ft. lbs. and use a new self-locking nut.

d. Drive a new lockplate into the brake disc with 33 4 050 and 00 5 500. Torque the nut to 181 ft. lbs.

e. Replace the drain plug and refill the final drive unit with the required lubricant.

Hub and Bearings

REMOVAL & INSTALLATION

➡️**A number of special tools are required to perform this operation. Read through the procedure and procure these before attempting to start work. Factory part numbers for tools are given, but it is possible to shop for equivalent tools, using these part numbers, in the aftermarket.**

1. Raise the car and support it securely. Remove the output halfshaft as described above. Then, remount the control arm with nuts just finger tight, to keep the spring strut in position.

2. Remove the upper and lower attaching bolts and remove the brake caliper, suspending it nearby with wire so that there is no tension on the brake hose.

3. Remove the allen bolt and remove the brake disc.

4. Bolt special tool 31 2 090 or equivalent to the knuckle with its 3 bolts. Then, mount 33 1 307 hooked around the tie rod arm and press the drive flange off. If it is scored, pull the bearing's inner race out of the drive flange with 33 1 307 and 00 7 500 or equivalent.

5. Compress the snapring with snapring pliers and remove it.

6. Remove 31 2 090 or the equivalent and replace 33 1 307 or its equivalent with a tool such as 31 2 070. Again install and use the combination, this time to press out the bearing.

7. Screw out the spindle of 31 2 090 and install 33 4 032 or equivalent so it is flush with the surface of 31 2 090. Use 33 4 034 and 33 4 038 to pull in the new bearing. Then, remove 31 2 090.

8. Install the snapring again, with snapring pliers, **making sure the open end faces downward.**

9. Pull the drive flange into place with 33 4 032 or equivalent, 33 4 038 or equivalent, 33 4 045 or equivalent, and 33 4 048 or equivalent.

10. Install the brake disc and caliper and the wheel in reverse order.

Final Drive

REMOVAL & INSTALLATION

➡ **A number of special tools are required to perform this operation. Use the BMW factory numbers given to shop for these from factory sources, or to cross-reference similar tools that may be available in the aftermarket. Use 33 4 050 and 00 5 500 to drive in a new lockplate for the brake disc. The tie rod must be pressed off with 342 2 070. Control arms are pressed off with 31 2 160. Use 33 2 112 and 33 2 113 to press the output shafts out of the brake discs and 33 2 112, 33 2 124 and 33 4 042 to press them back in. On the left side, the output shaft is pulled out of the drive axle with 31 5 011 and 30 31 581. On the right side, 31 5 011 and 31 5 012 are used to pull the output shaft out of the axle.**

1. Raise the car and support it securely. Remove the front wheels. Remove the drain plug and drain the lube oil from the front axle.

2. Remove the attaching nut from each tie rod and then press the rod off the steering knuckle with 33 2 070.

3. Remove the retaining nut and then press the control arm off the steering knuckle on either side.

4. To remove the drive axle from the differential on the left side: Install special tool 31 5 011 by bolting it together around the axle so that the ring on its inner diameter fits into the groove on the shaft. Install 30 31 581 onto the shaft so it will rest against the housing and the bolt heads of 31 5 011 will rest against it. Screw the 2 bolts in alternately in small increments to get even pressure on the shaft, pulling it out of the differential.

5. To remove the drive axle on the right side: Install 31 5 012 on the diameter of the shaft directly against the housing. Install 31 5 011 by bolting it together around the axle so that the ring on its inner diameter fits into the groove on the shaft. Screw the 2 bolts in alternately in small increments to get even pressure on the shaft, pulling it out of the differential.

6. Remove the front driveshaft flex coupling bolts and remove the driveshaft. Remove the mounting bolts for the final drive and lower the unit.

To install:

7. Install the final drive and torque the mounting bolts to 30 ft. lbs. (42 Nm). Replace the output flange seals at the side of the final drive case before installing the halfshafts.

8. Install the halfshafts, bearing the following points in mind:

   a. Install the shafts into the housing until the snapring inside engages in the groove of the shaft. It may be necessary to install the removal tool and tap against it with a plastic-headed hammer to drive the shaft far enough into the housing.

   b. Before installing the shafts into the steering knuckle, coat the spline with light oil.

   c. When installing the control arms onto the steering knuckle, torque the nut to 61.5 ft. lbs. and use a new cotter pin. When installing the tie rod onto the steering knuckle, torque to 61.5 ft. lbs. and use a new self-locking nut.

   d. Drive a new lockplate into the brake disc with 33 4 050 and 00 5 500. Torque the nut to 181 ft. lbs.

   e. Replace the drain plug and refill the final drive unit with the required lubricant.

REAR AXLE

Halfshaft

REMOVAL & INSTALLATION

E30 3 Series

1. Remove the rear wheel. Pull out the lockplate and remove the axle nut.

2. Remove the constant velocity joint bolts at the final drive output flange.

3. Use tool 33 2 110 or equivalent to press the axle through the bearing and out of the vehicle. Do not allow halfshaft to drop.

To install:

4. Place the halfshaft through the bearing and pull into place using tool 33 2 110 or equivalent.

5. Secure the constant velocity joint bolts at the final drive output flange and torque to 42 ft. lbs. (58 Nm).

6. Lubricate the axle nut with oil. Torque the axle nut to 145 ft. lbs. (200 Nm) and install the lockplate with tools 33 4 050 and 00 5 500 or equivalent. Install the rear wheel.

E36 3 Series

1. Remove the rear wheel. Remove the rear exhaust system at the rear axle. Disconnect the stabilizer bar and move down. Remove the ABS sensor. Pull out the lockplate and remove the axle nut.

2. Remove the constant velocity joint bolts at the final drive output flange.

3. Use tool 33 2 110 or equivalent to press the axle through the bearing and out of the vehicle. Do not allow halfshaft to drop.

To install:

4. Place the halfshaft through the bearing and pull into place using tool 33 2 110 or equivalent.

5. Secure the constant velocity joint bolts at the final drive output flange and torque to 42 ft. lbs. (58 Nm).

6. Lubricate the axle nut with oil. Torque the axle nut to 145 ft. lbs. (200 Nm) and install the lockplate with tools 33 4 050 and 00 5 500 or equivalent.

7. Install the ABS sensor, the stabilizer bar and the exhaust system. Install the rear wheel.

E34 5 Series

◆ See Figure 20

1. Remove the bolts from the constant velocity joints.

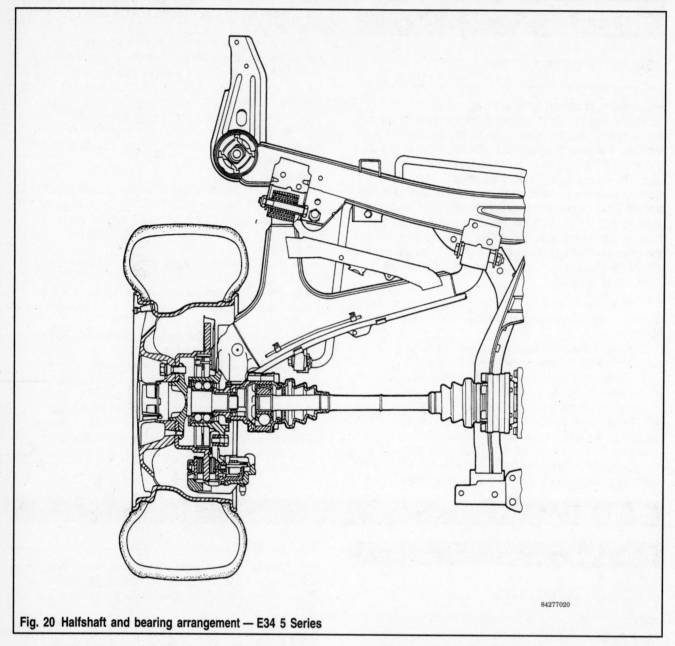

84277020

Fig. 20 Halfshaft and bearing arrangement — E34 5 Series

2. Separate the flanges and remove the halfshaft.

3. Install the halfshaft and torque the bolts to 42 ft. lbs. (58 Nm).

Final Drive

REMOVAL & INSTALLATION

1. Disconnect the drive shaft from the input flange of the final drive. Support the driveshaft with wire.

2. Remove the constant velocity joint bolts and support the halfshafts from the body.

3. Disconnect the speed sensors, as equipped.

4. Support the unit and remove the front mounting bolts, then the rear mounting bolts. Lower the unit. The axle ratio is marked on the housing or cover.

To install:

5. Install the final drive. Install the front bolts to support, then the rear bolts. Torque the bolts to 80 ft. lbs. (110 Nm).

6. Install the halfshafts and the driveshaft.

TORQUE SPECIFICATIONS

Component	U.S.	Metric
Automatic transmission mounting bolts		
Hex head bolts		
M8:	17 ft. lbs.	24 Nm
M10:	33 ft. lbs.	45 Nm
M12:	60 ft. lbs.	82 Nm
Torx head bolts		
M8:	15 ft. lbs.	21 Nm
M12:	72 ft. lbs.	52 Nm
Automatic transmission rear extension mounting bolts		
4HP-22:	17–19 ft. lbs.	23–26 Nm
THM-R1:	20–25 ft. lbs.	28–35 Nm
Automatic transmission filter screen bolts		
4HP-22:	6 ft. lbs.	8 Nm
THM-R1:	13–15 ft. lbs.	18–21 Nm
Automatic transmission drain plug		
4HP-22:	11–12 ft. lbs.	15–17 Nm
THM-R1:	18 ft. lbs.	25 Nm
Automatic transmission filler pipe:	71 ft. lbs.	98 Nm
Automatic transmission toque converter mounting bolts		
4HP-22 — M8:	18.0–19.5 ft. lbs.	25–27 Nm
4HP-22 — M10:	34–37 ft. lbs.	47–51 Nm
THM-R1:	33 ft. lbs.	45 Nm
Automatic transmission selector mounting nut		
4HP-22:	6–7 ft. lbs.	8–10 Nm
THM-R1:	11–18 ft. lbs.	15–25 Nm
Manual transmission mounting bolts		
Hex head bolts		
M8:	16.0–19.5 ft. lbs.	22–27 Nm
M10:	34–37 ft. lbs.	47–51 Nm
M12:	48–59 ft. lbs.	66–82 Nm
Torx head bolts		
M8:	14.5–17 ft. lbs.	20–24 Nm
M10:	27.5–34 ft. lbs.	38–47 Nm
M12:	47–58 ft. lbs.	64–80 Nm
Manual transmission to clutch housing mounting bolts		
M12:	52–58 ft. lbs.	72–80 Nm
Manual transmission reinforcement mounting bolts		
M8:	16–17 ft. lbs.	22–24 Nm
Manual transmission drain plug:	29–43 ft. lbs.	40–60 Nm
Manual transmission mount bolts		
M10:	31–35 ft. lbs.	43–48 Nm
Manual transmission crossmember to body mounting bolts		
M8:	16–17 ft. lbs.	22–24 Nm
Manual transmission shifter arm console mounting bolts		
steel:	16–17 ft. lbs.	22–24 Nm
aluminum:	8 ft. lbs.	12 Nm
Flex coupling (Guibo disk)		
M10-8.8:	35 ft. lbs.	48 Nm
M10-10.9:	52 ft. lbs.	72 Nm
M12:	59 ft. lbs.	81 Nm

84277021

TORQUE SPECIFICATIONS

Component	U.S.	Metric
Driveshaft spline locking ring		
2 wheel drive:	12 ft. lbs.	17 Nm
4 wheel drive:	16 ft. lbs.	22 Nm
Driveshaft to differential flange bolts		
U-joint:	52 ft. lbs.	72 Nm
constant velocity joint		
M8:	23 ft. lbs.	32 Nm
M10:	46 ft. lbs.	64 Nm
Driveshaft U-joint at center bearing bolt		
with threadlocker:	70 ft. lbs.	97 Nm
Transfer case mounting bolts		
automatic transmission:	17 ft. lbs.	23 Nm
manual transmission:	30 ft. lbs.	42 Nm
Transfer case coupling bolts to manual transmission		
M12:	65 ft. lbs.	90 Nm
Transfer case output flange		
with threadlocker:	72–87 ft. lbs.	100–120 Nm
Transfer case plug		
M14:	22–25 ft. lbs.	30–35 Nm
M18:	14–18 ft. lbs.	20–25 Nm
M24:	22–25 ft. lbs.	30–35 Nm
Transfer case crossmember to mounts		
M12:	58 ft. lbs.	80 Nm
Front final drive		
mounting bolts:	30 ft. lbs.	42 Nm
filler plug:	38 ft. lbs.	53 Nm
drain plug:	14 ft. lbs.	20 Nm
Rear final drive		
mounting bolts:	89 ft. lbs.	123 Nm
rubber mount:	56 ft. lbs.	78 Nm
drain and filler plug:	36 ft. lbs.	50 Nm
axle nut		
E30 and E36 3 Series:	145 ft. lbs.	200 Nm
E34 5 Series:	179 ft. lbs.	248 Nm
Center bearing to body		
bolts:	16–17 ft. lbs.	21–23 Nm
Manual transmission case mounting bolts:	16 ft. lbs.	22 Nm
Manual transmission clutch release bearing sleeve mounting bolts		
M6:	7 ft. lbs.	10 Nm
M8x22:	13 ft. lbs.	18 Nm
M8x30:	18 ft. lbs.	25 Nm

84277022

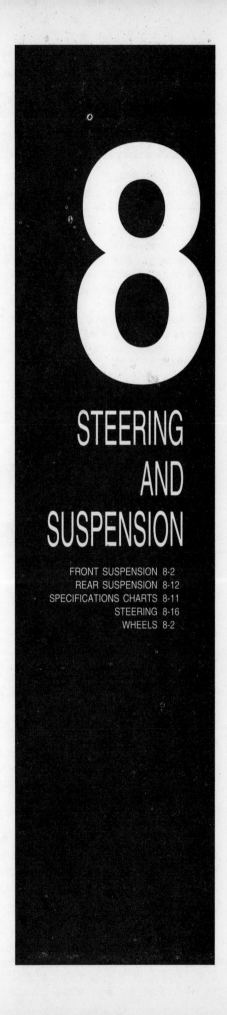

8

STEERING AND SUSPENSION

WHEELS

Wheel Assembly

REMOVAL & INSTALLATION

1. With the vehicle resting on the ground and the parking brake set, break loose the lug bolts but do not remove.
2. Block the wheel at the opposite corner of the vehicle with a chock. Raise the vehicle at the jacking point.
3. Place a jackstand under the vehicle at the jacking point before continuing work.
4. Mark the relationship of the wheel to the hub to maintain the finish balance. Remove the lug bolts and remove the wheel.

To install:

5. Clean the surfaces of the wheel and the hub where they meet. Coat the hub with a thin layer of antiseize.
6. Place the alignment tool provided in the vehicles too kit into one of the bolt holes. This tool is the metal rod with the plastic fitting on the end. Slide the wheel over the alignment tool and onto the hub. The alignment tool matches the lug holes in the wheel with the threaded holes in the hub.
7. Install the lug bolts and remove the alignment tool. Snug the lug bolts.
8. Lower the vehicle and torque the lug bolts to 65-79 ft. lbs. (90-110 Nm) in a crisscross pattern. On the 1991-92 M5, torque the vane bolts to 2 ft. lbs. (3 Nm).

INSPECTION

With the wheel removed, check for obvious bends, dents or chip missing from the rim. Check for cracks at the spokes, inside and outside. With the wheel installed, spin the wheel on the hub to check for bends and wobbles not noticeable with the wheel removed.

Do not try to repair a damaged wheel by hammering it straight. Have an alloy wheel professionally repaired or replace it. Replace damaged steel wheels. Use only OEM approved replacement wheels and check BMW NA or your dealer for approved makes of wheels. Do not change the size, width or offset without first checking if the change is acceptable.

FRONT SUSPENSION

▶ See Figure 1

Struts

REMOVAL & INSTALLATION

E30 3 Series

2 WHEEL DRIVE

1. Disconnect the negative battery cable.
2. Raise and safely support the vehicle. Remove the tire and wheel assembly.
3. Disconnect the brake pad wear indicator plug and ground wire. Pull the wires out of the holder on the strut. Remove the ABS pulse sender, if equipped.
4. Unbolt the caliper and pull it away from the strut, suspending it with a piece of wire from the body. Do not disconnect the brake line.
5. Remove the attaching nut and then detach the push rod on the stabilizer bar at the strut.
6. On the M3 remove the bolts holding the steering knuckle to the strut and remove strut. On others, unscrew the attaching nut and press off the ball joint stud with the proper tool.
7. Unscrew the nut and press off the tie rod joint.

➡**Do not turn the steering rack to full lock or damage to the seals can occur.**

8. Press the bottom of the strut outward and push it over the ball joint stud. Support the bottom of the strut.
9. Unscrew the nuts at the top of the strut, from inside the engine compartment, then remove the strut.

To install:

10. Install the strut into the wheel housing and install the nuts. On the M3, install the steering knuckle bolts coated with threadlocker and torque to 22 ft. lbs. (30 Nm). On others, press down on the control arm and install the ball joint stud into the strut bore. Using new nuts, torque the ball joint to 61 ft. lbs. (85 Nm) and the top strut mounting nuts to 16-17 ft. lbs. (21-23 Nm).
11. Install the tie rod into the steering arm and torque the new nut to 26 ft. lbs. (37 Nm).
12. Install the stabilizer bar link and torque to 43 ft. lbs. (59 Nm).
13. Install the brake caliper and torque to 80 ft. lbs. (110 Nm).
14. Install the ABS sensor, the brake pad wear sensor and the brake hose. Connect the negative battery terminal. Have the alignment checked.

4 WHEEL DRIVE

1. Disconnect the negative battery cable.
2. Raise and safely support the vehicle. Remove the front tire and wheel assembly. Unplug the ABS pulse transmitter.
3. Lift out the lock plate at the center of the brake disc with a small prybar. Unscrew the collar nut.
4. Disconnect the brake pad wear indicator plug and the ground wire. Pull the wires and brake hose out of the clip on the spring strut. Then, disconnect the small rod at the strut.
5. Remove the brake caliper mounting bolts and support the assembly with a piece of wire, keeping stress off the brake hose.
6. Remove the attaching nut from the tie rod end. Then press the stud off the knuckle with the proper tool.

➡**Do not turn the steering rack to full lock or damage to the seals can occur.**

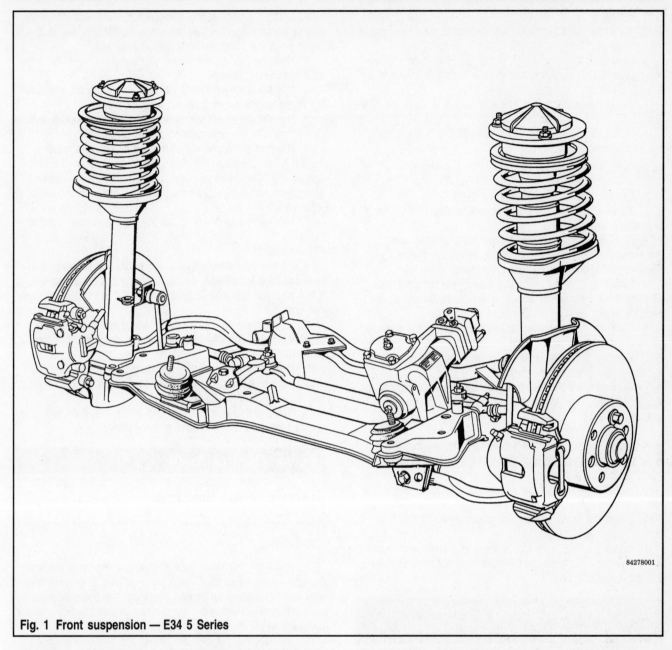

Fig. 1 Front suspension — E34 5 Series

84278001

7. Remove the attaching nut for ball joint and then press the stud off the knuckle with an appropriate tool.

8. Press the output shaft out of the center of the knuckle.

9. Support the spring strut from underneath. Remove the 3 bolts from the upper mount at the wheel housing. Remove the strut.

To install:

10. Install the strut into the wheel housing and install the nuts. Press down on the control arm and install the ball joint stud into the strut bore. Using new nuts, torque the ball joint to 61 ft. lbs. (85 Nm) and the top strut mounting nuts to 16-17 ft. lbs. (21-23 Nm).

11. Pull the axle through the bearing. Install a new nut and torque to 180 ft. lbs. (250 Nm). Install a new lockplate.

12. Install the tie rod into the steering arm and torque the new nut to 26 ft. lbs. (37 Nm).

13. Install the stabilizer bar link and torque to 43 ft. lbs. (59 Nm).

14. Install the brake caliper and torque to 80 ft. lbs. (110 Nm).

15. Install the ABS sensor, the brake pad wear sensor and the brake hose. Connect the negative battery terminal. Have the alignment checked.

E36 3 Series

1. Remove the wheel assembly. Disconnect the brake line and the wires from the holders on the strut, but do not disconnect from the caliper.

2. Install a lug bolt into the hub and attach a piece of wire to the bolt and to the body. This will support the hub assembly once it is removed from the strut.

3. Disconnect the stabilizer bar link from the strut. Remove the 3 bolts holding the hub assembly to the strut.

4. Remove the 3 nuts at the top of the strut assembly and remove the strut from the vehicle.

To install:

5. Install the strut to the vehicle and torque the new mounting nuts to 16-17 ft. lbs. (21-23 Nm).

6. Clean the threaded holes in the hub. Install new micro-encapsulated hub mounting bolts to the strut and torque to 58 ft. lbs. (80 Nm).

7. Install the stabilizer bar link and torque to 43 ft. lbs. (59 Nm).

8. Install the brake hose and wires into the holders. Have the alignment checked.

E34 5 Series

1. Disconnect the negative battery cable.

2. Raise and safely support the vehicle. Remove the tire and wheel assembly.

3. Disconnect the brake pad wear indicator plug and ground wire. Pull the wires out of the holder on the strut. Remove the ABS pulse sender, if equipped.

4. Unbolt the caliper and pull it away from the strut, suspending it with a piece of wire from the body. Do not disconnect the brake line.

5. Remove the attaching nut and then detach the push rod on the stabilizer bar at the strut.

6. Remove the bolts at the lower end of the strut connecting the steering arm to the strut.

7. Support the bottom of the strut. Unscrew the nuts at the top of the strut, from inside the engine compartment, then remove the strut.

To install:

8. Install the strut into the wheel housing and install the nuts. Using new nuts, torque the top strut mounting nuts to 16-17 ft. lbs. (21-23 Nm).

9. Install the stabilizer bar link and torque to 43 ft. lbs. (59 Nm).

10. Install the brake caliper and torque to 80 ft. lbs. (110 Nm).

11. Install the ABS sensor, the brake pad wear sensor and the brake hose. Connect the negative battery terminal. Have the alignment checked.

Strut Cartridge, Spring & Strut Mount/Bearing

REMOVAL & INSTALLATION

▶ See Figures 2 and 3

❊❊CAUTION

This procedure calls for the spring to be compressed. A compressed spring has high potential energy and if released suddenly can cause severe damage and personal injury. If not comfortable with dealing with a compressed spring, have a professional technician remove the spring from the strut for you.

1. Remove the strut from the vehicle and mount in a vise using a strut holder. This will prevent damage to the strut tube.

2. Using a proper spring compressor, compress the spring and lock into place. Use all the safety hooks provided and never point the compressed spring at a person.

3. Remove the top nut of the strut mount. Counterhold the strut rod during removal.

4. Pull the strut mount off the strut rod. Note the positioning of the spacers and washer for replacement.

5. Pull the spring off the strut and place somewhere safe. Do not release the compression of the spring.

6. Remove the gland nut at the top of the strut housing. Turn the nut and allow the pressure to bleed off on the M5. A special tool is sometimes needed to remove the nut. Some aftermarket strut manufacturers provide a tool with the replacement cartridges.

7. Pull the old cartridge out of the strut and pour out the oil.

To install:

8. Fill the strut tube with enough engine oil so when the new cartridge is installed, oil fills the tube but doesn't overflow. If the strut rod diameter is greater than 1.299 in. (33 mm) do not use oil.

9. Install the new cartridge and any spacers that where provided by the manufacturer. Install the gland nut and torque to 94 ft. lbs. (130 Nm).

10. Install the spring and strut mount with all the spacers and washers in their original positions. Torque the new strut rod nut to 47 ft. lbs. (65 Nm).

11. Release the spring slowly and check that it seats in the spring holders. Install the strut in the vehicle.

Lower Control Arms

REMOVAL & INSTALLATION

E30 3 Series

1. Raise and safely support the vehicle. Remove the front tire and wheel assembly. Use a piece of wire to prevent the strut from extending to far and damaging the brake hose.

2. Disconnect the rear control arm bushing bracket where it connects to the body by removing the bolts.

3. Remove the nut and disconnect the link on the front stabilizer bar where it connects to the stabilizer bar.

4. Unscrew the nut which attaches the control arm to the crossmember and remove the nut from above the crossmember. Then, use a plastic hammer to knock the stud out of the crossmember.

5. Unscrew the nut and press off the ball joint where the control arm attaches to the lower end of the strut, using the proper tool.

To install:

6. Make sure the ball joints studs and the bores in the crossmember and strut are clean before inserting the studs. Replace the original nuts with replacement nuts and washers. Torque the ball joint nut to 47 ft. lbs. (65 Nm) for 2 wheel drive and 61.5 ft. lbs. (93 Nm) for 4 wheel drive. Torque the control arm to subframe nut to 61 ft. lbs. (85 Nm) for 2 wheel drive and 72 ft. lbs. (100 Nm) for 4 wheel drive.

7. Install the control arm bushing bracket and torque the bolts to 30 ft. lbs. (42 Nm).

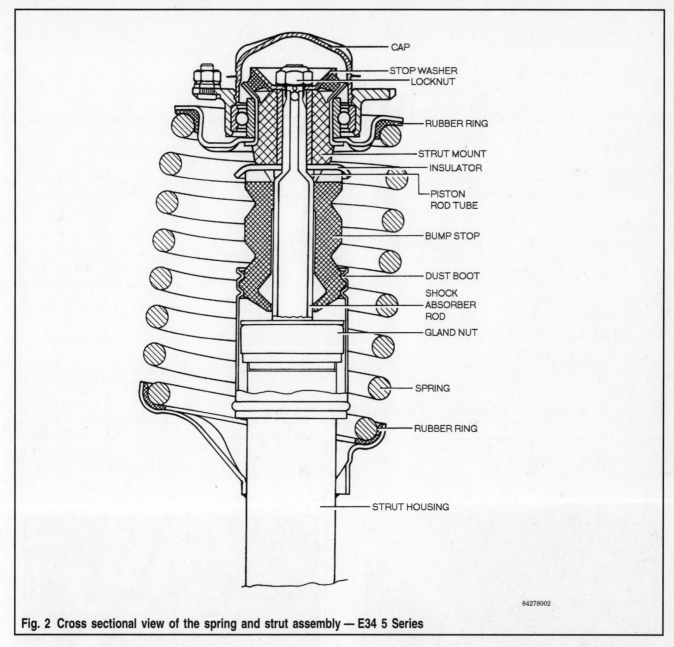

CAP
STOP WASHER
LOCKNUT
RUBBER RING
STRUT MOUNT
INSULATOR
PISTON ROD TUBE
BUMP STOP
DUST BOOT
SHOCK ABSORBER ROD
GLAND NUT
SPRING
RUBBER RING
STRUT HOUSING

84278002

Fig. 2 Cross sectional view of the spring and strut assembly — E34 5 Series

8. Install the stabilizer bar link and torque to 43 ft. lbs. (59 Nm).

E36 3 Series
▶ See Figures 4 and 5

1. Raise and safely support the vehicle. Remove the front tire and wheel assembly. Use a piece of wire to prevent the strut from extending to far and damaging the brake hose.

2. Disconnect the rear control arm bushing bracket where it connects to the body by removing the bolts.

3. Remove the nut and disconnect the link on the front stabilizer bar where it connects to the control arm.

4. Unscrew the nut which attaches the control arm to the crossmember and remove the nut from above the cross-member. Then, use a plastic hammer to knock the stud out of the crossmember.

5. Unscrew the nut to the point it contacts the strut housing. Remove the bolts connecting the hub to the struts. Press off the ball joint where the control arm attaches to the lower end of the strut, using the proper tool.

To install:

6. Clean the threaded holes in the hub. Install new micro-encapsulated hub mounting bolts to the strut and torque to 58 ft. lbs. (80 Nm).

7. Make sure the ball joints studs and the bores in the crossmember and strut are clean before inserting the studs. Replace the original nuts with replacement nuts and washers. Torque the ball joint nut to 47 ft. lbs. (65 Nm) for 2 wheel drive. Torque the control arm to subframe nut to 61 ft. lbs. (85 Nm) for 2 wheel drive.

8. Install the control arm bushing bracket and torque the bolts to 30 ft. lbs. (42 Nm).

9. Install the stabilizer bar link and torque to 43 ft. lbs. (59 Nm).

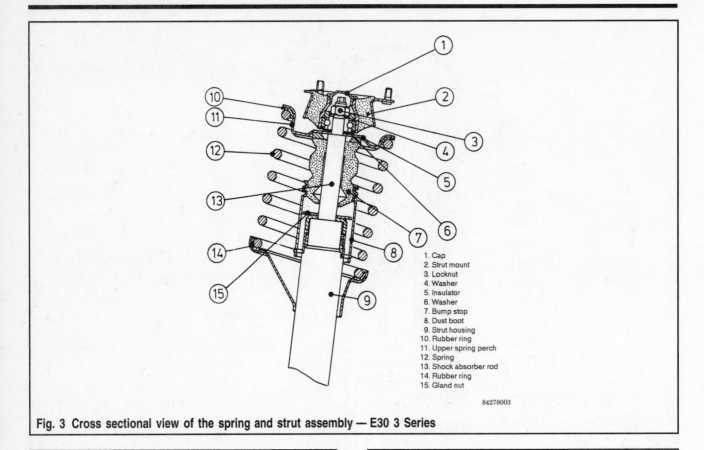

1. Cap
2. Strut mount
3. Locknut
4. Washer
5. Insulator
6. Washer
7. Bump stop
8. Dust boot
9. Strut housing
10. Rubber ring
11. Upper spring perch
12. Spring
13. Shock absorber rod
14. Rubber ring
15. Gland nut

84278003

Fig. 3 Cross sectional view of the spring and strut assembly — E30 3 Series

84278004

Fig. 4 Control arm bracket mounting. Matchmark the control arm position before pressing the bushing off during replacement — E36 3 Series shown, E30 3 Series uses the same design

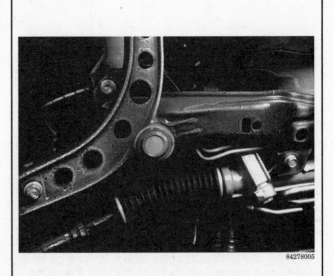

84278005

Fig. 5 Control arm to subframe mount ball joint — E36 3 Series shown, E30 3 Series uses the same design

E34 5 Series

1. Raise and safely support the front end. Do not place the jackstands under any suspension parts. Remove the wheel.

2. Remove the 3 bolts holding the steering knuckle to the bottom of the strut.

3. Remove the ball joint nut and press the stud out of the steering knuckle with a ball joint remover tool.

4. Remove the nut and bolt at the subframe end of the control arm. Remove the control arm.

To install:

5. Install the control arm to the subframe using a new nut and washer on both sides. Do not torque at this point.

6. Clean the grease and dirt off of the ball joint stud and bore. Install the ball joint stud into the steering knuckle and torque the new nut to 67 ft. lbs. (93 Nm).

7. Clean the threads and bores of the steering knuckle mounting bolts and the strut housing. Install the bolts, using threadlocker, and torque to 80 ft. lbs. (110 Nm). There is a groove that will align the strut and knuckle.

8. Install the wheel and lower the vehicle to the ground. Load 150 lbs. into each of the front seats and in the center of the rear seat. Torque the control arm to subframe bolt to 56 ft. lbs. (77.5 Nm).

BUSHING REPLACEMENT

▶ **See Figures 6 and 7**

The bushings must be pressed out of the housing bores. BMW bushings are notoriously hard to press out of the housings. Use a high capacity hydraulic press, penetrating lubricant and the proper sized mandrels for the press. Do not use

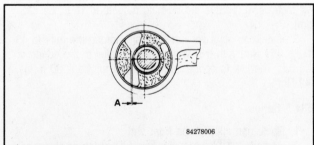

84278006

Fig. 6 With the vehicle loaded and at normal ride height, the gap at A in the lower control arm bushing should be 0.028-0.067 in. (0.7-1.7 mm) — E30 3 Series

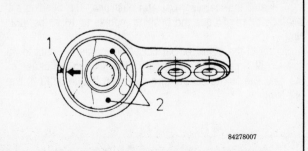

84278007

Fig. 7 The lower control arm bushing arrow should match the cast boss on the bracket — E30 3 Series

sockets to try to replace the bushings. Mark the relationship of the bushing to the bore for correct replacement positioning.

Thrust Rod

REMOVAL & INSTALLATION

E34 5 Series

▶ **See Figure 8**

The E34 5 Series uses a multi-link type suspension. There is a lower control arm to support the strut housing and a thrust rod to control fore and aft motion. The thrust rod is not used on 3 Series vehicles.

Always replace the strut rods in pairs. If the strut rods are not replaced in pairs, uneven driving response may result.

1. Raise and safely support the front end. Do not place the jackstands under any suspension parts. Remove the wheel.

2. Remove the thrust rod ball joint nut and press the stud out of the steering knuckle with a ball joint remover tool.

3. Remove the nut and bolt at the subframe end of the strut rod. Remove the strut rod.

To install:

4. Install the strut to the subframe using a new nut and washer on both sides. Do not torque at this point.

5. Clean the grease and dirt off of the ball joint stud and bore. Install the ball joint stud into the steering knuckle and torque the new nut to 67 ft. lbs. (93 Nm).

6. Install the wheel and lower the vehicle to the ground. Load 150 lbs. into each of the front seats and in the center of

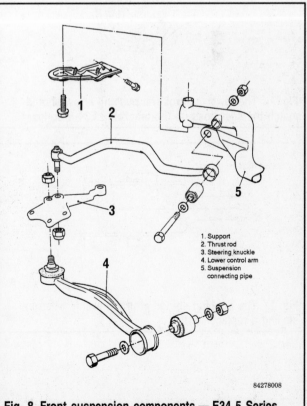

1. Support
2. Thrust rod
3. Steering knuckle
4. Lower control arm
5. Suspension connecting pipe

84278008

Fig. 8 Front suspension components — E34 5 Series

the rear seat. Torque the control arm to subframe bolt to 92 ft. lbs. (127 Nm).

BUSHING REPLACEMENT

▶ **See Figures 9, 10 and 11**

The bushings must be pressed out of the housing bores. BMW bushings are notoriously hard to press out of the housings. Use a high capacity hydraulic press, penetrating lubricant and the proper sized mandrels for the press. Do not use

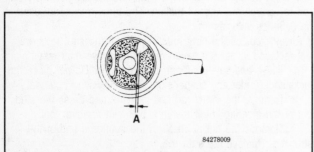

Fig. 9 With the vehicle loaded and at normal ride height, the gap at A in the lower control arm bushing should be 0.039-0.079 in. (1.0-2.0 mm) — E34 5 Series

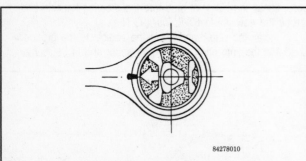

Fig. 10 The lower control arm bushing arrow should match the cast boss on the bracket — E34 5 Series

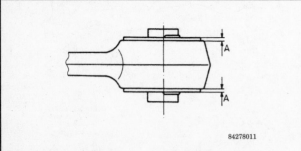

Fig. 11 The bushing should protrude evenly when installing a replacement

sockets to try to replace the bushings. Mark the relationship of the bushing to the bore for correct replacement positioning.

Stabilizer Bar

REMOVAL & INSTALLATION

E30 3 Series

1. Raise and support the front end.
2. Remove the stabilizer bar link nuts at the stabilizer bar. Disconnect the links from the bar on both sides.
3. Remove the bolts holding the left control arm bracket.
4. Remove the bolts holding the stabilizer bar and bushings to the body. Remove the stabilizer bar out from the left side.
   To install:
5. Install the stabilizer bar and bushings. Torque the bushing mounts to 16 ft. lbs. (22 Nm) with the wrench flats parallel to the edges of the bar. Install the left control arm bracket and torque the bolts to 30 ft. lbs. (42 Nm).
6. Install the stabilizer bar links and torque the nuts to 43 ft. lbs. (59 Nm). The link to control arm mounting torque is 30 ft. lbs. (42 Nm).

E36 3 Series

1. Raise and support the front end.
2. Remove the stabilizer bar link nuts at the stabilizer bar. Disconnect the links from the bar on both sides.
3. Remove the bolts holding the stabilizer bar and bushings to the body. Remove the stabilizer bar.
   To install:
4. Install the stabilizer bar and bushings. The bushing slit will face down. Torque the bushing mounts to 16 ft. lbs. (22 Nm).
5. Install the stabilizer bar links and torque the nuts to 43 ft. lbs. (59 Nm) with the wrench flats parallel to the edges of the bar. The link to control arm mounting torque is 30 ft. lbs. (42 Nm).

E34 5 Series

1. Raise and support the front end.
2. Remove the stabilizer bar link nuts at the stabilizer bar. Disconnect the links from the bar on both sides.
3. Remove the bolts holding the stabilizer bar and bushings to the body. Remove the stabilizer bar.
   To install:
4. Install the stabilizer bar and bushings. The bushing slit will face down. Torque the bushing mounts to 16 ft. lbs. (22 Nm).
5. Install the stabilizer bar links and torque the nuts to 43 ft. lbs. (59 Nm) with the wrench flats parallel to the edges of the bar. The link to control arm mounting torque is 30 ft. lbs. (42 Nm).

Wheel Bearings

REMOVAL & INSTALLATION

▶ **See Figure 12**

This procedure is for 2 wheel drive vehicles. For removal and installation for 4 wheel drive vehicles, refer to Section 7.

➡**The wheel bearings are only removed if they are worn. They cannot be removed without destroying them (due to side thrust created by the bearing puller). They are not periodically disassembled, repacked and adjusted.**

1. Remove the front wheel and support the car. Remove the attaching bolts and remove and suspend the brake caliper, hanging it from the body so as to avoid putting stress on the brake line.
2. Remove the brake disc setscrew with an Allen wrench. Pull off the brake disc and pry off the dust cover with a small prybar.
3. Using a chisel, knock the tab on the collar nut away from the shaft. Unscrew and discard the nut.
4. Pull off the bearing with a puller set such as 31 2 101/102/104 and discard it. On the M3, use a puller set such as 31 2 102/105/106. On the M3, install the main bracket of the puller with 3 wheel bolts.
5. If the inside bearing inner race remains on the stub axle, unbolt and remove the dust guard. Bend back the inner dust guard and pull the inner race off with a special tool capable of getting under the race (BMW 00 7 500 and 33 1 309 or equivalent). Reinstall the dust guard.

To install:

6. If the dust guard has been removed, install a new one. Install a special tool (BMW 31 2 120 or equivalent; on M3, use 31 2 110 or equivalent) over the stub axle and screw it in for the entire length of the guide sleeve's threads. Press the bearing on.
7. Reverse the remaining removal procedures to install the disc and caliper. Torque the wheel hub collar nut to 210 ft. lbs. (290 Nm). Lock the collar nut by bending over the tab.

Front End Alignment

CASTER

▶ **See Figure 13**

Caster is the tilt of the axis that the strut rotates about. The axis, called the king pin inclination, allow the tires to be pushed as opposed to being dragged by the car. Caster allows the wheels to self-center and return to the straight ahead position after the wheels have been turned. Excessive caster will numb the steering response of the vehicle.

Caster is not adjustable. If the caster measurement is not correct, a suspension part is bent or broken, or the body has been damaged.

KING PIN INCLINATION

▶ **See Figure 14**

The king pin is an imaginary line drawn from the top of the strut bearing to the ball joint at the base of the strut. This is the axis that the strut rotates about. The angle at which it makes with true vertical is the inclination.

The king pin inclination allows for road shock transmission to the steering wheel to be reduced, lower the amount of effort required to turn the wheels and also provides self returning force to straighten the vehicle after a turn. King pin inclination in addition to camber determines the contact patch of the tire on the ground.

King pin inclination is not adjustable and usually is not measured.

3
4
5
6

1
2

1. Grease cap
2. Collar nut
3. Bearing unit
4. ABS sensor pulse teeth
5. Inner dust cover
6. Spindle

84278012

Fig. 12 Wheel bearings can not be adjusted. The bearings must be replaced as a unit and never be reused once removed from the spindle

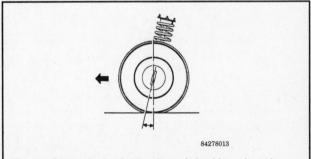

84278013

Fig. 13 Caster is the inclination of the king pin axis versus true vertical

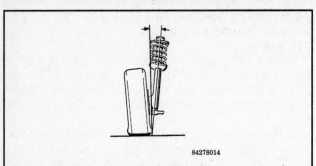

84278014

Fig. 14 King pin inclination is the angle the strut rotational axis makes with true vertical

CAMBER

▶ **See Figure 15**

Camber is the inclination of the wheel to true vertical. Camber allows the tire to place a larger contact patch on the ground as the vehicle rolls. Camber can be negative with the top of the wheel tilted in towards the vehicle or positive with the top of the wheel tilted out. Excessive negative camber will wear the tire on the inside edge and on the outside edge if the camber is too far positive.

High performance and racing tires tend to need more negative camber then a standard street tire. A race prepared vehi-

cle may have up to 3 degrees negative camber to compensate for roll. In a high performance application, the camber should be adjusted as many degrees negative as there are degrees body roll. This will cause the tire to be straight up and down at maximum roll and have a tire contact patch that is flat to the ground. If these levels of camber where used on a street car, the tires would wear the inside edges of the front tires in a very short period of time, plus exhibit twitchy steering response.

Camber is adjusted by moving the top of the strut mount in or out as needed. There are offset strut mounts available to change the camber.

TOE

▶ **See Figure 16**

Toe is measured with the wheels in the straight ahead position and is the difference between distances between the front of the wheels and at the rear of the wheels. Toe is considered toe-in if the tires are closer at the front of the wheels than at the back of the wheels. Toe-out is when the wheels are closer at the front than at the rear. Toe-in allow stability and toe-out causes a very sharp and unpredictable turn-in response if it is excessive.

Toe is adjusted by changing the length of the tie rods. The tie rods are adjusted evenly with the steering box centered.

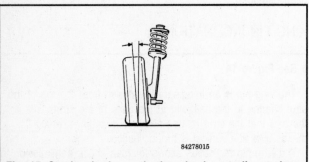

84278015

Fig. 15 Camber is the angle the wheel centerline makes with true vertical

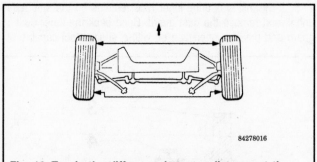

84278016

Fig. 16 Toe is the difference between distance at the front of the wheels and the rear of the wheels

FRONT WHEEL ALIGNMENT

Year	Model	Caster Range (deg.)	Caster Preferred Setting (deg.)	Camber Range (deg.)	Camber Preferred Setting (deg.)	Toe-in (in.)	Steering Axis Inclination (deg.)
1989	325i E30	$8^{1}/_{2} \pm {}^{1}/_{2}$	$8^{1}/_{2}$	$-{}^{2}/_{3} \pm {}^{1}/_{2}$	$-{}^{2}/_{3}$	0.08 ± 0.024	$13^{5}/_{6} \pm {}^{1}/_{2}$
	325iC E30	$8^{1}/_{2} \pm {}^{1}/_{2}$	$8^{1}/_{2}$	$-{}^{2}/_{3} \pm {}^{1}/_{2}$	$-{}^{2}/_{3}$	0.08 ± 0.024	$13^{5}/_{6} \pm {}^{1}/_{2}$
	325iX E30	$1^{1}/_{2} \pm {}^{1}/_{2}$	$1^{1}/_{2}$	$-1 \pm {}^{1}/_{2}$	-1	0.08 ± 0.024	$12^{2}/_{3} \pm {}^{1}/_{2}$
	M3 E30	$9^{2}/_{15} \pm {}^{1}/_{2}$	$9^{2}/_{15}$	$-{}^{7}/_{10} \pm {}^{1}/_{2}$	$-{}^{7}/_{10}$	0.08 ± 0.024	$14^{1}/_{6} \pm {}^{1}/_{2}$
	525i E34	$7^{13}/_{15} \pm {}^{1}/_{2}$	$7^{13}/_{15}$	$-{}^{7}/_{32} \pm {}^{1}/_{2}$	$-{}^{7}/_{32}$	0.08 ± 0.024	$12^{1}/_{15} \pm {}^{1}/_{2}$
	535i E34	$7^{13}/_{15} \pm {}^{1}/_{2}$	$7^{13}/_{15}$	$-{}^{7}/_{32} \pm {}^{1}/_{2}$	$-{}^{7}/_{32}$	0.08 ± 0.024	$12^{1}/_{15} \pm {}^{1}/_{2}$
1990	325i E30	$8^{1}/_{2} \pm {}^{1}/_{2}$	$8^{1}/_{2}$	$-{}^{2}/_{3} \pm {}^{1}/_{2}$	$-{}^{2}/_{3}$	0.08 ± 0.024	$13^{5}/_{6} \pm {}^{1}/_{2}$
	325iC E30	$8^{1}/_{2} \pm {}^{1}/_{2}$	$8^{1}/_{2}$	$-{}^{2}/_{3} \pm {}^{1}/_{2}$	$-{}^{2}/_{3}$	0.08 ± 0.024	$13^{5}/_{6} \pm {}^{1}/_{2}$
	325iX E30	$1^{1}/_{2} \pm {}^{1}/_{2}$	$1^{1}/_{2}$	$-1 \pm {}^{1}/_{2}$	-1	0.08 ± 0.024	$12^{2}/_{3} \pm {}^{1}/_{2}$
	M3 E30	$9^{2}/_{15} \pm {}^{1}/_{2}$	$9^{2}/_{15}$	$-{}^{7}/_{10} \pm {}^{1}/_{2}$	$-{}^{7}/_{10}$	0.08 ± 0.024	$14^{1}/_{6} \pm {}^{1}/_{2}$
	525i E34	$7^{13}/_{15} \pm {}^{1}/_{2}$	$7^{13}/_{15}$	$-{}^{7}/_{32} \pm {}^{1}/_{2}$	$-{}^{7}/_{32}$	0.08 ± 0.024	$12^{1}/_{15} \pm {}^{1}/_{2}$
	535i E34	$7^{13}/_{15} \pm {}^{1}/_{2}$	$7^{13}/_{15}$	$-{}^{7}/_{32} \pm {}^{1}/_{2}$	$-{}^{7}/_{32}$	0.08 ± 0.024	$12^{1}/_{15} \pm {}^{1}/_{2}$
1991	318i E30	$8^{1}/_{2} \pm {}^{1}/_{2}$	$8^{1}/_{2}$	$-{}^{2}/_{3} \pm {}^{1}/_{2}$	$-{}^{2}/_{3}$	0.08 ± 0.024	$13^{5}/_{6} \pm {}^{1}/_{2}$
	318iC E30	$8^{1}/_{2} \pm {}^{1}/_{2}$	$8^{1}/_{2}$	$-{}^{2}/_{3} \pm {}^{1}/_{2}$	$-{}^{2}/_{3}$	0.08 ± 0.024	$13^{5}/_{6} \pm {}^{1}/_{2}$
	318iS E30	$8^{1}/_{2} \pm {}^{1}/_{2}$	$8^{1}/_{2}$	$-{}^{2}/_{3} \pm {}^{1}/_{2}$	$-{}^{2}/_{3}$	0.08 ± 0.024	$13^{5}/_{6} \pm {}^{1}/_{2}$
	325i E30	$8^{1}/_{2} \pm {}^{1}/_{2}$	$8^{1}/_{2}$	$-{}^{2}/_{3} \pm {}^{1}/_{2}$	$-{}^{2}/_{3}$	0.08 ± 0.024	$13^{5}/_{6} \pm {}^{1}/_{2}$
	325iC E30	$8^{1}/_{2} \pm {}^{1}/_{2}$	$8^{1}/_{2}$	$-{}^{2}/_{3} \pm {}^{1}/_{2}$	$-{}^{2}/_{3}$	0.08 ± 0.024	$13^{5}/_{6} \pm {}^{1}/_{2}$
	325iX E30	$1^{1}/_{2} \pm {}^{1}/_{2}$	$1^{1}/_{2}$	$-1 \pm {}^{1}/_{2}$	-1	0.08 ± 0.024	$12^{2}/_{3} \pm {}^{1}/_{2}$
	M3 E30	$9^{2}/_{15} \pm {}^{1}/_{2}$	$9^{2}/_{15}$	$-{}^{7}/_{10} \pm {}^{1}/_{2}$	$-{}^{7}/_{10}$	0.08 ± 0.024	$14^{1}/_{6} \pm {}^{1}/_{2}$
	525i E34	$7^{13}/_{15} \pm {}^{1}/_{2}$	$7^{13}/_{15}$	$-{}^{7}/_{32} \pm {}^{1}/_{2}$	$-{}^{7}/_{32}$	0.08 ± 0.024	$12^{1}/_{15} \pm {}^{1}/_{2}$
	535i E34	$7^{13}/_{15} \pm {}^{1}/_{2}$	$7^{13}/_{15}$	$-{}^{7}/_{32} \pm {}^{1}/_{2}$	$-{}^{7}/_{32}$	0.08 ± 0.024	$12^{1}/_{15} \pm {}^{1}/_{2}$
1992-93	318i E36	$3^{2}/_{3} \pm {}^{1}/_{2}$	$3^{2}/_{3}$	$-{}^{2}/_{3} \pm {}^{1}/_{2}$	$-{}^{2}/_{3}$	0.08 ± 0.024	$15^{1}/_{2} \pm {}^{1}/_{2}$
	318iS E36	$3^{2}/_{3} \pm {}^{1}/_{2}$	$3^{2}/_{3}$	$-{}^{2}/_{3} \pm {}^{1}/_{2}$	$-{}^{2}/_{3}$	0.08 ± 0.024	$15^{1}/_{2} \pm {}^{1}/_{2}$
	318iC E30	$8^{1}/_{2} \pm {}^{1}/_{2}$	$8^{1}/_{2}$	$-{}^{2}/_{3} \pm {}^{1}/_{2}$	$-{}^{2}/_{3}$	0.08 ± 0.024	$15^{1}/_{2} \pm {}^{1}/_{2}$
	325i E36	$3^{2}/_{3} \pm {}^{1}/_{2}$	$3^{2}/_{3}$	$-{}^{2}/_{3} \pm {}^{1}/_{2}$	$-{}^{2}/_{3}$	0.08 ± 0.024	$15^{1}/_{2} \pm {}^{1}/_{2}$
	325iS E36	$3^{2}/_{3} \pm {}^{1}/_{2}$	$3^{2}/_{3}$	$-{}^{2}/_{3} \pm {}^{1}/_{2}$	$-{}^{2}/_{3}$	0.08 ± 0.024	$15^{1}/_{2} \pm {}^{1}/_{2}$
	325iC E30	$8^{1}/_{2} \pm {}^{1}/_{2}$	$8^{1}/_{2}$	$-{}^{2}/_{3} \pm {}^{1}/_{2}$	$-{}^{2}/_{3}$	0.08 ± 0.024	$15^{1}/_{2} \pm {}^{1}/_{2}$
	525i E34	$7^{13}/_{15} \pm {}^{1}/_{2}$	$7^{13}/_{15}$	$-{}^{7}/_{32} \pm {}^{1}/_{2}$	$-{}^{7}/_{32}$	0.08 ± 0.024	$12^{1}/_{15} \pm {}^{1}/_{2}$
	525iT E34	$7^{13}/_{15} \pm {}^{1}/_{2}$	$7^{13}/_{15}$	$-{}^{7}/_{32} \pm {}^{1}/_{2}$	$-{}^{7}/_{32}$	0.08 ± 0.024	$12^{1}/_{15} \pm {}^{1}/_{2}$
	535i E34	$7^{13}/_{15} \pm {}^{1}/_{2}$	$7^{13}/_{15}$	$-{}^{7}/_{32} \pm {}^{1}/_{2}$	$-{}^{7}/_{32}$	0.08 ± 0.024	$12^{1}/_{15} \pm {}^{1}/_{2}$
	M5 E34	$8^{1}/_{6} \pm {}^{1}/_{2}$	$8^{1}/_{6}$	$-{}^{1}/_{2} \pm {}^{1}/_{2}$	$-{}^{1}/_{2}$	0.08 ± 0.024	$12^{45}/_{64} \pm {}^{1}/_{2}$

84278025

REAR SUSPENSION

▶ See Figures 17 and 18

Coil Springs

REMOVAL & INSTALLATION

E30 3 Series

1. Disconnect the rear portion of the exhaust system and hang it from the body.
2. Disconnect the final drive rubber mount, push it down, and hold it down with a wedge.
3. Remove the bolt that connects the rear stabilizer bar to the strut on the side being worked on. Be careful not to damage the brake line.

➡Support the lower control arm securely with a jack or other device that will permit it to be lowered gradually, while maintaining secure support.

4. Then, to prevent damage to the output shaft joints, lower the control arm only enough to slip the coil spring off the retainer.
   To install:
5. Make sure, in replacing the spring, that the same part number, color code, and proper rubber ring are used. Install the spring, making sure that the spring is in proper position.

6. Keep the control arm securely supported while raising and replace the shock bolt. Install the bolts in the final drive rubber mount and torque to 69 ft. lbs. (95 Nm).
7. Torque the stabilizer bolt to 16 ft. lbs. (21.5 Nm), and the shock bolt to 63 ft. lbs. (87 Nm) with the control arm in the normal ride position. Install the exhaust system.

E36 3 Series

1. Raise the rear of the vehicle and support securely. Do not support on the suspension parts.
2. Support the lower trailing arm at the hub and disconnect the stabilizer bar at the control arm and the subframe.
3. Remove the shock absorber lower mounting bolt. Lower the trailing arm slowly and remove the spring to the side.
   To install:
4. Install the spring with the bushing in place and the top of the lubricated.
5. Raise the trailing arm to a level where the bolt can be replaced in the lower shock mount. Connect the stabilizer bar.
6. Torque the stabilizer bolt to 16 ft. lbs. (21.5 Nm), and the shock bolt to 63 ft. lbs. (87 Nm) with the control arm in the normal ride position.

E34 5 Series
▶ See Figure 19

1. Raise and support the rear of the vehicle.
2. Remove the rear seat cushion and backrest. Remove the trim panel over the strut mount.

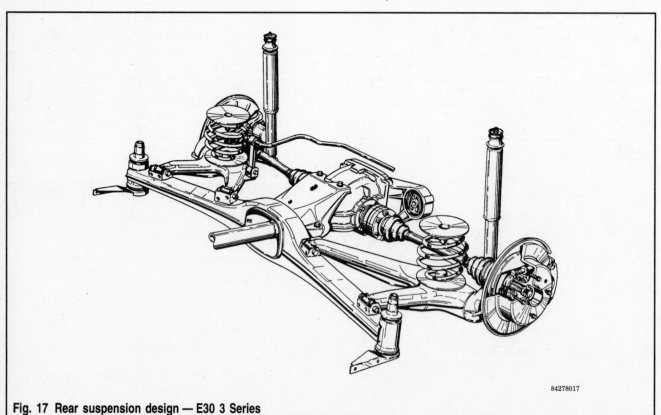

84278017

Fig. 17 Rear suspension design — E30 3 Series

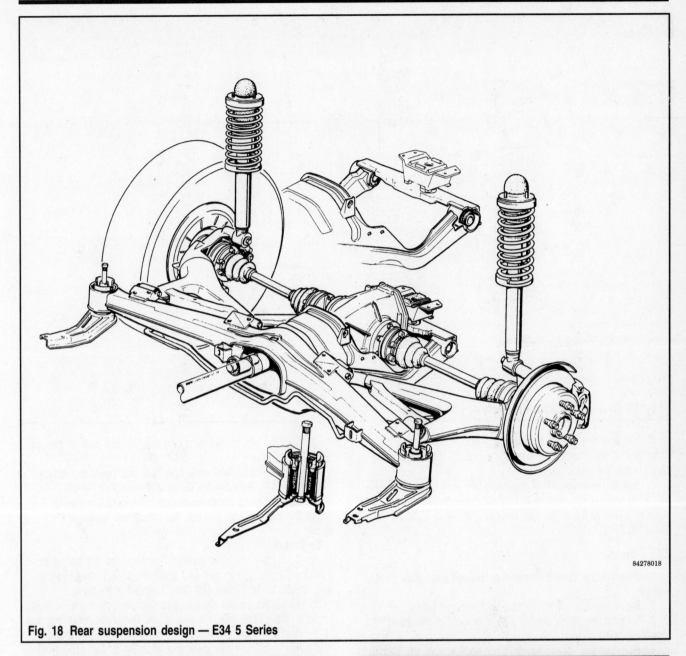

Fig. 18 Rear suspension design — E34 5 Series

3. Support the control arm and remove the nuts at the top of the strut mount.

4. Remove the lower mounting bolt and lower the spring strut assembly. Remove the assembly from the vehicle.

5. Use a spring compressor and compress the spring. Remove the top nut and pull the top mount off. Remove the spring.

To install:

6. Compress the new spring or replace the old spring on the strut. Install the mount and washers. Use a new locknut and torque to 18 ft. lbs. (25 Nm). Release the spring.

7. Install the spring strut and torque the upper mount nuts to 16 ft. lbs. (21.5 Nm). Loosely install the lower mounting bolt.

8. With the vehicle lowered to the ground and at standard riding height, torque the lower mount to 94 ft. lbs. (130 Nm).

9. Install the trim and seat cushions.

Shock Absorbers

REMOVAL & INSTALLATION

E30 3 Series

1. Remove the trunk trim panel to expose the upper shock mounts.

2. Raise the rear of the vehicle and support safely.

3. Support the lower control arm and remove the lower mounting bolt.

4. Remove the upper mounting nut and remove the shock from the vehicle.

To install:

5. Exchange or replace the upper shock mount and torque the upper shock nut to 11 ft. lbs. (15 Nm).

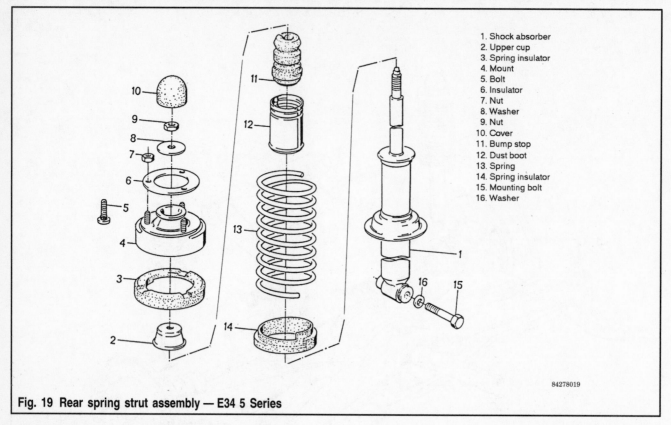

1. Shock absorber
2. Upper cup
3. Spring insulator
4. Mount
5. Bolt
6. Insulator
7. Nut
8. Washer
9. Nut
10. Cover
11. Bump stop
12. Dust boot
13. Spring
14. Spring insulator
15. Mounting bolt
16. Washer

84278019

Fig. 19 Rear spring strut assembly — E34 5 Series

6. Replace the gasket between the shock mount and the body. Install the shock and torque the nuts to 11 ft. lbs. (15 Nm). Install the trunk panel.

7. Install the lower shock mounting bolt and lower the vehicle. With the vehicle resting at standard ride height, torque the mounting bolt to 63 ft. lbs. (87 Nm) or if marked 10.9, 94 ft. lbs. (130 Nm).

E36 3 Series

1. Remove the trunk trim panel to expose the upper shock mounts.

2. Raise the rear of the vehicle and support safely.

3. Support the lower control arm and remove the lower mounting bolt.

4. Remove the upper mounting nut and remove the shock from the vehicle.

To install:

5. Exchange or replace the upper shock mount and torque the upper shock nut to 11 ft. lbs. (15 Nm).

6. Replace the gasket between the shock mount and the body. Install the shock and torque the nuts to 11 ft. lbs. (15 Nm). Install the trunk panel.

7. Install the lower shock mounting bolt and lower the vehicle. With the vehicle resting at standard ride height, torque the mounting bolt to 63 ft. lbs. (87 Nm) or if marked 10.9, 94 ft. lbs. (130 Nm).

E34 5 Series

▶ See Figure 19

1. Raise and support the rear of the vehicle.

2. Remove the rear seat cushion and backrest. Remove the trim panel over the strut mount.

3. Support the control arm and remove the nuts at the top of the strut mount.

4. Remove the lower mounting bolt and lower the spring strut assembly. Remove the assembly from the vehicle.

5. Use a spring compressor and compress the spring. Remove the top nut and pull the top mount off. Remove the spring.

To install:

6. Compress the new spring or replace the old spring on the strut. Install the mount and washers. Use a new locknut and torque to 18 ft. lbs. (25 Nm). Release the spring.

7. Install the spring strut and torque the upper mount nuts to 16 ft. lbs. (21.5 Nm). Loosely install the lower mounting bolt.

8. With the vehicle lowered to the ground and at standard riding height, torque the lower mount to 94 ft. lbs. (130 Nm).

9. Install the trim and seat cushions.

TESTING

The shock absorbers, more properly called suspension dampers, should be checked on a regular basis. Visual inspection for leaking oil and damage is a primary indicator of worn or broken shocks. A quick glance at the shocks will provide advance warning of shocks in need of replacement. If oil is visible in any amount more than a very slight coating, the shock need to be replaced. If any visible physical damage is noted, the shock should also be replaced.

The old time method of checking shocks by bouncing the corner of the vehicle is being outmoded by the use of gas pressure and deflecting disk technology shock absorbers. By the time the vehicle does bounce more than once during this type of test, the shocks have been in need of replacement for a long time. A gradual reduction in the handling capacity may not be noticed as it occurs over a long period of time. Some manufactures of shock absorbers use a design called deflecting disk. This design is inherently self-adjusting for wear and use. An indicator of worn shocks is uneven tire wear and a lack of suspension dampening while traveling over rough roads.

The shocks should always be replaced in pairs. It is also recommended to replace the springs on high mileage vehicles to restore original handling characteristics. Replace the shock mounts and rubber bushings. Check the condition of the stabilizer bar and the mounts

Rear End Alignment

The rear wheel alignment use many of the same parameters as the front end of the vehicle. The independent rear suspension exhibits changing camber, caster and toe as the wheels move up and down.

Camber, or the angle the wheel makes with true vertical, can be adjusted with special tools and techniques. The same is true for toe adjustments. It is best left to a properly equipped alignment specialist to perform any adjustments.

To properly align a fully independent suspension as all BMW's are equipped with, both the front and rear settings must be checked and adjusted to compensate for any differences at the front and rear axles. This is called a 4-wheel alignment and allows the front and rear suspensions to work in unison and not work against each other. If the front axle wants to travel in one direction and the rear works on another geometric axis, the vehicle will tend to crab or feel unstable. The front and rear suspensions have to be set to work on a common axis.

REAR WHEEL ALIGNMENT

Year	Model	Caster Range (deg.)	Caster Preferred Setting (deg.)	Camber Range (deg.)	Camber Preferred Setting (deg.)	Toe-in (in.)
1989	325i E30	NA	NA	$-2 \pm 1/2$	-2	0.08 ± 0.031
	325iC E30	NA	NA	$-1 5/6 \pm 1/2$	$-1 5/6$	0.08 ± 0.031
	325iX E30	NA	NA	$-2 \pm 1/2$	-2	0.08 ± 0.031
	M3 E30	NA	NA	$-2 1/2 \pm 1/2$	$-2 1/2$	0.09 ± 0.031
	525i E34	NA	NA	$-2 1/3 \pm 1/2$	$-2 1/3$	0.09 ± 0.031
	535 E34	NA	NA	$-2 1/3 \pm 1/2$	$-2 1/3$	0.09 ± 0.031
1990	325i E30	NA	NA	$-2 \pm 1/2$	-2	0.08 ± 0.031
	325iC E30	NA	NA	$-1 5/6 \pm 1/2$	$-1 5/6$	0.08 ± 0.031
	325iX E30	NA	NA	$-2 \pm 1/2$	-2	0.08 ± 0.031
	M3 E30	NA	NA	$-2 1/2 \pm 1/2$	$-2 1/2$	0.09 ± 0.031
	525i E34	NA	NA	$-2 1/3 \pm 1/2$	$-2 1/3$	0.09 ± 0.031
	535i E34	NA	NA	$-2 1/3 \pm 1/2$	$-2 1/3$	0.09 ± 0.031
1991	318i E30	NA	NA	$-2 \pm 1/2$	-2	0.08 ± 0.031
	318iC E30	NA	NA	$-1 5/6 \pm 1/2$	$-1 5/6$	0.08 ± 0.031
	318iS E30	NA	NA	$-2 \pm 1/2$	-2	0.08 ± 0.031
	325i E30	NA	NA	$-2 \pm 1/2$	-2	0.08 ± 0.031
	325iC E30	NA	NA	$-1 5/6 \pm 1/2$	$-1 5/6$	0.08 ± 0.031
	325iX E30	NA	NA	$-2 \pm 1/2$	-2	0.08 ± 0.031
	M3 E30	NA	NA	$-2 1/2 \pm 1/2$	$-2 1/2$	0.09 ± 0.031
	525i E34	NA	NA	$-2 1/3 \pm 1/2$	$-2 1/3$	0.09 ± 0.031
	535i E34	NA	NA	$-2 1/3 \pm 1/2$	$-2 1/3$	0.09 ± 0.031
1992-93	318i E36	NA	NA	$-1 1/2 \pm 1/6$	$-1 1/2$	0.09 ± 0.031
	318iS E36	NA	NA	$-1 1/2 \pm 1/6$	$-1 1/2$	0.09 ± 0.031
	318iC E30	NA	NA	$-1 5/6 \pm 1/2$	$-1 5/6$	0.08 ± 0.031
	325i E36	NA	NA	$-1 1/2 \pm 1/6$	$-1 1/2$	0.09 ± 0.031
	325iS E36	NA	NA	$-1 1/2 \pm 1/6$	$-1 1/2$	0.09 ± 0.031
	325iC E30	NA	NA	$-1 5/6 \pm 1/2$	$-1 5/6$	0.08 ± 0.031
	525i E34	NA	NA	$-2 1/3 \pm 1/2$	$-2 1/3$	0.09 ± 0.031
	525iT E34	NA	NA	$-2 3/4 \pm 1/2$	$-2 3/4$	0.09 ± 0.031
	535i E34	NA	NA	$-2 1/3 \pm 1/2$	$-2 1/3$	0.09 ± 0.031
	M5 E34	NA	NA	$-2 1/4 \pm 1/2$	$-2 1/4$	0.09 ± 0.031

NA—Not available

84278026

STEERING

Steering Wheel

REMOVAL & INSTALLATION

Without SRS Air Bag

1. Unlock the steering column with the ignition key.
2. Carefully pry the center emblem out of the steering wheel.
3. Hold the steering wheel and remove the nut from the steering shaft.
4. Mark the relationship of the steering wheel to the shaft and pull the steering wheel off the shaft.
   To install:
5. Install the steering wheel in its original position. Install the washer and a new locknut. Torque the nut to 58 ft. lbs. (80 Nm). Do not use the steering column lock to hold the steering wheel against the torque. Hold the wheel during torquing.
6. Install the center emblem by pressing down into the opening. Check for smooth rotation of the wheel and operation of the horn.

With SRS Air Bag

✳✳CAUTION

All precautions must be adhered to or premature deployment of the air bag may occur causing personal injury. If the air bag system is damaged or rendered inoperative, the additional protection an air bag provides in a frontal collision will not be available and may lead to greater injury in an accident. Refer to Section 6 for SRS precautions and procedures.

1. Disarm the SRS and disconnect the negative battery terminal. Remove the lower steering column trim or the small panel and disconnect the orange connector.
2. Use tool 00 2 110 or equivalent, to remove the air bag module bolts from behind the steering wheel. Remove the air bag module and disconnect the wire on the back. Place the air bag module in the trunk with the pad facing up.
3. Unlock the steering column with the ignition key. Turn the steering wheel to the straight position.
4. Hold the steering wheel and remove the nut from the steering shaft.
5. Mark the relationship of the steering wheel to the shaft and pull the steering wheel off the shaft.
   To install:
6. Install the steering wheel in its original position with the lock pin in the bore. Install the washer and a new locknut. Torque the nut to 58 ft. lbs. (80 Nm). Do not use the steering column lock to hold the steering wheel against the torque. Hold the wheel during torquing.
7. If the contact ring has moved out of position and needs to be return to the center, press the spring and rotate the ring completely left or right to the stop. Turn the ring in the opposite direction 3 turns to align the marks.
8. Install the air bag module and connect the wires. Torque the mounting bolts to 6 ft. lbs. (8 Nm), right side first. Check for smooth rotation of the wheel and operation of the horn.

Turn Signal Switch

REMOVAL & INSTALLATION

E30 3 Series

1. Disconnect the negative battery terminal. Remove the steering wheel.
2. Remove the trim panel at the bottom left of the instrument panel and the lower steering column casing.
3. Remove the screws holding the switch. Remove the switch and disconnect the plug.
   To install:
4. Install the switch and connect the plug. The ground wire must be connected and the retainers must fit into the holes.
5. Install the trim panels and steering wheel. Connect the negative battery terminal.

E36 3 Series

1. Remove the lower dashboard trim panel at the left. Remove the lower section of the steering column casing.
2. Remove the steering wheel. Remove the screw and compress the clip to release the switch. Disconnect the plug.
3. Install the switch and connect the plug. Install the steering wheel and trim panels.

E34 5 Series

1. Remove the lower dashboard trim panel at the left. Remove the lower section of the steering column casing.
2. Remove the steering wheel and compress the clip to release the switch. Disconnect the plug.
3. Install the switch and connect the plug. Install the steering wheel and trim panels.

Ignition Switch

REMOVAL & INSTALLATION

1. Disconnect the negative battery terminal. Disarm the SRS when working on the steering column, if equipped.
2. Remove the steering wheel, the trim panel below steering column and the steering column lower casing.
3. Disconnect the ignition switch harness and press the clips in securing the switch. Pull the switch off the lock assembly.
4. Check the position of the switch and install in reverse order.

Ignition Lock Cylinder

REMOVAL & INSTALLATION

1. Insert the ignition key and turn 60 degrees.
2. Use a 3/64 inch (1.2mm) wire to press down into the small bore on the face of the lock.
3. Pull the lock cylinder out.
4. If there is no bore, remove the steering column trim and press the bore on the side of the cylinder with punch to remove the cylinder.
5. Installation is the reverse of removal.

Steering Column

✳✳CAUTION

On vehicles equipped with an air bag, the negative battery cable must be disconnected, before working on the system. Failure to do so may result in deployment of the air bag and possible personal injury.

REMOVAL & INSTALLATION

1. Disconnect the negative battery cable. Remove the steering wheel.
2. Remove the lower instrument trim panel. Disconnect the steering column casing.
3. Disconnect the electrical connections. Press down on the steering spindle, remove the bolt and the spindle.
4. Remove the shear-off bolts with a proper chisel. Remove the mounting nuts/bolts.
5. Press down and remove the steering column.
6. The installation is the reverse of the removal procedure. Install new bolts.

Steering Linkage

REMOVAL & INSTALLATION

Tie Rod

E30 3 SERIES

1. Raise and support them front of the vehicle.
2. Remove the tie rod nut at the steering arm. Disconnect the tie rod from the steering arm with a tie rod end removal press.
3. Remove the straps around the rack dust boot and push the boot back to expose the rack connection.
4. Use pliers to push back the lock plate. Use tool 32 2 100 or equivalent, to loosen and remove the tie rod from the rack.
   To install:
5. Install a new lock plate. Install a new dust boot, if necessary. Torque the tie rod joint to 54 ft. lbs. (75 Nm). The boss must fit into the groove on the rack. Use pliers to bend the lock plate over the flats on the nut.
6. Install new straps to hold the dust boot in place.
7. Install the tie rod to the steering knuckle. Clean the bore and the stud before assembly. Torque the nut to 23-29 ft. lbs. (33-40 Nm). Do not use a locknut on a tie rod that has a hole for a cotter pin. If originally equipped with a locknut, use a new locknut for installation.
8. Have the alignment check and adjusted.

E36 3 SERIES

1. Raise and support them front of the vehicle.
2. Remove the tie rod nut at the steering arm. Disconnect the tie rod from the steering arm with a tie rod end removal press.
3. Remove the straps around the rack dust boot and push the boot back to expose the rack connection.
4. Use pliers to push back the lock plate. Use tool 32 2 100 or equivalent, to loosen and remove the tie rod from the rack.
   To install:
5. Install a new lock plate. Install a new dust boot, if necessary. Torque the tie rod joint to 54 ft. lbs. (75 Nm). The boss must fit into the groove on the rack. Use pliers to bend the lock plate over the flats on the nut.
6. Install new straps to hold the dust boot in place.
7. Install the tie rod to the steering knuckle. Clean the bore and the stud before assembly. Torque the nut to 23-29 ft. lbs. (33-40 Nm). Do not use a locknut on a tie rod that has a hole for a cotter pin. If originally equipped with a locknut, use a new locknut for installation.
8. Have the alignment checked and adjusted.

E34 5 Series

1. Raise and safely support the front end. Do not place the jackstands under any suspension parts. Remove the wheel.
2. Remove the 3 bolts holding the steering knuckle to the bottom of the strut.
3. Remove the tie rod nut and press the stud out of the steering knuckle with a tie rod remover tool.
4. Remove the tie rod nut and press the stud out of control arm with a tie rod remover tool.
   To install:
5. Clean the grease and dirt off of the ball joint stud and bore. Install the tie rod stud into the steering knuckle and control arm. Torque the new nut to 67 ft. lbs. (93 Nm).
6. Clean the threads and bores of the steering knuckle mounting bolts and the strut housing. Install the bolts, using threadlocker, and torque to 80 ft. lbs. (110 Nm). There is a groove that will align the strut and knuckle.
7. Install the wheel and lower the vehicle to the ground. Have the alignment checked and adjusted.

Center Link

1. Raise and support the front end of the vehicle.
2. Remove the joint nuts and press the studs out of the center link with a tie rod removal tool.
3. Check the length between the studs. It should be 21.023 in. (534mm).
4. Install the center link. Clean the bores and studs. Use new nuts and torque to 23-29 ft. lbs. (33-40 Nm). Do not use

a locknut on a tie rod that has a hole for a cotter pin. If originally equipped with a locknut, use a new locknut for installation.

5. Have the alignment checked and adjusted.

Idler Arm

1. Raise and support the front end of the vehicle.
2. Remove the center link ball joint nut and press the stud out of the center link with a tie rod removal tool.
3. Remove the nut and bolt holding the idler arm. Remove the idler arm taking note of the positioning of the washer between the arm and the subframe. The bushing can be pressed out and replaced.

To install:

4. Install the idler arm and torque the nut to 30 ft. lbs. (42 Nm) if it is M10 or 61 ft. lbs. (85 Nm) if it is M12.
5. Clean the bores and studs. Use new nuts and torque the center link ball joint to 23-29 ft. lbs. (33-40 Nm). Do not use a locknut on a joint that has a hole for a cotter pin. If originally equipped with a locknut, use a new locknut for installation.
6. Have the alignment checked and adjusted.

Power Steering Rack/Gear

REMOVAL & INSTALLATION

E30 3 Series
▶ See Figures 20 and 21

2 WHEEL DRIVE

1. Raise and support the front end of the vehicle. Remove the front wheels.
2. Remove the steering wheel. Remove the steering rack coupling bolt. Loosen the upper bolt so the coupling can be disconnected from the steering rack.
3. Remove the power steering fluid from the reservoir and discard. Disconnect and plug the fluid return line from the rack. Remove the pressure line hollow bolt from the rack and plug.
4. Disconnect the tie rods from the steering knuckles. Remove the steering rack mounting bolts. Note which holes the steering rack was mounted to. If equipped, disconnect the engine mounts located above the steering rack.
5. Raise the engine about 2 in. (50mm) and remove the steering rack.

To install:

6. Install the steering gear. Use the rear holes in the crossmember or the ones originally used if not the rear holes. Lower the engine.
7. Torque the steering gear bolts to 30 ft. lbs. (42 Nm). Torque the engine mount nuts to 16 ft. lbs. (22 Nm) for M8 bolts and 30 ft. lbs. (42 Nm) for M10 bolts.
8. Connect the tie rods to the steering knuckles and torque the nuts to 23-29 ft. lbs. (33-40 Nm). Do not use a locknut on a joint that has a hole for a cotter pin. If originally equipped with a locknut, use a new locknut for installation.
9. Connect the return line to the steering rack. Connect the pressure line to the steering rack using new crush washers.

Torque the hollow bolt to 7 ft. lbs. (10 Nm) for M10 bolts and 14.5 ft. lbs. (20 Nm) for M12 bolts.

10. Align the mark on the steering rack shaft with the mark on the rack housing. Align the slot of the universal joint with the shaft and housing marks. This is the centered position. Install the bolts and torque to 16 ft. lbs. (22 Nm).
11. Install the steering wheel in the centered position.
12. Fill and bleed the power steering reservoir. Have the alignment checked.

4 WHEEL DRIVE

➡**To remove the steering gear on 4WD vehicles, use a special tool to support the engine via the body. It is also advisable to use a special tool to support the front axle carrier without damaging it. It is necessary to remove the entire front axle carrier to gain access to the mounting bolts for the steering gear on this vehicle.**

1. Raise the vehicle and support it securely. Remove the splash guard. Remove the front wheels.
2. Remove the air cleaner. Use a clean syringe to remove the power steering fluid from the pump reservoir.
3. Attach the support tool and connect it to the engine hooks to be sure the engine is securely supported.
4. Remove the through bolts from the right and left engine mounts.
5. Disconnect both the hydraulic lines running from the power steering pump to the steering gear, and then plug the openings.
6. Loosen both the retaining bolts and then disconnect the steering column spindle off the steering gear.
7. Remove the retaining nuts on both sides and then press the tie rod ends off the steering knuckles with the proper tools. Be careful to keep grease out of the bores and off the tie rod ball studs.
8. Remove the cotter pins, remove the retaining nuts on both sides and then use the proper tool to press the control arm ball joint studs out of the steering knuckles. Be careful to keep grease out of the bores and off the control arm ball studs.
9. Remove the bolts on either side attaching the control arm brackets to the body.
10. Remove the bolts and remove the stabilizer bar mounting brackets from the front axle carrier on both sides.
11. Support the front axle carrier with a suitable jacking device. Then, remove the mounting bolts on either side and remove the axle carrier. Remove the mounting bolts and remove the steering gear from the axle carrier.

To install:

12. Install in reverse order, noting these points:
    a. Clean the bores into which the axle carrier bolts are mounted. Use some sort of locking sealer and torque the bolts to 30 ft. lbs. (41 Nm).
    b. Torque the mounting bolts holding the steering gear to front axle carrier to 30 ft. lbs. (41 Nm).
    c. Install new cotter pins on the retaining nuts for the control arm ball studs. Torque to 61.5 ft. lbs. (84 Nm).
    d. Replace the self-locking nuts on the tie rod end ball studs and connecting the steering column spindle to the steering box. Torque tie rod ball stud nuts to 24-29 ft. lbs. (33-40 Nm).
    e. Replace the gaskets on power steering hydraulic lines.

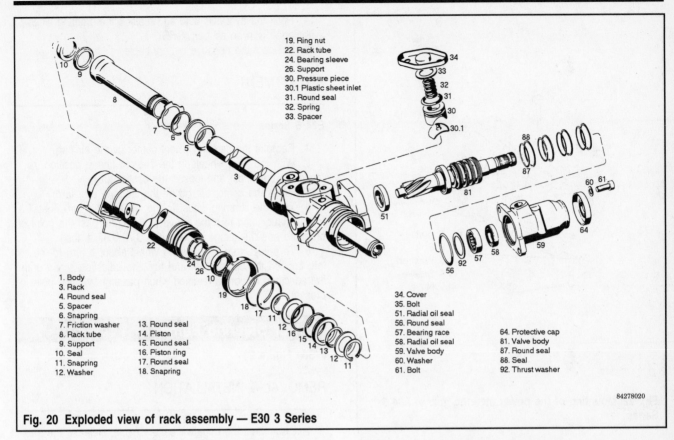

19. Ring nut
22. Rack tube
24. Bearing sleeve
26. Support
30. Pressure piece
30.1 Plastic sheet inlet
31. Round seal
32. Spring
33. Spacer

1. Body
3. Rack
4. Round seal
5. Spacer
6. Snapring
7. Friction washer
8. Rack tube
9. Support
10. Seal
11. Snapring
12. Washer

13. Round seal
14. Piston
15. Round seal
16. Piston ring
17. Round seal
18. Snapring

34. Cover
35. Bolt
51. Radial oil seal
56. Round seal
57. Bearing race
58. Radial oil seal
59. Valve body
60. Washer
61. Bolt

64. Protective cap
81. Valve body
87. Round seal
88. Seal
92. Thrust washer

84278020

Fig. 20 Exploded view of rack assembly — E30 3 Series

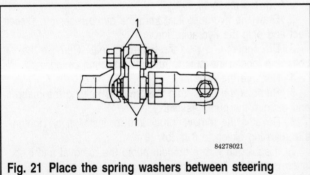

84278021

Fig. 21 Place the spring washers between steering coupling and joint — E30 3 Series

13. Refill the fluid reservoir with specified fluid. Idle the engine and turn the steering wheel back and forth until it has reached right and left lock 2 times each. Then, turn off the engine and refill the reservoir.

E36 3 Series

1. Raise and support the front end of the vehicle. Remove the front wheels.

2. Remove the steering wheel. Remove the steering rack coupling bolt. Loosen the upper bolt so the coupling can be disconnected from the steering rack.

3. Remove the power steering fluid from the reservoir and discard. Disconnect and plug the fluid return line from the rack. Remove the pressure line hollow bolt from the rack and plug.

4. Disconnect the tie rods from the steering knuckles. Remove the steering rack mounting bolts. Note which holes the

steering rack was mounted to. If equipped, disconnect the engine mounts located above the steering rack.

5. Raise the engine about 2 in. (50mm) and remove the steering rack.

To install:

6. Install the steering gear. Use the rear holes in the crossmember or the ones originally used if not the rear holes. Lower the engine.

7. Torque the steering gear bolts to 30 ft. lbs. (42 Nm). Torque the engine mount nuts to 16 ft. lbs. (22 Nm) for M8 bolts and 30 ft. lbs. (42 Nm) for M10 bolts.

8. Connect the tie rods to the steering knuckles and torque the nuts to 23-29 ft. lbs. (33-40 Nm). Do not use a locknut on a joint that has a hole for a cotter pin. If originally equipped with a locknut, use a new locknut for installation.

9. Connect the return line to the steering rack. Connect the pressure line to the steering rack using new crush washers. Torque the hollow bolt to 7 ft. lbs. (10 Nm) for M10 bolts and 14.5 ft. lbs. (20 Nm) for M12 bolts.

10. Align the mark on the steering rack shaft with the mark on the rack housing. Align the slot of the universal joint with the shaft and housing marks. This is the centered position. Install the bolts and torque to 16 ft. lbs. (22 Nm).

11. Install the steering wheel in the centered position.

12. Fill and bleed the power steering reservoir. Have the alignment checked.

E34 5 Series

▶ See Figure 22

1. Disconnect the negative battery cable.

2. Remove the steering wheel, if equipped with an air bag (SRS).

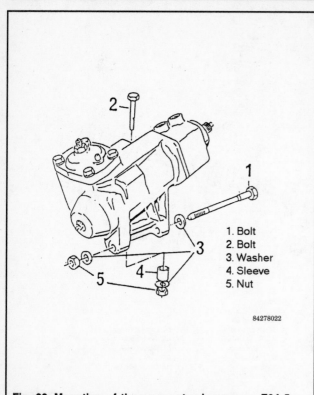

Fig. 22 Mounting of the power steering gear — E34 5 Series

1. Bolt
2. Bolt
3. Washer
4. Sleeve
5. Nut

84278022

3. Discharge the pressure reservoir by pushing in on the brake pedal about 10 times or until the pedal feels hard. Draw off hydraulic fluid in the supply tank.

4. Unscrew the bolt and press the tie rod off the steering drop arm with the proper tool.

5. Remove the heat shield on the steering gear and disconnect the ride level height control pipes, if equipped.

6. Remove the bolt and push the U-joint from the steering gear. Disconnect and plug the hydraulic lines.

7. Unscrew the steering gear mounting bolts and remove the steering gear.

➡**If necessary, move the steering drop arm by turning the steering stub to enable the removal of the gear assembly.**

To install:

8. Install the steering gear and tighten the mounting bolts. Torque the M10 bolts to 30 ft. lbs. (42 Nm) and the M12 bolts to 52-64 ft. lbs. (72-88 Nm).

9. Connect the hydraulic lines, using new seals. Torque the M14 bolts to 25 ft. lbs. (35 Nm) and the M16 bolts to 29 ft. lbs. (40 Nm).

10. Turn the steering wheel counterclockwise or clockwise against the stop and then it back about 1.7 turns until the marks are aligned.

11. Connect the U-joint to the steering gear making sure the bolt is in the locking groove of the steering stub.

12. Install the tie rod to the steering drop arm and replace the self locking nut.

13. Replace the heat shield on the steering gear and connect the ride level height control pipes if equipped.

14. Refill the hydraulic fluid and replace the steering wheel, if equipped with an air bag (SRS).

15. Connect the negative battery cable.

ADJUSTMENT

E34 5 Series

1. Remove the steering wheel center or the air bag.

2. With the front wheels in the straight ahead position, remove the cotter pin and loosen the castle nut.

3. Press the center tie rod off the steering drop arm.

4. Turn the steering wheel to the left about 1 turn. Install a friction gauge and turn the wheel to the right, past the point of pressure and the gauge should read 0.72-0.87 ft. lbs.

5. To adjust, turn the steering wheel about 1 turn to the left. Loosen the counter nut and turn the adjusting screw until the specified friction is reached when passing over the point of pressure.

Power Steering Pump

▶ **See Figure 23**

REMOVAL & INSTALLATION

1. Disconnect the negative battery cable. Release the pressure from the reservoir.

2. Draw the hydraulic fluid from the pump reservoir. Disconnect and plug the hydraulic lines.

3. Disconnect and plug the hydraulic lines. Remove the bolts and loosen the nuts to turn the adjusting pinion.

4. Remove the drive belt.

5. Remove the bolts from the brackets holding the pump and remove the pump assembly.

6. Reverse the removal procedure for installation. Tighten the adjusting pinion to 6 ft. lbs. (8 Nm).

7. If equipped with a tandem pump the removal and installation procedure is the same.

SYSTEM BLEEDING

Without Ride Height Control

1. Fill the reservoir to the **MAX** mark on the oil stick.

2. Rotate the steering in both directions fully, to each stop, until all the air is removed from the fluid.

3. Check the oil level and fill to the specified mark, if necessary.

With Ride Height Control

1. Fill the reservoir to the level of the strainer.

2. Rotate the steering in both directions fully at least 2 times.

3. Raise the vehicle so the rear wheels are off the ground.

4. Check the oil level. The level should be about ¼ in. (5 mm) above the strainer after 2 minutes. Fill to the specified mark, if necessary.

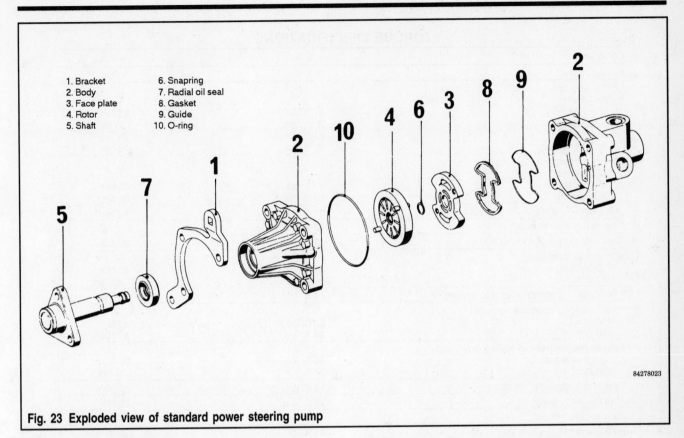

1. Bracket
2. Body
3. Face plate
4. Rotor
5. Shaft
6. Snapring
7. Radial oil seal
8. Gasket
9. Guide
10. O-ring

84278023

Fig. 23 Exploded view of standard power steering pump

With ASC+T Traction Control

1. Check the brake fluid reservoir and top off if necessary.

2. Turn the ignition switch to the **OFF** position. Remove the electronics box cover in the rear right of the engine compartment. Disconnect the plug from the forward control unit. Fill the reservoir with hydraulic fluid.

3. Connect the control unit and run the engine for 1 minute.

4. Connect tool 34 3 110 or equivalent, to the plunger-type hydraulic control unit bleeder screw. Place the hose into the reservoir and loosen the bleeder screw. Allow fluid to flow for 15 seconds or until the flow is without bubbles.

TORQUE SPECIFICATIONS

Component	U.S.	Metric
Air bag to steering wheel:	7 ft. lbs.	10 Nm
Control arm to subframe		
E30 3 Series		
2 wheel drive:	61 ft. lbs.	85 Nm
4 wheel drive:	72 ft. lbs.	100 Nm
E36 3 Series:	61 ft. lbs.	85 Nm
E34 5 Series:	56 ft. lbs.	78 Nm
Control arm to strut		
E30 3 Series		
2 wheel drive:	47 ft. lbs.	65 Nm
4 wheel drive:	62 ft. lbs.	85 Nm
Control arm bushing bracket to subframe:	30 ft. lbs.	42 Nm
Connecting pipe to body:	92 ft. lbs.	127 Nm
Connecting pipe support to body:	42 ft. lbs.	59 Nm
Idler arm to subframe		
M10 bolt:	30 ft. lbs.	42 Nm
M12 bolt:	52–64 ft. lbs.	72–88 Nm
Power steering pump bracket to engine:	16 ft. lbs.	22 Nm
Power steering hose connections		
M14 bolt:	25 ft. lbs.	35 Nm
M16 bolt:	29 ft. lbs.	40 Nm
Rear shock absorber to trailing arm		
Except 10.9 bolt:	63 ft. lbs.	87 Nm
10.9 bolt:	94 ft. lbs.	130 Nm
Rear shock absorber mounts:	16 ft. lbs.	22 Nm
Strut mount to body:	16 ft. lbs.	22 Nm
Strut to strut mount:	47 ft. lbs.	65 Nm
Strut gland nut:	94 ft. lbs.	130 Nm
Stabilizer bar mount to body:	16 ft. lbs.	22 Nm
Stabilizer bar link to strut or control arm:	43 ft. lbs.	59 Nm
Stabilizer bar link pivot to control arm:	30 ft. lbs.	42 Nm
Steering knuckle to strut		
E30 M3:	22 ft. lbs.	30 Nm
E34 5 Series:	80 ft. lbs.	110 Nm
Steering knuckle to control arm		
E30 M3:	48 ft. lbs.	64 Nm
E34 5 Series:	67 ft. lbs.	93 Nm
Steering column disk and joint bolts:	16 ft. lbs.	22 Nm
Steering wheel nut:	58 ft. lbs.	80 Nm
Steering gear to subframe		
M10 bolt:	30 ft. lbs.	42 Nm
M12 bolt:	52–64 ft. lbs.	72–88 Nm
Steering gear adjusting locknut:	20 ft. lbs.	27 Nm
Steering gear oil drain plug:	30 ft. lbs.	42 Nm
Steering arm to steering gear:	43 ft. lbs.	59 Nm
Subframe to body		
M10 9.8 bolts:	34 ft. lbs.	47 Nm
M10 8.8 bolts:	30 ft. lbs.	42 Nm
M12:	56 ft. lbs.	77 Nm
Tie rod to rack:	54 ft. lbs.	75 Nm
Tie rod stud nuts:	23–29 ft. lbs.	33–40 Nm
Tie rod adjustment nuts:	10 ft. lbs.	14 Nm
Thrust arm to steering knuckle:	67 ft. lbs.	93 Nm
Thrust arm to connecting pipe:	92 ft. lbs.	127 Nm
Wheels		
Lug bolts:	65–79 ft. lbs.	90–110 Nm
Vane bolts:	2 ft. lbs.	3 Nm
Wheel hub nut		
2 wheel drive:	210 ft. lbs.	290 Nm
4 wheel drive:	181 ft. lbs.	250 Nm

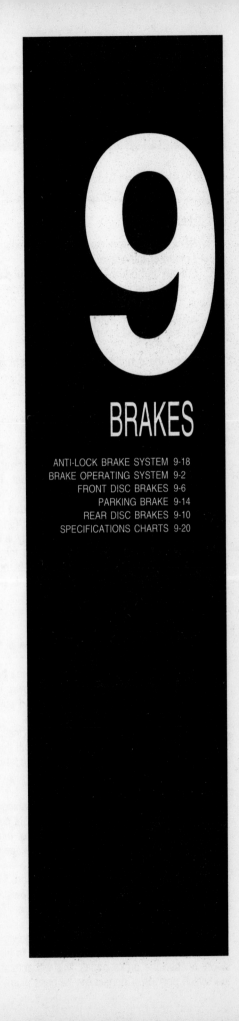

9

BRAKES

BRAKE OPERATING SYSTEM

Brake Pedal

REMOVAL & INSTALLATION

E30 3 Series

1. Remove the lower dashboard trim panel to access the upper portion of the brake pedal.
2. Unhook the brake pedal and clutch pedal return springs.
3. Unclip the retainer from the brake pedal to linkage pin and pull the pin out.
4. Remove the nut from the pivot shaft and pull the shaft out. Remove the brake pedal.
   To install:
5. Check the condition of the pedal bushing and replace if necessary. Lubricate the bushing with a light coating of grease.
6. Install the pedal and replace the pivot. Use a new locknut and torque to 20 ft. lbs. (27 Nm).
7. Install the pin and retainer at the linkage. Connect the pedal return springs.
8. Adjust the pedal height at the pushrod. The height should be 9.25 inches (235mm) from the lower edge of the pedal to the firewall, not including the carpet. Torque the locknut to 20 ft. lbs. (27 Nm).
9. If the brake light switch has a threaded body, adjust the brake light switch so there is 0.236 inches (6mm) from the pedal to the edge of the switch. If the body is not threaded, adjustment is automatic. Depress and hold the brake pedal down. Pull the sleeve and plunger to the full out position. Install in the holder and slowly release the brake pedal.
10. Install the lower trim.

E36 3 Series

1. Remove the lower dashboard trim panel to access the upper portion of the brake pedal.
2. Disconnect the wiring harness from the brake light switch. Press the brake pedal and hold down. Pull the plunger and sleeve of the brake switch forward and pull the switch out of the holder.
3. Disconnect the pedal return spring. Unclip the retainer from the brake pedal to linkage pin and pull the pin out.
4. Unclip the retainer from the brake pedal pivot pin and pull the pedal off.
   To install:
5. Check the condition of the pedal bushing and replace if necessary. Lubricate the bushing with a light coating of grease.
6. Install the pedal and replace the pivot retainer clip.
7. Install the pin and retainer at the linkage. Connect the pedal return springs.
8. Adjust the pedal height at the pushrod. The height should be 8.85 inches (225mm) from the lower edge of the pedal to the firewall, not including the carpet. Torque the locknut to 20 ft. lbs. (27 Nm).
9. Depress and hold the brake pedal down. Pull the sleeve and plunger to the full out position. Install in the holder and slowly release the brake pedal. This will automatically adjust the switch position. Connect the harness plug.
10. Install the lower trim.

E34 5 Series

1. Remove the lower dashboard trim panel to access the upper portion of the brake pedal.
2. Unhook the brake pedal return spring.
3. Unclip the retainer from the brake pedal to linkage pin and pull the pin out.
4. Remove the nut from the pivot shaft and pull the shaft out to the clutch pedal. Remove the brake pedal complete with spacers and spring.
   To install:
5. Check the condition of the pedal bushing and replace if necessary. Lubricate the bushing with a light coating of grease.
6. Install the pedal and replace the pivot shaft. Use a new locknut and torque to 20 ft. lbs. (27 Nm).
7. Install the pin and retainer at the linkage. Connect the pedal return spring.
8. Adjust the pedal height at the pushrod. The height should be 9.65 inches (245mm) from the lower edge of pedal to the firewall, not including the carpet. Torque the locknut to 20 ft. lbs. (27 Nm).
9. If the brake light switch has a threaded body, adjust the brake light switch so there is 0.236 inches (6mm) from the pedal to the edge of the switch. If the body is not threaded, adjustment is automatic. Depress and hold the brake pedal down. Pull the sleeve and plunger to the full out position. Install in the holder and slowly release the brake pedal.
10. Install the lower trim.

ADJUSTMENT

▶ **See Figure 1**

E30 3 Series

1. Remove the lower dashboard trim panel to access the pedal.
2. Adjust the pedal height at the pushrod. The height should be 9.25 inches (235mm) from the lower edge of the pedal to the firewall, not including the carpet.
3. Torque the locknut to 20 ft. lbs. (27 Nm). Install the trim.

E36 3 Series

1. Remove the lower dashboard trim panel to access the pedal.
2. Adjust the pedal height at the pushrod. The height should be 8.85 inches (225mm) from the lower edge of the pedal to the firewall, not including the carpet.
3. Torque the locknut to 20 ft. lbs. (27 Nm). Install the trim.

E34 5 Series

1. Remove the lower dashboard trim panel to access the pedal.
2. Adjust the pedal height at the pushrod. The height should be 9.65 inches (245mm) from the lower edge of the pedal to the firewall, not including the carpet.
3. Torque the locknut to 20 ft. lbs. (27 Nm). Install the trim.

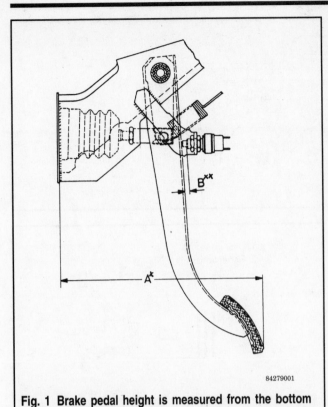

Fig. 1 Brake pedal height is measured from the bottom of the pedal to the firewall

84279001

Brake Light Switch

The brake light switch is located at brake pedal. There are different styles of switches. If there is a single threaded body switch, the switch will need to be manually adjusted. If the body is not threaded, it only has to be adjusted once during installation. If there are 2 switches at the brake pedal, one threaded and one that is not, the non-threaded unit operates the brake lights and the threaded body switch is the test switch.

REMOVAL & INSTALLATION

Threaded Body

1. Remove the lower dashboard trim to access the brake light switch.
2. Pull the wire connectors off the switch.
3. Loosen the switch lock nuts and thread the switch out of the holder.
4. Install in reverse order. Adjust the switch there is 0.236 inches (6mm) from the pedal to the edge of the switch threads.
5. Connect the wires and install the trim.

Non-Threaded Body

1. Disconnect the wiring harness from the brake light switch.
2. Press the brake pedal and hold down. Pull the plunger and sleeve of the brake switch forward and pull the switch out of the holder.

3. Depress and hold the brake pedal down. Pull the sleeve and plunger to the full out position. Install in the holder and slowly release the brake pedal. This will automatically adjust the switch position.
4. Connect the harness plug.

ADJUSTMENT

Threaded Body

1. Remove the lower dashboard trim to access the brake light switch.
2. Pull the wire connectors off the switch.
3. Loosen the switch lock nuts.
4. Adjust the switch there is 0.236 inches (6mm) from the pedal to the edge of the switch threads.

Non-Threaded Body

1. Disconnect the wiring harness from the brake light switch.
2. Press the brake pedal and hold down. Pull the plunger and sleeve of the brake switch forward and pull the switch out of the holder.
3. Depress and hold the brake pedal down. Pull the sleeve and plunger to the full out position. Install in the holder and slowly release the brake pedal. This will automatically adjust the switch position.
4. Connect the harness plug.

Brake Master Cylinder

▶ **See Figure 2**

REMOVAL & INSTALLATION

1. Remove the brake fluid from the reservoir. Disconnect the clutch hose from the reservoir if equipped. Clean all the brake line connections.
2. Pull the reservoir off the master cylinder. On the E36 3 Series, turn the ignition switch to **OFF** and disconnect the harness connectors next to the master cylinder to gain more working room.
3. Using a line or flare wrench, remove the line connections from the master cylinder. Plug the lines to prevent the ingress of contaminants.
4. Remove the mounting nuts and pull of the booster.
To install:
5. Check the condition of the O-ring at the mounting flange of the master cylinder. Clean the mounting surfaces.
6. Install the master cylinder. On E30 and E36 3 Series, torque the nuts to 14.5 ft. lbs. (20 Nm). On E34 5 Series, torque the nuts to 18-21 ft. lbs. (25-29 Nm).
7. Install the brake lines and torque the connections to 10 ft. lbs. (14.2 Nm). Connect the harness connectors on the E36 3 Series.
8. Install the reservoir and clutch hose. Fill the reservoir and bleed the system.

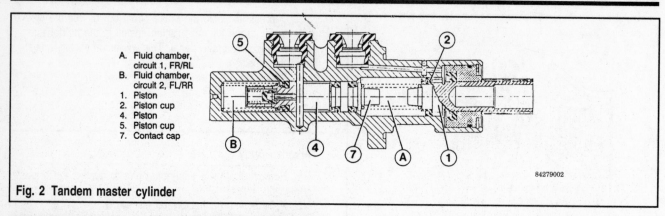

A. Fluid chamber, circuit 1, FR/RL
B. Fluid chamber, circuit 2, FL/RR
1. Piston
2. Piston cup
4. Piston
5. Piston cup
7. Contact cap

84279002

Fig. 2 Tandem master cylinder

Power Brake Booster

REMOVAL & INSTALLATION

1. Disconnect the negative battery cable. Draw off brake fluid in the reservoir and discard.
2. Remove the reservoir and disconnect the clutch hydraulic hose.
3. Disconnect all brake lines from the master cylinder.
4. Remove the instrument panel trim from the bottom/left inside the passenger compartment.
5. Remove the return spring from the brake pedal. Press off the clip and remove the pin which connects the booster rod to the brake pedal.
6. Remove the 4 nuts and pull the booster and master cylinder off in the engine compartment.

To install:

7. If the filter in the brake booster is clogged, it will have to be cleaned. To do this, remove the dust boot, retainer, damper, and filter, and clean the damper and filter. Make sure when reinstalling that the slots in the damper and filter are offset 180 degrees.
8. Install the brake booster and torque the nuts to 16-17 ft. lbs. (22-24 Nm). Connect the brake lines and torque to 10 ft. lbs. (14.2 Nm).
9. Connect the reservoir and lines. Connect the brake pedal to the pushrod. Adjust the pedal height. Adjust the brake light switch. Fill and bleed the system.

Brake Force Regulator Valve

♦ See Figure 3

REMOVAL & INSTALLATION

1. Disconnect the negative battery cable. Draw off hydraulic fluid from the master cylinder with a syringe or hose used only with clean brake fluid.
2. Disconnect the brake lines at the top and bottom of the proportioning valve.
3. Remove the clamp from the valve and disconnect the pressure connection at the union.

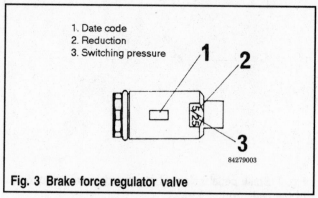

1. Date code
2. Reduction
3. Switching pressure

84279003

Fig. 3 Brake force regulator valve

4. Check day/year codes, reduction factor, and switch-over pressure to make sure the new valve is identical.
5. Install in reverse order. Bleed the system.

Brake Hoses & Pipes

REMOVAL & INSTALLATION

When removing or installing the brake pipes, line or hoses, always use a backup wrench on the fitting to prevent twisting. Avoid bending the lines or damaging the coating. Use a tubing bender if the line needs to be bent. Use premade lines with the flare already constructed. Torque all fittings to 10 ft. lbs. (14.2 Nm).

Bleeding & Fluid Change

♦ See Figures 4 and 5

To ensure continued proper operation of the braking system, the brake fluid must be changed at least every 2 years. If the vehicle is used for heavy duty use, change the fluid at least once a year. If the vehicle is used in competition or drivers schools, bleed the system before and after each event.

Use a quality, name brand DOT 4 brake fluid. Use fluid from sealed, unused cans. Buy the fluid in quantities that you expect to use. Buying a large container of fluid and only using a small portion can lead to the remaining fluid to become con-

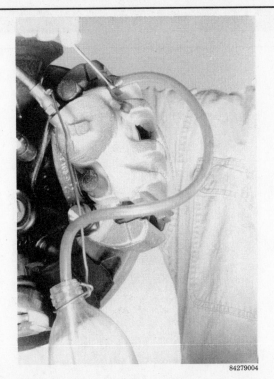

Fig. 4 Bleeding the front brakes. Replace the bleeder cover when done

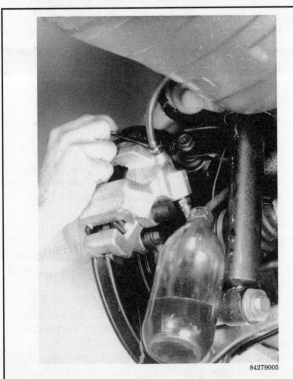

Fig. 5 Bleeding the rear brakes. Replace the bleeder cover when done

taminated over time. Brake fluid absorbs moisture and can lead to system corrosion.

➡**Always use clean, factory approved brake fluid.**

❋❋CAUTION

This procedure is valid for E30 3 Series with or without ABS. The procedure also is valid for E34 5 Series without ASC+T. To bleed the E36 3 Series or the E34 5 Series with ASC+T special tools and procedures are required. If the special procedures are not performed in accordance to BMW requirements, the brake system may not completely bleed. This will lead to improper brake system operation and potential injury or death.

1. Fill the master cylinder to the maximum level with the proper brake fluid.

2. Raise and safely support the vehicle. Remove the protective caps from the bleeder screws.

3. The proper bleeding sequence always start with the brake unit farthest from the master cylinder. The proper bleeding sequence is: right rear, left rear, right front and left front.

4. Insert a tight fitting plastic tube over the bleeder screw on the caliper and the other end of the tube in a transparent container partially filled with clean brake fluid.

5. Depress the brake pedal and loosen the bleeder screw to release the brake fluid. Pump the brake pedal to the stop at least 12 times. Tighten the bleeder screw when the escaping brake fluid is free of air bubbles.

6. Repeat this step on all 4 wheels. Torque the 7mm bleeders to 3.5 ft. lbs. (5 Nm) and the 9mm bleeders to 4.3 ft. lbs. (6 Nm). Replace the bleeder dust covers. Lower the vehicle and check the brake fluid level.

FRONT DISC BRAKES

▶ See Figure 6

❋❋CAUTION

Most BMW original equipment brake pads are a non-asbestos formulation. If the brake pads have been changed or it is unknown the history of the brake pads, take all precautions as if the pad are asbestos type. Asbestos can cause lung disease and cancers. Never clean the brake surfaces with compressed air and avoid breathing brake dust. Use a commercial brake cleaner and dispose of any rags contaminated with brake dust.

BMW's are equipped with some of the finest braking equipment found on production cars. When replacing any portion of the braking system, use original quality parts. Use components approved by BMW to maintain the high standards set by the manufacturer. Brakes are no place to skimp on quality.

Brakes have more power than the engine. This is best demonstrated by the fact that a vehicle can stop in a shorter distance from a given speed than the vehicle took to accelerate to that speed. Examining the capacity of the braking system to dissipate energy from this point of view gives a new respect for the incredible job the braking system must perform and the reasons the braking system should be maintained to the highest standards.

BMW does not recommend the use of brake dust shields. The shields that mount between the wheel and the hub can block the flow of cooling air. All the energy dissipated by the brake rotors is in the form of heat. Air flow must be maintained through the wheel to prevent warping of the rotors and fading of the brakes. If brake dust on the wheels is a problem, there are high quality, high performance brake pads available from the aftermarket that give off less brake dust than original equipment brake pads.

New materials and construction of brake pads have allowed racing levels of brake performance from street usable brake pads. Carbon formulations and metallic brake pads have shown exceptional levels of performance with few of the drawbacks once found in high performance brake pads. Old style, high performance brake pad formulations needed to be heated by use before they would start to give any performance. These old style pads would hardly stop the car on a cold day until brake application brought the pad temperature up to the working range. The new formulations work hot and cold and wear the rotor little.

Brake rotors are a wear item and should be replaced if found to grooved, warped or worn below the minimum thickness. The more metal a rotor has, the more heat the rotor can absorb, then reject without warping. As the rotor wears, the amount of metal in the rotor is reduced along with the heat absorbing capacity. Rotors can be ground to restore a smooth surface, but it is better to replace the rotors with new. Always replace the rotors and pads in pairs to maintain braking balance.

84279006

Fig. 6 The 12.8 inch front brake rotors of the M5

Brake Pads

REMOVAL & INSTALLATION

E30 3 Series

1. Raise and support the vehicle. Remove the front wheels.
2. Disconnect the brake pad wear sensor from the harness.
3. Hold the flats of the pin slide and remove the lower pivot bolt.
4. Rotate the caliper up and remove the brake pads.

To install:

5. Clean the brake caliper and all sliding surfaces. Press the caliper piston fully back into the caliper housing. Check for leaking fluid, damaged dust boots and frozen pistons.
6. Install a new brake pad wear sensor in the pad if the plastic part has been worn through on the old sensor. New sensors are not required unless the wire inside the plastic part has been exposed.
7. Install the brake pads in the caliper mount. Lower the caliper over the brake pads. Install a new bolt and torque to 25 ft. lbs. (35 Nm). Check that the pad springs are correctly seated.
8. Connect the brake pad wear sensor to the harness. Check for a good connection as most problems with the sensor circuit are caused by faulty connections. Check that the wire is held by the loop in the dust cover and the connector is held at the clips.

9. Install the wheels and torque to 65-79 ft. lbs. (90-110 Nm).

E36 3 Series

♦ See Figures 7, 8, 9, 10 and 11

1. Raise and support the vehicle. Remove the front wheels.
2. Disconnect the brake pad wear sensor from the harness.
3. Carefully pry the pad retainer spring out from the hub side and remove.
4. Remove the plastic plugs from the caliper slide bolts and remove the bolts. Remove the caliper and the pads from the caliper.

To install:

5. Clean the brake caliper and all sliding surfaces. Press the caliper piston fully back into the caliper housing. Check for leaking fluid, damaged dust boots and frozen pistons.
6. Install a new brake pad wear sensor in the pad if the plastic part has been worn through on the old sensor. New sensors are not required unless the wire inside the plastic part has been exposed.
7. Install the brake pads in the caliper. Lower the caliper over the caliper mount. Install the bolts and torque to 18-22 ft. lbs. (25-30 Nm). Install the retainer spring.
8. Connect the brake pad wear sensor to the harness. Check for a good connection as most problems with the sensor circuit are caused by faulty connections. Check that the wire is held by the loop in the dust cover and the connector is held at the clips.
9. Install the wheels and torque to 65-79 ft. lbs. (90-110 Nm).

Fig. 8 Remove the spring by prying the bottom side out

Fig. 7 Caliper mounting on the E34 5 Series. The E36 3 Series is similar

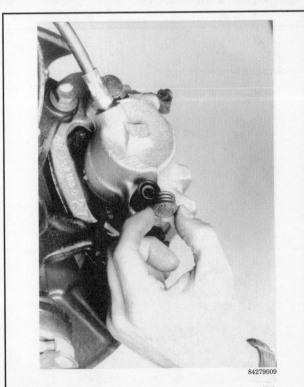

Fig. 9 Remove the plastic plugs to access the slide bolts

E34 5 Series

♦ See Figures 12, 13, 14, 15, 16 and 17

1. Raise and support the vehicle. Remove the front wheels.

Fig. 10 Slide bolts have a internal hex and should be tightened with a torque wrench

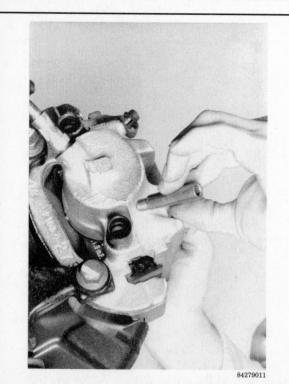

Fig. 11 Slide bolts should have a unblemished, smooth surface to ensure proper operation of the caliper

Fig. 12 Pull the caliper off the mount. Note the anti-noise compound used on the brake pad

Fig. 13 Pull the pads out of the grooves. Support the caliper so not to put tension on the brake hose

4. Remove the plastic plugs from the caliper slide bolts and remove the bolts. Remove the caliper and the pads from the caliper.

To install:

5. Clean the brake caliper and all sliding surfaces. Press the caliper piston fully back into the caliper housing. Check for leaking fluid, damaged dust boots and frozen pistons.

6. Install a new brake pad wear sensor in the pad if the plastic part has been worn through on the old sensor. New sensors are not required unless the wire inside the plastic part has been exposed.

7. Install the brake pads in the caliper. Lower the caliper over the caliper mount. Install the bolts and torque to 18-22 ft. lbs. (25-30 Nm). Install the retainer spring.

8. Connect the brake pad wear sensor to the harness. Check for a good connection as most problems with the sensor circuit are caused by faulty connections. Check that the wire is held by the loop in the dust cover and the connector is held at the clips.

Fig. 14 Press the piston back into the caliper. Use an old brake pad if available between the clamp foot and the piston

2. Disconnect the brake pad wear sensor from the harness.

3. Carefully pry the pad retainer spring out from the hub side and remove.

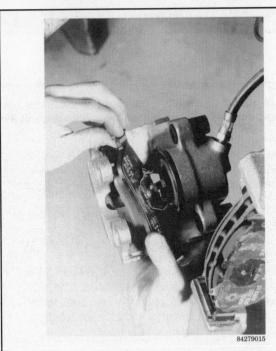

Fig. 15 The inner pad has springs to retain the pad to the caliper. Make sure the spring fits into the piston and a light coating of anti-noise compound is used at the piston

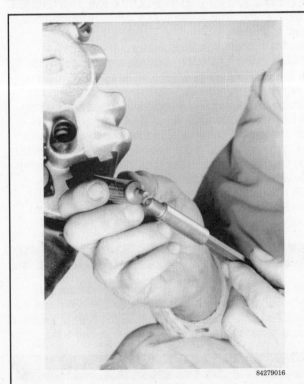

Fig. 16 Coat the slide bolt with a high temperature lubricant made for disc brake use

9. Install the wheels and torque to 65-79 ft. lbs. (90-110 Nm).

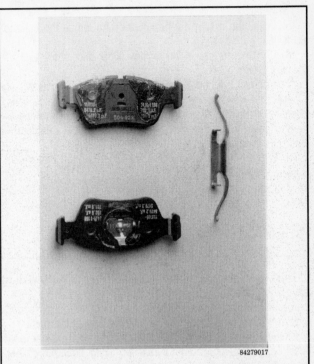

Fig. 17 The upper brake pad is the outer pad and the lower pad, with the spring, is the inner pad. Replace the mounting spring if loose

INSPECTION

1. Check the pad for thickness. The minimum friction material thickness allowed by BMW is 0.08 in (2.0mm).
2. Check the condition of the friction material. If the friction material is cracking or coming loose from the backing plate, replace the pads.
3. Check the pattern of wear of the friction material. If the pads are wearing unevenly or on an angle, there may be a problem with the caliper hanging up on its slides.
4. If the inside pad is worn more than the outside pad, the caliper may not be sliding on the pins. Clean and check for free movement of the caliper.
5. If one sides set of pads wear more than the other, the caliper with the unworn pads may be frozen. Check that the piston retracts smoothly and that the dust boot is intact.

Brake Caliper

REMOVAL & INSTALLATION\

1. Raise and support the vehicle. Remove the front wheels.
2. Disconnect the brake pad wear sensor from the harness.
3. If the caliper is to be replaced, draw off the brake fluid from the reservoir and fix the brake pedal in the depressed position. This will prevent brake fluid from draining out of the brake lines while the line is disconnected form the caliper. Disconnect the line from the caliper.
4. Remove the caliper to knuckle mounting bolts and pull the caliper off.

To install:

5. Install the caliper on the knuckle and torque the bolts to 89 ft. lbs. (123 Nm).

6. Connect the brake line to the caliper and torque to 10 ft. lbs. (14.2 Nm).

7. Connect the brake wear sensor wire to the harness. Check for a good connection as most problems with the sensor circuit are caused by faulty connections. Check that the wire is held by the loop in the dust cover and the connector is held at the clips.

8. Clip the brake line into the holder. Bleed the brake system.

9. Install the wheels and torque to 65-79 ft. lbs. (90-110 Nm).

OVERHAUL

The overhaul procedure covers replacement of the seal, dust boot and guide sleeves. If the piston or bore is found to be pitted or corroded, replacement of the caliper is recommended. Use a original manufacturer overhaul kit. Use all the parts contained in the kit. Work in a clean, dust free area. Use only alcohol and non-lubricated compressed air to clean the caliper and parts.

1. Remove the caliper and brake pads. Remove the plastic caps and the guide bolts or slide pins.

2. Clean the exterior before further disassembly.

3. Place a piece of wood in the caliper and use compressed air at the hose connection to extend the piston out of the caliper body. Remove the piston.

4. Use a plastic pick to remove the seal from the bore.

5. Clean the bore and piston with alcohol and dry with non-lubricated compressed air.

6. Lubricate the parts with brake assembly paste. Install the new seal in the groove. Install the dust boot on the piston and slide the piston into the bore. Seat the boot into the grooves.

7. Install new guide bushing sleeves at the slides.

8. Assemble the caliper and install.

Brake Rotor

REMOVAL & INSTALLATION

➡**The balancing clips in the venting of the rotor must not be moved or removed. This will cause an imbalance of the rotor.**

1. Raise and support the vehicle. Remove the front wheels.

2. Remove the caliper without disconnecting the brake line. Hang the caliper with a piece of wire so no tension is put on the brake line.

3. Remove the internal hex bolt from the hub and pull the rotor off the hub.

4. Check the rotor and replace as necessary. Install the rotor and caliper. Install the wheels.

5. Burnish the rotors by making 5 full stops from 30 mph (50 km/h), then allow the brakes to cool. Make 5 additional stops from 30 mph (50 km/h) and allow the brakes to cool again. This will burnish the rotors and allow full braking efficiency.

INSPECTION

1. Use a micrometer to measure the thickness of the rotor at 8 points around the circumference. The rotor measurements should not deviate more than 0.0008 inches (0.02mm) from largest to smallest.

2. The minimum machining thickness is 0.803 inches (20.4mm) except for the M3 which has a machining thickness of 0.921 inches (23.4mm) and the M5 whose rotors must not be machined. The minimum wear thickness is 0.787 inches (20.0mm) except for the M3 which is 0.906 inches (23.0mm) and the M5 which is 1.039 inches (26.4mm).

3. Remove the caliper or retract the brake pads. Bolt the rotor to the hub. Install a dial indicator with the tip perpendicular to the friction surface of the rotor. With the wheel bearings in serviceable condition, the axial runout must not exceed 0.008 inches (0.2mm).

4. Replace or machine the rotors on both sides if found defective.

REAR DISC BRAKES

▶ See Figure 18

✳✳CAUTION

Most BMW original equipment brake pads are a non-asbestos formulation. If the brake pads have been changed or it is unknown the history of the brake pads, take all precautions as if the pad are asbestos type. Asbestos can cause lung disease and cancers. Never clean the brake surfaces with compressed air and avoid breathing brake dust. Use a commercial brake cleaner and dispose of any rags contaminated with brake dust.

The rear disc brakes utilize sliding caliper similar to the front disc brakes. The parking brake assembly is mounted in the brake rotor hat. This is known a drum in disc design. This allows a simpler caliper design than those that incorporate the parking brake mechanism in the rear caliper. Most of the maintenance procedure are the same as the front disc brakes.

Brake Pads

▶ See Figures 19, 20, 21, 22, 23, 24, 25 and 26

REMOVAL & INSTALLATION

1. Raise and support the vehicle. Remove the rear wheels.

2. Disconnect the brake pad wear sensor from the harness.

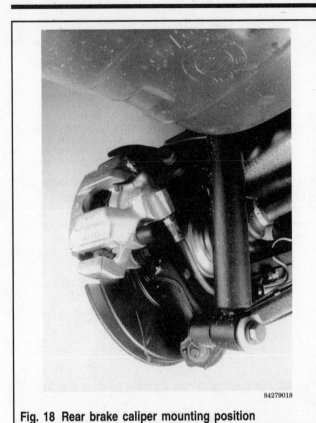

Fig. 18 Rear brake caliper mounting position

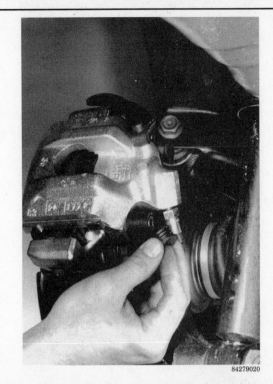

Fig. 20 Remove the caps to expose the internal hex slide pins

Fig. 19 Remove the clip spring before removing the slide pins

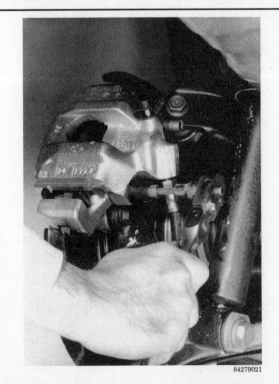

Fig. 21 Make sure the wrench is fully seated in the slide pin to prevent stripping internal hex

3. Carefully pry the pad retainer spring out from the hub side and remove.

4. Remove the plastic plugs from the caliper slide bolts and remove the bolts. Remove the caliper and the pads from the caliper.

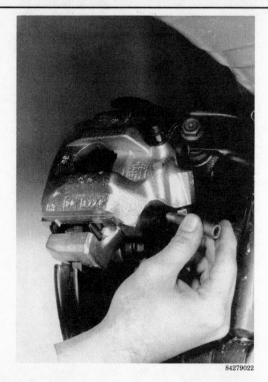

Fig. 22 Inspect the slide pins for corrosion and pitting once removed

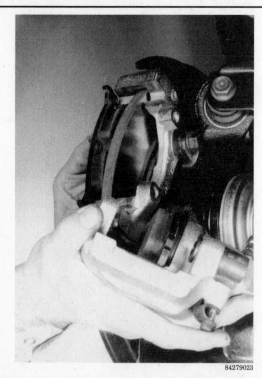

Fig. 23 The inside pad will stay with the caliper and the outside pad will stay with the lower mount

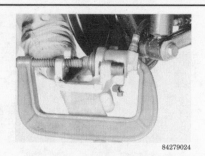

Fig. 24 Press the piston back in the caliper. Use an old pad to protect the piston when using a C-clamp

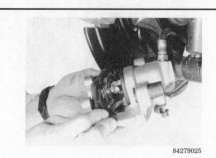

Fig. 25 The inside pad has a spring holding it in the piston bore

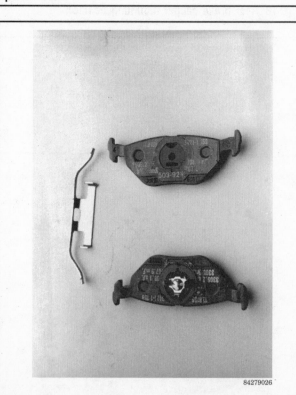

Fig. 26 The upper pad is the outside pad and the lower pad with the spring is the inside pad

To install:

5. Clean the brake caliper and all sliding surfaces. Press the caliper piston fully back into the caliper housing. Check for leaking fluid, damaged dust boots and frozen pistons.

6. Install a new brake pad wear sensor in the pad if the plastic part has been worn through on the old sensor. New sensors are not required unless the wire inside the plastic part has been exposed.

7. Install the brake pads in the caliper. Lower the caliper over the caliper mount. Install the bolts and torque to 18-22 ft. lbs. (25-30 Nm). Install the retainer spring.

8. Connect the brake pad wear sensor to the harness. Check for a good connection as most problems with the sensor circuit are caused by faulty connections. Check that the wire is held by the loop in the dust cover and the connector is held at the clips.

9. Install the wheels and torque to 65-79 ft. lbs. (90-110 Nm).

INSPECTION

1. Check the pad for thickness. The minimum friction material thickness allowed by BMW is 0.08 inches (2.0mm).

2. Check the condition of the friction material. If the friction material is cracking or coming loose from the backing plate, replace the pads.

3. Check the pattern of wear of the friction material. If the pads are wearing unevenly or on an angle, there may be a problem with the caliper hanging up on its slides.

4. If the inside pad is worn more than the outside pad, the caliper may not be sliding on the pins. Clean and check for free movement of the caliper.

5. If one sides set of pads wear more than the other, the caliper with the unworn pads may be frozen. Check that the piston retracts smoothly and that the dust boot is intact.

Brake Caliper

REMOVAL & INSTALLATION

▶ **See Figure 27**

1. Raise and support the vehicle. Remove the rear wheels.
2. Disconnect the brake pad wear sensor from the harness.
3. If the caliper is to be replaced, draw off the brake fluid from the reservoir and fix the brake pedal in the depressed position. This will prevent brake fluid from draining out of the brake lines while the line is disconnected form the caliper. Disconnect the line from the caliper.
4. Remove the caliper to knuckle mounting bolts and pull the caliper off.

To install:

5. Install the caliper and torque the bolts to 89 ft. lbs. (123 Nm).

6. Connect the brake line to the caliper and torque to 10 ft. lbs. (14.2 Nm).

7. Connect the brake wear sensor wire to the harness. Check for a good connection as most problems with the sen-

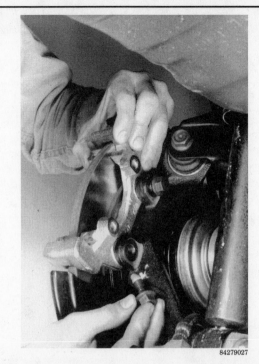

84279027

Fig. 27 Removing the caliper mount. The upper housing of the caliper does not have to be removed from the mount to dismount the caliper

sor circuit are caused by faulty connections. Check that the wire is held by the loop in the dust cover and the connector is held at the clips.

8. Clip the brake line into the holder. Bleed the brake system.

9. Install the wheels and torque to 65-79 ft. lbs. (90-110 Nm).

OVERHAUL

The overhaul procedure covers replacement of the seal, dust boot and guide sleeves. If the piston or bore is found to be pitted or corroded, replacement of the caliper is recommended. Use a original manufacturer overhaul kit. Use all the parts contained in the kit. Work in a clean, dust free area. Use only alcohol and non-lubricated compressed air to clean the caliper and parts.

1. Remove the caliper and brake pads. Remove the plastic caps and the guide bolts or slide pins.

2. Clean the exterior before further disassembly.

3. Place a piece of wood in the caliper and use compressed air at the hose connection to extend the piston out of the caliper body. Remove the piston.

4. Use a plastic pick to remove the seal from the bore.

5. Clean the bore and piston with alcohol and dry with non-lubricated compressed air.

6. Lubricate the parts with brake assembly paste. Install the new seal in the groove. Install the dust boot on the piston and slide the piston into the bore. Seat the boot into the grooves.

7. Install new guide bushing sleeves at the slides.

8. Assemble the caliper and install.

Brake Rotor

REMOVAL & INSTALLATION

▶ See Figure 28

1. Raise and support the vehicle. Remove the rear wheels.
2. Remove the caliper without disconnecting the brake line. Hang the caliper with a piece of wire so no tension is put on the brake line.
3. Remove the internal hex bolt from the hub and pull the rotor off the hub.

84279028

Fig. 28 Remove the screw before attempting to remove the rotor

4. Check the rotor and replace as necessary. Install the rotor and caliper. Install the wheels. Adjust the parking brake.
5. Burnish the rotors by making 5 full stops from 30 mph (50 km/h), then allow the brakes to cool. Make 5 additional stops from 30 mph (50 km/h) and allow the brakes to cool again. This will burnish the rotors and allow full braking efficiency.

INSPECTION

1. Use a micrometer to measure the thickness of the rotor at 8 points around the circumference. The rotor measurements should not deviate more than 0.0008 inches (0.02mm) from largest to smallest.
2. The minimum machining thickness is 0.330 in (8.4mm) except for the M5 which has a machining thickness of 0.725 inches (18.4mm). The minimum wear thickness is 0.315 inches (8.0mm) except the M5 which is 0.709 inches (18.0mm).
3. Remove the caliper or retract the brake pads. Bolt the rotor to the hub. Install a dial indicator with the tip perpendicular to the friction surface of the rotor. With the wheel bearings in serviceable condition, the axial runout must not exceed 0.008 inches (0.2mm).
4. Replace or machine the rotors on both sides if found defective.

PARKING BRAKE

Cables

REMOVAL & INSTALLATION

▶ See Figures 29 and 30

E30 3 Series

1. Raise and safely support the vehicle. Remove the rear tire and wheel assembly. Remove the rear brake rotors.
2. Pull the rubber parking brake boot up at the front and lift off at the rear. Pull out the rear ashtray and remove the bolt. Pull the console back and remove.
3. Remove the adjuster nuts from the cables. Remove the 3 bolts securing the lever. Remove the lever.
4. Using brake spring pliers, disconnect the lower return spring for the parking brake shoes. Then, using the proper tool, turn the retaining springs for the parking brake shoes 90 degrees to unlock them and remove.
5. Separate the parking brake shoes at the bottom and remove from above.
6. Disconnect the spreader locks from the backing plates: first, rock the lower end of the spreader lock outward, and then pull out the pin. Press the cable connection out of the spreader lock. Pull the spreader lock out of the housing.
7. Disconnect the parking brake cable at the trailing arm and the backing plate. Remove the cable.

To install:

8. Install the support for the parking brake cable on the backing plate. Install the cable into potion and connect the housing to the trailing arm.
9. Install the cable into the tubes going to the parking brake lever. Install the parking brake lever.
10. Connect the parking brake cable to the spreader lock. Apply a light grease to the mechanism. Install the brake shoes, retainers and return spring.
11. Install the brake rotor and wheel. Adjust the shoes, the adjust the cables. Install the console and boot for the parking brake lever.

E36 3 Series

1. Raise and safely support the vehicle. Remove the rear tire and wheel assembly. Remove the rear brake rotors. Remove the rear muffler and heat shield.
2. Pull up and out the parking brake lever dust cover trim.
3. Remove the adjuster nuts from the cables using tool 34 1 030 or equivalent.
4. Using brake spring pliers, disconnect the lower return spring for the parking brake shoes. Then, using the proper tool, turn the retaining springs for the parking brake shoes 90 degrees to unlock them and remove.
5. Separate the parking brake shoes at the bottom and remove from above.
6. Disconnect the spreader locks from the backing plates: first, rock the lower end of the spreader lock outward, and then pull out the pin. Press the cable connection out of the spreader lock. Pull the spreader lock out of the housing.

7. Disconnect the parking brake cable at the trailing arm and the backing plate. Remove the cable.

To install:

8. Install the support for the parking brake cable on the backing plate. Install the cable into potion and connect the housing to the trailing arm.

9. Install the cable into the tubes going to the parking brake lever. Install the parking brake lever cable nuts.

10. Connect the parking brake cable to the spreader lock. Apply a light grease to the mechanism. Install the brake shoes, retainers and return spring.

11. Install the brake rotor and wheel. Adjust the shoes, the adjust the cables. Install the console and boot for the parking brake lever.

E34 5 Series

1. Raise and safely support the vehicle. Remove the rear tire and wheel assembly.

2. Remove the rear brake discs.

3. Using brake spring pliers, disconnect the upper return spring for the parking brake shoes. Then, using the proper tool, turn the retaining springs for the parking brake shoes 90 degrees to unlock them and then disconnect them.

4. Separate the parking brake shoes at the top and then remove them from below.

5. Disconnect the spreader locks from the backing plates: first, rock the lower end of the spreader lock outward, and then pull out the pin. Press the cable connection out of the spreader lock. Pull the spreader lock out of the housing. Pull the cable through the backing plate.

6. Disconnect the parking brake cable at the trailing arm.

7. Working inside the vehicle, remove the console cover as follows:

　a. Lift out the air grille and remove the nuts underneath.

　b. Remove the cap and unscrew the mounting bolt that's located at the forward end of the console on the right side. Lift out the cover that the bolt retains.

　c. Remove the bolt on the left side of the forward end of the console. If the vehicle has power windows, disconnect the plugs. Then, lift the console and remove air ducts.

　d. Turn the retainer 90 degrees and peel the rubber cover downward. Now, unscrew the adjusting nuts on the parking brake cables and pull them out.

8. Remove the cable from the vehicle.

To install:

9. Install the support for the parking brake cable on the backing plate. Install the cable into potion and connect the housing to the trailing arm.

10. Install the cable into the tubes going to the parking brake lever. Install the parking brake lever cable nuts.

11. Connect the parking brake cable to the spreader lock. Apply a light grease to the mechanism. Install the brake shoes, retainers and return spring.

12. Install the brake rotor and wheel. Adjust the shoes, the adjust the cables. Install the console and boot for the parking brake lever.

ADJUSTMENT

E30 3 Series

1. Remove 1 lug bolt from the wheel and turn the opening so it is positioned to the rear approximately 30 degrees from the top. This is the location of the star adjuster for the brake shoes.

2. Use a thin bladed adjustment tool or equivalent to turn the star adjuster. On the left side, turn the star up to tighten. On the right side, turn the star down to tighten.

3. Turn the star until the wheel will not turn. Loosen the star 3-4 threads. Check that the wheel turn freely.

4. Pull the parking lever boot up in the front and pull out from the rear. Remove the rear ashtray and the underlying bolt. Pull the console back and out.

5. Pull the parking brake lever up 5 notches. Adjust the cables with the nuts so that the wheels can just barely be turned. Release the lever and check that the wheels spin freely. Both sides must be adjusted evenly.

6. The parking brake indicator lamp should extinguish when the lever is released otherwise adjust the switch so it does. Install the console and the lug bolt.

E36 3 Series

1. Remove 1 lug bolt from the wheel and turn the opening so it is positioned to the rear approximately 65 degrees from the top. This is the location of the star adjuster for the brake shoes.

2. Use a thin bladed adjustment tool or equivalent to turn the star adjuster. On the left side, turn the star up to tighten. On the right side, turn the star down to tighten.

3. Turn the star until the wheel will not turn. Loosen the star 18 notches. Check that the wheel turn freely.

4. Pull the parking lever dust cover trim up.

5. Pull the parking brake lever up 6 notches. Adjust the cables with the nuts so that the wheels can just barely be turned. Release the lever and check that the wheels spin freely. Both sides must be adjusted evenly.

6. The parking brake indicator lamp should extinguish when the lever is released otherwise adjust the switch so it does. Install The dust cover and the lug bolt.

E34 5 Series

1. Remove 1 lug bolt from the wheel and turn the opening so it is positioned to the rear approximately 45 degrees from the bottom. This is the location of the star adjuster for the brake shoes.

2. Use a thin bladed adjustment tool or equivalent to turn the star adjuster. On the left side, turn the star up to tighten. On the right side, turn the star down to tighten.

3. Turn the star until the wheel will not turn. Loosen the star 18 notches. Check that the wheel turn freely.

4. Pull the parking lever dust cover trim up.

5. Pull the parking brake lever up 6 notches. Adjust the cables with the nuts so that the wheels can just barely be turned. Release the lever and check that the wheels spin freely. Both sides must be adjusted evenly.

6. The parking brake indicator lamp should extinguish when the lever is released otherwise adjust the switch so it does. Install The dust cover and the lug bolt.

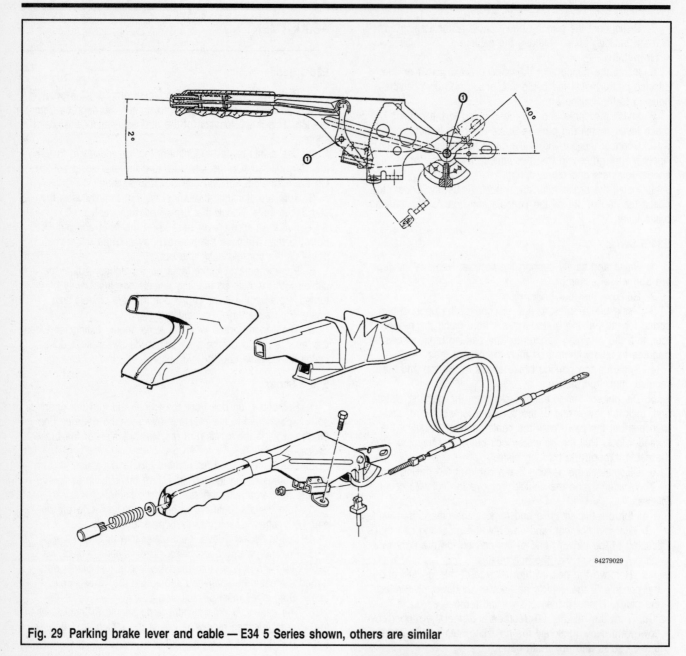

Fig. 29 Parking brake lever and cable — E34 5 Series shown, others are similar

BURNISHING

The parking brake is subjected to only limited wear and use. Often the friction surfaces become corroded and cause a loss of braking performance. This can often be cured by burnishing the parking brakes and the performance will return.

This procedure should also be performed whenever new shoes or rotors are installed and before the parking brake adjustment is made.

1. While driving the car at 25 mph (40 km/h) pull the parking brake lever until braking is felt. Pull the lever 1 more notch and drive the car 1300 ft. (400 m) to the working area.
2. Adjust the parking brake.
3. Check the performance of the parking brake.

Brake Shoes

REMOVAL & INSTALLATION

▶ **See Figures 31, 32, 33, 34 and 35**

E30 3 Series

1. Raise and safely support the vehicle. Remove the rear tire and wheel assembly. Remove the rear brake rotors.
2. Using brake spring pliers, disconnect the lower return spring for the parking brake shoes. Then, using the proper tool, turn the retaining springs for the parking brake shoes 90 degrees to unlock them and remove.
3. Separate the parking brake shoes at the bottom and remove from above. Separate the shoes from the adjuster and spring.

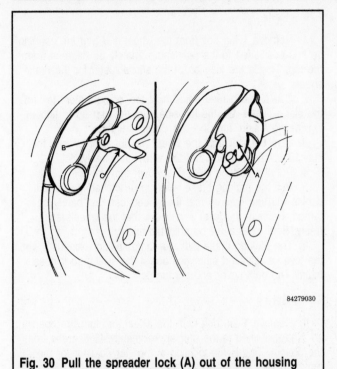

Fig. 30 Pull the spreader lock (A) out of the housing and remove the pin at the lower end. Disconnect the cable at (B) and pull the inner portion out of the housing

Fig. 31 Disconnect the return spring at the spreader

Fig. 32 Pull the shoes apart at the spreader

To install:

4. Install the adjuster and spring at the shoes. Install the shoes from the top to the backing plate.

Fig. 33 Turn the retainer springs 90 degrees to release

5. Install the retainer locks and the return spring. Install the rotor. Burnish and adjust the parking brake.

E36 3 Series

1. Raise and safely support the vehicle. Remove the rear tire and wheel assembly. Remove the rear brake rotors.

2. Using brake spring pliers, disconnect the lower return spring for the parking brake shoes. Then, using the proper tool, turn the retaining springs for the parking brake shoes 90 degrees to unlock them and remove.

3. Separate the parking brake shoes at the bottom and remove from above. Separate the shoes from the adjuster and spring.

To install:

4. Install the adjuster and spring at the shoes. Install the shoes from the top to the backing plate.

5. Install the retainer locks and the return spring. Install the rotor. Burnish and adjust the parking brake.

Fig. 34 The retainers are located on each brake shoe

E34 5 Series

1. Raise and safely support the vehicle. Remove the rear tire and wheel assembly. Remove the rear brake rotors.

2. Using brake spring pliers, disconnect the upper return spring for the parking brake shoes. Then, using the proper tool, turn the retaining springs for the parking brake shoes 90 degrees to unlock them and remove.

3. Separate the parking brake shoes at the top and remove from below. Separate the shoes from the adjuster and spring.

To install:

4. Install the adjuster and spring at the shoes. Install the shoes from the bottom to the backing plate.

5. Install the retainer locks and the return spring. Install the rotor. Burnish and adjust the parking brake.

ADJUSTMENT

E30 3 Series

1. Pull the parking lever boot up in the front and pull out from the rear. Remove the rear ashtray and the underlying bolt. Pull the console back and out. Loosen the brake cables.

2. Remove 1 lug bolt from the wheel and turn the opening so it is positioned to the rear approximately 30 degrees from the top. This is the location of the star adjuster for the brake shoes.

3. Use a thin bladed adjustment tool or equivalent to turn the star adjuster. On the left side, turn the star up to tighten. On the right side, turn the star down to tighten.

4. Turn the star until the wheel will not turn. Loosen the star 3-4 threads. Check that the wheel turn freely.

5. Pull the parking brake lever up 5 notches. Adjust the cables with the nuts so that the wheels can just barely be turned. Release the lever and check that the wheels spin freely. Both sides must be adjusted evenly.

6. The parking brake indicator lamp should extinguish when the lever is released otherwise adjust the switch so it does. Install the console and the lug bolt.

84279035

Fig. 35 Layout of the parking brake components

E36 3 Series

1. Remove 1 lug bolt from the wheel and turn the opening so it is positioned to the rear approximately 65 degrees from the top. This is the location of the star adjuster for the brake shoes.

2. Use a thin bladed adjustment tool or equivalent to turn the star adjuster. On the left side, turn the star up to tighten. On the right side, turn the star down to tighten.

3. Turn the star until the wheel will not turn. Loosen the star 18 notches. Check that the wheel turn freely.

4. Pull the parking lever dust cover trim up.

5. Pull the parking brake lever up 6 notches. Adjust the cables with the nuts so that the wheels can just barely be turned. Release the lever and check that the wheels spin freely. Both sides must be adjusted evenly.

6. The parking brake indicator lamp should extinguish when the lever is released otherwise adjust the switch so it does. Install The dust cover and the lug bolt.

E34 5 Series

1. Remove 1 lug bolt from the wheel and turn the opening so it is positioned to the rear approximately 45 degrees from the bottom. This is the location of the star adjuster for the brake shoes.

2. Use a thin bladed adjustment tool or equivalent to turn the star adjuster. On the left side, turn the star up to tighten. On the right side, turn the star down to tighten.

3. Turn the star until the wheel will not turn. Loosen the star 18 notches. Check that the wheel turn freely.

4. Pull the parking lever dust cover trim up.

5. Pull the parking brake lever up 6 notches. Adjust the cables with the nuts so that the wheels can just barely be turned. Release the lever and check that the wheels spin freely. Both sides must be adjusted evenly.

6. The parking brake indicator lamp should extinguish when the lever is released otherwise adjust the switch so it does. Install The dust cover and the lug bolt.

BURNISHING

The parking brake is subjected to only limited wear and use. Often the friction surfaces become corroded and cause a loss of braking performance. This can often be cured by burnishing the parking brakes and the performance will return.

This procedure should also be performed whenever new shoes or rotors are installed and before the parking brake adjustment is made.

1. While driving the car at 25 mph (40 km/h) pull the parking brake lever until braking is felt. Pull the lever 1 more notch and drive the car 1300 ft. (400 m) to the working area.

2. Adjust the parking brake.

3. Check the performance of the parking brake.

ANTI-LOCK BRAKE SYSTEM

Description & Operation

One of the greatest contributions to automotive safety was the advent of anti-lock braking systems. Anti-lock braking systems (ABS) allows maintaining directional control of the vehicle during braking. While benefits from ABS can be derived on dry pavement driving, the most substantial benefits are witnessed under adverse traction conditions.

Braking systems operate on the principle that motion energy is removed from the vehicle in the form of heat and dissipated. The brake calipers squeeze the brake pads against the rotors and slow the rotors. This does not stop the vehicle; the friction of the road surface against the tires is what actually slows the vehicle. The brakes merely provide the retarding force for the tires. If the tires can not maintain a level of traction with the road surface, the best braking system can not slow the vehicle.

If during braking, 1 or more tires hit a section of low traction, the braking force applied by the calipers will overwhelm the available traction at the tire contact patch. As a result the tire will slide instead of roll. If we look at the contact patch of the tire as the car rolls down the road, we would see that the tire has a relative speed of zero compared to the ground. Under braking the relative may increase so there is a slight percentage of slip between the tire and the road surface. A small percentage of slip is acceptable and friction force will rise, slowing the car. If the percentage rises too high and the tire is no longer rolling, the friction force drops tremendously and the tire can not provide lateral or longitudinal traction.

Driving in the wet or snow, loose gravel or sand, or any other kind of low traction surface can cause the tires to lock and loose directional stability. ABS monitors the rotation of the tires and compares the speed of each. If the speed of 1 or more tires drop drastically below that of the others during braking, the ABS controller will cut hydraulic pressure to that wheel until it is rotating at the same speed as the others. This will provide the best chance of maintaining directional control of the vehicle.

In the case of the 325iX, four wheel drive vehicle, a deceleration sensor is needed to sense the relative motion of the car. Since the possibility exists that 1 or more wheels can be spinning due to acceleration, not braking, a sensor independent of the wheel speed sensors is needed.

ABS can not perform miracles. If the laws of physics are exceeded, the car can leave the roadway. ABS can only help to maintain control. Go too fast into a turn and mash the brakes, ABS or not, the tires can only do so much and control may be lost. Driving too fast in the rain or snow is a recipe for trouble. ABS is a tool to make driving safer, not a cure-all for bad driving habits.

ABS can be useful in dry ground driving in the same way it is in low traction situations. ABS, once eschewed by the racing world, has now been gladly accepted and used on vehicles ranging from rally cars, World Touring Car Championship M3's and Formula 1 cars.

COMPONENTS

Speed Sensors

The speed sensors are located at each wheel and provide the speed reference to the control unit. The speed sensors are permanently magnetized inductive sensors that read pulses from a tooth wheel on each hub. A voltage signal is generated as each tooth passes through the magnetic field. The sensors are replaceable. The tooth wheels are integral with the wheel hubs and are replaced with the complete hub.

Control Unit

The control unit contains all the signal conditioning circuitry and the output circuits. The output circuits control the hydraulic unit to adjust the line pressure to each caliper. The unit is located under the dash panel on the left side in the E30 3 Series, above the glove compartment in the E36 3 Series and in the forward position of the electronics box in the engine compartment of the E34 5 Series. If a problem is sensed, the control unit will light the instrument panel warning lamp.

Hydraulic Unit
▶ See Figure 36

The hydraulic unit, located in the engine compartment contains valves and a pump. The valves have 3 positions; pressure build-up, pressure hold and pressure drop. As the tires locks, the control unit informs the valve to hold the pressure. If the tire remains locked, the control unit will allow the valve to drop the pressure until the tire starts to turn. The control unit will allow the valve to start building pressure to start the cycle over again.

The pump returns the brake fluid taken from the wheel cylinder while the pressure is lowered. The pump is designed to maintain separation of the 2 braking circuits.

During operation of the anti-lock system, a pulsing may be felt at the brake pedal and a clicking heard from the hydraulic unit. This is normal and informs the operator that the ABS is in the functioning mode.

SERVICING

While parts of the of the ABS system can be removed and replaced by the owner of the vehicle, special tool, technique and procedure are needed to check the operation and performance of the system once repairs are completed.

To bleed the hydraulic system, a necessary step after the hydraulic system has been repaired, the BMW Diagnostic Tester or equivalent must be utilized to electronically open the internal valve. Only this way can the system be completely bled.

To check the operation of the ABS system after any of the electronic portions have been replaced or disconnected, the BMW Diagnostic Tester or equivalent must be used.

It is recommended to allow a licensed and trained professional to complete repairs on the ABS system. Most repairs are straightforward, but the diagnosis and testing of the system can enter a different realm. The safety and integrity of the braking system is at stake.

BRAKE SPECIFICATIONS

All measurements in inches unless noted.

| Year | Model | Front Brake Disc | | | | Rear Brake Disc | | | | Minimum Lining Thickness | | |
		Diameter	Machining① Thickness	Wear② Thickness	Maximum Runout	Diameter	Machining① Thickness	Wear② Thickness	Maximum Runout	Front	Rear	Parking
1989	325i E30	10.24	0.803	0.787	0.008	10.16	0.330	0.315	0.008	0.08	0.08	0.06
	325iC E30	10.24	0.803	0.787	0.008	10.16	0.330	0.315	0.008	0.08	0.08	0.06
	325iX E30	10.24	0.803	0.787	0.008	10.16	0.330	0.315	0.008	0.08	0.08	0.06
	M3 E30	11.00	0.921	0.906	0.008	11.10	0.330	0.315	0.008	0.08	0.08	0.06
	525i E34	10.89	0.803	0.787	0.008	11.81	0.330	0.315	0.008	0.08	0.08	0.06
	535i E34	10.89	0.803	0.787	0.008	11.81	0.330	0.315	0.008	0.08	0.08	0.06
1990	325i E30	10.24	0.803	0.787	0.008	10.16	0.330	0.315	0.008	0.08	0.08	0.06
	325iC E30	10.24	0.803	0.787	0.008	10.16	0.330	0.315	0.008	0.08	0.08	0.06
	325iX E30	10.24	0.803	0.787	0.008	10.16	0.330	0.315	0.008	0.08	0.08	0.06
	M3 E30	11.00	0.921	0.906	0.008	11.10	0.330	0.315	0.008	0.08	0.08	0.06
	525i E34	10.89	0.803	0.787	0.008	11.81	0.330	0.315	0.008	0.08	0.08	0.06
	535i E34	10.89	0.803	0.787	0.008	11.81	0.330	0.315	0.008	0.08	0.08	0.06
1991	318i E30	10.24	0.803	0.787	0.008	10.16	0.330	0.315	0.008	0.08	0.08	0.06
	318iC E30	10.24	0.803	0.787	0.008	10.16	0.330	0.315	0.008	0.08	0.08	0.06
	318iS E30	10.24	0.803	0.787	0.008	10.16	0.330	0.315	0.008	0.08	0.08	0.06
	325i E30	10.24	0.803	0.787	0.008	10.16	0.330	0.315	0.008	0.08	0.08	0.06
	325iC E30	10.24	0.803	0.787	0.008	10.16	0.330	0.315	0.008	0.08	0.08	0.06
	325iX E30	10.24	0.803	0.787	0.008	10.16	0.330	0.315	0.008	0.08	0.08	0.06
	M3 E30	11.00	0.921	0.906	0.008	11.10	0.330	0.315	0.008	0.08	0.08	0.06
	525i E34	10.89	0.803	0.787	0.008	11.81	0.330	0.315	0.008	0.08	0.08	0.06
	535i E34	10.89	0.803	0.787	0.008	11.81	0.330	0.315	0.008	0.08	0.08	0.06
1992–93	318i E36	11.26	0.803	0.787	0.008	11.02	0.330	0.315	0.008	0.08	0.08	0.06
	318iS E36	11.26	0.803	0.787	0.008	11.02	0.330	0.315	0.008	0.08	0.08	0.06
	318iC E30	10.24	0.803	0.787	0.008	10.16	0.330	0.315	0.008	0.08	0.08	0.06
	325i E36	11.26	0.803	0.787	0.008	11.02	0.330	0.315	0.008	0.08	0.08	0.06
	325iS E36	11.26	0.803	0.787	0.008	11.02	0.330	0.315	0.008	0.08	0.08	0.06
	325iC E30	10.24	0.803	0.787	0.008	10.16	0.330	0.315	0.008	0.08	0.08	0.06
	525i E34	10.89	0.803	0.787	0.008	11.81	0.330	0.315	0.008	0.08	0.08	0.06
	525iT E34	10.89	0.803	0.787	0.008	11.81	0.330	0.315	0.008	0.08	0.08	0.06
	535i E34	10.89	0.803	0.787	0.008	11.81	0.330	0.315	0.008	0.08	0.08	0.06
	M5 E34	12.75	③	1.039	0.008	11.81	0.725	0.709	0.008	0.08	0.08	0.06

① Minimum thickness after machining
② Minimum thickness at which point the rotor
   should be replaced
③ Machining not recommended

84279037

1. Hydraulic control unit
2. Valve relay
3. Motor relay
4. Cover
5. ABS control unit

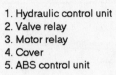
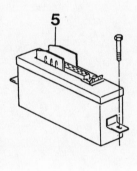
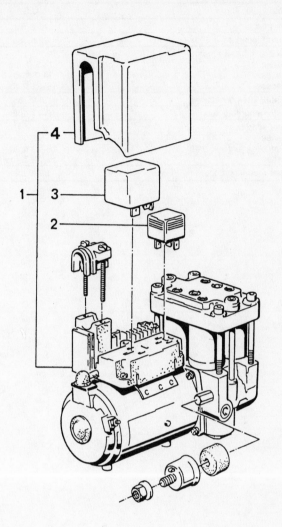

84279036

Fig. 36 Hydraulic unit of the anti-lock brake system

TORQUE SPECIFICATIONS

Component	U.S.	Metric
Pedal pivot shaft nut	20 ft. lbs.	27 Nm
Brake pushrod locknut	20 ft. lbs.	27 Nm
Master cylinder mounting nuts		
E30 3 Series	14.5 ft. lbs.	20 Nm
E36 3 Series	14.5 ft. lbs.	20 Nm
E34 5 Series	18–21 ft. lbs.	25–29 Nm
Master cylinder line connections	10 ft. lbs.	14.2 Nm
Brake booster mounting nuts	16–17 ft. lbs.	22–24 Nm
Brake caliper slide bolts		
E30 3 Series	25 ft. lbs.	35 Nm
E36 3 Series	18–22 ft. lbs.	25–30 Nm
E34 5 Series	18–22 ft. lbs.	25–30 Nm
Brake caliper mounting bolts	89 ft. lbs.	123 Nm

84279038

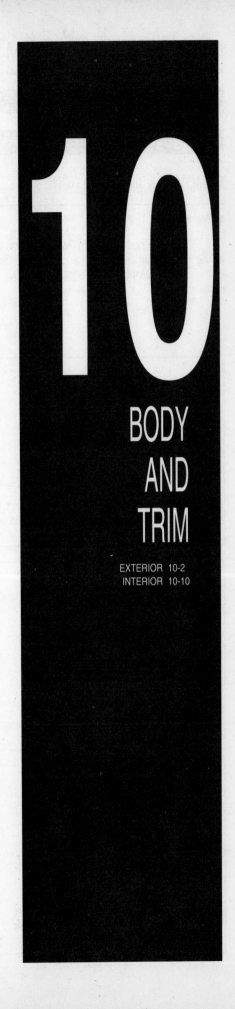

10

BODY AND TRIM

EXTERIOR

Doors

REMOVAL & INSTALLATION

▶ **See Figures 1, 2 and 3**

1. Open the door to the full wide position to make working at the hinges easier. Place a support under the bottom edge of the door to support the weight of the door. Roll down the window.

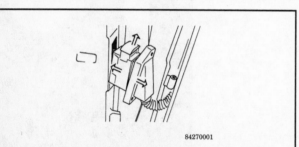

Fig. 1 Unbolt the connector and pull out of the door. Pull up on the clamp to separate the halves of the connector

Fig. 2 Remove the retainer and the press out the pin from he door brake

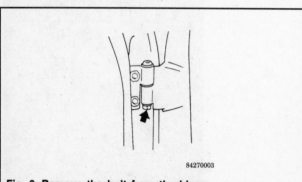

Fig. 3 Remove the bolt from the hinge

2. On the E30 3 Series, depress the clips on the electrical connection on the pillar and remove. On the E36 3 Series and the E34 5 Series, remove the 2 bolts holding the connector to the door. Pull the connector out of the opening and pull up on the clip of the interior portion of the connector body. Separate the connector.

3. Remove the clip on the bottom of the door brake pin. Push the pin out of the bore.

4. Support the door and remove the bolts from the door hinges. The upper hinge will have the bolt at the bottom of the hinge and the lower hinge will have the bolt at the top of the hinge. Pull the door off the hinges and place upright on a padded surface.

To install:

5. Check the door hinge bushing and replace if necessary. Lubricate the hinge. Place the door back on the hinges and replace the bolts.

6. Connect the door brake pin and retainer. Connect the electrical plug.

7. Close the door and check the alignment. Correct as necessary.

ADJUSTMENT

1. Check the gaps around the door. The gaps should be even.

2. Adjust the gap spacing by loosening the hinge mounting bolts and moving the door in the direction necessary to even out the gap.

3. Adjust the panel height at the front edge of the door by inserting hinge shims between the hinge mount and the body. The hinges are available in 0.020 inch (0.5mm) and 0.039 inch (1.0mm) thicknesses. It is acceptable to have the front door edge set lower than the front fender by up to 0.039 inches (1.0mm). This will help prevent wind noise and stone chips.

4. Adjust the rear edge of the door by moving the door striker in or out.

5. After adjustment is completed, some area without paint may be noticed. This is due to the way the vehicle was manufactured. The doors are hung and adjusted before the vehicle is painted. By moving the hinge or striker, an unpainted area may be uncovered. Touch up this area with matching body paint.

HINGE BUSHING REPLACEMENT

▶ **See Figures 4, 5 and 6**

1. Remove the door from the hinge.

2. Remove the snapping and washer from the hinge pin. Press the hinge pin out of the hinge.

3. Press the hinge bushing out of the hinge.

4. Install a new hinge bushing by pressing in. Use tool 41 5 010 or equivalent to press the bushing into place.

5. Install the hinge pin and lubricate. Install the door.

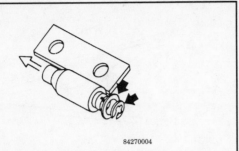

Fig. 4 Remove the snapring and the washer to release the hinge pin during bushing replacement

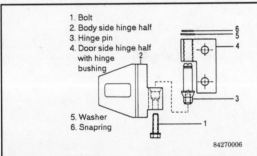

Fig. 5 Press the new bushing into place

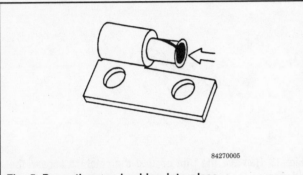

1. Bolt
2. Body side hinge half
3. Hinge pin
4. Door side hinge half with hinge bushing
5. Washer
6. Snapring

Fig. 6 Exploded view of the hinge assembly. Upper hinge is shown; lower is reverse

Hood

REMOVAL & INSTALLATION

E30 3 Series

1. Open the hood. Disconnect the windshield washer hoses and the wiring for the heated washer jets, if equipped.
2. If equipped with hood prop rods or gas springs, disconnect at the hood attachment point by pulling out the retainer and pin.
3. If equipped with removable hinge pins, remove the retainer and pull the hood off the body.
4. If not equipped with removable hinge pins, mark the alignment of the hinge on the hood and remove the hinge

mounting bolts from the hood side. Remove the hood from the body.
5. Install in reverse order and check the adjustment.

E36 3 Series

1. Open the hood. Disconnect the windshield washer hoses and the wiring for the heated washer jets and the underhood lights.
2. Disconnect the hood gas props at the hood attachment point by pulling out the retainer and pin.
3. Mark the alignment of the hinge on the hood and remove the hinge mounting bolts from the hood side. Remove the hood from the body.
4. Install in reverse order and check the adjustment.

E34 5 Series

1. Open the hood. Disconnect the windshield washer hoses and the wiring for the heated washer jets and the underhood lights.
2. Disconnect the hood gas props at the hood attachment point by pulling out the retainer and pin.
3. Remove the hood hinge pin retainer and remove the hinge pin.
4. Remove the hood from the body.
5. Install in reverse order and check the adjustment.

ADJUSTMENT

▶ **See Figures 7, 8, 9, 10 and 11**

E30 3 Series

1. Screw in the hood stoppers on the body fully.
2. Adjust the side gaps by loosening the hinge mounting bolts on the hood and moving side to side.
3. Adjust the front hood height by loosening the bolts on the body side of the hood hinge and moving up and down. The hood should rest 0.039 inches (1.0mm) below the fenders with the hood stoppers fully retracted.
4. Adjust the rear roller so it matches the catch and slides in with no lateral force.
5. Adjust the rear catch so the rear hood height is equal with the fenders.
6. Adjust the hood stoppers so the hood slightly presses against the stoppers while in the closed position and the hood is on the same level as the fenders.

Fig. 7 Hood hinge bolt locations for side gap adjustment — E34 5 Series

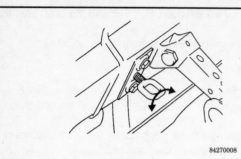

84270008

Fig. 8 Hood lock ring adjustment for hood height — E34 5 Series

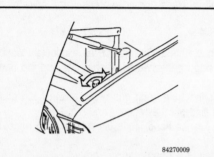

84270009

Fig. 9 Hood stopper pads. Adjust so the hood is flush with the fenders after all other adjustments are made

84270010

Fig. 10 Adjust the roller bracket so the roller is perfectly aligned with the catch

84270011

Fig. 11 Adjust the rear catch for rear hood height

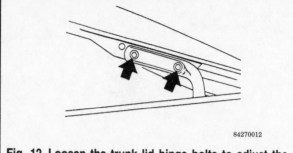

84270012

Fig. 12 Loosen the trunk lid hinge bolts to adjust the side gaps

84270013

Fig. 13 Remove the trim around the catch to access the adjustment bolts

84270014

Fig. 14 Move the catch to adjust the location of the trunk lid

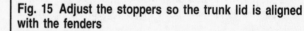

84270015

Fig. 15 Adjust the stoppers so the trunk lid is aligned with the fenders

E36 3 Series

1. Remove the center grilles by knocking them out from behind. Remove the hood lock cable and adjust so there is no play.

2. Adjust the hood side gaps by loosening the hood hinge bolts on the hood and moving the hood side to side.

3. Adjust the hood locks by loosening the bolts and raising and lowering the hood, without allowing it to lock, to align the catches. Install 1 of the bolts with threadlocker and torque to 7.2 ft. lbs. (10 Nm).

4. Adjust the hood height at the front with the spring stopper. Loosen the bolt and adjust so the hood is equal height with the fenders.

5. Adjust the headlights so the upper edge of the housing is recessed 0.060 inches (1.5mm) from the edge of the hood. Loosen the headlight mounting screws and turn the expansion nuts. Have the headlights aimed after this adjustment.

E34 5 Series

1. Remove the center and side grilles.

2. Loosen the bolts on the hood lock ring mounted on the hood. Screw in the hood stopper pads on the body.

3. Adjust the hood side gaps by loosening the hinge mounts accessible through the grille openings.

4. Adjust the hood height by screwing in or out the hood lock ring so the hood is recessed 0.039 inches (1.0mm) from the fenders. The lock is automatically adjusted in the fore and aft direction when the hood is closed and the bolts are tightened.

5. Adjust the hood height with the hood stopper pads so the hood is even with the fenders when closed.

6. Adjust the rear roller so it matches the catch and slides in with no lateral force.

7. Adjust the rear catch so the rear hood height is equal with the fenders.

Trunk Lid

REMOVAL & INSTALLATION

1. Open the trunk lid and disconnect the wiring.

2. Disconnect the trunk lid props from the trunk lid.

3. Loosen, then remove the trunk hinge bolts from the trunk lid side of the hinge. Remove the trunk lid.

4. Install in reverse order and adjust.

ADJUSTMENT

▶ See Figures 12, 13, 14 and 15

1. Adjust the height of the trunk lid at the hinge end by placing shims between the trunk lid and the hinge.

2. Adjust the side gaps by loosening the hinge bolts to the trunk lid and the catch bar mounting bolts. Align the lid and tighten the bolts.

3. Screw in the stopper pads and adjust the trunk lid height at the catch with the locking bar length. Screw the locking bar in or out so the trunk lid sit 0.039 inches below the fenders.

4. Adjust the stopper pads so the trunk lid sits flush with the fenders.

Bumpers

REMOVAL & INSTALLATION

Front

E30 3 SERIES

1. Disconnect the wiring from the turn signals. On the M3 unscrew the splash shield.

2. Remove the covers to access the bumper shock to bumper mounting bolts. The mounting hardware on the M3 is a nut instead of a bolt.

3. Remove the mounting hardware and remove the bumper.

4. Install in reverse order. Torque to 35 ft. lbs. (48 Nm).

E36 3 SERIES

1. Pull the left side rubber bumper trim strip off the bumper. Remove the nuts.

2. Remove the right side towing eye cover and remove the nuts.

3. Disconnect the outside temperature sensor.

4. Remove the bolts holding the covers at both sides, bottom of the bumper.

5. Remove the bolts in the wheel wells and remove the bumper.

6. Replace the bumper brackets if damaged.

To install:

7. Install the bumper and replace the wheel well bolts. Install the bottom covers.

8. Connect the temperature sensor. Install the nuts and the towing eye cover. Torque the nuts to 35 ft. lbs. (48 Nm).

9. Install the nuts and the left side rubber bumper trim strip with new mounting tape. Torque the nuts to 35 ft. lbs. (48 Nm).

E34 5 SERIES

▶ See Figures 16 and 17

1. Remove the rubber bumper guards from both side of the bumper. Remove the bolts from beneath the strips.

2. Pull the bummer off and disconnect the wires and headlight washer tubes.

3. Install in reverse order. Adjust the bumper so the gap is even. Torque the bolts to 35 ft. lbs. (48 Nm).

Rear

E30 3 SERIES

1. Remove the bumper mounting bolts.

2. Pull the bumper up and off.

3. Install in reverse order. Torque the bolts to 35 ft. lbs. (48 Nm).

E36 3 SERIES

1. Remove the screws from the lower rear panel and pull the panel off towards the rear.

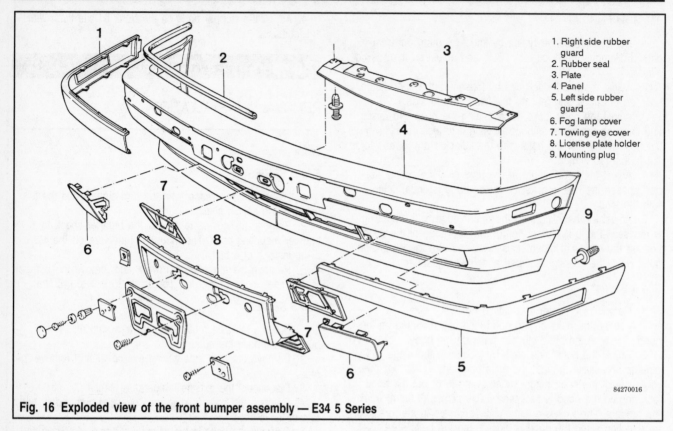

1. Right side rubber guard
2. Rubber seal
3. Plate
4. Panel
5. Left side rubber guard
6. Fog lamp cover
7. Towing eye cover
8. License plate holder
9. Mounting plug

Fig. 16 Exploded view of the front bumper assembly — E34 5 Series

2. Remove the bumper cover bolts from inside the rear wheel wells.

3. Remove the bumper mounting bolts and pull the bumper off.

4. Install in reverse order. Use new coated bolts or apply threadlocker to the old bolts. Torque the bolts to 35 ft. lbs. (48 Nm).

E34 5 SERIES

▶ See Figures 18 and 19

1. Remove the center and side rubber guards.
2. Remove the mounting bolts.
3. Pull the bumper out and off.
4. Install in reverse order. Torque the mounting bolts to 35 ft. lbs. (48 Nm).

Grilles

REMOVAL & INSTALLATION

E30 3 Series

1. Open the hood and pull off the center grille clips. Pull the center grille out of the opening.
2. Pull off the side grille clips. Remove the screws and the grille.
3. Install in reverse order.

E36 3 Series

1. From behind the grille, knock the grille out at the center to bottom third. The grille will move back.

2. Pull the chrome surround out of the opening.
3. Assemble the grille and install in the opening.

E34 5 Series

1. Open the hood and remove the screws and clips holding the headlight covers. Remove the covers.
2. Remove the screw at the center of the nose holding the grille.
3. Press down the clips accessible at the outside of the headlights and pull the grilles forward. Press the clips for the center grille down and remove the center grille.
4. Remove the screw, depress the clips and remove the side grilles.
5. Install in reverse order.

Outside Mirrors

REMOVAL & INSTALLATION

1. Remove the mirror mounting trim on the interior of the door by pulling it off towards the rear, except on the E36 3 Series which pull off from the top after the top is pull out slightly.
2. Support the mirror and remove the bolts. Disconnect the plug and remove the mirror.
3. On the E30 3 Series and E34 5 Series, remove the mirror glass by inserting a thin tool into the opening at the bottom, center of the mirror. Rotate the locking ring to the outside of the mirror to remove. On the E36 3 Series, protect the edge of the mirror and pry the glass out of the mount clips at the bottom edge.

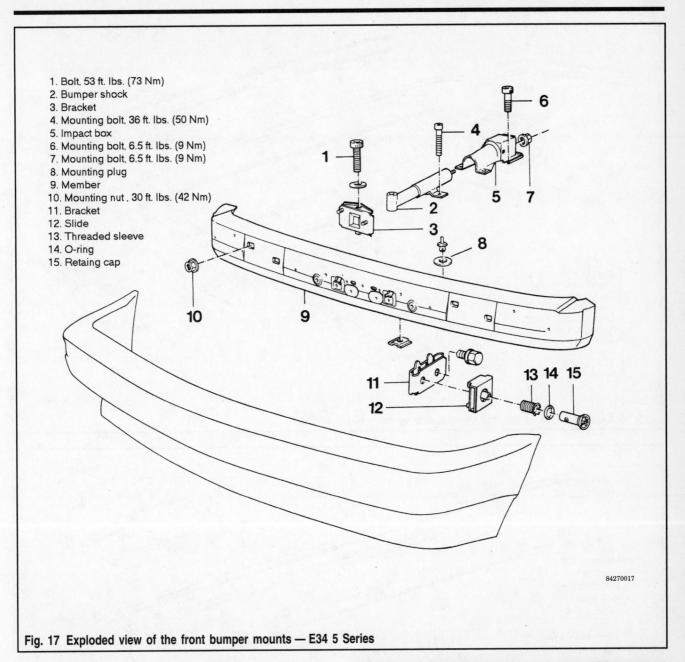

1. Bolt, 53 ft. lbs. (73 Nm)
2. Bumper shock
3. Bracket
4. Mounting bolt, 36 ft. lbs. (50 Nm)
5. Impact box
6. Mounting bolt, 6.5 ft. lbs. (9 Nm)
7. Mounting bolt, 6.5 ft. lbs. (9 Nm)
8. Mounting plug
9. Member
10. Mounting nut , 30 ft. lbs. (42 Nm)
11. Bracket
12. Slide
13. Threaded sleeve
14. O-ring
15. Retaing cap

84270017

Fig. 17 Exploded view of the front bumper mounts — E34 5 Series

4. Install the mirror and connect the plug. Install the mounting trim.

Front Fenders

The front fenders are a bolted on design. By removing any connecting body trim and removing the mounting bolts, the front fender can be replaced. Use only factory approved replacement panels to maintain rust-through warranties and original body appearance quality. Have the new panel finished using original factory methods by a facility capable of duplicating the factory paint.

Sunroof

REMOVAL & INSTALLATION

E30 3 Series
▶ See Figures 20 and 21

1. Open the sunroof lid 2-4 inches (5-10cm).
2. Unclip the roof liner frame and push back into the opening.
3. Close the sunroof lid and loosen the screws on each end of the gates.
4. Pull in the retainers, remove the center screws and lift off the lid.
5. Remove the cover over the motor and gearbox. Close the sunroof lid, if not already closed.

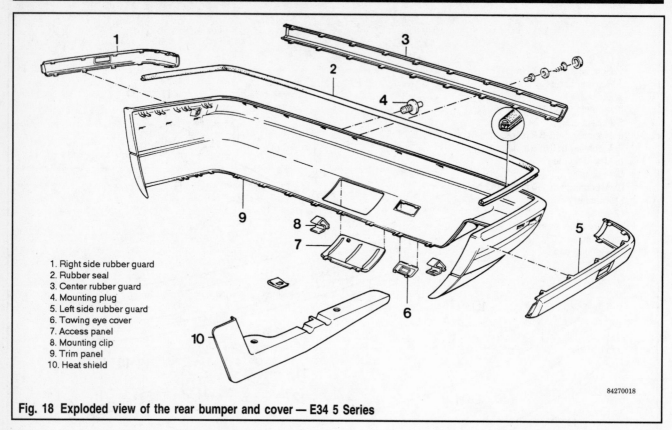

1. Right side rubber guard
2. Rubber seal
3. Center rubber guard
4. Mounting plug
5. Left side rubber guard
6. Towing eye cover
7. Access panel
8. Mounting clip
9. Trim panel
10. Heat shield

84270018

Fig. 18 Exploded view of the rear bumper and cover — E34 5 Series

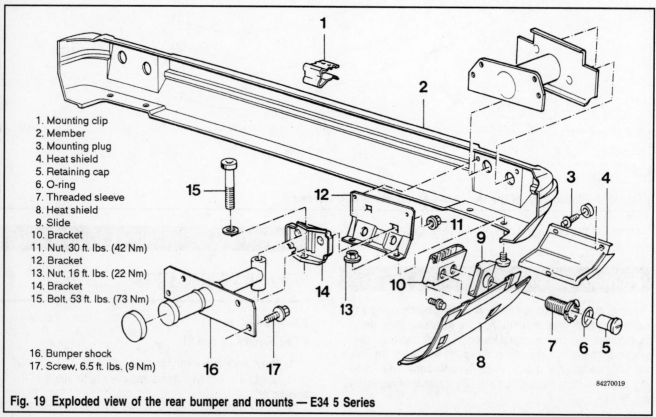

1. Mounting clip
2. Member
3. Mounting plug
4. Heat shield
5. Retaining cap
6. O-ring
7. Threaded sleeve
8. Heat shield
9. Slide
10. Bracket
11. Nut, 30 ft. lbs. (42 Nm)
12. Bracket
13. Nut, 16 ft. lbs. (22 Nm)
14. Bracket
15. Bolt, 53 ft. lbs. (73 Nm)

16. Bumper shock
17. Screw, 6.5 ft. lbs. (9 Nm)

84270019

Fig. 19 Exploded view of the rear bumper and mounts — E34 5 Series

6. Disconnect the wiring harness and remove the 3 mounting screws. Remove the motor and gearbox.

7. Push the cables back evenly on both sides. Remove the rail covers and pull the cables out of the guides.

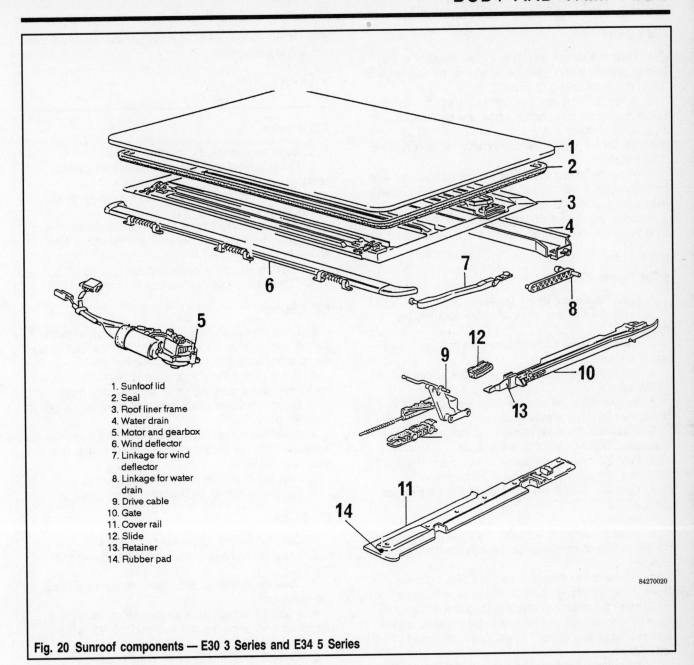

1. Sunfoof lid
2. Seal
3. Roof liner frame
4. Water drain
5. Motor and gearbox
6. Wind deflector
7. Linkage for wind deflector
8. Linkage for water drain
9. Drive cable
10. Gate
11. Cover rail
12. Slide
13. Retainer
14. Rubber pad

84270020

Fig. 20 Sunroof components — E30 3 Series and E34 5 Series

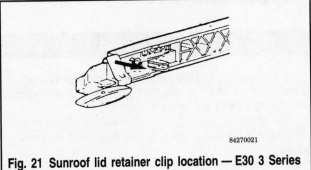

84270021

Fig. 21 Sunroof lid retainer clip location — E30 3 Series and E34 5 Series

8. Place the cable in the center position of the gate and press off.

To install:

9. Install the cables to the gate. The cable are marked with the proper side of installation. Do not lubricate fabric covered cables.

10. Pull the cables through guides and align the cables. Insert a hex key through the gate and cable at the 0 position.

11. Install the motor and gearbox. The motor and gearbox must be synchronized with the hole in the drivegear aligned between the centers of the 2 gears. Torque the bolts to 2.0 ft. lbs. (2.8 Nm).

12. Install the sunroof lid. Use new screws and torque to 2.5 ft. lbs. (3.5 Nm).

13. Adjust the sunroof lid. Pull the roof liner frame into position and clip into place.

E36 3 Series

1. Close the sunroof fully. With a quick actuation of the sunroof opening button, open the sunroof so the back edge of the lid depresses 0.08-0.12 inches (2-3mm).

2. Slowly push the roof liner panel back into the roof. Do not force or use a quick motion or damage could occur.

3. Remove the mounting screws and pull the lid off at the rear side. Do not operate the sunroof with the panel removed.

To install:

4. Install the lid and check that the hooks and levers align. Install the screws with threadlocker or use new micro-encapsulated screws. Torque to 2.5 ft. lbs. (3.5 Nm).

5. Adjust the sunroof lid. Lower the rear of the lid by operating the motor. Pull the liner forward and clip into place.

E34 5 Series

▶ **See Figures 20 and 21**

1. Open the sunroof lid 2-4 inches (5-10cm).

2. Unclip the roof liner frame and push back into the opening.

3. Close the sunroof lid and loosen the screws on each end of the gates.

4. Pull in the retainers, remove the center screws and lift off the lid.

5. Remove the cover over the motor and gearbox. Close the sunroof lid, if not already closed.

6. Disconnect the wiring harness and remove the 3 mounting screws. Remove the motor and gearbox.

7. Push the cables back evenly on both sides. Remove the rail covers and pull the cables out of the guides.

8. Place the cable in the center position of the gate and press off.

To install:

9. Install the cables to the gate. The cable are marked with the proper side of installation. Do not lubricate fabric covered cables.

10. Pull the cables through guides and align the cables. Insert a hex key through the gate and cable at the 0 position.

11. Install the motor and gearbox. The motor and gearbox must be synchronized with the hole in the drivegear aligned between the centers of the 2 gears. Torque the bolts to 2.0 ft. lbs. (2.8Nm).

12. Install the sunroof lid. Use new screws and torque to 2.5 ft. lbs. (3.5 Nm).

13. Adjust the sunroof lid. Pull the roof liner frame into position and clip into place.

ADJUSTMENT

E30 3 Series

1. Open the sunroof lid 2-4 inches (5-10cm).

2. Unclip the roof liner frame and push back into the opening.

3. Close the sunroof lid and loosen the screws on each end of the gates.

4. Adjust the sunroof panel so the front of the panel is depressed 1mm below the roof level and the rear is 1mm above the roof level.

5. Align the lid so it is centered in the opening.

6. Tighten the screws and replace the liner.

E36 3 Series

1. Close the sunroof fully. With a quick actuation of the sunroof opening button, open the sunroof so the back edge of the lid depresses 0.08-0.12 inches (2-3mm).

2. Slowly push the roof liner panel back into the roof. Do not force or use a quick motion or damage could occur.

3. Loosen the adjustment screws and move the wedges to move the panel.

4. Adjust the sunroof panel so the front of the panel is depressed 1mm below the roof level and the rear is 1mm above the roof level.

5. Align the lid so it is centered in the opening.

6. Tighten the screws and replace the liner.

E34 5 Series

1. Open the sunroof lid 2-4 inches (5-10cm).

2. Unclip the roof liner frame and push back into the opening.

3. Close the sunroof lid and loosen the screws on each end of the gates.

4. Adjust the sunroof panel so the front of the panel is depressed 1mm below the roof level and the rear is 1mm above the roof level.

5. Align the lid so it is centered in the opening.

6. Tighten the screws and replace the liner.

INTERIOR

INSTRUMENT CLUSTER

REMOVAL & INSTALLATION

E30 3 Series

1. Remove the lower dash trim from under the steering column.

2. Remove the trim from above the steering column.

3. Remove the 2 screws from the top of the instrument panel hood and the 4 screws from below. Note the positions of the screws as they are different lengths.

4. Remove the screws from the instrument cluster and pull forward. Pull the clip off the plug and disconnect from the cluster.

5. Install in reverse order.

E36 3 Series

If the instrument cluster is disconnected from the harness, the cluster must be recoded using the BMW Diagnostic Tester or equivalent. Arrange to have the cluster recoded.

1. Remove the steering wheel.

2. Remove the screws from the instrument cluster at the top.

3. Pull the instrument cluster forward. Push the levers up to disconnect the harness.

4. Install in reverse order.

E34 5 Series

1. Remove the steering wheel.

2. Remove the screws from the instrument cluster at the top.

3. Pull the instrument cluster forward. Push the levers up to disconnect the harness.

4. Install in reverse order.

Center Console

REMOVAL & INSTALLATION

E30 3 Series

1. Disconnect the negative battery cable.

2. Remove the lower dash trim from under the steering column.

3. Pull out the ashtray from the rear of the console. Remove the screw underneath. Pull the console back and off the brake lever. Disconnect the wiring.

4. Pull the manual transmission shift knob off the shift lever. Pull the shifter boot up and off. On automatic equipped vehicles unclip the trim on the right side of the shifter. Remove the screws exposed.

5. Pull out and disconnect the window switches.

6. Remove the screws from the forward ashtray console and lift out. Disconnect the wiring for the lighter.

7. Remove the bolts below the heater controls. Rotate the retainers on the sides of the consoles to release. Pull the console out.

8. Install in reverse order.

E36 3 Series

1. Remove the ashtray, cover and the hazard switch.

2. Remove the console and glove compartment.

3. Remove the lower dash trim. Remove the gear shifter handle and the clock.

4. Remove the center console.

5. Install in reverse order.

E34 5 Series

1. Remove the trim from under the steering column.

2. Remove the rear trim plate and disconnect the wires. Remove the screws from underneath.

3. Pull out the cassette holder, if equipped, and disconnect the wiring for the lights.

4. Remove the brake lever boot and the screw in the compartment next to the lever.

5. Remove the switches and disconnect the wiring. Remove the screw. Pull off the manual gear shift knob or remove the screw from the automatic transmission shifter and remove.

6. Remove the center cover from the console horizontal section. Remove the radio and pull out the heater controls.

7. Disconnect the clips and screws. Remove the console.

8. Install in reverse order.

Door Panels

REMOVAL & INSTALLATION

1. Remove the power mirror switch. Remove the screw underneath the switch and the screw under the armrest. Remove the armrest.

2. Remove the door lock button. Pull the interior door handle cups out. Lower the window.

3. Pull the panel out from the bottom and unclip from the top except on the rear doors of the E36 3 Series which unclip from the top first.

4. Check the clips and seals when replacing. Press down and in to seat.

Door Glass

REMOVAL & INSTALLATION

E30 3 Series

1. Remove the door panel and water shield.

2. Remove the inside access panel, if equipped.

3. Remove the window trim at the bottom of the window opening.

4. Remove the glass fastening screws and pull the glass out of the guide roller. Remove the glass out of the door.

5. Install the glass and adjust the window guides to align. Install the door water shield and panel.

E36 3 Series

2 DOOR

1. Remove the door panel, water shield and the upper trim strip from the glass opening.

2. Lower the glass about 6 inches (152mm) and remove the screws on the rear guide rail holder.

3. Lower the glass another 4 inches (102mm) and push the retainers at the bottom guide out.

4. Disconnect the motor connector. Loosen the screw at the bottom of the rear guide and remove the screw above it. Remove the rear stop holder.

5. Disconnect the regulator arm while holding the glass from falling. Remove the screw at the front guide and loosen the screw at the front stop. Remove the front stop holder and pull the window glass out of the door.

6. Install in reverse order.

4 DOOR

1. Remove the door panel and water shield. Lower the window about 1 ft. (approx. 300mm).

2. Disconnect the window motor. Disconnect the clips on the lower guide rail. On the rear windows, remove the weather-stripping and trim from around the window opening.

3. Disconnect the lifting arms from the guide while lifting the window out of the door opening. The glass will remove to the outside.

4. Install in reverse order.

E34 5 Series

1. Remove the door mirror, door panel and the water shield. Lower the window.

2. Disconnect the window motor. Disconnect the clips on the lower guide rail.

3. Disconnect the lifting arms from the guide while supporting the window.

4. Remove the trim strips from the around the window opening. Remove the screws and the trim plate at the rear of the window opening. Pry the trim from the outside, bottom of the window opening.

5. Pull the door glass out of the door opening.

6. Install in reverse order.

Window Regulator & Motor

REMOVAL & INSTALLATION

E30 3 Series

1. Remove the door panel.
2. Remove the window glass.
3. Disconnect the wiring harness from the regulator motor.
4. Remove the mounting screws from the door panel.
5. Pull the regulator out of the door cutout.
6. Install in reverse order.

E36 3 Series

1. Remove the door panel. On the 4 door, remove the window. On the 2 door, disconnect the window glass from the regulator and block up to support.

2. Remove the interior door handle. Grind out the regulator mounting rivets and remove the screw at the end of the arm.

3. Remove the regulator.

4. Install in reverse order. Replace the rivets with M6x10 bolts with 6.4mm washers and matching nuts.

E34 5 Series

1. Remove the door panel. Disconnect the window glass from the regulator and block up to support.

2. Remove the microswitch. Grind out the regulator mounting rivets and remove the screw at the end of the arm.

3. Remove the regulator.

4. Install in reverse order. Replace the rivets with M6x10 bolts with 6.4mm washers and matching nuts.

Door Lock Actuators

REMOVAL & INSTALLATION

E30 3 Series

1. Remove the door panel and the water shield.

2. Disconnect the wiring from the actuator. Remove the screws and pull the actuator off the linkage.

3. When installing, move the actuator and linkage to the locked position.

4. Connect the linkage to the actuator and loosely install with the screws.

5. Compress the actuator drive to take out any play in the linkage and tighten the screws.

6. Test the locks and install the door panel.

E36 3 Series

1. Remove the door panel and water shield.

2. On the front doors, remove the guide rail nut and pull the guide rail down. Disconnect the wiring and the linkage from the actuator.

3. On the rear doors, remove the window and the access panel. Disconnect the wiring and the linkage from the actuator.

4. Remove the 3 bolts holding the latch and actuator to the door structure.

5. Install in reverse order using threadlocker on the bolts.

E34 5 Series

1. Remove the door panel and the water shield.

2. Disconnect the wiring from the actuator. Remove the screws and pull the actuator off the linkage.

3. When installing, move the actuator and linkage to the locked position.

4. Connect the linkage to the actuator and loosely install with the screws.

5. Compress the actuator drive to take out any play in the linkage and tighten the screws.

6. Test the locks and install the door panel.

Front Seats

REMOVAL & INSTALLATION

E30 3 Series

1. Slide the seat to the full back position. Remove the covers and the forward bolts.

2. Slide the seat to the full forward position. Remove the covers and the rear bolts.

3. On 4 door vehicles, remove the cap covering the seat belt bracket. Remove the bolt and bracket.

4. Disconnect the wiring and remove the seat. Be careful not to damage the interior trim while removing.

5. Lubricate the rails and install in reverse order.

E36 3 Series

1. Move the seat up and full forward. Remove the rear bolts.

2. Turn the seat belt tensioner lock cable toggle a quarter turn to disconnect. It is accessible from the front of the seat.

3. Move the seat back and remove the front bolts.

4. On the 4 door vehicles, lift the seat and disconnect the seatbelt bolt.

5. Remove the seat. Be careful not to damage the sills or trim while removing.

To install:

6. Lubricate the rails. Install the seat and bolts, but do not tighten.

7. Move the seat full forward then move back to the second catch from the full forward position. Check that the catches have engaged properly.

8. Push the seat forward a few times from the back seat and tighten the rear bolts.

9. Move the seat back and check that the catches engage at each position. Tighten the front bolts.

E34 5 Series

1. On manual seats, disconnect the seatbelt tensioner lock cable to deactivate. On power seats, turn in the screw at the rear of the lock assembly.

2. Remove the headrest by pulling out.

3. If the power seat does not work via the switch, the seat can be move fore and aft by inserting a screwdriver in the motor drive at the front of the seat and turning.

4. Move the seat forward and remove the rear bolts.

5. Move the seat to the high position and disconnect the seatbelt height adjustment. Disconnect the seatbelt.

6. Lift the rear of the seat and pull out of the holders. Disconnect the wiring and remove the seat.

7. Install in reverse order.

Rear Seat

REMOVAL & INSTALLATION

E30 3 Series

1. Pull the front of the seat cushion up to disengage from the clips.

2. Pull the cushion out from under the backrest and remove from the vehicle.

3. Remove the bolts from the brackets at the bottom of the backrest.

4. Remove the backrest from the vehicle.

5. Install in the reverse order.

E36 3 Series

1. Pull the front of the seat cushion up to disengage from the clips.

2. Pull the cushion out from under the backrest and remove from the vehicle.

3. On vehicles without folddown seats, pull the top of the backrest forward and lift out of the vehicle.

4. When equipped with the folddown rear seat, unscrew the seat belt lower bolt, fold the seat down and remove the hinge cover. Press the lock in and remove the backrest.

5. Install in the reverse order.

E34 5 Series

1. Pull the front of the seat cushion up to disengage from the clips. Remove the cushion from the vehicle.

2. Except M5, lower the armrest and remove the nuts. Pull out the seat belt strap covers. Lift out the backrest.

3. On the M5, remove the headrests by pulling out. Turn the retainers a quarter turn and remove the covers. Open the console and press in the tabs to remove. Pull out the seat belt strap covers. Remove the 4 bolts and the backrest.

4. Install in reverse order.

Power Seat Motor

REMOVAL & INSTALLATION

E34 5 Series
▶ See Figure 22

1. Remove the seat from the vehicle. Disconnect the side panels by unclipping and removing the screws. Disconnect the switches.

2. Remove the seat control unit from under the seat. Use tool 52 1 100 or equivalent to drive out the 4 bearing pins.

3. Drill out the rivets and remove the base plate.

4. Remove the front seat height motor and remove the rails.

5. Remove the fore/aft motor.

6. Remove the backrest cover by removing the 2 screw at the sides, if equipped, and pushing the cover up to disengage the clips. Pull the cover off and disconnect the wiring.

7. At the lowers sides, press the levers down to disconnect the backrest. Pull the headrest out.

8. Loosen the headrest gearbox cover. Remove the bolts and take off the gearbox. Remove the motor from the gearbox.

9. Loosen the bottom seat cushion cover. Remove the bolts at the cable shaft retainer plate on the motor and remove the shafts.

10. Remove the screws and the snapring at the backrest fittings. Remove the motors.

To install:

11. Install the motors. The black plug is for the backrest position motor and the white plug is for the seat up/down motor.

12. Lubricate the splines for the backrest fittings and install the sleeve. Install the fittings and snapring.

13. Install the motor shaft and retainer plate. Install the seat cover.

14. Install the headrest motor and gearbox. Install the headrest.

15. Install the backrest on the seat bottom. Connect the electrical leads. The plug colors will match.

16. Install the backrest cover and screws.

17. Lubricate the splines and install the fore/aft motor. Connect the spring at the fore/aft motor before tightening the mounting nuts.

18. Install the seat front height motor. Check that the linkage is in the same position on both sides. Lubricate the splines and install the sleeves.

19. Install the base plate with new rivets or bolts. Install the 4 bearing pins with tool 52 1 100 or equivalent. Check that the retainer and stops are not damaged.

20. Install the control unit and the side panels.

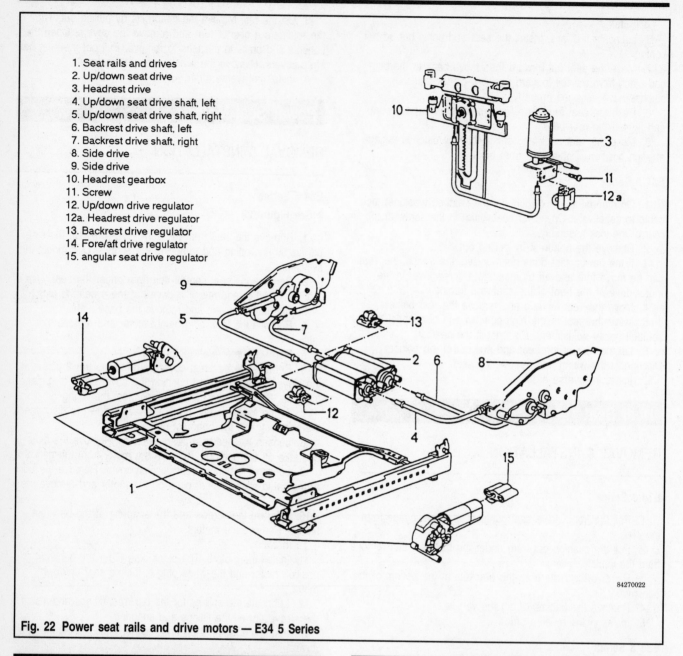

1. Seat rails and drives
2. Up/down seat drive
3. Headrest drive
4. Up/down seat drive shaft, left
5. Up/down seat drive shaft, right
6. Backrest drive shaft, left
7. Backrest drive shaft, right
8. Side drive
9. Side drive
10. Headrest gearbox
11. Screw
12. Up/down drive regulator
12a. Headrest drive regulator
13. Backrest drive regulator
14. Fore/aft drive regulator
15. angular seat drive regulator

Fig. 22 Power seat rails and drive motors — E34 5 Series

Seat Belts

REMOVAL & INSTALLATION

▶ See Figure 23

E30 3 Series

FRONT

1. Remove the front seat to access and unscrew the lower seat belt receptacle.
2. 2 Door: Pull the side panel trim over the seat belt retractor out. There are 3 clips. Pull the cover off the upper seat belt mount and unscrew the bolt. Disconnect the slide by pressing in the pin body remove the bolts for the retractor and the bottom anchor.

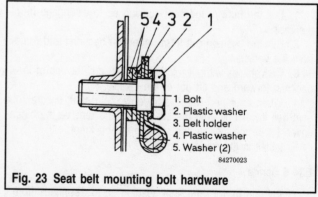

1. Bolt
2. Plastic washer
3. Belt holder
4. Plastic washer
5. Washer (2)

Fig. 23 Seat belt mounting bolt hardware

3. 4 Door: Remove the caps on the upper and lower seat belt mounts and unscrew the bolts. Unclip or unscrew the B

pillar cover and remove the seat belt through the trim. Remove the bolt and the retractor.

4. Convertible: Remove the cover plate over the lower anchor and unscrew the bolt. Remove the rear seat and the side trim panel over the retractor assembly. The side trim panel is held by screws under the speaker grille at the arm rest and the door weather-stripping. Remove the upper mount and the retractor bolts.

To install:

5. Install the retractor assembly and the lower anchors.

6. Install the upper mount. There are 2 mounting bosses for the upper mount. The mount can be installed in either depending on the height and preference of the driver. A new hole may need to be made if the nonstock boss is utilized.

7. Torque the bolts to 35 ft. lbs. (48 Nm). Install the trim panels and seats.

REAR

1. Remove the cover at the upper mount. Remove the back tray. On the convertible remove the backseat completely and the side trim panel.

2. Remove the bolt holding the retractor.

3. Remove the seat cushion and unbolt the lower mount.

4. Install in reverse order. Torque the bolts to 35 ft. lbs. (48 Nm).

E36 3 Series

FRONT

1. Deactivate the belt tensioner by turning the cable perpendicular to the seat cushion plane. Remove the front seat and unscrew the bolt for the lower anchor receptacle.

2. Remove the bolt holding the seat belt tensioner. Remove the cap over the upper mount and unscrew the bolt.

3. Unscrew the belt holder and the retractor.

4. Install in reverse order. Torque the bolts to 35 ft. lbs. (48 Nm).

REAR

1. If equipped with fold down rear seat, remove the rear seat. If not equipped with the fold down rear seat, remove the back tray.

2. Remove the bolts for the lower anchors and the receptacles.

3. Without fold down seats: Remove the bolts for the retractors.

4. With fold down seats: Remove the cap over the bolt for the retractor on the back of the seat section. Remove the bolt and the end plate. Slide the retractor out of the seat.

5. Install in reverse order. Torque the bolts to 35 ft. lbs. (48 Nm).

E34 5 Series

FRONT

▶ See Figure 24

1. Disconnect the negative battery cable. Deactivate the seat belt tensioner by disconnecting the cable on manual seats or screwing in the screw on power seats.

2. Raise the seat to the highest position. Unbolt and disconnect the cables to the tensioners.

3. Remove the side panel by pulling back the trim and pulling up. Remove the screws holding the door jamb plugs.

4. Remove the seat belt bolts and the retractor. Remove the guide.

5. If the seat belt need to be replaced, the entire system including the height control must be replaced. Install in reverse order. Torque the bolts to 35 ft. lbs. (48 Nm).

REAR

1. Remove the back seat. Unscrew and remove the lower anchors.

2. Remove the C-pillar trim panel by unclipping and pulling out.

3. Remove the clips and pull out the back tray.

4. Remove the bolt and the retractor.

5. Install in reverse order. Torque the bolts to 35 ft. lbs. (48 Nm).

Inside Mirror

REMOVAL & INSTALLATION

The mirror is held with either a spring clip if mounted in the roof and pulls out or it mounts to a pad cemented to the windshield. If it is windshield mounted, rotate the mirror and pull off to the rear. Match the mount and press into place.

Windshield

REMOVAL & INSTALLATION

This procedure for removing and installing the windshield requires special tools and techniques. If you are not comfortable with your ability to complete this procedure, allow a glass professional to replace the windshield. An incorrectly installed windshield can leak and cause wind noise.

E30 3 Series

This procedure does not include the M3. The M3 uses a windshield mounting scheme similar to that of the E34 5 Series. The M3 uses a square cross section cement bead as opposed to the triangle shaped cross section of the E34 5 Series.

1. Pull out the trim strips from around the windshield. Loosen the gaskets grip on the windshield and body opening.

2. Press the windshield out of the gasket starting at an upper corner. Sit in the passenger seat and use you feet to press on the glass. Guide the glass out of the gasket.

To install:

3. Install the new gasket in the body opening. Place the seam at the bottom center.

4. Use a non-petroleum lubricant on the glass edge and the gasket. Press the glass into the gasket starting at the center.

5. Use a flat bladed tool and push the gasket over and around the glass.

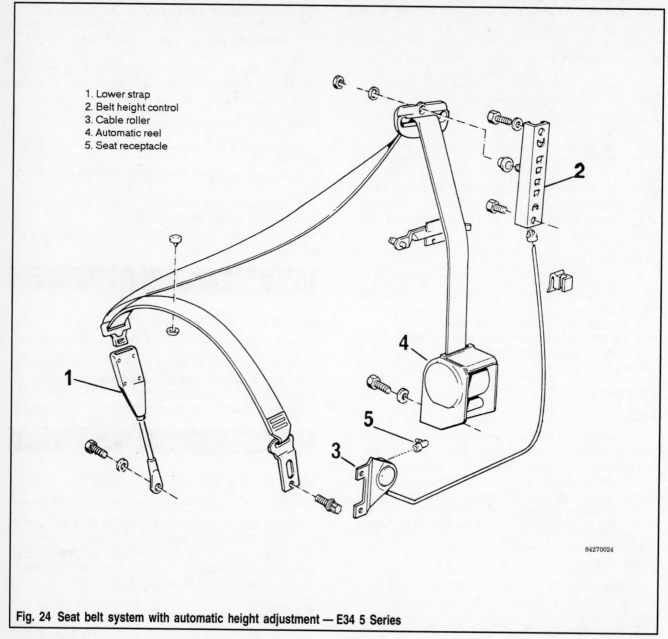

1. Lower strap
2. Belt height control
3. Cable roller
4. Automatic reel
5. Seat receptacle

84270024

Fig. 24 Seat belt system with automatic height adjustment — E34 5 Series

6. Install the trim strips into the gasket and press into place. Start at the center. Check for leaks.

E36 3 Series

1. Remove the hood and cowl covers beneath the windshield.

2. Pull out the seals from around the windshield. Apply protective tape to the finish around the windshield.

3. Remove the inside mirror and the A-pillar trim panels.

4. Use a cement cutting tool to cut the cement bead around the windshield. Remove the windshield.

To install:

5. Reduce the thickness of the remaining cement to 0.020 inches (0.5mm). This is true for the remaining cement on the body opening and for the cement on the windshield if the windshield is being reused.

6. Touch-up any paint chips with anti-rust primer. Install the upper seal onto the windshield.

7. Check the condition of the rubber pads and replace if necessary. Apply primer from the cement kit to the windshield and body opening. Allow to dry for 10 minutes.

8. Remove the protective tape from the finish. Install the hood and align. Install tools 51 3 032 or equivalent, into the cowl and tools 51 3 032 or equivalent, to the frame with the doors open.

9. Cut a notch into the cement cartridge nozzle to produce a right triangle of cement with a base width of 0.275 inches (7mm) and a height of 0.433 inches (11mm). Apply cement to the windshield 0.354 inches (9mm) from the bottom, 0.196 inches. (5mm) from the sides and 0.157 inches (4mm) from the top. Install the glass quickly into the opening.

10. Press the glass up to meet the roof. Use tape to secure the glass from sliding down. Allow the cement to dry and remove the tools. Check for leaks.

E34 5 Series

▶ **See Figure 25**

1. Remove the windshield wipers and the cowl cover.

2. Remove the outer windshield trim, the inside visors and clips. Pull down the door trim and the A-pillar trim. Remove the mirror and pull down the headliner in the front.

3. Remove the cement on the body and the windshield clips. Cut the cement bead and remove the windshield.

To install:

4. Reduce the thickness of the remaining cement to 0.020 inches (0.5mm). This is true for the remaining cement on the body opening and for the cement on the windshield if the windshield is being reused.

5. Touch-up any paint chips with anti-rust primer. Install the upper seal onto the windshield.

6. Check the condition of the clips and replace if necessary. Mount the clips to match the clip openings in the ornamental trim strips. Apply primer from the cement kit to the windshield and body opening. Allow to dry for 10 minutes.

7. Place the windshield in the opening and align. Check the alignment of the clips. Lift out the window and cut off the tabs on the clips.

8. Apply a bead of cement around the window at a distance of 0.197 inches (5mm) from the edge. Press the window in place and apply pressure during the curing time. Check for leaks.

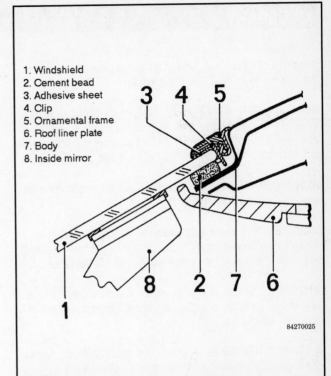

1. Windshield
2. Cement bead
3. Adhesive sheet
4. Clip
5. Ornamental frame
6. Roof liner plate
7. Body
8. Inside mirror

84270025

Fig. 25 Cross-section of the windshield mounting — E34 5 Series

TORQUE SPECIFICATIONS

Component	U.S.	Metric
Bumper to bumper shock:	35 ft. lbs.	48 Nm
Hood lock catch mounting bolts:	7.2 ft. lbs.	10 Nm
Sunroof motor mounting bolts:	2.0 ft. lbs.	2.8 Nm
Sunroof lid mounting screws:	2.5 ft. lbs.	3.5 Nm
Seat belt mounting bolts:	35 ft. lbs.	48 Nm
Seat belt height control mounting bolts:	17 ft. lbs.	24 Nm

84270026

GLOSSARY

AIR/FUEL RATIO: The ratio of air to gasoline by weight in the fuel mixture drawn into the engine.

AIR INJECTION: One method of reducing harmful exhaust emissions by injecting air into each of the exhaust ports of an engine. The fresh air entering the hot exhaust manifold causes any remaining fuel to be burned before it can exit the tailpipe.

ALTERNATOR: A device used for converting mechanical energy into electrical energy.

AMMETER: An instrument, calibrated in amperes, used to measure the flow of an electrical current in a circuit. Ammeters are always connected in series with the circuit being tested.

AMPERE: The rate of flow of electrical current present when one volt of electrical pressure is applied against one ohm of electrical resistance.

ANALOG COMPUTER: Any microprocessor that uses similar (analogous) electrical signals to make its calculations.

ARMATURE: A laminated, soft iron core wrapped by a wire that converts electrical energy to mechanical energy as in a motor or relay. When rotated in a magnetic field, it changes mechanical energy into electrical energy as in a generator.

ATMOSPHERIC PRESSURE: The pressure on the Earth's surface caused by the weight of the air in the atmosphere. At sea level, this pressure is 14.7 psi at 32{248}F (101 kPa at 0{248}C).

ATOMIZATION: The breaking down of a liquid into a fine mist that can be suspended in air.

AXIAL PLAY: Movement parallel to a shaft or bearing bore.

BACKFIRE: The sudden combustion of gases in the intake or exhaust system that results in a loud explosion.

BACKLASH: The clearance or play between two parts, such as meshed gears.

BACKPRESSURE: Restrictions in the exhaust system that slow the exit of exhaust gases from the combustion chamber.

BAKELITE: A heat resistant, plastic insulator material commonly used in printed circuit boards and transistorized components.

BALL BEARING: A bearing made up of hardened inner and outer races between which hardened steel balls roll.

BALLAST RESISTOR: A resistor in the primary ignition circuit that lowers voltage after the engine is started to reduce wear on ignition components.

BEARING: A friction reducing, supportive device usually located between a stationary part and a moving part.

BIMETAL TEMPERATURE SENSOR: Any sensor or switch made of two dissimilar types of metal that bend when heated or cooled due to the different expansion rates of the alloys. These types of sensors usually function as an on/off switch.

BLOWBY: Combustion gases, composed of water vapor and unburned fuel, that leak past the piston rings into the crankcase during normal engine operation. These gases are removed by the PCV system to prevent the buildup of harmful acids in the crankcase.

BRAKE PAD: A brake shoe and lining assembly used with disc brakes.

BRAKE SHOE: The backing for the brake lining. The term is, however, usually applied to the assembly of the brake backing and lining.

BUSHING: A liner, usually removable, for a bearing; an anti-friction liner used in place of a bearing.

CALIPER: A hydraulically activated device in a disc brake system, which is mounted straddling the brake rotor (disc). The caliper contains at least one piston and two brake pads. Hydraulic pressure on the piston(s) forces the pads against the rotor.

CAMSHAFT: A shaft in the engine on which are the lobes (cams) which operate the valves. The camshaft is driven by the crankshaft, via a belt, chain or gears, at one half the crankshaft speed.

CAPACITOR: A device which stores an electrical charge.

CARBON MONOXIDE (CO): A colorless, odorless gas given off as a normal byproduct of combustion. It is poisonous and extremely dangerous in confined areas, building up slowly to toxic levels without warning if adequate ventilation is not available.

CARBURETOR: A device, usually mounted on the intake manifold of an engine, which mixes the air and fuel in the proper proportion to allow even combustion.

CATALYTIC CONVERTER: A device installed in the exhaust system, like a muffler, that converts harmful byproducts of combustion into carbon dioxide and water vapor by means of a heat-producing chemical reaction.

CENTRIFUGAL ADVANCE: A mechanical method of advancing the spark timing by using flyweights in the distributor that react to centrifugal force generated by the distributor shaft rotation.

CHECK VALVE: Any one-way valve installed to permit the flow of air, fuel or vacuum in one direction only.

CHOKE: A device, usually a moveable valve, placed in the intake path of a carburetor to restrict the flow of air.

CIRCUIT: Any unbroken path through which an electrical current can flow. Also used to describe fuel flow in some instances.

CIRCUIT BREAKER: A switch which protects an electrical circuit from overload by opening the circuit when the current flow exceeds a predetermined level. Some circuit breakers must be reset manually, while most reset automatically

COIL (IGNITION): A transformer in the ignition circuit which steps up the voltage provided to the spark plugs.

COMBINATION MANIFOLD: An assembly which includes both the intake and exhaust manifolds in one casting.

COMBINATION VALVE: A device used in some fuel systems that routes fuel vapors to a charcoal storage canister instead of venting them into the atmosphere. The valve relieves fuel tank pressure and allows fresh air into the tank as the fuel level drops to prevent a vapor lock situation.

COMPRESSION RATIO: The comparison of the total volume of the cylinder and combustion chamber with the piston at BDC and the piston at TDC.

CONDENSER: 1. An electrical device which acts to store an electrical charge, preventing voltage surges.
2. A radiator-like device in the air conditioning system in which refrigerant gas condenses into a liquid, giving off heat.

CONDUCTOR: Any material through which an electrical current can be transmitted easily.

CONTINUITY: Continuous or complete circuit. Can be checked with an ohmmeter.

COUNTERSHAFT: An intermediate shaft which is rotated by a mainshaft and transmits, in turn, that rotation to a working part.

CRANKCASE: The lower part of an engine in which the crankshaft and related parts operate.

CRANKSHAFT: The main driving shaft of an engine which receives reciprocating motion from the pistons and converts it to rotary motion.

CYLINDER: In an engine, the round hole in the engine block in which the piston(s) ride.

CYLINDER BLOCK: The main structural member of an engine in which is found the cylinders, crankshaft and other principal parts.

CYLINDER HEAD: The detachable portion of the engine, fastened, usually, to the top of the cylinder block, containing all or most of the combustion chambers. On overhead valve engines, it contains the valves and their operating parts. On overhead cam engines, it contains the camshaft as well.

DEAD CENTER: The extreme top or bottom of the piston stroke.

DETONATION: An unwanted explosion of the air/fuel mixture in the combustion chamber caused by excess heat and compression, advanced timing, or an overly lean mixture. Also referred to as "ping".

DIAPHRAGM: A thin, flexible wall separating two cavities, such as in a vacuum advance unit.

DIESELING: A condition in which hot spots in the combustion chamber cause the engine to run on after the key is turned off.

DIFFERENTIAL: A geared assembly which allows the transmission of motion between drive axles, giving one axle the ability to turn faster than the other.

DIODE: An electrical device that will allow current to flow in one direction only.

DISC BRAKE: A hydraulic braking assembly consisting of a brake disc, or rotor, mounted on an axle, and a caliper assembly containing, usually two brake pads which are activated by hydraulic pressure. The pads are forced against the sides of the disc, creating friction which slows the vehicle.

DISTRIBUTOR: A mechanically driven device on an engine which is responsible for electrically firing the spark plug at a predetermined point of the piston stroke.

DOWEL PIN: A pin, inserted in mating holes in two different parts allowing those parts to maintain a fixed relationship.

DRUM BRAKE: A braking system which consists of two brake shoes and one or two wheel cylinders, mounted on a fixed backing plate, and a brake drum, mounted on an axle, which revolves around the assembly.

DWELL: The rate, measured in degrees of shaft rotation, at which an electrical circuit cycles on and off.

ELECTRONIC CONTROL UNIT (ECU): Ignition module, module, amplifier or igniter. See Module for definition.

ELECTRONIC IGNITION: A system in which the timing and firing of the spark plugs is controlled by an electronic control unit, usually called a module. These systems have no points or condenser.

ENDPLAY: The measured amount of axial movement in a shaft.

ENGINE: A device that converts heat into mechanical energy.

EXHAUST MANIFOLD: A set of cast passages or pipes which conduct exhaust gases from the engine.

FEELER GAUGE: A blade, usually metal, of precisely predetermined thickness, used to measure the clearance between two parts.

FIRING ORDER: The order in which combustion occurs in the cylinders of an engine. Also the order in which spark is distributed to the plugs by the distributor.

FLOODING: The presence of too much fuel in the intake manifold and combustion chamber which prevents the air/fuel mixture from firing, thereby causing a no-start situation.

FLYWHEEL: A disc shaped part bolted to the rear end of the crankshaft. Around the outer perimeter is affixed the ring gear. The starter drive engages the ring gear, turning the flywheel, which rotates the crankshaft, imparting the initial starting motion to the engine.

FOOT POUND (ft.lb. or sometimes, ft. lbs.): The amount of energy or work needed to raise an item weighing one pound, a distance of one foot.

FUSE: A protective device in a circuit which prevents circuit overload by breaking the circuit when a specific amperage is present. The device is constructed around a strip or wire of a lower amperage rating than the circuit it is designed to protect. When an amperage higher than that stamped on the fuse is present in the circuit, the strip or wire melts, opening the circuit.

GEAR RATIO: The ratio between the number of teeth on meshing gears.

GENERATOR: A device which converts mechanical energy into electrical energy.

HEAT RANGE: The measure of a spark plug's ability to dissipate heat from its firing end. The higher the heat range, the hotter the plug fires.

HUB: The center part of a wheel or gear.

HYDROCARBON (HC): Any chemical compound made up of hydrogen and carbon. A major pollutant formed by the engine as a byproduct of combustion.

HYDROMETER: An instrument used to measure the specific gravity of a solution.

INCH POUND (in.lb. or sometimes, in. lbs.): One twelfth of a foot pound.

INDUCTION: A means of transferring electrical energy in the form of a magnetic field. Principle used in the ignition coil to increase voltage.

INJECTOR: A device which receives metered fuel under relatively low pressure and is activated to inject the fuel into the engine under relatively high pressure at a predetermined time.

INPUT SHAFT: The shaft to which torque is applied, usually carrying the driving gear or gears.

INTAKE MANIFOLD: A casting of passages or pipes used to conduct air or a fuel/air mixture to the cylinders.

JOURNAL: The bearing surface within which a shaft operates.

KEY: A small block usually fitted in a notch between a shaft and a hub to prevent slippage of the two parts.

MANIFOLD: A casting of passages or set of pipes which connect the cylinders to an inlet or outlet source.

MANIFOLD VACUUM: Low pressure in an engine intake manifold formed just below the throttle plates. Manifold vacuum is highest at idle and drops under acceleration.

MASTER CYLINDER: The primary fluid pressurizing device in a hydraulic system. In automotive use, it is found in brake and hydraulic clutch systems and is pedal activated, either directly or, in a power brake system, through the power booster.

MODULE: Electronic control unit, amplifier or igniter of solid state or integrated design which controls the current flow in the ignition primary circuit based on input from the pick-up coil. When the module opens the primary circuit, the high secondary voltage is induced in the coil.

NEEDLE BEARING: A bearing which consists of a number (usually a large number) of long, thin rollers.

OHM:(Ω) The unit used to measure the resistance of conductor to electrical flow. One ohm is the amount of resistance that limits current flow to one ampere in a circuit with one volt of pressure.

OHMMETER: An instrument used for measuring the resistance, in ohms, in an electrical circuit.

OUTPUT SHAFT: The shaft which transmits torque from a device, such as a transmission.

OVERDRIVE: A gear assembly which produces more shaft revolutions than that transmitted to it.

OVERHEAD CAMSHAFT (OHC): An engine configuration in which the camshaft is mounted on top of the cylinder head and operates the valve either directly or by means of rocker arms.

OVERHEAD VALVE (OHV): An engine configuration in which all of the valves are located in the cylinder head and the camshaft is located in the cylinder block. The camshaft operates the valves via lifters and pushrods.

OXIDES OF NITROGEN (NOx): Chemical compounds of nitrogen produced as a byproduct of combustion. They combine with hydrocarbons to produce smog.

OXYGEN SENSOR: Used with the feedback system to sense the presence of oxygen in the exhaust gas and signal the computer which can reference the voltage signal to an air/fuel ratio.

PINION: The smaller of two meshing gears.

PISTON RING: An open ended ring which fits into a groove on the outer diameter of the piston. Its chief function is to form a seal between the piston and cylinder wall. Most automotive pistons have three rings: two for compression sealing; one for oil sealing.

PRELOAD: A predetermined load placed on a bearing during assembly or by adjustment.

PRIMARY CIRCUIT: Is the low voltage side of the ignition system which consists of the ignition switch, ballast resistor or resistance wire, bypass, coil, electronic control unit and pick-up coil as well as the connecting wires and harnesses.

PRESS FIT: The mating of two parts under pressure, due to the inner diameter of one being smaller than the outer diameter of the other, or vice versa; an interference fit.

RACE: The surface on the inner or outer ring of a bearing on which the balls, needles or rollers move.

REGULATOR: A device which maintains the amperage and/or voltage levels of a circuit at predetermined values.

RELAY: A switch which automatically opens and/or closes a circuit.

RESISTANCE: The opposition to the flow of current through a circuit or electrical device, and is measured in ohms. Resistance is equal to the voltage divided by the amperage.

RESISTOR: A device, usually made of wire, which offers a preset amount of resistance in an electrical circuit.

RING GEAR: The name given to a ring-shaped gear attached to a differential case, or affixed to a flywheel or as part a planetary gear set.

ROLLER BEARING: A bearing made up of hardened inner and outer races between which hardened steel rollers move.

ROTOR: 1. The disc-shaped part of a disc brake assembly, upon which the brake pads bear; also called, brake disc.
 2. The device mounted atop the distributor shaft, which passes current to the distributor cap tower contacts.

SECONDARY CIRCUIT: The high voltage side of the ignition system, usually above 20,000 volts. The secondary includes the ignition coil, coil wire, distributor cap and rotor, spark plug wires and spark plugs.

SENDING UNIT: A mechanical, electrical, hydraulic or electromagnetic device which transmits information to a gauge.

SENSOR: Any device designed to measure engine operating conditions or ambient pressures and temperatures. Usually electronic in nature and designed to send a voltage signal to an on-board computer, some sensors may operate as a simple on/off switch or they may provide a variable voltage signal (like a potentiometer) as conditions or measured parameters change.

SHIM: Spacers of precise, predetermined thickness used between parts to establish a proper working relationship.

SLAVE CYLINDER: In automotive use, a device in the hydraulic clutch system which is activated by hydraulic force, disengaging the clutch.

SOLENOID: A coil used to produce a magnetic field, the effect of which is produce work.

SPARK PLUG: A device screwed into the combustion chamber of a spark ignition engine. The basic construction is a conductive core inside of a ceramic insulator, mounted in an outer conductive base. An electrical charge from the spark plug wire travels along the conductive core and jumps a preset air gap to a grounding point or points at the end of the conductive base. The resultant spark ignites the fuel/air mixture in the combustion chamber.

SPLINES: Ridges machined or cast onto the outer diameter of a shaft or inner diameter of a bore to enable parts to mate without rotation.

TACHOMETER: A device used to measure the rotary speed of an engine, shaft, gear, etc., usually in rotations per minute.

THERMOSTAT: A valve, located in the cooling system of an engine, which is closed when cold and opens gradually in response to engine heating, controlling the temperature of the coolant and rate of coolant flow.

TOP DEAD CENTER (TDC): The point at which the piston reaches the top of its travel on the compression stroke.

TORQUE: The twisting force applied to an object.

TORQUE CONVERTER: A turbine used to transmit power from a driving member to a driven member via hydraulic action, providing changes in drive ratio and torque. In automotive use, it links the driveplate at the rear of the engine to the automatic transmission.

TRANSDUCER: A device used to change a force into an electrical signal.

TRANSISTOR: A semi-conductor component which can be actuated by a small voltage to perform an electrical switching function.

TUNE-UP: A regular maintenance function, usually associated with the replacement and adjustment of parts and components in the electrical and fuel systems of a vehicle for the purpose of attaining optimum performance.

TURBOCHARGER: An exhaust driven pump which compresses intake air and forces it into the combustion chambers at higher than atmospheric pressures. The increased air pressure allows more fuel to be burned and results in increased horsepower being produced.

VACUUM ADVANCE: A device which advances the ignition timing in response to increased engine vacuum.

VACUUM GAUGE: An instrument used to measure the presence of vacuum in a chamber.

VALVE: A device which control the pressure, direction of flow or rate of flow of a liquid or gas.

VALVE CLEARANCE: The measured gap between the end of the valve stem and the rocker arm, cam lobe or follower that activates the valve.

VISCOSITY: The rating of a liquid's internal resistance to flow.

VOLTMETER: An instrument used for measuring electrical force in units called volts. Voltmeters are always connected parallel with the circuit being tested.

WHEEL CYLINDER: Found in the automotive drum brake assembly, it is a device, actuated by hydraulic pressure, which, through internal pistons, pushes the brake shoes outward against the drums.

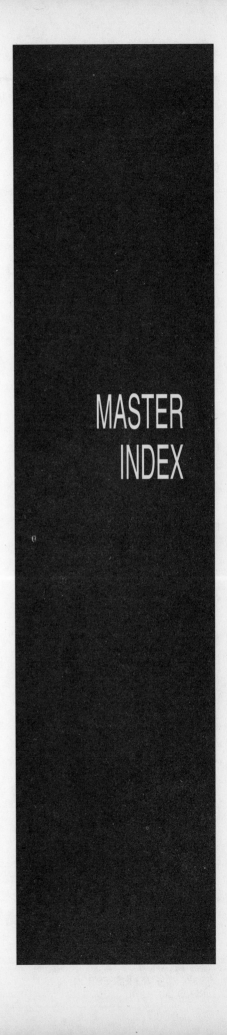

MASTER INDEX